MW00737707

Christoph Willibald Gluck

Iphigénie en Tauride
Iphigenie auf Tauris

Partitura

Könemann Music Budapest
K 1024

PERSONNAGES

Iphigénie, grande Prêtresse de Diane	*Soprano*
Oreste, Frère d'Iphigénie	*Basse élevé*
Pylade, Prince Grec, ami d'Oreste	*Ténor*
Thoas, Roi de la Tauride	*Basse élevé*
Diane	*Soprano*
Ministre de Thoas	*Basse*
Un Scythe	*Basse*
Une Femme Grecque	*Soprano*

Prêtresses, Scythes, Gardes de Thoas, Euménides et Démons,
Grecs de la suite de Pylade

INDICE

ACTE I

ACTE II

ACTE III

ACTE IV

PERSONEN

Iphigenie, Oberpriesterin der Diana	*Sopran*
Orest, Bruder der Iphigenie	*Hoher Bass*
Pylades, griechischer Prinz, Freund des Orest	*Tenor*
Thoas, König von Tauris	*Hoher Bass*
Diana	*Sopran*
Ein Aufseher des Thoas	*Bass*
Ein Scythe	*Bass*
Eine Griechin	*Sopran*

Priesterinnen, Scythen, Leibwache des Thoas, Eumeniden und Dämonen,
Griechen im Gefolge des Pylades

INDEX

AKT I

AKT II

AKT III

AKT IV

Iphigénie en Tauride   Iphigenie auf Tauris

ACTE I.

Le Théâtre représente, dans le fond, l'entrée du Temple de Diane; sur le devant, le Bois Sacré qui le précède et l'entoure.
Im Hintergrunde der Bühne die Vorhalle zu dem Tempel der Diana; im Vordergrunde der heilige Hain, welcher denselben umgiebt.

SCENE I.

Iphigénie, Prêtresses.
Iphigenie, Priesterinnen.

Nº 1. Introduction und Chor.

Christoph Willibald Gluck
(1714 - 1787)

Fl.
Ob.
Cor.
Tr.
Vl. I
Vl. II
Vle
B.
a 2.
p
Allegro moderato.
Timp.
sf
Tempête de loin.
Gewitter von ferne.

a 2.
Ob.
Cor.
Timp.
Vl. I
Vl. II
Vle
B.
Tempête un peu plus rapprochée.
Gewitter etwas näher.
cresc.
Fl.
Cl.
Fg.
Tr.
divisi
Tempête très fort.
Gewitter sehr stark.

Fl.
Ob.
Cl.
Fg.
Cor.
Tr.
Timp.
Vl. I
Vl. II
Vle
B.
a 2.
a 2.
f
p

Fl.
Ob.
Cl.
Fg.
Cor.
Tr.
Timp.
Vl. I
Vl. II
Vle
B.
Fl.
Ob.
Cl.
Fg.
Cor.
Tr.
Timp.
Vl. I
Vl. II
Vle
B.
a 2.
a 2.

Fl. picc.
Fl.
Ob.
Cl.
Fg.
Cor.
Tr.
Vl. I
Vl. II
Vle
B.

Fl. picc.
Fl.
Ob.
a 2.
Cl.
Fg.
Cor.
Tr.
Vl. I
Vl. II
Vle
Iphigenie.
Iph.
Grands Dieux! soyez-nous secou-
All - mächti-ge, des Fre - vels
B.
La Tempête cesse.
Das Gewitter lässt nach.
ra - bles, détour - nez vos fou - dres vengeurs; ton - nez sur les tê - tes coupa - bles, l'in - no-
Rä - cher! Ent - flammt der Blitz sich uns al - lein? Er töd - te strafend den Verbre - cher, doch

Fl.
Ob.
Cl.
Fg.
Cor.
Tr.
Vl. I
Vl. II
Vle
Iph.
cen-ce ha - bi - te en nos cœurs, l'in-no - cen - ce ha - bi-te en nos cœurs.
Unschuld lasst verschonet sein, doch Unschuld lasst verscho - net sein!
B.
Prêtresses · Priesterinnen
Coro
(Pr.)
Grands Dieux! soyez-nous secou - ra - bles, détour - nez vos fou - -dres vengeurs; ton -
All - mäch-tige, des Fre - vels Rä - cher! Ent - flammt der Blitz sich uns al-lein? Er

Fl.
Ob.
Cl.
Fg.
Cor.
Tr.
Vl. I
Vl. II
Vle
Coro
(Pr.)
B.
a 2.
nez sur les tê - tes coupa - bles, l'in-no - cen-ce ha-bi- - te en nos coeurs, l'in-no - cen- - ce ha - bi-te en nos
töd - te strafend den Verbre - cher, doch Unschuld lasst verschonet sein, doch Unschuld lasst verscho- - net
sempre cresc.
coeurs.
sein!
Tempête.
Gewitter.

Fl. picc.
Fl.
Ob.
Cl.
Fg.
Cor.
Tr.
Vl. I
Vl. II
Vle
Iph.
B.

a 2.

Iphigenie.

Si ces bords cru - els et si - nis - tres sont l'ob-
Seid ihr dem schrecklichen Gesta - de zu heissem

La Tempête cesse.
Das Gewitter lässt nach.

Fl.
Ob.
Cl.
Fg.
Cor.
Tr.
Vl. I
Vl. II
Vle
Iph.
B.
f p ff
a 2.
jet de vo-tre cour-roux, dai-gnez à vos fai-bles mi-nis-tres of-frir des a-
Feu-er-zorn ent-brannt, so leit' uns wal-tend eu-re Gna-de nun end-lich
si-les plus doux, of-frir des a-si-les plus doux.
in ein mil-des Land, nun endlich in ein mil-des Land.

Fl.
Ob.
Cl.
Fg.
Cor.
Tr.
Vl. I
Vl. II
Vle
Coro
(Pr.)
B.
a 2.
Grands Dieux! soyez-nous secou - ra - bles, détour-nez vos fou- - dres vengeurs; ton-
All- -mäch-tige, des Fre - vels Rä - cher! Ent - flammt der Blitz sich uns al - lein? Er
nez sur les tê- -tes cou-pa - bles, l'in-no - cen-ce ha - bi - te en nos cœurs, l'inno - cen- - ce ha - bi-te en nos
töd - te strafend den Ver-bre - cher, doch Unschuld lasst verschonet sein, doch Unschuld lasst verscho - net

Fl. picc.
Fl.
Ob.
Cl.
Fg.
Cor.
Tr.
Vl. I
Vl. II
Vle
Coro
(Pr.)
B.
a 2.
cœurs.
sein!
Tempête.
Gewitter.
sempre cresc.

Fl.
Ob.
Cl.
Fg.
Cor.
Tr.
Vl. I
Vl. II
Vle
B.

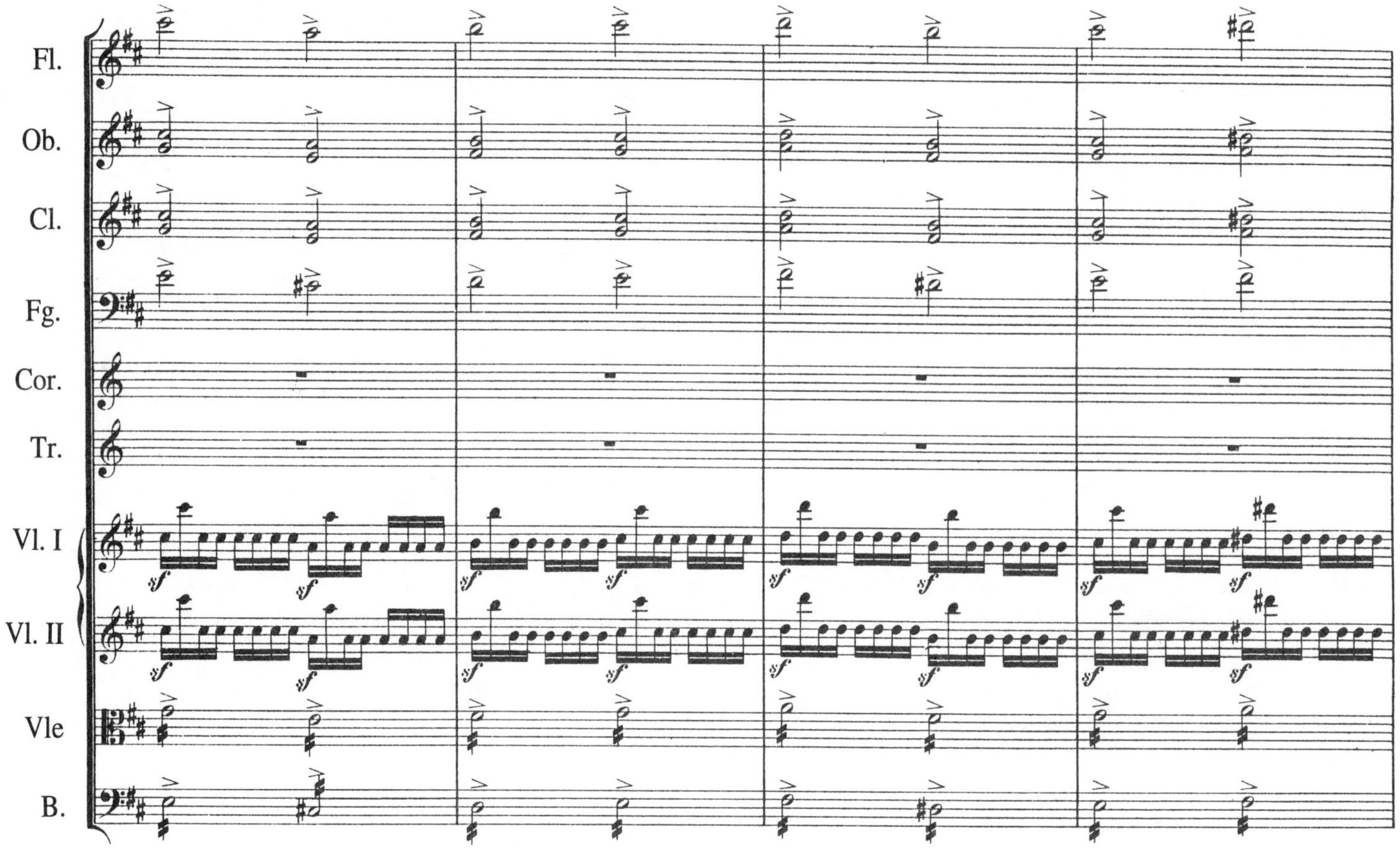

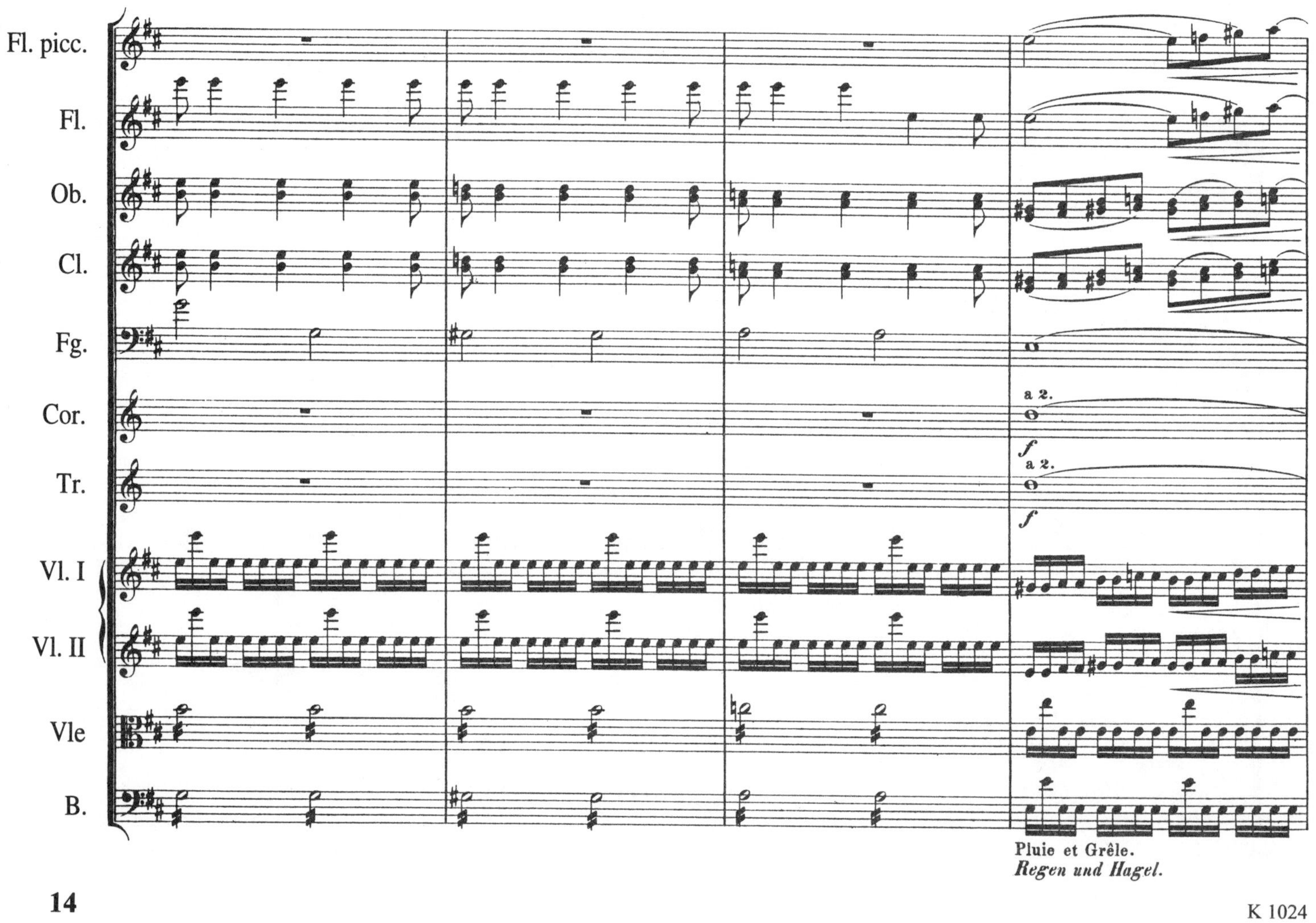

Fl. picc.
Fl.
Ob.
Cl.
Fg.
Cor.
a 2.
Tr.
a 2.
Vl. I
Vl. II
Vle
B.
Pluie et Grêle.
Regen und Hagel.

Fl. picc.

Fl.

Ob.

a 2.

Cl.

Fg.

Cor.

Tr.

Vl. I

Vl. II

Vle

Iphigenie.

Iph.

Que nos mains, saintement bar - ba - res, n'ensan-

Lasst weiter nicht__ die rei - nen Hän - de mit

B.

La Tempête cesse.

Das Gewitter lässt nach.

Fl.
Ob.
Cl.
Fg.
Cor.
Tr.
Vl. I
Vl. II
Vle
Iph.
glan-tent plus vos au-tels! Rendez ces peu-ples plus a - va-res du sang des malheu-
Blut der Brü-der uns ent-weih'n! Ach, dieses Vol-kes Wild-heit en - de! Ihr Göt-ter, lehrt es
B.
Fl.
Ob.
a 2
Cl.
Fg.
Cor.
Tr.
Vl. I
Vl. II
Vle
Iph.
reux mor-tels, du sang des mal-heu - reux mor-tels!
mensch-lich sein, ihr Göt-ter, lehrt es mensch - lich sein!
B.
Tempête.
Gewitter.

Fl.
Ob.
Cl.
Fg.
Cor.
Tr.
Vl. I
Vl. II
Vle
Coro
(Pr.)
B.
Grands Dieux! soyez-nous secou-ra-bles, détour-nez vos fou-dres vengeurs; ton-
All-mäch-tige, des Fre-vels Rä-cher! Ent-flammt der Blitz sich uns al-lein? Er
La Tempête cesse tout à fait.
Das Gewitter verschwindet gänzlich.
nez sur les tê-tes cou-pa-bles, l'in-no-cen-ce ha-bi-te en nos coeurs, l'in-no-cen-ce ha-bi-te en nos
töd-te stra-fend den Verbre-cher, doch Unschuld lasst verschonet sein, doch Unschuld lasst ver-scho-net

Fl.
Ob.
Cl.
Fg.
Cor.
Tr.
Vl. I
Vl. II
Vle
Coro
(Pr.)
B.
sempre diminuendo
p
smorzando
coeurs.
scin!
Timpani coperti
Timp.
p assai

Fl.
Ob.
Cl.
Fg.
Cor.
Tr.
Timp.
Vl. I
Vl. II
Vle
Iphigenie.
Iph.
Ces Dieux que no-tre voix im-plo- - -re,
Ja seht! Sie bli-cken huld-reich nie- - -der,
B.
a 2.
a-pai-sent en-fin leur ri-gueur:
nun schweigt ihr schrecken-vol-les Droh'n.
Le
Die

Fl.
Ob.
Cl.
Fg.
Cor.
Tr.
Vl. I
Vl. II
Vle
Recitativo.
Iph.
calme re-pa-raît. Le calme re-paraît, mais au fond de mon coeur, hé-las! l'o-ra- -ge habi-te enco-re!
Ruhe kehrt zu-rück. Die Ruhe kehrt zurück, doch mir__ bleibt sie ent-floh'n, und ach! ach! mir kehrt sie niemals wieder!
B.
1ère Prêtresse · 1. Priesterin
2ème Pr. · 2. Pr.
Iphigenie.
Pr.
Iphi-gé-nie, ô ciel! craindrait-el-le un malheur? D'où naît le trouble affreux dont vo- -tre â-me est saisi-e? Ju- -ste
Ihr Götter! Fürchtet I-phi-ge-nia ein Unglück? Wo-her das grau-se Schrecken, das deine See-le so ergreift? Ach, welch ein
1ère Pr. · 1. Pr.
ciel! Ah, parlez! di- -vi-ne Iphi-gé-ni-e, nos malheurs sont communs; loin de no-tre pa-tri-e, con-
Traum! Entdecke dich, erhab'ne Tochter A-gamemnons! Wir lei-den ja mit dir, dem Va-terland ent-fernt; ver-

Vl. I
Vl. II
Vle
Pr.
B.
pp
duites avec vous sur ce funeste bord, n'avons-nous pas toujours partagé votre sort?
schlagen, so wie du, an diese rauhe Küste, ertrugen wir nicht stets mit dir ein gleiches Loos?
Iphigenie.
Iph.
Cette nuit... j'ai revu le palais de mon père; j'allais jouir de ses embrassements.
Ich sah in dieser Nacht die Burg der Ahnen wieder; ich fühlt' im Traume schon des Vaters Segens-Kuss.
tremolo
f
p
J'oubliais, en ces doux moments, ses anciennes rigueurs, et quinze ans de misère... La
Vergessen waren in diesem süssen Augenblick sein strenger Zorn, und fünfzehn Jahre voller Elend. Die
Andante.
mf
cresc.
terre tremble sous mes pas; le soleil indigné fuit ces lieux qu'il abhorre; le feu brille dans
Erd' erbebet unter mir; die Sonne flieht erzürnt aus der verhassten Gegend; vom Feuer flammt die

Vl. I
Vl. II
Vle
Iph.
l'air, et la fou - - dre en é - clats tom - be sur le pa -
Luft, und furcht - bar stürzt ein Blitz her - ab auf den Pa -
B.
ff
Presto.
lais, l'em - bra - - se et le dé - vo - re.
last, ent - zün - - det ihn... er ist ver-nich-tet!
Lento.
Ob.
Cl.
Du mi-lieu des dé-bris fu-mants sort u-ne voix plain-ti-ve et ten - dre: jusqu'au
Aus der Mit - te der Trümmer naht mei - nem Ohr ein Ton des Jam - mers, durch-
p

Presto.
Ob.
Cl.
Vl. I
Vl. II
Vle
Iph.
B.
fond de mon cœur el-le se fait enten - dre. Je vo-le à ces tris - tes ac-cents: à mes yeux aussi -
dringt mein Herz, und tief wird es erschüt-tert. Ich ei-le hin, wo diese Stimme klagt: vor meinen Au - gen
tôt se pré-sen-te mon pè - re, sanglant, per-cé de coups, et d'un spec-tre in-humain
steht mein er-ha-be-ner Va - ter, mit Blut bedeckt, durchbohrt von Wunden. Er fliehet schnell und weit
fuyant la ra-ge meur-tri - è - re. Ce spectre af-freux... c'é-tait ma mè - re! El-le
vor ei-ner mör-de - ri-schen Fu-ri-e. Und die - se Fu-ri-e war mei-ne Mut - ter! Sie
tremolo

Ob.
Cl.
Vl. I
Vl. II
Vle
Iph.
B.
m'ar- -me d'un glai - ve, et dis - pa - raît soudain... Je veux fuir... On me crie: Ar-rê - -
reicht mir ei - nen Dolch, und dann verschwindet plötzlich sie. Ich will entflieh'n... Man ruft mir zu: Verweil'!
te! C'est O - res - - te: Je vois un mal - heu - reux, et je lui tends la main, je veux le se - cou -
Es ist O - rest: Er war es, wild und bleich; ich reich' ihm mei - ne Hand, ich will sein Lei - den
rir; un as - cen - dant fu - nes - - te for - çait mon bras à lui per - cer le sein.
mil - dern; un - wi - der - steh - lich treibt mich ei - ne höh' - re Macht, das Herz ihm zu durch - boh - ren.
Elle tombe sur l'autel.
Sie sinkt auf dem Altare nieder.

Nº 2. Chor.

Lento.
2 Oboi
2 Clarinetti in Do
2 Fagotti
Violini I
Violini II
Viole
Coro
(Prêtresses)
(Priesterinnen)
Soprano I.
Ô songe af-freux! nuit ef-froy - a-ble! Ô dou - leur! ô mor - tel ef - froi! Ton cour-
Soprano II.
O wel-che Nacht! Was droht uns Ar-men! Welch' banges Grau'n, o welch' Traumge - sicht! Gro - sse
Bassi
Ob.
Cl.
Fg.
Vl. I
Vl. II
Vle
Coro
(Pr.)
roux est - il im-pla - ca-ble? En-tends nos cris, ô ciel! a - pai - se - toi, ô ciel! a - pai - se - toi!
Göt - ter, schenkt uns Er - bar-men! Er-hört dies Fleh'n, und zür - net län - ger nicht, und zür - net län - ger nicht!
B.

Violini I
Violini II
Viole
Recitativo.
Iphigenie
Bassi
Ô ra-ce de Pé-lops! ra-ce toujours fa - ta - le! Jus - - que dans ses der-niers neveux le
Ach, ar-me Pe-lo - pi-den! du unglück-se- - li-ges Ge-schlecht! Bis zu der En-kel fern-sten hin straft
Vl. I
Vl. II
Vle
Iph.
B.
ciel poursuit en-co-re le cri-me de Tan-ta-le! Le Roi des Rois, le sang des Dieux, A-gamem-non des-
Tan-ta-lus, den Frevler, des Him-mels Zürnen noch! Der Fürsten Erster, vom Stamm der Götter, A- - -ga-memnon sinkt
cend dans la nuit in-fer- -na- -le. Son fils res-tait à ma dou-leur, j'at-ten-dais de lui
hin zur Nacht des Gra- -bes. Sein Sohn blieb mei-ner Hoff-nung noch: Er, sagt' ich trö-stend
seul la fin de ma mi- sè- -re. Ô mon cher O- -res - te! ô mon frè - re! Tu ne sé-che-ras
mir, wird dei-ne Lei-den en-den. Ge-lieb-te-ster O- -rest! mein theu - rer Bru-der! Du trocknest nim- -mer
p
f

Vl. I
Vl. II
Vle
Iph.
B.
2ème Pr.
2. Pr.
pas les lar-mes de ta soeur! Calmez ce dés-es-poir où vo-tre â-me est li-vré-e; les Dieux conser-ve-
nun der Schwester Thränen ab! Gebeut dem bangen Schmerz, der dei-ne Brust er-greift; ge-wiss, der Göt-ter
Pr.
Iphigenie.
ront cet-te tê-te sa-cré-e; o-sez tout es-pé-rer! Non, je n'es-pè-re
Huld beschützt sein theu-res Le-ben; drum ver-trau' ih-rer Macht! Nein, län-ger hoff' ich
plus! De-puis que je res-pi-re, en but-te à leur co-lè-re, d'op-pro-bre et de mal-
nicht! So lang' ich ath-me, hat ihr Zorn mich stets ver-folgt; mein Le-ben ist der
heurs tous mes jours sont tis-sus; ils y met-tent le com-ble: ils m'en-lè-vent mon frè-re!
Schmach, dem Unglück dar-ge-bracht; nun fül-let sich das Maass: geraubt wird mir mein Bru-der!

Nº 3. Arie.

Moderato, con espressione.
2 Oboi
Violini I
Violini II
Viole
Iphigenie
Bassi
Ô toi qui pro-lon-geas mes
O du, die mir einst Hül-fe
Ob.
Vl. I
Vl. II
Vle
Iph.
B.
jours, reprends un bien que je dé-tes-te! Di-a-ne, je t'im-plo-re, je t'im-plo-re, arrê-tes-en le
gab, nimm dies Ge-schenk, o nimm es wieder! Di-a-na, zu dir fleh' ich, lass sin-ken mich in's
cours! je t'im-plo-re, ar-rê-tes-en le cours!
Grab! zu dir fleh' ich, lass sin-ken mich in's Grab!

Ob.
Vl. I
Vl. II
Vle
Iph.
B.
Rejoins I-phi-gé - ni - e, re-joins I-phi-gé - ni - e au mal-heureux O - res - te, hé -
Gieb jen-seits dieses Grabes, gieb jen-seits dieses Grabes mich meinem Bruder wie - der! Weh'
las! tout m'en fait u-ne loi! La mort me de-vient néces-sai - re; j'ai
mir, der Tod nur ret - tet mich! Sonst hoff'ich kei - nen an - dern Ret - ter; denn wider
vu s'é-le-ver contre moi les Dieux, ma pa-trie et mon pè - - re.
mich em-pör - ten sich mein Volk, mein Va - ter und die Göt - - ter!

Ob.
Vl. I
Vl. II
Vle
Iph.
B.
Ô toi qui pro-lon-geas mes jours, reprends un bien que je dé-tes-te! Di-
O du, die mir einst Hül-fe gab, nimm dies Ge-schenk, o nimm es wie-der! Di-
a-ne, je t'im-plo-re, je t'im-plo-re, ar-rê-tes-en le cours! je t'im-
a-na, zu dir fleh' ich, lass sin-ken mich in's Grab! zu dir
plo-re, ar-rê-tes-en le cours!
fleh' ich, lass sin-ken mich in's Grab!
sf
p
f

Nº 4. Chor.

Largo.
2 Oboi
2 Clarinetti in Do
2 Fagotti
Violini I
Violini II
Viole
Coro
(Prêtresses)
(Priesterinnen)
Bassi
Soprano I.
Quand verrons-nous ta - rir nos pleurs? La sour-ce en est - el - le in-fi - ni - - e?
Soprano II.
Wann trocknen un - sre Thrä-nen ab? Drückt Lei - den denn e - wig un-ser Le - - ben?
Ob.
Cl.
Fg.
Vl. I
Vl. II
Vle
Coro
(Pr.)
B.
Ah, dans un cer - cle de dou - leurs le ciel mar - qua le cours de no - tre vi - - e!
Ach, soll al - lein das stil - le Grab die lang' ent - floh'- ne Ruh' uns wie-der - ge - - ben?

SCÈNE II.

Iphigénie, Prêtresses, Thoas, Gardes.

Iphigenie, Priesterinnen, Thoas, Wache.

Thoas s'arrête et paraît effrayé des cris de douleur des Prêtresses.

Thoas bleibt, bestürzt von dem Wehklagen der Priesterinnen, stehen.

Vl. I
Vl. II
Vle
Iph.
B.
Thoas.
Iphigenie.
ciel est sourd, hé-las! Eh! ce n'est pas des pleurs, c'est du sang qu'il deman-de. Quelle ef-froy-able offran-de! A-
Jungfrau hei-ssem Fleh'n! Thränen nicht wol-len sie, nur Blut kann sie versöh-nen. O welch' ein grauses O-pfer! Ver-
pai-se-t-on les Dieux par des as-sas-si-nats? Le ciel par d'é-cla-tants mi-ra-cles
söhnt die Göt-ter Blut, ver-söhnt sie Mord-be-gier? Der Him-mel, er liess durch ein Zei-chen
Th.
a dai-gné s'ex-pli-quer à vous: Mes jours sont me-na-cés par la voix des O-
mich in die Nacht der Zu-kunft seh'n: Be-dro-het wird mein Le-ben durch un-srer Göt-ter
ra-cles, si d'un seul é-tran-ger, re-lé-gué par-mi nous, le sang é-chappe à leur courroux.
Spruch, wenn von den Frem-den al-len, die unsrer Kü-ste nah'n, nur Ei-ner ih-rem Zorn entrinnt.

Nº 5. Arie.

Andante.

2 Oboi
2 Fagotti
2 Corni in Re
Violini I
Violini II
Viole
Thoas
Bassi

a 2.

De noirs pres-senti-ments mon âme in-ti-mi-dé-e, de si-nis-tres ter-reurs est sans
Der Ahnung bange Furcht, das Grau'n der Zukunft wecken in meinem Her-zen Angst und

Ob.
Fg.
Cor.
Vl. I
Vl. II
Vle
Th.
B.

Fag. I.

ces-se obsé-dé-e; le jour bles-se mes yeux et sem-ble s'ob-scur-cir, j'é
nie gefühl-te Schrecken; für mich glänzt nie ein Tag, rings um mich ist nur Tod: ich

Ob.
Fg.
Cor.
Vl. I
Vl. II
Vle
Th.
B.

a 2.

prou-ve l'ef-froi des cou-pa-bles; je crois voir sous mes pas la ter-re s'entr'ouvrir, et l'en-fer
muss die Qual der Höll' em-pfin-den! Schon seh' ich dort das Grab! Wie furchtbar es mir droht! Schon öff-net

Ob.
Fg.
Cor.
Vl. I
Vl. II
Vle
Th.
B.
prêt à m'englou-tir dans ses a-bî-mes ef-froy-a- bles, dans ses a-bî-mes ef-froy-
sich's! Seht, wie es winkt! Schon fasst es mich mit off'nen Schlün - den, schon fasst es mich mit off'-nen
ff
a - bles.
Schlünden!
Je ne sais quelle voix crie au fond de mon cœur:
O welch'ein ban - ger Ruf mir durch die See - le dringt: Er-
p
Lento.
Tempo I.
a 2.
Trem-ble, ton sup-pli - ce s'ap-prê - te! La nuit de ces tourments re-double encor l'hor-reur, et les
be - be den ge-rech - ten Göt-tern! Ver-mehrt wird von der Nacht die grau-en-vol - le Pein! Dann dringen
f

Ob.
Fg.
Cor.
Vl. I
Vl. II
Vle
Th.
B.
fou-dres d'un Dieu ven - geur semblent sus-pen-dus sur ma tê - te, sem-blent sus-pen-
Gei-ster auf mich ein, und Bli-tze sind be-reit mich zu zer-schmet-tern, Bli - tze sind be-
dus sur ma tê - - te! Et les fou-dres d'un Dieu ven - geur semblent sus-pen-dus sur ma
reit mich zu zerschmet - - tern! Dann drin-gen Gei-ster auf mich ein, und Bli - tze sind be-reit mich zu zer-
tê - te, semblent sus-pen-dus sur ma tê - te!
schmettern, Bli - tze sind be - reit mich zu zer-schmet-tern!

SCENE III.

Les Acteurs précédents, Scythes entrant en foule.

Die Vorigen, Scythen in Menge auftretend.

Fl. picc.
Ob. e Cl.
Fg.
Tamb.
Ptti
Vl. I
Vl. II
Vle
Coro (Sc.)
B.

a 2 — tr

mes; les Dieux a - pai - sent leur courroux, ils nous a - mènent des vic - ti - - mes: à ces

den; be - sänf - tigt ist der Göt - - ter Wuth, da sie uns selbst das O-pfer sen - - den: ver -

mes; les Dieux a - pai - sent leur courroux, ils nous a - mènent des vic - ti - - mes: à ces

Fl. picc.
Ob. e Cl.
Fg.
Tamb.
Ptti
Vl. I
Vl. II
Vle
Coro (Sc.)
B.

tr — a 2.

jus - tes ven-geurs des cri - - mes, que leur sang soit of - fert pour nous, que leur sang soit of - fert pour nous!

spritzt mit heil'- gen Hän - - den, ver-spritzt sei beider Frem-den Blut, ja, verspritzt sei beider Frem-den Blut!

jus - tes ven-geurs des cri - - mes, que leur sang soit of - fert pour nous, que leur sang soit of - fert pour nous!

Violini I
Violini II
Viole
Iphigenie
Thoas
Scythe
Bassi
Recitativo. Thoas.
Iph. à part. bei Seite.
Malheu-reuse! Grands Dieux, re-ce-vez nos offrandes! Moins je les espérais, plus vos faveurs sont grandes.
Ich zitt're! Ihr Götter, nehmt das Opfer gnädig an! Wie gross ist eure Huld, und o wie un-verhofft!
Vl. I
Vl. II
Vle
Un Scythe
Ein Scythe
Sc.
B.
Deux jeunes Grecs, é-chou-és sur ces bords, ont longtemps contre nous ten-té de se dé-fendre; ils viennent en-fin de se
Zwei junge Griechen, die der Sturm ver-schlug, ver-theidigten sich lang' und tapfer gegen uns; doch dann sank ih-re
ren-dre a-près de pé-ni-bles ef-forts. L'un d'eux é-tait rem-pli d'un dés-espoir fa-rou-che: les mots de
Kraft nach ei-nem schwe-ren Kampf. Den ei-nen quäl-te wild die schreck-lich-ste Ver-zweiflung: Er sprach ohn'
cri-me, de remord, étaient sans cesse dans sa bou-che: il détestait la vi-e, il ap-pelait la mort.
Un-terlass von Greuelthat, von wilder Qual der Fu-rien: er fluchte seinem Leben und wünsch-te sich den Tod.

Allegro.
Fl. picc.
a 2.
Ob. e Cl.
a 2.
Fg.
Tamb.
Ptti
Allegro.
Vl. I
f staccato
Vl. II
f staccato
Vle
Coro (Sc.)
Les Dieux a - pai - sent leur cour - roux, ils nous a - mènent des vic - ti - mes:
Be - sänf - tigt ist der Göt - ter Wuth, da sie uns selbst das O-pfer sen - den: ver-
Les Dieux a - pai - sent leur cour - roux, ils nous a - mènent des vic - ti - mes:
B.
Fl. picc.
Ob. e Cl.
Fg.
Tamb.
Ptti
Vl. I
Vl. II
Vle
Coro (Sc.)
que leur sang soit of - fert pour nous à ces jus - tes ven - geurs des cri - mes. Les
spritzt sei bei - der Frem - den Blut, verspritzt mit heil' - gen Hän - den. Be
que leur sang soit of - fert pour nous à ces jus - tes ven - geurs des cri - mes. Les
B.

Fl. picc.
Ob. e Cl.
Fg.
Tamb.
Ptti
Vl. I
Vl. II
Vle
Coro
(Sc.)
B.
a 2.
Dieux a - pai - sent leur cour-roux, ils nous a - mènent des vic - ti - mes: à ces jus - tes ven -
sänf - tigt ist der Göt - ter Wuth, da sie uns selbst das Opfer sen - den: ver-spritzt mit
Dieux a - pai - sent leur cour-roux, ils nous a - mènent des vic - ti - mes: à ces jus - tes ven -
geurs des cri - mes, que leur sang soit of - fert pour nous, que leur sang soit of - fert pour nous!
heil'- gen Hän - den, verspritzt sei bei-der Frem - den Blut, ja, verspritzt sei beider Frem-den Blut!
geurs des cri - mes, que leur sang soit of - fert pour nous, que leur sang soit of - fert pour nous!

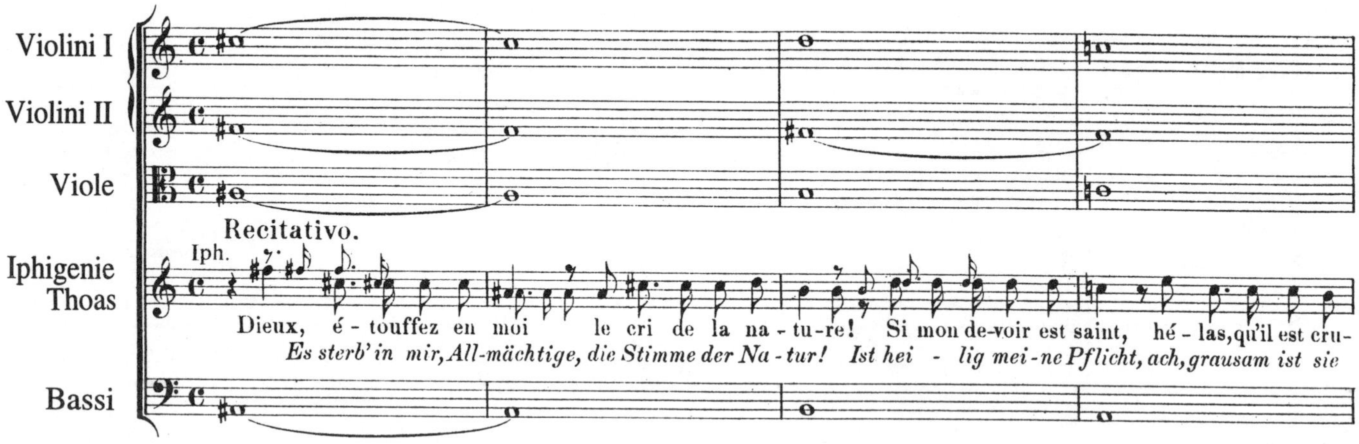

Violini I
Violini II
Viole
Iphigenie
Thoas
Bassi
Recitativo.
Iph.
Dieux, é - touffez en moi le cri de la na - tu-re! Si mon de-voir est saint, hé - las, qu'il est cru-
Es sterb' in mir, All-mächtige, die Stimme der Na - tur! Ist hei - lig mei-ne Pflicht, ach, grausam ist sie

Vl. I
Vl. II
Vle
Iph.
B.
Thoas. à Iphigénie. zu Iphigenie.
el! Al - lez; et les cap - tifs vont vous sui - vre à l'au-tel. Pour moi, qu'un trop si - nis-tre au-
auch! Geht nun; euch fol-gen bald die O-pfer zum Al - tar. Doch ich, dem grau - en-vol - le

Vl. I
Vl. II
Vle
Th.
B.
gu - re me-na-ce du cour-roux des Dieux, ma pré-sen - ce pour-rait nui-re à vos saints mys - tè - res.
Zei - chen mit al-ler Göt - ter Ra - che droh'n, ich will nicht durch mei - ne Nä - he das O - pfer stö - ren.

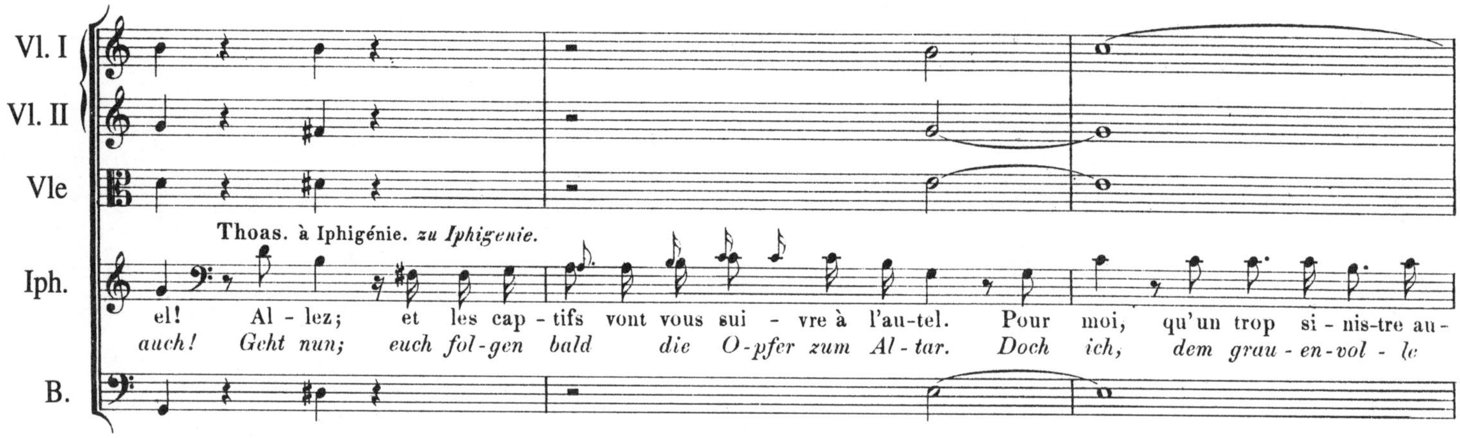

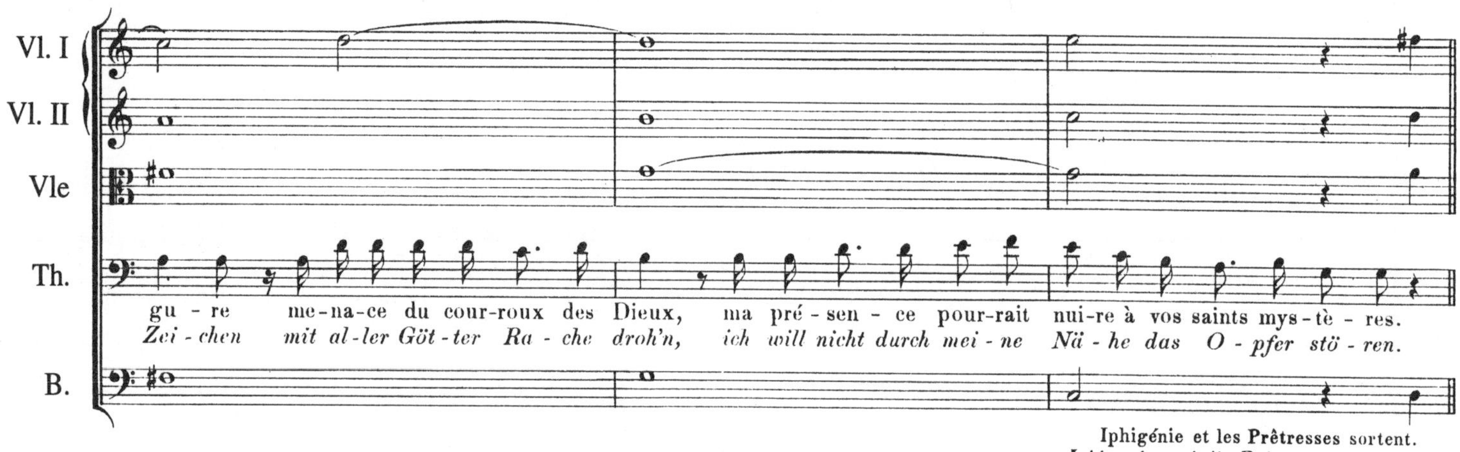

Iphigénie et les Prêtresses sortent.
Iphigenie und die Priesterinnen gehen ab.

SCÈNE IV.

Thoas, Scythes, Gardes.
Thoas, Scythen, Wache.

in tempo.
Vl. I
Vl. II
Vle
Th.
B.
au Peuple. zum Volk.
Et vous, à nos Dieux tu-té - lai - res adressez vos chants bel-liqueux! Que vos jus - tes transports pé-nètrent jusqu'aux cieux!
Den Göttern, die uns schützen, stimmt ihr indess ein Lied des Sieges an! Zum Himmel stei-ge laut der Lobge-sang em - por!

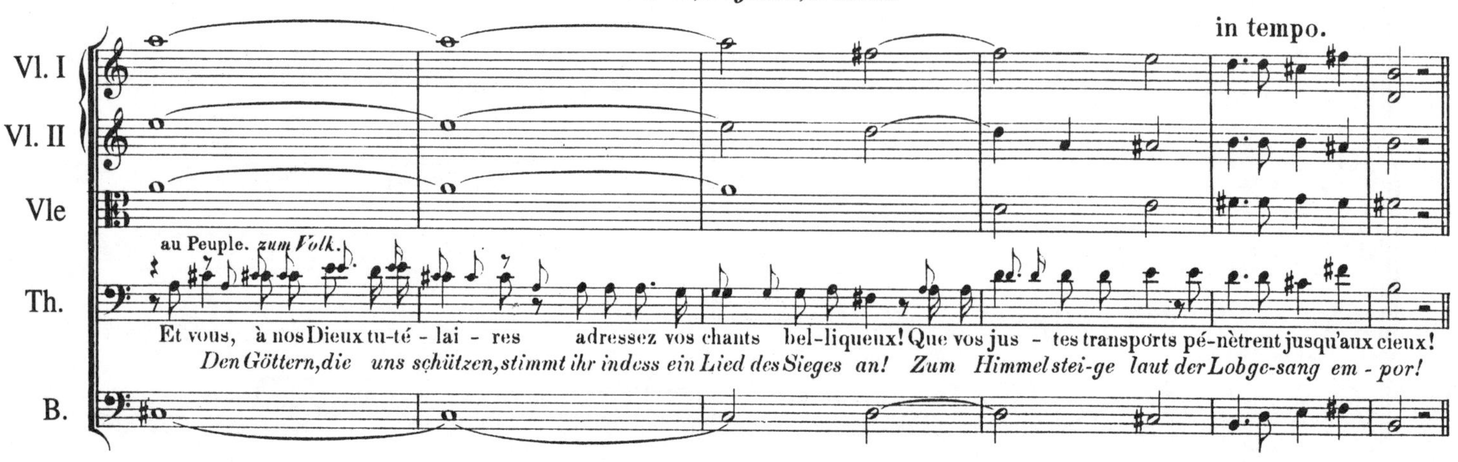

Nº 7. Chor.
Allegro.
2 Flauti piccoli
2 Oboi, e 2 Clarinetti in Do
2 Fagotti
Triangolo e Tamburo
Piatti
Violini I
Violini II
Viole
Coro (Scythes) (Scythen)
Bassi
ten.
Peuple exprimant sa joie barbare.
Volk im Ausbruch wilder Freude.
Tenore I.
Tenore II.
Basso.
Il nous fal-lait du sang pour ex-pi-er nos cri-mes; les cap - tifs sont aux fers,
Blut kann des Vol-kes Schuld, Blut kann allein sie bü-ssen. Schon sind die O - pfer da,
Fl. picc.
Ob. e Cl.
Fg.
Trg. e Tamb.
Ptti
Vl. I
Vl. II
Vle
Coro (Sc.)
B.
et les au-tels sont prêts. Les Dieux nous ont eux-mê-me a-me - né les vic - ti - mes: que la re-con-nais-
schon flammt der Fest-Al - tar. Lasst zu der Göt-ter Preis nun Blut in Strö-men flie-ssen: so herrlich sei der

Fl. picc.
Ob. e Cl.
Fg.
Trg. e Tamb.
Ptti
Vl. I
Vl. II
Vle
Coro (Sc.)
B.

a 2.

san - ce é - ga - le les bien-faits! Sous le cou-teau sa - cré que leur sang re-jail - lis - se!

Dank, wie ih - re Wohlthat war! Bald wird der heil'- ge Stahl nun Beider Herz durch - drin-gen!

san - ce é - ga - le les bien-faits! Sous le cou-teau sa - cré que leur sang re-jail - lis - se!

Fl. picc.
Ob. e Cl.
Fg.
Trg. e Tamb.
Ptti
Vl. I
Vl. II
Vle
Coro (Sc.)
B.

sf

a 2.

Que leur as-pect im - pur n'in - fec-te plus ces lieux! Of-frons leur sang en sa-cri - fi - ce:

Ja, die-ser Fremden Blut ver-söh-ne un-sre Schuld! Den Göt-tern wol-len wir es bringen:

Que leur as-pect im - pur n'in - fec-te plus ces lieux! Of-frons leur sang en sa-cri - fi - ce:

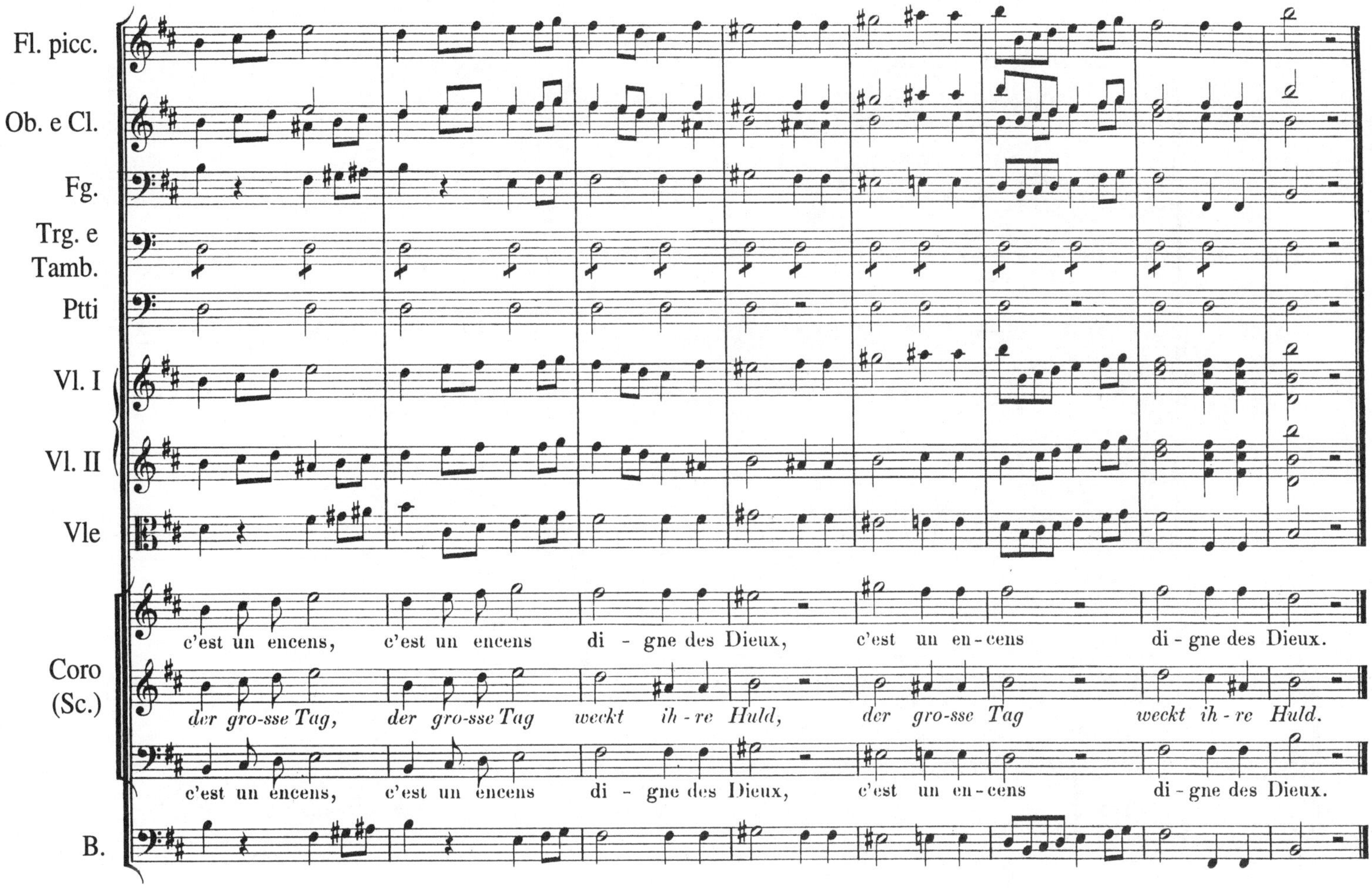

Fl. picc.
Ob. e Cl.
Fg.
Trg. e Tamb.
Ptti
Vl. I
Vl. II
Vle
Coro (Sc.)
c'est un encens, c'est un encens di - gne des Dieux, c'est un en-cens di-gne des Dieux.
der gro-sse Tag, der gro-sse Tag weckt ih-re Huld, der gro-sse Tag weckt ih-re Huld.
c'est un encens, c'est un encens di - gne des Dieux, c'est un en-cens di-gne des Dieux.
B.

№ 8. Ballet.

L'istesso tempo. (Un poco animato.)
a2
2 Fagotti
Violini I
marcato
Violini II
marcato
Viole
Bassi

Fg.
Vl. I
Vl. II
Vle
B.

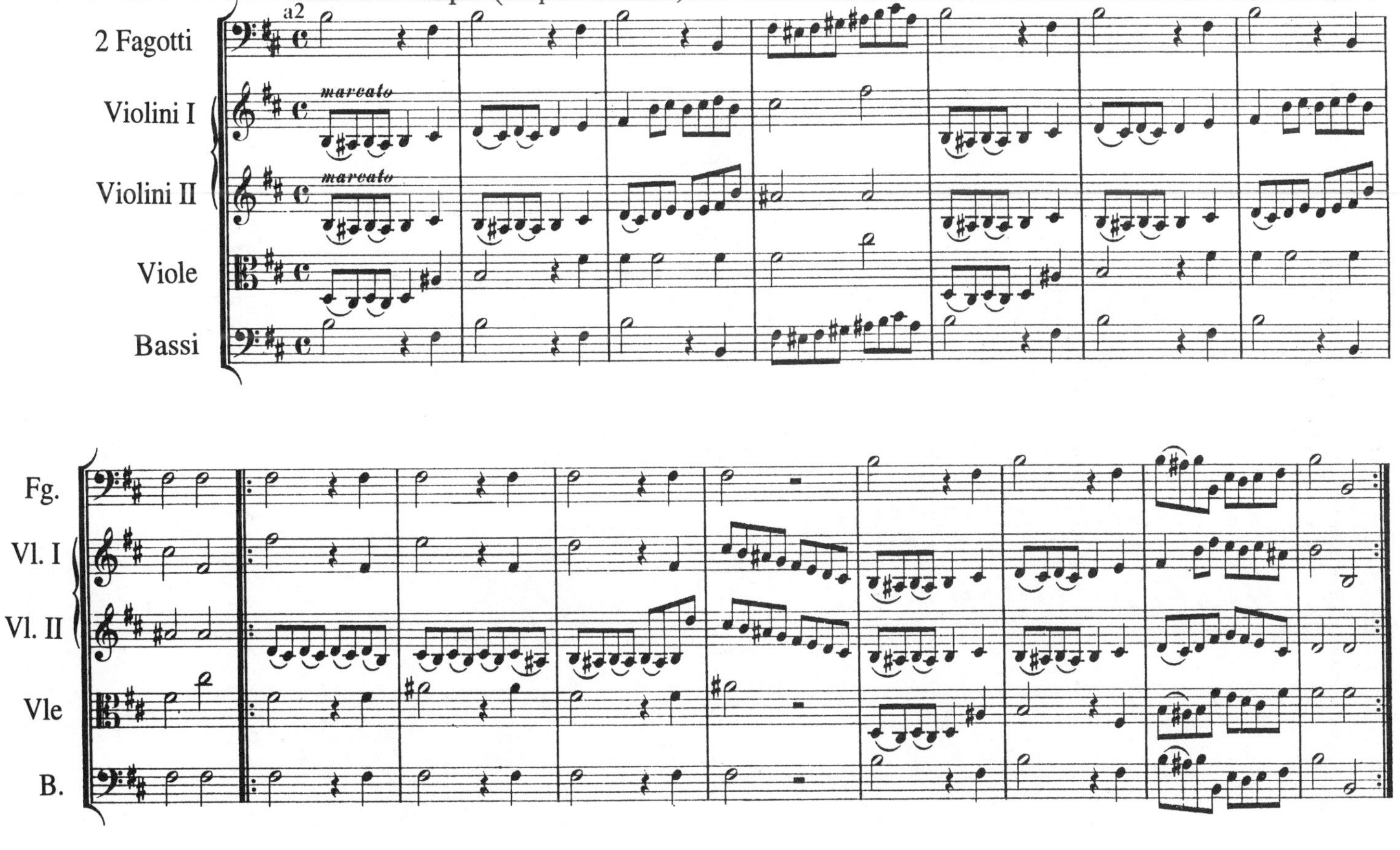

Nº 9. Ballet.

K 1024

Nº 10. Ballet, Scene und Chor.

L'istesso tempo.
2 Oboi
2 Fagotti
Violini I
Violini II
Viole
Bassi

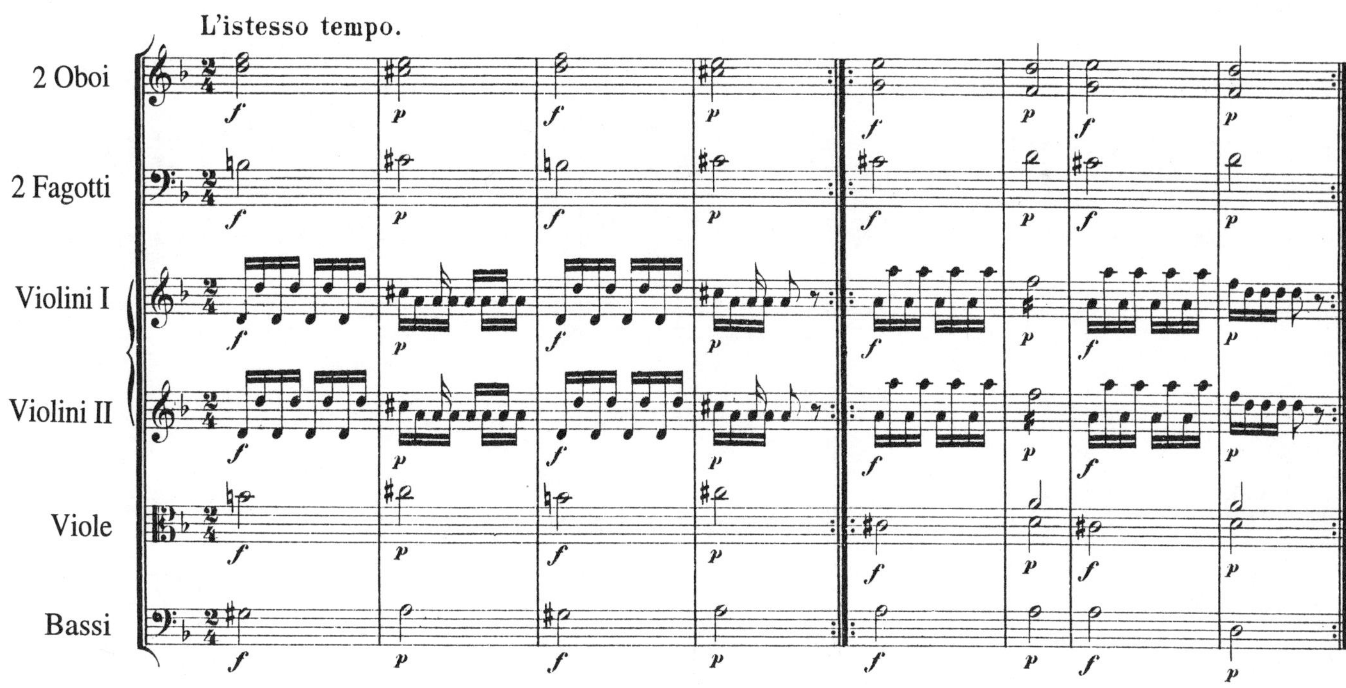

L'istesso tempo.
2 Flauti piccoli
2 Oboi
2 Fagotti
2 Corni in Re
Tamburino
Piatti
Violini I
Violini II
Viole
Bassi

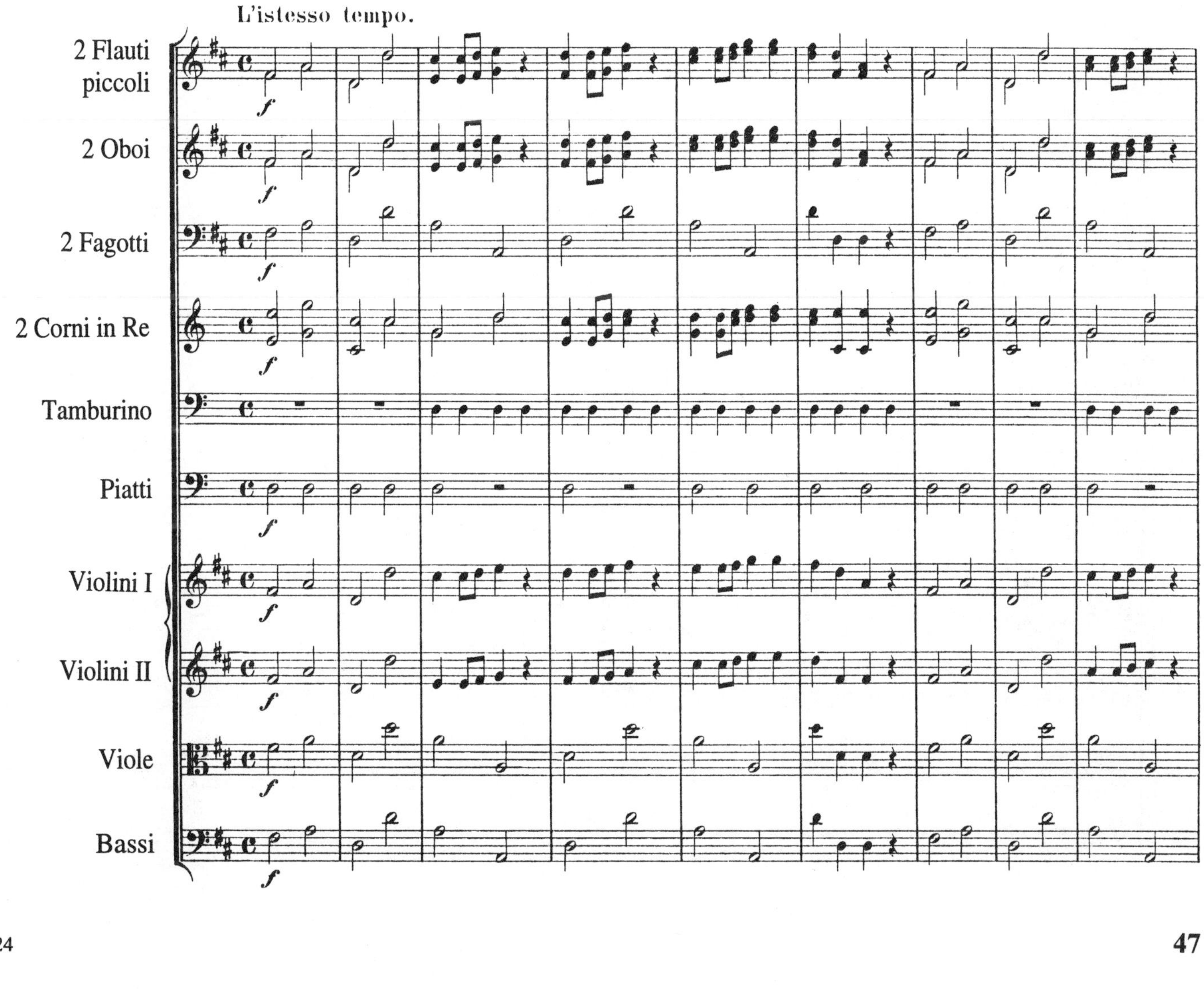

Fl. picc.
Ob.
Fg.
Cor.
Tamb.
Ptti
Vl. I
Vl. II
Vle
B.

Fl. picc.
Ob.
Fg.
Cor.
Tamb.
Ptti
Vl. I
Vl. II
Vle
B.

SCÈNE V.

Les Acteurs précédents; Oreste et Pylade, enchaînés.

Die Vorigen; Orest und Pylades, in Fesseln.

Oreste a les yeux fixés à terre et paraît accablé.

Orest schlägt schwermuthsvoll die Augen nieder.

Chor № 7. Da Capo. (Pag. 43.)

Fin de l'acte 1ère.

Ende des ersten Actes.

ACTE II.

Le Théâtre représente un Appartement intérieur du Temple destiné aux Victimes. Sur un des côtés est un Autel.
Innerer Raum des Tempels, für die Opfer bestimmt. Auf der einen Seite ein Altar.

SCÈNE I.

Oreste et Pylade, enchaînés.
Orest und Pylades, in Fesseln.
Oreste a les yeux baissés vers la terre et paraît comme abîmé dans sa douleur.
Orest schlägt die Augen nieder und scheint ganz in seinen Schmerz versunken.

Nº 11. Recitativ.

Ob.
Fg.
Vl. I
Vl. II
Vle
Pyl.
Orest.
la - de, et n'es-tu plus O - res-te? Dieux! à quel-les horreurs m'a-viez-vous ré-ser-vé? D'un a-
Py - lades, bist du nicht mehr O - rest? Göt-ter! Wel - chen Gräueln habt ihr mich aufgespart? Des
B.
Or.
veu - gle des-tin déplo - ra - ble vic - ti - me, par-tout er-rant et par-tout réprou-vé, mon
zür-nenden Ge-schick's be - kla-genswer-thes O - pfer, wo-hin ich ir-re, ver - worfen ü-ber-all, mein
Pylades.
sort est ac-com-pli. J'é - tais né pour le cri - me. Que dis - tu? Quel est ce re -
Schicksal ist er-füllt. Ich bin ge - bo - ren zum Ver-bre - chen. O - rest! Was quält von Neu-em
mord, quel nouveau crime en-fin? Je t'ai don-né la mort! Ce n'é-tait pas as-sez que ma
dich, und welche That hast du ge - than? Ich gab auch dir den Tod! Es war noch nicht genug, dass

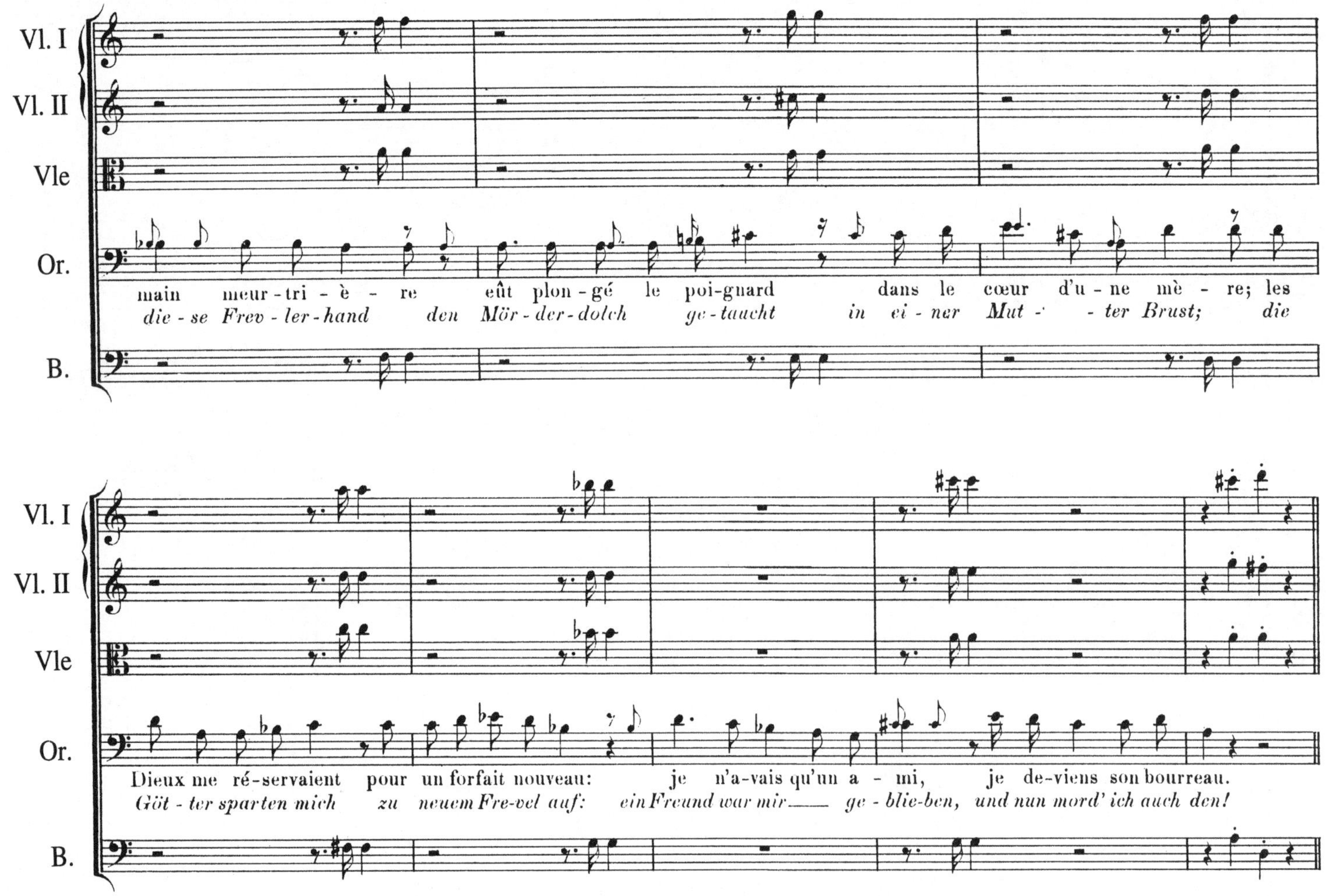

Vl. I
Vl. II
Vle
Or.
main meur-tri-è-re eût plon-gé le poi-gnard dans le cœur d'u-ne mè-re; les
die-se Frev-ler-hand den Mör-der-dolch ge-taucht in ei-ner Mut-ter Brust; die
B.
Vl. I
Vl. II
Vle
Or.
Dieux me ré-servaient pour un forfait nouveau: je n'a-vais qu'un a-mi, je de-viens son bourreau.
Göt-ter sparten mich zu neuem Fre-vel auf: ein Freund war mir ge-blie-ben, und nun mord' ich auch den!
B.

Nº 12. Arie.

Allegro.
2 Oboi, e
2 Clarinetti in Do
2 Fagotti
2 Corni in Re
2 Trombe in Re
Timpani in Re, La
Violini I
Violini II
Viole
Orest
Dieux! qui me pour-sui-vez, Dieux! auteurs de mes
Ihr, die ihr mich ver-folgt, ihr, meiner Fre-vel
Bassi

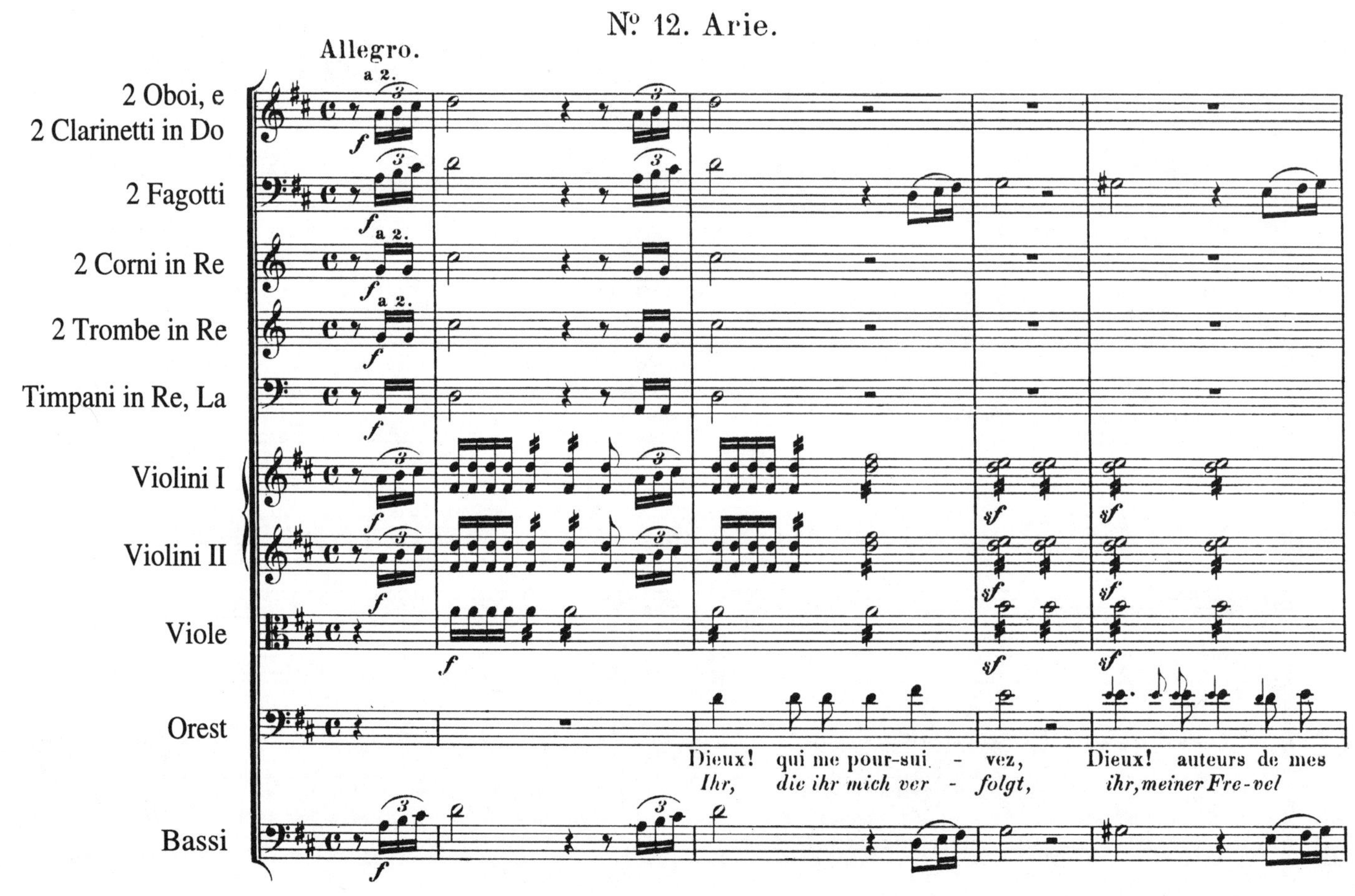

Ob. e Cl.
Fg.
Cor.
Tr.
Timp.
Vl. I
Vl. II
Vle
Or.
B.

cri - mes, de l'en - fer sous mes pas entr'ou - vrez les a - bî - mes!
Schö - pfer, rei - sset auf un - ter mir eu - rer Nacht grau - se Schlün - de!

Ob. e Cl.
Fg.
Cor.
Tr.
Timp.
Vl. I
Vl. II
Vle
Or.
B.

p *cresc.* *sf* *f*

Ses sup - pli - ces pour moi se - ront en - cor trop doux, ses sup - pli - ces pour moi se - ront en - cor trop
Ih - re här - te - ste Pein wird noch zu mil - de sein, ih - re här - te - ste Pein wird noch zu mil - de

Ob. e Cl.
Fg.
Cor.
Tr.
Timp.
Vl. I
Vl. II
Vle
Or.
B.

a 2.

doux, se - ront en-cor trop doux!
sein, wird noch zu mil - de sein!

Ob. e Cl.
Fg.
Cor.
Tr.
Timp.
Vl. I
Vl. II
Vle
Or.
B.

J'ai tra-hi l'a-mi-tié, j'ai tra-hi la na-tu-re, des plus noirs at-ten-tats j'ai com-blé la me-
Ich ver-rieth meinen Freund, ich verrieth die Na-tur, von dem hei-ligsten Blut träuft meiner Schritte

Ob. e Cl.

Fg.

Cor.

Tr.

Timp.

Vl. I

Vl. II

Vle

Or.

B.

a 2.

su - re. Dieux! frap - pez, frap-pez le cou - pa - - ble, et jus - ti - fi - ez - vous! Dieux! frap-

Spur! Auf! be - straft, be-straft den Ver - bre - - cher, Göt - ter, rä - chet euch! Auf! be-

Ob. e Cl.

Fg.

Cor.

Tr.

Timp.

Vl. I

Vl. II

Vle

Or.

B.

a 2.

pez, frappez le cou-pa-ble, et jus - ti - fi - ez-vous, et jus-ti - fi - ez - vous!

straft, bestraft den Ver-bre-cher, Göt - ter, rä - chet euch, Göt - ter, rä - chet euch!

Ob. e Cl.

Fg.

Cor.

Tr.

Timp.

Vl. I

Vl. II

Vle

Or.

B.

sf *p*

J'ai tra-hi l'a-mi - tié, j'ai tra-hi la na-
Ich verrieth meinen Freund, ich verrieth die Na-

Ob. e Cl.

Fg.

Cor.

Tr.

Timp.

Vl. I

Vl. II

Vle

Or.

B.

f

tu-re, des plus noirs at-ten - tats j'ai com-blé la me - su-re, des plus noirs at-ten - tats j'ai com-blé,
tur, von dem hei - lig-sten Blut träuft mei-ner Schrit-te Spur, von dem hei - lig-sten Blu - te träuft

Ob. e Cl.
Fg.
Cor.
Tr.
Timp.
Vl. I
Vl. II
Vle
Or.
B.

a 2.

j'ai comblé la me - su - re. Dieux! qui me poursui - vez, Dieux! auteurs de mes

mei-ner Schrit - te Spur! Ihr, die ihr mich ver - folgt, ihr, meiner Fre-vel

Ob. e Cl.
Fg.
Cor.
Tr.
Timp.
Vl. I
Vl. II
Vle
Or.
B.

cri - mes, de l'en - fer sous mes pas entr'ou - vrez les a - bî - mes!

Schö - pfer, rei - sset auf un - ter mir eu - rer Nacht grause Schlün - de!

Ob. e Cl.
Fg.
Cor.
Tr.
Timp.
Vl. I
Vl. II
Vle
Or.
B.

Ses sup-pli-ces pour moi se-ront en-cor trop doux, ses sup - pli - ces pour moi se - ront en-cor trop

Ih - re här - te - ste Pein wird noch zu mil - de sein, ih - re här - te - ste Pein wird noch zu mil - de

Ob. e Cl.
Fg.
Cor.
Tr.
Timp.
Vl. I
Vl. II
Vle
Or.
B.

doux, se - ront en-cor trop doux!

sein, wird noch zu mil - de sein!

Violini I
Violini II
Viole
Recitativo.
Pylades
Quel lan-ga - ge acca-blant pour un a-mi qui t'ai-me! Reviens à toi, mourons di-gnes de
Wie kränken die-se Wor-te den Freund, der so dich liebt! Auf, fas-se dich, lass unser werth uns
Bassi
Vl. I
Vl. II
Vle
Pyl.
nous! Ces - se, dans ta fu-reur ex-trê-me, d'ou-trager et les Dieux, et Py - la - de, et toi-mê - me!
sterben! Nicht län-ger schmäh' in dei-ner Wuth die hoch-er-hab' - nen Göt-ter, deinen Freund und auch dich selber! Muss
B.
Si le tré-pas nous est in - é - vi - ta - ble, quel-le vai - ne ter - reur te fait pâ - lir pour
je - der denn von uns des To-des O-pfer sein, wa-rum macht ban-ge Furcht für dei - nen Freund dich
moi? Je ne suis pas si mi-sé - ra-ble, puis-qu'en-fin je meurs près de toi.
bleich? Ist Py - la-des be-kla-gens - werth, da er an dei-ner Sei - te stirbt?

Nº 13. Arie.

Andante grazioso.
2 Fagotti
Violini I
Violini II
Viole
Pylades
Bassi
Fg.
Vl. I
Vl. II
Vle
Pyl.
B.
U-nis dès la plus ten - dre enfan-ce, nous n'a-vions qu'un mê-me dé-
Nur ei- nen Wunsch, nur ein Ver-langen hatt' ich mit dir, mein
sir, nous n'a-vions qu'un mê-me dé - sir: ah! mon cœur applau-dit d'a- -van-ce au
Freund, hatt' ich mit dir, mein Freund: will froh den Streich em- -pfan-gen, der

Fg.
Vl. I
Vl. II
Vle
Pyl.
coup qui va nous ré - u - nir, ah! mon coeur applau-dit d'a - van-ce au coup qui va nous ré-u -
e - wig uns ver - eint, will froh den Streich em - pfan-gen, der e - wig uns ver -
B.
nir, au coup qui va nous ré - u - nir, qui va nous ré - u - nir.
eint, der e - wig, e - wig uns ver - eint, der e - wig uns ver - eint.
Le sort nous fait pé-rir en - sem - ble, n'en ac-cu-se point la ri -
Mag das Schick - sal uns be - trü - gen, folg' ge-lassen, wenn es

Fg.
Vl. I
Vl. II
Vle
Pyl.
B.
gueur: la mort mê-me est u-ne fa-veur, puisque le tom-beau nous ras-sem- -ble, la mort
ruft, denn es wird in ei-ner Gruft un-ser Staub___ beisammen lie- - - -gen, denn es
mê-me est u- -ne fa-veur, puis-que le tom-beau, puisque le tom-beau nous ras- -sem- - - -
wird in ei-ner Gruft un- -ser Staub, un- -ser Staub___ bei-sammen lie- - - -
ble. Le sort nous fait pé-rir en-sem-ble,
gen. Mag das Schick- -sal uns be-trü-gen,

Fg.
Vl. I
Vl. II
Vle
Pyl.
n'en ac-cu-se point la ri-gueur: la mort mê - me est u - ne fa - veur, puisque le tom-beau nous ras-
folg' ge-lassen, wenn es ruft, denn es wird in ei - ner Gruft un - ser Staub bei-sammen
B.
sem - - - - ble, la mort mê - me est u - ne fa - veur, puisque le tom-beau, puisque le tom-
lie - - - - gen, denn es wird in ei - ner Gruft un - ser Staub, un - ser
beau nous ras - sem - - ble.
Staub beisammen lie - - gen.

SCÈNE II.

Oreste, Pylade, un Ministre du Sanctuaire, Gardes du Temple.
Orest, Pylades, ein Aufseher des Heiligthums, Tempelwache.

Vl. I
Vl. II
Vle
Pyl.
deux! Vos glai-ves, vos bûchers sont cent fois moins af-freux que le moment qui nous sé - pa - re.
trifft! Der Dolch und der Al - tar sind minder grau - en - voll, als die-ser Au-gen-blick der Tren-nung!
Der Aufseher.
Or.
deux! Vos glai-ves, vos bûchers sont cent fois moins af-freux que le moment qui nous sé - pa - re. J'o-bé-is à nos
trifft! Der Dolch und der Al - tar sind minder grau - en - voll, als die-ser Au-gen-blick der Tren-nung! So will es das Ge-
B.
Allegro.
Pylade, s'arrachant avec peine des bras d'Oreste.
Pylades, mit Mühe den Armen Orest's sich entreissend.
Hé - las!
O Schmerz!
aux Gardes. zu der Wache.
Orest.
Min.
lois, j'o-bé-is à nos Dieux. Qu'on le con-dui-se! Ar-rê-te! Mons-tres sau-
setz, die Göt-ter wol-len's so. Führt ihn hin-weg! Halt' ein! Fluch euch, ihr
Lento.
va - ges!
Un-geheu-er!
On te l'en-lève, hé-las! Py-la-de est mort pour toi!
Man reisset ihn hin-weg, auch Py-la-des ist todt für mich!
Pylade, le Ministre et les Gardes sortent.
Pylades, der Aufseher und die Wache gehen ab.

SCÈNE III.

Oreste, seul.

Orest, allein.

Ob. e Cl.
Fg.
Cor.
Vl. I
Vl. II
Vle
Or.
Il tombe. Fällt zu Boden.
Tonnez! é - cra - sez - moi!
Heran, zerschmettert mich!
é - cra - sez - moi!
zerschmettert mich!
B.
Lento.
Fg.
Vl. I
Vl. II
Vle
Or.
Où suis - je? À l'hor - reur qui m'ob - sè - de quel - le tran - quil - li - té suc - cè - de?
Wo bin ich? Auf die Qual, die mich um - ring - te, folgt nun so plötz - lich Ruh' und Stil - le?
B.
Nº 14. Arie.
Andante.
Oboe 1.
Violini I
Violini II
Viole
Orest
Le cal - - me ren - tre dans mon
Die Ru - - he keh - ret mir zu -
Bassi

Ob.
Vl. I
Vl. II
Vle
Or.
coeur... Mes maux ont donc las-sé la co-lè-
rück... So konn-te mei-ne Qual euch, ihr Göt-
B.

Ob.
Vl. I
Vl. II
Vle
Or.
re cé-les-te,... je tou-che au ter-me du mal-
ter, er-mü-den,... so en-det hier mein Miss-ge-
B.

Ob.
Vl. I
Vl. II
Vle
Or.
heur? Vous lais-sez res-pi-rer le par-ri-ci-de O-res-
schick,... so gön-net ihr ein-mal dem Mat-ter-mör-der Frie-
B.

Ob.
Vl. I
Vl. II
Vle
Or.
B.
te? Dieux jus - tes! Ciel ven - geur!
den? O Göt - ter! Welch' ein Glück!
Oui, oui, le cal - - me ren - tre dans mon
Ja, ja, die Ru - - he keh - - ret mir zu -
Il s'endort d'accablement.
Er schläft vor Ermattung ein.
coeur...
rück...

SCÈNE IV.

Oreste, les Euménides.
Orest, die Eumeniden.

Les Euménides sortent du fond du Théâtre, et entourent Oreste. Les unes exécutent autour de lui un Ballet-Pantomime de terreur, les autres lui parlent. Oreste est sans connaissance pendant toute cette scène.

Die Eumeniden erscheinen aus dem Hintergrunde der Bühne und umringen Orest. Die einen führen ein Schreckens-Pantomimenballet um ihn aus, die anderen reden auf ihn ein. Orest ist während der ganzen Scene ohne Bewusstsein.

Ob. e Cl.
Fg.
Trb.
Vl. I
Vl. II
Vle
B.

Ob. e Cl.
Fg.
Trb.
Vl. I
Vl. II
Vle
B.

Nº 15. Chor.

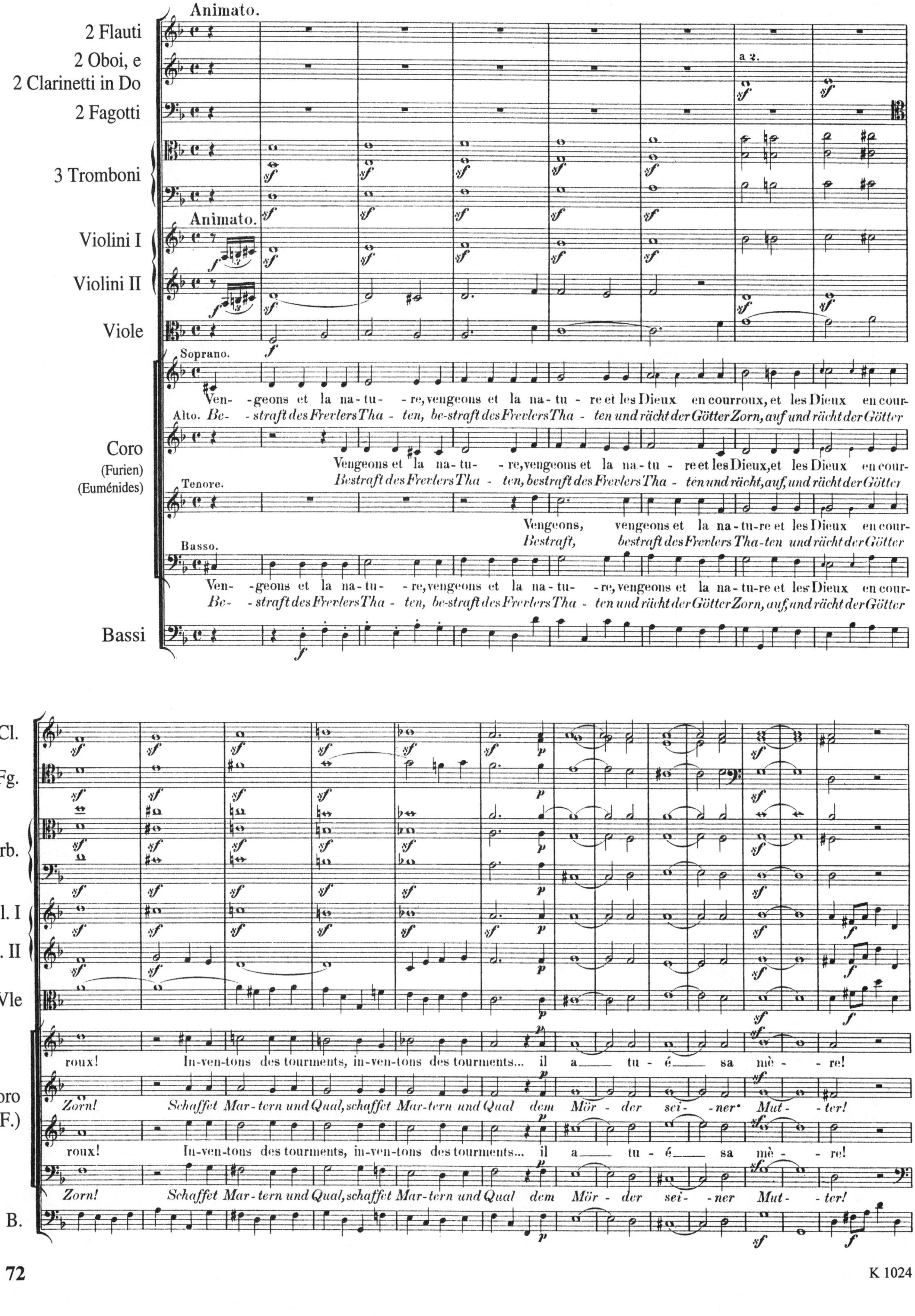

Animato.

2 Flauti

2 Oboi, e 2 Clarinetti in Do

a 2.

2 Fagotti

3 Tromboni

Animato.

Violini I

Violini II

Viole

Coro (Furien) (Euménides)

Soprano.

Ven- geons et la na- tu- re, vengeons et la na- tu- re et les Dieux en courroux, et les Dieux en cour-

Alto. *Be- straft des Frevlers Tha- ten, be-straft des Frevlers Tha - ten und rächt der Götter Zorn, auf und rächt der Götter*

Vengeons et la na- tu- re, vengeons et la na- tu- re et les Dieux, et les Dieux en cour-

Bestraft des Frevlers Tha - ten, bestraft des Frevlers Tha - ten und rächt, auf, und rächt der Götter

Tenore.

Vengeons, vengeons et la na- tu- re et les Dieux en cour-

Bestraft, bestraft des Frevlers Tha- ten und rächt der Götter

Basso.

Ven- geons et la na- tu- re, vengeons et la na- tu- re, vengeons et la na- tu- re et les Dieux en cour-

Be- straft des Frevlers Tha - ten, be-straft des Frevlers Tha - ten und rächt der Götter Zorn, auf, und rächt der Götter

Bassi

Fl.
Ob. e Cl.
Fg.
Clarinetti
Ob. e Clar.
a 2.
Vl. I
Vl. II
Vle
Coro
(F.)
B.
Orest.
Point de grâ - ce, il a tu - é sa mè - re!
Schafft ihm Qual, dem Mör - der sei - ner Mut - ter!
Vengeons et la na-
Bestraft des Frevlers
Ah! ah! ah!
Ach! ach! ach!
Trb.
I.
tu - re et les Dieux en courroux!
Tha - ten, auf, und rächt der Götter Zorn!
tu - re et les Dieux en cour - roux!
Tha - ten und rächt der Göt - ter Zorn!
Ah, quels tourments! Ah, quels tourments!
Ach, wel - che Qual! Ach, wel - che Qual!
Ils sont en - cor trop doux! Ven-
Für dich noch nicht ge - nug! Be-
Ils sont en - cor trop
Für dich noch nicht ge-

Fl.
Ob. e Cl.
Fg.
Trb.
Vl. I
Vl. II
Vle
Coro (F.)
B.

geons et la na - tu - re et les Dieux en courroux! Il a — tu - é — sa mè - re!
straft des Frevlers Tha - ten und schafft, schafft ihm Qual, dem Mör - der sei - ner Mut - ter!

doux, ils sont en - cor trop doux! Il a - tu - é - sa mè - re!
nug! Auf, schafft ihm, schafft ihm Qual, dem Mör - der sei - ner Mut - ter!

geons et la na - tu - re et les Dieux en courroux! Il a - tu - é - sa mè - re!
straft des Frevlers Tha - ten und schafft, schafft ihm Qual, dem Mör - der sei - ner Mut - ter!

Orest.

doux, ils sont en - cor trop doux! Il a — tu - é — sa mè - re! Un
nug! Auf, schafft ihm, schafft ihm Qual, dem Mör - der sei - ner Mut - ter! Ent-

L'Ombre de Clytemnestre paraît au milieu des Furies, et s'abîme aussitôt.
Der Schatten Klytemnestra's erscheint mitten unter den Furien und verschwindet sofort wieder.

Fl.
Ob. e Cl.
Fg.
Trb.
Vl. I
Vl. II
Vle
Coro (F.)
B.

I. Clarinetti Ob. e Clar. Clar.

Point de grâ - ce, il a tu - é sa mè - re!
Neu - e Qual dem Mörder sei - ner Mut - ter!

Point de grâ - ce, il a tu - é sa mè - re!

Orest.

spec - tre! Ah! Ah! Ayez pi - tié! Ay - ez pi - tié!
se - tzen! Weh! Weh! Neu - e Qual dem Mörder sei - ner Mut - ter! Erbarmet euch! Erbarmet euch!

Fl.
Ob. e Cl.
Fg.
Trb.
Vl. I
Vl. II
Vle
Coro (F.)
B.

a 2.

De la pi-tié? Le monstre! il a tu-é sa mè-re! Ven-geons et la na-
Be-straft des Frevlers
Erbarmen dir? dem Frev-ler? dem Mör-der sei-ner Mut-ter? Be-straft des Frevlers Tha-ten und
De la pi-tié? Le monstre! il a tu-é sa mè-re! Ven-geons et la na-tu-re et les
Erbarmen dir? dem Frev-ler? dem Mör-der sei-ner Mut-ter? Be-straft des Frevlers Tha-ten und

Fl.
Ob. e Cl.
Fg.
Trb.
Vl. I
Vl. II
Vle
Coro (F.)
B.

Clarinetti

tu-re et les Dieux en courroux, et les Dieux en courroux!
Tha-ten und rächt der Götter Zorn, auf, und rächt der Götter Zorn!
rächt der Götter Zorn, bestraft des Frevlers Tha-ten und rächt der Götter Zorn!
Dieux en courroux, vengeons et la na-tu-re et les Dieux en courroux!
rächt der Götter Zorn, bestraft des Frevlers Tha-ten und rächt der Götter Zorn!
Orest.
Ay-ez pi-tié! Ah, quels tourments!
Erbarmet euch! Er-bar-met euch!

Fl.
Ob. e Cl.
Fg.
Trb.
Vl. I
Vl. II
Vle
Coro (F.)
B.

Ob. e Clar. a 2.

Ah, quels tourments!
Er- bar-met euch!

É-ga-lons, s'il se peut, sa ra-ge meurtri-è- - -re, ce cri- -me af-
Machet gleich sei-ne Pein, vermögt ihr's, sei-ner wil- -den Wuth, doch kei- -ne

Fl.
Ob. e Cl.
Fg.
Trb.
Vl. I
Vl. II
Vle
Or.
Coro (F.)
B.

apercevant Iphigénie.
bemerkt Iphigenie.

Ay-ez pi-tié! Dieux cruels! Ma mè-re! Ciel!
Erbarmet euch! Grau-same! Die Mutter! Weh'!

freux ne peut ê-tre ex-pi-é, ne peut ê-tre ex-pi-é, ton for-fait ne peut ê-tre ex-pi- -é!
Qual söh-net sein Verbre-chen aus, nichts söhnt sein Ver-bre-chen aus, keine Qual, kei-ne Qual söhnt es aus!

SCÈNE V.

Oreste, Iphigénie, Prêtresses.
Orest, Iphigenie, Priesterinnen.

Les portes de l'Appartement s'ouvrent, les Prêtresses paraissent; les Furies s'abîment sans en pouvoir être aperçues.
Die Thüren des Tempelraumes öffnen sich, die Priesterinnen erscheinen; die Furien verschwinden unbemerklich.

Vl. I
Vl. II
Vle
Or.
B.
Iphigenie.
Orest.
Iphig.
Dieux! D'où vient que vo-tre cœur sou-pi - re? Qu'ê - tes-vous? Malheureux. C'est as - sez vous en di - re. De
Göt-ter! Ein Seufzer dringt aus dei-ner Brust hervor? Wer bist du? Un - glück-lich; das sei dir ge-nug! Ver-
Iph.
Orest.
Iphigenie.
grâce, ré-pondez: de quels lieux venez-vous, quel sang vous donna l'ê - tre? Vous le vou-lez? My-cè - ne m'a vu naître. Dieux! qu'en-
hehle mir es nicht: wo kamst du her, und welch' ein Land hat dich erzeugt? Du willst es denn: My-cen gab mir das Leben. Was
ben marcato
tends-je? Ache-vez... di-tes... in-formez-nous du sort d'Agamemnon, de ce - lui de la Grè - ce.
hör' ich! Rede mehr, voll - en-de... be - leh-re mich vom Schicksal A - ga-memnons und Grie - chenlands.
A-gamemnon? D'où naît la dou - leur qui vous presse? A-gamem - non... Je vois cou - ler vos pleurs. ..sous un
A-ga-memnon? Wo-her der Schmerz, der dich ergreift? A - ga - memnon... Dein Au-ge schwimmt in Thränen!..ward von

Vl. I
Vl. II
Vle
Or.
B.
Iphigenie.
Orest. à part. für sich.
Iphigenie.
fer parri-ci-de est tombé... Je me meurs! Quel-le est donc cette femme? Et quel mon-stre e-xé-cra - ble a sur un roi si
Mör - derhänden erschlagen! Weh! Ent-se-tzen! Ha! wer ist dieses Weib? Und welch' ein Unge-heu'r er-kühnte sich, dem ersten al-ler
tremolo
Orest.
Iphigenie.
Orest.
Iph.
grand o-sé le-ver le bras? Au nom des Dieux, ne m'inter-rogez pas! Au nom des Dieux, parlez! Ce mon-stre a-bomina-ble,
Könige den Dolch in's Herz zu stossen? Bei al-len Göt-tern, fra-ge weiter nicht! Bei al-len Göt-tern, rede! Dies schwar-ze Un-geheuer
Iphigenie.
Orest.
Iphigenie.
Orest.
c'est... A-che-vez: vous me fai - tes fré-mir! ..son é - pou-se. Grands Dieux! Cly-tem-nes-tre? El-le-mê-me.
war... Voll- en-de: mich er-greift ein Todesschauer! ..sei-ne Gat-tin. Ihr Götter! Kly-tem-nes-tra? Ja, sie sel-ber.
Vivace.
posément. gewichtig.
Orest.
Et des Dieux vengeurs la jus-ti- ce su-prême a vu ce cri- me a-tro-ce? El-le a su le pu-
Und straf - te nicht der all-ge-rechten Götter Rache den schwarzen, grauenvollen Frevel? Er blieb nicht un-ge-
(Prêtresses)
(Priesterinnen)
Coro
(Pr.)
Ciel!
Weh!

Allegro.
Vl. I
Vl. II
Vle
Iphigenie.
Orest.
Or.
nir: son fils... Ô ciel! il a ven-gé son pè - re.
straft: der Sohn... O Göt-ter! er räch-te sei-nen Va-ter!
B.
Lento.
Iph.
De for-faits sur for-faits quel as-sem-bla-ge af-freux! Et ce fils qui du Ciel a ser-vi la co-
Ach, wie fürch-ter-lich folgt hier ein Gräu'l dem an-dern nach! Und dieser Sohn, dess sich der Göt-ter Zorn be-
De mes for-faits quel as-sem-bla-ge af-freux!
Ja, schrecklich folgt ein Gräu'l dem an-dern nach!
Coro
(Pr.)
De for-faits sur for-faits quel as-sem-bla-ge af-freux!
Ach, wie fürch-ter-lich folgt hier ein Gräu'l dem an-dern nach!
lè-re, ce fa-tal instru-ment des vengean-ces des Dieux... A rencon-tré la mort qu'il a longtemps cherché-e. É-
die-net, der von des Him-mels Rach' ein traurig' Beispiel war... Fand endlich auch den Tod, den er so lang' ge-suchet. E-

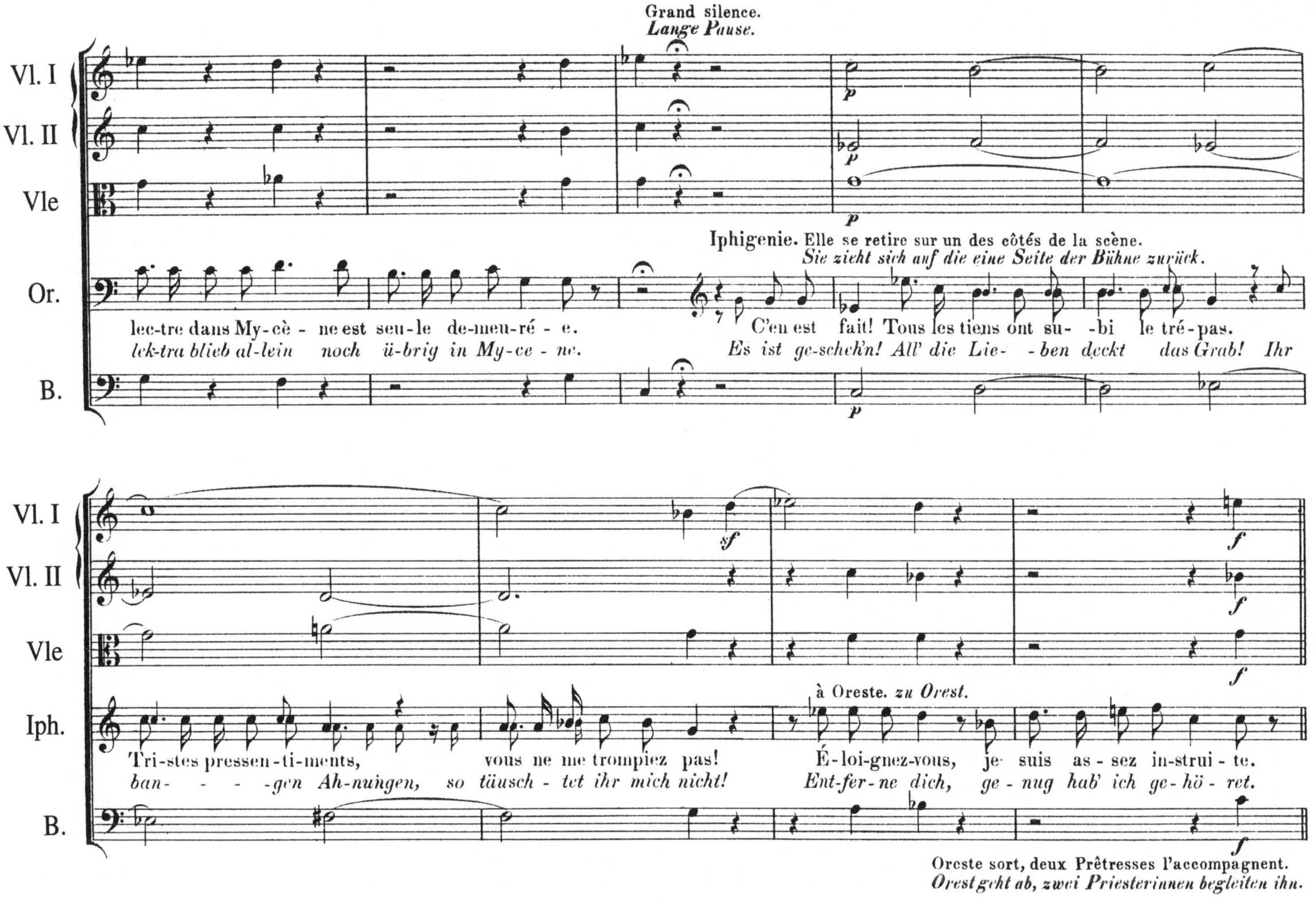

Grand silence.
Lange Pause.

Vl. I
Vl. II
Vle

Iphigenie. Elle se retire sur un des côtés de la scène.
Sie zieht sich auf die eine Seite der Bühne zurück.

Or.

lec-tre dans My-cè - ne est seu-le de-meu-ré - e. C'en est fait! Tous les tiens ont su- bi le tré-pas.
lek-tra blieb al-lein noch ü-brig in My-ce - ne. Es ist ge-scheh'n! All' die Lie- - ben deckt das Grab! Ihr

B.

Vl. I
Vl. II
Vle

à Oreste. *zu Orest.*

Iph.

Tri-stes pressen-ti-ments, vous ne me trompiez pas! É-loi-gnez-vous, je suis as-sez in-strui - te.
ban- - - -gen Ah-nungen, so täusch - tet ihr mich nicht! Ent-fer-ne dich, ge - nug hab' ich ge-hö - ret.

B.

Oreste sort, deux Prêtresses l'accompagnent.
Orest geht ab, zwei Priesterinnen begleiten ihn.

SCÈNE VI.

Iphigénie, Prêtresses.
Iphigenie, Priesterinnen.

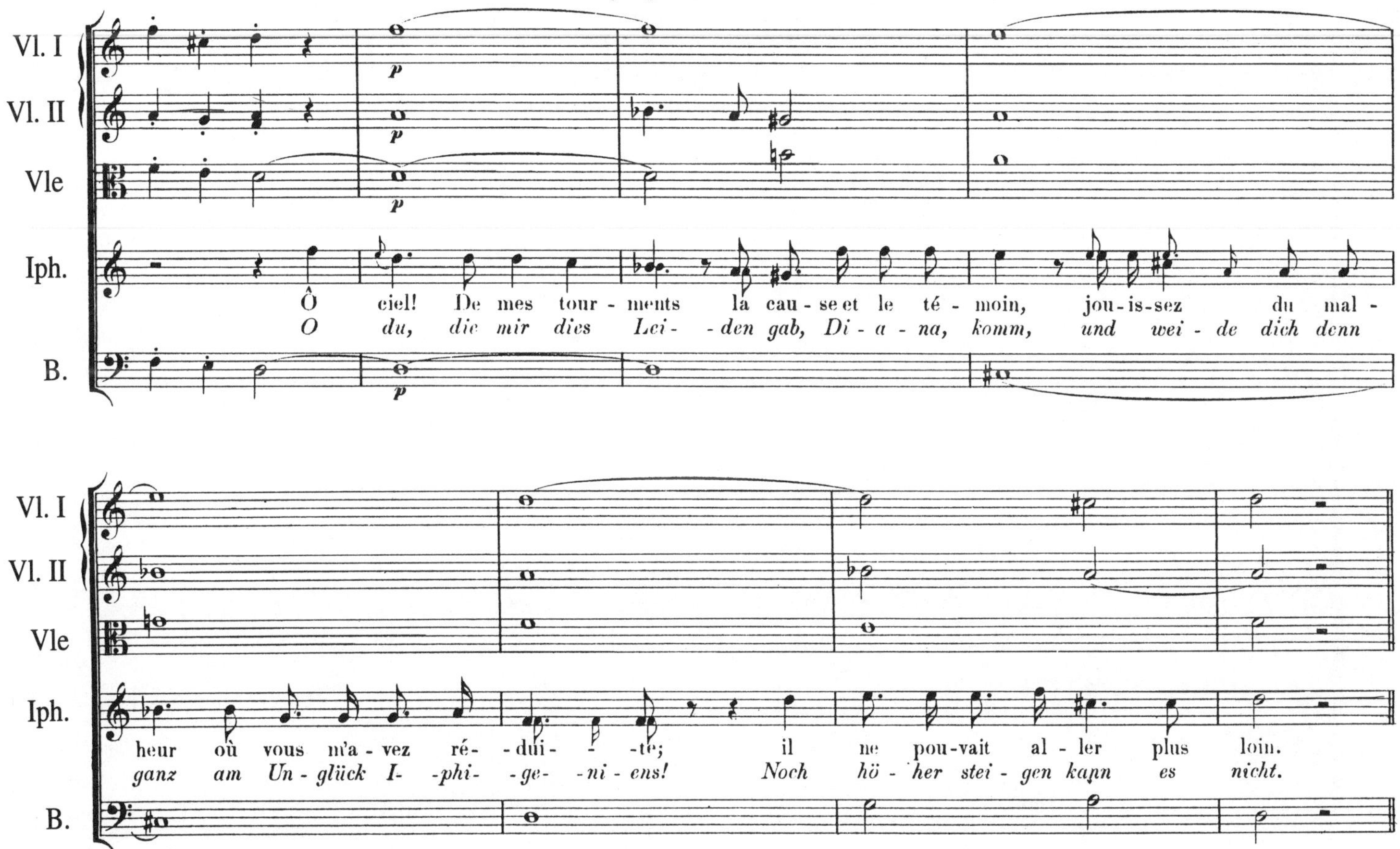

Nº 16. Chor.

Andante.
2 Clarinetti in Do
2 Fagotti
Violini I
Violini II
Viole
Coro
(Prêtresses)
(Priesterinnen)
Soprano I.
Pa - trie in-for-tu - né - e, où par des nœuds si
Soprano II.
Lasst Gram uns e-wig näh-ren, da je-de Hoff-nung
Bassi
mf

Cl.
Fg.
Vl. I
Vl. II
Vle
Coro
(Pr.)
doux no-tre â-me est enco-re enchaî - né - e, vous a - vez dis-pa-ru pour nous, vous a - vez dis - pa - ru pour nous!
schwand, und wir dich stets ent- - beh - ren, dich, o theu - res Va - ter - land, dich, o theures, theures Va- - ter - land!
B.

Nº 17. Arie.

Andante moderato.
Oboe I. Solo
2 Oboi
Solo
Fagotto
a 2.
2 Corni in Sol
Andante moderato.
Violini I
Violini II
Viole
Iphigenie
Violoncelli
pizz.
Bassi

Ob.
Fg.
Cor.
Vl. I
Vl. II
Vle
Iph.
Ô mal-heu-reu- - se I-phi- - gé-ni- - - e! Ta fa-
O lasst mich Tief- - ge-beug- - te wei- - - nen! Da-hin, da-
Vlc.
B.

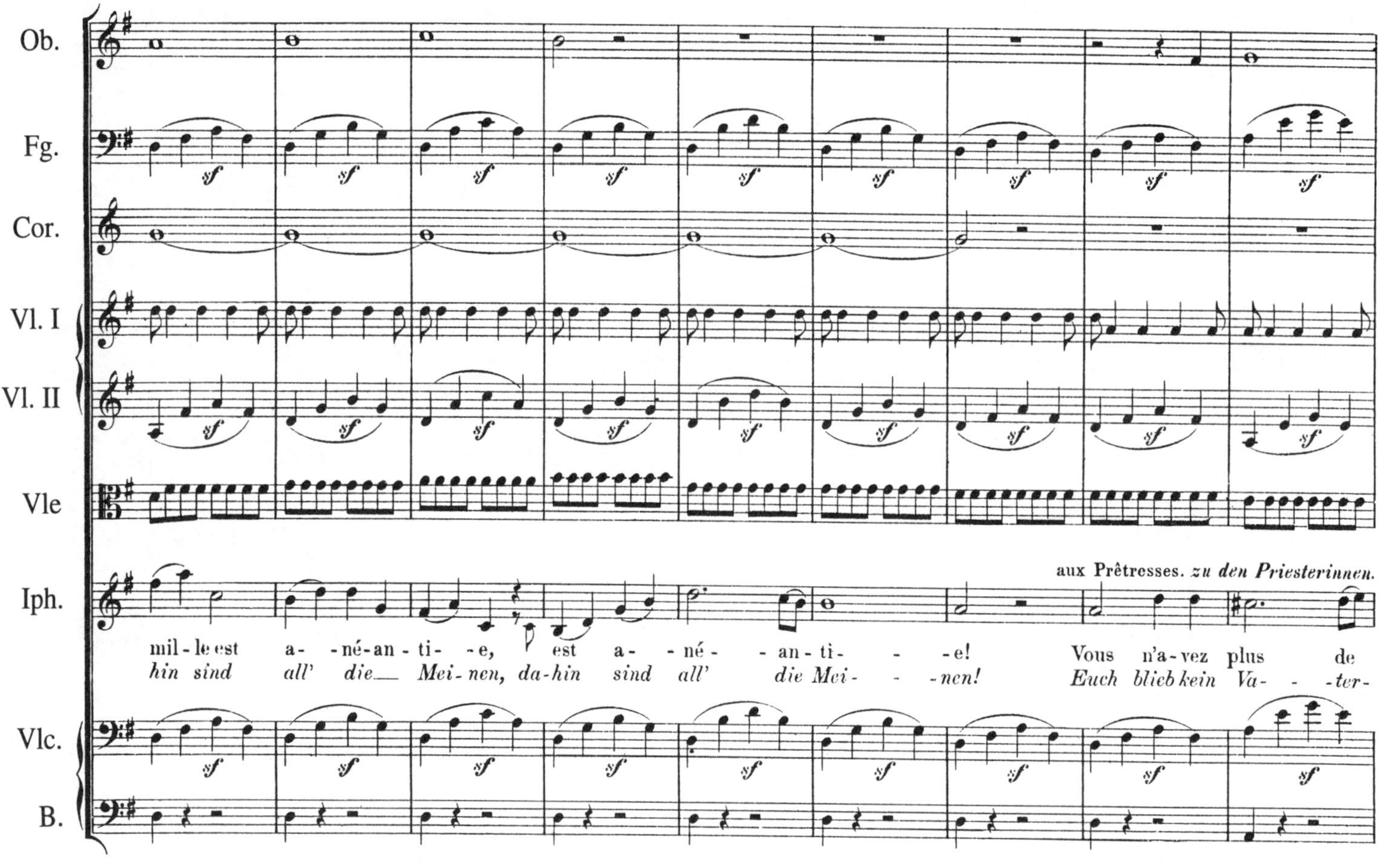

Ob.
Fg.
Cor.
Vl. I
Vl. II
Vle
Iph.
aux Prêtresses. zu den Priesterinnen.
mil-le est a-né-an-ti--e, est a-né-an-ti--e! Vous n'a-vez plus de
hin sind all' die Mei-nen, da-hin sind all' die Mei--nen! Euch blieb kein Va--ter-
Vlc.
B.
Ob.
Fg.
Cor.
Vl. I
Vl. II
Vle
Iph.
Rois, je n'ai plus de pa-rents. Mê-lez vos cris plain-tifs à mes gé-mis-se-
land, kein Freund, kein Ret-ter mir! Ihr lei-det wie ich selbst, so weint, so klagt auch
Vlc.
B.

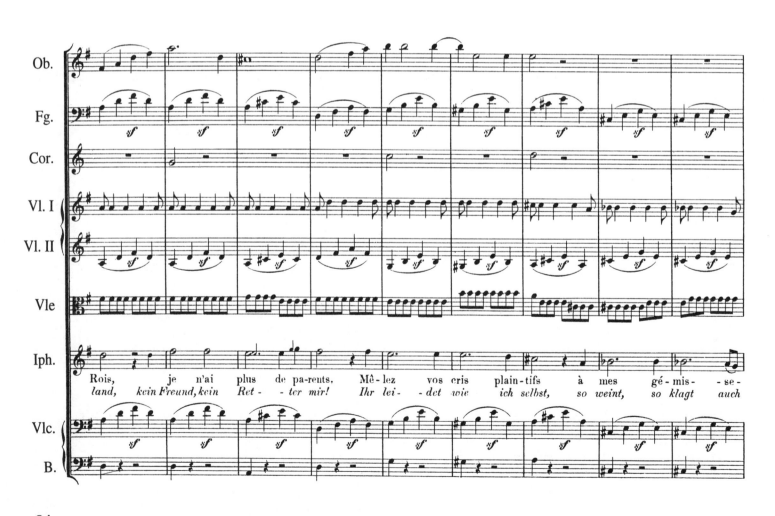

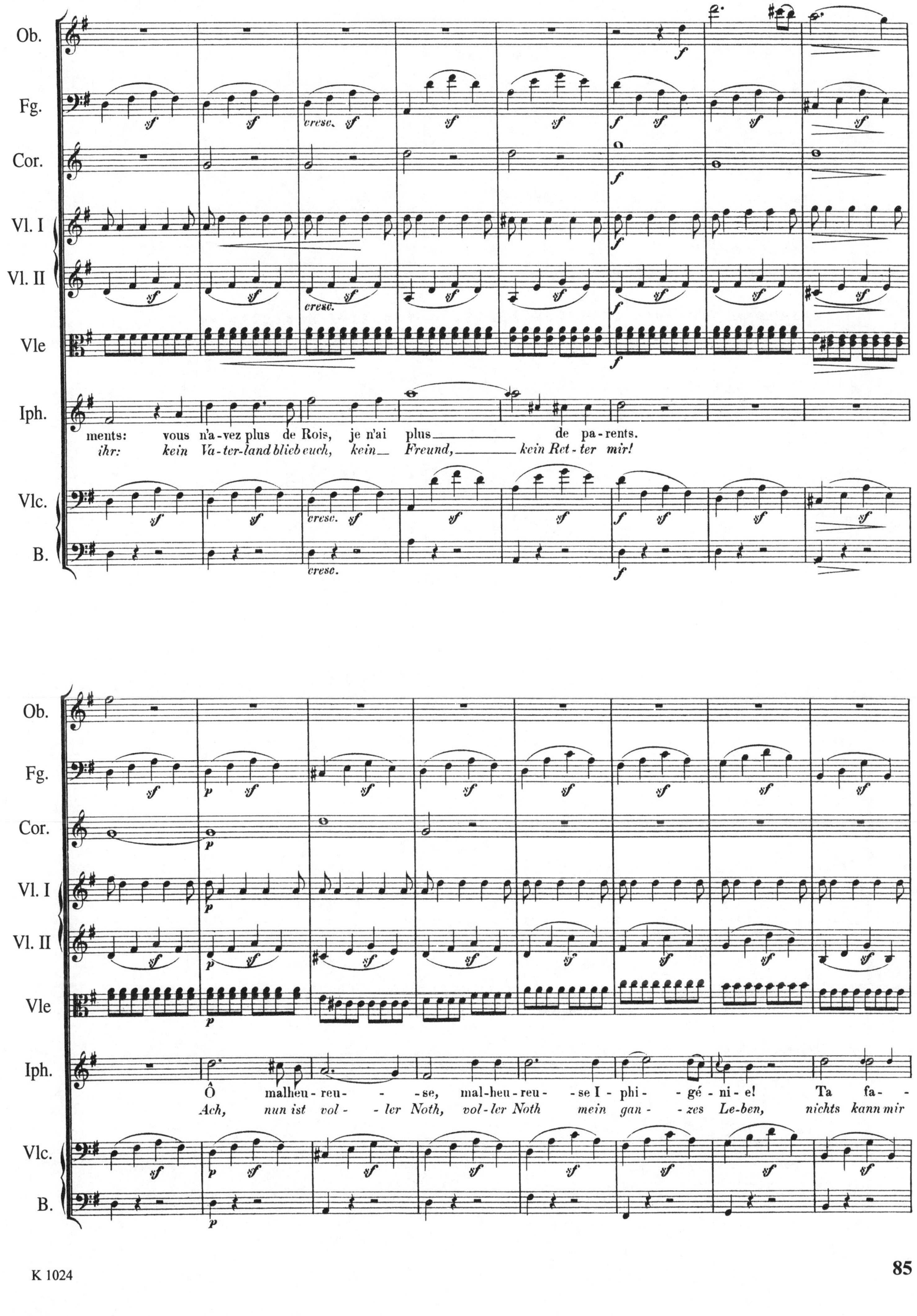

Ob.
Fg.
Cor.
Vl. I
Vl. II
Vle
Iph.
Vlc.
B.

ments: vous n'a-vez plus de Rois, je n'ai plus de pa-rents.

ihr: kein Va-ter-land blieb euch, kein Freund, kein Ret-ter mir!

Ob.
Fg.
Cor.
Vl. I
Vl. II
Vle
Iph.
Vlc.
B.
Ô malheu-reu- - se, mal-heu-reu- - se I - phi- gé-ni-e! Ta fa-
Ach, nun ist vol- - ler Noth, vol-ler Noth mein gan- - zes Le-ben, nichts kann mir

Ob.
Fg.
Cor.
Vl. I
Vl. II
Vle
Iph.
Vlc.
B.
mil - le est a - né - an - ti - e, ta fa - mil - le est a - né - an - ti - e! Vous n'a - vez
Ar - men Freu - de ge - ben, nun ist voll Noth mein gan - zes Leben! Euch blieb kein

Ob. Oboe I. Oboe II. p cresc. p
Fg. cresc. p
Cor. cresc. p
Vl. I cresc. p
Vl. II cresc. p
Vle cresc. p
Iph.
plus de Rois, je n'ai plus de pa - rents. Mê - lez vos cris plain - tifs, vos cris plain-
Va - ter - land, kein Freund, kein Ret - ter mir! Ihr lei - det wie ich selbst, so wie ich
Vlc. cresc. p
B. arco cresc. p

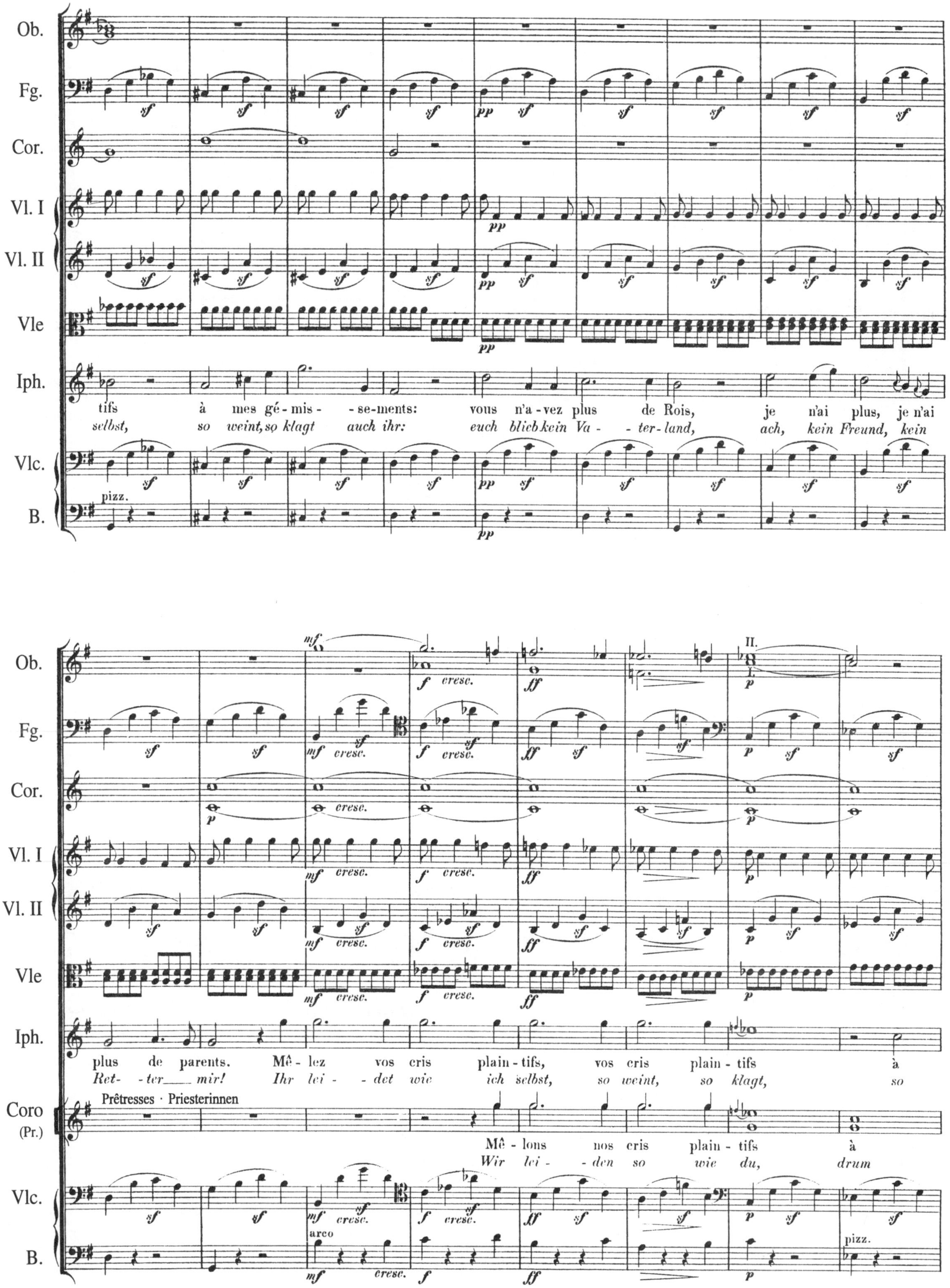

Ob.
II.
Fg.
Cor.
Vl. I
Vl. II
Vle
Iph.
plus de parents. Mê - lez vos cris plain - tifs, vos cris plain - tifs à
Ret- - ter___ mir! Ihr lei - - det wie ich selbst, so weint, so klagt, so
Coro (Pr.)
Prêtresses · Priesterinnen
Mê - lons nos cris plain - tifs à
Wir lei - - den so wie du, drum
Vlc.
arco
pizz.
B.

Ob.
Fg.
Cor. a 2.
Vl. I
Vl. II
Vle
Iph.
mes gé-mis- se-ments: vous n'a-vez plus de Rois, je n'ai plus, je n'ai plus de pa-
weint, so klagt auch ihr: euch blieb kein Va- -ter - land, ach, kein Freund, ach, kein Ret- -ter
Coro (Pr.)
ses gé-mis- se - ments!
kla- - gen wir mit dir!
Vlc.
B. arco

Ob. a 2.
Fg.
Cor. a 2.
Vl. I
Vl. II
Vle
Iph.
rents.
mir!
Coro (Pr.)
Nous n'a- vions d'espé - ran- -ce, hé-las! que dans O- -res- -te: Nous a-vons
Einst würd'O-rest, so hoff- -ten wir, uns noch er- -ret- -ten. Wer bricht, da
Vlc.
B.

On apporte la coupe, et l'on commence les cérémonies funèbres.
Man bringt die Opferschale und beginnt die Trauerfeierlichkeiten.

Nº 18. Chor.

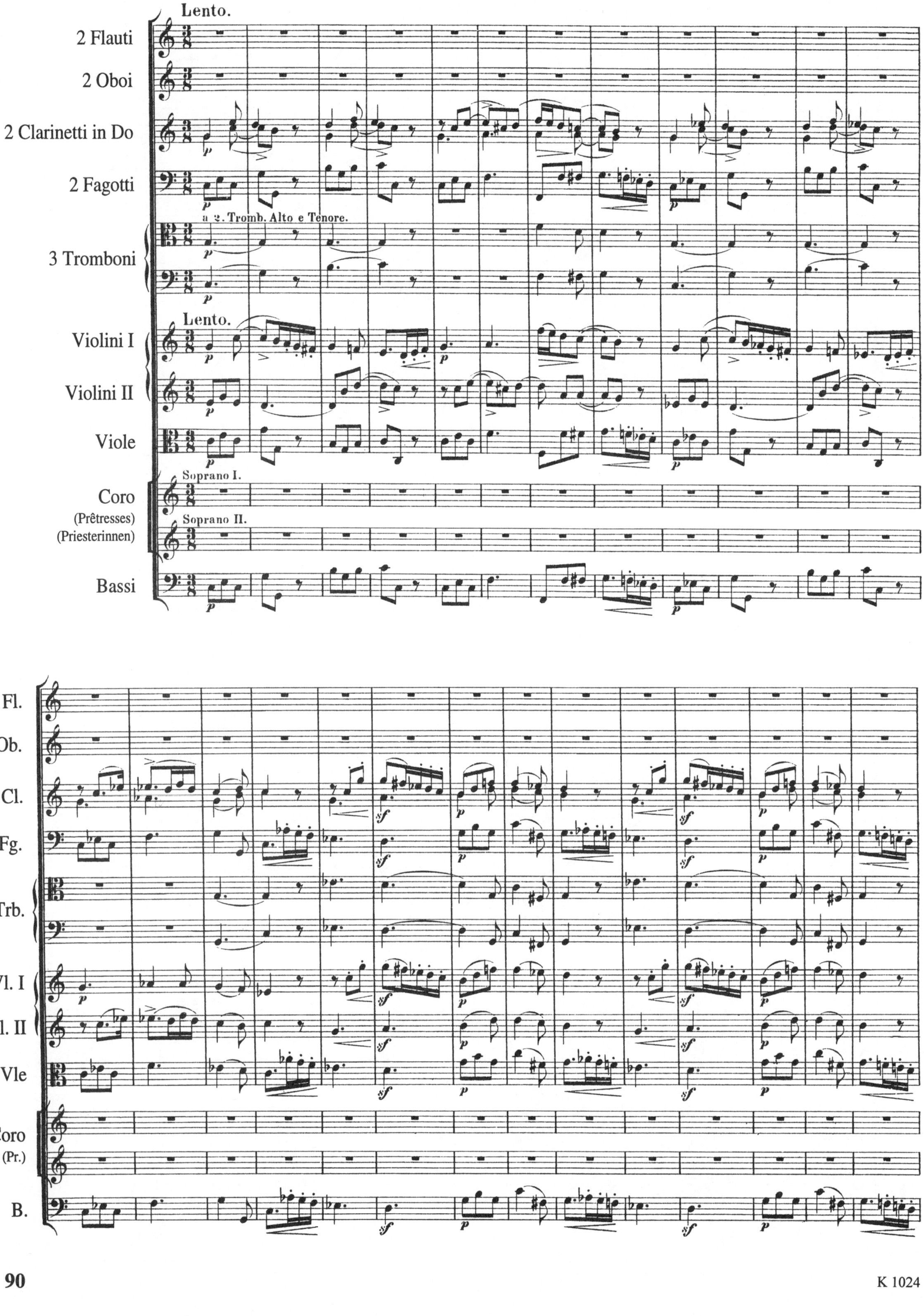

Lento.
2 Flauti
2 Oboi
2 Clarinetti in Do
2 Fagotti
a 2. Tromb. Alto e Tenore.
3 Tromboni
Lento.
Violini I
Violini II
Viole
Soprano I.
Coro
(Prêtresses)
(Priesterinnen)
Soprano II.
Bassi
Fl.
Ob.
Cl.
Fg.
Trb.
Vl. I
Vl. II
Vle
Coro
(Pr.)
B.

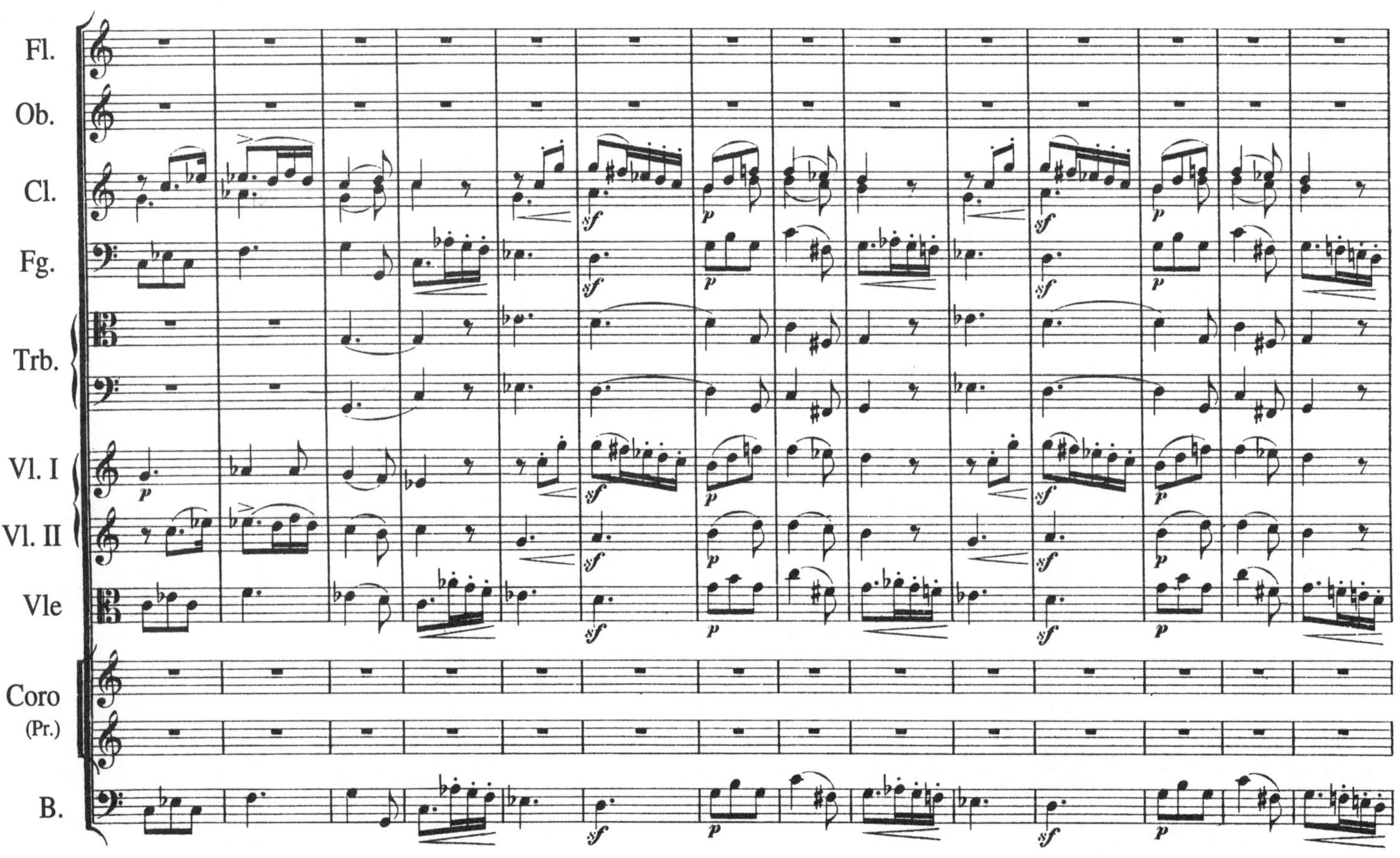

Fl.
Ob.
Cl.
Fg.
Trb.
Vl. I
Vl. II
Vle
Coro
(Pr.)
Con - tem - plez ces tristes ap - prêts, mânes sa - crés, ombre plain - ti - ve; que nos larmes, que nos re - grets
Kannst du noch aus je - ner Welt wie - der zu der Er - - de dringen, sich' uns dann, ge - fall' - ner Held,
B.
Fl.
Ob.
a 2.
Cl.
Fg.
Trb.
Vl. I
Vl. II
Vle
Coro
(Pr.)
pé - nè - trent l'in - ferna - le ri - - ve!
dir ge - rech - te Opfer brin - gen!
B.

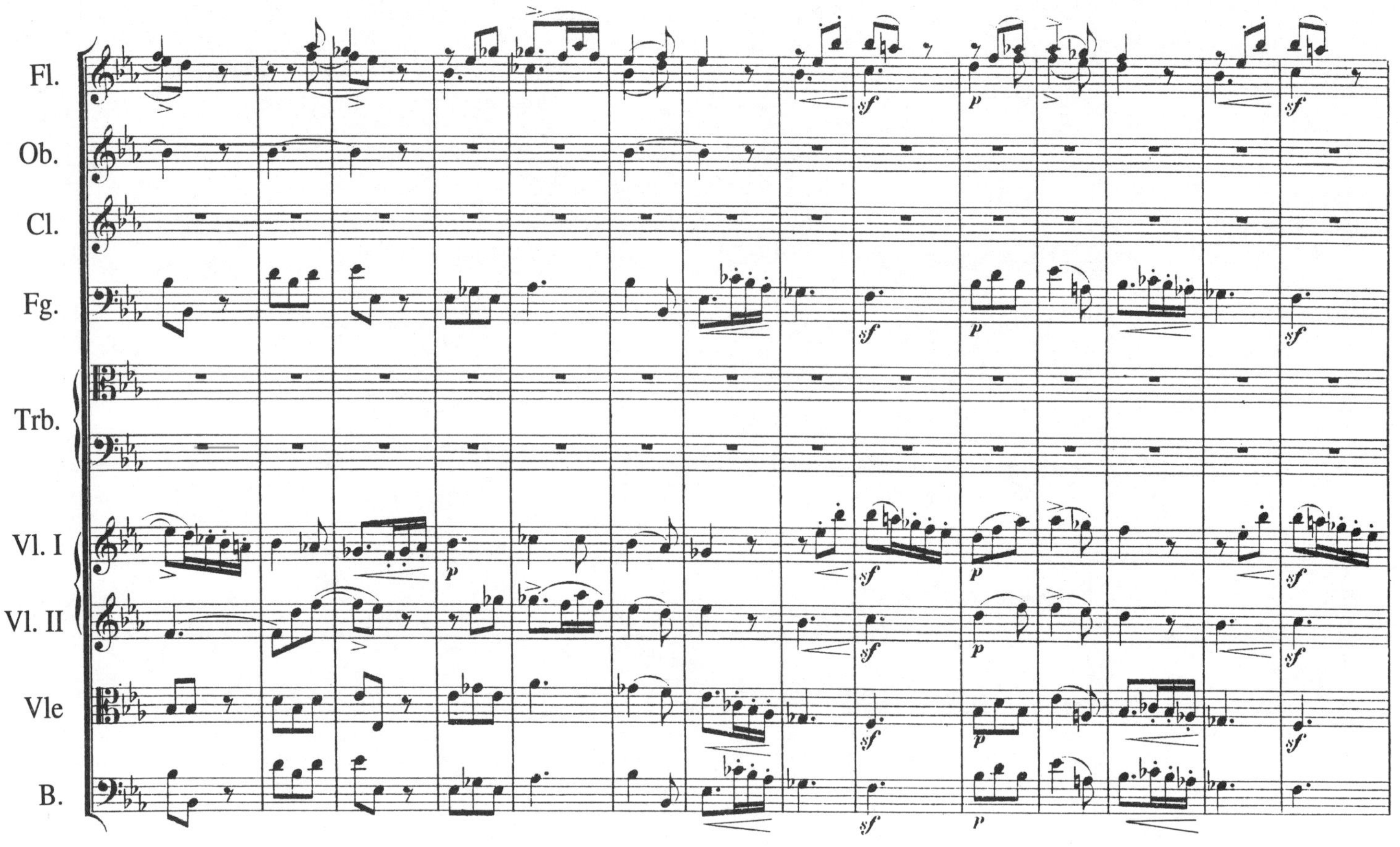

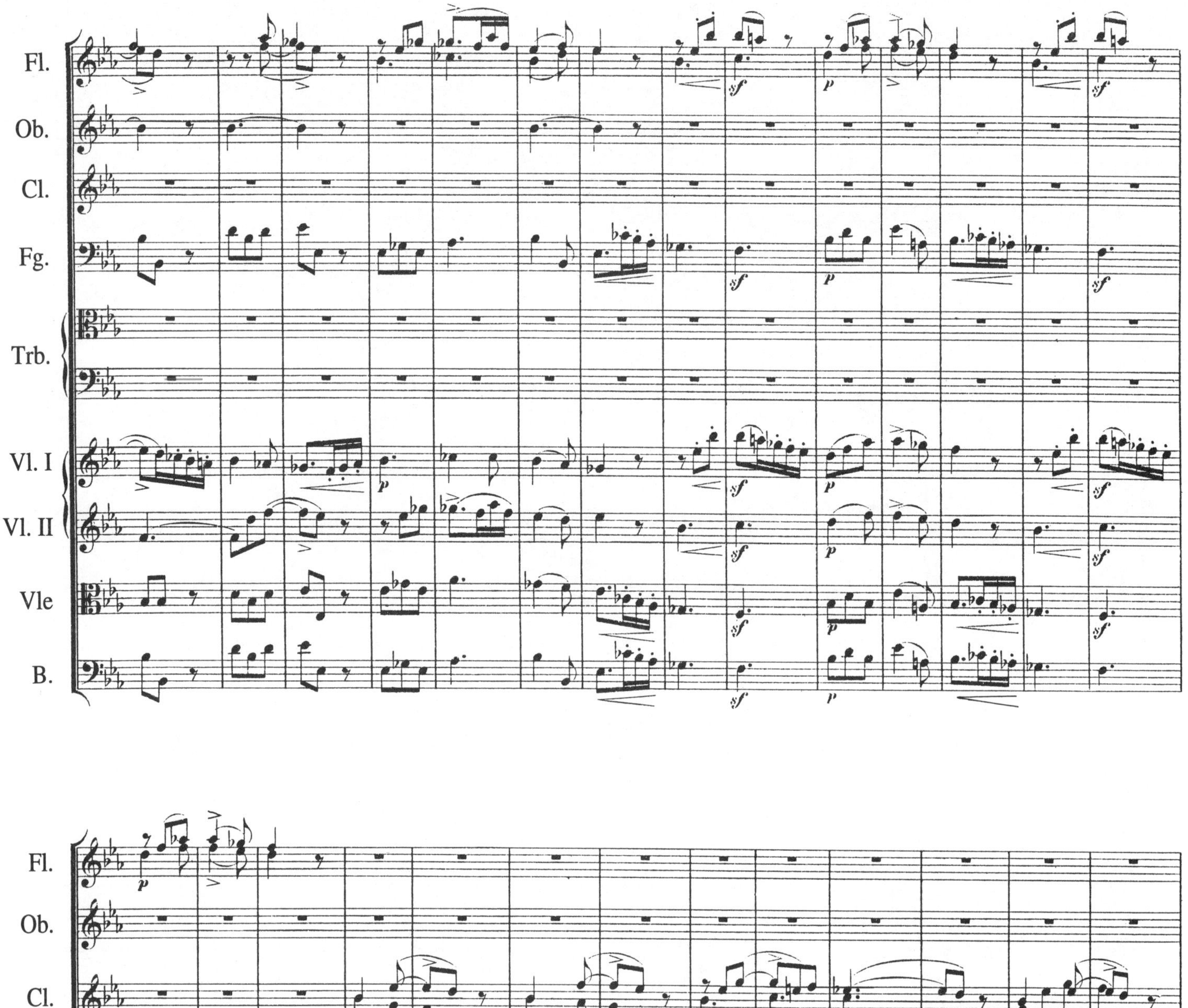

Fl.
Ob.
Cl.
Fg.
Trb.
Vl. I
Vl. II
Vle
B.
Fl.
Ob.
Cl.
Fg.
Trb.
Vl. I
Vl. II
Vle
Iph.
Ô mon frè-re, daignez en-tendre les ac-cents de ma dou-leur: que les re-grets
O mein Bruder, die- -se Thränen wei-net dir voll Schmerz die Pflicht, doch um-sonst,
B.

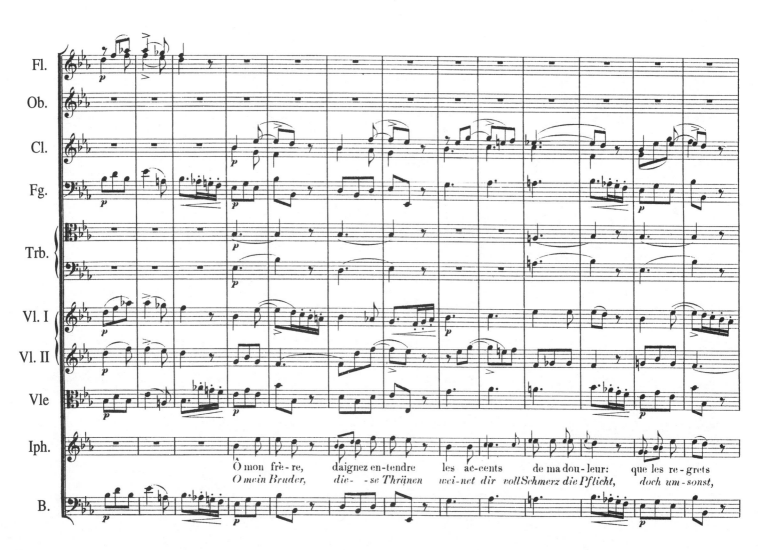

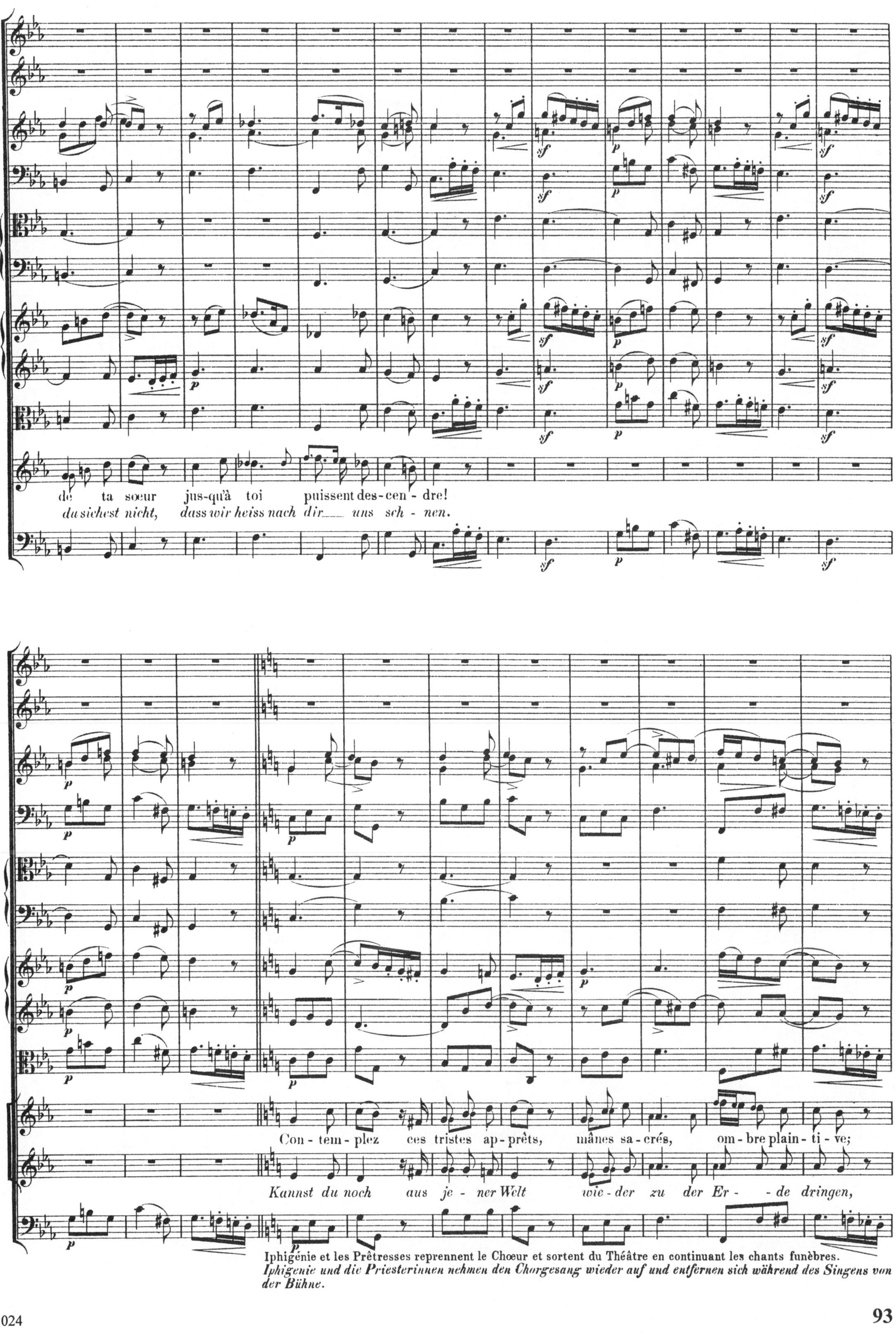

Fl.

Ob.

Cl.

Fg.

Trb.

Vl. I

Vl. II

Vle

Coro (Pr.)

Con - tem - plez ces tristes ap - prêts, mânes sa - crés, om - bre plain - ti - ve;

Kannst du noch aus je - ner Welt wie - der zu der Er - de dringen,

B.

Iphigénie et les Prêtresses reprennent le Chœur et sortent du Théâtre en continuant les chants funèbres.
Iphigenie und die Priesterinnen nehmen den Chorgesang wieder auf und entfernen sich während des Singens von der Bühne.

Fl.
Ob.
Cl.
Fg.
Trb.
Vl. I
Vl. II
Vle
Coro (Pr.)
B.

que nos lar-mes, que nos re - grets pé - nè - trent l'in - ferna - le ri - - ve!

sich' uns dann, ge - fall' - ner Held, dir— ge- - rech - te Opfer brin - gen!

Fin de 2ème Acte.
Ende des zweiten Actes.

ACTE III.

Le Théâtre représente l'Appartement d'Iphigénie.
Das Gemach der Iphigenie.

SCÈNE I.

Iphigénie, Prêtresses.
Iphigenie, Priesterinnen.

Nº 19. Recitativ und Arie.

Allegro maestoso.
Violini I
Violini II
Viole
Iphigenie
Bassi
Recitativo.
Je cè-de à vos dé-sirs: du
Nun wohl, so sei es denn! Das

Vl. I
Vl. II
Vle
Iph.
B.
sort qui nous op-pri-me in-strui-sons É-lec-tre, ma sœur! Aux hor-reurs du tré-pas j'ar-ra-che u - ne vic-
Lei-den, das uns drückt, erfahr' E - lektra, mei - ne Schwester! Dem To - de wird so ein O - pfer auch ent-

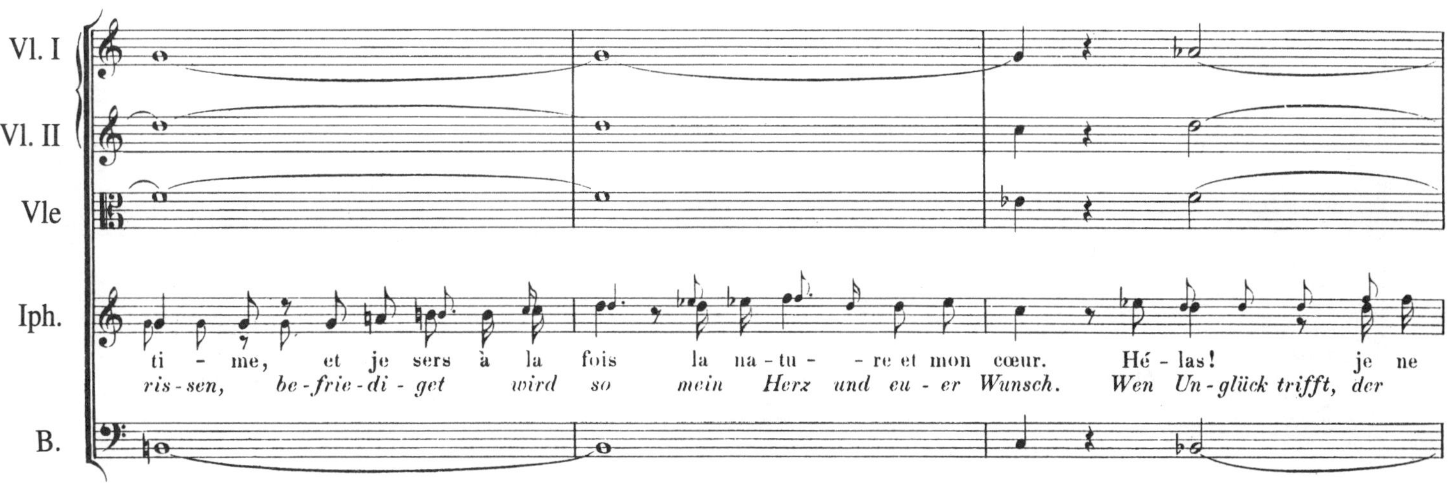
Vl. I
Vl. II
Vle
Iph.
B.
ti - me, et je sers à la fois la na-tu - re et mon cœur. Hé - las! je ne
ris-sen, be-frie-di-get wird so mein Herz und eu - er Wunsch. Wen Un-glück trifft, der

Vl. I
Vl. II
Vle
Iph.
puis m'en dé-fen-dre; pour l'un de ces infor-tu-nés, par nos bar-ba- -res lois à la mort condam-
kann nicht grausam sein: für Ei-nen die- -ser Fremdlinge, die un-ser schreckliches Ge-setz dem To- -de
B.
Vl. I
Vl. II
Vle
Iph.
nés, je sens la pi- tié la plus ten-dre. Mon cœur s'u-nit à lui
weiht, em-pfind' ich jetzt, was ich noch nie ge-fühlt; ver-eint ist ihm mein Herz durch
B.
Vl. I
Vl. II
Vle
Iph.
par des rap-ports se-crets... O-res-te se-rait de son â-ge: ce cap-tif mal-heu-
ein ge-hei-mes Band... In sei- -nem Al-ter war O-rest! sein Bild- -niss
B.
Vl. I
Vl. II
Vle
Iph.
reux m'en rap-pel- -le l'i-ma-ge, et sa no-ble fier-té m'en re-tra- -ce les traits.
ruft der ar-me Fremdling mir zu-rück; ach, beseelt war auch er von sol-chem ed-len Stolz.
B.

Arie.

Andante poco lento.
Violini I
Violini II
Viole
Iphigenie
Bassi
mf
p
pp
sf
D'une i-
E-wig
Vl. I
Vl. II
Vle
Iph.
B.
ma-ge, hé-las! trop ché-ri-e, j'aime en-co-re à m'en-tre-te-nir; mon â-me se plait à nour-
werd' ich sein, sein ge-den-ken, sein, den ich so früh ver-lor; ach, sein Bild-niss schwebt mir
rir l'es-pé-ran-ce qui m'est ra-vi-e. In-u-ti-les et chers trans-ports! Chas-
vor, meinem Her-zen Trost zu schen-ken. Welch' ein Traum ist die-sem gleich, a-ber
sons u-ne vai-ne chi-mè-re! Ah! ce n'est plus qu'aux som-bres bords que je puis re-trou-
schon ent-eilt er wieder! Ar-me! ach, nur im Schat-ten-reich sie-hest du den

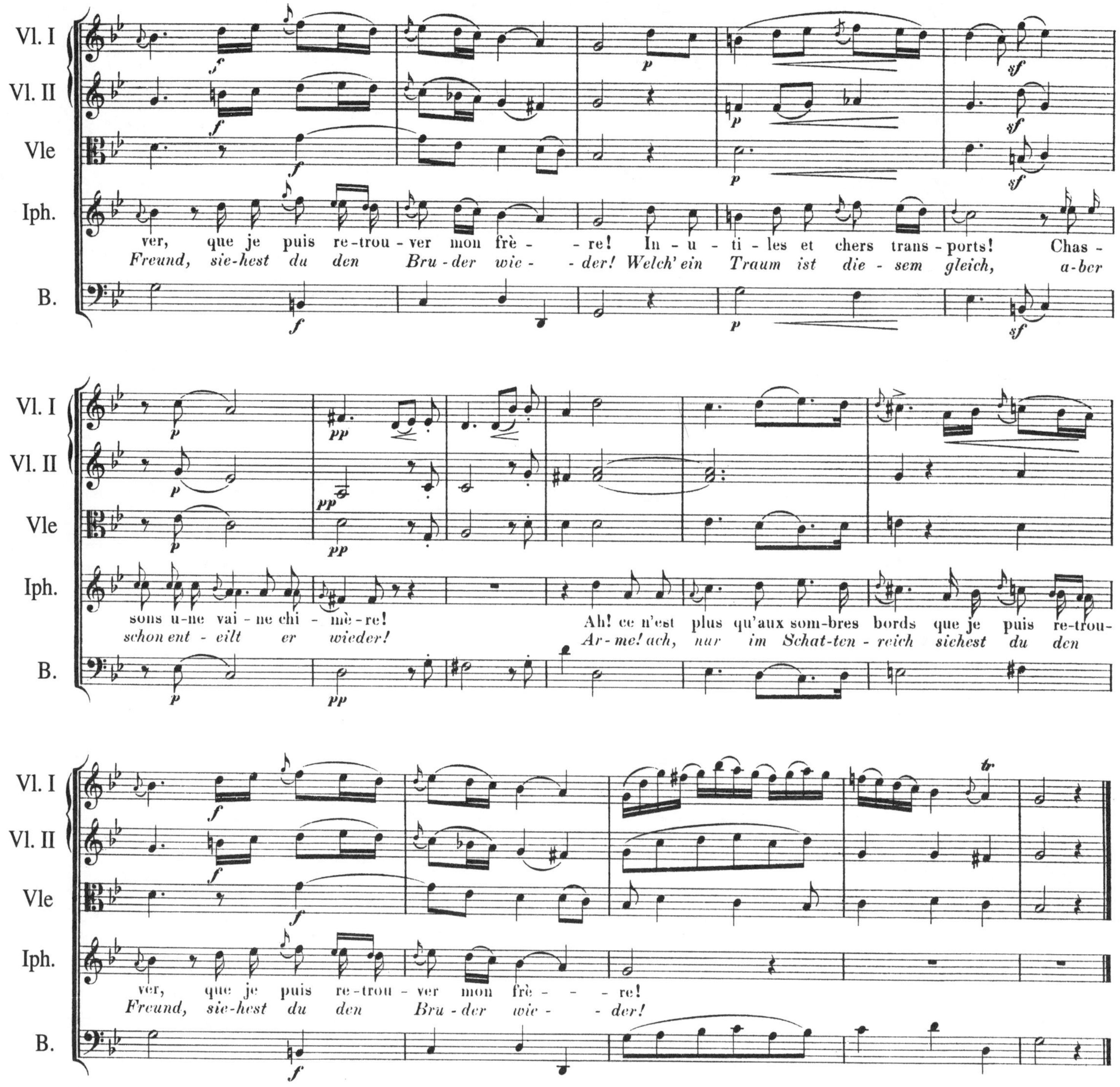

Vl. I
Vl. II
Vle
Iph.
B.

ver, que je puis re-trou - ver mon frè - - re! In - u - ti - les et chers trans - ports! Chas -
Freund, sie-hest du den Bru - der wie - - der! Welch' ein Traum ist die - sem gleich, a-ber

Vl. I
Vl. II
Vle
Iph.
B.

sons u-ne vai - ne chi - mè - re! Ah! ce n'est plus qu'aux som-bres bords que je puis re-trou-
schon ent - eilt er wieder! Ar - me! ach, nur im Schat-ten - reich siehest du den

Vl. I
Vl. II
Vle
Iph.
B.

ver, que je puis re-trou - ver mon frè - - - re!
Freund, sie-hest du den Bru - der wie - - der!

SCÈNE II.

Iphigénie, Prêtresses, Oreste, Pylade.
Iphigenie, Priesterinnen, Orest, Pylades.

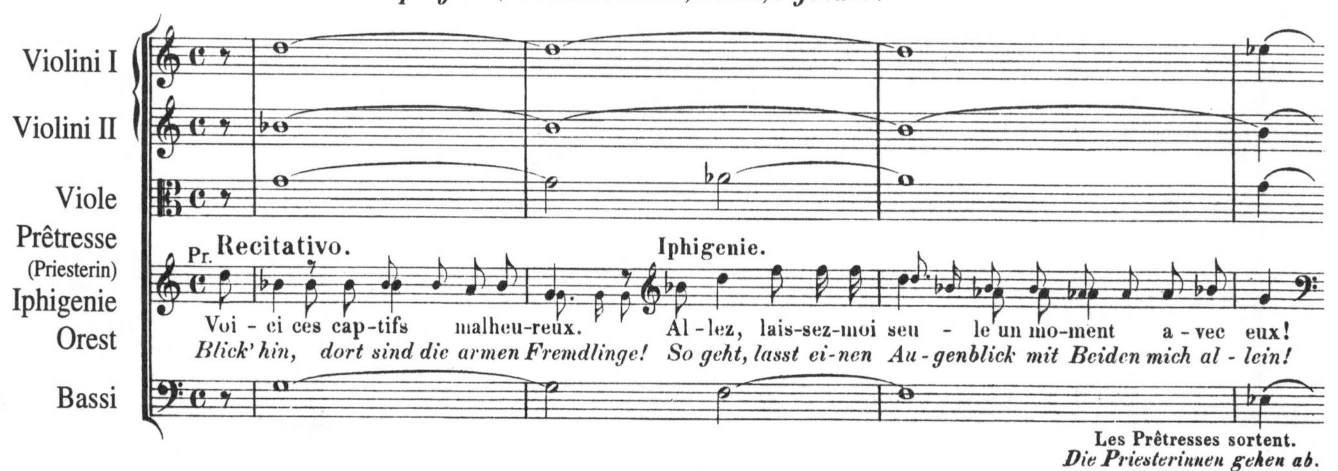
Violini I
Violini II
Viole
Prêtresse
(Priesterin)
Iphigenie
Orest
Bassi
Pr. Recitativo.
Iphigenie.
Voi - ci ces cap-tifs malheu-reux. Al - lez, lais-sez-moi seu - le un mo-ment a - vec eux!
Blick' hin, dort sind die armen Fremdlinge! So geht, lasst ei-nen Au - genblick mit Beiden mich al - lein!

Les Prêtresses sortent.
Die Priesterinnen gehen ab.

SCÈNE III.

Iphigénie, Oreste, Pylade.
Iphigenie, Orest, Pylades.

Vl. I
Vl. II
Vle
Iph.
ciel fi - xa nos pas, nous a - vons vu le jour dans de plus doux cli - mats, et la Grèce est no - tre pa - tri - e.
wil - den Scythen hin, das Le - ben gab uns einst ein sanf - ter Him - melsstrich, und Grie - chen - land ge - bar uns.
B.
Vl. I
Vl. II
Vle
Pyl.
Iphigenie.
Quoi? des mains d'u - ne Grec - que il faut per - dre la vi - e? Ah! pour sau - ver vos
So wer - den Grie - chen denn durch ei - ne Grie - chin ster - ben! Ge - wiss, ich gä - be
B.
Vl. I
Vl. II
Vle
Iph.
jours, je don - ne - rais les miens; mais Tho - as veut du sang: Sa pi - é - té bar -
gern, euch zu be - frei'n, mein Le - ben! Doch Tho - as for - dert Blut: mit wil - der Ty - ran -
B.
Vl. I
Vl. II
Vle
Iph.
ba - re a - jou - te - rait aux maux qu'on vous pré - pa - re, si de tous deux je bri - sais les li - ens.
nei vermehrt er noch die Qual, die er be - rei - tet, wenn ich die Band' euch Bei - den lö - sen will.
B.

Nº 20. Terzett.

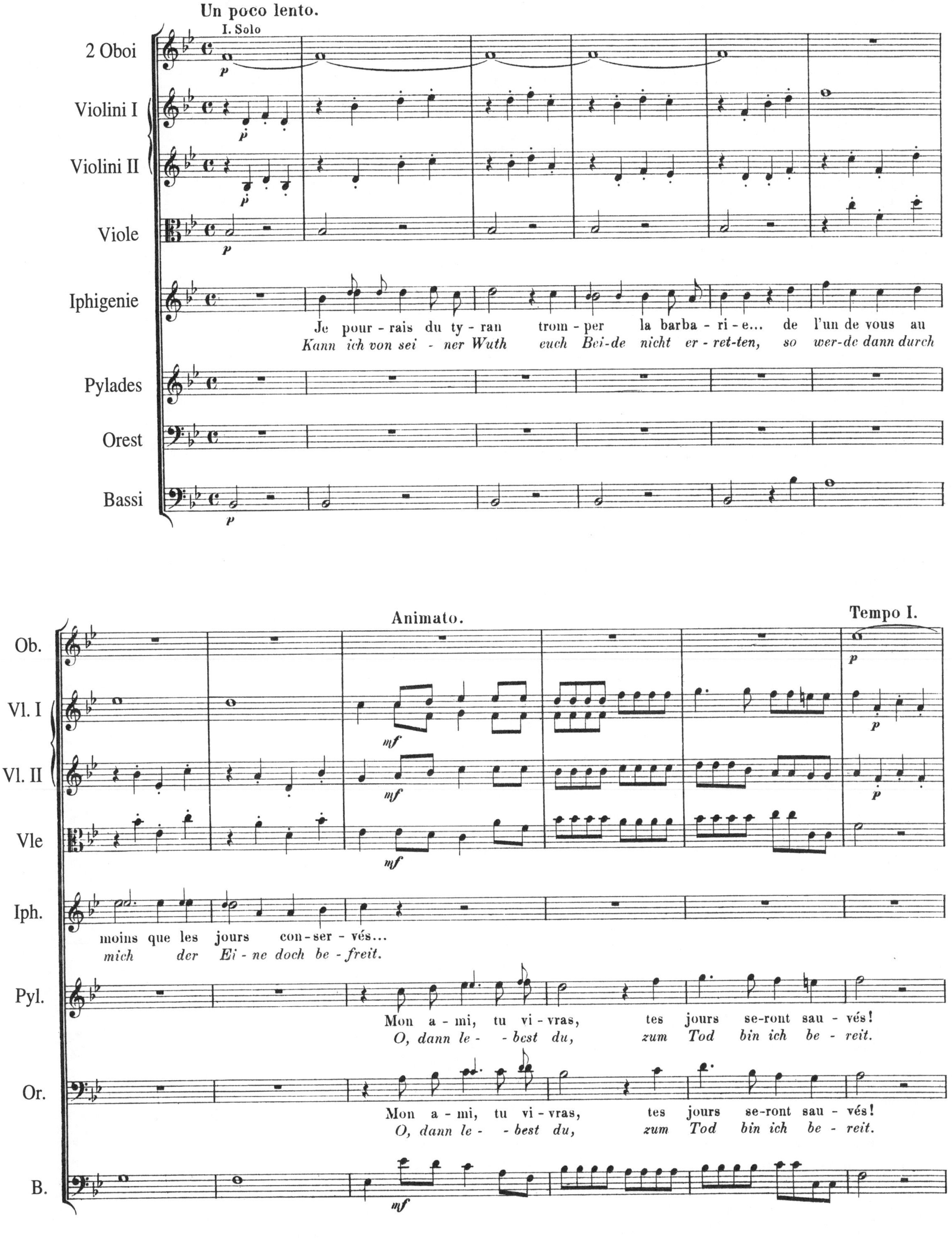

Animato. Tempo I.

Ob.
Vl. I
Vl. II
Vle
Iph.
moins que les jours con-ser - vés...
mich der Ei - ne doch be - freit.
Pyl.
Mon a - mi, tu vi - vras, tes jours se-ront sau - vés!
O, dann le - best du, zum Tod bin ich be - reit.
Or.
Mon a - mi, tu vi - vras, tes jours se-ront sau - vés!
O, dann le - best du, zum Tod bin ich be - reit.
B.

Ob.
Vl. I
Vl. II
Vle
Iph.
Pyl.
Or.
B.
Animato.
De ce - lui de vous deux qui me devra la vi - e, pourrais - je at - ten - dre un ser - vi - ce?
Doch nehm' ich Ei - nem dann von euch die har - ten Ketten, wird dann auch Dankbarkeit mich loh - nen?
A - che - vez! Je vous ré - ponds de sa re - connais - san - ce.
Ja, ge - beut! Er wird für dich sein Le - ben freudig wa - gen.
Tempo I.
Dans Ar - gos, comme vous, j'ai re - çu la nais - san - ce il m'y res - te encor des a - mis. Jurez - moi qu'un bil - let, fi -
In A - gamem - nons Stadt sah einst auch ich das Licht: mich knüpft an sie ein theures Band. So schwö - ret mir, dass treu ein

Animato.
Tempo I.
Ob.
Vl. I
Vl. II
Vle
Iph.
dè - le-ment re - mis...
Blatt von mei-ner Hand...
Pyl.
J'en at-tes - te les Dieux: vos vœux se-ront rem - plis.
Bei al-len Göt - tern ja, er täuscht dich wahr - lich nicht.
Or.
J'en at-tes - te les Dieux: vos vœux se-ront rem - plis.
Bei al-len Göt - tern ja, er täuscht dich wahr - lich nicht.
B.
Il faut donc en - tre vous choi-sir u - ne vic - ti - me...
So muss ich, muss ich denn aus euch ein O-pfer wäh-len...
Hé - las! dans le
Wie wird die har - te
soin qui m'a - ni - me, que ne puis-je à tous deux rendre un ser-vi-ce é - gal!
Pflicht mich quä - len, wie möcht' ich von dem Tod euch Bei-de gern be-frei'n!
Il
Dem

Vl. I
Vl. II
Vle
Iph.
B.
à part. bei Seite.
faut que l'un des deux ex - pi - - re... Mon â - me se dé - chi - re, mon â - me se dé - chi - re!
Le - ben muss der Ein' ent - sa - - gen... Wie kann mein Herz es' tra - gen, wie kann mein Herz es tra - gen!
dolcissimo
Mais, puis-qu'il faut en - fin faire un choix si fa - tal,
Doch ach, die schwere Wahl, sie muss getrof-fen sein:
Or.
colla voce
à Oreste. zu Orest.
c'est vous qui par - ti - rez.
so ge - he du von hier!
Ré - pon - dez à mes
Ja, das Leben geb' ich
Que je par - te? qu'il meure? Ô ciel!
Ich soll ge - hen? er sterben? Nein, nein!
Animato.
vœux: soyez prêt à par - tir, je cours en pres - ser l'heu - re.
dir! ja, sei zum Entflieh'n be - reit! Lass nicht umsonst mich ei - len!
Elle sort.
Sie geht ab.

SCÈNE IV.
Oreste, Pylade.
Orest, Pylades.

Nº 21. Duett.

Fiero ed animato.
2 Oboi
2 Fagotti
2 Corni in Do
Violini I
Violini II
Viole
Pylades
Orest
Bassi
a 2.
Et tu prétends en - co - re que tu m'ai - mes?
Und du ver-si-cherst doch, dass du mich lie - best?
Lors-qu'au mé-pris des Dieux
Du beut'st den Göt-tern Trotz,

Ob.
Fg.
Cor.
Vl. I
Vl. II
Vle
Pyl.
Or.
B.
Ils veil-lent sur les tiens, ils pro-tè-gent leur cours; je rem -
Ja, mein O - rest, lass mich, lass mich das O - pfer sein: die Götter
sa - cri - fi - ant tes jours...
willst dich zum O - pfer weih'n!

Ob.
Fg.
Cor.
Vl. I
Vl. II
Vle
Pyl.
plis leurs de-crets su-prê - mes.
ha - - ben mich er - ko - ren.
Or.
À ces Dieux con-ju-rés pré-tends - tu donc t'u - nir, pour a - - jou-
Den feind - lichen Göt - tern willst du dich ver - bin - - den, die
B.

Ob.
Fg.
Cor.
Vl. I
Vl. II
Vle
Pyl.
Que me de-mandes - tu?
Was forderst du von mir?
Or.
ter aux tour-ments que j'en - du - re? De me lais-ser mou-
Ta - ge mei - ner Qual zu ver - meh - ren? Mich sollst du ster-ben
B.

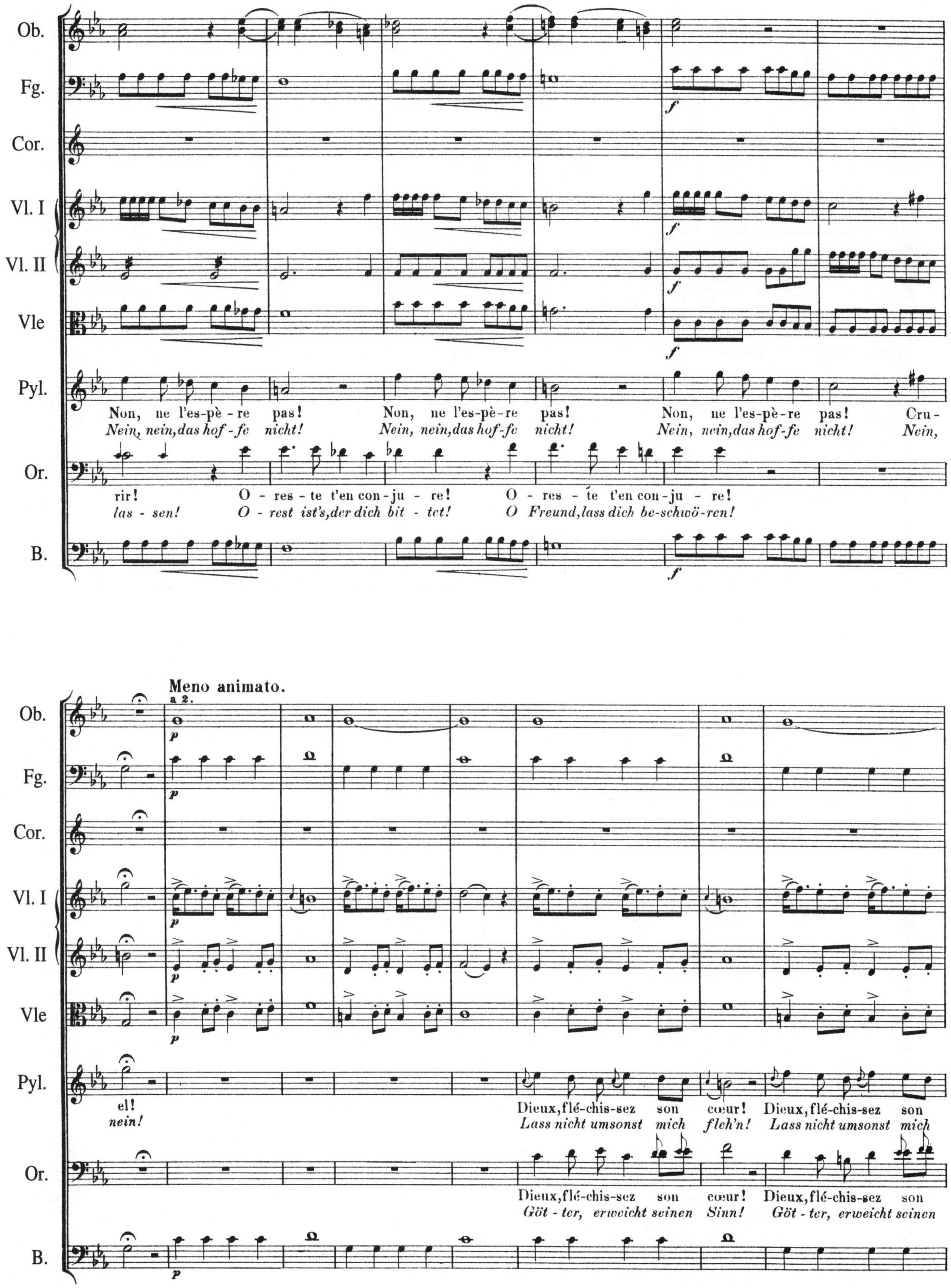

Meno animato.

a 2.

Ob.
Fg.
Cor.
Vl. I
Vl. II
Vle
Pyl.

el! Dieux, flé-chis-sez son cœur! Dieux, flé-chis-sez son
nein! Lass nicht umsonst mich fleh'n! Lass nicht umsonst mich

Or.

Dieux, flé-chis-sez son cœur! Dieux, flé-chis-sez son
Göt-ter, erweicht seinen Sinn! Göt-ter, erweicht seinen

B.

Ob.
Fg.
Cor.
Vl. I
Vl. II
Vle
Pyl.
cœur! Ren-dez - moi mon a - - mi, qu'il m'ac - cor - de sa grâ - ce,qu'il m'ac - cor - - de sa
fleh'n! Sei, was du warst, sei mein Freund! Dir weih'ich gern, dir mein Le - ben, dir weih'ich gern mein
Or.
cœur! Ren-dez - moi mon a - - mi, qu'il m'ac - cor - de,qu'il m'ac - cor - - de sa
Sinn! Gebt mir mei-nen Freund zu - - rück, lasst, o Göt - ter,lasst ihn meinen Wunsch er -
B.

Ob.
Fg.
Cor.
Vl. I
Vl. II
Vle
Pyl.
grâ - ce. Que tout mon sang vous sa - tis - fas - - se, qu'il suf - - fi - - se à
Le - ben; kann das der Göt - ter Huld dir ge - - ben, dann sollst du noch sie
Or.
grâ - ce. Que tout mon sang vous sa - tis - fas - - se, qu'il suf - - fi - - se à
fül - len!Kann all' mein Blut eu'r Zür - nen stil - - len, nehmt es zur Ver -
B.

Ob.
Fg.
Cor.
Vl. I
Vl. II
Vle
Pyl.

vo - tre ri - gueur! Dieux, flé - chis - sez, flé - chis - sez son cœur! Ren - dez -
gnä - - dig seh'n. Lasst nicht um - sonst, nicht um - sonst mich - fleh'n! Sei, was du

Or.

vo - tre ri - gueur! Dieux, fléchis - sez son cœur, Dieux, fléchis - sez son cœur!
söh - - nung hin! Göt - ter, erweicht seinen Sinn, Göt - ter, erweicht seinen Sinn!

B.

Ob.
Fg.
Cor.
Vl. I
Vl. II
Vle
Pyl.

moi mon a - mi, qu'il m'ac - cor - de sa grâ - ce, qu'il m'ac - cor - de sa grâ - ce. Que
warst, sei mein Freund! Dir weih' ich gern mein — Le - ben, dir weih' ich gern mein Le - ben; kann

Or.

Ren - dez - moi mon a - - mi, qu'il m'ac - cor - de, qu'il m'ac - cor - de sa grâ - ce.
Gebt mir mei - nen Freund zu - - rück, lasst, o Göt - ter, lasst ihn mei - nen Wunsch er - fül - len!

B.

Ob.
Fg. a 2.
Cor.
Vl. I
Vl. II
Vle
Pyl.

tout mon sang vous sa - tis - fas - se, qu'il suf - fi - se à vo - tre ri -
das der Göt - ter Huld dir ge - ben, dann sollst du noch sie gnä - dig

Or.

Que tout mon sang vous sa - tis - fas - se, qu'il suf - fi - se à vo - tre ri -
Kann all' mein Blut eu'r Zürnen stil - len, nehmt es zur Ver - söh - nung

B.

Ob.
Fg.
Cor.
Vl. I
Vl. II
Vle
Pyl.

gueur! Que tout mon sang vous sa - tis - fas - se, qu'il suf - fi - se à
seh'n; kann das der Göt - ter Huld dir ge - ben, dann sollst du noch sie

Or.

gueur! Que tout mon sang vous sa - tis - fas - se, qu'il suf - fi - se à
hin! Kann all' mein Blut eu'r Zür - nen stil - len, nehmt es zur Ver -

B.

Ob.
Fg.
Cor.
Vl. I
Vl. II
Vle
Pyl.

vo - tre ri - gueur, qu'il suf - fi - se à vo - tre ri - gueur, qu'il suf - fi - se à vo - tre ri -
gnä - dig seh'n, dann sollst du sie gnä - dig seh'n, dann sollst du sie gnä - dig

Or.

vo - tre ri - gueur, qu'il suf - fi - se à vo - tre ri - gueur, qu'il suf - fi - se à vo - tre ri -
söh - nung hin, all' mein Blut, o nehmt es hin, zur Ver - söh - nung nehmt es

B.

Ob.
Fg.
Cor.
Vl. I
Vl. II
Vle
Pyl.

gueur!
seh'n.

Or.

gueur!
hin!

B.

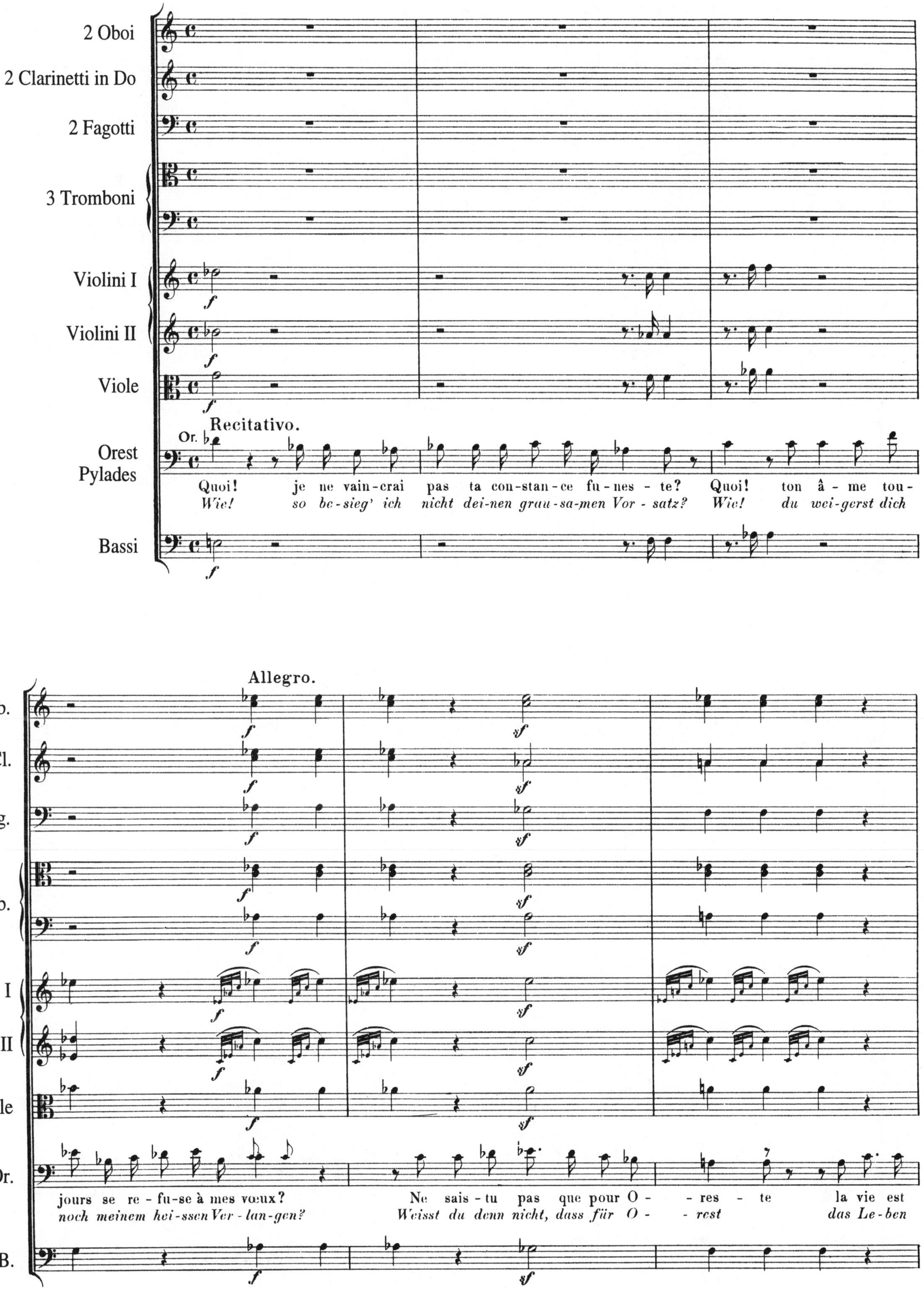

Allegro.

Ob.
Cl.
Fg.
Trb.
Vl. I
Vl. II
Vle
Or.

jours se re - fu-se à mes vœux? Ne sais - tu pas que pour O - - res - te la vie est
noch meinem hei-ssen Ver - lan-gen? Weisst du denn nicht, dass für O - - rest das Le-ben

B.

Ob.
Cl.
Fg.
Trb.
Vl. I
Vl. II
Vle
Or.

un sup-pli-ce af-freux? Ne sais-tu pas que ces mains par-ri - - ci - - des fu-ment en-cor du

ei - ne Mar-ter ist? Weisst du denn nicht, dass die - se Mör-der-hand noch von dem Blu-te

B.

Ob.
Cl.
Fg.
Trb.
Vl. I
Vl. II
Vle
Or.

sang que j'ai ver - sé? Ne sais-tu pas que l'en-fer cour-rou - - cé ras-semble au-tour de

raucht, das sie ver - goss? Weisst du es nicht, dass der Or-kus, em - - pört, ver-sam-melt rings um

B.

Ob.
Cl.
Fg.
Trb.
Vl. I
Vl. II
Vle
Or.
moi ses noi - res Eu-mé - - ni - des, qu'el-les m'ob - sè-dent en tous lieux?
mich die schwarzen Eu-me - - ni - den, dass ü - ber - all sie mich um - steh'n?
B.

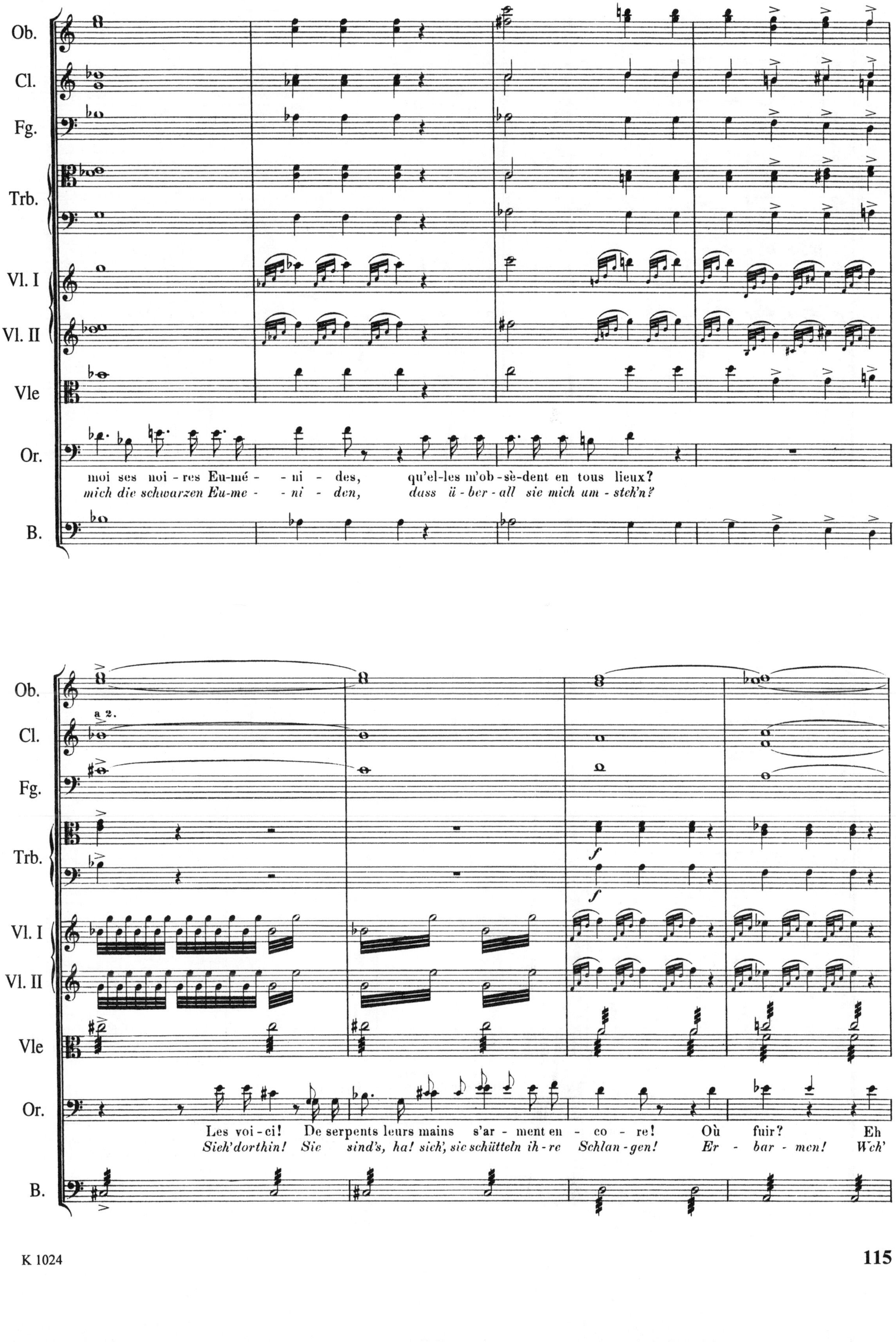

Ob.
a 2.
Cl.
Fg.
Trb.
f
f
Vl. I
Vl. II
Vle
Or.
Les voi - ci! De serpents leurs mains s'ar - ment en - co - re! Où fuir? Eh
Sieh' dorthin! Sie sind's, ha! sieh', sie schütteln ih - re Schlan - gen! Er - bar - men! Weh'
B.

Ob.
Cl.
Fg.
Trb.
Vl. I
Vl. II
Vle
Or.
B.

cresc.

quoi! Py - la - de me fuit et m'ab - hor - re? Il me li - vre à leurs coups!... Ar-rê-

mir! Auch Py-lades entflieht mit Ab - scheu, ü-ber-giebt mich ih-rer Wuth!... Haltet

Ob.
Cl.
Fg.
Trb.
Vl. I
Vl. II
Vle
Or.
B.

ff

Il tombe dans les bras de Pylade.

Er fällt Pylades in die Arme.

Pylades.

tez... ah, grands Dieux! — Eh quoi! Méconnais - tu Py - la - de qui t'im-

ein... ew'- ge Göt - ter! O - rest! Verkennst du mich, der stets dich

Vl. I
Vl. II
Vle
Pyl.
B.
in tempo.
Orest. revenant à lui. zu sich kommend.
Pylades.
plo-re? Eh bien, Py-la-de, est-ce à toi de mou-rir? O Dieux! Vo-tre cour-roux ne peut-il se flé-
lieb-te? Da sieh', o Py-lades, for-dert mich nicht der Tod? So währt, ihr Göt-ter, e-wig eu-er
Orest. accable. niedergeschlagen.
chir? La mort à mes tourments est l'u-ni-que re-lâ-che; je l'ob-te-nais: Py-la-de me l'ar-ra-che!
Zorn! Der Tod nur en-det mild die Qualen, die ich tra-ge; schon war er mein, und Py-lades ent-reisst ihn mir!
Nº 22. Arie.
Allegro.
Andante.
Oboe 1.
Violini I
Violini II
Viole
Pylades
Orest
Bassi
Pyl.
Ah! mon a-mi, j'im-plo-re ta pi-tié, O-res-te, hé-las! peut-
O theurer Freund, um Mitleid fleh' ich dich! Kannst du, O-rest, kannst
Ritenuto.
Tempo I.
Andante.
Ob.
il me mécon-naî-tre? Qu'il s'at-ten-dris-se aux pleurs de l'a-mi-tié! Ton cœur au mien
du mich so ver-ken-nen? Sieh' meinen Schmerz, in Thrä-nen siehe mich! Soll ich, O-rest,

Tempo I.
Ob.
Vl. I
Vl. II
Vle
Pyl.
n'est pas fer - mé peut - ê - tre, ton cœur au mien n'est pas fer - mé peut - ê - tre? Cet a -
nicht länger Freund dich nen - nen, soll ich, O - rest, nicht länger Freund dich nen - nen? Er, den du
B.
mi qui te fut si cher, Py - la - de est à tes pieds; il con - ju - re, il te pres - se; à tes fu - reurs laisse -
einst so treu ge - liebt, er fleht im Stau - be hier; lass ihn Er - hörung, Er - hö - rung hof - fen! Nimm, was der Spruch der
Andante.
Ritenuto.
Lento.
Orest.
moi t'ar - ra - cher, sous - cris au choix dic - té par la Prê - tres - se, sous - cris, sous - cris! Py -
Prie - sterin dir giebt; folg' ih - rer Wahl, sie ist ge - recht ge - trof - fen. O - rest, O - rest! O

Allegro.
Andante.
Ritenuto.
Ob.
Vl. I
Vl. II
Vle
Or.
B.
Pylades.
la - de! Ah! mon a - mi, j'im-plo-re ta pi - tié, O - res-te, hé - las! peut - il me mécon - naî -
Py - la-des! O theurer Freund, um Mitleid fleh' ich dich! Kannst du, O - rest, kannst du mich so ver - ken -
Tempo I.
Andante.
Orest.
Pylades.
Pyl.
tre? Grands Dieux! Qu'il s'atten - dris - se aux pleurs de l'ami - tié! Ton cœur au mien n'est pas fer -
nen? O Zeus! Sieh' meinen Schmerz, in Thrä-nen siehe mich! Soll ich, O - rest, nicht länger
Tempo I.
mé peut-ê - tre, ton cœur au mien n'est pas fer - mé peut-ê - tre?
Freund dich nen - nen, soll ich, O - rest, nicht länger Freund dich nen - nen?

SCENE V.

Oreste, Pylade, Iphigénie, Prêtresses.
Orest, Pylades, Iphigenie, Priesterinnen.

Animato.
Violini I
Violini II
Viole
Orest
Iphigenie
Pylades
Bassi
Relevant Pylade avec un mouvement de fureur.
Mit heftiger Bewegung Pylades bestürmend.
Or.
Recitativo.
Malgré toi, je sau-rai t'arracher au tré-pas!
Und dennoch ent-reiss' ich dich dem Tod!
Ritenuto.
Lento.
Iphigenie. à Pylade. zu Pylades.
aux Prêtresses.
zu den Priesterinnen.
Orest.
Que je vous plains! Vous, con-dui-sez ses pas! Non, Prêtres-se, ar-rê-
O wie be-klag' ich dich! Führt ihn zum Hei-lig-thum! Nein, Prie-ste-rin, halt'
tez! Vo-tre pi-tié s'é-ga-re. Que di-tes-vous? C'est à moi de mou-rir. Mon a-
ein! Dein Mit-leid täu-schet dich. Was sa-gest du? Nur mir ge-hört der Tod. Mein Freund er-
Iphigenie.
Orest.
mi pour-ra vous ser-vir; qu'il soit le digne ob-jet d'un ser-vi-ce si ra-re! N'é-cou-tez
fül-let, was du forderst; ihn weih', er ist es werth, dem mir be-stimm-ten Dienst! Nein, hör' ihn
Pylades.

Vl. I
Vl. II
Vle
Pyl.
B.
Iphigenie. à Oreste. zu Orest.
Orest.
Pylades.
point ses transports fu-ri-eux! Vi - vez et me ser-vez! Je ne le puis sans cri - me. Cru-
nicht in sei-nem Ra-sen! Leb' du, und die-ne mir! Ich kann es nicht oh-ne Fre-vel. Du
Iphigenie.
Orest. à Py- zu Py-
el! quel-le fu-reur t'a - ni - me? Ah! je sens que mon choix est dic - té par les Dieux. C'en est
Grausamer! Noch im-mer muss ich fle-hen? Die Göt - ter selbst be - - stimm - ten mei - - ne Wahl. Nun
lade avec vitesse.
lades mit Lebhaftigkeit.
Or.
Pylades.
Orest. à Iphigénie. zu Iphigenie.
Pylades.
fait: i - ci même, à l'instant, je dé - cla - re... Ar - rê - te! Eh bien, sa - chez... Ar - rê - te, jus-tes
wohl: in diesem Au - gen-blick er - klär' ich... Halt' ein! So wis - se denn... Halt' ein, gerech-te
Iphigenie. à Oreste. zu Orest.
Orest. à Iphigénie. zu Iphigenie.
Dieux! Quel-le sou-dai-ne hor-reur de vo-tre â - me s'em - pa - re? Pronon - cez, que ma
Göt-ter! O wel-che Ra - se - rei fasst so plötz-lich dei - ne See - le? Ge - beut denn, dass mein

Vl. I
Vl. II
Vle
Iphigenie.
Or.
mort… Non, ne l'es-pé-rez pas: un pou-voir in-con-nu, puis-sant, ir-ré-sis-
Tod… Nein, das hof-fe nicht: ich weiss, es hielt' ein Gott, zwar un-bekannt, doch
B.
Vl. I
Vl. II
Vle
Iph.
ti-ble, sur l'au-tel des Dieux mê-me ar-rê-te-rait mon bras.
mäch-tig, auch selbst an dem Al-tar, den Arm mir noch zu-rück!
B.
Lento.
Vivace.
Violini I
Violini II
Viole
Orest
Iphigenie
Or.
Quoi! Tou-jours à mes vœux vous ê-tes in-fle-xi-ble? Mais c'est en
Wie! Noch immer bleibst du taub bei meinem heissen Fle-hen? Doch nur um-
Bassi
Tempo I.
Vl. I
Vl. II
Vle
Or.
vain, j'en at-tes-te les Dieux: Si mon a-mi n'é-chappe au sort qu'on lui pré-pa-re, je vais, m'immo-
sonst, bei den Göt-tern, um-sonst! Wenn nicht mein Freund dem To-des-loo-se ent-ge-het, so tödt' ich mich
B.
cresc.

Vivace.
Vl. I
Vl. II
Vle
Or.
Iphigenie.
lant à vos yeux, ré-pan-dre tout ce sang dont le ciel est a - va - - - re. O
selbst hier vor euch, ver-strö-mend all' das Blut, das der Him - mel sich spa - - - ret. O
B.
Lento.
Vivace.
Iph.
Dieux! Eh bien, cru-el, rem-plis-sez vos dé-sirs!
Schmerz! Nun wohl, du Grau-sa-mer, so sei dein Wunsch gewährt!
Orest. vivement à Pylade. lebhaft zu Pylades.
Vis, mon a - mi, cours ser-vir la Prêtres - se! D'u-ne sœur qui m'est
Le - be, mein Freund, ge-hor-che dei - ner Rette-rin! Der heiss - ge - lieb-ten
chè - re, a - dou-cis la tris - tes - se, por - te - lui mes der-niers sou - pirs! A - dieu!
Schwester gieb Trost in ih - rem Schmerze, bring' ihr den letz - ten Seuf - zer mei - ner Brust! Leb' wohl!
Il sort.
Geht ab.

SCÈNE VI.

Iphigénie, Pylade.
Iphigenie, Pylades.

Lento.
Vl. I
Vl. II
Vle
Iph.
B.
Puis-que le ciel à vos jours s'in - té - res - se, prê - tez - moi le se-cours que
Der Himmel selbst hat dich in Schutz ge - nom-men. Nun, so er-fül - le denn, was
vous m'a-vez pro-mis: Por-tez cet é-crit dans la Grè-ce, qu'en-tre les mains d'É-lec-tre il soit par vous re-mis.
du versprochen hast: nach Grie-chen-land bring' die-ses Schreiben; dort sprich E - lek-tra selbst, und ü-berreich' es ihr!
Pylades.
Qu'en-tends-je? et quel rap-port l'u-ne à l'au - tre vous li - e?
Was hör' ich? Welch' ein Ge - schick ver - ei - net dich mit ihr?
Pyl.
Iphigenie.
J'ai res - pec - té vo - tre se - cret: n'e-xi-gez rien de plus!
Ich ehr - te dein Ge - heim-niss, so frag' auch du mich nicht!
Pylades.
Vous se-rez o - bé - i - e, je rem-pli-rai vos voeux, si le ciel le per-met.
Wohl! ich ge-hor-che dir, er-fül-le dei-nen Wunsch, wenn es die Göt - ter wol-len.

Iphigénie sort.
Iphigenie geht ab.

SCÈNE VII.

Pylade, seul.

Pylades, allein.

Ob.
Fg.
Vl. I
Vl. II
Vle
Pyl.
res - te, ou cou-rir au tré-pas, ou cou-rir au tré-pas. A - mi - tié,
rest, ihm geweiht sei mein Blut, ihm geweiht sei mein Blut! Freundschaft, komm!
Bassi.
Vlc. e B.
a - mi - tié, viens, viens ar - mer mon bras!
Freundschaft, komm! komm, komm, und gieb mir Muth!
Rem - plis mon cœur de tes cé - les - tes flam - mes, rem - plis mon cœur de tes cé -
Ent-flammt lass mich von dei-nem Feu - er wer - den, ent-flammt lass mich von dei-nem

Ob.
Fg.
Cor.
Tr.
Timp.
Vl. I
Vl. II
Vle
Pyl.

les - - tes flam - mes, je vais sau-ver O-res - te, ou cou-rir au tré - pas, ou cou-rir au tré-
Feu - - er wer - den! Ge - ret - tet sei O-rest, ihm geweiht sei mein Blut, ihm geweiht sei mein

Vlc. e B.

Ob.
Fg.
Cor.
Tr.
Timp.
Vl. I
Vl. II
Vle
Pyl.

pas. Je vais sau-ver O - res-te, ou cou-rir au tré-pas, ou cou-rir au tré -
Blut! Ge-ret - tet sei O - rest, ihm ge-weiht mein Blut, ihm ge-weiht sei mein

Vlc. e B.

Ob.
Fg.
Cor.
Tr.
Timp.
Vl. I
Vl. II
Vle
Pyl.
Vlc. e B.

pas, ou cou-rir au tré - pas.
Blut, ihm ge-weiht sei mein Blut!

Ob.
Fg.
Cor.
Tr.
Timp.
Vl. I
Vl. II
Vle
Pyl.
Vlc. e B.

Fin du 3ème acte

Ende des dritten Aktes

K 1024

ACTE IV.

Le Théâtre représente l'intérieur du Temple de Diane; la Statue de la Déesse, élevée sur une estrade, est au milieu; en avançant sur un des côtés, on voit l'Autel des Sacrifices.

Das Innere des Tempels der Diana. In der Mitte, auf einer Erhöhung, die Bildsäule der Göttin; auf der einen Seite im Vordergrunde der Opferaltar.

SCÈNE I.

Iphigénie, seule.

Iphigenie, *allein.*

Nº 24. Recitativ und Arie.

Fieramente, un poco animato.
Arie.
2 Oboi
2 Fagotti
2 Corni in Sol
Violini I
Violini II
Viole
Iphigenie
Bassi
a 2.
Ob.
Fg.
Cor.
Vl. I
Vl. II
Vle
Iph.
B.
Iphigenie.
au pied de l'autel.
am Fusse des Altars.
Je t'im-plo-re et je trem-ble, ô Dé-es-se impla-
Er-be-bend fleh' ich dir, o Göttin voll vom
ca-ble! Dans le fond de mon coeur mets la fé-ro-ci-té: é-touf-fe de l'hu-ma-ni-
Grimme, er-fül-le mei-ne Brust mit düst'-rer Grausam-keit: sie hö-re, deinem Dienst ge-

Ob.
Fg.
Cor.
Vl. I
Vl. II
Vle
Iph.
B.
a 2.
té la voix plain - ti-ve et la-men - ta - ble! Hé - las! et quel-le est
weiht, nicht mehr der Menschheit sanf-te Stim - me! O Schmerz! was hast du
donc la ri - gueur de mon sort? D'un sanglant mi-nis - tè-re vic - ti-me in-vo-lon - tai - re,
mir, Di - a - na, auf - er - legt! Ich muss den wilden Horden so vie - le O-pfer morden! Die
j'o - bé - is; et mon cœur est en proie, est en proie au re - mord, et mon cœur est en
Hand ge - horcht; doch ach! dass es mein Herz, dass es mein Herz nicht trägt! doch ach! dass mein

Ob.
Fg.
Cor.
Vl. I
Vl. II
Vle
Iph.
B.
proie au re - mord, est en proie au re - mord, en proie au re - mord, en proie au, re
Herz es nicht trägt, dass mein Herz es nicht trägt, doch ach! dass mein Herz, mein Herz es nicht
a 2.
mord!
trägt!
Je t'im-plo - re et je tremble, ô Dé-es - se im-pla - ca-ble! Dans le fond de mon cœur
Ich fle-he dich er - bebend, o Göttin voll vom Grimme, er - fül-le mei-ne Brust, er -

Ob.
Fg.
Cor.
Vl. I
Vl. II
Vle
Iph.
B.
mets la fé-ro-ci-té, mets la fé-ro-ci-té: é-touf-fe de l'hu-ma-ni-té la
fül-le mei-ne Brust mit düst'rer Grausam-keit; sie hö-re, dei-nem Dienst ge-weiht, nicht
voix plain-ti-ve et la-men-ta-ble! Dans le fond de mon cœur mets la fé-ro-ci-
mehr der Mensch-heit sanf-te Stim-me! Er-fül-le mei-ne Brust mit düst'-rer Grausam-
a 2.
té, mets la fé-ro-ci-té! Hé-las! et quel-le est donc la ri-
keit, mit düst'-rer Grausam-keit! O Schmerz! was hast du mir, Di-

Ob.
Fg.
Cor.
Vl. I
Vl. II
Vle
Iph.
gueur de mon sort? D'un sang-lant mi-nis-tè-re vic-ti-me in-vo-lon-tai-re, j'o-bé-
a-na, auf-er-legt! Ich muss den wilden Horden so vie-le O-pfer morden! Die Hand ge-
B.
a 2.
is; et mon cœur est en proie, est en proie au re-mord, et mon cœur est en proie au re-
horcht; doch ach! dass es mein Herz, mein Herz nicht trägt! doch ach! dass mein Herz es nicht
mord, est en proie au re-mord, en proie au re-mord, en proie au re-mord!
trägt, dass mein Herz es nicht trägt, dass mein Herz es nicht trägt, dass mein Herz es nicht trägt!

 K 1024

SCÈNE II.

Iphigénie, Prêtresses, Oreste au milieu d'elles.
Iphigenie, Priesterinnen; Orest *inmitten unter ihnen.*

Nº 25. Chor.

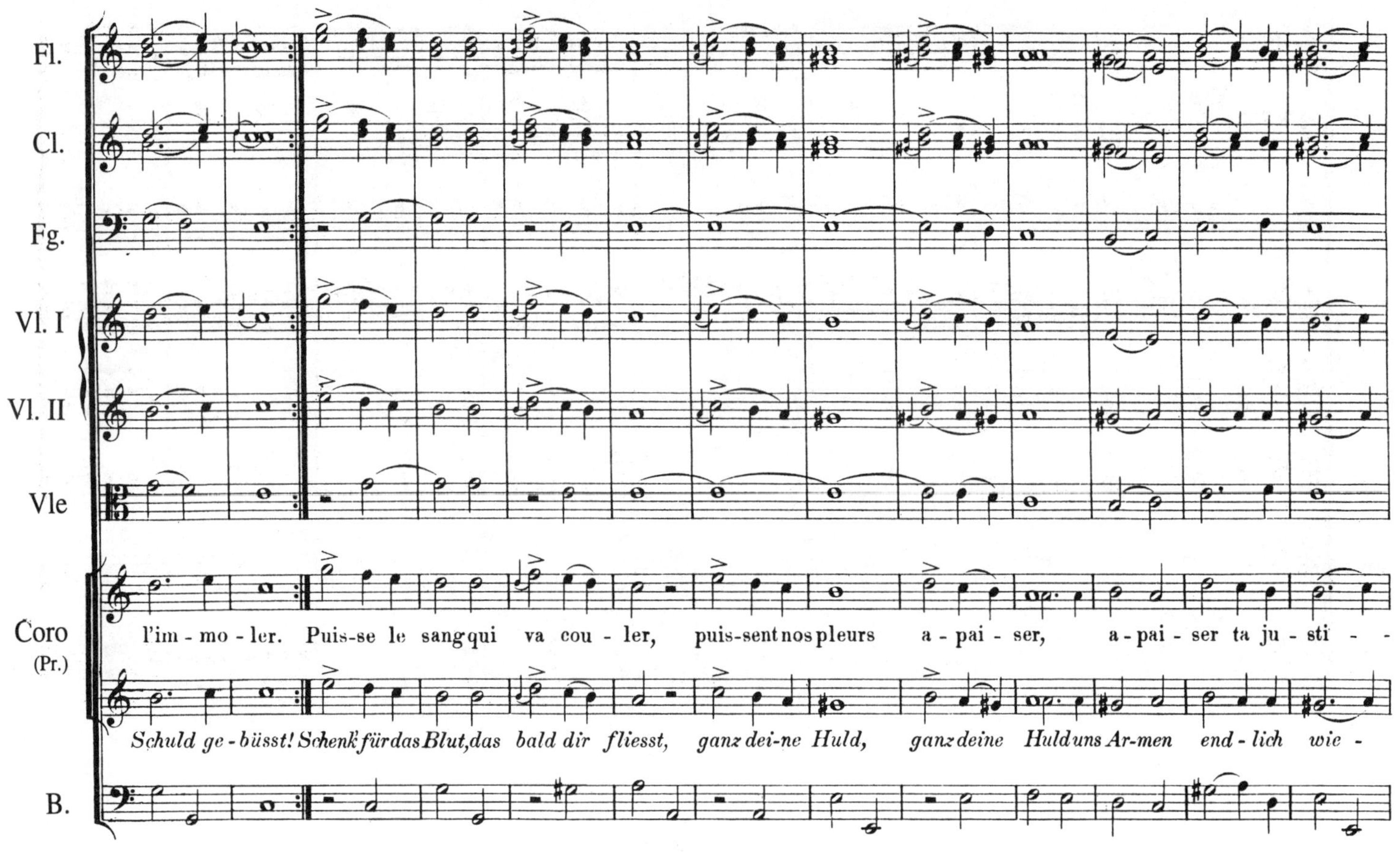

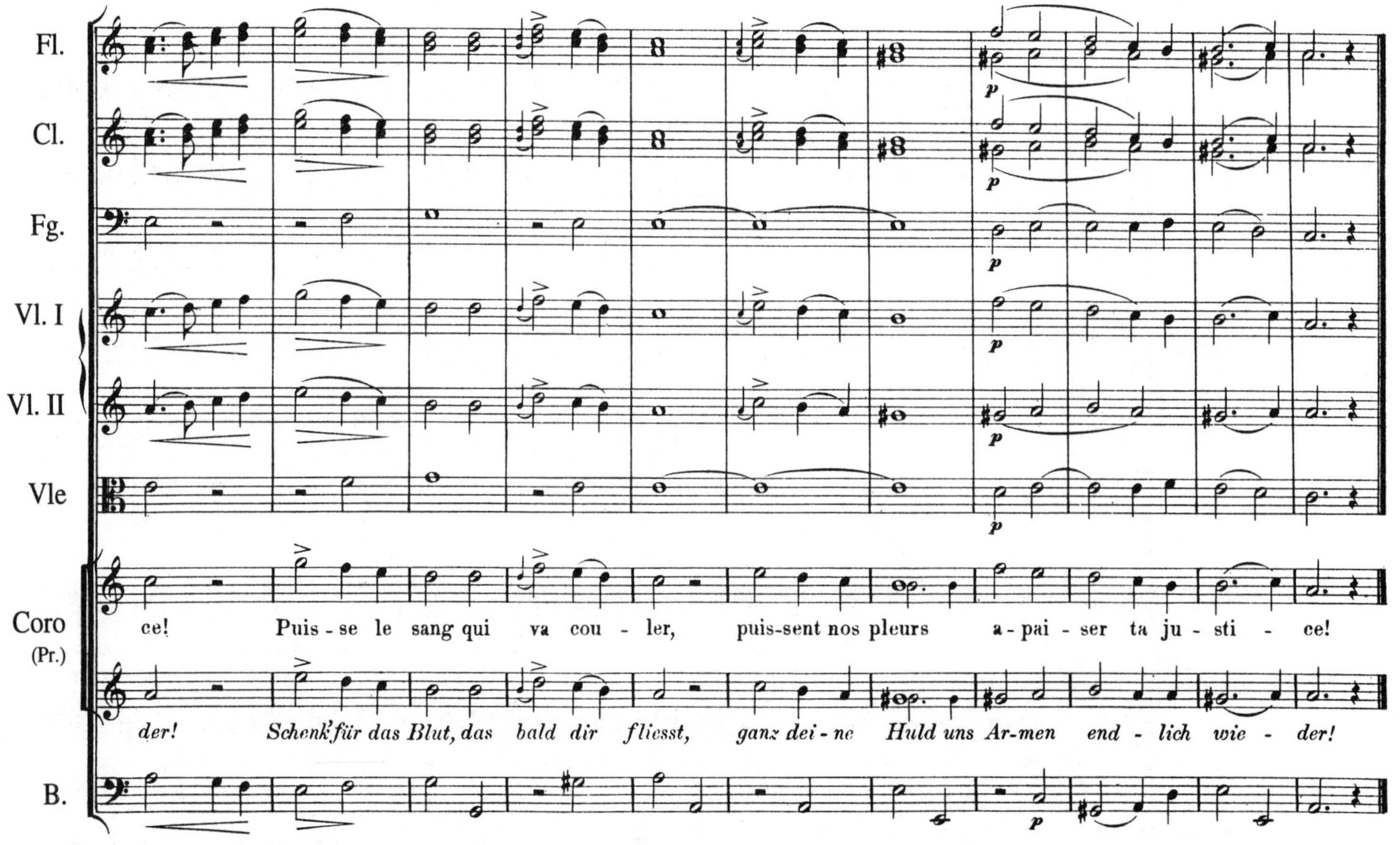

Fl.
Cl.
Fg.
Vl. I
Vl. II
Vle
Coro
(Pr.)
l'im - mo - ler. Puis-se le sang qui va cou - ler, puis-sent nos pleurs a - pai - ser, a - pai - ser ta ju - sti - -
Schuld ge - büsst! Schenk' für das Blut, das bald dir fliesst, ganz dei-ne Huld, ganz deine Huld uns Ar-men end - lich wie -
B.

Fl.
Cl.
Fg.
Vl. I
Vl. II
Vle
Coro
(Pr.)
ce! Puis - se le sang qui va cou - ler, puis-sent nos pleurs a - pai - ser ta ju - sti - ce!
der! Schenk' für das Blut, das bald dir fliesst, ganz dei - ne Huld uns Ar-men end - lich wie - der!
B.

Violini I
Violini II
Viole
Iphigenie
Orest
Bassi
Recitativo.
Elle tombe sur un siège.
Iph. Sie fällt auf einen Sessel nieder.
La for - ce m'a - ban - don - ne; ô mo - ment dou - lou - reux!
Die Kräf - te schwin - den mir; o ban - ger, qua - len - vol - ler Au - gen - blick!
Vl. I
Vl. II
Vle
Orest.
Or.
Voi - là le ter - me heu - reux de mes lon - gues souf - fran - ces: puis - se - t - il l'ê - tre aus -
So wer - den end - lich hier sich mei - ne Lei - den en - den: möch - te doch end - lich
B.
si, grands Dieux, de vos ven - gean - ces! Ô ciel! Sé - chez les pleurs qui
auch, o Göt - ter, sich eu - re Ra - che wen - den! O Schmerz! Ge - beut der Thrä - ne,
Iphigenie.
cou - lent de vos yeux; ne plai - gnez point mon sort, la mort fait mon en - vi - e. Frap -
die dein Au - ge weint; be - kla - ge nicht mein Loos, der Tod ist mei - ne Lust. Voll -

Vl. I
Vl. II
Vle
Or.
B.
Iphigenie.
pez! Ah, ca - chez - moi cet - te hor - ri - ble ver - tu! Les Dieux pro - té - geaient vo - tre
en - de! Birg die - se schre - cken - vol - le Tu - gend! Wir al - le bo - ten
Iph.
Orest.
vi - e; mais vous al - lez mou - rir, et vous l'a - vez vou - lu! Ces Dieux m'en a - vaient
Ret - tung dir; doch nun ist dein der Tod, nur du hast ihn ge - wollt! Die Göt - ter hat - ten
fait un de - voir né - ces - sai - re. En vou - lant pro - lon - ger mon sort, vous com - met -
mir als Pflicht ihn auf - er - legt. Wenn du das Le - ben mir er - hiel - test, dich mach - te
Iphigenie.
tiez un cri - me in - vo - lon - tai - re. Un cri - me? Ah! c'en est un de vous don - ner la mort.
dann dein Mit - leid zur Ver - bre - che - rin. Ver - bre - che - rin? Das werd' ich jetzt, da ich dein Le - ben en - den muss!

Lento. Solo
Flauto 1.
Violini I
Violini II
Viole
Orest
Iphigenie
Or.
Que ces re - grets tou - chants pour mon cœur ont de char - mes! qu'ils a - dou -
Wie die - se Kla - gen doch mein Herz so trö - stend grü - ssen, wie mil - dern
Bassi
Fl.
Vl. I
Vl. II
Vle
Or.
cis - sent mes tour - ments! De - puis l'in - stant fa - tal... hé - las! de - puis long - temps, per -
sie mein her - bes Leid! Seit je - nem schwarzen Tag, weh' mir! so lan - ge Zeit, sah
B.
Fl.
Vl. I
Vl. II
Vle
Or.
son - ne à mes mal - heurs n'a - vait don - né de lar - mes. Hé - las!
ich bei mei - ner Qual, ach, kei - ne Thrä - ne flie - - ssen! Weh' mir!
Iphigenie.
B.

Les Prêtresses environnent Oreste en chantant le Chœur suivant; elles le conduisent dans le Sanctuaire, où elles l'ornent de bandelettes et de guirlandes.

Die Priesterinnen umgeben Orest, während sie den folgenden Chor singen; sie führen ihn in das innere Heiligthum, wo sie ihn mit Bändern und Blumengewinden schmücken.

Nº 26. Hymne.

Andante.
2 Clarinetti in Do
2 Fagotti
Violini I
Violini II
Viole
Coro
(Prêtresses)
(Priesterinnen)
Bassi
dolce
p
Soprano I.
Chaste fil-le de La - to - ne, prê - te l'o - reil-le à nos chants! Que nos vœux, que
Soprano II.
Du, o Tochter der La - to - ne, lei - he die-sem Flehn dein Ohr! Un-ser Weihrauch

Cl.
Fg.
Vl. I
Vl. II
Vle
Coro
(Pr.)
B.
p
no-tre en - cens s'é - lè - vent jus-qu'à ton trô - ne. Dans les cieux et sur la ter-re
steig' em - por bis zu deinem Göt - ter - thro - ne! Wie im wei-ten Kreis der Er-de,

Cl.

Fg.

Vl. I

Vl. II

Vle

Coro (Pr.)

tout est sou-mis à ta loi. Tout ce que l'É-rè-be en - ser-re, à ton nom pâ - lit d'ef - froi.

was nur le - bet, dir — sich beugt, Al - les in des Or - kus Näch-ten schon vor dei - nem Wink er - bleicht.

B.

Cl.

Fg.

Vl. I

Vl. II

Vle

Coro (Pr.)

En tout temps on te con - sul - te, dans la paix, dans les com - bats; et l'on t'of - fre le seul

Dir ist ganz die Zu-kunft hel - le, gleich der Zeit, die längst ver - rann; schon an dei - nes Tem-pels

B.

Pendant le Chœur, lorsqu' Oreste est paré de guirlandes, on le conduit derrière l'Autel, qui est sur un des côtés; on brûle des parfums autour de lui, on le purifie en faisant des libations sur sa tête.

Noch während des Chores führt man Orest, nachdem er mit Blumengewinden geschmückt ist, hinter den auf der einen Seite befindlichen Altar; man zündet Weihrauch um ihn an und ergiesst, um ihn zu reinigen, Weihwasser über sein Haupt.

Un poco animato.
Violini I
Violini II
Viole
Recitativo.
toujours assise sur le devant du Théâtre.
immer im Vordergrunde der Bühne sitzend.
Iph.
Iphigenie
Orest
Quel mo-ment! Dieux puissants, se-cou-rez-moi!
Di-a-na! Welch' ein Augenblick! ach, stär-ke mich!
Soprano I.
Coro
(Prêtresses)
(Priesterinnen)
Quatre Prêtresses viennent chercher Iphigénie.
Vier Priesterinnen kommen, um Iphigenie zum Opfer zu geleiten.
Ap-pro-chez, sou-ve-rai-ne Prê-
Soprano II.
So na-he nun, er-hab'-ne
Bassi
Vl. I
Vl. II
Vle
se traînant avec peine à l'Autel.
mühsam zum Altar schreitend.
Iph.
Bar-ba-res, ar-rê-tez, res-pec-tez ma fai-
Ihr Grau-sa-men, ver-weilt, und scho-net mei-nes
Coro
(Pr.)
tres-se, remplis-sez vo-tre au-gus-te em-ploi!
Priesterin, er-fül-le dei-ne gro-sse Pflicht!
B.
Lento.
Vl. I
Vl. II
cresc.
Vle
cresc.
Elle frémit en fixant Oreste. Une Prêtresse lui présente le couteau sacré.
Sie schaudert bei Orest's Anblick. Eine Priesterin überreicht ihr das heilige Opfermesser.
prenant le couteau.
das Messer ergreifend.
Iph.
bles-se! Dieux! Tout mon sang se gla-ce dans mon coeur... je
Herzens! Ach! All' mein Blut er-starret in den Adern... ich
Coro
(Pr.)
B.

Vl. I
Vl. II
Vle
Iph.
trembl... et mon bras plus ti - mi-de...
be - be... die - ser Arm, so ban-ge...
Mon
Mein
Or.
Ain - si tu pé - ris en Au - li - de, I - phi - gé - nie, ô ma
So sankest du in Au - lis, I - phi - ge - ni - e, mei-ne
Coro (Pr.)
Frap-pez!
Voll - en - de!
B.
Animato.
a 2.
Ob. e Cl.
Fg.
frè - re!... O - res - te!...
Bruder! mein Orest!
soeur!
Schwester!
se prosternant.
niederfallend.
O - res - te?.. no - tre Roi!
O - rest? un - ser Kö - nig?
Oui, c'est
Ja, er
Où suis-je! se peut-il?...
Wo bin ich? wär's mög-lich?..
lui, c'est mon frè - re!
ist's, er ist mein Bruder!
Oui, c'est el - le, qu'aux fu - reurs d'un
Ich bin's, die von des Va - ters
Ma soeur!... I - phi - gé - ni - e!... Est ce el - le que je vois?
O Schwe - ster! I - phi - ge - ni - e! Ich se - he wirklich dich?

Vl. I
Vl. II
Vle
Iph.
pè - re, qu'à la ra - ge des Grecs Di - a - ne a su sous-trai - re.
Zorn und von der Wuth der Grie - chen Di - a - nens Hand geret - tet hat.
se jetant dans les bras
Orest in die Arme fallend.
Ô mon frè - re!
Mein Bruder!
Coro (Pr.)
Oui, c'est I - phi - gé - ni - e!
Ja, es ist I - phi - ge - ni - e!
B.
Un poco animato.
Ob.
d'Oreste.
Ô mon frè - re! ô mon cher O - res -
Ach, O - re - stes! ach, mein theu - rer Bru -
Or.
Ô ma sœur! Oui, c'est vous: oui, tout mon cœur me l'at - tes - te!
O mei - ne Schwester! Ja, du bist es, mein Herz be - zeugt es mir laut!
Andante.
te!
der!
Ah! lais - sons là ce sou - ve - nir fu -
Ach! lass nun ganz den ban - gen Gram ver -
Quoi! vous pou - vez m'ai - mer, vous n'a - vez point hor - reur?..
Wie! du, du kannst mich lieben, du fühl - test kei - nen Abscheu?..

Ob.
Vl. I
Vl. II
Vle
Iph.
B.
nes - te, lais-sez-moi res-sen-tir, lais-sez-moi res-sen-tir l'ex-cès de mon bon-heur!
schwinden! Komm, o komm, komm, o komm, komm und thei - le jetzt dies Won - ne-fest mit mir!
p
f
Sans te con-naî-tre en - cor, je t'a - vais dans mon cœur; au
Kaum hatt' ich dich ge - sehn, doch sehnt' ich mich nach dir! Ich
ciel, à l'u - ni - vers je de-man-dais mon frè - re, je de - man - dais mon
rief zum Him-mel auf: Wann werd' ich einst ihn fin - den, wann werd' ich einst ihn
frè - re! Le voi-là! je le tiens! il est en-tre mes bras!... Mais que vois - je?
fin - den! Nun bist du da! da, und mein! um - ar - met halt' ich dich! Doch ach! was seh' ich?

SCÈNE III.

Les Acteurs précédents, une Femme Grecque.
Die Vorigen, eine Griechin.

Ob. e Cl.
Fg.
a2
Vl. I
Vl. II
Vle
Gr.
ran fu - ri - eux vient de l'au - tre à l'in - stant pres - ser le sa - cri - fi - ce!
hört' ihn schrecklich droh'n: nun wird des Andern Tod der Grausa - me ge - bie - ten!
Coro
(Pr.)
Grands Dieux, se - cou - rez - nous!
Ihr Göt - ter, schützet uns!
Vlc.
e B.
Violini I
Violini II
Viole
Recitativo.
Iphigenie
aux Prêtresses.
zu den Priesterinnen.
Il ne se fe - ra pas ce sa - cri - fi - ce a - bo - mi - na - ble, im - pi - e... Vous, sau - vez vo - tre
So werd'es nie denn wie - der gebracht, das blu - ti - ge, ver - hass - te O - pfer! Auf, si - chert
Bassi
Vl. I
Vl. II
Vle
Iph.
Roi des fu - reurs de Tho - as! Il est du sang des Dieux, ils dé - fen - dront sa vi - e.
ihn vor Tho - as' Wuth! Er ist vom Stamm der Göt - ter, sie sel - ber sind sein Schutz.
B.
Elle met Oreste sous la garde du Sanctuaire.
Sie stellt Orest unter die Obhut des Heiligthums.

SCÈNE IV.

Les Acteurs précédents, Thoas, Gardes.
Die Vorigen, Thoas, Wachmannschaft.

Nº 27. Arie und Scene.

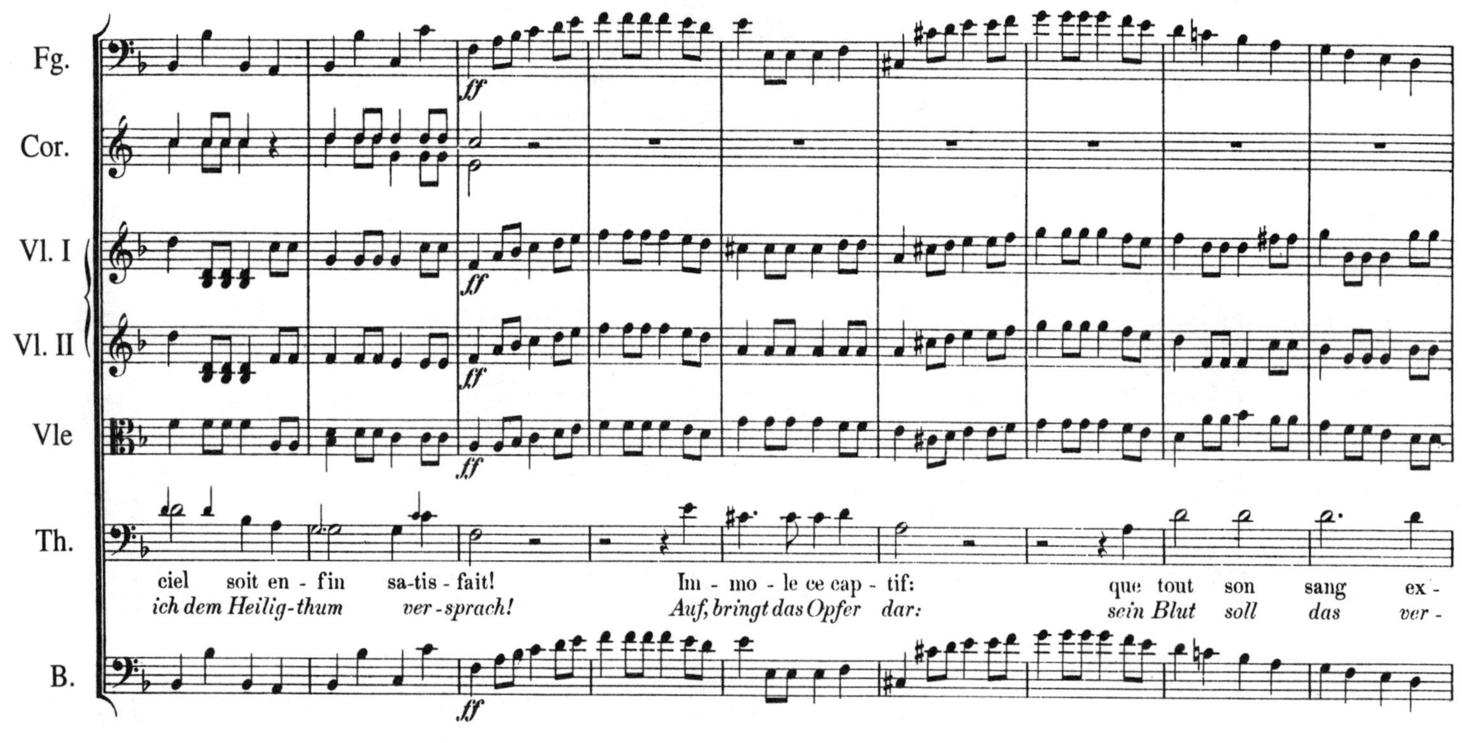

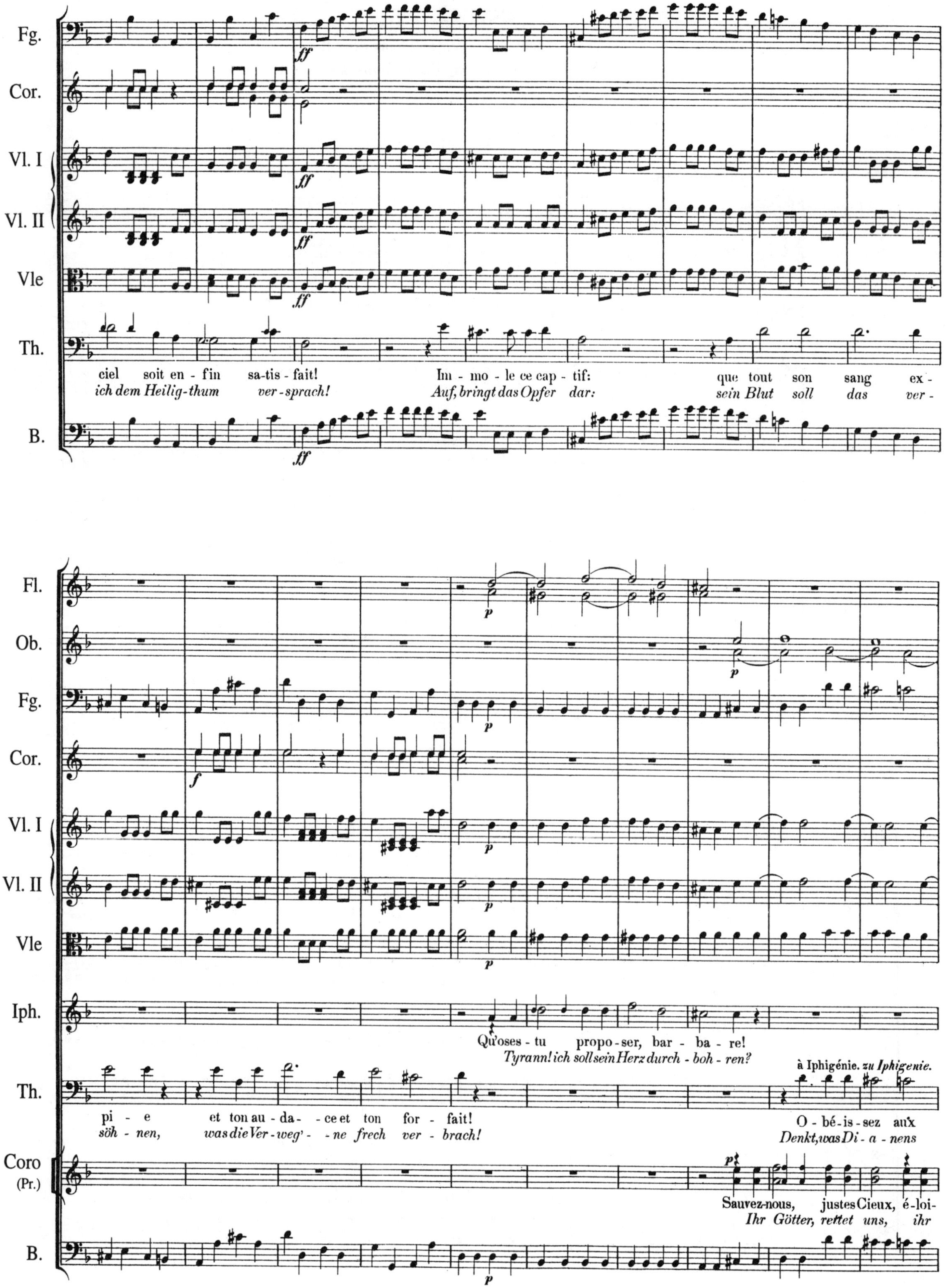

Fg.
Cor.
Vl. I
Vl. II
Vle
Th.
B.
ff
ciel soit en - fin sa-tis - fait! Im - mo - le ce cap - tif: que tout son sang ex -
ich dem Heilig-thum ver-sprach! Auf, bringt das Opfer dar: sein Blut soll das ver -
Fl.
Ob.
Fg.
Cor.
Vl. I
Vl. II
Vle
Iph.
Th.
Coro (Pr.)
B.
p
f
Qu'oses - tu propo - ser, bar - ba - re!
Tyrann! ich soll sein Herz durch - boh - ren?
à Iphigénie. zu Iphigenie.
pi - e et ton au - da - ce et ton for - fait! O - bé - is - sez aux
söh - nen, was die Ver - weg' - - ne frech ver - brach! Denkt, was Di - a - nens
Sauvez-nous, justes Cieux, é - loi -
Ihr Götter, rettet uns, ihr

Fl.
Ob.
Fg.
Cor.
Vl. I
Vl. II
Vle
Iph.
Th.
Coro (Pr.)
B.
aux Prêtresses.
zu den Priesterinnen.
aux Gardes.
zu der Wache.
Ô ciel! qu'o - ses-tu
Tyrann! was wagest du zu
Dieux, le ciel par - le, il suf-fit! Gar - des, se-con-dez - moi! Qu'on le sai - sis - se! Qu'on le
Spruch dem Reich und mir gedroht! Wohlan, ehrt mein Ge - bot! Reisst zum Al - tar ihn hin! Da
gnez les horreurs que ce moment pré - pa - re!
Götter, rettet uns, wir al - le sind ver - lo - ren!
Cl.
Or.
se précipitant au devant des Gardes.
sich der Wache entgegen stürzend.
fai - re? Cru - el! il est mon frè - re! C'est mon frè - re et mon
spre - chen? Ty-rann! es ist mein Bruder! Ja, mein Bru - der, sein ein
Oui, je le suis!
Ja, ja, ich bin's!
traî - ne à l'au - tel! Ton frè - re?
treff' ihn Qual und Tod! Dein Bru - der?

Fl.
Ob.
Fg.
Cor.
Vl. I
Vl. II
Vle
Iph.
Th.
B.

avec feu aux Gardes. *mit Feuer zu der Wache.*

aux Prêtresses. *zu den Priesterinnen.*

Iph.: Roi, le fils d'A - ga - mem - non! N'approchez pas! Et
Thron, er A - ga - memnons Sohn! Zurück, zu - rück! Und

Th.: Frap - pez, quel qu'il puis - se ê - tre!
Schont nicht, ich muss Di - a - nen rä - chen!

Lento. Tempo I.

Fl.
Ob.
Fg.
Cor.
Vl. I
Vl. II
Vle

Les Prêtresses forment un cercle et placent Oreste entre elles dans le Sanctuaire.
Die Priesterinnen schliessen einen Kreis um Orest in dem Heiligthum.

Iph.: vous, dé - fen - dez vo - tre maî - tre!
ihr, ver - hindert das Ver - bre - chen!

aux Gardes qui balancent.
zu der Wache, welche schwankt.

Th.: Lâ - ches! vous re - cu - lez d'ef - froi?.. J'im - mo - le - rai moi -
Ihr Fei - gen! lähmt die Furcht euch schon? So führ' ich sel - ber

B.

Fl.
Ob.
Fg.
Cor.
muta in Re
Vl. I
Vl. II
Vle
Or.
L'immo - ler? qui, ma soeur?
Meine Schwester? Wie, zum Al - tar?
Th.
mê - me, aux yeux de la Dé - es-se, et la vic - ti-me et la Prê - tres - se!
denn ihn und die Prie-sterin zum blu - tigen Al - ta - re hin!
Oui, je
Ja, zur
B.
sf
On entend un grand bruit derrière le Théâtre.
Man hört grossen Lärm hinter der Bühne.

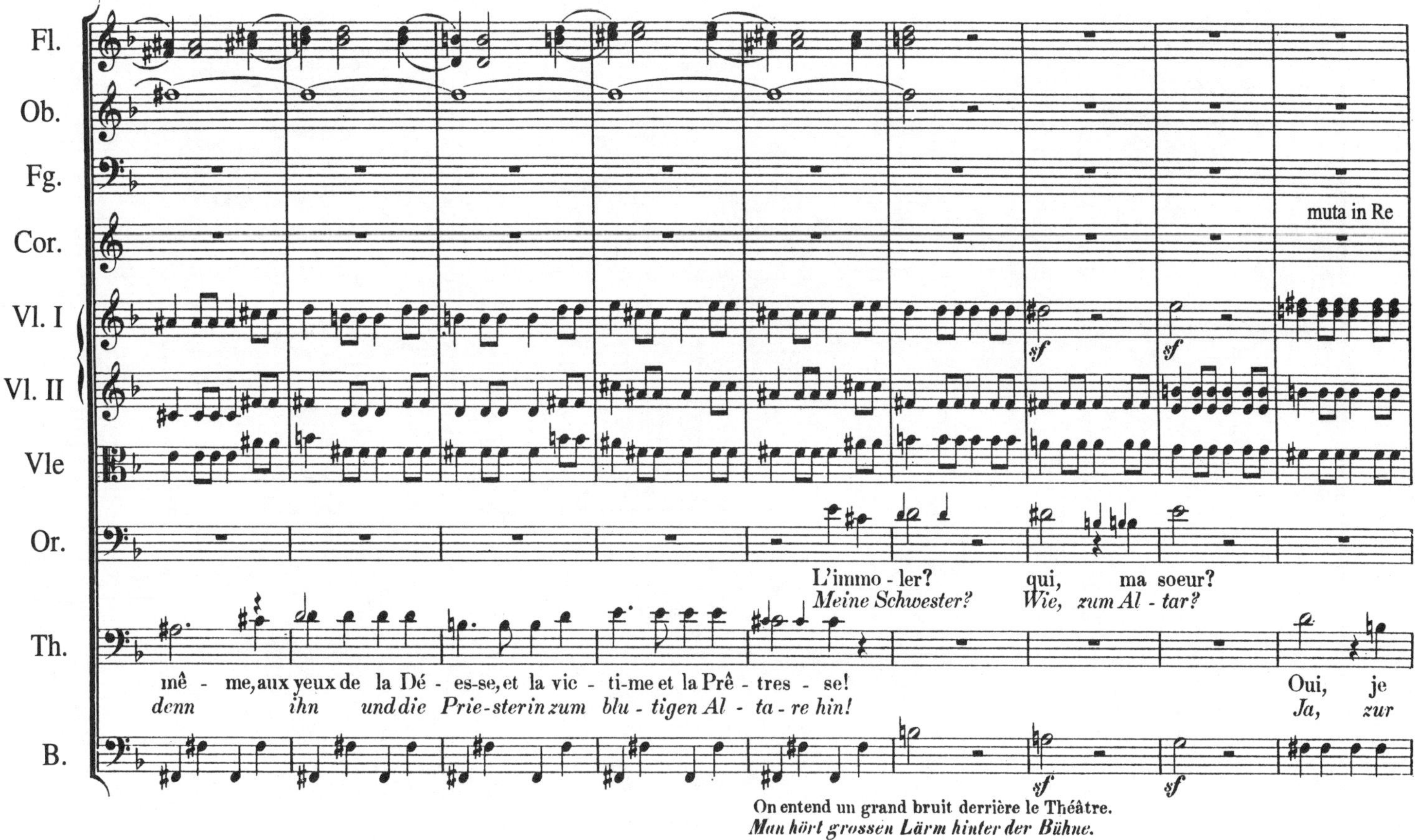

SCÈNE V.

Pylade, Troupe de Grecs, les Acteurs précédents.
Pylades, Schaar von Griechen, die Vorigen.

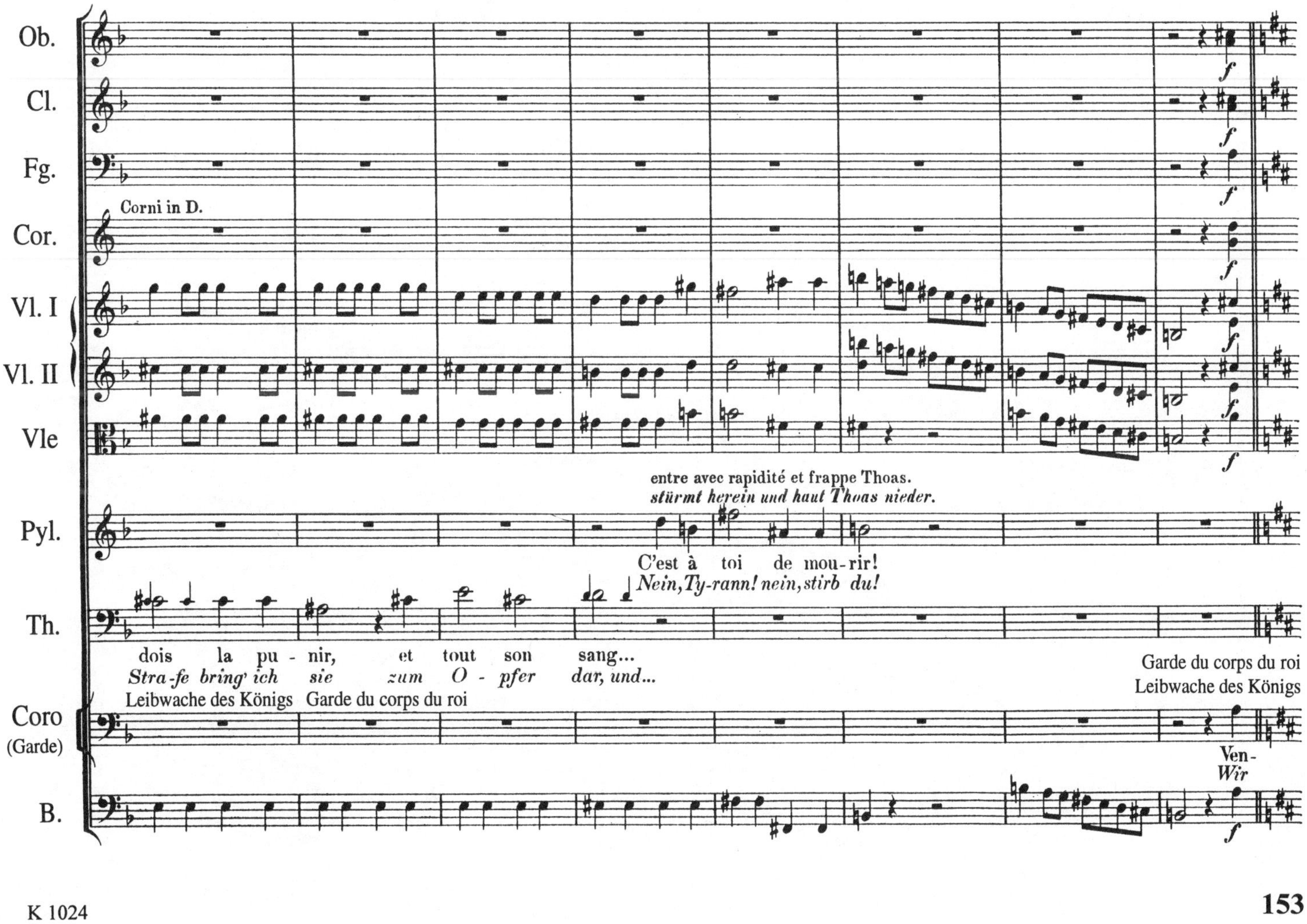

Ob.
Cl.
Fg.
Cor.
Corni in D.
Vl. I
Vl. II
Vle
entre avec rapidité et frappe Thoas.
stürmt herein und haut Thoas nieder.
Pyl.
C'est à toi de mou-rir!
Nein, Ty-rann! nein, stirb du!
Th.
dois la pu - nir, et tout son sang...
Stra-fe bring' ich sie zum O - pfer dar, und...
Leibwache des Königs Garde du corps du roi
Garde du corps du roi
Leibwache des Königs
Coro
(Garde)
Ven-
Wir
B.
f

Allegro moderato.
Ob.
a2.
Cl.
Fg.
Cor.
a2.
Vl. I
Vl. II
Vle
Iph.
Grands Dieux, sau-vez mon frè - re!
Be - schü - tzet ihn, ihr Göt - ter!
Pyl.
Cou - ra - ge, mes a - mis, et sui-vez-
Ihr Freun-de, fol-get mir mit kühnem
(Prêtresses)
(Priesterinnen)
Coro (Pr.)
Grands Dieux, sau-vez son frè - re!
Be - schü - tzet ihn, ihr Göt - ter!
Coro (Garde)
geons le sang de no-tre Roi!
rä - - chen unsers Königs Blut!
Frap - pons!
Hin - zu!
B.
Ob.
Cl.
Fg.
Cor.
Vl. I
Vl. II
Vle
Pyl.
moi!
Muth!
Ô mon u - ni - que a - mi!
O du, mein einz' - ger Freund!
Or.
Py - la - de! ô mon. Dieu tu-té - lai - re!
O Py - la-des, mein Freund, o mein Ret - ter!
B.

Ob.
Cl.
Fg.
Cor.
Vl. I
Vl. II
Vle
Iph.
Grands Dieux, se - cou - rez - nous!
Ihr Göt - - ter, schü - tzet ihn!
Coro (Pr.)
Grands Dieux, se - cou - rez - nous!
Ihr Göt - - ter, schü - tzet ihn!
B.
Ob.
Cl.
Fg.
Cor.
Vl. I
Vl. II
Vle
Iph.
Grands Dieux, sau - vez mon frè - re!
Ach, schü - - tzet ihn, ihr Göt - ter!
Coro (Pr.)
Grands Dieux, sau - vez son frè - re!
Ach, schü - - tzet ihn, ihr Göt - ter!
Grecs
Griechen
Coro (Grecs)
Ten. I
Ten. II
De ce peu-ple o - di - eux
Lasst die ver - hass - te Brut
B.

Ob.
Cl.
Fg.
Cor.
Vl. I
Vl. II
Vle
Coro (Grecs)
ex - - ter - minons jus - - - qu'au moin - dre res - - - - - te, ser - vons la vengean - ce cé -
uns nun bis zu der letz - - - ten Spur zer - stö - - - - - ren, die Gottheit wird uns sie - - gen
Coro (Garde)
Fuy - ons de ce lieu fu - nes - - te! Sauvons-
Scht Schre - - cken sie ver - brei - - ten! Auf, und ent-
B.
les - - - - - - - - te! et pu - ri - fions ces lieux au nom de Py - la - - de et d'O -
leh - - - - - - - - ren! Ja, grauser Mord und Blut soll län - - ger sie nicht mehr ent -
nous, é - vi - tons leurs coups! é - vi - tons leurs coups, les Dieux com - bat - tent pour O -
flieht, ent - flie - het ih - rer Wuth! ih - rer Wuth ent - flieht, da Göt - - ter sel - ber für sie

SCÈNE VI.

Les Acteurs précédents, Diane.

Die Vorigen, Diana.

Diane descend dans un nuage au milieu des Combattants. Les Scythes et les Grecs tombent à genoux à la voix de la Déesse; Iphigénie et les Prêtresses lèvent les mains vers elle.

Diana steigt in einer Nebelwolke unter die Kämpfenden hernieder. Die Stimme der Göttin vernehmend, fallen die Scythen und Griechen auf die Kniee; Iphigenie und die Priesterinnen heben die Hände ihr entgegen.

Ob.
Vl. I
Vl. II
Vle
D.
B.
ces cli-mats sau-va-ges, dés-ho-no-ré mon cul-te et mes au-tels.
eu-erm rau-hen Lan-de ent-wei-het mei-nen Dienst, ent-wei-het den Al-tar.
Grave.
a 2.
à Oreste. zu Orest.
Je prends soin de ta des-ti-né-e, O-res-te:
O- -rest, ich schü-tze selbst dich nun:
tes re-mords ef-fa-cent tes for-faits.
durch Reu' ist dei-ne That ver-söhnt.
My-cè-ne at-tend son
My-ce-ne war-tet
Roi, vas y régner en paix, et rends I-phi-gé-ni-e à la Grè-ce é-ton-né- - -
dein, be-herrsch' es nun in Frie-den, und stau-nend se-he Grie- -chen-land von Neu- -em I-phi-
Diane remonte au Ciel.
Diana steigt wieder den Himmel.

SCÈNE DERNIÈRE.

Iphigénie, Oreste, Pylade, Prêtresses, Scythes, Grecs.

Iphigenie, Orest, Pylades, Priesterinnen, Scythen, Griechen.

Nº 28. Schlusschor.

Fl.
Ob.
Cl.
Fg.
Cor.
Tr.
Timp.
Vl. I
Vl. II
Vle
Coro
B.
1.
2.
sta - cles,un jour plus pur luit sur nous. nous. U - - ne paix dou-ce et pro-fon - de
schwunden, dichter Nacht folgt Son-nen-licht. -licht. Se - - het, wie des Mee - - res Wel - len
sta - cles,un jour plus pur luit sur nous. nous. U - - ne paix dou-ce et pro-fon - de
schwunden, dichter Nacht folgt Son-nen-licht. -licht. Se - - het, wie des Mee - - res Wel - len

Fl.
Ob.
Cl.
Fg.
Cor.
Tr.
Timp.
Vl. I
Vl. II
Vle
Coro
B.
rè - - gne sur le sein de l'on - - de: la mer, la ter - - - re et les cieux, tout
schon von sanf - ten Win - - den schwel - len: nun füh - ret bald der Göt - ter Hand be -
rè - - gne sur le sein de l'on - - de: la mer, la ter - - - re et les cieux, tout
schon von sanf - ten Win - - den schwel - len: nun füh - ret bald der Göt - ter Hand be -

K 1024

Fl.
Ob.
Cl.
Fg.
Cor.
Tr.
Timp.
Vl. I
Vl. II
Vle
Coro
B.
1.
2.
a2.
p
fa - vo - ri - se nos voeux, tout fa - vo - ri - se, tout fa - vo - ri - se nos voeux. voeux, la
bald führt sie uns, uns beglückt nach Griechen - land. -land, ja, bald
glückt uns hin nach Griechen - land, bald führt sie uns beglückt, be - glückt nach Griechen - land. -land, ja, bald
fa - vo - ri - se nos voeux, tout fa - vo - ri - se, fa - vo - ri - se nos voeux. voeux, la
glückt uns hin nach Griechen - land, bald führt sie uns beglückt, be - glückt nach Griechen - land. -land, ja, bald

Fl.
Ob.
Cl.
Fg.
Cor.
Tr.
Timp.
Vl. I
Vl. II
Vle
Coro
B.
a2.
a2.
a2.
a2.
mer, la ter - re et les cieux, tout fa - vo - ri - se nos voeux, tout fa - vo - ri - se nos voeux.
führt der Göt - ter Hand uns beglückt nach Griechen - land, uns beglückt nach Griechen - land.
führt der Göt - ter Hand uns hochbeglückt nach Griechen - land, uns hochbeglückt nach Griechen - land.
mer, la ter - re et les cieux, tout fa - vo - ri - - se nos voeux, tout fa - vo - ri - - se nos voeux.
führt der Göt - ter Hand uns hochbeglückt nach Griechen - land, uns hochbeglückt nach Griechen - land.

Fin
Ende

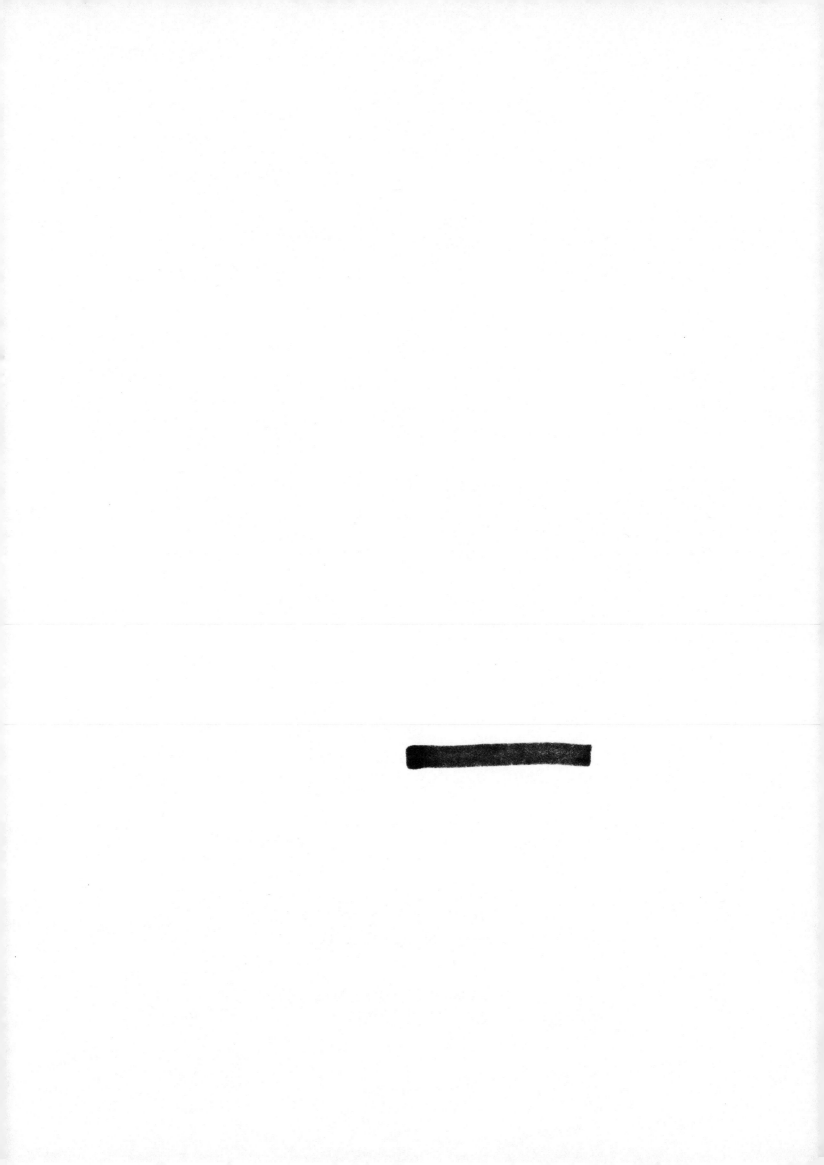

This publication is a reprint of an early edition.

K 1024

Distributed worldwide by
Könemann Verlagsgesellschaft mbH, Bonner Str. 126.
D-50968 Köln

Responsible editor: István Máriássy
Production: Detlev Schaper
Cover design: Peter Feierabend
Technical editor: Dezső Varga

Printed by: Kner Printing House Gyula
Printed in Hungary

ISBN 963 8303 99 9

CW00683596

SPACE FOR FREEDOM
THE SEARCH FOR
ARCHITECTURAL EXCELLENCE
IN MUSLIM SOCIETIES

"From the travails and labours of thousands, humble masons or expensive experts, there have emerged those works made by us and for us which we can present as a being, all together, as an aggregate, as a group, the statement of our hopes and of our expectations as much as of our achievements. This is indeed the way in which Pakistan's beloved poet, Muhammad Iqbal, put it in two quotations that say what the Awards can mean.

Speaking of Islam in his vision for tomorrow, he wrote that it was

> *A world eternal, with renewing flames and renewing leaves,*
> *fruit and principles.*
> *With an immoveable inside and an outside of*
> *Changing, continuous revolutions.*

And then, in another poem he said:

> *The journey of love is a very long journey.*
> *But sometimes with a sign you can cross that vast desert.*
> *Search and search again without losing hope.*
> *You may find sometime a treasure on your way.*

On behalf of the Master Jury and of the Award Committee, it is to this search for our new environment that I wish to invite the immense community of Muslim, and the whole world as well."

– His Highness the Aga Khan

SPACE FOR FREEDOM

THE SEARCH FOR ARCHITECTURAL EXCELLENCE IN MUSLIM SOCIETIES

BY ISMAIL SERAGELDIN

THE AGA KHAN AWARD FOR ARCHITECTURE

BUTTERWORTH ARCHITECTURE

London • Boston • Singapore • Sydney • Toronto • Wellington

BUTTERWORTH ARCHITECTURE
is an imprint of Butterworth Scientific

 **PART OF REED INTERNATIONAL P.L.C.**

British Library Cataloguing in Publication Data
Serageldin, Ismail, 1944–
Space for freedom: the search for architectural excellence in Muslim societies.
1. Islamic structure, to 1977
I. Title
723' .3
Library of Congress Cataloguing in Publication Data applied for
ISBN 0–408–50049–2

Design by Hui-Huy Ko.
Production supervision by Patricia Theseira.
Typesetting and composition by Superskill Graphics Pte Ltd, Singapore.
Colour and duotone separation by Colourscan Pte Ltd, Singapore.
Printing by Tien Wah Press, Singapore.

Most of the photographic material was contributed by Kamran Adle, Chant Avedissian, Jacques Bétant, Argun Dündar, Reha Günay, Christian Lignon and Pascal Maréchaux (see complete list of photographic credits on page 304). Darab Diba and Houshang Amir Ardalan produced the drawings.

Frontispiece, overleaf: Mostar Old Town, Mostar, Yugoslavia.

CONTRIBUTORS

Ismail Serageldin, Architect and Planner, the World Bank, Washington D.C. Mohammed Arkoun, Professor of History of Islamic Thought, University of Paris III, Paris. Author of *Arab Thought*. Oleg Grabar, Aga Khan Professor of Islamic Art, Director of the Fogg Museum. Author of *The Formation of Islamic Art*. Charles Correa, Architect, recipient of the RIBA Gold Medal. Author of *The New Landscape*. William Porter, Professor of Architecture and Planning, former Dean and present Chairman of the Massachussetts Institute of Technology, School of Architecture and Planning. Hasan-Uddin Khan, Architect. Editor in Chief of *Mimar, Architecture in Development*. Suha Özkan, Architect, Deputy Secretary General of the AKAA, former Professor of History of Architecture, METU, Ankara. Saïd Zulficar, Historian and Conservationist, Secretary General of the AKAA, former Programme Specialist at the Division of Cultural Heritage, UNESCO. Mona Serageldin, Professor of Planning, Graduate School of Design, Harvard University. Serge Santelli, Architect, Paris. Recipient of an AKAA Award in 1983. Rasem Badran, Architect, Amman. Winner of the Baghdad State Mosque Competition. Halim Abdel-Halim, Architect, Cairo. Abdel Wahed El-Wakil, Architect, Egypt and England. William J.R. Curtis, Architectural Historian. Author of *Modern Architecture since 1900*.

ACKNOWLEDGEMENTS

This book represents the activities of The Aga Khan Award for Architecture during its third cycle, from 1984 to 1986, which culminated in the recognition of a number of contemporary building projects as well as the lifetime works of a single individual.

Many people deserve credit for bringing this book to fruition. First and foremost is His Highness The Aga Khan, whose vision, leadership, and generosity have made the Award the distinguished organisation it is today. My colleagues on the 1986 Steering Committee initiated and fostered the dialogue which characterised the rich intellectual search during this cycle: Oleg Grabar, Charles Correa, William Porter, Mohammed Arkoun, and Hasan-Uddin Khan. I have learnt from each of them. The title, *Space for Freedom*, is derived from an expression coined by Mohammed Arkoun, who made valuable comments on the early draft of this volume. Hasan-Uddin Khan also reviewed the manuscript in its completed form, and made useful suggestions on its presentation and layout. The Award's Secretary General, Saïd Zulficar, and Deputy Secretary General, Suha Özkan, greatly contributed to the deliberations of the Steering Committee and forged much of the character of the current cycle. They were supported by an efficient and devoted staff, led by Jack Kennedy, Executive Officer, and Farrokh Derakhshani, Co-ordinator of Award Procedures who admirably guided the architectural department of the Award and whose assistance in the preparation of this volume merits acknowledgement and gratitude.

The Master Jury responsible for the designation of the 1986 Award recipients which are featured in Part II of this volume comprised: Soedjatmoko, Mahdi Elmandjra, Abdel Wahed El-Wakil, Hans Hollein, Zahir Ud-Deen Khwaja, Ronald Lewcock, Fumihiko Maki, Mehmet Doruk Pamir, and Robert Venturi.

The Technical Review Team comprised of Abdelhalim I. Abdelhalim, Samir Abdulac, Selma Al-Radi, William J.R. Curtis, Darab Diba, Romi Khosla, Okan Üstünkök, Fernando Varanda, Dorothée Vauzelles, Kenneth Yeang King Mun, and Atilla Yücel. Their reports provided an inestimable resource on which I have drawn heavily in preparing the sections on each of the Award recipients. At the Award office in Geneva, Quayny Porter undertook research for the appendices.

The actual production of this book benefited from the input of many additional individuals, and I would like to specifically recognise the contributions of six persons in Washington: Tania Kamal Eldin, who provided editorial support, Adoración Morao, whose tireless efforts and organisational skills made it possible to produce the manuscript on schedule, and Song-Li Tifone, who was always there to provide additional support when needed. Samir El-Sadek, Rawia Fadel and Nevine Madkour all read the manuscript and provided precious comments.

Special recognition is due to Hui-Huy Ko, the graphic consultant who designed the layout of this book and contributed to all phases of its final production. Robert Powell and Shantheni Chornalingam ably undertook technical editing, and Pat Theseira coordinated the many and varied aspects in Singapore.

Finally, the encouragement and confidence of Michael Spens and Nicola Hamilton were most appreciated, as were the efforts of Nicholas Bulloch and Christopher Curtis who helped put in place the arrangements for publication and distribution.

An expression of special gratitude is due to Suha Özkan, who deployed indefatigable efforts to see this project through. From brainstorming to acting as sounding board, from critical review to administration and logistics, and from research to graphic design, I have benefitted from his wise counsel, endless stamina, and unremitting commitment.

Much of whatever credit this book possesses belongs to my friends and colleagues; any shortcomings are entirely my own.

Ismail Serageldin

CONTENTS

The Social Security Complex, Istanbul, Turkey.

Dar Lamane Housing Community, Casablanca, Morocco.

PART TWO

MILESTONES AND LANDMARKS

THE 1986 WINNERS AND HONOURABLE MENTIONS

Mostar Old Town, Mostar, Yugoslavia.

Al-Aqsa Mosque, al-Haram al-Sharif, Jerusalem.

Yaama Mosque, Yaama, Niger.

PART THREE

A RISING EDIFICE

CONTRIBUTIONS TOWARDS A BETTER UNDERSTANDING OF ARCHITECTURAL EXCELLENCE IN THE MUSLIM WORLD

Bhong Mosque, Bhong, Pakistan.

Waqaf Building, Baghdad. (Etching from the portfolio of Rifat Chadirji).

The Award Logo

The name of Allah

in Kufic Script,

reflecting itself,

forms the basis

of the logo design.

Design: Karl Schlamminger

INTRODUCTION: THIS BOOK

"The Aga Khan Award for Architecture is intended to encourage an understanding and awareness of the strength and diversity of Muslim cultural traditions which, when combined with an enlightened use of modern technology for contemporary society, will result in buildings more appropriate for the Islamic world of tomorrow."[1]

– *His Highness the Aga Khan*

In pursuit of that lofty vision, the Aga Khan Award for Architecture (AKAA) has embarked on a far ranging search to understand the present and interpret the past, to seek out the best in the contemporary, avoiding both dogma and lack of rigour. This search leads to a series of awards every three years, when U.S. $500,000 in prizes are distributed to the projects selected by a distinguished international jury.

This book is an account of this magnificent search for excellence that, over the last ten years, has succeeded in creating a unique *space of freedom* for inquiry into the architectural activity of the Muslim world. It focuses primarily on the third Aga Khan Award for Architecture, awarded in Marrakesh on November 25, 1986, but relates these to the preceding awards of 1980 and 1983, and more importantly, to the ongoing intellectual search that has underpinned these awards, and maps out the directions of concern in the years to come.

This book, which is the third in the series *Building in the Islamic World Today*, comes as a complement to *Architecture and Community*[2] which covered the 1980 Award and *Architecture in Continuity*[3] which covered the 1983 Award. Yet this book should be somewhat different in its overall tone. Since the Award is now ten years old, it is appropriate that any discussion of the last round of winners be put in the context of a retrospective as well as a prospective outlook. There is thus an element of stocktaking in this volume, as well as an attempt to map out an agenda for the next decade. To remain true to the spirit of the intellectual pursuits of the Award, the presentation of the retrospective and stocktaking are intended as much to be an auto-critique of the Award activities as an overview for the reader of the events leading to the 1986 Award and their significance.

This book is organised in three parts: the first part is an introductory essay that sets the stage for the better appreciation of the 1986 awards. This is followed by a second part which includes a detailed presentation of the 1986 winners: six Award winners, five honourable mentions and the Chairman's Award to Iraqi architect, critic and teacher, Rifat Chadirji. The presentations are preceded by the Steering Committee's statement and the Master Jury's report.

Finally, the third part provides a sample of some of the intellectual papers, reports and seminar interventions that have taken place during the third award cycle indicating the thrust of the ongoing activities.

PART ONE

SPACE FOR FREEDOM

THE SEARCH FOR ARCHITECTURAL EXCELLENCE IN MUSLIM SOCIETIES

THE AGA KHAN AWARD FOR ARCHITECTURE

His Highness the Aga Khan: a bold vision for the future of the built environment of Muslim societies.

AN EARLY VISION

Confronted with the deteriorating built environment in most Muslim countries, His Highness the Aga Khan resolved to awaken the cultural consciousness of Muslims and to sensitise those who would build in the Muslim world to the unique heritage of Muslim art and architecture that they may produce a more relevant, culturally sensitive and effective contemporary architecture. His instrument to achieve this ambitious goal was the creation of a triennial prize, to honour and make known, worthy exemplars that demonstrate this appropriate mix of cultural authenticity and appropriate response to contemporary life. Thus, the Aga Khan Award for Architecture (AKAA) was launched in 1977.

At the outset, there was the idea that the AKAA should present five awards of up to U.S. $100,000 each, to projects which "demonstrate architectural excellence at all levels. Since architecture cannot be isolated from the society in which it is created, the Award will consider the context in which architecture is practiced and the processes of design, research and evaluation through which it is achieved. The social, economic, technical, physical and environmental challenges to which the projects respond must be important factors in any assessment of their success.

Projects will thus be chosen as much for their catalytic value in the evolution of a new cultural and environmental sensibility, as for their individual design merits. The aim is to nurture within the architectural profession and related disciplines a heightened awareness of the roots and essence of Muslim culture, and a deeper commitment to finding meaningful expressions of the spirit of Islam within the context of modern life and technology.

Consideration will be given particularly to those projects which use local initiatives and resources creatively, which meet both the functional and cultural needs of their users and have the potential to stimulate related developments elsewhere in the Muslim world."[1]

It was assumed that one of these awards would go to each of the areas of concern, identified as housing, public buildings and spaces, community planning, and restoration and reuse It was clear, however, that the subject matter was so vast and the situations confronted in the Muslim world so diverse, that the activities of the Award must include further study of key ideas that were loosely defined, and concepts that were dimly perceived. This, plus a systematic exploration of the reality of the Muslim world and its rapidly evolving built environment were to accompany the identification and study of specific projects as potential award recipients.

ORGANISATION AND PROCEDURES

His Highness the Aga Khan established a committee which he chairs, of prominent intellectuals and practitioners to help him undertake this enterprise. It was to become the *Steering Committee* of the Aga Khan Award for Architecture. This distinguished group was to be supported by a full-time person who would convene the committee meetings. "The convener" (Renata Holod) and her deputy (Hasan-Uddin Khan) were the nucleus of what was to become the *Secretariat* of the AKAA.

It was decided however, that there was a need to have an independent body make the final selection of the winners. The independent *Master Jury* was to be selected by the Steering committee to represent both western and Muslim practitioners and to include disciplines other than architecture. The interaction between the Steering Committee, the Master Jury, and the Secretariat was to remain the main instrument for the promotion of the Award.

From the start, the main intellectual task of the Steering Committee and the Secretariat was to try to define the scope and the field encompassed by the Award, and the criteria for nomination, evaluation and selection. The corollary to this was the need to set up a methodology for nomination, documentation, analysis, and evaluation as well as to set up the mechanisms of choice.

The mechanisms have evolved into a triangular relationship between the Steering Committee, the Secretariat, and the Master Jury. To this triumvirate must be added a vast and vital complement of dedicated individuals: the nominators and the technical review teams. The nominators are about 300 to 400 highly competent individuals throughout the world who are asked to identify worthy projects for consideration. Their identities remain confidential. This widespread network is essential to supplement the knowledge of the Secretariat and the Steering Committee, and to consistently bring to the forefront little known efforts in distant places.

The process starts with the receipt of nominations. The Secretariat then sorts them out, rejecting any that do not conform to the eligibility criteria, which are:

- The project must have been built no less than two years and no more than 25 years ago;
- The project must be located in a predominantly Muslim society *or* be designed for or used by a Muslim community in a non-Muslim society *or* be predominantly inspired by and respectful of the Muslim architectural heritage;
- For restoration work, the monument(s) being restored should be a recognisable part of the Muslim heritage, and the technical work being evaluated should fall within the same 2 to 25 year period; and
- All work done by anyone on the Steering Committee, the Master Jury, or the Secretariat or commissioned by His Highness the Aga Khan cannot be considered.

The Secretariat then contacts architects and clients of nominated projects, and prepares detailed dossiers on each accepted nomination.

Along with these tasks the Steering Committee and the Secretariat undertake three streams of activities:

- A constant review of the incoming nominations and further contacts with nominators to encourage a broad geographic and building type coverage.
- Continuing discussions and seminars to sharpen the issues and deepen the analysis of the challenges the Award seeks to respond to;
- Selection of a well-balanced Master Jury of international standing.

The Master Jury is briefed by the Steering Committee but retains its independence of judgement. The Master Jury elects its chairman from among its members, and establishes its own working procedures. The Jury then reviews the 200 to 250 project dossiers prepared for the cycle. These are then shortlisted to 25 to 35 projects. For each of these finalists, they prepare detailed questions which serve as an additional brief to the *Technical Review* teams. Technical Review teams comprise of specialists in architecture and photographers, who spend several days on each project conducting interviews and gathering critical evidence and extensive visual documentation. These highly trained specialists then visit each of the short listed projects and prepare meticulously detailed technical dossiers about each project, including interviews with the users and relevant actors. The Technical Review

The Master Jury of 1980, from left to right: Soedjatmoko (back to camera), De Carlo, Islam, Tange, Kuran, Cantacuzino, Mona Serageldin, Burckhardt.

teams then make their reports, in writing and in person, to the Master Jury, which makes its final selection and prepares a report explaining the reasons for its choices. The allocation of prize money between architect, client, builder, and craftsmen is also at the discretion of the Jury, subject to a limit of U.S. $100,000 for a single award and an overall limit of U.S. $500,000.

The Steering Committee reviews the report and adds any comments it considers appropriate. The Steering Committee also makes nominations for the Chairman's Award, which is given to an individual for a lifetime's work rather than any specific project. His Highness the Aga Khan then reviews and approves the recommendations for the Chairman's Award.

THE INTELLECTUAL SEARCH

If these procedures seem the most thorough and complete yet devised for an architectural prize, it is the intellectual search that has accompanied it that remains the AKAA's most unique and worthwhile contribution, not only to the Muslim world, but also to the contemporary reflection on the meaning of architecture and culture worldwide.

The Award's philosophy is a balanced one: while searching for the best in the modern, it still seeks to acknowledge conservation and preservation. The Award also recognises examples that reinterpret the lessons of the past in contemporary terms, and that find and enhance the elements of cultural continuity in a particular area. The Award also seeks to recognise efforts that are innovative in their approaches to coping with the unique problems of their locales. In doing so, the Award has also reflected the remarkable diversity that exists within the Muslim world.

This broad endeavour transcends the limits of what is conventionally thought of as an award for architecture. Thus, the Aga Khan Award seeks to embrace buildings produced by non-architects, recognising that 90% of the built environment of Muslims is in fact dependent upon non-architects. The Award also recognises the social aspects of the efforts of those concerned with the environment by premiating such worthy schemes as the Kampung Improvement Programme in Jakarta, regardless of the absence of notable physical architectural achievement. This is intended as a counterpoint to the conventional vision of architecture as the creation of interesting and inspiring monuments for a changing contemporary society, or as a continuation and a reinterpretation of a vernacular architecture.

This search has been characterised primarily by openness, lack of dogma and scrupulous attention to scholarship that create a *space of freedom* wherever the Award holds it activities. Here, interested parties can make their contributions without restriction other than common courtesy, orderly presentation and respect for the rights of others to be heard. So firm has this commitment to the integrity of the process become that even in disagreement between key participants there is no effort to ensure that one view prevails. Thus, in 1986, the differences in opinion both within the Master Jury and between the Master Jury and the Steering Committee could not be easily bridged given the depth and importance of the issues that underlie these differences. All views were given a chance to be heard, and it is a measure of the success of the Award that, in this third cycle, both by the substance of the issues that they address and by the institutional self-confidence of the enterprise, the Award presents to the world questions as well as answers, worthy winners and missing elements. It is an appropriate and less simplistic response to the complexity of our times, even if it disappoints some who would have preferred a more definitive though more simplified view of the subject. But the story deserves to be told from the beginning...

The intellectual search. Members of the first Steering Committee posed some hard questions, left to right: Ardalan, Correa and Kuban.

THE FIRST CYCLE: 1977–1980

Setting the agenda at the first Steering Committee: His Highness the Aga Khan, Holod (Convenor) and Porter.

Members of the first Steering Committee, from left to right: Grabar, Campbell, Casson and Fathy with Khan (Deputy Convenor).

The first cycle of the Award was critical in translating the Aga Khan's vision into a reality. A distinguished and diverse group of individuals were responsible for this notable achievement. The Steering Committee, under the chairmanship of His Highness the Aga Khan comprised eight members, drawn from leading practitioners and scholars whose work relates to Islamic architecture. These were Nader Ardalan, a distinguished architect and planner; Garr Campbell, a landscape architect and planning consultant to the Aga Khan Foundation; Sir Hugh Casson, architect and President of the Royal Academy of Arts in England; Charles Correa, one of the leading architects in India; Hassan Fathy, a renowned Egyptian architect and proponent of vernacular architecture; Oleg Grabar, Chairman of the Department of Fine Arts at Harvard University and a specialist in Islamic art and architecture; Doğan Kuban, architect and architectural historian, Director of the Institute of History of Architecture and Restoration at Istanbul Technical University; and William Porter, architect and planner, Dean of the School of Architecture and Planning at the Massachusetts Institute of Technology.

The Secretariat comprised of Renata Holod, first Convener and subsequently Consultant to the Award, and specialist in Islamic art and architecture at the University of Pennsylvania and Hasan-Uddin Khan, architect and planner from Pakistan, who was first Deputy Convener and subsequently Convener of the Award Steering Committee.

The 1980 Award Master Jury included Muslims and non-Muslims, architects and non-architects. It comprised nine members: Titus Burckhardt, a Swiss philosopher, architectural historian and oriental art expert; Sherban Cantacuzino, Chairman of the Master Jury, architect, Secretary of the British Royal Fine Art Commission, and former Executive Editor of *The Architectural Review;* Giancarlo De Carlo, a prominent Italian architect, Director of the International Laboratory of Architecture and Urban Design at Urbino and Professor at the Institute of Architecture and Urbanism, University of Venice; Mahbub ul Haq, a noted economist, Director of Policy Planning and Programme Development for the World Bank in Washington, D.C.; Muzharul Islam, architect and president of the Institute of Architects in Bangladesh; Aptullah Kuran, Chairman of the Department of Humanities at Bogazici University, Istanbul, author and architect; Mona A. Serageldin, Egyptian architect, planning consultant, and an expert in demographic analysis and programming with special experience in low cost housing in the Middle East; H.E. Soedjatmoko, an Indonesian sociologist and historian, advisor on Social and Cultural Affairs to the National Development Planning Agency (BAPPENAS) in Jakarta, and former Ambassador to the United States; and lastly, Kenzo Tange, Japanese architect and planner of international repute, and Professor Emeritus of Architecture and Urban Design at Tokyo University.

These then were the individuals on whose labours the credibility of the Award was to rest. It is their endeavours which helped to establish the Award and its most vital tradition: the *space of freedom* for an ongoing dedicated search into the built environment of the Muslim world.

SEMINARS AND PUBLICATIONS

The first cycle was launched with exceptional dynamism. It included an intensive series of seminars, five in three years, that covered:

- "Toward Architecture in the Spirit of Islam" (France, April 1978).
- "Conservation as Cultural Survival" (Turkey, September 1978).
- "Housing Process and Physical Form" (Indonesia, March 1979).
- "Architecture as Symbol and Self-Identity" (Morocco, October 1979).
- "Places of Public Gathering in Islam" (Jordan, May 1980).

These seminars, subsequently published as a series entitled "Architectural Transformations in the Islamic World", established the pattern of the AKAA seminars, and the format of their publication, including the commentary of the participants. The result of these initial seminars was manifold:

- They helped establish an important network of interested intellectuals, practitioners, and decision-makers who were made aware of the presence of the Award and its concerns.
- They helped map out the intellectual terrain in which this network operates, identifying very rapidly the dearth of much badly needed data and analysis, which led to research visits by the secretariat and the Steering Committee to some 30 Muslim countries thereby developing an invaluable store of data on architectural issues in these countries.
- They helped identify three main areas of concern of the Award, that were to be echoed again in subsequent cycles, even if they were not specifically identified as such. These were: the historical, social, and architectural premises on which interventions in the built environment of Muslims are based.

A Sense of Unity — study of the structure of a dome. Bu Ali Sina University, Hamadan, Iran.

Qarawiyyin Mosque, Fez, decorative details.

The impact of that first seminar at Aiglemont in April of 1978 should not be underestimated. It was at that gathering that a number of important approaches were established; approaches that were to become characteristic of the Award's work in the years to come.

First, the breadth of the seminar's coverage, from symbolism to new towns, to the economics of traditional buildings in Yemen, to restoring old quarters in Cairo, all staked out a domain that far exceeds the concerns of more conventional architectural prizes. Secondly, the high calibre of the participants, each an authority in his or her field established the Award's unwavering commitment to excellence in every facet of its work. Thirdly, the variety of disciplines represented among the participants established an important feature of the Award's future work. Fourthly, and most importantly, the invitation of widely divergent views and the encouragement of debate. The opening essay at that meeting, by S.H. Nasr which emphasises the spiritual regeneration on Muslim architects is severely critisised by Doğan Kuban's commentary which takes a diametrically opposed view emphasising the universality of the trends affecting the Muslim world today.

But it was His Highness the Aga Khan's opening remarks that defined the range of interests and clearly spelled out the commitment to this *space of freedom* for the unbounded search for creative solutions to the problems of the built environment of the Muslim world.

> *"It would be tempting ... to propogate a particular type of design solution, but this we have absolutely rejected. Similarly, it is not our intention ... to found a particular school of architectural thought."*[2]

From that first seminar, the various strands of the Award's many functions were launched. These were developed in the other four seminars of this first cycle.

Of these seminars, the one with the most ambitious intellectual objectives was that held in Fez in 1979 on "Architecture as Symbol and Self-Identity". It was a small gathering of philosophers, historians, architects, planners and critics who for several days grappled with the most daunting agenda the Award had set since its initial meeting in Aiglemont: "Islam as Symbol and Self-Identity". The background materials were well prepared as were the set responses by the appointed discussants. As one of the participants, I can attest that the intellectual debate was exhilarating. Yet, one must acknowledge that the absence of closure on most questions was not solely due to the complexity of the subject matter, but also to the absence of a commonly accepted terminology, analytical method, and contextual framework. The philosophers (Arkoun and Mahdi) clearly could share both references and method, even if their views were frequently at odds, but they lacked familiarity with contemporary architectural practice and its issues. The historians (for example, Raymond) were unable or unwilling to translate their analytical insights into relevant bridges to the better understanding of the present. The planners (William Porter, Mona Serageldin and myself) were more concerned with relating ideas, be they philosophical or architectural, to the broad changes that were affecting Muslim societies as we saw them. The art historians and critics (Grabar, Holod, and Kuban) were able to provide the link between conceptual and visual, while Burckhardt, Fathy and Ardalan emphasised the mystical and the spiritual.[3] The architects and planners made valiant attempts at mastering the concepts of semiotics, but clearly felt more comfortable in the visual and descriptive. On the positive side, however, all were enriched by this excellent inter-disciplinary exchanges. The quality of these exchanges was excellent as can be seen from the ensuing publications, and the Award could be satisfied with achieving a substantial enrichment of that intellectual search that had become its vocation.

Despite these important achievements, the first five seminars did not treat all the aspects they covered with equal profundity or intensity. They nevertheless had an important innovative edge to them, as well as some truly inspired momentary insights. But a candid and objective overview must conclude that, while the areas of concern were well defined, the seminars left some important issues relatively untouched. One was the urban dimension of the problem of building, i.e. the city planning aspects, as opposed to urban design or large scale architecture. This is particularly evident in the seminar on public spaces, where it would have fitted rather naturally. Glimpses of aspects of the problem can be found in a variety of papers in the different seminars (for example Mona Serageldin with William Doebele and Kadri El Araby on "Land Tenure Systems and Development Controls in the Arab countries of the Middle East", delivered at the Housing Seminar in Jakarta).

Another gap in terms of systematic study, though certainly not in terms of recall and concern, is the issue of poverty, its unique needs of mass shelter, and its milieu of environmental degradation and socio-economic particularities. The link was only partially made between a Muslim world whose overwhelming reality is one of mass poverty, and an architectural language whose key exemplars and the very components of its symbolic language derive from monuments of extraordinary opulence and impressive proportions. The intellectual constructs to link these two realities and to provide a historical dimension to this interaction thus providing context and continuity to a contemporary paradigm, were barely broached, despite passionate pleas to breach this gap (for example, Mahbub ul Haq in the Amman seminar on Public Spaces and Mohammed Arkoun in the Fez seminar on Symbolism) and the constant reminder by Hassan Fathy of the importance of vernacular architecture.

Another lacuna was the absence of a systematic look at the rural habitat in which the vast majority of Muslims still live, or at the links between architecture and the urban context; the evolving bustling cities of the Muslim world, with their unique characteristics and problems that clearly affect the possibilities of architectural expression. These lacunae were to become the agenda for the second cycle's series of seminars, and the impressive intellectual ground covered by this first round of seminars should not be underestimated.

It must be recognised, however, that despite the occasional insight and incisive comment most of the treatment of the subject matter remained descriptive rather than analytical. On those occasions where the subject matter itself was deeply analytical, such as the Fez seminar of 1979, on "Architecture as Symbol and Self-Identity", one of the best ever held, the results did not go as far as one would have hoped. This may well have been the unavoidable price of being at the forefront of the multi-disciplinary thinking on a complex subject.

On the whole, however, the outstanding contribution of the first cycle's seminars was to have indicated to the world at large that the AKAA was much more than a series of prizes, important as these are. They clearly demonstrated the seriousness, breadth and depth of the intellectual search that would henceforth be an inseparable part of the enterprise.

THE 1980 WINNERS

The culmination of the AKAA cycle is the premiation of the winners. By the time the 1980 Master Jury met, they had the important body of literature already produced by the Award in the form of the proceedings of the five seminars and other internal documents. At that point, however, neither the seminars nor the internal documentation had produced either a systematic categorisation of the vast array of possible choices to be put before the Master Jury or a set of specific operational criteria that the Master Jury should use in its selection of winners. The question of categorisation, having been debated and rejected, left the absence of operational criteria all the more troublesome. Indeed, in the first Award cycle the Steering Committee, for considerations of time, inter alia, short listed the projects and the Master Jury was given 35 technically reviewed projects to choose from. Here, the absence of operational criteria resulted in the Master Jury re-thinking the basic criteria of the Award and ultimately proposing 15 winners under seven "categories" of search. The themes they chose, and which the winners manifested, were:

- Social Premises for Future Architectural Development
- Search for Consistency with Historical Context
- Search for Preservation of Traditional Heritage
- Restoration
- Search for Contemporary Use of Traditional Language
- Search for Innovation
- Search for Appropriate Building Systems

The prizewinners selected highlighted two important points:

First: the Award demonstrated its openness to a variety of solutions. Here was an award for architecture that premiated slum-upgrading schemes devoid of the physical aesthetics that one normally attributes to works of architectural excellence, as well as high-tech engineering (the Kuwait Water Towers) and restoration.

The Kuwait Tower group is regarded as a national landmark.

Second: That at this stage, the winners were worthy efforts in an ongoing search and were not to be considered definitive solutions.

These two points were eloquently expressed by the Master Jury in their report:

> "... *the projects presented to us reflected the present stage of transition, experimentation and continued search in Muslim societies. In most instances they represented not the ultimate in architectural excellence, but steps in a process of discovery, still an incomplete voyage towards many promising frontiers. Although we have selected some of the projects for their excellence in architecture, many of them stand as accomplishments in this continuing search for relevant forms and designs which has already started and which must be supported. For this reason we have deliberately chosen a fairly broad sample of projects for the Award, rather than only up to five*

Aerial view of a typical kampung in Jakarta.

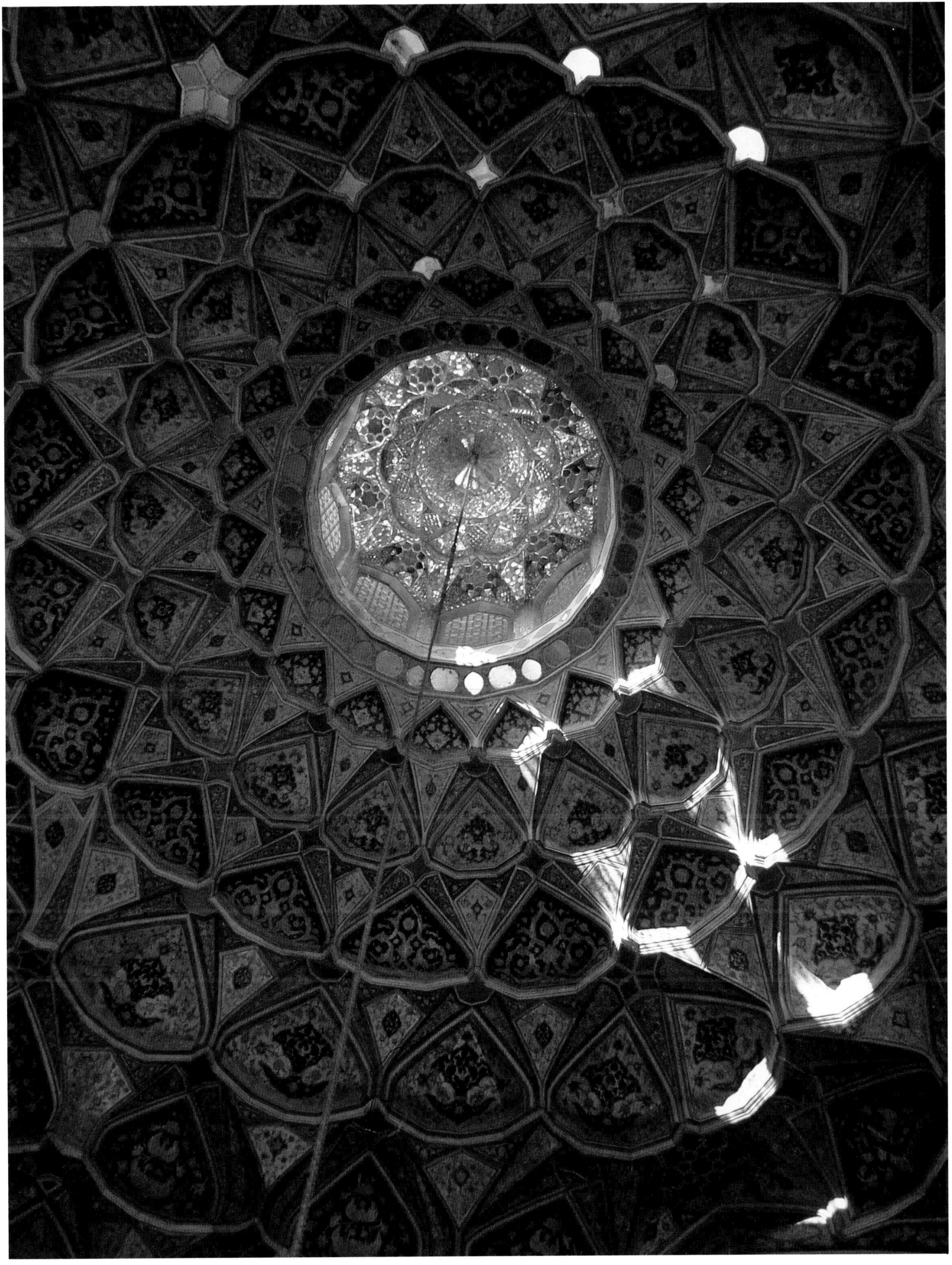

Muqarnas of the dome of Hasht Behesht, Isfahan, Iran.

projects, since few projects really meet all the criteria for a creative and socially responsive Islamic architecture, yet each presents an important facet of the ongoing search for an ideal."[4]

When his Highness the Aga Khan not only endorsed these choices, but also decided to create the Chairman's Award and designated as its first recipient Hassan Fathy, champion of indigenous buildings, self-help and architecture for the poor, the image of the Award was established as something unique, transcending the conventional notion of prizes of architecture, be they avant-garde or establishmentarian. Indeed, the 1980 presentation ceremonies at the Shalimar Gardens in Lahore, Pakistan, marked a very significant event: the AKAA had made the successful transition from idea to reality. And what a reality! This was the first international Award for architecture that was about and for a non-western context. Yet it eschewed chauvinism and xenophobia and welcomed Westerners both in its organisation and among its winners. It was the first international award to recognise the contributions of builders, craftsmen and clients, as well as the architects and the engineers in the creation of the built environment. One must not underestimate the symbolic significance of the master mason Alladin Moustafa receiving an architecture award from the hand of the Aga Khan in the presence of the president of Pakistan and so many luminaries of the international architectural world. Finally, the Award's recognition of both social and historic dimensions of the built environment in addition to architectural excellence in contemporary buildings provided a redefinition of the interlinked nature of these three areas of concern. This was the same Jury, the same Award recognising merit in different facets of the same reality, thereby breaking the compartmentalisation which had hitherto characterised these activities.

HASSAN FATHY

Hassan Fathy.

The creation of a special "Chairman's Award" to honour the great Egyptian architect Hassan Fathy was universally well received. His profound influence throughout the Third World was well known. Recently he had come to be recognised in the West as well.[5] This was the first international prize to honour Fathy, and was to be followed by others a few years later when the first International Gold Medal Award of the International Union of Architects was also awarded to him, a signal honour for the Third World generally and Fathy specifically.

Fathy's undeviating dedication to a clear vision that many had branded as overly romantic was buttressed by deep beliefs in concepts that today have become so widely accepted that their revolutionary character is frequently forgotten.[6] Ideas, such as the importance of learning from vernacular architecture, using local materials, self-help, and architecture for the poor, are not accepted as conventional wisdom. The unpopularity of those views among the international architectural establishment at the time he presented them in the 1940's, should not be forgotten.

In terms of the Award's intellectual search, Hassan Fathy's contributions are essentially a profound humanism that transcends the forms and methods of his buildings, and opens up broad avenues of awareness in areas badly needed in the Muslim world today. The true contributions of Hassan Fathy are not just the quaint mud brick structures he built with such elegance and refinement, but ideas: the idea of empowering the disenfranchised to express themselves with the architect as catalyst for the refining of local sensibility; the idea of rooting architectural expression in the local and regional context to ensure both relevance and authenticity; the use of rational, scientific methods to accept or reject elements of both the old and the new;[7] and the idea of the architect as a decoder of a past legacy and the articulator of a new, symbolically charged environment.

Fayoum (Gouache by Hassan Fathy).

THE FIRST AWARD BOOK

The handsome volume entitled *Architecture and Community: Building in the Islamic World Today* edited by Renata Holod and Darl Rastorfer, was a superb summary of the first award cycle.[8] It was introduced by His Highness the Aga Khan, who explained the vision that motivates the Award. He emphasised that the search itself, the unfettered intellectual pursuit of excellence in architecture, is at the heart of the enterprise.

The rest of the volume, after an introduction by the editors comprised selections from the first five seminars, then a detailed presentation of the fifteen winning projects, and a commentary on and by Hassan Fathy, first winner of the Chairman's Award for a lifetime's achievements in areas relevant to the Award's objectives. The book remained true to the spirit of the Award. It provided a superb recapitulation of the successful launch of a most ambitious enterprise.

The presentations in the book did not, however, try to provide for a categorisation different than that proposed by the Master Jury, not did it acknowledge or take on frontally those critics, especially in some quarters of the western architectural media, who were stunned by the number and diversity of the awards and who accordingly found "the message" of the awards to be unfocused and unclear. The clarity of the award to Hassan Fathy was recognised as championing indigenous architecture, but wrongly perceived by many as being exclusive of architecture with a capital "A". This became a red-herring that was to dog the external debates about the Award, but not debates within the Award's discussions, for years to come.

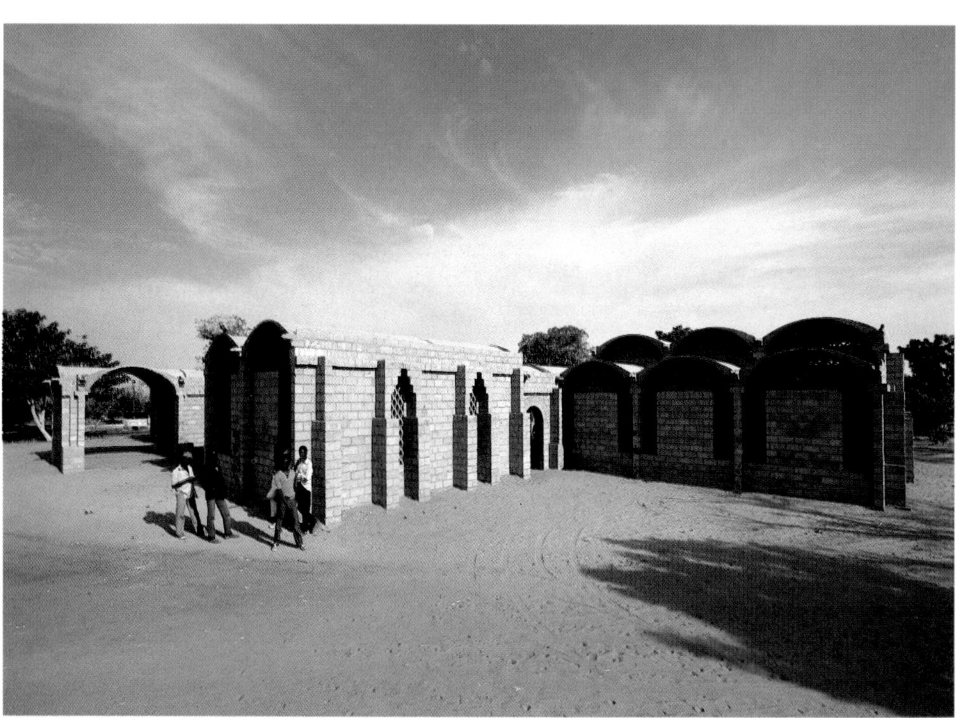

Agricultural Training Centre, Nianing, Senegal.

THE SECOND CYCLE: 1980–1983

The Secretariat and the Steering Committee for the second cycle, from left to right, rear row: Curtis, Makiya and Correa; second row: Cantacuzino, Mumtaz and Kuban; third row: Porter, Grabar, Arkoun, Khan and Casson; front row: Holod, His Highness the Aga Khan, Zulficar and Özkan.

The Master Jury of 1983, from left to night: Fida Ali, Stirling, Chadirji, Simounet, Sudi, Cansever, Moore, Kiray and Serageldin.

The first cycle thus created an invaluable framework for the second cycle, in terms of process as well as mandate. It also helped define the agenda for the next seminars directing attention to some of what it had left untouched: the rural habitat and the city. The transition from the first to the second cycle also established an integral part of the AKAA's tradition, the restructuring of both the Steering Committee and the Master Jury for the new cycle, to promote renewal while retaining continuity.

Eleven members in addition to His Highness the Aga Khan made up the new Steering Committee: Mohammed Arkoun, a specialist in Arabic and Arabic literature at the Sorbonne; Sherban Cantacuzino, an architect and editor, Secretary of the Royal Fine Art Commission in Great Britain; Sir Hugh Casson, an architect and president of the Royal Academy of Arts in Great Britain; Charles Correa, a leading architect from India; Oleg Grabar, a specialist in Islamic art and architecture at Harvard Univerity; Renata Holod, former Award Convenor and specialist in Islamic art and architecture at the University of Pennsylvania; Hasan-Uddin Khan, former Award Convenor, architect and planner, and editor of *Mimar;* Doğan Kuban, an architect and architectural historian, director of the Institute of History of Architecture and Restoration at Istanbul Technical University; Mohammed Makiya, architect; Kamil Khan Mumtaz, an architect and planner from Pakistan; and lastly William Porter, Professor of architecture and planning at the Massachusetts Institute of Technology.

The Master Jury again comprised of nine members: Turgut Cansever, architect, Istanbul; Rifat Chadirji, architect, Baghdad; Habib Fida Ali, architect, Karachi; Mubeccel Kiray, urban sociologist, Istanbul; Charles Moore, architect, Los Angeles; Parid Wardi bin Sudin, architect and university lecturer, Kuala Lumpur; Ismail Serageldin, Chairman of the Master Jury, architect and planner, Washington D.C.; Roland Simounet, architect, Paris; and lastly James Stirling, architect, London.

The Secretariat was restructured. The office of the Convener, first held effectively by Renata Holod and briefly by Hasan-Uddin Khan (who had now both joined the Steering Committee), was replaced by a Secretary General and a Deputy Secretary General. Saïd Zulficar, conservationist and historian, former Programme Specialist, Division of Cultural Heritage, UNESCO, became Secretary General. Suha Özkan, architect, Professor of Theory of Architecture at the Middle East Technical University, Ankara, became Deputy Secretary General.

SEMINARS AND PUBLICATIONS

The seminars of the second cycle were marked by a shift in scale and context. They dealt with "The Changing Rural Habitat" (China, 1981), "Reading the Contemporary African City" (Senegal, 1982), and "Development and Urban Metamorphosis" (Yemen, 1983). The locations of the Award seminars were new to the core group which had become identified with the Award during the first cycle and thus helped to expand their horizons and enrich their appreciation of the diverse realities of

Muslim societies as well as extending the network of contacts that the Award was building throughout the Muslim world.

The new secretary general, and his deputy, were prime movers in the push to expand the contacts of the Award, not just in terms of seeking new seminar locations, but also by translating the seminar proceedings into French, Arabic and Chinese. They also extended contacts with diverse international and professional associations in the Muslim world.

The series of seminars took the Award's search further afield from the recognised domain of architectural criticism to explore the rural and urban settings of buildings. The material presented, although rich in content and vast in coverage, did not produce the kind of intellectual breakthrough that some had hoped for. Instead, it consolidated the intellectual foundations established in the first cycle and filled in the lacunae that had not been covered. It was to prove salutary in providing a truly broad foundation for later work during the third cycle. But more importantly, these seminars established contacts with professional groups and Muslim communities outside the mainstream of existing contacts and transactions. This enhanced the understanding of the Award's principal bodies about the diverse realities of the Muslim world, its problems and what the local inhabitants were doing to cope with them. It also helped the rest of the world, especially those concerned with building in the Muslim world, to realise the treasures of Yemen, the wonders of Muslim China and the unique reality of Sub-Saharan African Islam.[9]

China: The changing rural habitat — massive four storey school carved in the hillside in Shaanxi province.

The African city: Beni Izguen, Mzab, Algeria.

Yemen's unique architectural heritage.

In terms of content, the three seminars, published in five volumes, provide an impressive addition to the body of knowledge, analysis and opinions generated by the Award. In terms of intellectual constructs, or critical theory, it brought little new except for the Dakar seminar. The Dakar seminar had different objectives which were emphasised, even in its title, by addressing the notion of "reading" an urban environment. This meant decoding an intricate set of symbols and signs of an established traditional order which was rapidly being changed by socio-economic and demographic forces and the political discourse that invariably accompanies such transformations. The symbols were being degraded into signs or worse, ideologically charged signals. This theme is one which we shall return to as it clearly appears to be one of the dominant issues confronting the Muslim world and its elites today. Although the objectives of the Dakar seminar aimed in that direction, the results were inconclusive. It was a milestone on the part of the Award's ongoing search for understanding this important subject rather than an effectual breakthrough. Again, the reasons were similar to those encountered in the Fez seminar when the question of a multi-disciplinary probing of "symbol" and "identity" was broached. More preparatory groundwork was needed to establish a common terminology, methodology and analytic framework before the results of such encounters could be realised.

In their more modest objectives, the other two seminars were quite successful. In the case of China, this was guaranteed by the novelty of both context (Muslim regions of China) and material (an architectural study of the changing rural habitat). The Sana'a seminar (May 1983) effectively tackled many themes[10] that had come up time and again in the Award's deliberations, and which continue to do so until now. These include :

- The dichotomy between "modernity" *(al-hadatha)* and "tradition" *(al-turath)*,[11] which on closer, more reasoned scrutiny are terms fraught with problems, carrying an intellectual baggage of considerable proportions. The dichotomy itself is also too simplified as a construct to deal with the underlying issue of cultural continuity and rupture.
- The role of conservation in a rapidly growing city with its evolving, modernising economic base and the necessary changes in its infrastructure.

- The image of progress that elites in Muslim countries (and more generally less developed countries) hold, and the role of architects in shaping that image as well as in responding to it.
- Islam and technology and whether there are inherent contradictions between the two. It is surprising how much discussion can be generated by such a patently ahistorical and demonstrably loose and erroneously structured dichotomy.
- The role of the architect in bringing about changes in a society's environment.

The regional seminar at Kuala Lumpur in July 1983, the first in a projected series on "Exploring Architecture in Islamic Cultures", dealt with "Architecture and Identity". It was an important event, to be repeated in the third cycle. At the Kuala Lumpur gathering, Charles Correa in his essay and comments, underlined the pluralistic character of the expression of identity, a concept central to the Award's understanding of this area. Mona Serageldin's paper on "New Popular Housing in the Middle East"[12] addressed the question of popular taste already evoked brilliantly by Jean-Jacques Guibbert's article, "Symbols, Signs, Signals: Walls of the City" in the Dakar Seminar on "Reading the African City".[13] At the time, the issue of "populism" in architectural expression had not yet emerged. Not until the 1986 awards, were the differences between "populism" and the "popular" to be extensively debated.

PARALLEL EFFORTS ELSEWHERE

The themes addressed in the Award seminars were also being treated effectively and with considerable depth in two other fora which complemented the Award activities and involved many of the same individuals. By 1983, *Mimar*, produced in Singapore and edited by Hasan-Uddin Khan, was rapidly becoming the intellectual journal for architects of the Third World. It treated some of these themes from a more "architectural" perspective, in short essays, emphasising their physical manifestation and visual evidence.

Halfway around the world, the Aga Khan Program for Islamic Architecture (AKPIA) at Harvard and MIT was undertaking basic research and teaching in subjects relevant to the Award. More immediate in its impact, however, were the outreach seminars. Under AKPIA sponsoring, Mona Serageldin organised an impressive series of such seminars that addressed practitioners and decision-makers as well as academics on comparable issues. Here, however, the coverage tended to be more socio-economic than architectural, and more pragmatic and problem solving than intellectual and theoretical.

The seminar topics dealt with: "Higher-Education Facilities", "Urban Housing", "Adaptive Reuse", "Continuity and Change", and "Large Housing Projects". It was perhaps the only forum where the implementation aspects, namely institutional and financial considerations, were given as much weight as the socio-cultural aspects of design solutions. As such they provided an interesting and complementary stream of thinking that slightly preceded the second Award cycle and extended into the third.

The presence of William Porter and Oleg Grabar on both the AKAA Steering Committee and the AKPIA helped bridge the two activities. These bridges were enhanced by the frequent participation of the same major group of interested parties (a solid core group of 10 to 20 individuals) in both the AKPIA seminars and the AKAA activities.

ISSUES BEFORE THE MASTER JURY OF 1983

The 1983 Jury selections were the outcome of a long drawn-out discussion among the Jury members, which focused essentially around four questions:

- Should the winners include restoration and conservation projects as well as contemporary designs?
- Should the social merit of schemes be given weight in the Jury's evaluation or should evaluation be strictly limited to the architectural aspects of the project?
- Should the 1983 selections be seen as independent of or complementary to the 1980 winners?
- Should the number of premiated projects be limited to say 3 to 5 projects thereby focusing the message of the Award?

It is a tribute to the workings of the AKAA and to the constructive approach of all the members of the Jury that a satisfactory, albeit grudging, consensus could be reached on these difficult questions, many of which were to be evoked again in 1986. Since the 1983 Jury did not prepare a detailed report to document its views, it is perhaps pertinent to comment briefly about these four issues, thereby setting the stage for a better appreciation of how these same issues were treated in 1986.

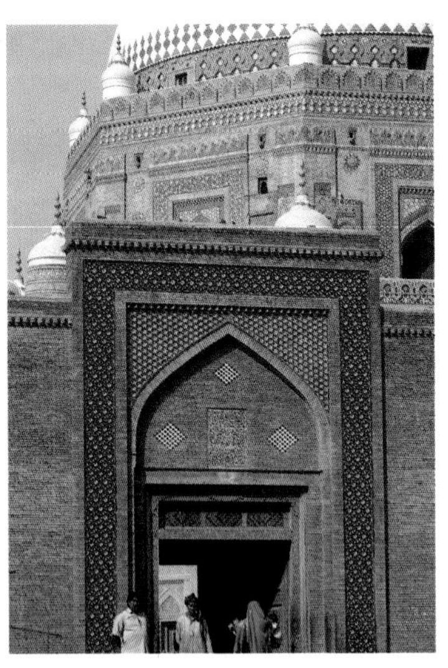

Shah Rukn-i-'Alam, Multan, Pakistan: an outstanding example of restoration.

On the Question of Restoration/Conservation Projects. Most of the Jury agreed that the skills required to undertake successful and effective restoration projects were substantially different from those involved in the creative process of designing a new building. Clearly, the emphasis on faithfulness to the original, the technical complexity of the work, and the premium placed on the quality of the historical scholarship, and the technical know-how of materials and past building methods are mostly at odds with the creative elan that marks much of the most innovative and interesting contemporary designs. Indeed, the most effective restoration/conservation efforts are those where the practitioner purposely effaces his or her own presence to enhance the work of the original designer. The personality of the contemporary designer not only comes through in most contemporary works of excellence, but it is frequently the "trademark" of the artist that imprints the work.

Despite these real distinctions, it was felt that the AKAA *must* acknowledge worthy efforts of conservation of the architectural heritage. At a time when this heritage is threatened with destruction in every part of the Muslim world and where contemporary Muslim societies are struggling to define their identity in a rapidly changing environment, their attention to exemplars of a worthy past, and the preservation of a continuum of historical evidence that traces an evolving and authentic identity, is all the more essential. This recognised and valued heritage can then serve as a springboard for modernist reinterpretation of the past, and for the definition of a contemporary aesthetic that is rooted in the cultural norms and social values of these rapidly evolving societies.

Accordingly, the 1983 Jury felt the necessity of maintaining these conservation efforts and chose to premiate three projects in this domain. Each one represented a different philosophy and one which requires recognition in its own right.

The Social Merit of Projects. The social merit of projects has probably been the most recurrent issue in the AKAA debates.[14] To simplify to the extreme, the arguments fall along a spectrum the poles of which can be defined as follows:

- *The social view:* Architectural projects do not exist in a vacuum. Architecture is the physical manifestation of the cultural, social, economic, legal, geographic, climatic and other factors that define a society. Hence, any effort to judge an architectural work outside of that context, is bound to be purely formalistic and sterile. Therefore, the question of the social impact of a project, and the relevance of a particular solution to the prevalent social and economic problems of the society where that project is found, remain important for assessing any project that is to be held up as an exemplar for others to learn from, and emulate.

This approach provides the justification for the selection of such projects as the Kampung Improvement Programme and the Pondok Pesantren Pebalen Project in the 1980 awards which, without strong visual content, significantly broadened the horizons of architects encouraging them to look beyond their concerns and interests with the monumental and the expensive structures for wealthy or large institutional clients.

- *The architectural view:* Architects are form-givers. They respond to the society's needs in a manner that transcends the responses of those who are not concerned with shaping the physical world. Their primary responsibility is to articulate an aesthetic, and provide working solutions in tune with a people; solutions which help them find themselves and define their identity. They must also provide a physical interpretation of that which is best in a contemporary society.

  Architectural excellence by such criteria cannot be ignored in the choice of any winning project. If the most noble and successful social schemes lack the physical attributes of aesthetic appeal that a true design of excellence must impart, they cannot and should not be considered for an award.

  If this approach leads to the premiation of only those buildings which happen to deal with particular types of commissions, so be it. It must be recognised that some of the greatest architectural exemplars that we use today to define the meaning of Islamic architecture were projects of relatively limited social merits, for example the Taj Mahal. Yet no one today will contest that the Taj Mahal is one of the universal achievements of all mankind and one of the jewels of world architecture as well as a great centre-piece of Islamic architectural heritage.

Great Mosque of Niono, Mali.

Between these two extremes, much has been said and remains to be said. But the 1983 Jury found that in taking its selected winners in conjunction with the 1980 awards the total set of winners served best to define the full message of the Aga Khan Award for Architecture. In this context, the 1983 selections when seen alone could be considered as tilting towards Architecture (with a capital "A") albeit without totally excluding the social dimensions. Indeed in both the Hafsia Project and the Ramses Wissa Wassef Arts Centre, one can easily find social dimensions reflecting the deep concerns of the architects involved, but without compromising the aesthetic standards or loss of architectural sensitivity and creativity.

In the Great Mosque of Niono, specially when coupled with the Sherefudin White Mosque of Yugoslavia, one has a statement of the social relevance of architecture be it ultra-modern or mostly traditional and vernacular. In both cases there is an authentic resonance which helps the community that built the mosque find itself and define its self-image through the creative act of a talented architect.

The balance sought between these two objectives, the purely social and the purely architectural, is obviously overdrawn in this simplistic statement. It does not do justice to the richness of the debate that animated the deliberations of the Jury as well as the many discussions of the Steering Committee. The Award's seminars which broadened the scope of this search to include the views and contributions of many professinals, practitioners, academics, critics, and concerned citizens, also covered the same ground. There is no simple way to convey the reams of research, debate and discussion that go into seeking this sensitive balance. Balanced it must be, for the Award has consistently refused to reject any of the multiple facets of the prismatic reality of the built environments of the Muslims.

Sherefudin White Mosque, Visoko, Yugoslavia.

Were the 1983 Awards Independent of the 1980 Awards? Each cycle allows a new Jury to select new winners and thus a Jury's judgments should be assessed on their own merits. Any objective observer has however to recognise that the awards cannot be seen as completely independent. If no one would deny the intrinsic worth of the Kampung Improvement Programme (KIP), it would make little sense for the Award to premiate a KIP every three years. Thus, the body of winners over the years, builds up the comprehensive message of the Award. Clearly, however, there can and should be among the winners repetitions of the same themes, with some subtle variations, that would serve to enrich the overall message, just as reworking of musical themes is an inherent part of any symphonic work.

In this view, the absence among the 1983 winners of a self-help community improvement programme aimed at poor slum dwellers does not signify a shift of the Award's concern with poverty alleviation. Rather, it reflects the preference to premiate projects such as the Ramses Wissa Wassef Arts Centre and the Hafsia Housing Project, each of which treats with sensitivity, some aspects of the broader problem while retaining social concerns.

The Number of Winning Projects. The idea of restricting the number of winners to a select few, thereby adding to the lustre and impact of the message that the Award gives by selecting those winners, has been uppermost in the minds of many, especially the Western press that covered the architectural awards. The diversity that found expression in 15 winning projects in 1980, and 11 winning projects in 1983, made it difficult for many in the Western press to relate to the subtle message of the Award. They found this diversity difficult to grasp and categorise. This led to ambiguity in their interpretations of the Award's message.

Yet it is undeniable that situations in the Muslim world today are astoundingly diverse, and call forth equally diverse responses. The simple, elegant yet basic designs produced by societies at almost subsistence existence in the Sahelian countries of Africa are, and must be, very different from the massive mega-projects of oil rich Saudi Arabia. From the icy winters of eastern Turkey, to the tropical climates of Indonesia passing through the arid deserts of Arabia, different architectural solutions must be, and have been found. This incredible diversity cannot be captured by a few winners. In the final analysis, it was difficult to say in purely architectural terms, that the artistry of the Great Mosque of Niono in Mali was any less deserving of an award than the wizardry of the roof structure of the Hajj Terminal in Saudi Arabia. It is this diversity that forced the juries past and present to look beyond one or two projects and to bring to the attention of the world more structures and solutions, more building types and materials, and variety of approaches and techniques than has been the case with any other architectural award.

The Hajj Terminal's roof structure: a bold vision at the cutting edge of technological innovation.

In so doing the Award avoided the temptation of prescribing an approach, a method or a technique as being *the* correct one. The Award remained true to its concept of creating a *space of freedom* where all searchers of integrity can pursue their vision for a better future for the Muslim world.

THE 1983 WINNERS

The 1983 Jury selected 11 projects out of 216 candidates. Of these, three were restoration/conservation projects. The Azem Palace in Damascus, Syria, the Shah Rukn-i-'Alam Tomb in Multan, Pakistan and the Darb Qirmiz project in Cairo, Egypt.

Azem Palace, Damascus: more reconstruction than conservation, but a stunning result nonetheless.

Each of those three projects represented a different philosophical approach to conservation. Collectively, the Jury felt that they endorsed the different options that could usefully be pursued to face the different problems and opportunities confronting conservationists in the Muslim world today.

Thus, the Shah Rukn-i-'Alam Tomb in Multan, Pakistan, is an outstanding example of restoration of a monument with tremendous faithfulness to the original design. The guiding philosophy however, is to restore the monument to its original grandeur. Even though every piece of material that was introduced in the Shah Rukn-i-'Alam conservation/restoration project is clearly labelled so that future generations undertaking restoration will know exactly where original material ended and new material began, for the outside viewer it is difficult to make that distinction. Indeed, the monument stands in all its splendour as it must have when it was first built. The craftsmanship, attention to detail, and the skill required to execute a project of such a magnitude justified its being premiated as an outstanding exemplar of restoration work.

Conversely, the Darb Qirmiz project in Egypt, sought to relate two different concepts of conservation and restoration. First, the concern was for area preservation, using a complex of seven different structures as a starting point for a renewal of the whole district. The restoration of these seven monuments was undertaken also to exacting standards and superb technical skills, but there the philosophy that guided the work was to clearly distinguish between what is new and what is old. No effort was made to clean the old or to make the new similar to the old. The patina of age is obvious to the casual observer demarcating the old from the new. This approximate "filling-in" of the visual gaps restores the monuments to some of their former glory but still retains the veracity and authenticity of an older, if somewhat refurbished structure. Proponents of this approach argue that the older parts are all the more enhanced by their contrast with the distinctly, if discretely, new.

The third selected project reflects yet another approach which is more akin to reconstruction than to either conservation or restoration in a more conventional sense. The restoration of the Azem Palace in Damascus required reconstruction of entire sections of the palace without the benefit of detailed documentation of what existed there before. Furthermore, for purposes of recreating the ambience of that grandiose structure, the conservationist felt justified in taking entire sections, (the ceiling), from another structure of a contemporary period and placing it in the reconstructed palace.

The result is no less stunning than any of the other premiated conservation and restoration efforts, and it can justifiably be argued that the Azem Palace restored in this manner is preferred to one that would have remained in ruins. Some, however, have argued that this type of reconstruction, though imaginative and bold, is not fully in tune with the more conventional means of conservation/preservation of historical monuments that are favoured by the Venice convention.[15]

Of the remaining eight winners, one was clearly *sui generis* — the roof structure of the Hajj terminal building in Jeddah, Saudi Arabia. This huge structure is an outstanding effort at devising innovative technology for a unique (and uniquely Islamic) phenomenon: the hundreds of thousands of pilgrims that come through Jeddah Airport to visit Mecca.

Two other winners were mosques. One, the Great Mosque of Niono, Mali, is a traditional mud brick structure of poetic beauty and grace. The other, the Sherefudin White Mosque of Visoko, Yugoslavia, is an avant garde sculptural structure that provides a modern treatment for a key building in a community that adheres strongly to traditional values. That these two polar opposites in approach both worked well and that they were the first mosques to receive an award made the Award's message of openness to alternative solutions all the more forceful.

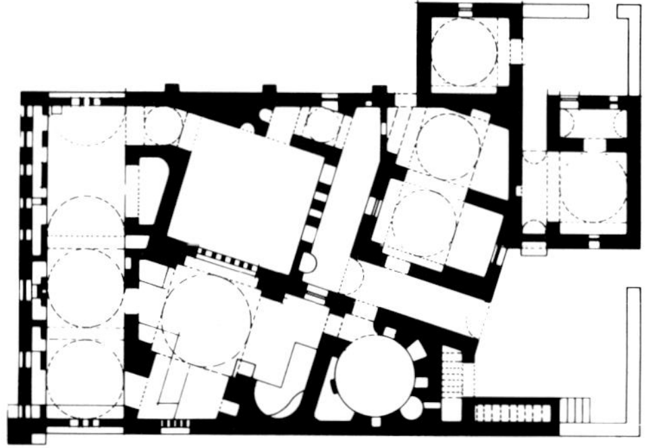

Ramses Wissa Wassef Arts Centre in Giza, Egypt: the sculpture museum's plan shows artful misalignment that creates a unique sequence of spaces, dramatically enhancing the experiential value of the building.

The Ramses Wissa Wassef Arts Centre in Egypt with its magnificent sculpture museum demonstrated the artistry of one of Egypt's great masters. A contemporary and friend of Hassan Fathy, Wassef who died in 1974 did not live to see his work recognised internationally. The deliberate casualness of his plans, the poetic simplicity and harmony of his structures and the dramatic use he made of natural light show how the humblest of materials (mud brick) can, in the hands of a master, create structures that soar above the norm.

The Hafsia Housing Project in the old *medina* in Tunis showed how modern buildings could be sensitively incorporated into the fabric of the old *medina*. If the project had flaws in its socio-economic aspects, these were useful lessons that the authorities intended to learn from and correct in the design and implementation of the second phase.[16]

Residence Andalous, Sousse, Tunisia: the use of water, appropriate scale and the echo of tradition in a thoroughly modern design.

Two hotels-cum-tourist complexes were also winners. In Malaysia, the Tanjong Jara Beach Hotel and Rantau Abang Visitors' Centre was commended for its ability to successfully adapt and develop traditional architecture and crafts while expressing a contemporary architecture. The project has revived a number of building-material industries, crafts, and traditional construction skills.

In Sousse, Tunisia, Serge Santelli's Residence Andalous was premiated for its contemporary expression of the structural principles underlying the traditional architecture. The simplicity and functional elegance of the design, the successful use of local architectural elements such as courtyards, interior gardens and especially water, represents an effective synthesis of the traditional and modern architectural vocabularies.

The last of the 11 winners, a small vacation house in Turkey, designed by journalist Nail Çakirhan, was to prove the most controversial decision of 1983. The house built in the traditional style of the Mugla region, sparked off a small revival of the local crafts as other wealthy Turks from Ankara and Istanbul built similar vacation houses. The fact that the outsiders did not build in "modern" materials or style also enhanced the value of the traditional architectural vocabulary in the eyes of the local inhabitants of the region.

The Turkish architectural establishment was incensed by this Award (the only winner in Turkey that year) which was given to a non-architect. This was considered all the more galling since the ceremonies were held in the Topkapı Palace in Istanbul. The Award seminar held in the Ibrahim Paşa Palace on September 4, 1983, was to prove a lively affair.

Once more, the freedom of exchanges between the Jury and the critics of the awards led to an enrichment for all concerned, and a grudging acceptance of the message of the Jury's decisions by the vast majority of those present. The issues were:

- The winner was a non-architect. It was explained that the winner is a structure and not a person. Only the Chairman's Award is to a person, and none were given in 1983.
- The structure was a tiny and insignificant one compared to the major buildings undertaken in Turkey in the last twenty five years. It was explained that the

scale of a building was in no way proportional to its architectural significance. Thus, three relatively small structures, Mies Van der Rohe's Barcelona Pavilion, Frank Lloyd Wright's Falling Water, and Le Corbusier's Notre Dame du Haut at Ronchamps, were undoubtedly among the most influential in the twentieth century. This was not to imply that the Çakirhan residence was in the same league, but merely to dismiss the issue of scale. Furthermore, the same Jury had also made an Award to the Hajj Terminal structure in Jeddah Airport arguably the largest piece of architecture in the world.

- The Jury displayed anti-modern bias reflected in its choices of the quaint, small traditional buildings. Again the Jury explained that the prizes given to the Yugoslav mosque, the Tunisian hotel and the Hajj Terminal were truly modern structures. The diversity of the prize winners was only a reflection of the diversity of meritorious solutions.

The Çakirhan Residence: a small, elegant building that generated much debate in 1983.

On the whole, this debate reaffirmed the objectives of the Award. It was instrumental in promoting a wider discussion of the issues that were raised rather than limiting the discussion to the physical attributes of the winners. This controversy, which had already erupted in 1980, over the Kampungs and the Water Towers, was now well established as an integral part of the AKAA tradition.

THE SECOND AWARD BOOK

Architecture in Continuity was the title selected for the beautiful volume produced by Sherban Cantacuzino to tell the story of the awards of 1983. Appropriately, the book included a thoughtful presentation by Cantacuzino followed by three fairly lengthy essays. Doğan Kuban treated the issue of modern expression in Turkish architecture in his essay entitled "A Survey of Modern Turkish Architecture", which gave a thorough and scholarly discussion of the many important issues touched upon ever so lightly in the sometimes vociferous debates in Istanbul.

In recognition that for the first time two mosques were among the winning projects, two essays on mosque architecture were included. Ihsan Fethi's "The Mosque Today" dealt with the mosque in contemporary Muslim societies and Robert Hillenbrand's essay addressed "The Mosque in the Medieval Islamic World".

The rest of the book followed the same format as that of the first Award book, with detailed presentations of the winners.

The book, though extremely elegant in format and presentation has not yet been sufficiently disseminated. Its publication marked an important milestone in the maturing of the Award process and the gradual establishment of a tradition of excellence in presentation, openness in expression, and freedom in exploration.

THE THIRD CYCLE: 1983–1986

For the third cycle, His Highness the Aga Khan decided to reduce the size of the Steering Committee which now included: Mohammed Arkoun, Professor of History of Islamic Thought, Sorbonne; Charles Correa, architect, Bombay; Hasan-Uddin Khan, architect, editor of *Mimar*, Paris; Oleg Grabar, Professor of Islamic Art, Harvard University; William Porter, Professor of Architecture and Planning, Massachusetts Institute of Technology; and, Ismail Serageldin, architect and planner, The World Bank, Washington D.C.

The Master Jury comprised of: Soedjatmoko (Chairman of the Master Jury), Development Specialist, Indonesia; Mahdi Elmandjra, economist, Morocco; Abdel Wahed El-Wakil, architect, Egypt; Hans Hollein, architect and designer, Austria; Zahir Ud-Deen Khwaja, architect and Planner, Pakistan; Ronald Lewcock (secretary of the Master Jury), architect, restoration specialist, Australia; Fumihiko Maki, architect, Japan; Mehmet Doruk Pamir, architect, Turkey; and, Robert Venturi, architect, United States.

The Secretariat added an additional member, Jack Kennedy, an architect, who became Executive Officer. Saïd Zulficar and Suha Özkan remained Secretary-General and Deputy Secretary-General respectively.

SEMINARS, PUBLICATIONS AND THINK TANKS

Despite the considerable work on the contextual framework in which architecture is practiced in the Muslim world, the Award had not yet confronted the key problems of urban explosion that characterise the growth of mega-cities such as Cairo, Jakarta, and Karachi. The scale of the problems, the speed of urbanisation, and the intensity of the socio-economic and demographic pressures generated by this urban growth pose problems for architects and planners, both in terms of their societal role and the influence of architectural work. These are problems that transcend anything Western cities experience today.

Thus, the third cycle launched its first international seminar, "The Expanding Metropolis: Coping with the Urban Growth of Cairo", in Cairo, Egypt, on November, 1984. Drawing heavily upon the Egyptian intellectual community, the Award seminar proved to be a major catalyst in joining disparate groups that seldom listen to each other. The *space of freedom* was manifest as decisions-makers, academics, practitioners, politicians, journalists and concerned citizens all joined in an inquiry revolving around four themes:

- The meaning of history in the context of present day Cairo. From A.K. Abul Magd's keynote speech via Oleg Grabar's thoughtful posing of the question to Arkoun's enunciation of the changeable and the permanent in the Muslim consciousness, Cairo's unique historical legacy weighed heavily on the concerns of participants. Both technical and philosophical issues of conservation were widely discussed, but the notion of historical legacy that concerned the participants transcended the issues of conservation of the Medieval Islamic city (which is on the world heritage list).

- The institutional context in which decisions affecting the urban environment are made. Mona Serageldin's presentation and the panels on housing and finance were the focus of lively exchanges, that explored the non-physical aspects of the planning and design processes.
- Alternatives to the urban growth of Cairo and the role of new towns. The allure of designing a new town, a physical utopia, has been the architects' fondest dream since time immemorial. Financial and political realities, however, have continued to thwart the noblest of dreams.[17] Social diversity and its physical reflection in individualised designs, are the quintessential qualities for an interesting sense of urban character. Yet these are precisely the qualities that are most difficult for state planning agencies to build into their programmes.
- The international character of the problems. This was highlighted by comparative studies of Casablanca, Bombay, and Karachi. To a lesser extent, these same problems are found in all Third World cities where urbanisation is a reality with urban population growth rates running up to six to eight per cent per year.

Cairo: an exploding modern metropolis underneath its Islamic skyline.

The seminar proceedings, published in Arabic and English, attest to the scope and content of the material covered. However, in my judgment, the singular success of this seminar was the extent of the participation of the Egyptians themselves and the degree and intensity of the interaction that took place among then. Never was the Award's *space of freedom* more clearly evident.

The second international seminar in the cycle witnessed a shifting of emphasis from the series of Sana'a, Dakar, and Cairo to a new subject for the AKAA: architectural education in the Muslim world.

Having defined the domain in the first cycle's five seminars, and extended it further to both rural and urban environments in the second cycle and the first seminar of the third, the Award now turned to the question of what underpinned the training of architects.

By now, the formula of the Award's international seminars was well established and continued to attract many international authorities. Although the subject of Architectural Education would naturally call forth the experience of the Aga Khan Program for Islamic Architecture (AKPIA), the link to AKPIA was not played up precisely to retain that by now invaluable *space of freedom*. Thus, the AKPIA was modestly presented as *one* of the valuable experiences to be reviewed.

The approach to the seminar was a telling one. The Steering Committee designed the seminar around the following conceptual sequence:

- What are the problems of architecture in the Muslim world today?
- What should architects do about them?
- What are the prerequisite skills neccessary to undertake this role?
- What sort of education is needed to prepare such architects?

It is important to note the Steering Committee's preference of this sequence over the alternative possibility, namely: what are the prevailing approaches to architectural education in the world today and which of them (or which features of each of them) is most suited to deal with the needs of the Muslim world.

This preference denotes the committee's conviction that the approach to the Muslim world's problems must start from those problems. In other words, the intellectual constructs developed for training architects in the Muslim world must emanate from a correct reading of that world and not from an adaption of an imported version of what is deemed "right" elsewhere. This does not preclude an opening to the outside world. Nor does it diminish the importance of having architects from the Muslim world go abroad for training and inter-cultural cross-fertilisation. The approach merely sets out the *problematique* of architectural education in the same context of needed self-knowledge and self-awareness that is considered essential for cultural continuity, regional identity, and innovative change in architecture (all recurrent themes in the Award's deliberations over the years).

The format selected was a well-tested one: a series of general papers followed by case studies, working groups, and a plenary session. The general papers were organised around four main themes:

- Islamic culture, modernity, and architecture;
- Architecture as art;
- Technology, form, and culture: exploring the links between technology and artistic expressions.[18]
- Architecture and society: exploring the links between architectural practice and society to devise some notions for the role of architects and hence their training.

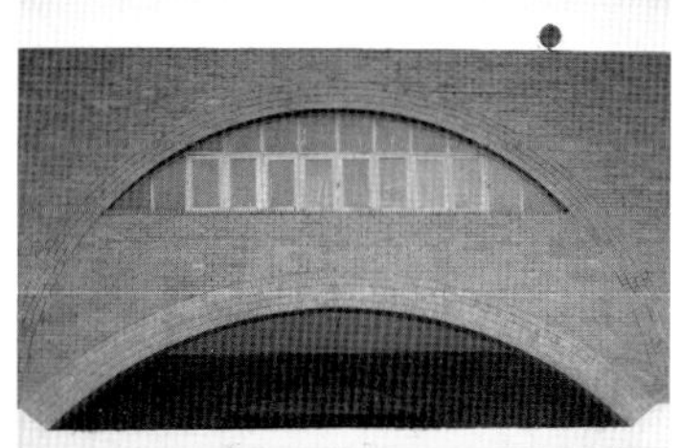

Dhaka: Cardiac Hospital.

The quality of the papers was high and the discussion open and candid. The tone was set by an excellent opening address by Spiro Kostoff. Except for an over-romanticised view of Islam and Islamic architecture presented by the distinguished Norberg-Schulz and a somewhat distressing but realistic assessment of conditions in the Muslim world by Gulzar Haidar, the discussion ran along anticipated lines within the four broad themes. The quality of the case-studies proved to be varied but they were enormously instructive in giving a firm base for the subsequent discussions. The working groups, once again, proved fertile ground for intense interaction and valuable networking.

Yet the nature of the enterprise was such that it raised as many questions as it answered. As expected, no conclusions were reached but there was sufficient interest in the questions raised by the seminar, and which the discussions enhanced, adumbrated, and developed further, that His Highness the Aga Khan, in his closing remarks, considered it appropriate to promise the gathering to revisit the subject in another seminar in a few years. This had never happened in an Award seminar before, and underlines the richness of the vein being mined in this discussion.

Regionalism in Architecture was the subject of the second AKAA regional seminar held in Dhaka, Bangladesh, (December, 1985). It was as successful as the first seminar held in Kuala Lumpur during the second cycle in expanding the scope of the search for a meaningful regionalism and in enhancing discourse among concerned architects of the region. The international participants, including four of the six members of the Award Steering Committee, provided a bridge to international experience and concerns and also acted as catalysts for the interaction between the regional participants.

However, the intellectual activities of the Award during this third cycle transcended these seminars, important as they were, and went beyond the patient, meticulous work of identification, documentation and analysis of scores of projects from all over the Muslim world. There were many reports, memoranda, and think tanks, that dealt with the recurrent themes of the Award's concerns, but added new dimensions to each of them. Some samples of this work will be found in the third part of this book. But the major contribution of the third Steering Committee was elsewhere. Challenged by His Highness the Aga Khan to go beyond the themes of the first six years to the core issues that must be confronted for the Award to continue to be a pathbreaker, the committee responded by addressing new issues that emerged from the Award's first two cycles and that are likely to shape the concerns of the fourth cycle (concluding with the awards of 1989). These two new concerns were: Firstly, what are the constituents of the mythical imagination and the creative processes that underlie the architecture design process generally and in the Muslim world specifically? and secondly, what are the elements of an expanded architectural criticism that is suited to, and meaningful in, the context of regionalism and cultural continuity that are central to Muslim societies of today?

The challenge of these issues requires a critical approach and an intellectual framework of analysis[19] that transcends what the seminars have produced to date, and which the work of the third cycle has barely started. How it might be approached is spelled out in the last section of this essay.

By 1986, the Steering Committee concluded that the body of the 26 premiated projects of 1980 and 1983 made a collective statement that identified both the direction to follow as well as the lacunae that needed attention. Of the former, a concern with *cultural continuity* (historic preservation, conservation), *cultural authenticity* (regionalism in modernity), *societal relevance* (issues of poverty, technology, or materials), as well as *architectural excellence* were coupled with concerns for *innovation* as a means of coping with the rapidly changing environment.[20] That all of these directions could be manifested in the most modest structures in Niger or Mali as well as the more sophisticated buildings in Saudi Arabia and Kuwait, was now well established. Although these directions will be reinforced by future awards, there were large gaps in the challenges that must be confronted by Muslim societies, and where our knowledge and appreciation of appropriate exemplars is sorely lacking. Among these, in terms of building types, one can identify industrial buildings, landscaping, and office buildings. All of these have remained under-represented among the winners that the Award could show the world. Much, therefore, remained to be done to ensure that appropriate exemplars can be found. A major effort to identify buildings in each of these categories was undertaken, and a special brief directing the attention of the Master Jury was prepared.

Industrial buildings and landscaping have been under-represented to date. Outstanding examples include Tekeli-Sisa's Lassa Tyre factory in Izmit Turkey (top) and Kamran Diba's Garden of Niavaran.

The brief emphasised what by now had emerged as the three main areas of concern of the Award: Firstly assessing efforts to preserve the Islamic architectural and urban heritage; secondly assessing social housing and community building efforts; and lastly assessing excellence in contemporary architecture.

In the latter category the brief argued that the Award had already premiated a number of projects in tourism and private residences but had as yet failed to recognise industrial buildings, public office buildings and public spaces (landscaping). The Steering Committee and the Secretariat had tried hard to look for potential candidates in these areas.

Besides the brief, the Steering Committee also provided the Master Jury with the proceedings of the seminars, the AKAA files, and a verbal briefing of the objectives and philosophy of the Award. In its outline of the issues, the Steering Committee shared with the Master Jury in only the most general terms the evolving concepts of its vision of architectural criticism that it has been developing through the think tanks, research reports and other unpublished documents. As it was still in the process of being elaborated, there was little to communicate in writing, but since a number of the Master Jury members had participated in the Award seminars and think tanks, they were contributors to the development of these ideas although they were not as involved with the research and the issues as the Steering Committee members, by the nature of their assignment, were.

The Steering Committee clearly hoped that its brief, the most detailed brief yet given to a Master Jury, would orientate the Master Jury to a set of award decisions that would complement and complete the first 26 winners by filling in the lacunae and enriching the Award's message. This was indeed to happen but in directions totally unexpected by the Steering Committee. The 1986 Master Jury, like preceding ones, is a sovereign body, and it can choose to reinterpret the problem and the mandate as it sees fit. This is at the very heart of the unfettered procedures that the Aga Khan Award for Architecture is committed to in the creation of this *space of freedom* that must govern our ongoing intellectual search. The Master Jury's report clearly states a sense of purpose that has manifested itself in the six winners and the five honourable mentions that were retained for 1986. Prominent and conspicuous by their absence are a number of modern projects that have captured the imagination of the architectural profession but which did not find favour with the 1986 Master Jury. Two members of the jury chose to dissent because of this omission.

THE 1986 WINNERS

The six winning projects comprised two restoration/conservation projects, two mosque complexes, and two projects that represent refined contemporary architectural expressions for the widely different problems of large public housing project and government offices.

In addition, the Master Jury decided to designate five "honourable mentions", which were believed to have merit but were lacking sufficient architectural excellence needed for an award. These included two "social" schemes dealing with community improvement, one public housing scheme, one modern mosque and one restoration/reuse project.

To explain these choices, the Master Jury made a lengthy statement. There were two dissenting reports and a separate statement by the Steering Committee. These are reproduced in full in Part Two of this book.

In the following discussion of the winners and honourable mentions, they are grouped by the broad issues they address and are discussed collectively. In Part Two of this book, each of the projects is presented separately.

On Conservation. The three projects that were selected in 1983 complemented the 1980 winners and made a strong statement about the Award's commitment to historic preservation and restoration. Nevertheless, the 1986 awards went further. With two outstanding winners, and one honourable mention, they brought new dimensions to the message of the AKAA; its respect for the historic heritage of Muslims and its encouragement of tenacity in the face of adversity and of innovation in the face of constraints.

The award winning scheme for the preservation of Mostar Old Town in Yugoslavia, introduced an institutional dimension into the awards for conservation, which had hitherto concentrated on the technical aspects of restoration. With the exception of the Sidi Bou Said award in 1980, which focused on the institutional measures adopted by an entire community to preserve the urban character of the environment, the other awards had mostly been given for the technical quality of the work or the importance of the effort in national terms. In the case of Mostar, the Jury premiated a scheme that showed innovation and an ability to re-channel resources generated by the old city to restore buildings within the same boundary, and thus rejuvenate the old city from the revenue of economic activities within its perimeter. This scheme, which belies the contentions by many that historic preservation is a hopelessly costly enterprise, has shown that some of the finest restoration work can be largely self-financing, and that with will and proper organisation, a substantial effort can be undertaken in this direction. Mostar is an outstanding winner in the institutional as well as the technical field and in the completeness with which it has addressed the renovation of an entire section of the old city.

The restoration of al-Aqsa Mosque, one of the holiest shrines of the Muslim world, has shown tremendous technical ability, outstanding sensitivity, and great tenacity and dedication in the face of a most difficult situation. The Award, in premiating these noble efforts, has recognised one of the more outstanding efforts in the Muslim world today.

The Touring Automobile Association of Turkey: a non-governmental organisation promotes the conservation and re-use of important historic buildings.

And yet, there was one more, perhaps even more interesting award, albeit given the status of honourable mention in 1986, which deserves to be discussed here. This is the Touring Club Restorations in Turkey. Although none of the structures in that project are particularly notable, and the technical work is not complex or outstanding, two features deserve special recognition: Firstly, this is an effort that was undertaken by the private sector and not by a government authority, and secondly, it included buildings of the 19th century, some of which are not recognised as Islamic. This latter point shows that Muslims, and Muslim societies at large, are recognising that there are no broken chains in the continuity between their past and their present, that all periods of their heritage are worthy of preservation, and that all exemplars of these periods contribute to fashioning the image that society holds of itself, its environment, and its character; that which we have come to cherish and accept as our own.

On the Social Dimensions of Design. Four projects fit in this grouping. The Dar Lamane Housing Project in Morocco (winner) and the Shushtar New Town project in Iran (honourable mention). They both represent thoughtful efforts at articulating an adequate urban environment for many inhabitants with modest economic means. Both projects were designed on original sites and the issues of integration with a surrounding urban fabric did not arise. They created their own environments.

Shushtar, Iran: an elegant and sensitively scaled new town.

The salient features of Dar Lamane are the presence of a pedestrian social street accentuated by occasional gateways that helps create the sense of place. The harsh geometry of the plan is softened by the mix of uses and people which bring the space dramatically to life.

The most prominent features of Shushtar are the exquisite brick work and the articulation of volumes to create an inviting, elegant environment of subtle shadings and humane dimensions. Given the dramatic and consistent failure of most public housing projects to create a decent and humane environment for its residents, both of these projects are signal successes. They manage to echo the architectural vocabulary of their regions with subtle resonances. This is a further tribute to the sensitivity of the architects.

The Kampung Kebalen Programme of Surabaya, Indonesia is a worthy successor to the Kampung Improvement Programme (KIP) of Jakarta which received an award in 1980. This time, the local university teachers and students were involved in the project and its very effectiveness shows the successful and large-scale replicability of the KIP approach. The honourable mention is thus a useful reminder of the importance that the Award attaches to the improvement of the built environment of the poor in the Muslim world.[21]

The Ismailiyya development project, on the other hand, marks an important shift in the Egyptian government's approach to the problem of mass housing, complementing an aggressive "new towns" policy and the forced reconstruction of Ismailiyya after it was destroyed in the 1967–1973 wars. It legitimises self-help, slum upgrading, and "sites and services" approaches, all of which were being undertaken on a pilot basis elsewhere in Egypt and which have since been adopted as part of the Egyptian government policy.

Although visually unattractive, because they are geared to process rather than product, both the Ismailiyya and Kampung projects are most striking when measuring the improvements on a "before and after" comparison. This indicates the effect of these projects on the inhabitants–the dignity and hope that have been imparted to the populations and which inspire them to upgrade their communities.

Three Mosques. The Bhong and Yaama Mosques (winners) and the Saïd Naum Mosque (honourable mention) raise interesting questions on the architectural expressions of the most Islamic of all structures, the mosque. Some of the issues echo those raised by the Niono and Sherefudin White Mosques (1983 winners).[22]

The Saïd Naum Mosque represents a serious attempt to reinterpret local architecture in a contemporary fashion. The adherence to the overall aesthetics of the local traditions sets it apart from the Sherefudin White Mosque in Yugoslavia where there was a very distinct break with the Bosnian architectural tradition. Yet the conscious effort that the architect makes to transcend the traditional and the vernacular, remaining almost self-consciously modern, underlines a personal, intellectual and effective combination of the architect as creator and innovator.

The Yaama Mosque on the other hand is a popular structure in the tradition of the region. It is the epitome of the vernacular architectural expression, and thus joins the Niono Mosque as one of the major exemplars of a great living traditional architecture. The specific innovations introduced in this project, while significant in the local context, do not detract from this broader judgement.

The Bhong Mosque is a special case, that sparked considerable debate during and after the Award ceremonies. While it aspires to represent a popular aesthetic, it is this writer's judgement, shared by others, that it is a model of populism applied to architecture. The exuberance of its plentiful, even excessive decoration, is reminiscent of the buses and jeepneys that are lovingly embellished by their owners with effusive and colourful designs and decoration. Whether the Bhong Mosque represents a distillation of a popular aesthetic or merely a manifestation of the semantic disorder that pervades the Muslim world today is at the heart of the ongoing debate. This question will be further developed later in this book.

On Contextualism and Modernity. For many, the most deserving architectural selection of 1986 was Sedad Eldem's social security complex which is an outstanding achievement of sensitive contextualism that does not compromise on its modernity. It is one of the few buildings likely to be considered a true "classic", an exemplar of an era when Muslim societies were groping with modernisation and self-identity vis-a-vis a hegemonic western culture whose paradigm of the modern movement in architecture reigned supreme. Its uncluttered simplicity and elegance is markedly different from much of the more playful attempts of post-modernists to introduce "historic references" in their work.[23]

RIFAT CHADIRJI

Rifat Chadirji.

The Chairman's Award for 1986 was given to Rifat Chadirji in recognition of his contribution to the architecture of the Muslim world. He is one of those rare architects who has imbued his work with a deep understanding of the roots of authentic regional expression and a true appreciation of modernism and its principles. Chadirji has shown a unique capacity for the synthesis of form and function that translates traditional architectural idioms into contemporary expressions. He has worked with materials of the twentieth century, and produced an architecture that is uniquely and distinctively recognisable as his own and as a Middle Eastern architecture, if not a universally Islamic one.

The Steering Committee felt that in Chadirji's work throughout his life there was more than just a capacity for avoiding eclecticism and eschewing pastiche. His work is the result of a patient and systematic search where the search is as important to the world of architecture as what he built in Iraq.

Indeed, Chadirji's contributions transcend a mere corpus of built work, important as that may be, for he is also a major figure in one of the most important and influential architectural schools in the Arab world. The Baghdad School of Architecture, where Chadirji taught for many years, was strongly influenced by him. Rejecting the use of the forms of the past that others espoused, Chadirji devised a synthesis of form that could translate into a new and contemporary urban aesthetics that would guide the articulation of a genuinely modern Iraqi townscape in the latter part of the twentieth century.

Not only has Chadirji influenced many younger architects in Iraq, Turkey, Egypt and elsewhere but he has also laboured long and hard at developing a deep and thoughtful critical sense of what constitutes architectural practice in today's Muslim world, particularly in Iraq. It is this critical faculty and his thoughtful approach to the intellectual basis of his architectural concepts that sets him apart from other practitioners in the Arab world. His description and understanding of the deep processes that underlie the intellectual enterprise of architectural design were central to his work. The originality of his work emanates from an understanding and discernment seldom encountered among architects in the region.

Important as these achievements are however, the Steering Committee felt that the recognition of Chadirji was due primarily because his entire career can be seen as a long and unbroken *search* for a better and deeper understanding of architecture. A pursuit of an elusive truth to which he dedicated his life. His long and distinguished career is thus marked by remarkable tenacity, determination, an uncompromising intellectual honesty and great capacity for self-denial. He is a man who never compromises on principle, who has eschewed lucrative commissions for the pursuit of a personal vision.

Central Post, Telephone and Telegraph building in Baghdad. (Etching from the portfolio of Rifat Chadirji).

At present, Chadirji has retired from private practice to devote himself to research and publication on architecture. Moving between Iraq, the U.S.A. and England, he pursues his vision of truth as he develops the corpus of his intellectual contribution in a series of publications. His two-volume autobiography in Arabic is appropriately subtitled: *An Inquiry into the Dialectics of Architecture*. His work on explaining his projects and the influences upon them, published under the title *Concepts and Influences*, is a testament to intellectual honesty and illustrative of the legacy of a distinguished career. His portfolio of etchings stands as a monument of artistry and draftsmanship.

A talented practitioner, an inspired and insightful teacher, a thoughtful critic and a discerning intellectual and theorist, Rifat Chadirji is a worthy recipient of the Aga Khan's "Chairman's Award" for 1986.

The award is particularly important as Chadirji represents a modernist trend not just in architecture, but in the general intellectual movement in the Arab world. In the 1950's and 1960's when these battles for a reinterpretation of self and society were joined, he was there as an advocate of a forward looking, culturally authentic vision rooted in a deep understanding of his society and its heritage.

The award to Chadirji complements the first Chairman's Award to Hassan Fathy in 1980. The major contribution of Fathy, made primarily in the 1940's was the first appeal for authenticity from a major Third World architect and intellectual. Chadirji's major contributions were crystallised in the 1950's and 1960's. They were forward looking, embracing and encompassing the modern movement and the teachings of Le Corbusier and other international masters. That embrace was a discriminating one that could interpret and adapt as well as adopt. More importantly, Chadirji is a thoroughly modern person, who is also an authentically Arab Muslim from Iraq, and one who makes his own creative and innovative contributions to the point where Robert Venturi wrote:

> *"Chadirji's analysis appears applicable in many ways to the rest of the world; to the so-called Western world as well as to the so-called developing world. For this reason it is a work which is revealing and compelling and in the end universally significant as architectural criticism of our time.*[24]

In terms of the 1986 awards, the prize to Chadirji also brings an interesting addition to the Award's message to the world. It honours the patient search for a modern contemporary expression rooted in a deep understanding of the past forms and cultural expressions.

It is an important message that the Award has consistently sought to promote, but which some might have given insufficient weight to if they looked only at the images of the six winners without delving deeper into the corpus of work that accompanies the awards, including the thoughtful statements of the Steering Committee, Master Jury and dissenting opinions.

A LIVELY DEBATE

The 1986 winners sparked a very lively debate, revolving primarily around the following themes:

- Why were particularly well-known buildings excluded even from honourable mentions? Did this reflect an ideological position in the Jury? Was the Jury biased against western architects practicing in the Muslim world? Did the choices reflect an "anti-modern" bias?
- What was the significance of the Bhong Mosque, which emerged as the most controversial of the choices?
  What is the collective message of these awards?
- Where does the AKAA go from here?
- A proper appreciation of the last two questions requires a synthesis based on an overview of the preceding awards, along with the 1986 winner, and is addressed in the next section. The first two questions are unique to the 1986 awards and are addressed here.

CONSPICUOUS ABSENCES

Louis Kahn's spectacular Parliament building at Dhaka, Bangladesh.

SOM's National Commercial Bank Building at Jeddah, Saudi Arabia.

A number of projects that captured the imagination of many architects and that were widely published and discussed among the architectural profession were conspicuous by their absence in the 1986 awards. Specifically, three projects had been widely regarded as strong contenders for recognition: Louis Kahn's Sher-E-Bangla-Nagar Parliament building in Dhaka, Bangladesh; the National Commercial Bank in Jeddah, Saudi Arabia, by SOM's Gordon Bunshaft; and finally Henning Larsen's building for the Ministry of Foreign Affairs in Riyadh, Saudi Arabia.

The exclusion of these buildings surprised many, especially the exclusion of Kahn's building, which is widely considered a masterpiece. The debate within the Jury on this building led to the majority of the Jury devoting a special section in their report to explain why they did not premiate the project. This was unprecedented for the Award. It led to two minority opinions by Hans Hollein and Doruk Pamir, recorded in two separate dissenting statements.

The reasons given in the majority report of the Jury left some unconvinced. Allegations of bias were made. It is to the credit of the Award's commitment to the *space of freedom* that these allegations and concerns found expression in the Award's ceremonies and were openly and courteously discussed. Some of the subsequent articles in the press were more vociferous and polemical, but essentially repeated the same concerns. Notable among the critics has been William Curtis, whose commitment to modern architecture was deeply slighted by the exclusion of these major projects.[25] One outstanding article by Mildred Schmertz in the *Architectural Record* recast these concerns in a constructive fashion in the form of questions and issues to be addressed by the Award and the profession at large.

There were two major concerns. The first was that the Jury had expressed an anti-modern bias. While the six winners certainly included the Social Security Complex and the Dar Lamane Housing project, these were not the exemplars of the bold and visionary modern architecture that contemporary architects are building throughout the Muslim world. The former is an outstanding exercise in contextualism. The latter is more functional than form-giving. The boldness, innovation and modernity found in such awards as the Mecca Intercontinental and the Kuwait Water Towers (1980) or the Hajj Terminal structure and the Sherefudin White Mosque (1983), were absent among the winners in 1986.[26] Those espousing the Jury's majority view argued that the National Commercial Bank in Jeddah is an arrogant building that does not deserve recognition, that Larsen's Ministry of Foreign Affairs is a weak and derivative building, and that only Kahn's building is truly deserving of consideration. Kahn's building, however, had not been in use long enough to qualify. This technicality outraged Kahn partisans. They felt that this was an evasion of the Jury's responsibilities, and a denial of a building worthy of recognition. Others found the critiques by the Jury of the two other buildings equally ill-founded, considering Larsen's building a sensitive reinterpretation of an established vocabulary, executed to the highest standards, and Bunshaft's National Commercial Bank in Jeddah, an outstanding and bold new concept for coping with the problems of tall buildings in such an environment.

Henning Larsen's elegant Ministry of Foreign Affairs at Riyadh, Saudi Arabia.

While there is always room for disagreement on such issues, it remains true that, among the winners, there was only one building (Eldem's Social Security Complex) that addressed the imperative needs of today's new societies: office buildings. But the Social Security Complex, like the Turkish Historical Society (1980 winner), are limited in scope vis-a-vis the giant requirements of today's offices, factories, and big public buildings. The Jury is undoubtedly entitled to consider that none of the available projects met its standards of architectural excellence. However, if one looks at some of the projects retained for honourable mentions, it is difficult to conclude that all three buildings had no place among the selections of 1986.

The second concern, is that the Jury exercised some "affirmative action", whereby only local architects working in their own countries and in their own traditions were selected. This was corroborated by the coincidence that the six winners were indeed in that category. The Jury clearly refutes such allegations and simply underlines that objective criteria of choice led to this particular selection of buildings and projects, which happened to have been designed by nationals. This was the starting point for speculation in some quarters as to whether the Jury's selection was sending a message about the inherent qualities of the designers who can produce culturally authentic architecture. Must they indeed have lived and internalised the experience of being Muslims in a Muslim community to produce an architecture that is culturally sensitive? Many doubt that. The previous winners show that sensitivity is not necessarily hostage to accidents of birth, geography, and language.

THE BHONG MOSQUE

The award to the Bhong Mosque was unquestionably the most controversial of all. It was discussed at length in specific and general terms. Specifically, the architectural merit of the scheme, or lack of it, was discussed in terms of composition, harmony, and derivative versus original thinking. Some were attracted by the exuberant baroque character of the decoration, and found the vivacious, uninhibited interplay of elements and materials indicative of self-assurance and lack of affectation. The amount of the decoration, was in the view of the majority a statement of appreciation of the central building in the community, whose greater glory and grandeur somehow reflects favourably on the whole community.

Those who dissented from this view were deeply disturbed by the disassociation of the decorative elements from their frame of reference; for example, the use of imported bathroom tiles in some places; and the use of overt signs, for example, the

Arabic inscriptions of *Muhammad* in marquee advertising type grafted on top of key architectural elements. Such features it was argued indicated that the architects had not mastered part of their function, to design a project which adds to the prevailing, socially accepted view of the desirable, and to elevate the aesthetic standards of the community instead of pandering to the most obvious and lowest common denominator of what "pleases the people."[27]

This latter point of view leads to another critique, of a more general nature, that of the intellectual context in which the Bhong Mosque must be seen. At this time, Muslim societies are deeply troubled by the historic rupture they have suffered.[28]

The Bhong Mosque: a highly ornamental structure, it was to generate considerable debate as the most controversial of the six winners of 1986.

The coherence of their cultural milieu and its orderly evolution has been shattered. A major task lies ahead of all Muslim intellectuals to take on the challenge of rebuilding their societies in terms of an integrated and integrating culture. Integrated in so far as its constituent elements are synchronically and diachronically coherent. Integrating in so far as its capacity to accept the new and evolve in a manner that does not fall prey to the semantic disorder that accompanies the discontinuities of an arrested development.

In this context, elites be they political, socio-economic or intellectual, have two alternatives. They can either opt for the arduous task of rebuilding their socio-cultural system on a sound basis of self-knowing re-ordering of the milieu; or they can take the easier ideologically charged approach of a populist appeal to the prevailing majority, with all its negative intellectual connotations.

Here it is important to distinguish between *popular* and *populist*. The former is an expression of a deep collective consciousness that responds to a well-established and well-understood set of symbols, and whose discourse is governed by agreed conventions. Thus the Niono and Yaama Mosques are examples of a vernacular architecture that is an expression of a coherent popular culture.

On the other hand, the culture of populism is ideologically charged. It seeks to reify the popular culture, to set it up as a legitimising force for attitudes that restrict the social discourse. When elites exercise their authority (indirect or derivative as it may be) they have a responsibility in the manner in which they address the broad population at a time of cultural crisis. Architects, and in this instance Rais Ghazi must be considered as an architect as well as a member of the elite, can base their concepts and designs on a set of popularly accepted codes; but the manner in which they interpret these codes is what will make the difference.

To many architects and intellectuals, the Bhong Mosque complex is a project that negates the very purpose of an architectural enterprise rooted in the deep understanding of the culture and the idiom and familiar with the instruments and possibilities of the time.[29] To many others it is a wonderful, exuberant structure that evokes an almost palpable *joie de vivre*, and that represents a bow to the prevailing taste of its users.[30]

On the whole, however, the Bhong Mosque complex sends a troubling message to thinking architects everywhere. Its very vitality and self-assured use and misuse of the architectural idioms, its total disregard for the stylistic and thematic discipline central to contemporary architectural theory and practice, its pursuit of excessive decoration (as if more were always better); all these aspects must be seen as a simple, even naive statement, that is clearly *understood and appreciated* by the population, both users and observers. Herein lies the troubling aspect. The message of the Bhong Mosque is one of a populist approach to architectural expression. It transcends the popular towards a disorderly amalgam of elements devoid of syntax. It reflects the semantic disorder from which many contemporary Muslim societies suffer. Its very success must therefore give pause to architects who have been following a different approach, where they conceived their role to be one of defining the future from a reinterpreted past. To them, the success of Rais Ghazi's enterprise must give pause.

Yet, it would be wrong to assume that popularity is the sole criterion for judging a creative work of art, which all great architecture must aspire to be. What is clear from the Bhong Mosque is that a tremendous task lies ahead for intellectuals generally and architects specifically. They must confront the present rupture in the coherent cultural development of Muslim societies. They must confront the semantic disorder of their societies by energetically redefining the symbolic content of contemporary expression.[31] Only then will they have fully responded to the challenge of a popular eclecticism that eschews selectivity and negates a deeper sense of evolving identity.

The award to the Bhong Mosque has thus raised many important issues that will undoubtedly enrich the debate and fuel the search for a culturally authentic contemporary architectural expression for rapidly evolving Muslim societies.

ONGOING DISCUSSIONS

The debates of the Marrakesh seminar were lively and candid. The themes explored have been summarised above and the queries raised by the decisions have given architects and critics much food for thought. Interesting essays have already been written about them, most noteably by Brian B. Taylor and Shanti Jayewadene in *Mimar*.[32] Engaging thinking persons into further thought rather than grafting on ready-made solutions is the most impressive achievement of any intellectual endeavour. In doing this, the 1986 selections have succeeded admirably. The debates they helped generate continue to nourish discussions among those concerned with the built environment in the Muslim world.

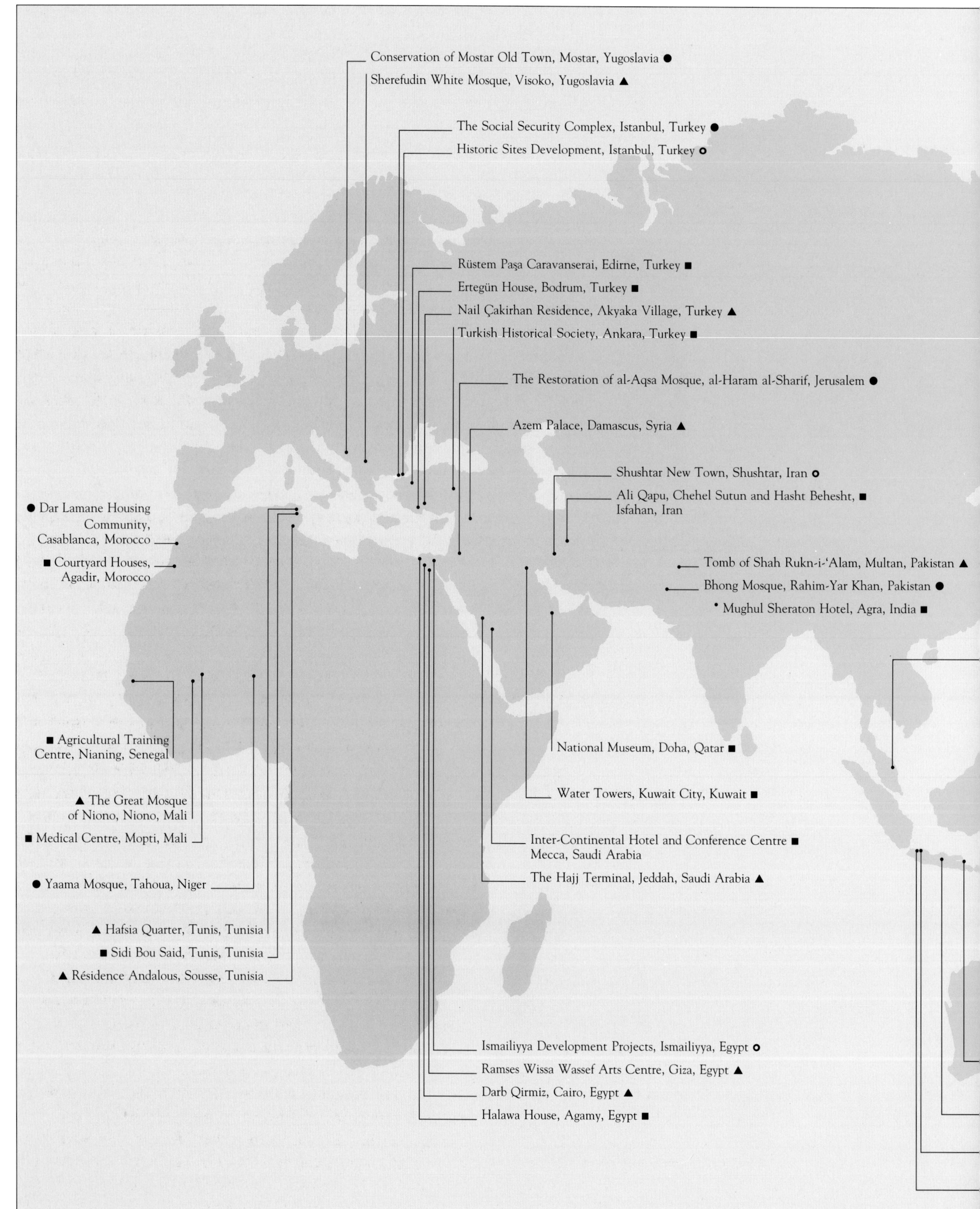

Conservation of Mostar Old Town, Mostar, Yugoslavia ●
Sherefudin White Mosque, Visoko, Yugoslavia ▲
The Social Security Complex, Istanbul, Turkey ●
Historic Sites Development, Istanbul, Turkey ○
Rüstem Paşa Caravanserai, Edirne, Turkey ■
Ertegün House, Bodrum, Turkey ■
Nail Çakirhan Residence, Akyaka Village, Turkey ▲
Turkish Historical Society, Ankara, Turkey ■
The Restoration of al-Aqsa Mosque, al-Haram al-Sharif, Jerusalem ●
Azem Palace, Damascus, Syria ▲
Shushtar New Town, Shushtar, Iran ○
Ali Qapu, Chehel Sutun and Hasht Behesht, ■ Isfahan, Iran
● Dar Lamane Housing Community, Casablanca, Morocco
■ Courtyard Houses, Agadir, Morocco
Tomb of Shah Rukn-i-'Alam, Multan, Pakistan ▲
Bhong Mosque, Rahim-Yar Khan, Pakistan ●
Mughul Sheraton Hotel, Agra, India ■
■ Agricultural Training Centre, Nianing, Senegal
National Museum, Doha, Qatar ■
▲ The Great Mosque of Niono, Niono, Mali
Water Towers, Kuwait City, Kuwait ■
■ Medical Centre, Mopti, Mali
Inter-Continental Hotel and Conference Centre ■ Mecca, Saudi Arabia
● Yaama Mosque, Tahoua, Niger
The Hajj Terminal, Jeddah, Saudi Arabia ▲
▲ Hafsia Quarter, Tunis, Tunisia
■ Sidi Bou Said, Tunis, Tunisia
▲ Résidence Andalous, Sousse, Tunisia
Ismailiyya Development Projects, Ismailiyya, Egypt ○
Ramses Wissa Wassef Arts Centre, Giza, Egypt ▲
Darb Qirmiz, Cairo, Egypt ▲
Halawa House, Agamy, Egypt ■

THE COLLECTIVE MESSAGE OF THE AWARD

The conclusion of the third cycle of the AKAA permits us to take stock of the collective message of the Award conveyed by the rich mosaic of the premiated winners that stretch back centuries into the Muslim past and span the Muslim world from Morocco to Indonesia.

It is pertinent to ask what the collective message of the Award is after its decade of existence. With 32 winning projects and five honourable mentions in over a dozen countries, not to mention the two Chairman's Awards, the complex mosaic reveals patterns that should not be obscured by the controversy surrounding the 1986 selected projects.

PATTERNS OF THE AKAA AWARDS

The awards have brought forth exemplars from practically every corner of the Muslim world (see map), thus underlining the richness and diversity that make up this world. Furthermore, it has been possible to group the projects in a number of ways to better assess their collective message. One such grouping which received wide attention at Marrakesh was the presentation made in *Mimar*.[33] Among other things, it provided a new category for "populism" in which the sole entry was the Bhong Mosque. After careful scrutiny however, I believe that the journey through space and time encapsulated in these awards is best appreciated in the grid proposed by the AKAA secretariat and presented at an exhibition in the U.K. in the summer of 1987. Under this classification, the awards can be seen as having defined three broad areas of concern, or premises, which coincide with the three main areas the Steering Committee highlighted in its brief for the 1986 Master Jury.

■ Awards 1980

▲ Awards 1983

● Awards 1986

○ Honourable Mentions

THE HISTORICAL PREMISES

The long standing concern of the Award with protecting the heritage as an integral part of the contemporary identity has been recently explained in an essay by Ismail Serageldin and Saïd Zulficar (see Part Three of this book). This approach recognises three broad types of intervention, examples of which have been acknowledged with awards:

Restoration Projects

The Restoration of al-Aqsa Mosque
al-Haram al-Sharif, Jerusalem,
completed 1983
1986 winner

The Tomb of Shah Rukn-i-'Alam
Multan, Pakistan, completed 1977.
1983 winner

Restoration of Ali-Qapu, Chehel Sutun and Hasht Behesht
Isfahan, Iran, major restoration completed 1977
1980 winner

Adaptive Reuse Projects

Historic Sites Development
Istanbul, Turkey, since 1974 and ongoing
1986 honourable mention

Azem Palace
Damascus, Syria, completed 1955
1983 winner

Rüstem Paşa Caravanserai
Edirne, Turkey, completed 1972
1980 winner

National Museum
Doha, Qatar, phase I completed 1975
1980 winner

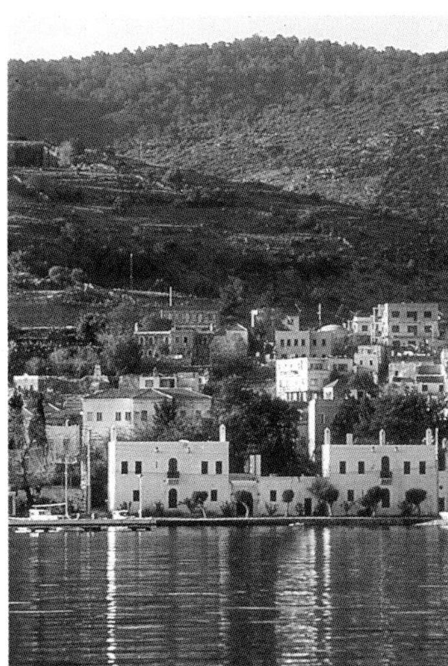

Ertegün House
Bodrum, Turkey, completed 1973
1980 winner

SOCIAL PREMISES

Under this broad heading two types of issues have been highlighted by the Award winners:

Preservation of Urban Heritage (Area Conservation) Projects

Conservation of Mostar Old Town
Mostar, Yugoslavia, since 1978 and ongoing
1986 winner

Darb Qirmiz Quarter
Cairo, Egypt, Phase I completed 1980
1983 winner

Sidi Bou Said
Tunis, Tunisia, ongoing since 1973
1980 winner

New Public Housing Projects

Dar Lamane Housing Community
Casablanca, Morocco, completed 1983
1986 winner

Shushtar New Town
Shushtar, Iran, phase I completed 1977 and ongoing
1986 honourable mention

Hafsia Quarter
Tunis, Tunisia, completed 1977
1980 winner

Community Improvement Projects

The Improvement of Kampung Kebalen
Surabaya, Indonesia, completed 1981
1986 honourable mention

Ismailiyya Development Projects
Ismailiyya, Egypt, since 1978, and ongoing
1986 honourable mention

Pondok Pesantren Pabelan
Central Java, Indonesia, ongoing since 1965
1980 winner

Kampung Improvement Programme
Jakarta, Indonesia, ongoing since 1969
1980 winner

ARCHITECTURAL PREMISES

Ultimately, the awards are for architecture, and the work that contributes most to the articulation of architectural designs of excellence has been recognised. For clarity, these very diverse approaches have been regrouped under five headings, which must be interpreted with caution since each of these projects transcend any single category.

Vernacular Architecture Projects

Yaama Mosque
Yaama, Tahoua, Niger, completed 1982
1986 winner

Bhong Mosque
Bhong, Rahim-Yar Khan, Pakistan, completed 1982
1986 winner

Nail Çakirhan Residence
Akyaka Yillage, Turkey, completed 1971
1983 winner

The Great Mosque of Niono
Niono, Mali, completed 1973
1983 winner

Ramses Wissa Wassef Arts Centre
Giza, Egypt, completed 1974
1983 winner

Halawa House
Agamy, Egypt, completed 1975
1980 winner

Contextualism

The Social Security Complex
Istanbul, Turkey, completed 1970
1986 winner

Medical Centre
Mopti, Mali, completed 1976
1986 winner

Courtyard Houses
Agadir, Morocco, completed 1964
1980 winner

Mughal Sheraton Hotel
Agra, India, completed 1976
1980 winner

Contemporary Language

Saïd Naum Mosque
Jakarta, Indonesia, completed 1977
1986 honourable mention

Résidence Andalous
Sousse, Tunisia, completed 1980
1983 winner

Tanjong Jara Beach Hotel/
Rantau Abang Visitors' Centre
Kuala Trengganu, Malaysia,
completed 1980
1983 winner

Turkish Historical Society
Ankara, Turkey, completed 1966
1980 winner

Innovation

Sherefudin White Mosque
Visoko, Yugoslavia, completed 1980
1983 winner

Inter-Continental Hotel and
Conference Centre
Mecca, Saudi Arabia, completed 1974
1980 winner

Appropriate Building Systems

The Hajj Terminal
King Abdul Aziz International
Airport, Jeddah, Saudi Arabia,
completed 1981 – 82
1983 winner

The Water Towers
Kuwait City, Kuwait, completed 1976
1980 winner

The Agricultural Training Centre
Nianing, Senegal, completed 1977
1980 winner

ON THE SPIRITUAL IN ARCHITECTURE

Relevant and clear as these patterns are, there is still a need to discuss the issue of 'the spiritual in Architecture'. The very fact that the Award is geared to the architecture of the Muslim world has led many to wonder whether it would honour only mosques and other distinctly Islamic buildings. The first cycle settled this issue decisively by defining the Award's concerns in the broadest possible terms, both by its publications and by its selections of the first fifteen winners (none of which were mosques). Yet, at the conclusion of the third cycle, there are at least six projects that deserve to be discussed collectively and separately from the rest of the winners, even though they each contribute something to one or other of the themes identified as the collective message of the Award. These are the Hajj Terminal, the Niono and Sherefudin Mosques (all three 1983 winners), the Yaama and Bhong Mosques (1986 winners) and the Saïd Naum Mosque, a 1986 honourable mention. These buildings, taken together, say much about key issues present throughout much of the Muslim world today, and how the symbols of an architectural vocabulary, whether traditional, modern or populist, manages to respond to the needs of the Muslim people to express the uniqueness and importance of such structures in both their community life and their self-image.

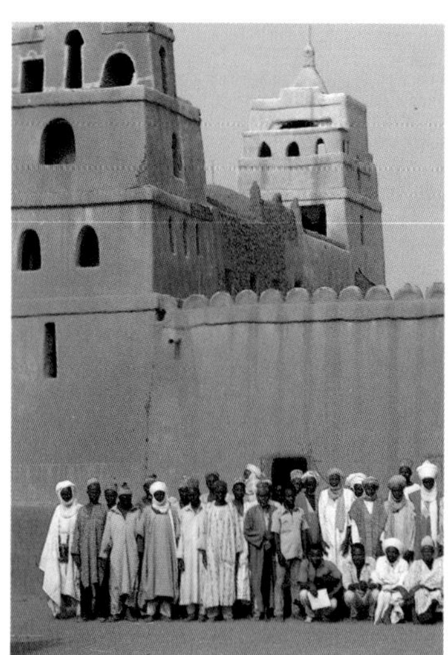

Yaama Mosque: the serene balance of the traditional is understood and appreciated by the community.

First and foremost the Hajj Terminal project was a brilliant technical solution to a formidable problem of scale. The elegance and aesthetics of the roofing structure stand out as a truly unique achievement. However, the rest of the project, the very building through which the pilgrims must pass, fails to complement the technical brilliance of the structural solution with an emotionally charged design that matches, or tries to match, the experiential phenomenon of pilgrimage. This is, after all, the antichamber through which the foreign pilgrims proceed to the elevating and enthralling experience of the Hajj. The building as it now stands is disorienting, and it is even difficult to know where the *Qibla* is located while inside the terminal. The pedestrian nature of the design led the Jury, quite rightly, to specify that the award was for the soaring and elegant roof structure not for the building underneath. This particular shortcoming can one day be remedied when these buildings will be considered obsolete and fit for replacement. There are many Saudi architects, as well as international architects, who could bring to the task the right balance of talent and emotion and provide the appropriate symbolically charged environment worthy of the Hajj, complementing the promise of an outstanding overall design.

If, however, the Hajj Terminal missed the opportunity of adequately responding to the need to create symbols in the contemporary Muslim world, how about the premiated mosques? Surely no structure can have as much symbolic content for a Muslim society than the mosque. Here the answer is both positive and enriching.

That the Muslim world has suffered a historic rupture has been discussed elsewhere in this essay. The result of this historic rupture, however, has been to leave Muslim communities an easy prey to the chaos of conflicting cultural messages. The inability of the contemporary semiotic frameworks to develop in keeping with these new messages has led to a semantic disorder with the degradation of symbols into signs and signals.[34] The mosque, most central of all buildings in the Muslim world, has, in many quarters fallen victim to this negative trend, and hence the importance of better underlining the distinct significance of the premiated mosques.

Let us first demonstrate briefly how this degradation of symbols into signs and, worse, into signals manifests itself. We can do this by examining some negative examples that highlight how some of the key elements of mosque design have been degraded: the minaret, the dome and the *mihrab*, which collectively constitute the image of the mosque for vast segments of the Muslim population. Indeed, in folkloric displays this stylised architecture of the mosque is interpreted as a symbol of religious feeling.

The Mihrab: By rights the essential part of any mosque (since it functionally indicated the direction of prayer) the *Mihrab* has evolved into a sort of niche, similar in some ways to an apse. This was the subject of learned scholastic debate, with an entire orthodox school of thought ruling the protruding niche heretical—a *bid'a!* Today in places like Egypt, this *bid'a* is so completely accepted that in the case of a mosque on the second floor of a building, a special cantilever was constructed to allow for the protruding niche of the *Mihrab*.

The Minaret: Long a symbol of Muslim architecture generally and of mosque architecture particularly, the minaret has acquired a very special position in the lexicon of architects working in the Muslim world. Oleg Grabar has devoted a distinguished article,[35] to the development of the minaret's significance. I will not try to summarise these learned arguments here, but the functional role of the minaret (the call to prayer) has been overtaken by the technology of loudspeakers. Its landmark function, however, has remained.

Yet today, in many cities, tall buildings make a mockery of its landmark function. Still the minaret is so deeply ingrained in the minds of the population that it has acquired the status of a *signal*. Minaret = mosque, ergo no minaret = no mosque! This has led to extremes such as piercing a balcony to allow a tiny minaret for a ground floor mosque and implanting a very tiny minaret when there were no funds to build any more.

The Dome: Although mosques do not have to have domes, they are again perceived as signals by the population in many Muslim countries. A most striking example is found in Cairo where a mosque was built with a dome over its central space. It was then noticed that the dome could not be seen from the street. Hence a second dome was added, whose only function was that it could be seen from the street and thus complete the mosque's facade!

Similarly in Lahore, Pakistan the Chughtaiyan Mosque has a "phony" minaret on top of the doorway, and a dome on top of a flat roof structure.

The premiated mosques show four distinct alternatives to coping with these types of problems. The Award was thus true to its philosophy of avoiding a narrow prescriptive approach that would pre-empt the creative search of architects for new and meaningful solutions, but enriches such a search by highlighting exemplars that illustrate some of the multiple facets of this complex problem.

The Traditional Solution: The Yaama and Niono Mosques have the serene balance of the traditional. Their message is clear and understood by the community they serve and there is no denying the authenticity which they exude, even to the foreign visitor. The only jarring note appears when in one part of the Niono mosque the mason tried to insert the modern material of corrugated tile. He himself saw it as incongruous and informed the attendees at the Istanbul seminar that he wanted to rectify it because it did not "fit well" with the composition. Although both of these mosques are the product of traditional builders, skilled architects such as Hassan Fathy and Abdel Wahed El-Wakil have shown that they can master this idiom producing elegant structures in the traditional mold, by rigorously respecting scale, technique and convention.

Bhong Mosque: an exuberant, vivacious and massive use of ornaments with clear populist appeal.

The Populist Approach: The exuberance and delight that characterise the mixture of crudeness and stylishness of the Bhong Mosque says much about the present semantic disorder. It is successful with the people it serves, and it raises key issues that architects must address fully if they are to do their share in re-symbolising the Muslim environment of today.

The Adaptive Modern Approach: The Saïd Naum Mosque demonstrates a serious effort to be both distinctly modern and yet echo the traditional vocabularly.

The Modernist Approach: The Sherefudin White Mosque of Visoko, Yugoslavia stands out as an attempt to truly break with the traditional Bosnian architecture surrounding it, while remaining a landmark building. This project which holds true to the modern movement has the unique distinction of having been commissioned and paid for by the users. The seven-year debate that preceded its construction and the subsequent use that the community makes of it shows that you can get traditional conservative communities to sponsor avant-garde works and later identify with them.

Saïd Naum Mosque: a serious effort to be modern while echoing the traditional vocabulary.

The winners and honourable mentions, therefore, tell us that there are many issues in approaching the problems of designing the key buildings of a Muslim community. The continuity of key symbolic elements (minaret, dome and *mihrab*) can be transformed without being degraded and can be retained while devoid of their content. It is the skill of the architects, the depth of their understanding and their affinity with the communities concerned that make the difference between Kitsch and creativity. The Award winners have shown that creativity can have multiple manifestations, but that each must be authentic and true to be effective in making a contribution towards providing better mosques and areas of congregation that respond to the need of Muslim societies to anchor their self-identity into structures built today and that speak to them and their children as eloquently as the symbols of the past did to their parents and grandparents. Only thus will this type of architecture make its all-important contribution to an integrated and integrating contemporary Muslim culture.

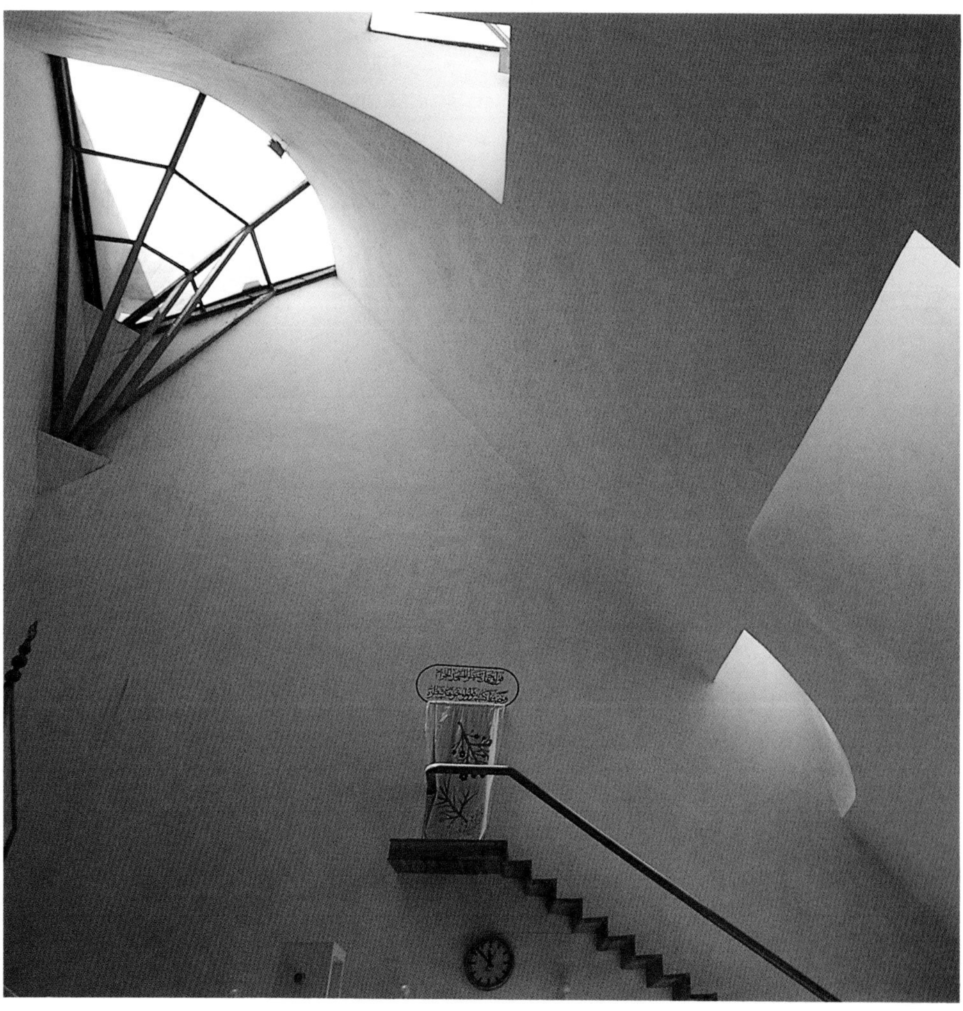

The interior of Sherefudin White Mosque shows the same modern and unconventional treatment as the outside form. Bold openings in the ceiling provide lights with dramatic effect.

A SUMMATION: CULTURAL CONTINUITY AND CULTURAL AUTHENTICITY

Running through the premises of excellence discussed above and highlighted with special force by the specific review of the religious buildings, are the primary concerns of architects practicing in Muslim societies today, namely the issues of cultural continuity and authenticity.

Few issues have affected contemporary Muslim societies as deeply, as the sense of loss of identity[36] and the corollary search for cultural authenticity which is seen by many as a return to the fountainhead of the Islamic faith to redefine the Muslim culture in its essential terms, thereby purging it of the "extraneous elements" that history, western hegemony and geographic realities have introduced.[37]

The AKAA rejects this approach as too narrow, overly romantic and fundamentally non-historical. Instead the Award approach recognises the need to thoroughly understand the past, and to decode its language through contemporary eyes that can sift the relevant from the timebound. The arsenal of contemporary analysis must be brought to bear on the reality of Muslim history as much as on the reality of Muslim societies today. We must come to grips with the historical rupture that characterises the evolution of Muslim cultural development, and by better understanding it, learn to transcend it.

This approach, though scientific and systematic is far from the arid scholastism of much academic research. It explores and revitalises the myths and images that nourish the creative imagination of contemporary artists and architects. It develops the iconography and enriches the symbols that punctuate their contemporary universe. Most importantly, it does so by grounding these expressions of culture in a deep and unhurried understanding of the essence of the culture in all its myriad manifestations, past and present.

We hope that the integrity of this approach will separate this search from the doomed attempts to escape a chaotic and unsettling present by a headlong flight into a romanticised past,[38] or the equally shortsighted approach that equates modernity with wholesale importation of western technology, aesthetics, and patterns of behaviour. The former is tantamount to a slow suicide, for no community can isolate itself from the present no matter how unpleasant its realities are. The latter approach is an agonising negation of self and identity, since no society can exclude its past from the constituents of its contemporary reality.

The pursuit of cultural continuity by maintaining the fragile links with a society's past has taken on several manifestations. Most direct of these is the preservation of historical vestiges, in this case, the protection of the architectural and urban heritage of the Muslim people. More subtle, but as direct, has been the attempt to protect the character of certain districts, that convey a sense of place, from encroachments upon that character even when such encroachments do not threaten a specific building. Area conservation has become increasingly recognised as an indispensible adjunct to preservation of particular monuments or complexes.

The Award has also promoted the scholarship needed to understand the legacy of the past, to learn to decode the historical symbols and to see them through contemporary eyes,[39] thus enhancing both the understanding and the appreciation of the heritage and making it more accessible to a modern public who has suffered from a rupture in its natural cultural evolution. Along with this deepening of our understanding, the Award has tried to broaden the awareness of the public, professional historians and conservationists, public officials and practicing architects and planners. This consciousness-raising has been done through publications, seminars, and lectures, and by bringing together disciplines that ordinarily do not interact, but whose interests overlap in the creative act of effective conservation. Thus sociologists, anthropologists, economists, philosophers, artists, writers, journalists and politicians have consistently rubbed shoulders with architects, engineers, planners and historians in meetings organised by the Award. These gatherings probe what constitutes appropriate conservation and what is essential in the Muslim legacy.

This probing into cultural continuity finds a corollary concern with cultural authenticity in new building. The issue is not whether the structure conforms exactly to the criteria of the past; it clearly cannot do so and remain relevant to today's concerns. Instead, the issue is whether the designer has learnt the lessons of the past, internalised them, and used them as an input, although partial, in defining the solution to a contemporary problem for contemporary clients.

Given the paucity of knowledge about the contemporary cultural scene throughout the diverse Muslim communities, and given the speed with which both physical development and socio-economic change are taking place, there is a monumental task ahead for Muslim intellectuals and for those who want their designs to be relevant to this rapidly changing world. The former must restate the basic questions that all societies ask so that their understanding of self will not be degraded into the mere modes of consumption of both materials and time. As Arkoun has said: Muslim intellectuals cannot afford to be alienated from their societies at present.[40]

Architects, must also learn to correctly decipher the past and the present.[41] Both the high technology of today and the socio-economic reality of their society must be integral parts of their present consciousness; and a proper understanding of their cultural past must be an integral part of their sense of self and society.

Together, architects and other intellectuals must dare to think the unthinkable and to go "where others fear to tread," in order not to fall prey to the prevalent mode of degraded thinking that has manipulated the symbols of the Muslim culture into debased ideologically charged signals that supplant critical appreciation by populist slogans. This is a tall order but it provides the springboard for the tasks ahead of the AKAA in its next decade.

AN AGENDA FOR THE FUTURE

ISSUES FROM THE FIRST DECADE

As the Award enters its second decade, it can look back on an impressive record of achievement. A stream of publications, research papers, and reports bear witness to the intensity, dedication, and freedom of the wide-ranging intellectual search undertaken under the Award's aegis. Resources that have been established include a library and documentation centre on the conditions of environment and building in the Muslim countries plus detailed documentation on some seven hundred projects in the Muslim world, an archive unmatched anywhere. Under the auspices of the AKAA, a *space of freedom* has been created for those professionals and intellectuals interested in joining this ongoing search.

Having established the terrain of its primary concerns, and mapped out its constituent parts, the Award must now move to a new level of critical analysis of the issues it confronts. To do so, it is essential that:

- The Award should develop a more systematic methodological basis for its appreciation of such key concepts as community, culture, Islam, society, identity, myth, imagination, creativity, and so on.

  This is not just an intellectual's request for esoteric discourse and hair-splitting definitions. This is an essential task that must be accomplished to construct a more sophisticated edifice for the theory and practice of architectural criticism in the Muslim world today. Without clearly understood and agreed concepts, terminology, and methodology, the inter-disciplinary discourse on these vital topics is bound to remain loose, unstructured, and possibly unconstructive. In fact this has been maintained by a number of Steering Committee members, and most vehemently by Arkoun throughout his tenure.[42]
- The Award must probe further into the reality of the architectural design and its constitutents; creativity, imagination, knowledge, experience, judgement and innate talent. The two think tanks organised during the third cycle constitute a good start for this complex endeavour.
- The Award must explore more thoroughly the problem of cultural continuity in today's Muslim societies. What is needed is not an endless array of descriptive monographs, useful as these may be, but a thorough analytical probing of the complex phenomena of an evolving culture and the way it is manifested, with a view to situating the role of the architect both as agent of change and a product of the milieu.
- Based on the preceding elements, the unifying theme of the next endeavours undertaken by the Award should be to establish the groundwork of an expanded and more thoughtful architectural criticism.

While the first of these four tasks is arduous, it is a pre-requisite for the successful implementation of the other three. Of these, the exploration of the design process has been initiated in the think tanks, abstracts of which are given in the third part of this book. The question of cultural continuity has been a constant theme running through the last three cycles. A recapitulation of its constituent elements has been given in the preceding chapter; but its rigorous and systematic exploration remains to be done on the basis of terminology, methodology and a conceptual framework to be established. The fourth, and last of these tasks deserves to be more broadly discussed here.

TOWARDS A BROADENED ARCHITECTURAL CRITICISM

Every architectural creation is a deliberate act to change the environment. Therefore, in the most direct sense, any building has a physical context within which it can be seen, understood, and evaluated. Topography, climate, materials, structure, proportions and surrounding physical environment both natural and man-made, are one set of dimensions developed to evaluate the "architectural quality" of a building above and beyond its ability to solve the utilitarian needs of a particular problem, essential as that dimension remains.

Architectural criticism has, however, gone beyond this level of appreciation to take account of the building's resonance with a collective societal heritage of artistic and aesthetic expression. Critics look at a building's ability to reflect and yet transcend these echoes of the past that preserve a collective sense of cultural identity for a society in the throes of rapid transformations.

Furthermore, in a rapidly shrinking world, communications have made us all subject to the influence of international currents of thought, perception and conduct. The creative architectural act is thus also assessed by its positioning amid these currents, as well as its contribution to the evolution of these currents. In other words, its international as well as its national or regional context is involved. Extreme cases of this cross-fertilisation, both negative and positive, can be found in the works of major western architects in the Muslim world: Le Corbusier's work in Chandigarh; Louis Kahn's work in Dhaka, and SOM's work in Saudi Arabia. Reverse influences can also be seen in Hassan Fathy's ideas being debated in western architectural schools. To the extent that each of these buildings addresses the key issues of contemporary architectural thought–modernism versus traditionalism, internationalism versus regionalism, or technology versus craft–each is a deliberate act that promotes one point of view over another.

This simple statement about expatriate interventions applies even more to the work of national architects, although the impact of their interventions is more subtle. There, we find architects such as Rifat Chadirji, whose entire life is devoted to the search for a suitable contemporary architectural expression that is inspired by the authentic heritage of his region. We find Hassan Fathy arguing for the nobility and wisdom of vernacular architecture in the face of imported models that are alien to the society. These are the gladiators in the arena of competing concepts of architecture in the Muslim world. They made their contributions and today many others, whose names and works are far less known, contribute daily to the evolving patterns of the built environment and the intellectual debate prevailing in the Muslim world, as well as to the architectural profession's image of its role as articulator and promulgator of societal values.

In this context, a more subtle and elevated form of architectural criticism is required. It is a criticism that functions on many levels:

- The building qua building: the simplest, most direct appreciation of the building's functional response and aesthetic qualities. Volume, space, light, materials, colours, and so on; the entire lexicon of studied architectural criticism is brought to bear on the building, taking it apart and putting it together again both in physical and experiential terms;
- The building in its physical context: harmony or discord, intentional or unintentional, can be either positive or negative. Its relation to its environment both natural and man-made can enhance or diminish the stature of the achievement;

- The building in its cultural context: its "fit" and appropriateness in the context of a cultural heritage expressed through a legacy of built forms that society's genius has produced through its history;
- The building in its international context: the positioning of the creative act as a part of the international network of currents, styles, schools and ideas, as well as the extent to which it contributes to the evolution of that debate, either by reinforcement or by innovation;
- The building in its own local/regional intellectual milieu: to what extent does it make a statement on the immediate level of the debate that presses upon the intelligentsia of the region? This is no mere reflection of the international context, although it could be. The local/regional intellectual milieu is much more concerned with issues of urgency and immediacy that are circumscribed geographically, even though they may have universal overtones.

This last level diverges from the more commonly accepted views of architectural criticism and deserves further elucidation.

Because the Muslim world is one with both a diverse regionalism and a unifying universal identity, it is one where local/regional issues can be, and are, overlain on the broader issues of the relationship of the Muslim identity vis-a-vis a rapidly westernising world. To varying degrees, the intellectuals and artists of the Muslim world confront the same issues: striking an appropriate balance between the demands of modernity and the requisites of tradition; reading their legacy and heritage through contemporary eyes; decoding the symbols of the past to identify and retain the elements of permanent value and to discard those of ephemeral or doubtful value; dealing with the tension between the integrative and disintegrative forces in society; accommodating and enabling the accession of the masses to the formation of, and identification with the total ethos of the societal cultural output; the allocation of priorities in their developmental efforts, and the preservation of a balance between the options and ligatures that circumscribe what Dahrendorf has called "life chances".[44]

Yet, for all its common threads, this debate acquires different flavours in different countries. The emphasis is different at different times. The issues in Turkey today are not the same as they were 30 years ago. And the issues in Turkey today are very different from those in Egypt, Saudi Arabia, Niger, or Indonesia. Diachronic and synchronic readings of the issues themselves are needed. Furthermore, the debate in each society, has accrued shorthand labels and interpretations of positions that load a particular creative artistic act, be it literary, sculptural, architectural or other type of artistic expression, with connotations unique to this particular intellectual milieu that are often obscured from the uninitiated outsider.

This line of argument can lead to two independent and equally erroneous conclusions. One erroneous view would hold that only the members of this intellectual milieu are qualified to pass judgments on the works of art that affect this milieu. This not only exacerbates xenophobic tendencies in society, but is also patently in error for at least two reason. First, local intellectuals are themselves part of the milieu and participants in the intellectual fray. Hence their judgement could be systematically impugned for bias, just as the outsider's could be impugned for lack of comprehension. Second, proper assessment of a work of art (the importance of the building in this case) should be multi-dimensional, with its reading in its intellectual milieu being only one dimension, and not necessarily the single most important one at that. Furthermore, with the perspective of time, the attitudes of intellectuals, both local and foreign, about particular buildings have evolved. Frequently, such evolutions are the result of the debates sparked by the building itself. Excluding foreign intellectual judgement from such a debate, even if it were possible, would not be desirable, since it would only impoverish the process.

The second erroneous conclusion that this line of argument could lead to would be to say that since outsiders will have difficulty in understanding the subtle ramifications of this cultural milieu, they would do best to ignore it in their evaluations of the building. Clearly, this means advocating a less complete, less thoughtful criticism of the work of art, in this case a deliberate act of architectural creation. Furthermore, outsiders cannot "assume away" the local cultural milieu. It exists. Any outside assessment of a notable building will be "read" by that milieu and the assessment itself will become a vector for change, in one way or another, that acts upon the milieu. This is particularly true of the attitudes of western observers, who represent the dominant culture of the world today, vis-a-vis Muslim intellectual elites who seek to redefine their identity in non-western terms in the face of a historic break in Muslim cultural continuity.

If we accept that the Award should be as thoughtful and discriminating as possible in its critical assessment of architectural output in the Muslim world, we should accept that this critical assessment should be multi-dimensional; and one of these dimensions should deal with the local intellectual milieu. A look at the concerns of this intellectual milieu is therefore pertinent at this point.

The societies of the Muslim world today are primarily poor, facing the physical needs of rapid modernisation, and the psychological needs of redefining their individual and collective identities in the face of a hegemonic world-dominating western culture. Their widespread poverty forces two issues to the fore: responding to the basic needs of the teeming millions of rural and urban poor that comprise the vast majority of these societies. Most pressing of these needs after food and clothing is shelter. From this point of view, the problems of mass housing predominate over those of individual (and luxury) residences or middle-class housing. Emphasising either of the last two without due weight to the former would trivialise the contribution of architecture and architects to the intellectual concerns of the key elements of their society. It would also seriously diminish the profession's influence on the built environment.

On another front, the issues of mass poverty have a more direct bearing on another aspect of architectural practice. The confrontation of elite perceptions of aesthetics and mass manifestations of popular taste have become ideologically charged. Elitism is confronted by populism. The latter, however, is a degraded form of the popular, a set of ideological concepts that are increasingly politicised in terms that reflect the cultural disintegration and uprooting found in contemporary Muslim societies. It is this phenomenon that intellectuals such as Arkoun have so cogently identified: an accelerated disintegration of the traditional semiotic frameworks in Third World countries generally, and the Muslim world specifically.[45]

This explosive reality requires a special understanding of how traditional symbols have degenerated into signs and signals and accordingly in Arkoun's phrase, "an intellectual commitment to re-symbolise the culture of today."

The manifestations of this cultural situation also include another significant front: the advancing insertion of a modern, rapidly changing technology into everyday lives traditionally governed by other concerns. The suitability of the technology, its adaptation to the needs of the population, and the societal context is only one part of the issue. This is the part that has usually concerned architectural critics when looking at buildings. For both building as a process and building as a product, the technology issue has invariably been addressed in terms of suitability and adaptation. In more sophisticated analyses, the intrusion of technology into aesthetic precepts and norms has also been addressed. But the present discussion would add that technology with its various facets and dimensions involves a rationalist ordered universe, whose frame of reference is governed by a reductionist logic. That in turn confronts a manifest reality of semantic disorder due to the disintegration of semiotic frameworks referred to above. This confrontation is resolved when the rationalist logic is used to provide new conditions that elicit a new set of cultural symbols, much as the modern movement in international (western and Japanese) architecture came into being, thus liberating and broadening the horizons of an authentic yet contemporary cultural response within the Muslim world.

Clearly, this type of interpretation of the creative acts of contemporary architects in the Muslim world entails a change in perceptions of many architects, critics, clients, and more generally, the intelligentsia of the Muslim world.

This broadened domain, which would undoubtedly enhance the quality of the intellectual discourse around issues relevant to the architectural profession (broadly defined) cannot be divorced from the content and practice of education in architecture and related disciplines. This links up with the themes covered in the Granada seminar. Consistent treatment of these themes within the context of expanding the *space of freedom* so ardently advocated by the Award, remains a vital part of the Award's ambitious enterprise.

ENVOI

This long retrospective and prospective on the Aga Khan Award for Architecture has highlighted the patient intellectual search of which the prizes are but a small, albeit very important, part. The rest of this book is dedicated to the 1986 winners, and to a sample of the work undertaken during the third cycle, 1983–1986. The future is replete with challenges, and the Award has shown that it can rise to them. The most important weapon in the Award's intellectual arsenal remains its unwavering dedication to the *space of freedom* in this ongoing search for culturally relevant architectural excellence in the built environment of the Muslim world.

Ceiling of the entrance doorway of the Sultan Hassan Mosque, Cairo, Egypt.

PART TWO

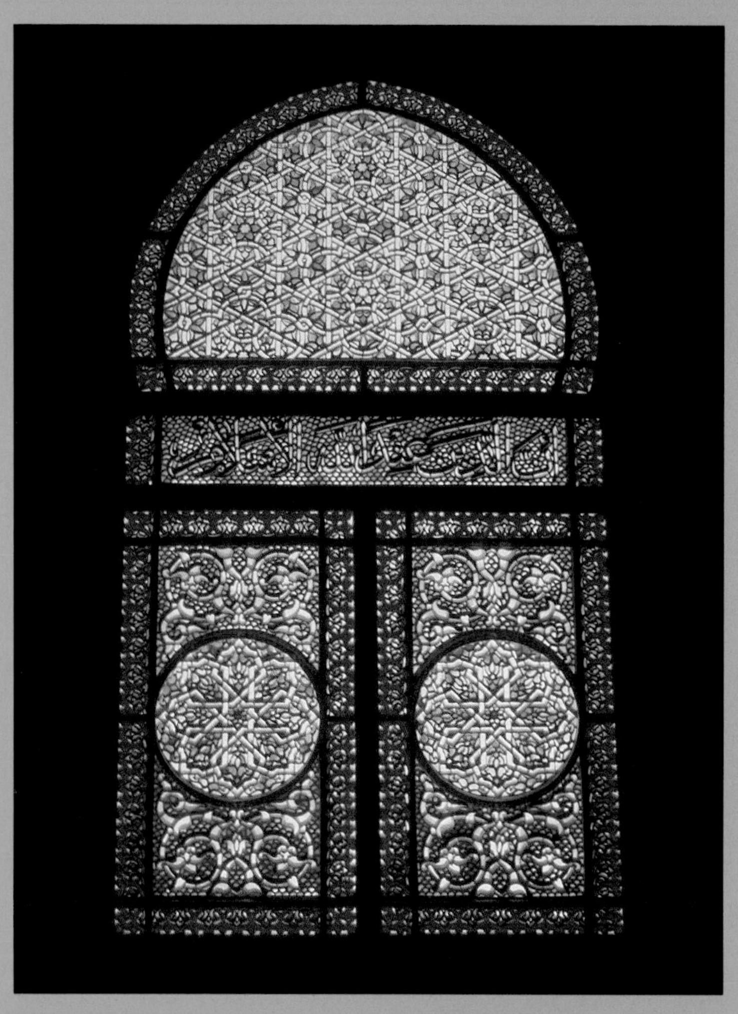

MILESTONES AND LANDMARKS

THE 1986 WINNERS AND HONOURABLE MENTIONS

STATEMENT OF THE AWARD STEERING COMMITTEE

His Highness the Aga Khan with Zulficar, Secretary General of the AKAA.

Serageldin, Grabar and Khan.

Throughout almost a decade of existence, the Aga Khan Award for Architecture has dedicated itself to the encouragement of an architecture in the spirit of Islam, an architecture that would improve and enrich the physical environment as well as the cultural evolution of the Islamic world. The Award recognises completed projects which successfully meet the challenges of today's needs while maintaining harmony with their culture and environment. The Award also encourages open debate, free discussion and thoughtful research on the key issues facing architecture in the Islamic world, for only through the intellectual endeavours of concerned practitioners, teachers, researchers and clients can the research for suitable architecture for the Islamic world be advanced.

From the enunciation of the Award's objectives in 1977, through the first Master Jury selection in 1980 and on to the present, the Award has been particularly careful to raise the issues, ask the questions and encourage the search for appropriate solutions to the challenges of the built environment of Muslims in the perspective of an integrating and integrated culture. At no time has the Award tried to endorse a particular "style", nor has it taken a position on an ideological plane that would exclude any dimension of this multi-faceted search. Thus, through its many activities, including research, seminars and publications as well as the project citations themselves, the Award has sought to create a *space of freedom* where intellectual debate among those concerned with the built environment of Muslims could proceed unhindered and uninhibited, dedicated to the purpose of enriching the dialogue, furthering the pursuit of excellence and a search for appropriate solutions.

A search it undoubtedly is, and no one would claim that even after ten years of debate and discussion the issues have yet been fully explored and every possible appropriate response exhausted. It is the considered judgement of the various Steering Committees, Master Juries, and Technical Review teams that have served the Award during these first nine years of existence that few of the building of the past twenty-five years have achieved the level of excellence that would mark them undeniably as true classics. They are all milestones on the paths of improvement in conception and practice towards a more enabling and human environment that allows contemporary Muslim societies to solve their problems and to express themselves in works of beauty and value.

The 1986 project awards continue to widen the range of issues that the Aga Khan Award for Architecture can address. What was not awarded in 1986 signals areas that would benefit from a substantial increase in the application of architectural talent, expertise and critical thought.

Today the Islamic world is a vast mosaic of different communities that confront many problems of wealth and poverty, of differences in terrain and climate, as well as the speed and content of the processes of change and modernisation. There are, therefore, multiple tendencies within such societies. The Award reflects these realities. With such a state of flux it is difficult to capture the diversity of the challenges and responses in six projects, no matter how excellent each one may be. Indeed, a minority of the Master Jury sought to promote projects other than those selected for recognition by the majority.

It is this same reality that has prompted the Award to provide, for the first time, a set of five honourable mentions along with the six Award winners. These are projects that were felt to deserve wider recognition for the values they embody and the issues that they address, but whose achievements in terms of architectural content were deemed by the Master Jury to fall short of the level of excellence sought in an Award winner.

The methodology of the Award Procedures is such that non-awarded projects from each Award cycle may be reconsidered by the juries of subsequent cycles. With additional distance, some projects acquire a greater stature as wider appreciation of their deep and lasting virtues matures with the perspective of time. This may well prove to be the case for some major efforts seeking the synthesis of modern and traditional forms, of which the recent years have given us some stellar examples and which some members of the Master Jury thought were already deserving of an award in 1986.

Correa, Porter and Arkoun.

Finally, 1986 is the second time that the Chairman's Award, established to honour achievements that fall outside the scope of the Master Jury's mandate, is being given. The first recipient, in 1980, was Hassan Fathy. This year's recipient is the distinguished Iraqi architect, teacher and critic, Rifat Chadirji. The Award salutes his lifetime commitment to the search for an authentic architectural regionalism that synthesises key elements of modernity and the traditional heritage into works of excellence and universal relevance.

REPORT OF THE MASTER JURY

As members of the Master Jury we have carefully considered the 213 nominations for the third Aga Khan Award for Architecture in two separate meetings in Geneva, in January and in June, 1986. At the first meeting, 25 projects were selected for detailed technical review. In the second meeting we selected the six Award winners. Both meetings were consistently well organised by the Secretariat staff. Without the thoroughness and technical competence of those who prepared the project dossiers and undertook the detailed technical reviews, and the outstanding support given to us by the Award office, the Award staff and the Secretary-General, our deliberations would have been more difficult and protracted.

The three-year period since the last awards has seen the culmination of a remarkable change in the climate of architectural opinion. In the Western world there have been emerging doubts that the earlier assurance of the Modern Movement was justified; at the same time nations in the Third World have begun to feel the need for architectures which express their own goals and identities.

In common with both these situations have been a number of significant developments. The accelerating urban growth has drawn attention to the plight of large sections of the population for whom adequate housing cannot possibly be provided by existing procedures. The decay of the historic centres has led to uncontrolled and unprincipled destruction and rebuilding. The deprivation and alienation experienced by the moving populations has been matched by the increasing validity given by designers to sociological issues and contextualism. Functionalism has been reassessed to include visual meaning and symbolism; human values balance technical values; a new critical spirit is reassessing the past.

In this third cycle of the Award, it is perhaps not surprising that the field was felt by the Jury to be somewhat reduced, and few projects excited any passions. The difficulties experienced by the Jury in agreeing on more than a small number of works of quality may also reflect the issues of doubt and reassessment mentioned above, and are an indication of a crisis in creativity and innovation.

The award of prizes is only part of the exercise of the Jury. Concern for vitality and quality have led us to look carefully at the reasons for the rejection of projects in the first round – and after this to reflect on problems that might be addressed by architects and clients in the Islamic world. The Jury has been only too aware of the difficult choices to be made and dilemmas to be faced by architects of the Islamic world over a wide spectrum of issues.

Many of the new buildings reflect the contradictory preferences that exist in countries of the Islamic world which are in a process of transformation or transition. There is no single sense of direction in which tastes are evolving, either with the general public or with the client or the architect. The distortion produced by external influences may interfere with cultural continuity, producing characteristics that are vulgar or ugly, but they can also be positive and enriching. The least we felt that we could do, as a jury, was to examine the submissions looking for works which illuminate the issues with genuine content and an absence of arrogance.

Public Awareness. In so doing, we felt that there was a great need for public debate about architecture within Islamic societies. The programmes of buildings and developments ought not to be left to public officials or powerful architectural firms to determine. A plea must be made for subjecting to public scrutiny all such proposals. The evolution of taste in societies that are transforming themselves should be a public affair, something of concern to every member of the community, about which the community should be able to speak: it should not be the sole prerogative of those in power, whether on the architectural side or on the client's side. A gestation period should also be built into the submission of such proposals to allow for public reaction and participation. Confusion of judgement and a breakdown of aesthetic standards are phenomena of transitional societies to which architects are as much subject as anyone else. By raising these issues, the Award Jury hopes to draw the attention of the architectural and non-professional communities to one process out of which a better design culture might begin to crystallise.

The reassessment of traditional values in modern contexts and in ways that respond to modern challenges is something that goes beyond questions of architectural aesthetics and functions, and becomes a key role in the professional ethics of the architect.

Cultural Continuity. To the above is related the important factor of cultural continuity. The whole crisis in Asia and Africa shows that when a nation loses its sense of identity, and therefore its pride in itself, it is deprived of creative genius; for this reason, it is essential that some sense of continuity is retained. Buildings may challenge this continuity, but they should not break with it completely, for then alienation sets in and antagonistic processes may result.

Two dangers threaten continuity. On the one hand, there are possibilities of distortion through the processes of reinterpretation and re-evaluation of cultures in the face of new challenges and opportunities, and of undue external influences, the latter sometimes introduced through such agencies as misdirected foreign aid. On the other hand, there is the extreme severity and urgency of the urban expansion in the Third World, so that architects have a new responsibility in their handling of socially oriented projects. Housing may now be the most important of the problems that architects in Islamic societies have to face: it challenges them not simply to emulate the standards by which professionals in the First World operate in working for the modern sector, but forces them to be critical of influences from the industrial world, and to face the issue of dealing with indigenous materials, the indigenous capacity for creativity and the special values of traditional societies. There is also the new ecological responsibility that the architect has to assume towards the countryside. Rural villages have grown so fast that urban responses are required; we have to search for new types of rural cities in the Third World capable of being viable at a very low level of income. These are new challenges to the architect which are expanding his ethics and his ethos and which are arising from a specific crisis in the Third World.

Education. Architectural education has a special role to play in preparing architects to deal with these new and major issues, especially, but not only, those of the Third World. The Jury has been only too aware of the dilemmas and of the difficult choices that Islamic architects will have to make across a wide spectrum of issues. It is to be hoped that the awards that we have recommended together with the recommendations of this report may help to draw attention to some of the categories now assuming such importance.

Soedjatmoko, Chairman of the Master Jury.

THE WORK OF THE AWARD JURY

In all these ways, architecture and urban design in the Islamic world are clearly in a state of transition. In recommending the awards the Jury has been considering signs of trends which might prove to be most useful or most desirable; these criteria have been carefully selected bearing in mind the diversity of Islamic cultures.

As a working method, the submitted projects were grouped under five headings and an endeavour was made to find at least one project which was judged worthy of an award in each group: mosques; public, commercial and industrial buildings; human settlements; rehabilitation and improvement; housing; and lastly conservation and adaptive re-use.

In the course of its task, the Award Jury was guided by the terms of reference for the Award which stress recognition of those projects "which demonstrate architectural excellence at all levels"; which respond to "social, economic, technical, physical and environmental challenges"; which nurture "a heightened awareness of the roots and essence of Muslim Culture"; which are concerned with the challenges of the future; and which have the potential to "stimulate related developments elsewhere in the Islamic world".

At the same time the Award Jury was aware that schemes might justify an award for quite different reasons. For instance, by serving as an example of the evolutionary process, or alternatively by serving as an example of a revolutionary process when appropriate. Throughout, the Jury placed emphasis in making its assessments on basic, elemental architectural qualities, as opposed to the over-simplistic, bombastic, or ideological qualities that are sometimes lauded in contemporary and "vernacular" architecture alike. In making its judgement the Jury was concerned to note conflicting philosophies between the approach of the "Modern Movement", which is often concerned with the search for a logical language of clarity and unity which might be universally applied, and the results of the continuing evolutionary process, which are frequently more concerned with diversity and vitality, with joy and engagement with the users.

In the judgement of the Award Jury its function was to assess not only the value and quality of a building complex but also its contextual significance. At this time in the Islamic world there is an important new category of buildings, those which are sophisticated and highly technical, but this fact should not lead to the neglect of their impact on the societies in which they are placed.

Nor should the development of new building types and technologies lead to the undervaluing of buildings which belong to the traditions of the people and have a naive vitality that is uniquely their own. A lively community has many levels of expression, and the creative vitality of craftsmen in society should be encouraged.

The Award Jury wishes to recognise in making the awards that the contributions of the client and the user were often of the greatest importance to the design process. When the process of design and building is correctly put in train, a true balance of contribution between the client, the user, the architects and the craftsmen is achieved. Such a framework allows the growth of a spontaneous vitality and creative energy. The process of designing constructions and the process of evolving communal action have to combine to generate projects which are within a framework for active use by the population.

In considering the category of sophisticated and highly technical buildings, the Jury observed with regret that few of the projects appeared to possess true inner conviction, let alone a vision for the future of architecture in the Islamic world. In selecting from the buildings nominated the Jury was keenly aware that its choice would be interpreted as "sending a message" of directions which architects in Islamic societies ought to follow. Few of the nominated projects could perform this role. In the final analysis, the most important criteria were felt to be:

- To what extent is the building expressive of a new vitality in the architecture of the Islamic world?
- Could the building stimulate local creativity, even if it is the work of a foreign architect, and thus point to new directions in architectural design?
- Will the solution adopted have a stimulating effect on identity formation?
- Does the building reveal a sense of purpose, social responsibility and conviction underlying its design?
- Is the claim that it is a functional solution truly sustainable?
- Is the attempt of the architecture to respond to the Islamic environment merely pompous and self-conscious?
- Is the building in scale with its environment, or does the handling of elements within the building produce a character that is arrogant and insensitive to the context in which it is placed?
- Is the building likely to induce alienation because of the difference between the image of the architecture and the expectations of the inhabitants of the area about their environment?

The relatively small number of buildings short-listed in this category is a reflection of the crisis in modern architecture in the Islamic world today and particularly in the contextual significance, or lack of it, in many of the approaches to architectural design being adopted by the profession. Nevertheless, the Jury would like to affirm its identification with the contemporary architectural efforts being made by many of the most sincere and committed designers.

Lewcock, Raporteur of the Master Jury.

The other side of the coin is that, in traditional societies, age-old architectural forms have reached such a state of high sophistication that even as they may slowly degenerate they remain more expressive and sympathetic to the aspirations of the people than all but the most perceptive of contemporary designs. Particularly in the hands of local craftsmen, the expressions of these surviving traditions sometimes have a vigour and conviction which truly celebrate devotion, contemplation or commemoration. The Jury felt that the success of these creations should be an object lesson to all interested in the art of architecture and the maintenance of a sense of identity, and that in a few important cases, the work of these humble designers reached a level of inspired expression, sensitivity and occasionally innovation, which merited recognition and encouragement with an award.

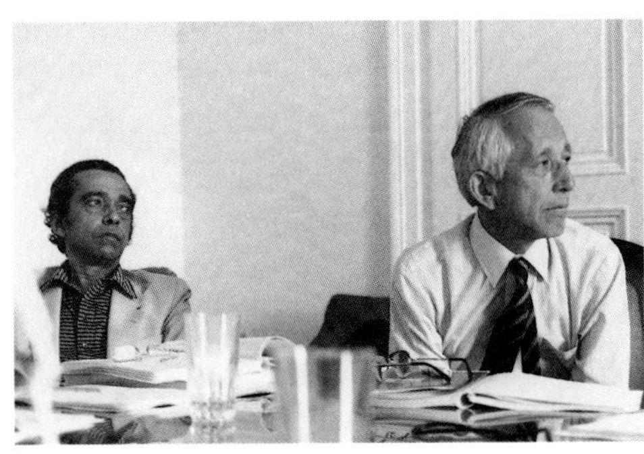

Elmandjra (left) and Maki.

The Award Jury felt that the quality of the awards might be enhanced by producing a wide-ranging list of recommendations that takes into account the vitality of the "popular" movement in architecture. There is an architecture which is expressive beyond our rational logical understanding. One of the responsibilities of the Award Jury was not to impose but to be alert and observant to what is there. Given the range of achievements in the world it is important for everyone to learn to adjust his values in order to be able to experience the full benefits of creative variety in each country and region.

One of the aspects of "popular" architecture that irritates sophisticated people is that it frequently takes elements and uses them in the "wrong ways", but history is full of examples in which such a process has led to important new developments, aesthetic and symbolic; "popular" art can be a source for "high" art and often has been in the history of art.

Architecture has a central role in creating and keeping alive a high level of taste. But this "popular" taste which is kept alive by the ingenuous craftsman may have equal significance for future vitality in the creative arts. In other words, there is a dualistic element of creativity in indigenous societies in the Third World that has tended to be eliminated by its Western-oriented component. Diversity is a necessary element for regeneration, reinterpretation and creation.

If we are called upon to find a direction that might be developed into a viable role for architects in the Islamic world, these divergent directions must be examined seriously. They possess pride and joy and essential, elemental qualities. It is a direction that is not always "nice" but it has this element of vitality.

Zahir Ud-Deen Khwaja.

The Award Jury was aware of the danger of bringing to its task a uniformity of approach and taste.

There should not be an imposition of middle-class tastes and styles all over the world but rather the acknowledgement of divergent tastes and styles, a situation which has existed in all creative periods.

The concern of the Jury with some projects for conservation is understandable in the light of the need to preserve and recover the past, particularly in the present state of rapid change in the Islamic world. In a global sense, much of what is happening in Islamic societies today is conservation or restoration in one sense or another. This is not a matter of nostalgia or sentiment, it is an intelligent assessment of the state of a civilisation.

Yet a number of the problems confronting the architect have only developed within recent times, so that precedent is no help in solving them. Nor can all questions be reduced to regional questions.

The Jury has felt the need to consider these issues in recommending projects. However, the Award Jury, while recognising the importance of awarding excellence and encouraging architects, was careful not to compromise the standard of its recommendations for excellence, for the sake of encouragement.

At this point, the Jury wishes to say explicitly that the apparent lack of balance in the range of its awards results, in its opinion, from the particular quality of the submissions and not from any bias on its part: social housing, and public and building types exhibiting modern architectural expression are especially relevant categories to be encouraged in the Islamic world and represented with a quality appropriate to their importance.

Six other aspects of the contemporary architectural situation in the Islamic world particularly attracted the attention of the Master Jury:

Tourism. The Jury felt that it had to acknowledge that there were different tastes among different cultures. While emphasising in its deliberations the importance of giving pre-eminence to the protection of the local cultures and the indigenous people from pollution by foreign tourism, and always considering domestic tourism as more important than tourism from outside, the Award Jury considered that the provision of tourist amenities did have important educational, culture-bridging and economic benefits.

The design of buildings for tourism was felt to involve quite different criteria from those involved in assessing any other architectures. One member of the Jury expressed this well during the deliberations: "Tourist architecture is scenic architecture, creating a scenic mood. Disney showed us the way. People escape, they play a role. We should be tolerant and show an understanding of this type of building ..."

The Jury therefore gave particularly careful consideration to the problem of designing architecture for tourism.

While mentioning tourism the Award Jury wished to praise the commendable conservation achievements of the Touring and Automobile Association of Turkey in undertaking the repair and adaptive re-use of a large number of important buildings, large and small, in and around Istanbul for the use of visitors and the public. One of the most noteworthy of the projects undertaken is the conservation and refitting of the Khedive Palace at Cubuklu for use as a hotel. The President of the Association has, by his driving force, achieved this remarkable programme which continues to engage ever more ambitious conservation projects and, at the same time, to serve the people of his country and tourism.

Airports. Airports were considered by the Jury to be of great importance to any nation. Apart from their functionality, they act as symbols of the society to strangers from abroad; they are gateways to the region they serve; they create images in the same way as the great railway stations in the cities of the nineteenth century.

These aspects were paramount in the minds of the Jury as they considered the nominated projects in this category which was felt to be a category of great importance in contemporary terms.

El-Wakil.

Venturi.

Industrial Architecture. The Award Jury resolved to place on record its view that architects in the Islamic world might pay more attention to the architectural design of industrial buildings. The Jury regretted that only one of the submitted industrial buildings was short-listed for the final round of the Jury. However, it was encouraging to note that this was of high merit.

Housing. The Jury noted with regret a detailed report on the failure of one well intentioned mass-housing project, initiated by agencies operating from abroad, due primarily to misjudgement of the priorities of the local population. In particular, the introduction of alien forms and materials of construction was a major cause of the rejection of the scheme by the people, because of adverse formal associations; they felt that the houses produced had nothing to do with their culture.

There was also a failure on the part of the architects to test, in the field, preliminary climatic studies. A further reason given for the cessation of the scheme was an unfortunate breakdown of communication among the agencies of external financing, the architects and urbanists, and national officials who combined some incompetence with some resistance to co-operation.

Such histories on the intervention of outsiders are unfortunately only too common, and the jury recommends that they be studied carefully by architects and international agencies, and that the practice of making case studies available for assessment be introduced, in the hope that the likelihood of such failures may be significantly reduced in future.

Human Settlements, Rehabilitation and Improvement. Throughout the Third World the booming expansion of cities is one of the most worrying prospects: at the present rate of growth, the urban poor of the Third World will form the majority of the world's population within 15 years.

In this situation the Award Jury gave the highest priority to making an award in the area of human settlements and rehabilitation. A number of projects were examined, and while the Jury noted with satisfaction that in some cases earlier awards had clearly encouraged further efforts along the same lines, their interventions were mainly of an infrastructural type. Schemes exhibiting the intervention of the skills of the architect to devise strategies by which the urban poor might be better served with housing and environmental amenities — other than those which are the normal responsibility of an efficient municipality — were felt to be in some cases flawed, and, in at least one case, of too recent a date for the Jury to be in a position to assess it.

Such schemes are endeavouring to provide permanence to human settlements: it has become clear that title to property in some form is an essential precondition of any successful scheme for revitalisation.

At the same time the economic implications of such an approach have to be fully worked out, and the long-term effects on the quality of life and social stability have to be clearly understood.

It was therefore with great regret the Jury felt that no award could be given in this category in this cycle. Nevertheless the Jury wish to stress their conclusion that this area of activity is one to which architectural schools and practitioners ought to be increasingly paying more attention, because of its urgency and its significance.

National Symbols and Patriotic Monuments. The Jury felt that any monuments which have a national patriotic meaning or symbolism, particularly mausoleums of recent leaders or martyrs, should be excluded from the competition. Whatever the decision of the Award Jury, whether positive or negative, it is bound to arouse feelings with respect to the Award. These symbols are so laden with emotions that any attempt to engage in judgement of them by the Award may lead to some misunderstanding; architectural judgements are only a minute part of the judgements that will eventually be made on the approval or rejection of such emotive monuments.

Before going on to list the citations of the Award, the Jury would like to comment on one project for which it is recommended that consideration for an award be postponed to the next cycle.

Sher-E-Bangla Nagar Capitol Complex, Dhaka. The Award Jury concluded that the time is not ripe to make an assessment on the Capitol Complex because the building has not so far been used fully enough to be tested socially and functionally. There is now some likelihood that this situation will be rectified soon, with the election of a new parliament. For this reason it was decided to recommend that the Complex be re-assessed by the next Award Jury.

The Jury's opinions have been sharply divided by its assessment of the significance of the project. Some members of the Jury agonised through a period of days over the dilemmas that they felt confronted by in these buildings. Since so much time was devoted to this task, it was felt worthwhile to record both the positive and negative conclusions of these deliberations.

Louis Kahn is one of the leading figures of our century; the complex is acknowledged to have outstanding quality and originality in many ways, to be most creative in its handling of scale, in the layering of space and in its original use of openings in walls. But it is also apparent that the Dhaka design contains some problems that are inherent to it; yet the problems were felt to be of a type that is almost inevitable in buildings that are so innovative — the sweat stains of struggle show.

Some Jury members did question certain qualities in the design: a tendency to over-formalism, a lack of connection with indigenous traditions and symbolism, a lack of connection to the city in which it is placed and finally the enormous expense in a country with very few resources and very low income levels. However, allowance ought also to be made for the great change that has taken place in the emphasis given to these factors in the twenty years since the building was designed. In addition, Kahn's architecture has entered the cycle of decline in prestige that almost inevitably follows a decade after an architect's death. A longer time-frame will undoubtedly rectify this to some extent. On the positive side, the building has made an invaluable contribution in the attention paid to the process of design and construction using rather simple materials yet achieving a design solution of high visual quality.

DISSENTING REPORTS

MEHMET DORUK PAMIR, *Member of the 1986 Master Jury*

The majority position of the Jury is a pre-meditated and clearly articulated defence of a severely limited set of options within the entire spectrum of possibilities which the Award might recognise. There is a romantic bias toward traditionalism, historicism and the vernacular. This reflects at least one dominant strain within the architectural discourse in Europe and America during the last decade. But the obvious question arises as to whether or not this one-dimensional message is a sufficient response to the complexities facing architects in the developing world. Most notably lacking is recognition of those projects which engage in the search for answers to the kind of technological issues which still face architects in regions where modern technical development cannot be taken from granted. Also curious was the tendency to suppress the creative hand of the architect through the predominance of awards to projects which involved a minimum of "design" concerns, at least in the strictest sense of self-conscious creative endeavour. Indeed, the projects seem to suppress these issues, relying on craft, folk-art and historic replication or preservation for aesthetic interest. For the large-scale projects, which are also well represented, the lumpen aesthetics of the marketplace or "kitsch" predominates. This is not to discount the sociological interest inherent to these projects, but again, for the architect as a professional there is a conspicuous absence of an aesthetic realm which one would hope is as important in the developing world as it is everywhere else.

The bias of the Jury did not accrue from a lack of endeavour. Projects were rejected which even by global standards represent major advances in high-rise design, for example, or in industrial prefabrication, or which involved creative transformation of regional building imperatives, while aspiring toward technological development. Beyond the polemical nature of the Jury's criteria lay a kind of professional discourse which is irrelevant to the high purpose of the Award. That the Sher-E-Bangla Nagar Capitol Complex in Dhaka should be excluded based on insufficient user evaluation does not succeed in overshadowing the less overt criteria, having to do, among other things, with the "prestige" of fashion. That the project is a masterpiece in the eyes of world architects can hardly be changed by the Jury's decision. But its exclusion does raise questions about the Jury's criteria which unfortunately are destined to remain obscure. The minority representation can take some reassurance from the hope that the next Award cycle will address some of the problems of balance and avoid fluctuations from one polemic to another, rather than aspiring to an even range of criteria within all cycles.

HANS HOLLEIN, *Member of the 1986 Master Jury*

The result of the judging does not reflect the opinion of a specific minority of jury members. It is clearly accepted that, in a democratic process, the majority wins. However, pluralistic tendencies are manifested in the fact that not one but several awards are attributed. An outsider would assume that the distribution to many diverse projects would reflect these pluralistic tendencies. The appointment of jurors of different persuasion seems to take care of having advocates for various opinions and secure such honouring of projects of different attitudes. This was not the case. Projects of unquestionable superior architectural merit and quality — such as the Sher-e-Bangla Nagar Capitol Complex in Dhaka — have been voted out because of a constant bias of the majority of the jury. In the light of history this judgement will be reversed. To the aims of the Aga Khan Award for Architecture, a judgement against architecture is a disservice.

WINNERS

THE SOCIAL SECURITY COMPLEX

DAR LAMANE HOUSING COMMUNITY

CONSERVATION OF MOSTAR OLD TOWN

THE RESTORATION OF AL-AQSA MOSQUE

YAAMA MOSQUE

BHONG MOSQUE

THE SOCIAL SECURITY COMPLEX
ISTANBUL, TURKEY

Completed 1970.
Client: The Social Security Organisation.
Architect: Sedad Hakki Eldem.

MASTER JURY'S CITATION. This submission engaged the interest and support of the Jury, from the beginning to the end of its deliberations, as a significant building in terms of its inherent architectural quality and its particular sensitivity to the urban context.

The quality of its architecture derives from its skilful and easy adaptation to modernist principles and industrial vocabulary; its exposed, reinforced concrete frame construction with infills of concrete block and metal sash windows are combined in a simple, repetitive manner and with a refinement of detail throughout. This design has particular originality and quality, derived from significant if slight variations within a conventional vocabulary and from the absence of any ideological bombast in its expression. Its original programme of an arcade with shops and courts on the ground floor and offices above, fits easily within its architectural form and relates well to the

Left: The rythm of the vertical elements highlights the purity of the treatment of the façade with its rigorous attention to scale.
Overleaf: The complex is inserted into the city at a visible intersection. Without compromising its modernity it blends in; respecting the historic landmarks around it and the Aqueduct in the distance.

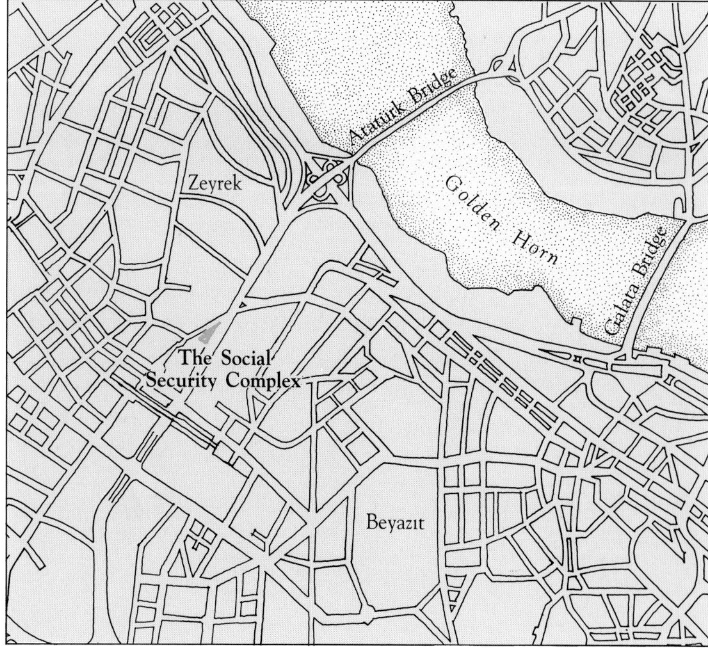

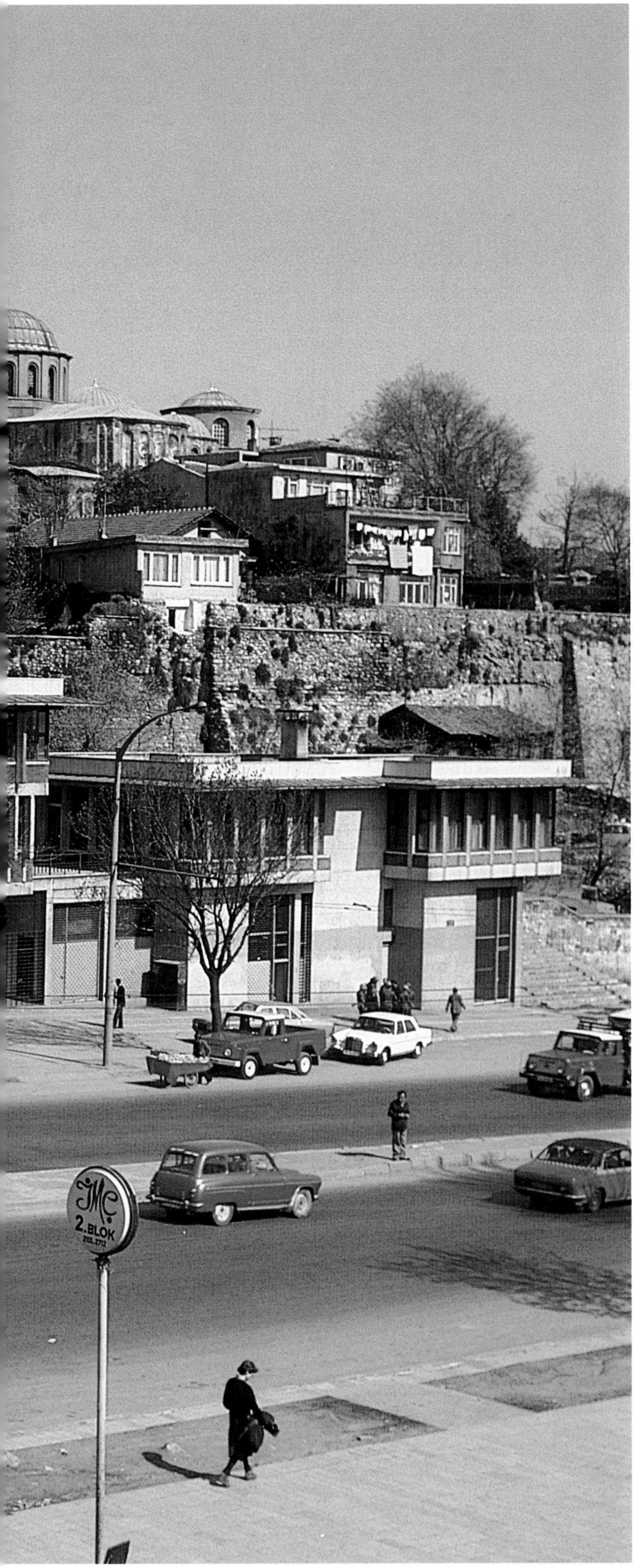

Left: The building fronts on a busy thoroughfare. Its low and cascading profile blends well with the surroundings and allows the dome of the Pantocrator to be seen behind it.
Above: The sideview of the building shows the same façade treatment with the characteristic extended roofline.

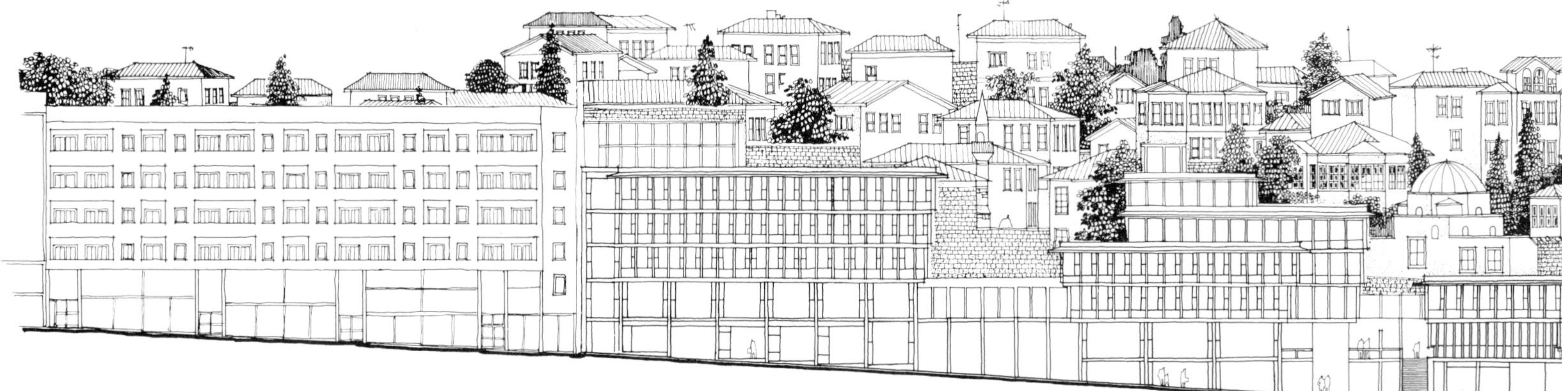

Urban elevation.

neighbourhood configuration in which it is situated. The Jury found the elemental sense of appropriateness in this building very moving.

This building must be one of the earliest and most refined examples of contextual architecture in the international Modern Movement, with its modulated forms, its scale and rhythms and its proportions, deriving as much from its exterior setting as from its interior determinants. At the time of its design, twenty years ago, the way to do an office building was to create a pure slab that dominated its setting. However, this building acts as a link between the dense and complex quarter containing traditional, small, wooden structures on the hill above and the open-spatial configuration of contemporary buildings along a modern boulevard below. While the style of the building is modern and connects with its foreground, its composition is articulated in a way that echoes its background. These qualities in combination work for a cultural synthesis which is formal and symbolic, evolutionary and revolutionary in its implications, and ends in a work of architecture that is sophisticated, artful and poignant.

Surrounding the building from the north is the old district separated only by a narrow street (below). Viewed from the Şebsafa Hatun Mosque the building blends unobtrusively into the landscape (right).

OBJECTIVES. In a neighbourhood being overwhelmed by concrete blocks and bulldozers, Eldem's building represents a deliberate attempt to reverse this trend. The area was devastated by a fire in the 1940's, followed by the construction of the Atatürk Boulevard in the 1960's. Eldem tried to make a gesture in harmony with the past while addressing the expansive continuity of the boulevard's edge. The success of the architect in meeting these objectives is apparent, in spite of the dramatic changes introduced by the tenants. This in turn has made the assessment of the internal performance difficult.

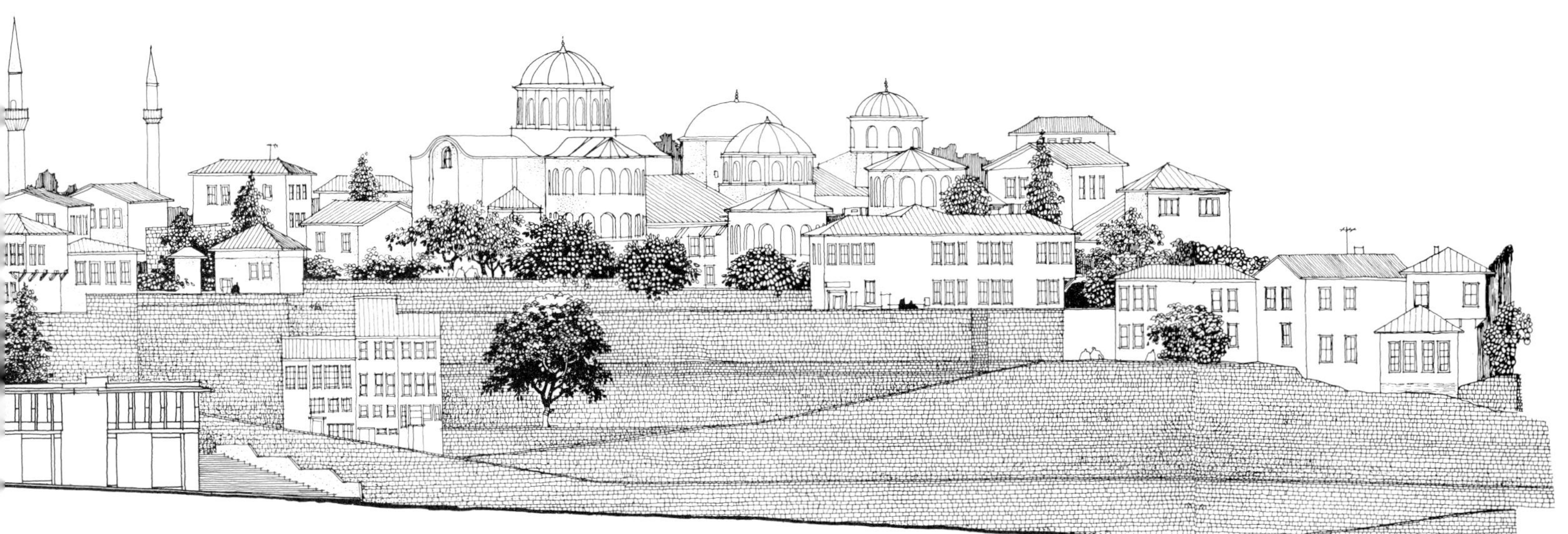

LOCATION. The Social Security Complex is in the Zeyrek district which until recent decades was an attractive residential area. The coming of the boulevard changed the nature to a commercial area with slum pockets. The dilapidated houses are being bought out by developers who are steadily replacing these wooden houses with "Jerry built" blocks of tenements. An Ottoman mosque, a tomb and a bath house *(hammam)* are nearby. Further up are the rapidly disintegrating remains of a Byzantine church. The terraces around this church were once surrounded by mansions and the palaces of the Ottoman aristocracy. The streets form irregular blocks that respond to the hilly topography. The triangular site of 3,537 square metres, faces the new boulevard on its front boundary, and the old quarter of Zeyrek on its rear boundary.

DESIGN. Shopping arcades and courtyards on the ground level link the complex with the surrounding urban fabric. This shopping arcade also extends to the first floor and conceptually resembles a *suq*. It connects four "pavilions"; a six-storey office building with shops on the ground level; a four-storey

The Social Security Complex is at the heart of a major intersection, but the design remained sensitive to the site, the tissue and the Çinili Hammam to the west and the Pantocrator to the east of it.

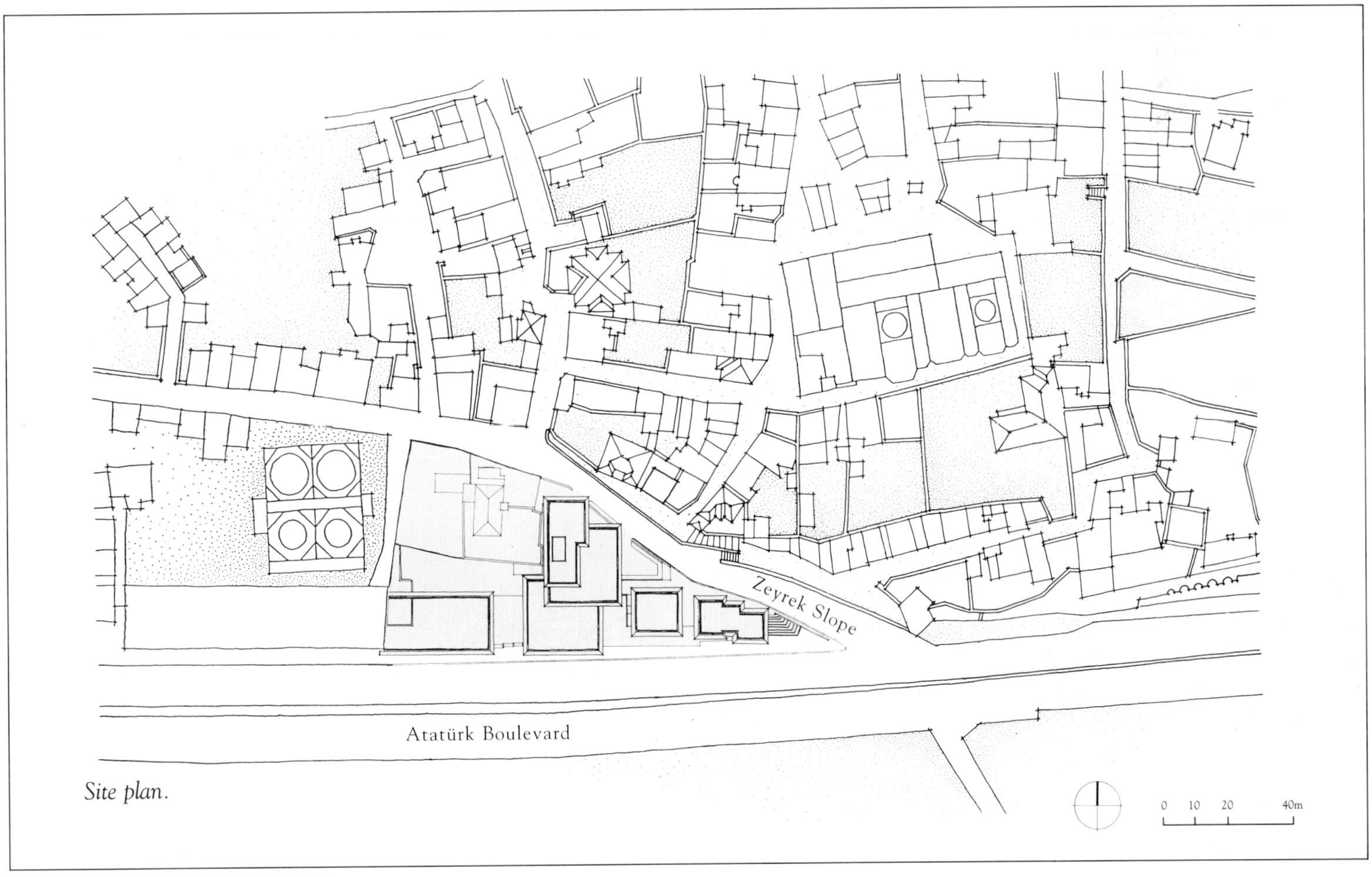

Zeyrek Slope

Atatürk Boulevard

0 10 20 40m

Site plan.

The broken façade of the building makes it appear as a group of individual structures and articulates its street frontage, where pedestrians can move with ease on the very wide sidewalk.

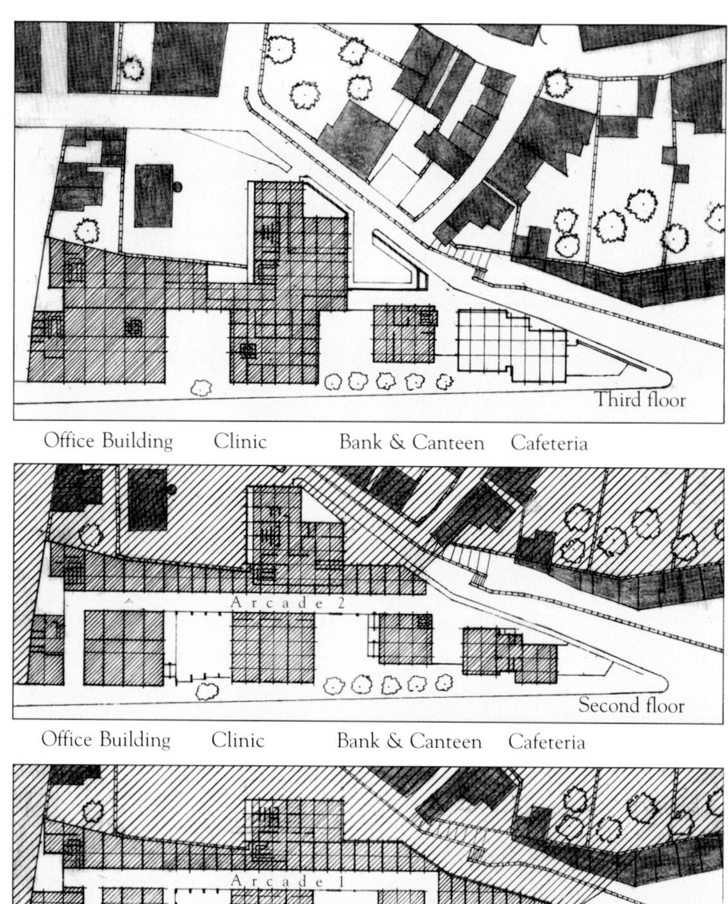

Diagrammatic plan of three levels.

clinic; a three-storey bank with a restaurant on the top floor; and a two-storey building with shops and a cafeteria. The graduated mass builds up the sloping site with the area used most by the public, the cafeteria and shops, at the lowest and most prominent point. The building is 114 metres long and begins at the southern end, at the same height as the adjacent houses. The pavilions enlarge in scale as they step up the slope, increasing the effect of terracing and giving the same sensibility found in the historic fabric of the neighbourhood. The building area is 10,163 square metres.

STRUCTURE, MATERIALS AND TECHNOLOGY. Not much importance is given to structure as an architectural element. It is made of a reinforced concrete frame with block infill and concrete slabs. Its technology is typical for buildings of its height in Istanbul. The overhanging roof eaves have protected the building from excessive weathering. Fins on the facade have been constructed with cantilevered concrete. The construction vocabulary is a familiar one–it is labour intensive. The building services and site utilities work well even if they are not specifically innovative. The use of a central heating system was perhaps ahead of its time when the building was completed. It is difficult to judge the adequacy of daylighting because of the partitions that have been put up and because of the drawn curtains and the fluorescent lighting.

TECHNICAL ASSESSMENT. It is difficult to assess most of this building in its current use. Perhaps only the medical centre, with its 100 employees, works as it was planned to. The five departments (general medicine, surgery, paediatrics, neurology and gynaecology) work in their planned spaces. Waiting spaces are well used. Doctors are pleased and do not criticise the functional use of the building. The cafeteria also continues to operate well. Divided into two parts, it is appropriated as a staff canteen for the Social Security staff,and therefore not open to the public. However, the kitchen requirements for the cafeteria were not adequate for its present use and a staircase was cut into the level below, and a "shop" at street level was converted into a kitchen. These changes were carried out by the in-house architect who did not consult the project architect.

The covered shopping arcades,and the open courtyards that give access to these arcades have been closed off. The open courtyards have been fenced off and enclosed for car parking and garbage collection. The bank and the shops were converted into offices or used to store files. On the upper level, a connection into the adjacent building has been made as the offices have expanded into the adjacent apartment block.

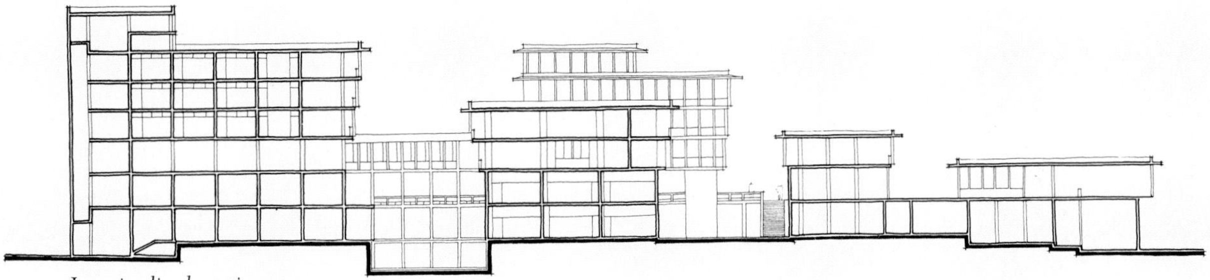

Longitudinal section.

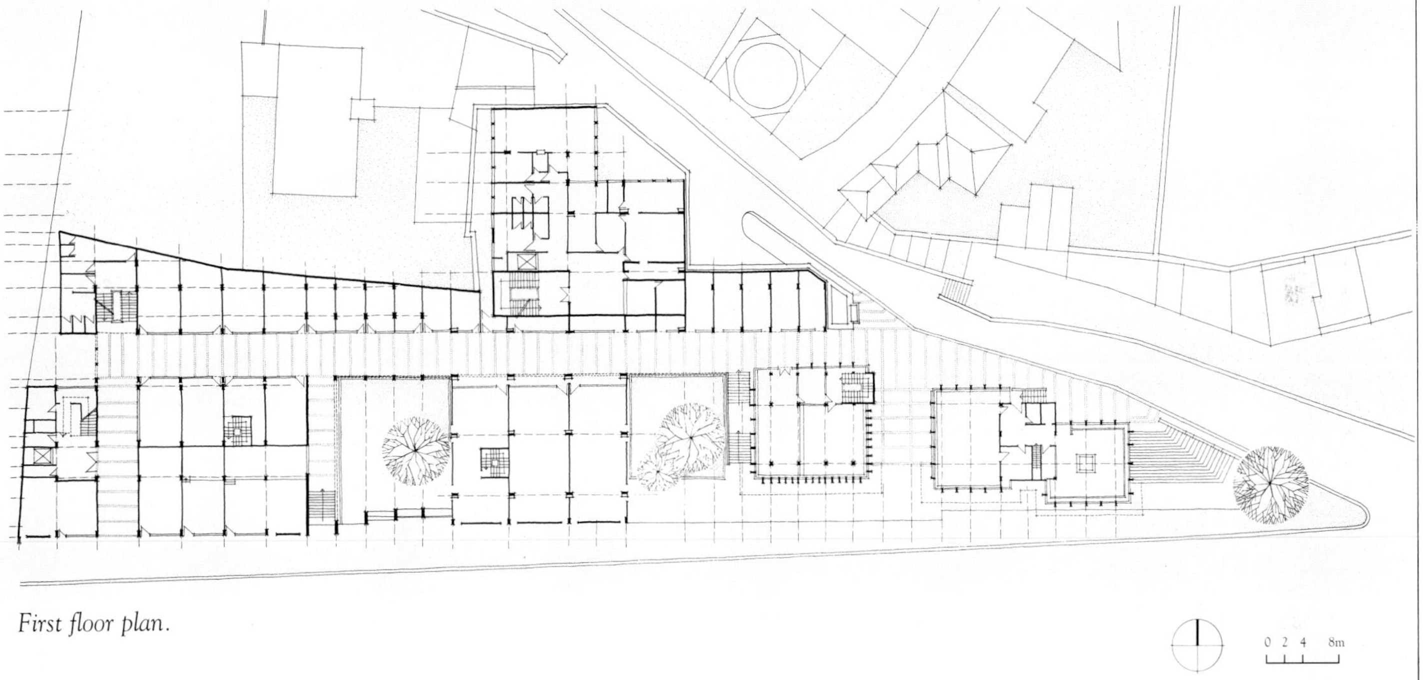

First floor plan.

0 2 4 8m

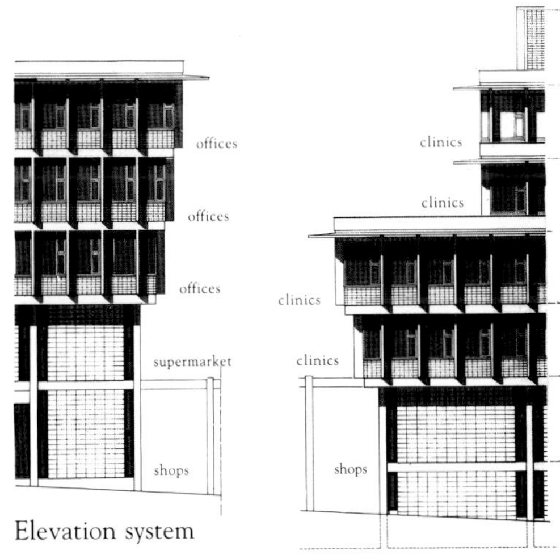

Elevation system

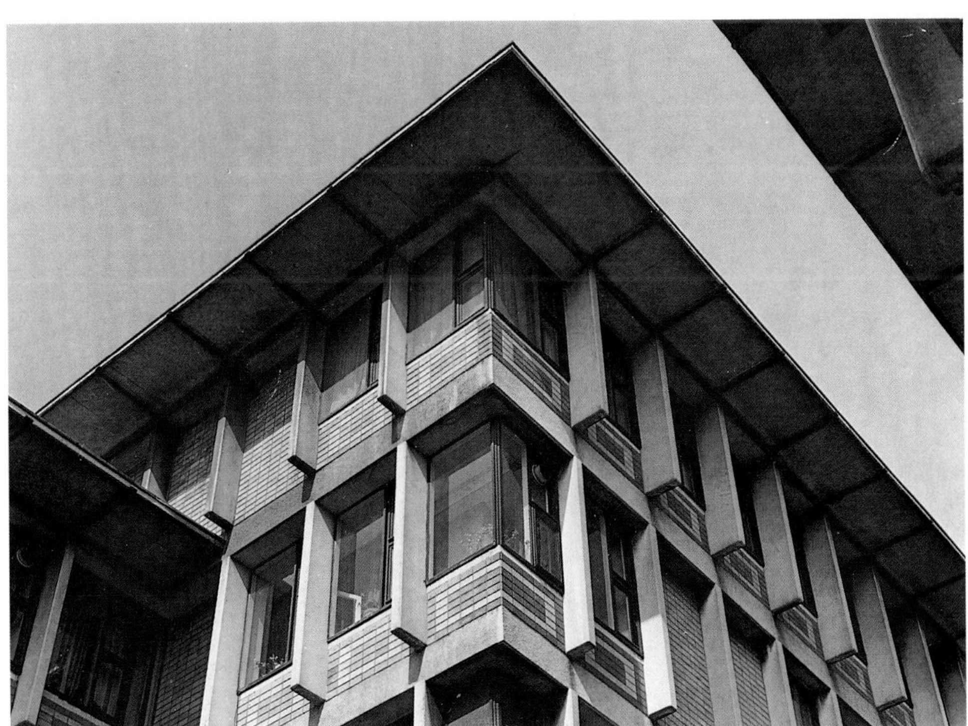

Above: Elevation showing treatment of vertical louvres and cement tiles.
Right: The purity of the angular connections can be seen at the different levels of interconnection.

AESTHETIC ASSESSMENT. A significant aesthetic symbol of the complex is its resistance to the insensitivity of much of the surrounding modern developments. It is an extraordinarily sensitive urban design by one of the great figures of contemporary architecture in Turkey. Eldem tried to extend the intimate character of the old fabric. His approach drew on the precedent of the traditional Ottoman *külliye*, a public building ensemble or urban sub-centre focused on internal public space. In this case, the internal space takes the form of a central covered "street" or arcade. The building has been abused by a government agency for several ad-hoc uses.

CONCLUSION. The project was never used the way it was originally intended. The client initially wanted a programme that could exploit the commercial potential of the land as an investment. The architect struggled to produce a building of high quality that would respond to these commercial considerations. After completion, the building was taken over by its present user, whose needs differed from those reflected in the architect's articulation of the spaces in response to the original programme. Large scale changes in use were introduced without consulting the architect. Only the clinic and cafeteria remain unchanged. Most of the public areas, including the arcades and shops were converted into storage for the agency's 16 million files. Obviously the building does not function well in its present use. The present users, however, are expected to move out in about three years time, creating the opportunity for the building to be restored to its intended purpose, or to be more imaginatively adapted to new and more compatible uses.

The significance of this building should be seen in a different context. In the 1960's, there was a heady debate in Turkey about finding a "new regionalism" in architectural expression and reassessing the international style of the 1950's. The Social Security building was a major intellectual statement in that it showed how a disciplined and talented architect could respond to both challenges. It displayed great sensitivity to both the physical and the historical context. The former in terms of topography and surrounding buildings, and the latter in its inspiration echoing the traditional Turkish architectural legacy. Yet Eldem achieved this without pastiche and without eschewing the rationalist disciplined approach that he, a truly modern architect, had made his own. Indeed, the vertically proportioned windows and the precast concrete elements could be seen as a distinctive Eldem signature, but relegated to the contextual framework in which this work was conceived. As a distinguished critic put it: *"If Eldem's individual buildings are the singular statements of his discourse, the Social Security Complex is, no doubt, a complete essay. The overall scheme illustrates that it is the modern architects' responsibility to engage in questions of scale and character, particularly in the Third World where the socio-economic dynamics gravely threaten the cultural continuity of the urban fabric."* [1]

The relevance of the project, however, has transcended the debate of the 1960's and addresses the concerns of the present generation of architects practicing in a rapidly evolving environment to satisfy societies in constant search for identity. As such, it has proven itself a true classic whose message and significance continue to have import through time despite the adverse uses it has been put to.

The rythm of the vertical elements in a horizontal building governs this composition and gives it its distinctive character:
Opposite: The purity of the rectilinear geometry is reflected in the interplay of light and shadow.
Below: The façades act as complementary and enhancing backdrop to older structures and arches.
Right: The modernity of the composition nicely frames the mosque.

DAR LAMANE HOUSING COMMUNITY
CASABLANCA, MOROCCO

Completed June, 1983.
Client: Compagnie Générale Immobilière.
Architects: Abderrahim Charai and Abdelaziz Lazrak.

MASTER JURY'S CITATION. At the time of its construction Dar Lamane was the largest single public housing project ever attempted in Morocco. It represents a successful example of housing for low-income families with great cohesion and character. The importance of urban public space is emphasised as an extension of the living space as well as for intensifying community life. Public space has thus been integrated within the housing in a harmonious manner which respects the cultural needs and aspirations of the population.

The project deserves praise not only because of its record low cost (U.S. $100 per square metre), its extremely short time of construction (30 months) and the size of the project (over 4000 housing units), but because of the authenticity of its ideas and the persistence of the designer, the manager and the client to work within a well defined cultural framework.

In many ways the physical organisation of Dar Lamane represents an innovative approach to planning. Gateways mark the entrances to the shopping streets and link the clusters of

Left: A massive gateway links the parallel buildings and defines a sense of place while lived in space above the street and the minaret in the background provide modern echoes of the traditional Medina.
Overleaf: The pedestrian street running throughout the scheme makes the project livable and humane. A wedding procession and daily encounters between neighbours make this street a key community building element.

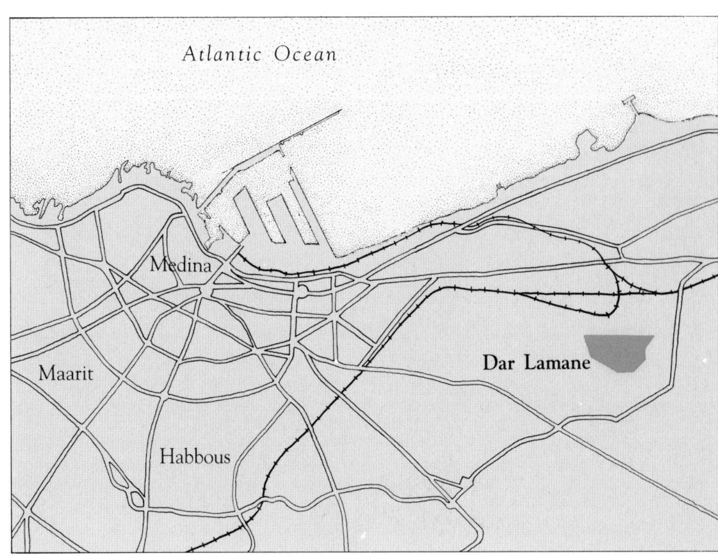

The project viewed from the central mosque (top) shows the buildings raised on an arcaded ground floor which provides for shops and shaded meeting space (detail above). The community mosque (left) is the central organising element of the whole project.

housing; their introduction is a brilliant device to provide a sense of territoriality which is fundamental to the success of a housing project. Even more important is that the gateway embodies many layers of meanings and functions that are deeply rooted in the Moroccan culture. The tremendously rich mix of public, semi-public and private activities around the gateway, and through it, makes a threshold to the cluster, a mark of separate territory, a sign for housing and domesticity, and a symbol for the quarter. It is more remarkable in that the architects chose to form the gateway by bridging between residential units on both sides of the street, to symbolise the solidarity and the sense of unity generated by the gateway.

Particular attention has been paid to the problems of safety and security especially with respect to children. The overall organisation and the design of the housing clusters recalls the traditional pattern of the Moroccan town and ensures a rich, continuous pedestrian network and a complementarity between formal and informal gardens.

Another feature of the form of housing in this project is the arrangement of two parallel rows of houses forming a group of clusters around the centre of the community, and at the same time housing enclosures on the periphery; these arrangements create at once a sense of introversion from within, and a wide and open sense of exposure from the outside. What is most significant here is the vital and dynamic pedestrian street as a consistent theme throughout the design.

The scheme presents a great variety of options in the arrangement of the housing units to the point where no two unit plans are identical. This has been made possible through an intelligent combination of design methodology, construction materials and techniques. The use of computer technology has helped to reduce the overall cost of providing such variety, as well as reducing the time of building.

The developing aesthetic of the project can be observed in the vital activity from within, even if the visual aspect which is an outcome of the construction process has not yet found its definitive expression. It will be the product of the people who inhabit it because it has been conceived as an open system.

This highly lauded project has been a learning experience for the client (Compagnie Générale Immobilière) which is now applying it to similar projects in Morocco.

The Dar Lamane Housing project represents, in many ways, a unique innovation and an important achievement in the area of public housing. It proves that a proper use of local human and material resources, combined with the mobilisation of the creative social, cultural and economic resources, can provide a workable answer to the challenge of housing low-income groups in an urban context.

OBJECTIVE. To plan, develop, and construct a residential community of over 4000 units with comprehensive facilities for low-income families.

The quality of Dar Lamane's housing contrasts sharply with the very poor dwellings surrounding it.

SITE. The housing complex was built on 37 hectares of reclaimed land in the industrial district of Casablanca about six kilometres from the city centre. The site was a stone quarry, exploited for many years by a national cement company and abandoned around 1935. Overflowing water from a spring created a huge swamp causing much pollution and illegal activities. The site was acquired by the client in 1979, reclaimed, and prepared for construction in 1980.

ACCESS. The site is accessible from the northwest side by a main road which connects the district to Casablanca and to the freeway. A loop road gives access to the centre of the community; the loop road is the only vehicular route inside the community. A service road encircles the site and is linked to the main and access roads.

LOCAL ARCHITECTURE. Industrial buildings and large warehouses are common features of the local architecture. Surrounding developments include four and five storey public housing apartment blocks to the north. They are arranged on a gridiron pattern with no amenities, and without any variety of expression. To the east, south, and west sides is a huge squatter settlement. Most constructions are shacks with deteriorating public facilities. There are no sewer systems or other essential services.

ARCHITECT'S BRIEF. In this project, the problems the architect faced included limits of scale, time, and budget. Over 4000 units were to be designed and constructed in less than 30 months. The client wanted the new community to relate to the surroundings and to the general cultural milieu of Morocco. In addition, the need for providing services and amenities was emphasised.

The architect saw the problem in its cultural context as a problem of defining a "form" for the housing of low-income, urban residents who were originally from rural or nomadic

Above left: The geometry of the façade provides a sense of balance while colour is provided by the inhabitants.
Above: Children at play on a makeshift soccer field, which is a paved parking lot located between the project and formal athletic facilities.

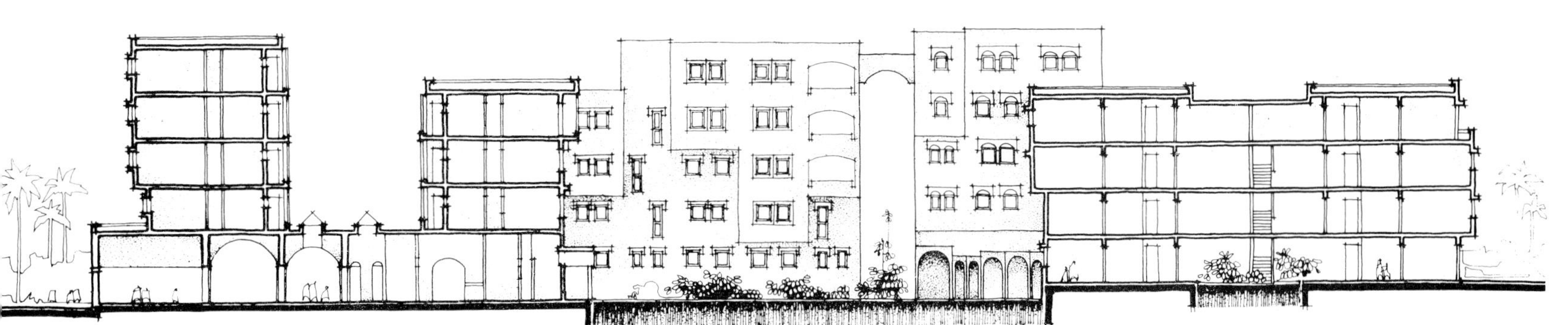

Typical section.

backgrounds. Public housing was restricted in "form" and informal housing lacked structure and services. Thus, neither option provided insight into this quest for "form".

Consequently, the planning and design approach was based on two observations: First, public space and the grouping of housing is more important to low-income groups than the design solution for individual units. Second, safety and security are more important features than possession and territoriality for newcomers to the city, especially those of rural or nomadic origin. These two observations led to the concept of Dar Lamane which means "safe or secure home." The architects referred to the concept of the *dar*, the traditional house for one or more families, and then drew a fairly elaborate scheme for the community, and for the individual housing.

DESIGN. The cohesion of urbanism depends on a complete hierarchy of public and private space. Thus, according to a hierarchy of public spaces and a re-definition of the housing form, a scheme was developed. Housing form was redefined so that public spaces would be within the domain of housing. The form of the housing would respond to the cultural needs of the different population groups as well as to the specific

Aerial view shows that Dar Lamane functions as a distinct community, whose scale and pattern is different from the surroundings.

0 2 4 8m

Cluster plan.

needs and aspirations of different age and social groups, among them children, mothers, the elderly, and so on.

The organisation resembles traditional Moroccan towns in structure but differs in form and expression. This can be illustrated by examining the organisation of public spaces, housing arrangements, and main networks.

The complex is organised around a large, central square that is reached from the main road by an access street. Six housing clusters surround this central space on three sides. The mosque, markets, and festival hall are along the northwest corner of the square. To the south, a vast sports field separates the community and the neighbouring squatter settlement. Five main gateways provide access from the central space to market streets and to the rest of the community with arcaded pavements.

The housing clusters are an arrangement of rows of attached apartment buildings separated by pedestrian streets which give access to all buildings. Entrances face each other and open staircases act as communal balconies. The apartment buildings are organised around service yards. These yards are accessible by car and serve shops, bakeries, a *hammam*, and a nursery school. An elementary school occupies the northwest corner of the site at the entrance and secondary schools are nearby. Nursery schools are provided in each cluster or housing street.

Housing unit plans are simple and flexible. Most of the apartments have three or four rooms and a few have five rooms. Many options are available to respond to various needs, as well as to respond to different layout arrangements such as corner sites, the gateway and the variety of floor levels. About 90 different apartment types are provided for and each of these has five possible arrangements.

FORMAL ASPECTS. When constructed, Dar Larmane was the largest single public housing project ever attempted in Morocco. The significance of this development is not in its size but in the model of organisation and form that it demonstrates. Despite its geometric layout, modern building techniques, and modern façades, Dar Lamane still echoes some aspects of the traditional Moroccan town with its characteristic spaces, buildings, and architectural expressions.

In spite of these echoes, the project is governed by a strict formal structure which can be seen as follows. Four storey height limits define the character of the buildings with slight variations on the roof top and in the profile of the buildings. Long walls of housing are formed by the arrangement of the apartment buildings in clusters. These create a sense of solidarity and cohesion. Arcades on the ground level not only give shade but a feeling of continuity as well. Units on the upper floors project to the outside with one or more rooms coordinated through a computerised scheme. This feature offers many choices in the apartment plans. Balconies, defined by large arched openings in the outside walls, provide an outdoor room for upper floor units. A three dimensional frame defines the window space. Metalwork, plaster, and overhangs are related to the windows. Exposed staircases act as vertical alleyways and are open to the pedestrian street. Gateways between clusters are made by projecting a room from two units on both sides of the street.

It is open to question whether the formalism of the layout, the uniformity of the heights, and the general dimensions of the spaces were not excessively constraining. For many visitors as well as residents, the overall effect, though formal, especially with its rectangular openings, remains rich with cultural references. Gateways to the cluster or to the street are simple, arched cappings to the tall opening between two buildings. A traditional minaret complements the different interpretations made throughout the complex.

MATERIALS AND TECHNOLOGY. The four storey height which defines the entire project was achieved using a structural skeleton of reinforced concrete post and beam, and bearing walls with brick and concrete block infill. Prefabricated elements for walls, beams, stairs, floors and arcades were used in combination with conventional cast-in-place construction.

Below: The space between the buildings is planted and utilised.
Bottom: Interior spaces have been individualised by the architects using computer aided designs.

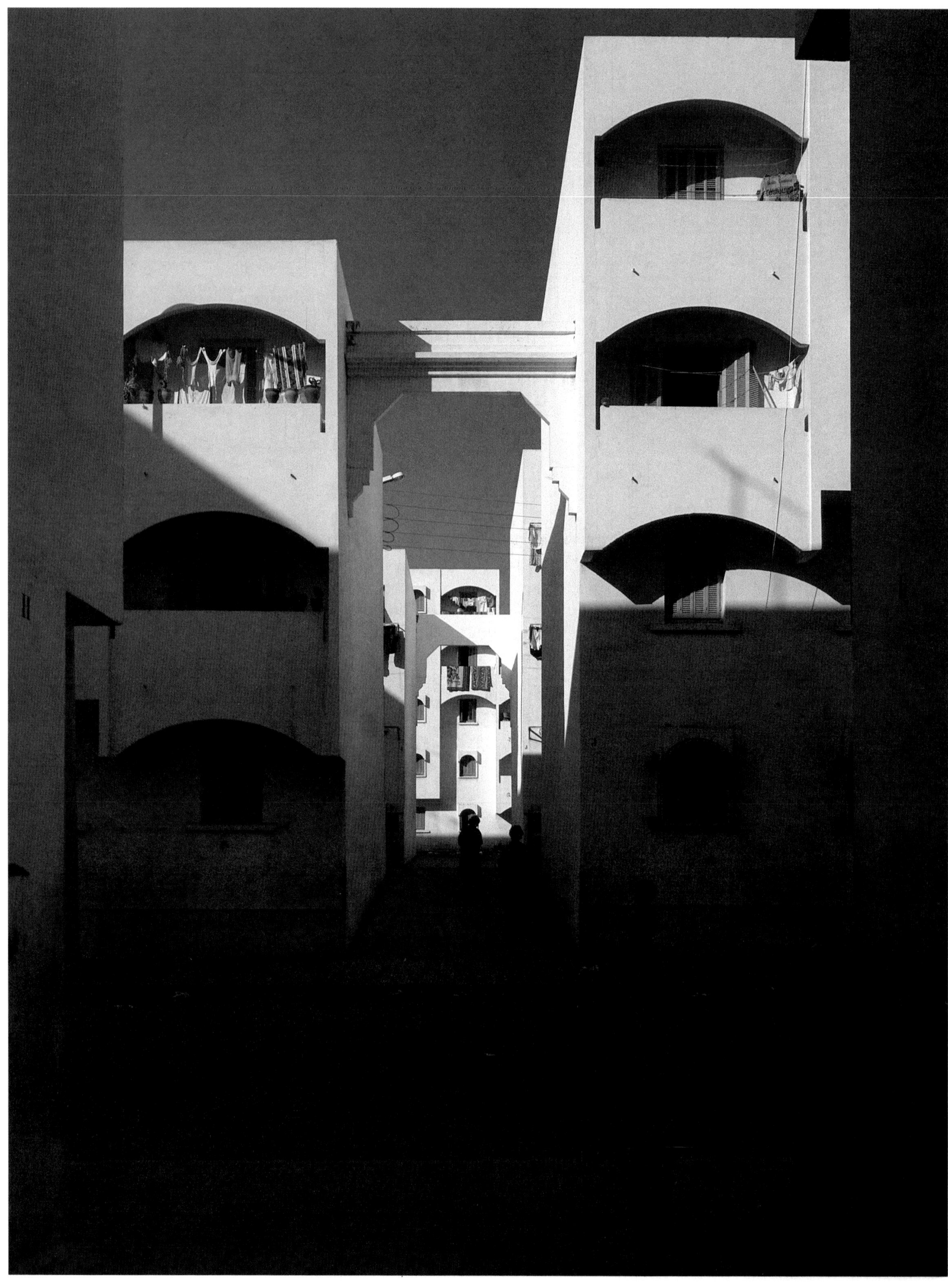

Plaster and paint were used for all exteriors. Simple ornaments, terracotta, and glazed tiles were used economically for decorative purposes.

Planning and design decisions as well as all tasks in the project were managed through a decision-making model aided by computer. Plans for housing were revised to produce maximum accuracy and efficiency of space, materials, and methods of construction.

Housing unit plans were coordinated through a computer aided model in which maximum variation was reached. Among the 4022 units in the complex, no two units are identical.

TECHNICAL ASSESSMENT. The project works well as a community. The arrangement of the clusters as well as the housing streets respond to cultural patterns. Shops, cafes, markets, and other social services are functioning efficiently and effectively.

Conventional as well as traditional technology was used for the construction. Sophisticated technology was used in planning, organisation, and construction management.

Dar Lamane has no signs of deterioration except for some leakage in the roof tops. Some cleaning problems are apparent especially in the central space. However, the community layout has helped people take charge of the public land. Pedestrian streets are well maintained, planted, and guarded. People pave the internal streets, organise the open space, and remove the accumulated garbage.

The complex has an impressive composition. The hierarchy of open spaces creates shaded and sunny spaces. Articulate massing contrasts with the dull public housing to the north of the main road. The whiteness of the wall receives a plethora of colours, shapes, and shadows either by design or by people's additions. Pedestrian streets are cool and shaded. Every unit has at least two orientations making natural ventilation and lighting quite agreeable.

CONCLUSION. The project clearly achieved its objectives and thus created a unique "form" for housing the low-income people in the city. The notion of Dar Lamane as a safe and secure community was realised. In less than 30 months, 4022 units were completed to provide housing for 25,000 people. Construction costs were 15 per cent less than initial estimates. All units were sold and inhabited by low-income families; workers, craftsmen and lower-level civil servants.

The diverse cultural origins of the residents are seen especially in their social habits and customs such as privacy, men/women relations, visiting activities, or in events such as weddings and religious or social festivals. Such events show how the buildings and the arrangement of spaces in Dar Lamane work in the cultural context.

A pre-wedding procession, for instance, takes several days in which the family of the bride shows off furniture and house appliances, gifts, cloth, and so on, to the community. This ritual is done on a horse carriage, creating huge crowds in the internal courtyards and all the way through the gateway to the pedestrian street.

The entire cluster shares in the festivities. Lines of well-wishers climb up and down the open staircases to give their greetings. The wedding party takes place in a large traditional tent erected by the community in the inner yard of the cluster.

The Dar Lamane residents clearly feel a sense of satisfaction. They are actively engaged in running and maintaining different aspects of community life. The grouping of the houses into clusters was conducive to this organised participation. Enthusiasm is also expressed towards their own individual units. Gardening, paving, repair work, remodelling, and various improvements are continually going on. This user sponsored vitality adds much to the value of the project.

Dar Lamane thus provides a rational, disciplined approach to the problem of providing humane, culturally sensitive public housing. The approach has had its impact on the client as well as other practitioners. Models developed for the design and the management of Dar Lamane are now used by the client with greater success, saving time and cost in other projects (Al-Fath: 4000 units) and in various cultural and economic contexts (Ben Mesik, minimal-income project: 4000 units).

The project's ultimate influence probably lies outside of the architectural forms it has generated. For officials responsible for designing and managing large housing projects, it shows a good balance between concern for the individual users and the needs for effective management of large public expenditures. It is not the only way to handle such problems. Clearly, guided self-help schemes are a distinct alternative deserving recognition, as demonstrated by previous Award winners (for example, the Kampung Improvement Programme in Jakarta, a 1980 winner). Professionals, be they architects or builders, will also find Dar Lamane a valuable prototype of efficient design and management techniques.

Opposite: The strong light and dark shadows heighten the impact of Dar Lamane's architectural geometry.
Below: The articulation of space and architectural detailing invites all sorts of use by the population.

CONSERVATION OF MOSTAR OLD TOWN

MOSTAR, YUGOSLAVIA

Completed 1978, and ongoing.
Client: The community of Mostar.
Conservator: Stari-Grad Mostar.

MASTER JURY'S CITATION. The Award is made for the remarkably conceived and realised conservation of the entire sixteenth century centre of this historic town.

The town of Mostar is situated 56 kilometres inland from the Adriatic Sea in the Neretva River Valley, some 150 kilometres north west of Dubrovnik on the Dalmatian Coast. It is the second largest town in the Republic of Herzegovina; 85,000 inhabitants live in the town, although the extended community numbers some 120,000.

Mostar originated as a small settlement some 500 years ago with a suspension bridge and a few houses. Its main period of expansion dates from the arrival of the Ottomans in Herzegovina and their building of a permanent bridge with flanking towers across the Neretva between the years 1557–1566. From this time a thriving business centre developed around this focal crossing point. It continued to flourish throughout the seventeenth century, by which time the town comprised over 1000 houses.

The community of Mostar founded Stari-Grad in 1977 as a work organisation set up to deal specifically with the restoration and preservation of the old town. The initiative was

Left: Buildings of Kujundžilik, mostly shops and offices, on the left bank of the Neretva River.
Overleaf: Aerial view of Old Mostar viewed from south west.

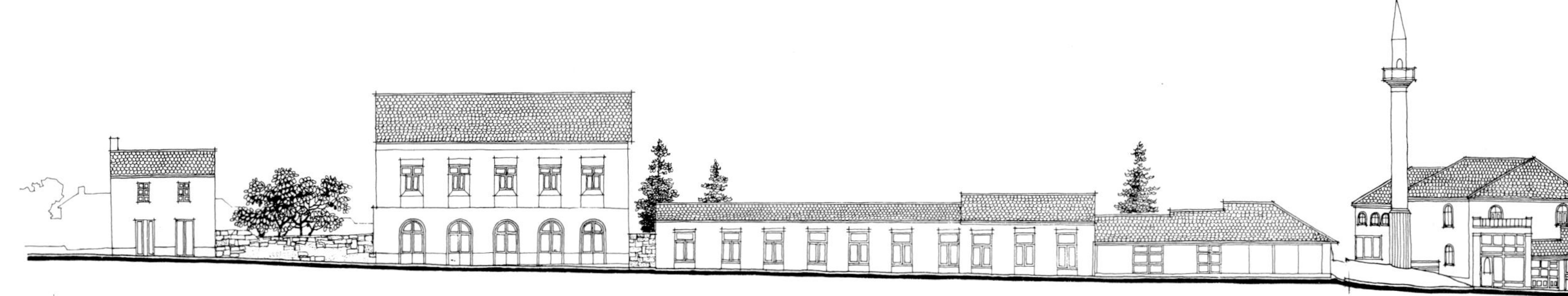

106 *Urban elevation.*

entirely taken by one man, Džihad Pašić, formerly a government Inspector of Monuments, who prepared all the documentation and who is still its director.

Stari-Grad is a semi-autonomous organisation approved and subsidised by the Ministry for the Protection of Monuments and Nature of the Republic of Herzegovina in Sarajevo. An area covering 742,000 square metres, i.e. the central core area of the old town, was given over to Stari-Grad: all the rents, taxes, dues and income from advertisement, cinemas, etc., collected from this zone go to the organisation and form the basic part of their annual budget. This inner zone is now being extended. An overall Four-Year Plan is prepared so that the organisation knows in advance the budget at its disposal and plans with priorities in mind. Methods of funding the work in the central area based on the extent of improvement in the rest of the city has recently been evolved.

The objectives of Stari-Grad are to restore the historical core of the town of Mostar and to revitalise and reactivate it as a thriving business centre. In seven years, they have resurrected the old town so that even in the off-season with no tourists, the level of activity is striking. The long waiting list for the finished shops/offices means that the old town centre is again commercially viable and alive.

The varied aspects of this restoration project, with many different types of buildings, from the central bridge, shops and private houses to public mosques, have been handled in an exemplary manner. All the restorations fit well into the general atmosphere of the old town and its homogeneous appearance is not disturbed; nothing is overdone or touristic. The re-use of old buildings is sensitively achieved, especially where mosques are concerned, and whenever possible the building is used for its original purpose. The overall impression is excellent.

In Yugoslavia, Stari-Grad has become a focus of attention especially among historic towns that need restoration. Two towns, Split and Novi Sad, have recently adopted a resolution to form an organisation similar to Stari-Grad, and Dubrovnik and Pula are also discussing this system.

OBJECTIVES. In Mostar, like many historic cities, the citizens wanted to preserve and protect their cultural heritage. Another corollary objective was revitalising Mostar's commercial and business centre through a programme of upgrading and re-use, or provision of modern facilities for the local and visiting population. Deterioration of the built fabric and commercial stagnation of the town centre were the principal motives for undertaking restoration; this was decided upon instead of indiscriminate destruction that often arises from commercial redevelopment and industrialisation.

TOPOGRAPHY, DESCRIPTION, AND HISTORICAL BACKGROUND. Mostar is the second largest town in the Republic of Herzegovina. It has 85,000 inhabitants divided almost equally among Muslims, Orthodox, and Catholics. Steep limestone mountains covered with scrub and fir trees tower over the townscape. The Neretva valley, widening out below Mostar, is agriculturally rich with many fruit orchards, farms, and vegetable gardens. Light industries found in the area include a hydro-electric plant, tobacco and cotton factories, an aluminum plant, a wine distillery, and many fruit juice factories. The region is famous for its crafts. Some are still practiced, including tanning and leather work, jewellery, filigree work, wood carving, coppersmithing, embroidery, blacksmithing, and *kilim* and saddle-making.

Five centuries ago, Mostar originated as a small settlement of a few houses with a suspension bridge; *Mostari* means bridgekeeper. Its main period of expansion was after the Ottomans arrived in Herzegovina and built a permanent bridge with flanking towers across the Neretva in 1557–1566. These developments caused the town and business centre to thrive. By the seventeenth century the town had over 1000 dwellings with a rich variety of private and public buildings. The period, under Austrian rule (1878–1918), is also well represented in Mostar by shops, public buildings, and an army barracks. By

the 1960's, however, many of these fine structures were deteriorating despite the efforts of the existing organisations to preserve and maintain their rich cultural heritage.

The community of Mostar had grown disenchanted with the inefficient bureaucracy that was responsible for the old town. Consequently, in 1977, it founded Stari-Grad. This organisation was set up to deal with the restoration and preservation of the historic centre of the town, and the documentation of its rich building heritage.

WORK PROCEDURES. Stari-Grad spent three years documenting the core of the old historical town, collecting and analysing historical data. It surveyed and, mapped the zone and produced measured plans, sections, and elevations for each building. All the data pertaining to a structure was collected; A dossier was compiled to include historic photographs, etchings and literary references. Archaeological and art historical on-site analysis and investigations were also conducted. Detailed examinations were made on the rate of deterioration and the state of repair for each building.

Before any restoration work can begin the following steps must be taken by Stari Grad: First, a detailed and analytical plan of action with plans of all reconstruction must be prepared. Second, questionnaires *(Anketni)* are distributed to the community; The responses are discussed at open meetings with community representatives. All resolutions passed at these meetings are published. Third, approval of the programme must be obtained from the Ministry for the Protection of Monuments in Sarajevo for certain buildings. Other buildings can be decided on by the community with the approval of the local Commission for Housing.

All restoration is done under the control and supervision of Stari-Grad. This ensures a consistent standard of workmanship. They also control the re-use of restored buildings with strict conditions and obligations for their upkeep. Rent from finished and renovated buildings goes back to Stari-Grad who reinvest it into subsequent restoration projects. Industries are frequently asked to donate their services and equipment for the restoration work.

BUDGET. The annual rents and dues from the zoned area are estimated and each year's work is planned in advance. A four year plan is made with estimates that have to be approved by Sarajevo and included in the city plan. Therefore, Stari-Grad knows its overall budget ahead of time and can plan accordingly. During implementation, however, since several projects go on simultaneously, it is difficult to separate the individual budgets.

Another problem is the high inflation rate in Yugoslavia. Inflation has to be estimated and included in the budget. Stari-Grad's forecasts have been fairly accurate so far. A special fund must also be set aside for rehousing or for buying a shop or house. Rehousing occupants while their building is being restored is usually easy. They are housed in local housing projects. Time estimates have also to be accurate and adhered to for the sake of inflation. In 1978, Stari-Grad started with an annual budget of U.S. $50,000. This figure currently exceeds U.S. $2 million. Recently, 40 per cent of the estimated revenues of any new building project outside the immediate zone was granted to Stari-Grad, as a form of tax to sustain the most interesting urban elements in the city. This new source of revenue will increase the potential for future projects.

CONSTRUCTION AND RESTORATION METHODS. All historic buildings in Mostar were built either of a conglomerate mixture of rock and river pebbles using a lime mortar, or with *teneliya* blocks, an oolitic limestone. Interior partition walls were sometimes made of baked bricks. The interior finish was done with lime plaster; the exterior facades were usually left unplastered except for houses. Many details were done in wood, especially the houses and shops. The materials are found locally and the *teneliya* mine is still operating. New roofing is done with traditional materials — slate tiles *(ploča)* on timber framing with overlaps sealed in lime.

1. Stari Most
2. Tara Tower
3. Halebija Tower
4. Tabhana
5. Hammam Ćejvan-beg
6. Prijećka Čaršija
7. Kujundžiluk
8. Sahat Kuly
9. Nasuh-age Vučjaković Mosque
10. Koski Mehmed Pasha Madrasa
11. Hadzi Mehmed Karadžozbeg Mosque
12. Hadzi Mehmed Karadžozbeg Madrasa
13. Roznamedži Ibrahim Efendi Mosque
14. Ćejvan-ćehajina Mosque
15. Biščević House
16. Kajtaz House
Neretva
0 10 20 40 80m

Site plan.

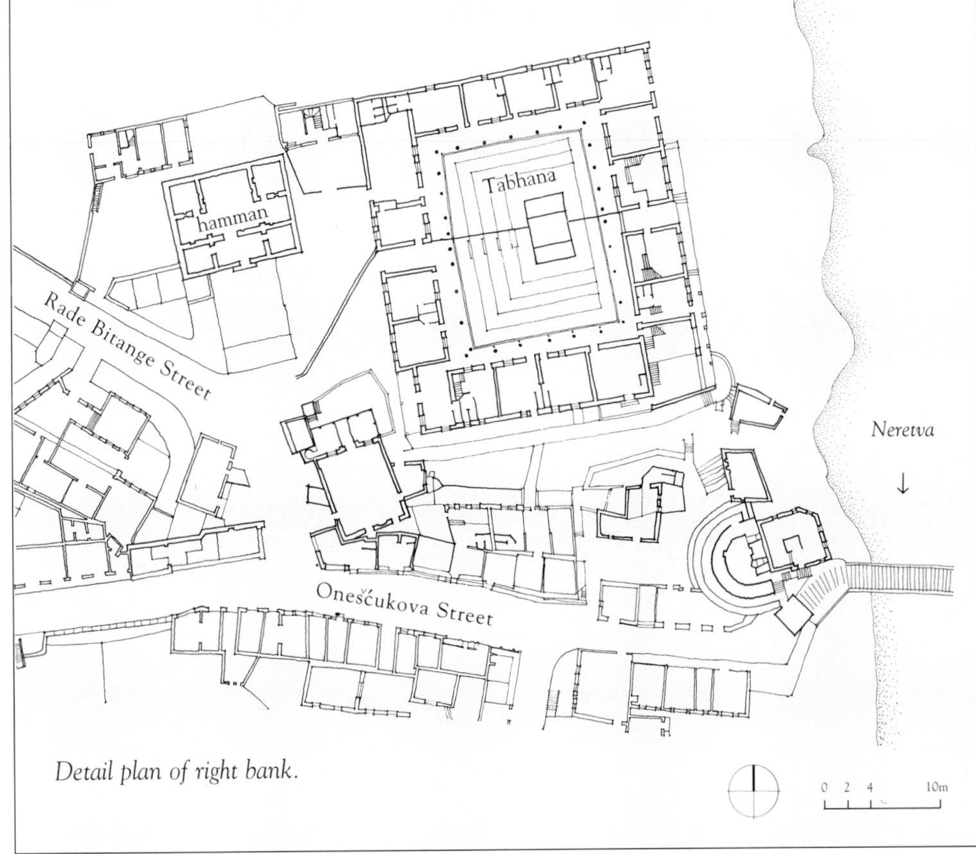

Detail plan of right bank.

Top: Tannery viewed from the north.
Centre: The Prijećka Čaršija business district.
Above: Restoring roof tiles.

When major rebuilding has been necessary, this has been done with a concrete frame, brick infill dividing walls and stone facing on the façades. The standard of workmanship has been high and maintenance conscientious.

RESTORATION AND RENOVATION.

The Bridge, Stari Most. Among Stari-Grad's long-term undertakings, the renovation and repair of the *Stari Most* bridge is still an ongoing project. The bridge is one of the most famous landmarks in Yugoslavia. It is a masterpiece of Ottoman architectural and engineering skill, and was completed in 1566 after nine years of construction. The architect who designed and built it was Khairuddin, a pupil of the great Ottoman architect, Sinan. *Stari Most* has a high arched span rising 27 metres above the river. It is four metres wide, 30 metres long and is built mainly of *teneliya* blocks. Raised bands of stones, about 60 centimetres apart, lead up the steep slopes of the bridge.

Repairs have been carried out in the past but scientific and systematic studies began only in 1970 when Džihad Pašić wrote the first major report. Drawings of the bridge were made and each stone numbered. In 1979, a preliminary underwater structural examination revealed major weakness in the natural rock under the footings of the bridge. The right bank had especially been eroded, creating caverns under the right foot. So with special divers and underwater equipment, the caverns were checked, drawn and core samples were taken for analysis. Steel bars were then driven into the bedrock. The overhang was thus strengthened and the area beneath was filled in with reinforced concrete.

Although the bridge is stable, it is constantly monitored and examined. (It survived World War II when the German army filled the steppings with sand and drove their tanks across it.) In 1985, small holes were discovered in the vaults. Water was seeping through the interstices and freezing in the hollows. This could have caused damage. It was therefore decided to waterproof the interstices between the stones on exposed surfaces. A bonding and waterproofing material was applied on the bridge in March 1986.

Tara Tower. In 1576, the tower on the left bank of the bridge complex was built. It was restored in 1737. Its interior deteriorated badly and in 1982, the walls were strengthened with reinforced concrete on the interior. The roof was completely redone and the interior spaces were redesigned as artists' ateliers. The studios are only used in the summer because there is no central heating.

Clock Tower, Sahat Kuly. Repairs on the seventeenth century clock tower carried out in 1982, involved restoration of the upper part, rebuilding the conical capping and replacing the lead sheathing. In addition, the interior stairs were completely rebuilt in oak and the Genoese clock was fixed. The garden near the tower was landscaped and the steps leading up to it were repaved.

Left: Stari-Most Bridge spans the Neretva River and is the focal point of the restoration areas on both sides of the river.
Below: The Stari-Most Bridge towards the Halebija Tower.
Opposite: View of the left bank with the Hadži Karadžozbeg Mosque and madrasa in the distance.

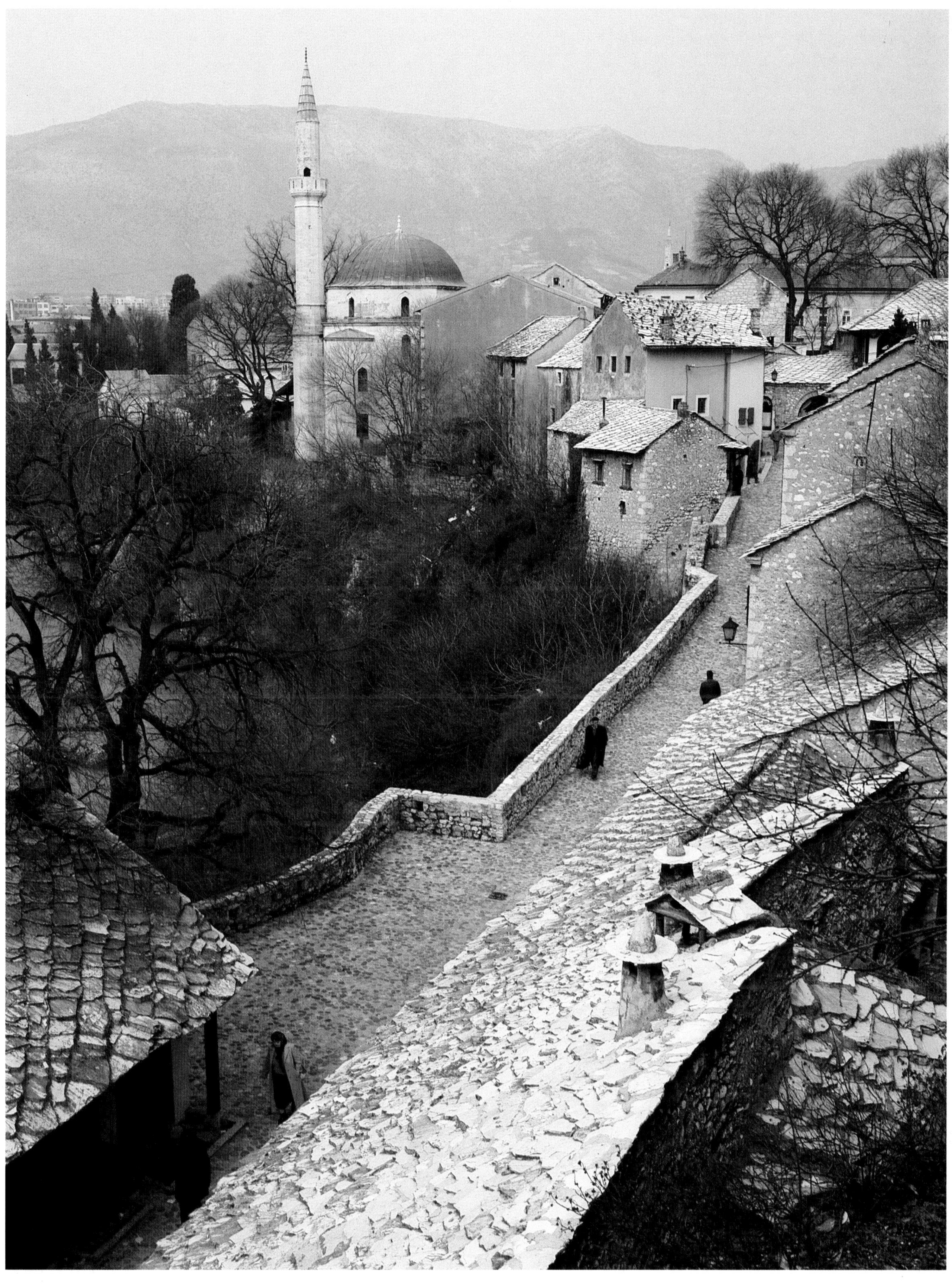

Hadži Mehmed Karadžozbeg Mosque and Madrasa. Sultan Suleiman the Magnificent ordered the mosque to be built. This classic Ottoman mosque was built in 1557 by the same masons who constructed the bridge. It is a square building with richly painted interiors. Stari-Grad had the open porch *hayat* repaired. The gardens and the cemetery were tidied and landscaped. The *madrasa* was built in the same complex in 1562. The wooden framework of the roof was rebuilt, the slates were replaced and new lead sheathing was put over the domes. Both the mosque and the *madrasa* continue to be used for prayer and study.

Roznamedži Ibrahim Efendi Mosque. Ibrahim Efendi who was *roznamedži* (controller/secretary) to Sultan Murad IV (1633–1640) built this mosque in 1621–1623. This small, square mosque has a single dome and an elegant minaret. In 1970, a section of the uppermost part of the minaret fell through the domed roof, damaging it. Pašić restored the minaret in 1970. Stari-Grad completed the restoration in 1978. They repaired and replaced the wooden panelling decorating the interior of the dome and redesigned the space inside for use as an exhibition hall or gallery. The roof was also repaired.

Shops and Offices, Kujundžiluk (left bank). Stari-Grad began renovation, still ongoing, of 30 shops and offices in the left bank business district. The shops are tiny wooden cubicles; the larger areas have been converted into restaurants. Restoration consists mainly of reconstructing the roofs. Modern facilities are provided for all the interiors. Details of the roofs, hinges, wooden slats, sills, overhangs, and so on, have been reproduced according to traditional methods. The shops have been rented out to locals. The interior decorations were done and paid for by the lessee's, after approval by Stari-Grad.

Top: Courtyard of Hadži Mehmed Karadžozbeg Mosque and madrasa with covered well.
Above: Portico (hayat) of the Hadži Mehmed Karadžozbeg Mosque.
Below: Ceiling of Roznamedži Mosque after restoration.

MAJOR REBUILDING PROJECTS.

Koski Mehmed Pasha Madrasa and Embankments. In 1979, Stari-Grad rebuilt the *Koski Mehmed Pasha Madrasa* and embankments on the left bank of the Neretva River. The *madrasa* was built in 1618–1619 by Mehmed Koski who was *roznamedži* to the Grand Vizier Lala Mehmed Sokolović (1604–1606). During World War II, the *madrasa* fell into a ruinous state and in the 1950's, it was razed. It was rebuilt from photographs taken of the original; the ground plan was excavated and the room divisions were kept. It was constructed with lime mortar and *teneliya* limestone blocks and was strengthened on the inside with reinforced concrete. Wooden details, chimneys, doors and windows were reproduced from photographic evidence. Modern facilities were incorporated without changing the floor plans. After completion, the building was rented by the Tourist Bureau. Coincidentally, the Assistant Director's father was the *imam* who taught at the *madrasa*. Stari-Grad also rebuilt the embankment and the ruined fountain in the courtyard was repaired.

Business District, Priječka Čaršija (right bank). About 30 shops dating from the eighteenth and nineteenth century were pulled down and completely rebuilt according to their original designs. All finishing and detailing were also replicated. The shops have been rented out as galleries, restaurants or as craft shops. The occupants include a blacksmith, a woodcarver and a shoemaker.

Tannery, Tabhana. This tannery was originally built in the sixteenth century as military barracks for Ottoman troops guarding the bridge. In the seventeenth century, it was turned into a tannery. When restoration work started, half of the quadrangle was still a working tannery. It will continue to operate as a tannery and will also house galleries, shops and space for leather work. The rebuilt half will have a restaurant and summer theatre.

Fruit vendors in front of Koski Mehmed Pasha Madrasa.

TECHNICAL AND AESTHETIC ASSESSMENT. The work is of a high standard. The finish is good, and so is the quality of the materials. The availability of traditional building materials obviously enhances restoration. There are no noticeable signs of ageing in any of the buildings. Nor are there any apparent problems with the restorations.

Maintenance is kept up and all the buildings are clean. Facilities function properly. If anything goes wrong, it is very quickly attended to.

The many aspects of this conservation project, involving different building types, from private houses to public mosques, have been handled very well. The restorations blend into the atmosphere of the old town and the homogeneous fabric is not disturbed. Nothing is overdone or artificial. The re-use of old buildings is sensitively done, and whenever possible the building is used for its original purpose.

CONCLUSION. Conservation efforts by the Stari-Grad organisation in Mostar varied from restoration and renovation to major rebuilding. In seven years, Stari-Grad made Mostar vibrant again. The significance of the project, aside from the conservation, is its popularity with the community and the democratic working methods that foster local participation.

Work is expanding for Stari-Grad although their major works are still in the zoned area of the old town. Many projects in the historic core and in the private residential district outside are planned between 1986–1990. The *Halebija* Tower on the right bank, completed in 1676, will be restored as ateliers for artists. Repair of interiors and the minaret of the Hadži Mehmed Karadžozbeg Mosque will go ahead. Stari-Grad also plans to replace the roof and repair the interiors in the Nasuhage Vičjaković Mosque. Built in 1528–1529, it is the oldest mosque in Mostar. Restoring and cleaning interiors and wall paintings is planned for the Koski Mehmed Pasha Mosque as well as repairing the roof. Hammam Ćejvan-beg, built in 1626, is the first *hammam* in Europe. Its domes, walls, and interior will be restored to function again as a *hammam*. Repairs are planned for the dome and interiors of the Cejvan Mosque, which dates from 1552 to 1558. It was restored during the Austrian period and in the 1970's was turned into a museum.

The main beneficiaries and users of the area are the townspeople and the tourists. Both groups seemed satisfied with the results. The Muslim community was especially enthusiastic. More communities in Mostar now want to be included in Stari-Grad's zoned area.

Whether an organisation like Stari-Grad could be duplicated outside the political circumstances peculiar to Yugoslavia is difficult to determine. The cooperation between the different agencies and the community needed to make an organisation like Stari-Grad effective, are not easily found in many countries. Nevertheless, the example of Stari-Grad should be a great encouragement for all those who are trying to establish a more effective means of revitalising the historic cores of their old cities.

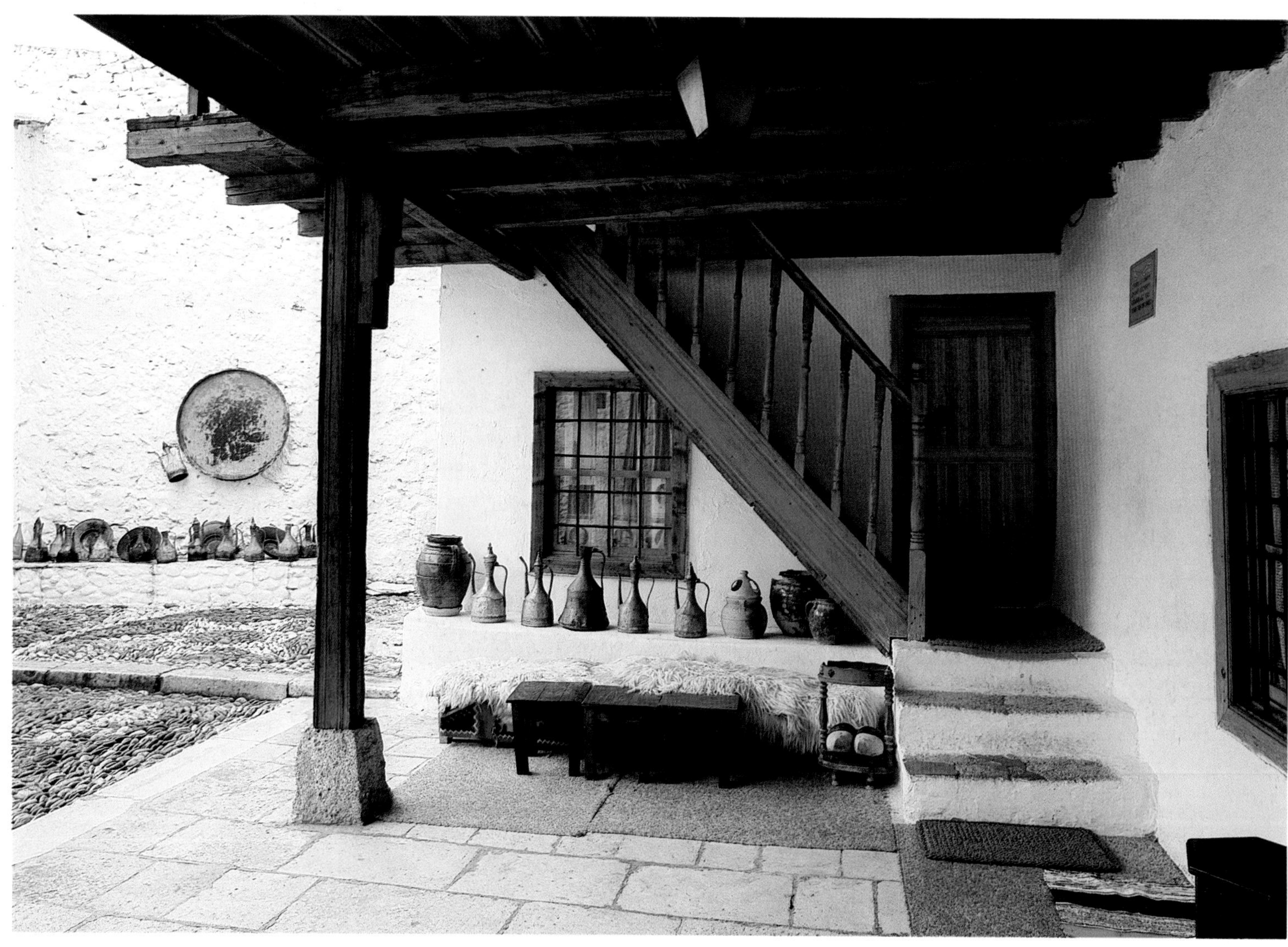

The Mostar restoration project included several sixteenth century houses of exceptional charm, such as the private Biščević House (above) and the Kajtaz House which has been converted to a museum (opposite and overleaf).

THE RESTORATION OF AL-AQSA MOSQUE

AL-HARAM AL-SHARIF, JERUSALEM

Completed 1983.
Client: Al-Aqsa Mosque and the Dome of the Rock Restoration Committee.
Restoration: The International Centre for the Conservation and Restoration of Monuments, ICCROM.

MASTER JURY'S CITATION. The Award is made for the high quality of the conservation work of this mosque and in the Haram al-Sharif generally.

Until recently the state of this, one of the three most important monuments of Islam, was a sorry one. Extensive alterations took place in the 1950's and 1960's in the name of "restoration", which only resulted in the creation of adverse conditions. In particular, the dome of the mosque was reconstructed in concrete and covered with anodised aluminium instead of the original ribbed lead sheeting.

Following explosions and fire in the mosque in 1969 which severely damaged the fourteenth-century paintings and the timber construction of the inner dome, together with the aluminium external cladding, al-Aqsa Mosque and Dome of the Rock Restoration Committee undertook, with the

Left: Al-Aqsa Mosque showing the courtyard and landscaped approach from the north-west.
Overleaf: Aerial view of al-Haram al-Sharif area with al-Aqsa in the foreground and the Dome of the Rock in the background.

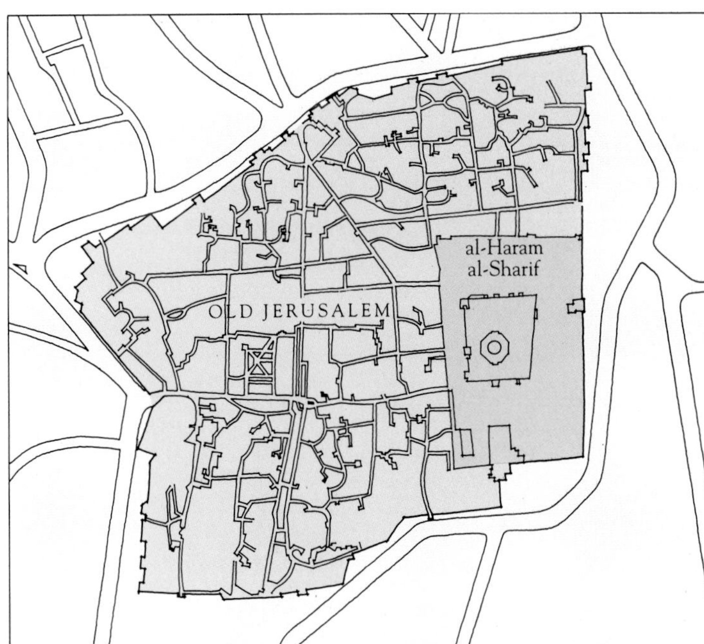

Exterior of dome before and after restoration.

continuous assistance and involvement of ICCROM in Rome, a programme of extensive conservation beginning with the damaged dome and its paintings.

From the purely technical point of view, taking into consideration the methodology, analytical precision, structural and constructional features, and criteria related to the principles of scientific restoration, most of the works which were done, and which are being done, are of very high quality (including the exterior works, mosaics, masonry work and windows). The ribbed outer covering of the dome was replaced in lead to match the original. The restoration of the inner decoration of the dome is exceptional and aesthetically satisfying.

In the courses of conservation, it was possible to bring to light the original painted decorations of the dome which were hidden under later layers and which at the outset seemed to be irreparably lost. It was thought necessary, because of the religious significance of the building, the repetitive nature of the decoration and the significance of the calligraphic inscriptions, to have a complete reconstruction of the paintings on the dome. The wooden inner dome construction was repaired, gaping holes closed with timber cladding, and a relief plaster surface to match the original was added. The missing paintings were executed using the *tratteggio* technique, a complete and exact reconstruction using fine vertical lines to distinguish reconstructed areas from original ones. For this purpose, water colour was employed as the medium.

Parallel to the works in the dome, other restoration works were done and these are still continuing. They consist of the consolidation and restoration of inner and outer wall surfaces; the restoration of columns and capitals which were either damaged by fire or ageing or badly restored during earlier works; the restoration of decorated marble panels; the decoration of the ceilings of the naves (mosaics and paintings); the restoration of leaded glass decoration windows; the restoration of marble mosaics and the restoration of pavements. Finally, work similar to that on the exterior dome is being done on the pitched roof of the nave. It consists of stripping the aluminium sheets and removing the heavy concrete roof construction which was introduced during the engineering "restoration" works of the 1950's and thereafter replacing the aluminium with lead.

Besides the ambitious restoration works in al-Aqsa Mosque, a series of other restorations have been done or are being done or are programmed within the Haram area.

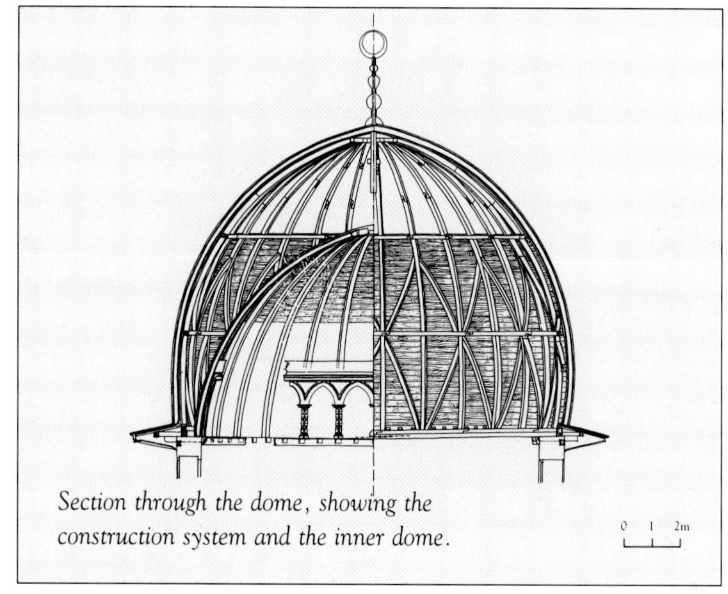

Section through the dome, showing the construction system and the inner dome.

OBJECTIVES. The main objectives included: rejuvenating the Haram area, by restoration, by landscaping, and by re-use of spaces and monuments that have symbolic value for the Muslim community; also improving the quality of the structures, including the covered mosque of al-Aqsa and the Dome of the Rock, that were menaced by careless restorations and damaged by fire in 1960.

SITE. Al-Aqsa Mosque is located within the Haram al-Sharif, the noble sanctuary which is in the south-eastern part of the Old City of Jerusalem. The Haram is about 140,000 square meters which represents one-sixth of the area of the Old City. It consists of the Dome of the Rock, al-Aqsa covered Mosque, the Dome of the Chain, other minarets, schools, Waqf and other old public buildings, fountains, *riwaqs* and *iwans*, *mastabas*, arches, and underground structures dating mostly from the Abassid, Fatimid, Mamluk or Ottoman periods. Monumental fortified gates give access to the holy site.

Courtyard on the western side of al-Aqsa.

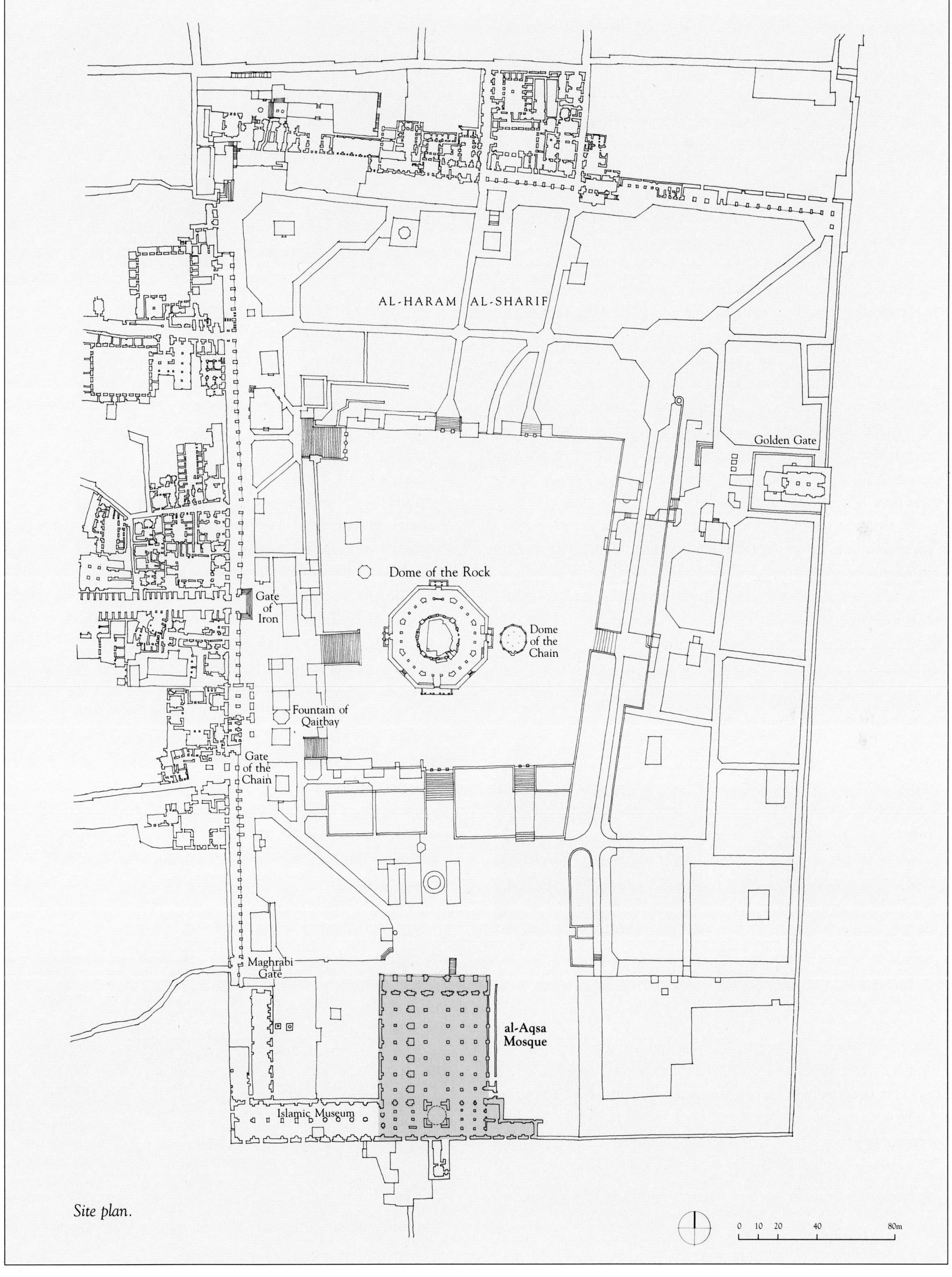
AL-HARAM AL-SHARIF
Golden Gate
Dome of the Rock
Gate of Iron
Dome of the Chain
Fountain of Qaitbay
Gate of the Chain
Maghrabi Gate
al-Aqsa Mosque
Islamic Museum
0 10 20 40 80m

Site plan.

HISTORICAL BACKGROUND OF THE SITE. Jerusalem has been fraught with battles, conquests, and occupations. After biblical times, the Romans, Byzantines, Arabs, Seljuks, Crusaders, Mamluks, Ottomans, and British reigned in succession. The Arabs and Israelis finally occupied both sides of the divided town. The Haram area was at the centre of the dispute. Despite the Israeli occupation, the area remained the heart of Muslim presence in the city.

The site and design of the Dome of the Rock and al-Aqsa Mosque originally had to do with conceptual/cosmological relationships from which these monuments and the Haram area took their historical symbolism and holiness for different religions: The Central Point, site of the sacrifice, source of the four rivers of paradise, and the site of Mohammed's night journey to Heaven *(miraj)*.

HISTORY OF THE BUILDING. Umayyad Khalif al-Walid built al-Aqsa Mosque in 711 A.D. After an earthquake, the Abbasid Khalif al-Mahdi rebuilt the mosque with major changes in its dimensions. The existing structure of the main building, the pendentives, and the drum of the dome are probably part of al-Mahdi's works. Fatimid Khalif al-Zahir restored the hypostyle structure in 1034 A.D. after another earthquake. The dome is on the eastern part of the central nave and comprises an inner and an outer timber structure.

Tremendous changes occurred during the Crusaders' occupation between 1099–1187. After Saladin's major restoration in the twelfth century, the size and plan of the building basically did not change.

Meticulous craftsmanship goes into reconstructing delicate mosaic work to restore it to its original splendor.

Reconstruction of the dome: before and after structural work.

CURRENT RESTORATION WORK. Al-Aqsa Mosque and the Dome of the Rock Restoration Committee makes decisions for the Haram area. It is a semi-governmental body established by Jordanian law. Five of its members live in Jordan, four in Jerusalem.

The Dome. Improvement of the outer dome covering has involved replacing the silver coloured aluminium sheets that were already damaged by the explosions during the fire, and putting back the original covering material which was lead.

Although the timber ribs were generally intact, some portions of the inner boards were seriously damaged by fire and explosions, with some holes exceeding one metre. Damage was also caused either by water or insects. This was all replaced in the first phase of the restoration of the inner dome. The seams between the boards were caulked with twist made from vegetable fibres soaked in glue. In the adjusted boards, epoxy glue was used for the joints and brass screws for the fixing to the timber ribs.

The Paintings. In their first inspection, international experts regarded the situation as hopeless because of the fire damage, but after the re-painted layers were completely removed it was

Painting severely damaged by the 1969 fire.

found that they had helped protect the inner layer from the fire, and it was decided to complete the work.

The restoration was carried out in four phases: The first phase was devoted to the consolidation and reattachment of the preparatory layers of plaster and flaking pictorial surface. The preparatory plaster composed of gypsum and glue presented serious problems of adhesion between the various layers and of separation of the whole from the wooden support. Dangerous loose areas were readhered with injections of a synthetic resin emulsion applied with hypodermic syringes. This work was coordinated with the restoration of the wooden elements.

During the second phase, there were problems encountered when removing the layers of repainting which completely covered the original pictorial surface. The superimposed layers were insoluble and therefore paint removing compounds had to be used. Old but relatively recent stuccoes obscuring original decoration were also removed.

During the third phase, consolidation and cleaning was done and then the missing areas of decoration were repaired. After the final consolidation of the surface, plastering of lost areas was carried out. The missing parts were reconstructed, the reliefs remodelled, and lacunae were filled. A technique similar to the original was used. Firstly, palm fibre was used to cover the wood surface, secondly a scratch coat of gypsum plaster was applied on which preparatory drawings were made,

thirdly brass screws were inserted to act as a mechanical key to attach areas in relief and lastly relief decoration was sculpted. In addition, other small lacunae were filled and the reconstructed reliefs were gilded with gold leaf.

The final phase consisted of pictorial reintegration. A thorough reconstruction of damaged paintings was carried out employing the *tratteggio* technique, an exact reconstruction using fine vertical lines to distinguish reconstructed areas from original ones. Water colour was used as the medium.

The restoration work throughout adheres to the most rigorous criteria of scientific restoration. The results (overleaf) are spectacular.

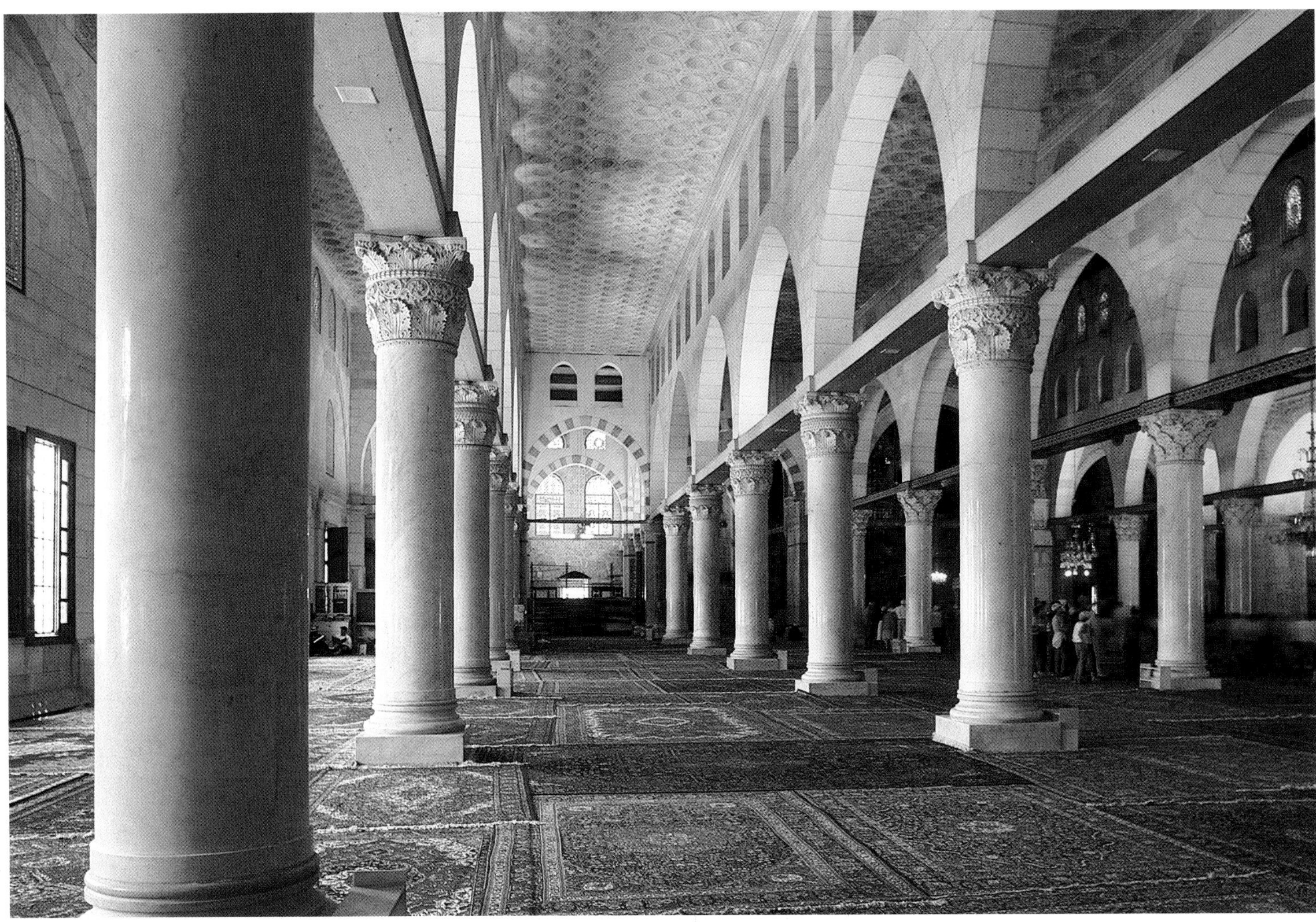

Above: The prayer space is imbued with serenity and spirituality.
Opposite: The interplay of light and shadow highlights the dramatic qualities of the structural system.

LANDSCAPING, REHABILITATION, AND RE-USE PROGRAMMES IN THE HARAM AREA AND OTHER RESTORATIONS. The Committee has enlarged the scope of the project beyond al-Aqsa's restoration to include other parts of the Haram. The annex building next to al-Aqsa was converted to an Islamic museum and library. The fortified gates of the enclosure (the Gate of the Chain, the Gate of Iron, the Maghrabi Gate and the Golden Gate) were restored, along with the Mamluk building façades on the inside. Underground structures were excavated and restored for re-use as the Committee's documentation centre and offices. Restoration work has begun on the structure and decoration at the Dome of the Chain. The women's mosque which is presently used for offices will be integrated with the complex and restored. Other restoration work now in progress includes foundations, *mastabas*, arches and other minor buildings. The development of a large-scale scientific restoration for the Dome of the Rock similar to al-Aqsa is also planned.

TECHNOLOGY, MATERIALS AND PERSONNEL. It is difficult to estimate the local and foreign contributions to this large, multi-faceted programme. The part played by the local team is very important and has been increasing. Two local experts, the resident architect and the master technician, have participated in educational restoration programmes abroad. The international teams set up workshops, which are still in operation, to train their local collaborators in building techniques and the latest scientific research methods. The international experts introduced sophisticated techniques of which the *tratteggio* technique brought by ICCROM is an example. Except for a few materials such as resins, adhesives, coatings, marble, some marble mosaics and gold leaves, most materials were obtained locally. Technology was also basically local. The local team is now able to undertake most types of restoration work on its own. Over a dozen local master craftsmen are now employed in ongoing restoration work such as gilding, masonry, mosaics, leaded-glass work, gypsum work, lead sheathing, drawing and painting. Training in these workshops has enabled the local team to develop large-scale restoration projects elsewhere. Some of the local craftsmen and artisans have moved on to other restoration projects.

TECHNICAL ASSESSMENT. According to all known criteria, related to scientific restoration, the work is of very high quality. It is impeccable in its thoroughness, precision, structural and construction features. The restoration of the inner decoration of the dome is particularly exceptional and aesthetically imposing. In addition, one must consider the less obvious but equally impressive achievements of the scientific approach, that is the training of the personnel, the improvement of their motivation and the systematic and scientific spirit which now pervades more and more new works.

The successful restoration of the dome decoration is an outstanding example of the application of *tratteggio* techniques.

Opposite: Other restoration and re-use programmes in the area include the Fakhriyya Minaret and Islamic Museum (top) and the Sabil of Qaytbay (with scaffolding) in the western courtyard (bottom).
Above: Installing marble wallfacings.

This is especially true when the extent of the damage being repaired is taken into account. The restoration programme and organisational framework are also worthy of commendation and emulation for other large scale operations. It is a further tribute to the managers of this enterprise that they were able to adhere so faithfully and sensitively to the lofty objectives while working in a delicate political context which was never allowed to mar the integrity of the undertaking.

CONCLUSION. The short term objectives of restoring the dome to the most exacting standards were achieved. More importantly, this success was conducive to achieving long term objectives. It enlarged the scale of interventions, built up an impressive local capability for state-of-the-art restoration work, and provided a boost to the participation of Muslims in the protection and conservation of their cultural heritage.

Positive commentary appeared in the local press during and after the restoration works but it still represents the attitudes of a cultural elite. Foreign visitors, especially professionals and scholars are increasingly attracted to and positively react to the works. The Committee and local Muslim community leaders are proud of the restoration. But these positive responses are still superficial, and there is still a long way to go before this appreciation is sufficiently broadly based, internationally as well as locally, so as to ensure that the gains made to date are not threatened, and that the systematic and scientific approach used here becomes the standard methods of approaching restoration work.

The restoration of al-Aqsa Mosque is not only an outstanding technical achievement representing the best of international and local cooperation, it is also an event of momentous religious and cultural import for Muslim communities everywhere. It is therefore all the more gratifying that under the able leadership of Isam Awwad, the Resident Architect, this enterprise has been so successfully undertaken.

YAAMA MOSQUE
YAAMA, NIGER

Completed 1982.
Client: The Muslim Community of Yaama.
Master Mason: Falké Barmou.

MASTER JURY'S CITATION. The Yaama Mosque is a vibrant expression of the total act of building. The community desired and was encouraged to achieve a splendid mosque that would be an appropriate rendering of their devotion to the Islamic faith. The architect, the master mason Falké Barmou, responded to, as well as nourished, these requirements through the use of more advanced techniques and great originality. There is a manifest will to use traditional techniques in a creative manner, to experiment with them and to achieve results that induce a new awareness of their possibilities. Within the local context this is a very striking element: almost everywhere traditional architecture is losing its momentum, but in this case it is very much alive and exploring its possibilities.

It is in such rare situations that the process of construction can be more critical than its accomplishment. It is the moment where the living tradition of that culture is revitalised. By reassessing the collective image within the community, the configuration of the sanctuary is developed. The productive force of the community is then activated and performed through an elaborate integration and coordination of tasks and duties.

Left: The setting sun illuminates the northern tower. The smaller mihrab tower is at the right. Yaama village is visible in the distance.
Overleaf: The striking architectural composition can be fully appreciated from the interplay of towers and roof lines.

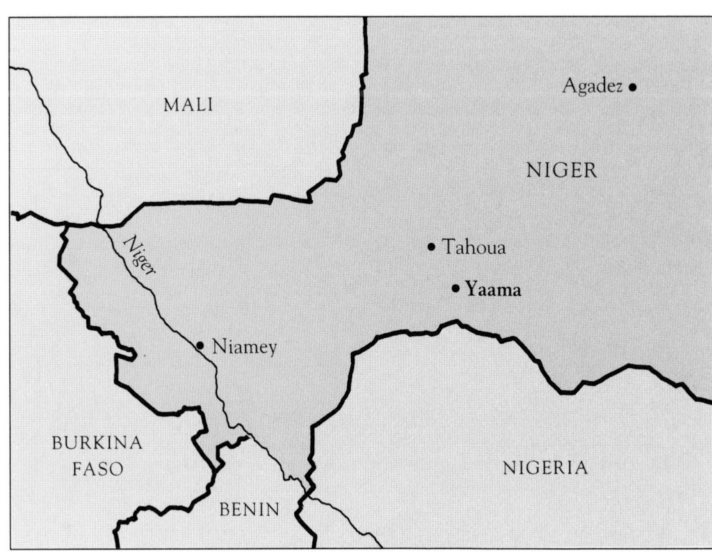

This symbiosis is generated more through a ritual than any rationale of project management and administration. Thus, the whole community participates in a ceremonial where every contribution becomes a sacrificial act to the Glory of God.

This ceremonial is re-enacted and perpetuated through the cyclic renovation, whether maintenance, alterations, or repairs of the edifice. This communal re-creation activates a productive energy which culminates in the contemplative moment of prayer. It is through this conformity, humility and reverence that the masterpiece gradually evolves.

There is an elemental beauty and integration in the whole complex, and a richness and depth in the profuse forms of the detailing. Exterior volumes and massing are simple, vigorous and effective. When the eye travels upwards along the walls of the towers, the growing freedom of plastic expression is very striking indeed and acquires an exuberant symbolic quality. The towers especially intrigued members of the Jury, combining as they do structural logic and discipline with extraordinary creativeness: this austerely functional basis grows into a sculptural manifestation of freedom.

In this architecture we do not see a "primitive" aspect, but a primordial state of being in which men are umbilically bound to Nature. The "regional" becomes intrinsic, and the "particular" extends to the universal. The "rational" is surpassed by the "intelligence of the heart". The "functional" becomes integral and appears in a wisdom that is reflected in the simplicity of operation and the attainment of grace throughout the process, where mastery of craft and perfection of technique result in an embellishment that is essential rather than superfluous. It is an architecture that contains the true symbol reflecting the magic of traditional cultures.

In this architecture, the issue of whether it is new or old becomes quite insignificant.

The members of the Jury are grateful to have an opportunity to recognise that divine spirit manifested within the work of such men.

That the quality of this work is appreciated even outside Yaama is clearly indicated by the enthusiasm with which other villages are seeking to follow its example and solicit the services of the same architect/mason. In an era when traditional architecture is losing ground, this is a remarkable feat.

OBJECTIVES. Until 1962, when the village elders decided to build a Friday mosque, only neighbourhood mosques existed. The village elders defined the major characteristics of the mosque. The structure was to be a simple, rectangular hypostyle prayer hall with the externally expressed *mihrab* as the only secondary volume. They appointed the local master mason, to carry out the construction as his share in the project.

SITE. The village of Yaama is in the Sahel region of Niger, near the northern limit of the rain dependent agricultural

Left: The gentle slope of the domical cupolas contrasts with the sharp edges of the towers.
Top: The fenestration is small but artistically grouped and varied.
Above: The sculptural quality of the material is evident in this elegant treatment of the staircase.

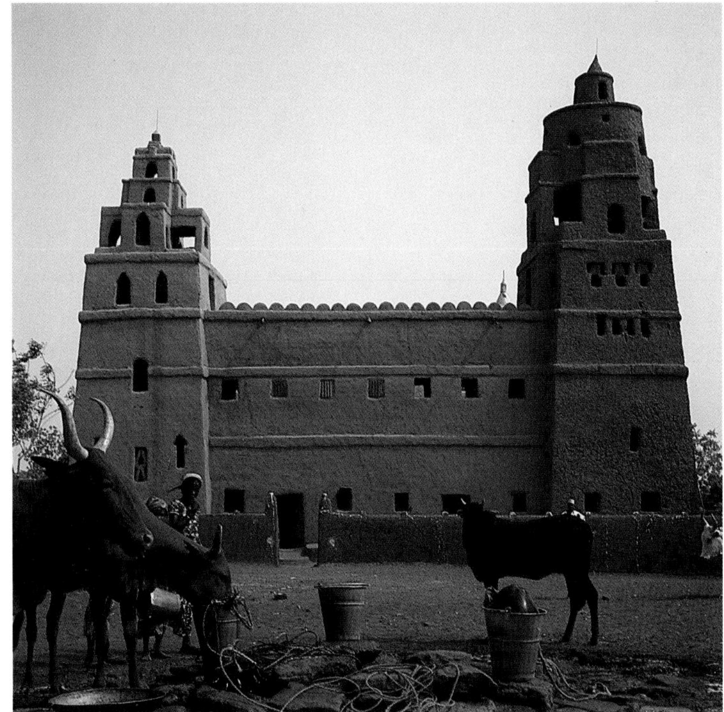

area. Vegetation is mostly sparse, consisting of scattered trees and shrubs.. Large areas hardly have any vegetation and are strewn with gravel and rocks. In the valleys and depressions the vegetation seems luxurious by comparison. The village site is flat but slopes slightly to the north towards a relatively fertile valley.

Village life in this settlement focuses around the Yaama Mosque which is centrally located. The mosque is set in a courtyard. Streets border two sides of the compound. A large open space is reserved for activities on the south side. And a smaller open space separates the east side from the compounds which face it.

HISTORICAL BACKGROUND. The region's present state belies its eventful history. For centuries it was the crossroads of large, autonomous and often conflicting states and interests — the Songhai and Kanem, Mali and Kanem/Borno, Songhai and Borno. Although independent, smaller states in the region and to the south sometimes became integrated into one of the greater powers' authority.

In the last decade of the sixteenth century, the Hausa, already commercially active, took advantage of the fall of the Songhai empire following the Moroccan invasion (1591). They increased their overall share in the trans-Saharan commercial and trade transactions.

Initial contact with Islam occured in 666 A.D. with the expedition of the Arab conqueror Oqba Ibn Nafi in the Kaouar (Bilma). Successive waves of Islamised Berbers spread Islam south. In the eighteenth century, reform movements developed, especially in the Hausa states. This was in reaction to the lifestyles of the ruling classes and the excessive taxes imposed on the poor. The most famous and successful reformer was Osman dan Fodio (1754–1817) who was born near Yaama. He succeeded in founding an Islamic state ranging from present day Burkina Faso to Lake Chad and the Cameroons, and from Birni Nkonni to the Benue river. Osman dan Fodio inspired similar movements in West Africa (Sekou Amadou, El Hadj Omar). His capital was Sokoto, in northern Nigeria about 140 kilometres south of Yaama.

When the dust settled, the frontier between the proponents and opponents of the Jihad was established between Niger and Nigeria. Presumably the area of Yaama-Illéla-Tahoua was outside the Sokoto empire but it was not far from major events or from the strong influence of its large and powerful neighbour.

After a bloody introduction to colonial ambitions (mission Voulet-Chanoine, 1899) the region was finally "pacified" at the beginning of this century. It was integrated into the French colonial empire first as a military territory and then as a colony in 1922. In 1960, the Republic of Niger gained its independence from France.

ACCESS. Yaama is reached by a half-hour drive on a dirt road branching off from the main road Niamey-Birni Nkonni-Tahoua-Agadez. This road becomes the village's main street. The first compound is a kind of youth and cultural centre. The street then meanders into the old village core. It passes near the village chief's compound and intersects another street where some modest shops are located. After the next turn, the mosque appears.

Access to the mosque is through four gates: a main gate with an entrance building in the northern enclosure wall, two closely placed gates in the western enclosure wall and another gate in the southern enclosure wall, facing the open space.

LOCAL ARCHITECTURE. Not far from Yaama, a modern building was constructed from plastered sand-cement blocks and covered with metal roofing sheets. Otherwise, the village

Upper left: The subtle proportions of the full structure can be appreciated from the sense of balance, stability and serenity it provides.
Below: Local village architecture uses the same vocabulary including the domical structures for the granaries.

is almost untouched by such materials and technology. Buildings are made from traditional materials using proven techniques from the past. Houses are made up of independent cells although these may be arranged in continuous clusters giving an urban aspect to the living quarters. The cells can function as a reception room, a sleeping room, a kitchen, a general store, or a shop. And sometimes more functions are served by the same cell. The cells are arranged in the compound so that a functional spatial arrangement is created — the courtyard is divided into outdoor areas that have specific functions: main courtyard, stable, fodder storage, kitchen courtyard, and so on.

Cells are square or rectangular. The rectangular bricks are made in wooden forms and reinforced with straw to avoid cracking. There is no evidence of the traditional pear or cone shaped bricks used in Hausa construction. The structures are built directly on the natural soil after removing the top soil when needed. The masonry is rendered with a straw-mud plaster that is often prepared with other inputs (cow dung, grain husks) and left to mature. Mud is extracted from different pits according to its specific qualities. Different mortar compositions may be used for exterior and interior plastering according to various considerations of suitability. For example, no cow-dung is used for the mosque's plastering since it is thought unsuitable for a cult building. Floors are made of compacted mud with a smooth finish.

The roofs of the main cells are made using two different techniques. In the first, a central wooden post is used to support a system of sloping wooden rafters on which branches or sticks are laid that carry the mud roof. In the second technique, arches made from bent sticks are placed in the walls to form the framework for a shallow dome that is covered with branches and mud mortar. Both techniques give a similar "camel's back" form when seen from the outside. Water from the roofs is evacuated through prominent gargoyles made from earthenware pipes, hollowed palm-wood planks, or hollow shaped pieces of corrugated iron.

Wall openings are few and small. Doors are generally low so adults have to bow to pass. Windows are so small that they are more like ventilation holes than openings for light. With a few exceptions, like the pinnacles on the corners of some buildings, or a modestly sculptured entrance to a house of an important family, the houses are without decoration.

The built environment is harmonious in its forms, its organisation, colours and textures. The most striking feature is formed by the granaries. These structures resemble giant earthenware pots resting on saddlestones raising them from the ground level. The granaries can be filled through an opening in the top, covered with a thatch cover that may be the size of the roof. Steps cut into a tree trunk give access to the top. The technique of making these granaries is more like that used in pottery than in buildings. A shell is made with sausage-like rolls of mud to form a spherical structure about 5.2 metres in diameter. The thickness of the mud shell varies from four to seven centimetres.

PLAN. The main prayer hall is a simple plan. In the east/west oriented rectangle of the outside walls there is a grid of squares: eight squares east-west, six squares north-south. Originally there were 30 columns in five rows (east-west), dividing the interior into six east-west or seven north-south corridors. The *mihrab* was placed on the axis of the central east-west row but slightly off to the south so that it can be seen from a corridor rather than be blocked by the first column facing it. During the 1975–1976 repairs, the third column of the central row, counting from the *mihrab*, was removed and the large square was covered with a dome-shaped roof. In the 1978–1982 dry seasons four corner towers were built at the extremities of the north and south walls. They enclose two galleries that each have a second floor with access through staircases in three of the towers. The staircase of the fourth tower starts on the second floor.

The span between the columns was determined by the length and bearing strength of the available beams for the original roof and by the spatial requirements for Muslim prayer.

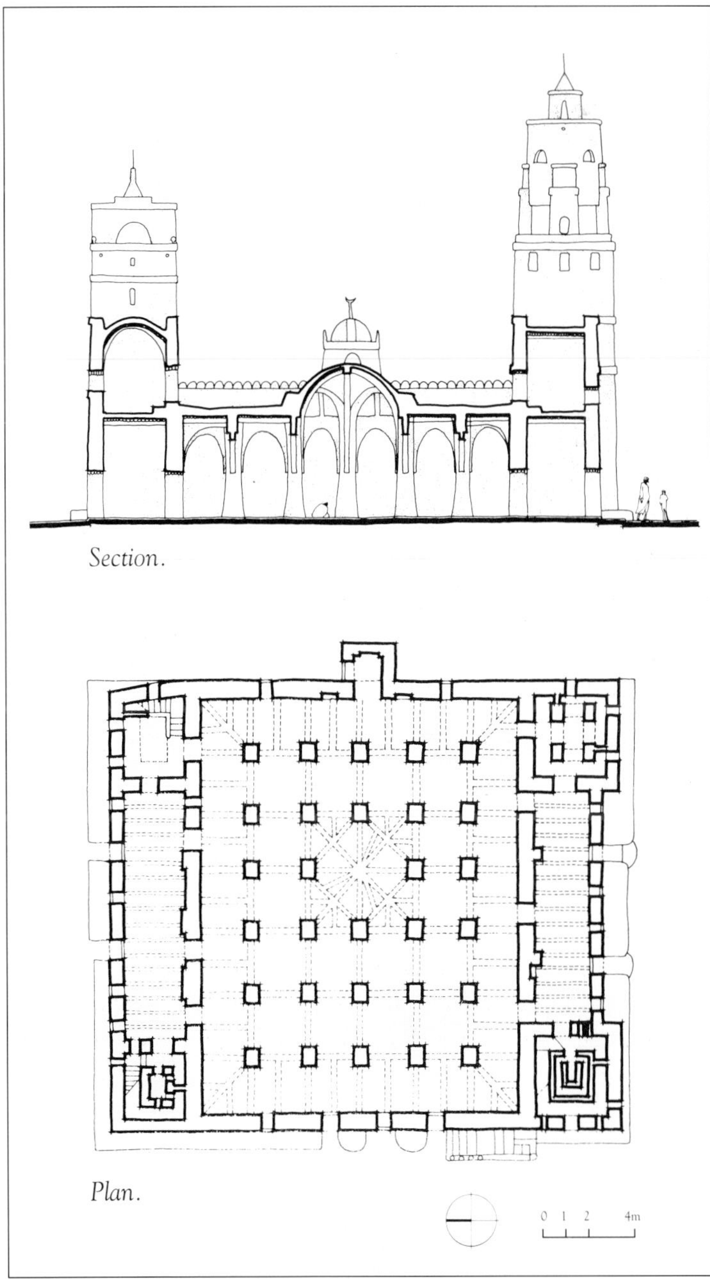

Section.

Plan.

People pray in rows running north-south and the span of the corridors accommodate a person kneeling in prayer and leaves a circulation space behind him. The dimensions of the columns along the east-west axis correspond to the space needed for a person kneeling down for prayer. The dimensions of the north and south galleries are less determined by the activity that occurs in them.

The outdoor space is an irregularly shaped courtyard in which the mosque is placed near the east wall, leaving a small passage between the *qibla* wall and the courtyard wall which is common in this type of mosque.

Religious activities can take place on the more spacious sides of the courtyard. The most important space is to the north, where the main entrance is. Banks are built along the walls inside the small entrance building. An exterior sculptural staircase is built against the west wall. It leads to a platform from which the *muezzin* usually calls. In the southwest corner of the courtyard stands a small building where water is kept in a jar for ablutions.

EVOLUTION OF DESIGN. About 12 years after its construction, the mosque needed repair. In 1975, Falké Barmou repaired and embellished the mosque. The opportunity was taken to instal a new arch supported roof and a dome. The addition involved removing a column, thus opening up a central square among the rows of columns, a striking feature in this type of mosque. The next step in the transformation of the mosque was the addition of four corner towers which enclose two-storey galleries. This work was accomplished during the 1978–1982 dry seasons. The entrance building was also built during this time.

From a severely sober structure it was transformed into a monumental building. The corner towers and the two-storey galleries changed its exterior appearance. The system of arches and half-arches and the dome, replacing the simpler horizontal beams as a roof support, changed the interior.

Below: Falké Barmou, the master mason, preparing mud bricks.
Opposite: Community pride is evident among the village population.

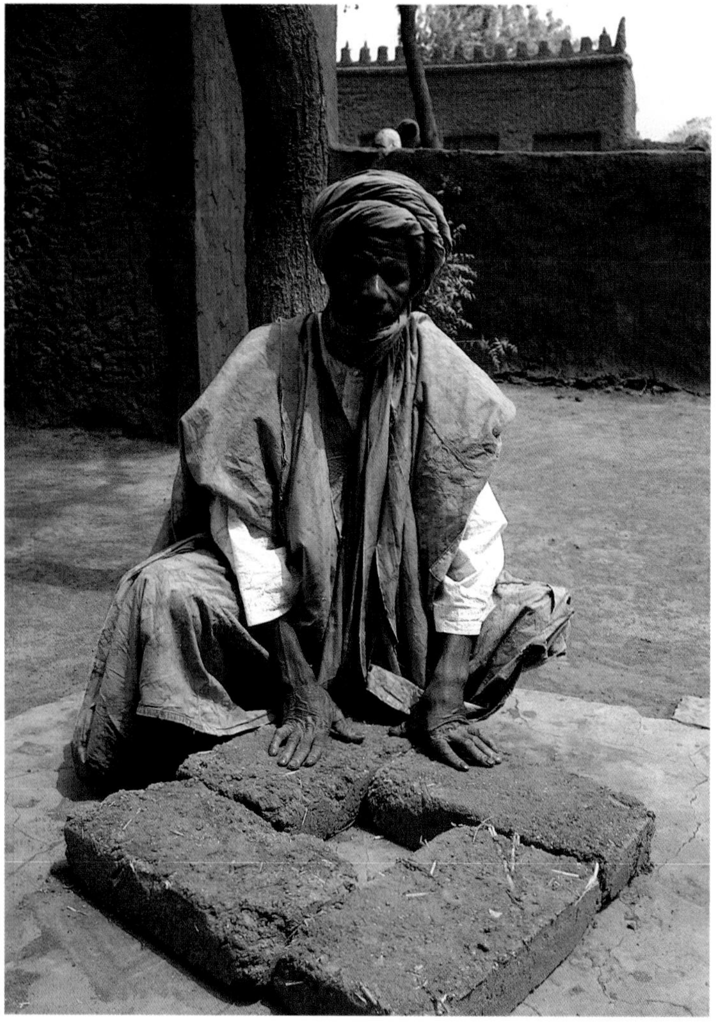

FORMAL ASPECTS. The mosque has a monolithic base, low on the east and west sides and high on the other sides. Towers project from the four corners. Each tower is a single form with heavy-set tapering walls crowned by a lighter sculptural element. The towers are reminiscent of the stepped minarets found in this area.

Frieze-like bands mark the elevations at irregular heights. They would seem to mark the levels of floors or roofs but this is not always the case. Crenellations of half circles decorate the parapets and rounded cones sometimes mark the corners. The *mihrab* has recently received a superstructure in the form of a crown.

MATERIALS AND TECHNOLOGY. Innovative use of traditional techniques and materials characterises the construction of the Yaama Mosque. Wood of any available kind was used as well as mud mortar and in some instances cement stabilised mortar finished with lime wash. Materials were local with the exception of a few minor items like nails and some wooden planks.

The technology employed is commonly used in the region and has been for generations. However, some of the applications of the general technology may have been developed by the mason/architect. Bricks were made by the villagers and brought to the site before and during construction. Mud for mortar was extracted and provided in the same way, then prepared on site. Wood was also furnished the same way. Scaffolding was simple and so were the mason's tools.

TECHNICAL ASSESSMENT. The mosque is accommodating and well conceived. Climatic performance is similar to that of other mosques. No special measures were taken to prolong physical comfort. The second floor galleries offer better conditions during the humid season since they are better ventilated. But this does not seem to have been a major consideration in their construction.

The choice of materials was traditional and therefore harmonious. Traditional techniques were used creatively.

The mosque faces similar maintenance problems as other mud buildings in the region. The mosque needs continual

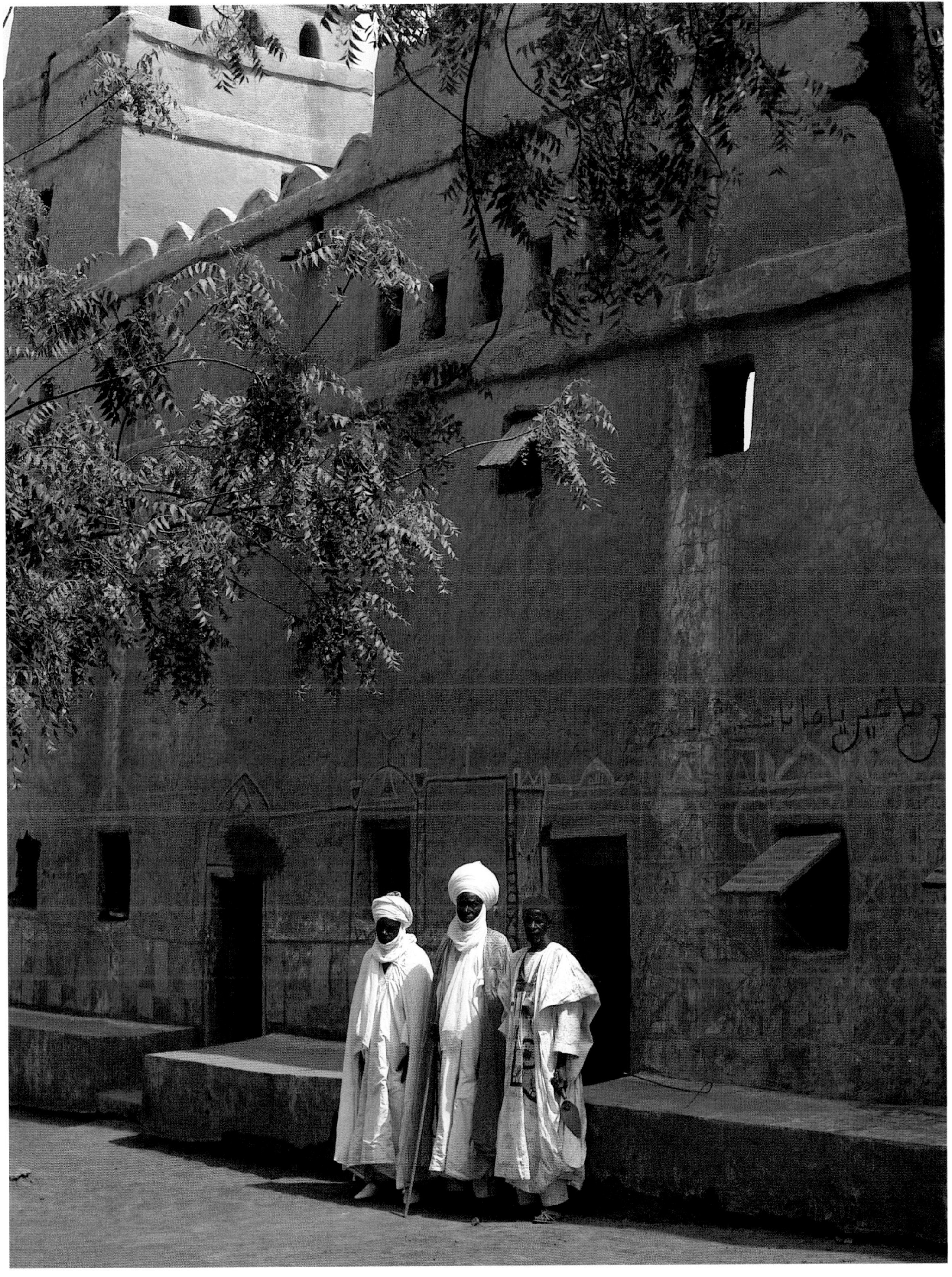

maintenance work, especially rendering. Large areas of the outside walls are eroded. Some parts have not been rendered at all, while other parts have been rendered with a cement stabilised mortar that does not hold up well. Some interior walls and part of the galleries' roofs have not been finished. The lack of finishing and maintenance is linked to the production process. The building's parts were constructed over a long period and consequently have varying maintenance needs. The work was carried out as a community project and not on a contractual basis. The architect/mason volunteered instead of being commissioned. In short, by the nature of its production process, the mosque is a permanent construction project. This ongoing process may be as important as its product.

The mosque's design is partly conventional and partly innovative. Its basic structure is simple and sound. And even if it was built by successive modifications and extensions, the result is homogeneous — as if a clear conception of the final stage existed from the beginning.

AESTHETIC ASSESSMENT. Treatment of masses and volumes is conventional and simple. Wall openings are few and small with no emphasis on their disposition in the base volume. This accentuates the monolithic character of the mass. In the middle part of the towers they become part of the composition and in the upper parts there is a balanced interplay of masses and voids.

Entering through one of the vestibules the quality of the sober spaces is marred because parts of the walls are unfinished. Nevertheless they are a pleasant, cool transition from the bright outside sun light to the comparative darkness of the interior of the main prayer hall.

The prayer hall gives the impression of a dimly lit forest of columns from which the arches spread like branches. The space below the dome enhances the interior by accentuating the troglodytic character of the corridors.

The dark interiors (opposite) contrast sharply with the brilliant outdoor light providing a sense of calm and mystery (below) and focusing attention on the imam near the mihrab during prayer times (right).

CONCLUSION. The project objectives were achieved. The mosque is functionally adequate and widely appreciated. Other villages seek to follow its example. The architect/mason has been called upon to assist neighbouring communities. The client/user response was positive and the entire process was adapted to the socio-economic situation.

Technology and architecture are local and regional. Some elements may have originated in northern Nigeria, others in the Sahelian region. Essentially it is a mosque in the tradition of Hausa Islamic architecture, though the technology used in making the arches may be unusual for this type of building.

The building was financed by the village community. Everyone contributed in proportion to their ability to do so. Some people made mud bricks; Others carried them to the building site. Women carried water for brick and mortar production while others cut and gathered wood. Those who could contribute cash were free to do so. Gifts of grain were also welcome and distributed to workers. The owner of the land where the mosque was built waived his rights to its use.

Making the Yaama Mosque more widely known could help maintain traditional architecture. The inevitable evolution towards modern construction techniques could become more gradual, allowing more scope for a transition with continuity, and safeguarding local and regional architectural vocabulary. Then craftsmen and users may integrate outside influences rather than have to adopt them in their entirety which results in a break with tradition.

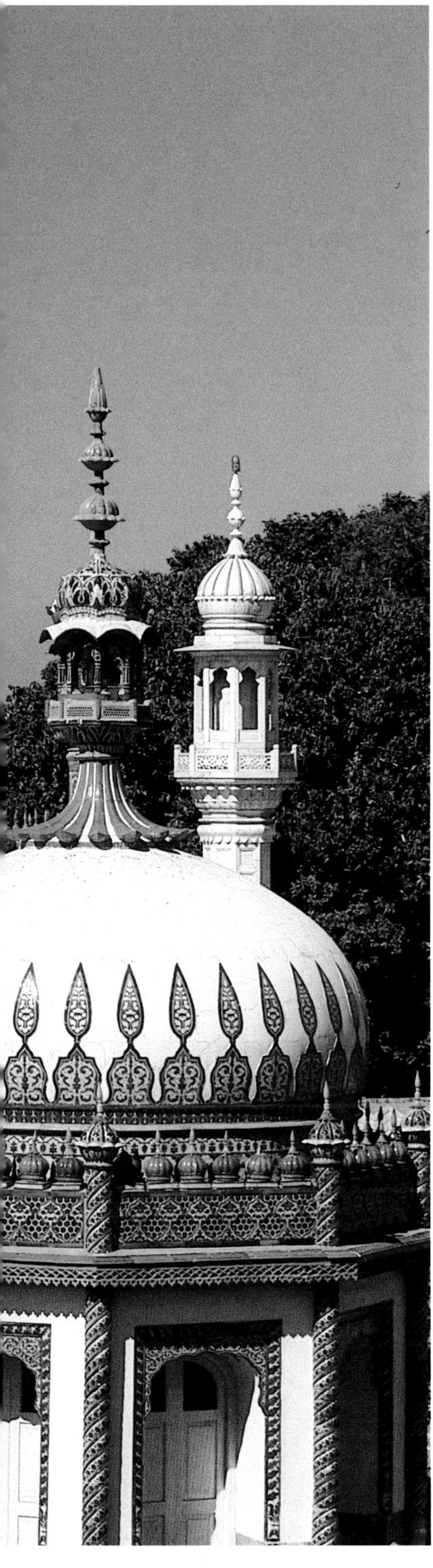

BHONG MOSQUE
BHONG, PAKISTAN

Completed 1982.
Patron: Rais Ghazi Mohammad.

MASTER JURY'S CITATION. The Award is made in recognition of a significant attempt by a single individual to create a local centre of learning and building crafts by establishing, in the village of Bhong, in the district of Rahimyar Khan, a complex of buildings consisting at first of a small mosque, later converted as a prayer hall and library for women, a *madrasa* and residential dormitories for students and visitors. All the infrastructure required to serve the complex, such as roads and irrigation channels, were also built by him for the use of the people. After some years the grand mosque was conceived and constructed.

The complex, as it stands today, is fully utilised by the local population and its acceptability by the people has been well established. The *madrasa* is still functioning, although with less importance than in the past; at its peak, students came from Turkey, Afghanistan and Iran.

This tremendous effort of Rais Ghazi Mohammad extended over a period of nearly 50 years from 1930 to 1980, during which time he engaged specialised craftsmen in various trades from all over Pakistan, and master masons to decorate the buildings of the complex. He patronised and encouraged these

Left: The domes of the main complex with the dome of the small mosque in the foreground make a dense and interesting composition.
Overleaf: Interior of portico leading to the main prayer hall shows rich and lavish detailing.

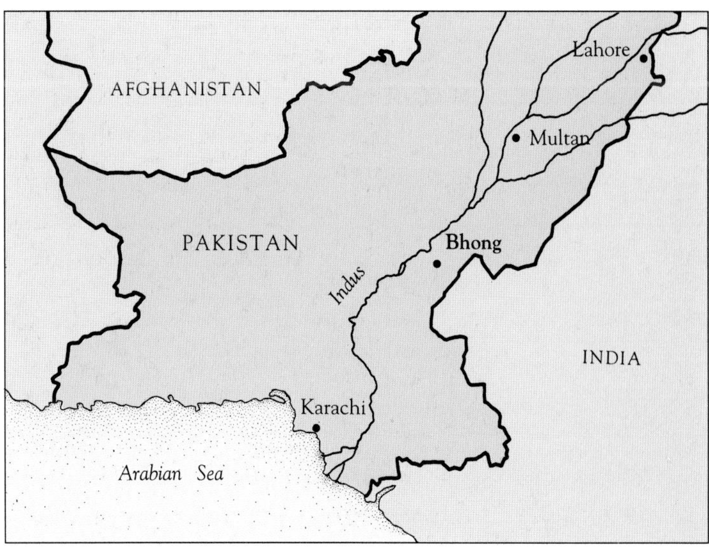

سورة الضحى
بسم الله الرحمن الرحيم والضحى والليل اذا سجى ما ودعك ربك وما قلى

Above left: Exuberance of decoration and attention to detail is evident in finials and parapets.
Above: View of main complex from the garden. The main prayer hall is on the right with the women's prayer-hall and library on the left.
Right: Cross section of the main complex matching the view shown above.

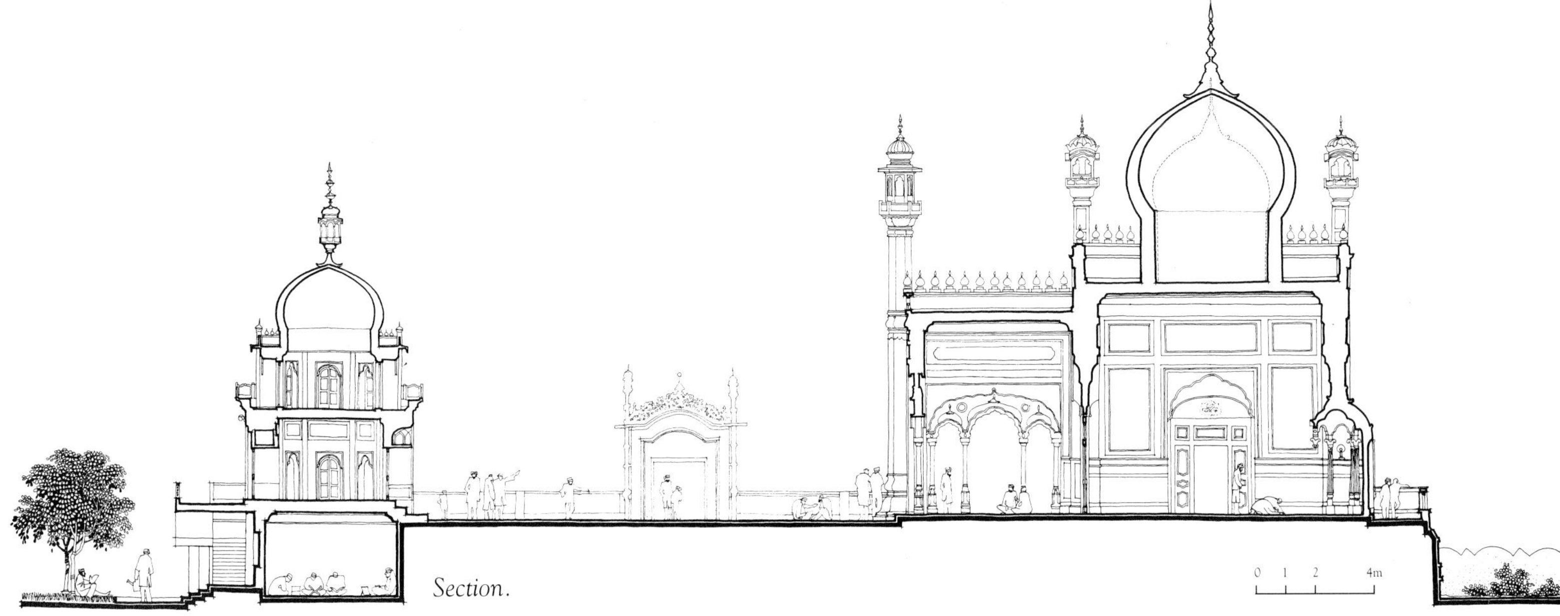

Section.

craftsmen and set up a workshop for their training; and a large number of these craftsmen have been subsequently employed in the restoration of monuments by the government. Thus he made a monumental effort in the revival of traditional crafts.

The achievements of the master craftsmen over two generations deserve to be recognised. It is sometimes thought that the quality of the architecture produced lacks authenticity in a country with a long historical and architectural tradition. But the buildings are of particular interest because of the skill with which the craftsmen have chosen and brought together vastly different materials and techniques. They have evolved a new kind of craftsmanship by choosing existing, manufactured elements and recombining them in original and judicious ways. This new creativity uses mass-produced elements to generate surprising meanings from new contexts and juxtapositions.

In giving the Award to this building complex the Jury wished to make an acknowledgement of the diversity that enriches society. "Popular" buildings might be a little different from buildings derived from indigenous craftsmanship. The populace might love them, and, therefore, they have an immense significance for ordinary people — in spite of the fact that architects might hate them.

Below: The main gate is covered with ceramic tiles of exceptional detailing. Below right: The rear (west side) of the building also shows significant attention to decoration.

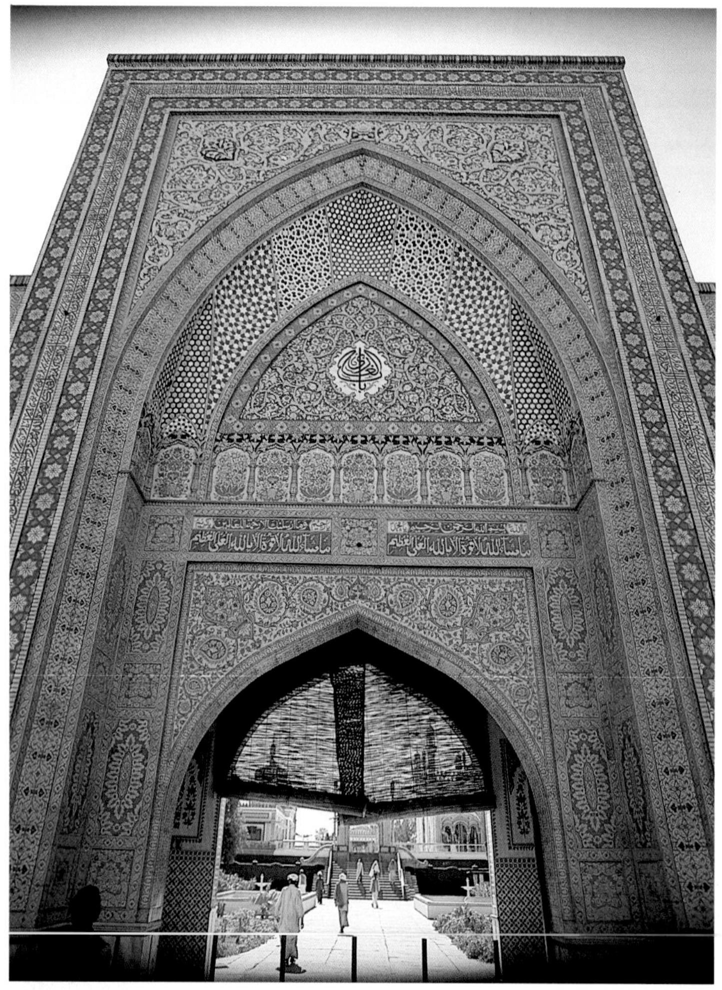

Bhong represents a monumental achievement in these terms. It enshrines and epitomises the "popular" taste in Pakistan with all its vigour, pride, tension and sentiment. Its use, and misuse, of signs and symbols expresses appropriate growing pains of an architecture in transition.

OBJECTIVES. Completion of the large mosque concluded the complex which was started in 1932. Rais Ghazi Mohammad intended to create a congregational mosque that would appear as an outstanding building, a centre of learning, and an employment centre for building craftspeople.

SITE. The Bhong estate is in southeast Punjab, Pakistan. It covers several scattered villages, the most important being Bhong village where the landlord, Rais Ghazi Mohammad, has his quarters. This is a region of large estates and powerful landlords. It is hot and dry, but where irrigated with river water, it is fertile.

A wall surrounds the village of 5,000 inhabitants, the mosque complex, and the landlord's compounds. Bhong is accessible by a small paved road and by train.

HISTORICAL BACKGROUND. Early in the 1930's, Rais Ghazi Mohammad built a small mosque on his property. Later he undertook the construction of a palace for himself. While the palace was being built, he decided to demolish the mosque and replace it with a larger one. This larger mosque was built on a raised platform to prevent moisture infiltration from the ground and so that the palace would not overpower it. This mosque now shelters the women's hall and the library. Rais Ghazi apparently felt that this building was not grandiose enough to compete with the palace and proceeded to build an even larger mosque on the same platform. This became the main prayer hall.

The great mosque was part of a complex conceived, directed and funded by Rais Ghazi over several decades. The development of this complex included the growth of infra-

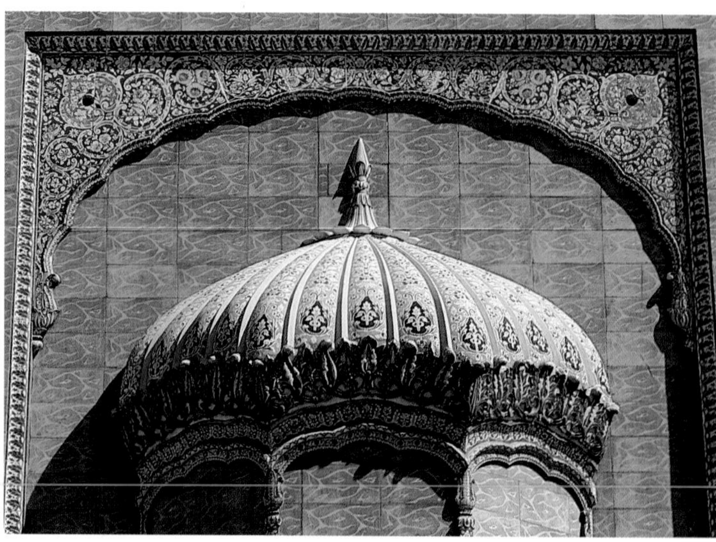

structure; a market, roads, installation of electricity, irrigation works and bus and railroad lines. In his compound, he built the palace, the mosques, a *madrasa*, and rooms for students, plus a house for family guests and service quarters.

Rais Ghazi wanted the mosque to be the most glorious of these buildings. Specialists were gathered from all over Pakistan and India. Master masons and craftsmen from Rajasthan; calligraphers and painters from Karachi. Craftsmen for the artificial stonework and most of the unskilled labourers were hired locally from Bhong.

LOCAL ARCHITECTURAL CHARACTER. Excluding the urban examples, regional architecture is characterised by a rural type of one room, one storey, mud or baked brick buildings opening to a court enclosed by high walls, which may take additional buildings if needed. Decoration on the houses is subdued. It consists of some treatment of the main facade and of the ventilation openings.

Villages are made of clusters of this type and their skylines are silhouetted with domes and small ornamental minarets of mosques. In contrast to the houses, these mosques have intricate and colourful decoration. Highly decorated, to the point

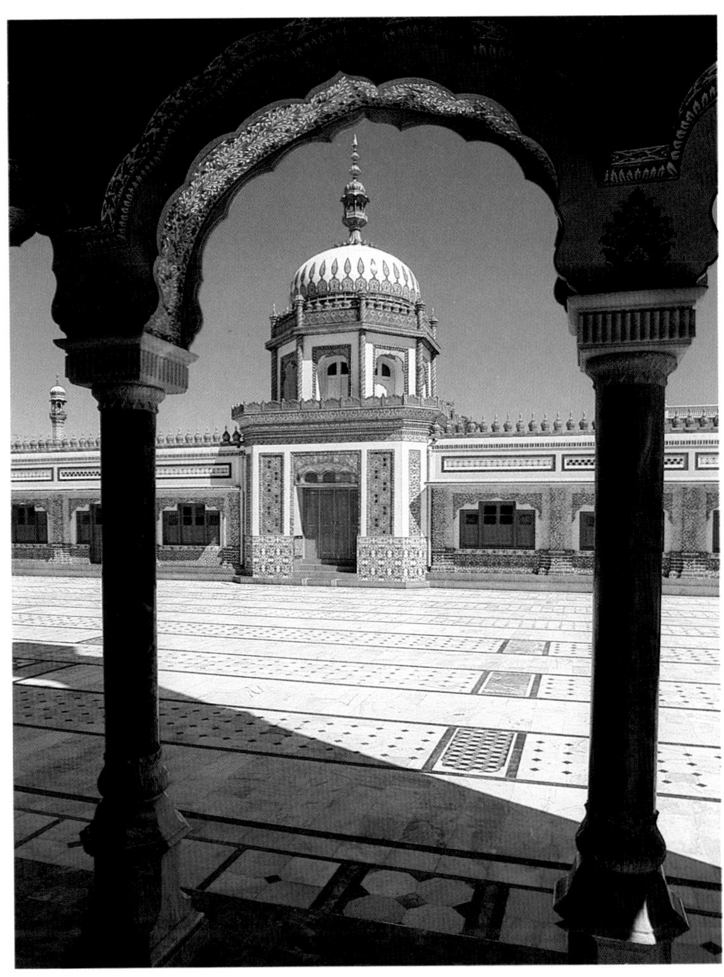

Right: The entrance to the small mosque, with the women's prayer hall and library, viewed from the portico of the main building across the courtyard. Below: Detail of porch decoration shows exquisite finishing.

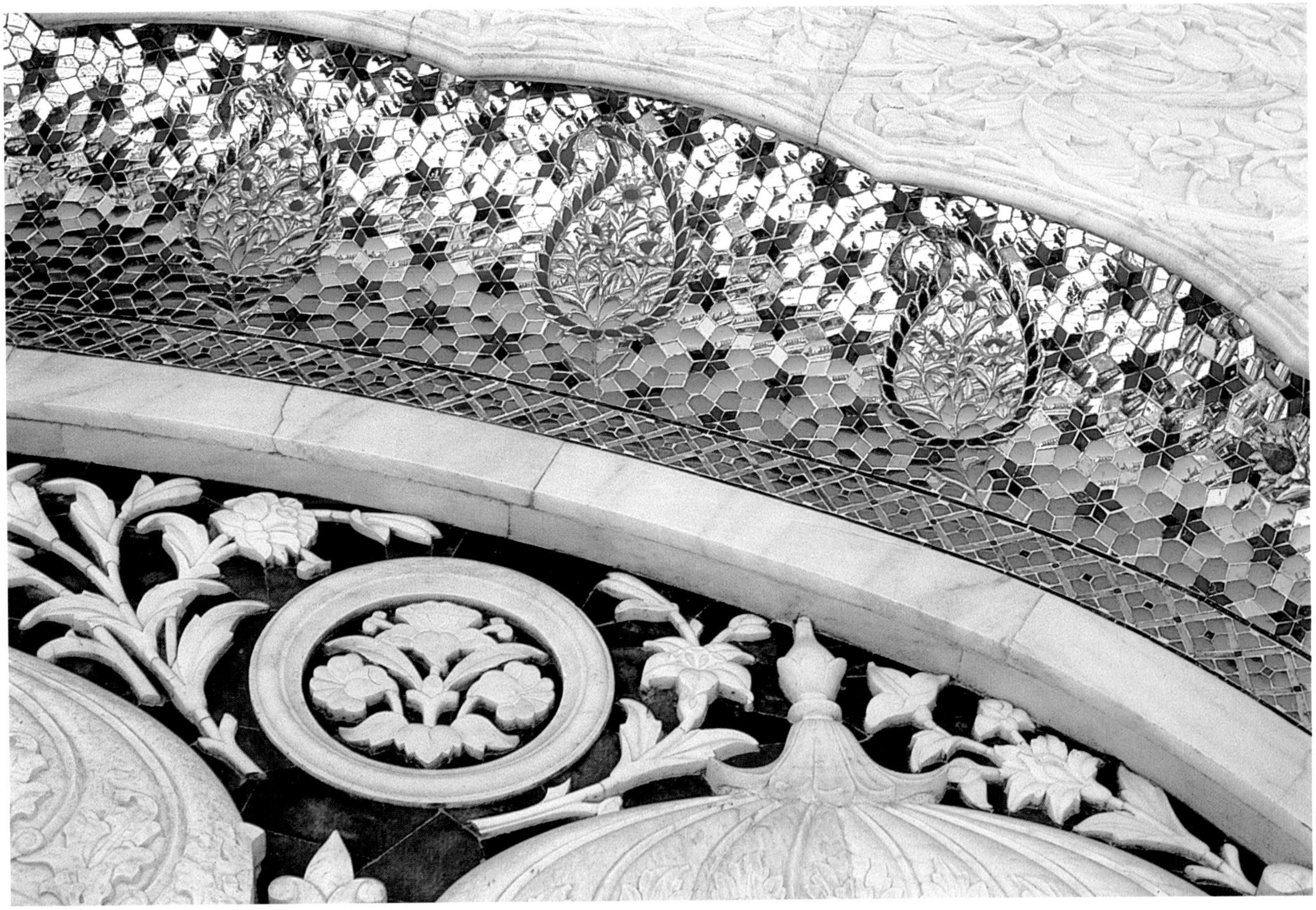

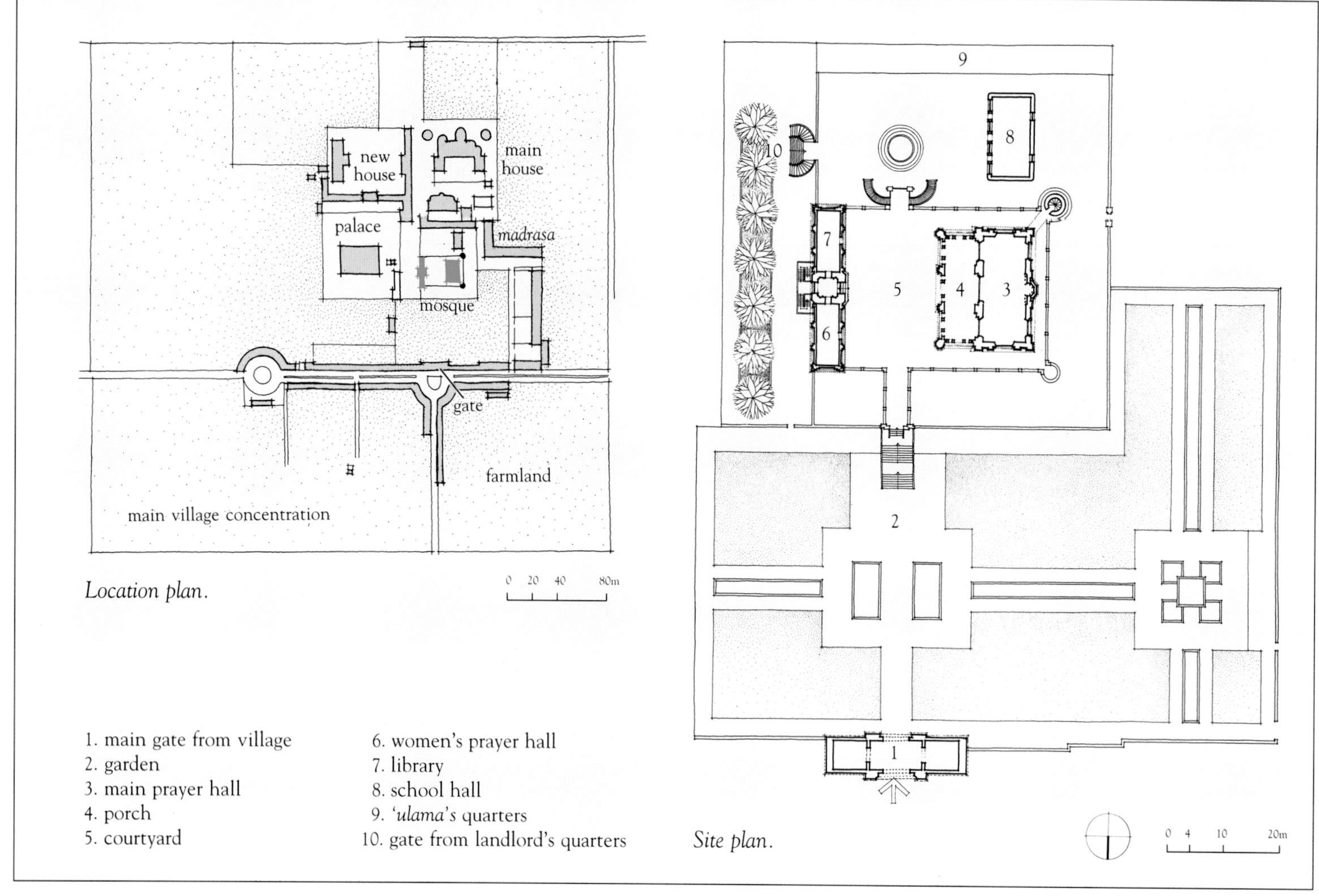

Location plan.

Site plan.

of saturation, three-domed mosques with many small ornamental minarets accenting the corners and entrance are common in the Islamic part of the Indian subcontinent.

DESIGN. The mosques are on a three metre high platform which contains storage space and workers' quarters. An ablutions pool, the school and guest accommodations are found at an intermediate level. The *madrasa* and student rooms are located even lower. The mosque garden surrounds the north and part of the east side of the complex. A private gate marks the entrance to the garden, along with a water channel which defines the main axis leading to the mosque.

The two mosques complement each other in terms of massing and shaping space. Some spatial relations are easily identified when looking at the plans. The proportion of the platform is based on a relation of 2:3, as is that of the courtyard in which the dimension "2" of the platform becomes the "3" of the courtyard. This and other relations are visible in the placing of the buildings and in their proportions.

Externally, the two mosques are treated differently. The small mosque is mostly covered with glazed tiles. The walls of the main mosque are lustreless materials — marble in the porch and marbleised cement tiles covering most of the building.

Internally, the mosques follow traditional models. In the smaller mosque, painted calligraphy and floral motifs on the walls and ceiling co-exist with marbleised industrial tiles. Coloured glass and mirrors are used in the stucco and wood tracery of the walls and ceilings of the main mosque.

The mosque garden is geometrically organised along two perpendicular axes defined by ponds. The main axis connects the courtyard with the main gate to the village and is intersected in the middle of the secondary axis which leads to the side entrance of the garden. The ablutions area is set in a covered recess of the wall to the left of the main entrance. It consists of a row of taps and footrests along a shallow trough.

MATERIALS AND TECHNOLOGY. When construction started, there were no roads, or electricity. Most of the materials were bought in bulk by river and then carried by ox cart to the construction site.

Materials and crafts ranged from the traditional (teak, ivory, marble, coloured glass, onyx, glazed tile work, fresco, mirror work, gilded tracery, ceramic, calligraphic work and inlay) to modern and synthetic (marbleised industrial tile, artificial stone facing, terrazzo, coloured cement tile and wrought iron). Bricks and wood, except for some Burmese teak, were locally aquired. Marble came from Peshawar and Quetta, except for black marble that was imported from Europe. Glass and mirrors came from Karachi; Multan supplied glazed tiles, mosaic, woodwork and painting.

Rais Ghazi used modern materials freely in the ancillary buildings, such as the gates, the small mosque and the porch of

Top: The richness of the decoration reaches a peak at the mihrab of the main prayer hall.
Left: The women's prayer hall is more simply, but elegantly, decorated.
Above: The details include complex floral patterns.

the large mosque. He applied only traditional materials to the mosque interiors. His intention was to represent as many forms of vernacular craft and Islamic religious architectural features as possible using a combination of traditional and modern materials. This intention was not founded on any specific theory of architecture or notion of a thematic treatment of materials and/or spaces. Rather, it was the articulation of one man's internal vision. His insights guided every selection of material, every step of the execution.

Reviving local craftsmanship was a major achievement of this project.

TECHNICAL ASSESSMENT. The mosque complex performs well as a religious centre and as a focal point for community activity.

There are ample openings in the mosque on all sides and they are oriented to catch prevailing winds. Ceiling fans are used in the main prayer hall. Direct light is regulated by wood shutters and fanlights with coloured glass on wood tracery in the western side of the main prayer hall.

Materials were chosen with attention to quality, sound performance and ornamental value. The marble balustrades of the roof on the main mosque are finished only on the outside. This is a common cost-cutting device.

The mosque requires continuous maintenance. Ageing has already taken its toll on the glazed tiles from Multan. A shortage of water in the pool and in the ponds in the garden (because of the limited supply of electricity to power the pumps) has impaired the visitor's appreciation of the building. This is especially unfortunate in the case of the forecourt pool since the water was to reflect the elaborate ceiling paintings.

Nevertheless, ongoing efforts to restore these elements are bound to enhance the overall effect of the composition.

AESTHETIC ASSESSMENT. The masses of the complex are imposing but do not overwhelm the neighbouring constructions. Creating a raised platform was a major achievement, since it provides a better scale for the relationships between the main and ancillary buildings. The overall conception, however, is quite eclectic in both design and style.

Rais Ghazi borrowed stylistic elements from monuments in Lahore, Iran, Spain and Turkey. He mixed these with the Western colonial elements of the 1940's, which appear in the guest houses and market. The borrowing from different sources is fanciful and unencumbered by any leitmotif or thematic structure. These are not cases of artful "resonances" or "echoes". They are the product of a boisterous gusto reminiscent of the vitality and vulgar insouciance of the self confident millionaires of nineteenth century America. Decorative materials and techniques are equally eclectic. The palace is a hybrid of colonial architecture, local decorative techniques and modern materials. The local decorative techniques and elements are clearly kindred to the very lively decoration found on buses and *jeepneys* in this part of the world.

At times, it seems there is a purposeful design against an established order. For example, some of the medallions in the courtyard floor, made in regular diamond patterns of black and white marble are juxtaposed with other marble elements disposed at random. This makes the pattern look as if it exploded.

The ultimate purpose of the whole design is grandiosity which is manifested among other things through size, and the excessive emphasis on decoration, the choices of materials, the complexity of technique, sheen, and colour.

There are unpleasant features such as the aborted minaret that stopped at being the staircase to the mosque roof. The buildings lack discipline of essentials that would make them model pieces of erudite architecture.

CONCLUSION. The project satisfies the needs of the local population and increasingly attracts visitors.

The effect on the local environment was tremendous especially considering that the mosques were part of a larger complex. Infrastructures were developed. Workshops were set up to train craftsmen in skills that had until now been passed down from father to son. At the peak of construction, the project employed 1,000 workers and trained up to 200 craftsmen. The workshops helped to revive and preserve these indigenous crafts and have contributed enormously to the government's conservation efforts.

Furthermore, it played an important role as a centre of learning especially before secular schools came to the region.

Rais Ghazi initiated *Lunger*, a practice that is continued by his family. It entails providing meals, and blankets for visitors to the mosque irrespective of their income as well as to students and to the poor of the village.

On the whole, the Bhong Mosque deserves attention, not so much for the architectural merits of composition or aesthetics, but because it reflects a statement of local, contemporary taste that runs counter to much that is dear to international and regional architectural theory and criticism. The issues it raises about the relevance of the intellectual pursuits of architects and critics as well as the inadequacy of unbridled populism help define an important agenda for practicing architects in the Muslim world today.

HONOURABLE MENTIONS

SHUSHTAR NEW TOWN

THE IMPROVEMENT OF KAMPUNG KEBALEN

ISMAILIYYA DEVELOPMENT PROJECTS

SAID NAUM MOSQUE

HISTORIC SITES DEVELOPMENT

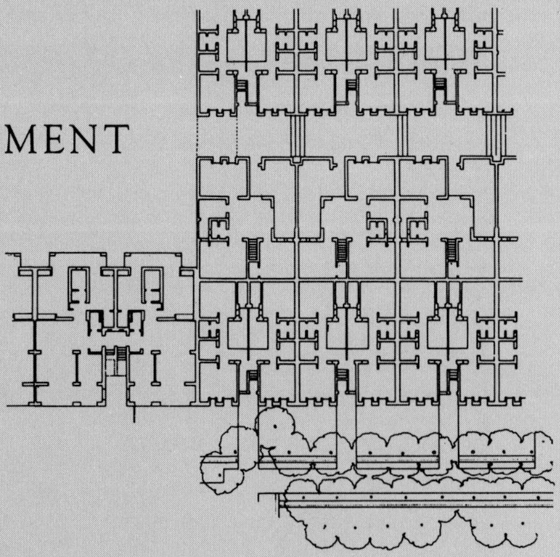

SHUSHTAR NEW TOWN
SHUSHTAR, IRAN

Completed 1977 (Phase I), and ongoing.
Client: Karoun Agro-Industries Corporation, and Iran Housing Corporation.
Architects: D.A.Z. Architects, Planners and Engineers.

OBJECTIVES. In 1973, the Karoun Agro-Industries Corporation decided to build a satellite town to house the employees of a sugar cane processing concern nearby. The inhabitants were to be provided with the advantages of individual housing as well as communal facilities and infrastructural services. Development of Shushtar New Town was also intended to revitalise the old town and to accommodate expansion generated by industrial growth in the region.

SITE. Shushtar New Town, in the Khuzestan Province in southwest Iran, is across the river from the old city. The site is exposed, undulating and bounded on the eastern and southern sides by the Shatit River. Most of the land is desert.

HISTORICAL BACKGROUND. Shushtar is one of the oldest fortress cities. It was an island city on the Karoun river during the Sassanian era when it also became the winter capi-

Left: The elegant brickwork frames the pedestrian street designed at a human and inviting scale. The streets are primarily for pedestrians and act as outdoor extensions of the homes where neighbours may interact in a peaceful atmosphere.
Overleaf: The rythmic geometry of the roofs captures the unifying theme of the underlying composition. Old Shushtar appears in the distance.

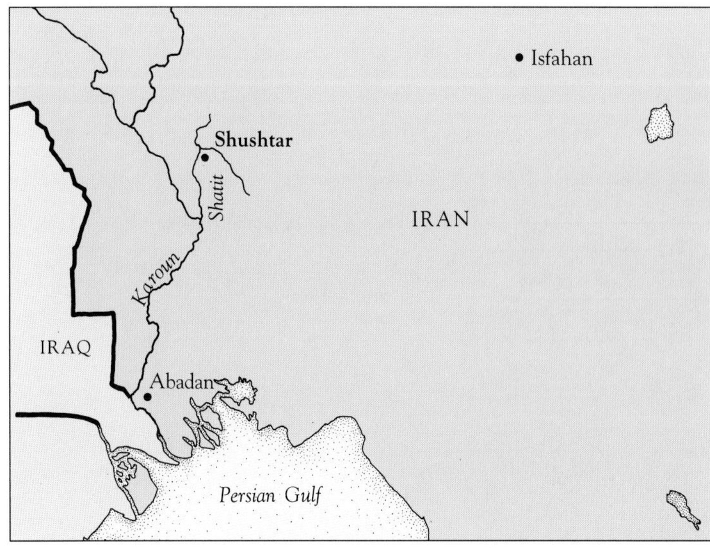

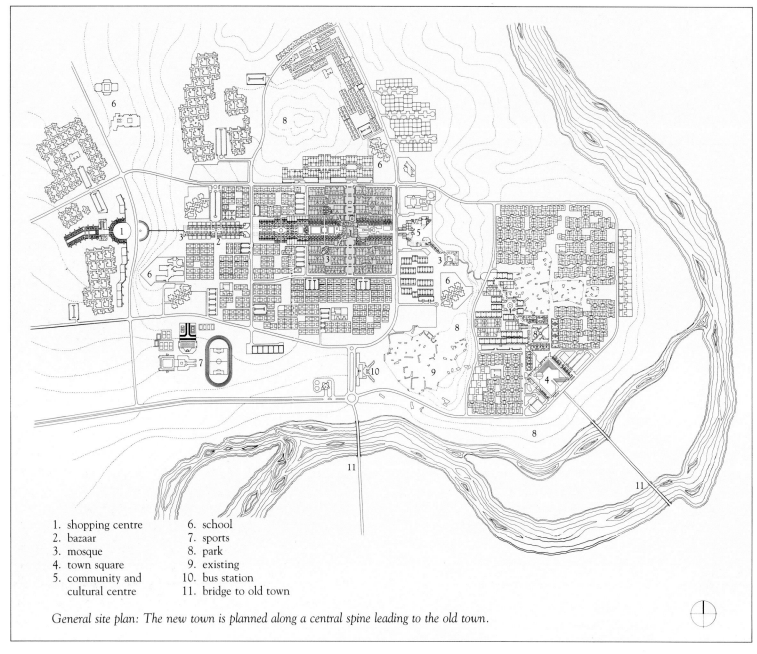

1. shopping centre
2. bazaar
3. mosque
4. town square
5. community and cultural centre
6. school
7. sports
8. park
9. existing
10. bus station
11. bridge to old town

General site plan: The new town is planned along a central spine leading to the old town.

Left: The neighbourhood pedestrian boulevard is defined with a brick wall and a row of trees. Above: Small private courtyards with open-to-sky space and greenery are woven into the fabric of the architectural composition.

tal. The fortress walls were destroyed at the end of the Safavid era from 1502 to 1722 A.D.

The river was channelled to form a moat around the city. Bridges and main gates into the city were built to the east, west and south of the city. Several rivers near Shushtar are conducive to the extension of agriculture. Sugar cane, the main crop, dates back to the Sassanian period, 226 to 641 A.D.

The system of channels and subterranean water, *qanat*, supplied water for domestic use and for irrigation. *Qanats* connected the river to the internal reservoirs of the assembled houses. Traces of these *qanats* are in the crypts of some houses. Subterranean channels were used to supply water during the war when the gates were closed.

LOCAL ARCHITECTURE. Most of the Shushtar's buildings belong to the Safavid era. The foundation of the city is attributed to the Abassid dynasty. Buildings are mostly of mudbrick. They became a formal arrangement of four rooms separated by the cross-formed barrel-vaulted *iwans*. The central intersection was an open courtyard. This form was also found in the layout of the fortress city with the fortress walls forming a square. The main streets, the transepts, and the houses occupied each quarter. The castle or administrative centre, mosque, baths and schools were at the geometric centre. The cross-form was also the symbol for the ancient Iranians.

The basic structural form during Zoroastrian times was the Fire Temple, usually built near a river or on top of a hill. This was a large, tall structure, square on plan, with each side open to the sky. The cross-form plan evolved from this "room" with *iwans* extending laterally to form barrel-vaulted passages leading to four domed rooms — one at each corner of a larger square plan as well as into the centre square courtyard.

In the desert, it was found that a dome over the central courtyard produced a pleasant cooling effect. The roofed patio, *tanabi*, became a place of general assembly. Consequently, the courtyard was moved to one side of the house. Depending on the climatic conditions, which vary north and south, the direction of access into the house, and the occupant's wealth, two courtyards were built — one on the hottest side and one on the coolest. The courtyard on the street side was usually lower than the street level. This facilitated the flow of rainwater into a central pond in the patio that stored water for drinking and irrigation.

The car and other modern innovations brought some changes. New roads, connecting the main gates and passing through the city neighbourhoods were built at the cost of old bazaars, caravanserais, and public baths. New buildings, now about ten per cent of the building stock, are constructed of materials such as steel, concrete and kiln fired bricks.

PLAN. The design of New Shushtar follows the pattern of traditional Iranian architecture which is introverted, taking its forms from climatic constraints, available local technology and the country's culture.

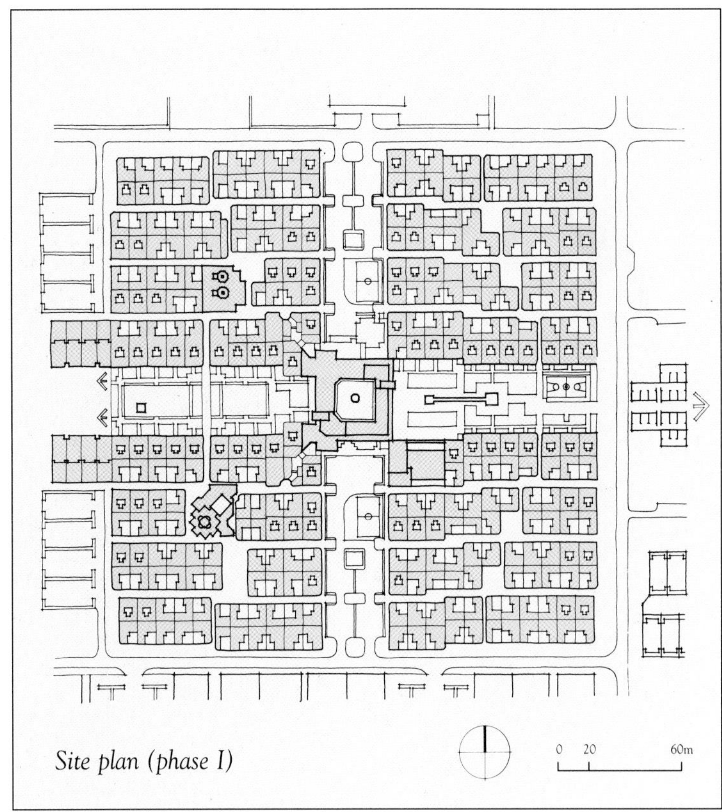

Site plan (phase I)

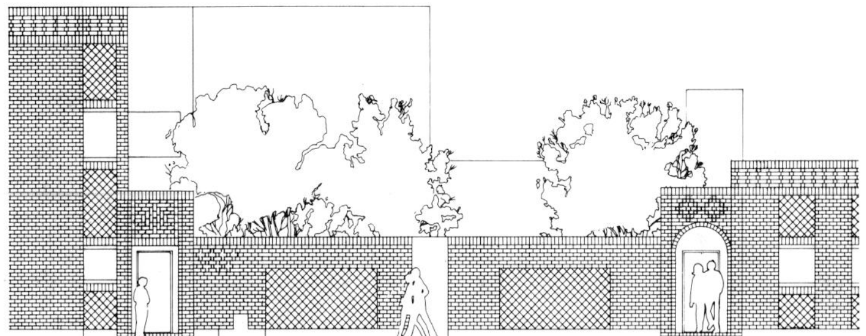

Internal street elevation.

The massing of the buildings is a parallel arrangement of mostly one and two storey houses that are clustered along narrow streets following traditional models for privacy. The treeless, narrow streets are paved in bricks. The top floor of the apartment houses is built along the street front to maximise shading. Most residential streets are east/west oriented so that houses catch the prevailing north wind. To further foster privacy and neighbourhood activity, automobile traffic is prohibited in the residential areas.

The public buildings grouped along the east/west pedestrian boulevard are designed to give neighbourhood identity to each block in the traditional manner. Public buildings are set at an angle to the grid, which organises the entire plan, to punctuate the dense residential fabric. In the residential clusters, each of the 650 units use the traditional organisation with multifunctional rooms arranged around a courtyard and roof terraces for sleeping. Most rooms in the two to four room houses are 5 metres x 5 metres; Smaller ones are 3 metres x 3 metres or 4 metres x 4 metres. Thick walls, small windows and

Above: Attention to proper use of materials, from street paving to walls and parapets provides a subtle setting in harmony with the climate and the environment.
Opposite: Individual residences demonstrate the same mastery of scale and massing that are found throughout the project.

street entry through a small protected space are also traditional features. Parapet walls surrounding the roof provide shade.

MATERIALS AND TECHNOLOGY. Traditional construction methods were used by the local contractor who used local materials and mostly local, unskilled labour.

Load-bearing walls are built of locally made bricks and footings are of concrete. Roofs are framed with steel beams supported by the walls or by engaged piers. Conventional shallow barrel vaults in brick span four metres between the beams. Ceilings are finished with plaster. Floor finishes are terrazzo tiles on concrete slabs. Wall finishings are mostly of brick but sometimes in kitchens and bathrooms, cement is used. Door and window openings are circular brick arches or lintels. Streets are paved in patterned brick with tile borders.

TECHNICAL ASSESSMENT. Residents are satisfied with the houses and the layout of the apartments. However, one of the problems is that some of the houses and apartments overlook each other which infringes upon privacy.

The houses were designed to cut down excessive heat and sunlight. The layout and natural lighting follows the local customs and architectural tradition. Inhabitants have installed air conditioning units or evaporation air coolers to cope with excessive summer heat and lack of air flow. Most of the roads are on an east-west axis. Thus, houses face either south or north which is conducive to shading. Other features that contribute to shading are the construction density, the spatial distribution of the houses, the varying dimensions of the streets, and the difference in height of the houses.

Technically, this complex follows the norms and standards of architectural production prevailing in the Third World. After eight years, ageing is average whilst maintenance and cleaning are mediocre.

AESTHETIC ASSESSMENT. The project is faithful to the traditional architecture of the region. It is reminiscent of traditional Islamic vernacular urban architecture, which encourages social interaction. By the design of its spaces, it generates a communal sense. The contrast between the vast public spaces and the dense fabric of the streets and residential neighbourhoods offers visual and spatial diversity.

The topography and slight slope of the ground allow the buildings to be arranged in a harmonious composition displaying an interesting variety of spaces.

Opposite: Public spaces are open and inviting to the residents. The connecting elements add architectural interest to the overall space.

Right above: The strong lights and deep shadows heighten the dramatic effect of the meticulously executed arches.

Right: Dramatically effective use of bricks is one of the hallmarks of this project. Note the treatment of the corner on the left and the lace-like tracery on the wall.

Perspectives change as the street and surrounding buildings step up towards the centre of town. Level changes vary the wall heights of the facing rows of houses. Decorative brickwork grilles beneath the windows, on the roof parapets, and the entry arcades also provide ventilation. Mosaic tiles mark entries to the houses and embellish street signs.

CONCLUSION. The project was planned in five stages, to be completed in 1985. Construction started in 1976, and most of the first stage was completed by 1978. The first stage was planned to function as an autonomous unit and accommodate about 4,000 inhabitants. Political unrest in 1979 disrupted the work. During the hiatus in construction, squatters and refugees moved into the complex, overcrowding and straining the infrastructure and services.

The remaining phases of the project are under way. Half of the site of phase three is now functioning and the work is ongoing depending on the availability of funding.

Shushtar New Town is relevant to the cultural values of Iran and maintains a continuity with the past, allowing cultural expression. Its example of urban housing is unique as a large scale new town conceived and produced by local designers and builders attempting to satisfy indigenous life styles and contemporary goals of industrial development.

THE IMPROVEMENT OF KAMPUNG KEBALEN
SURABAYA, INDONESIA

Completed 1981.
Client: The Municipal Government of Surabaya.
Planners: The Surabaya Kampung Improvement Programme, with the Surabaya Institute of Technology, and the Kampung Kebalen Community.

OBJECTIVES. Under severe demographic and economic pressure, the municipalities of Indonesia have sought a cost-effective way to upgrade the extremely dense, poor neighbourhoods known as kampungs. In the first Aga Khan Award Cycle in 1980, the Kampung Improvement Programme (KIP) of Jakarta was given an award in recognition of its widespread impact on the lives of so many by significantly improving their environment, and for having traced a replicable way to deal with this massive problem. The present programme in Surabaya shows the extension of the KIP to other areas of the country and reaffirms the Award's commitment to the social dimensions of interventions in the built environment of Muslim communities.

Left: Paved and drained streets are the backbone of the Kampung Improvement Programme. Residents tend to upgrade the houses fronting the street.

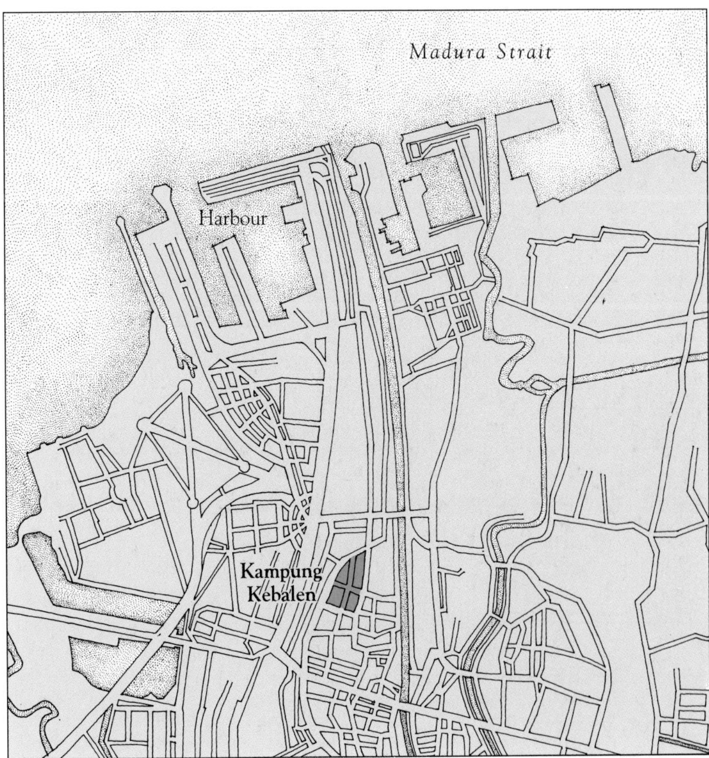

The involvement of university professors and students makes the Kampung Kebalen Improvement Programme particularly noteworthy.

People in Kampung Kebalen were poor and lived under flimsy shelters. Potable water, electricity, and sanitation, were lacking. Flooding of the passageways and houses during the rainy season exacerbated the problems. Thus, the goal was to alleviate the extremely low standard of living endemic to the kampung areas by providing badly needed basic infrastructure to the human settlements.

SITE. Surabaya is a major industrial city in the northeast corner of Java. It has a population of about 2.5 million. Almost one-quarter of the city area is covered by kampungs.

In urban areas of Indonesia, most of the low-income population lives in kampungs.

Kampung Kebalen is in the north of Surabaya, near the harbour. Its average density is 800 people per hectare and the average monthly household income is U.S. $35 to U.S. $65. Land belongs either to individuals or is rented to them by the government for 25 years, renewable under certain conditions.

The terrible and unsanitary conditions prevailing before upgrading (left above) have given way to functional streets with appropriate drainage and usable space after upgrading (left).
Below: The paved and upgraded streets are reclaimed for the people and become a major catalyst for upgrading deteriorated housing on either side.

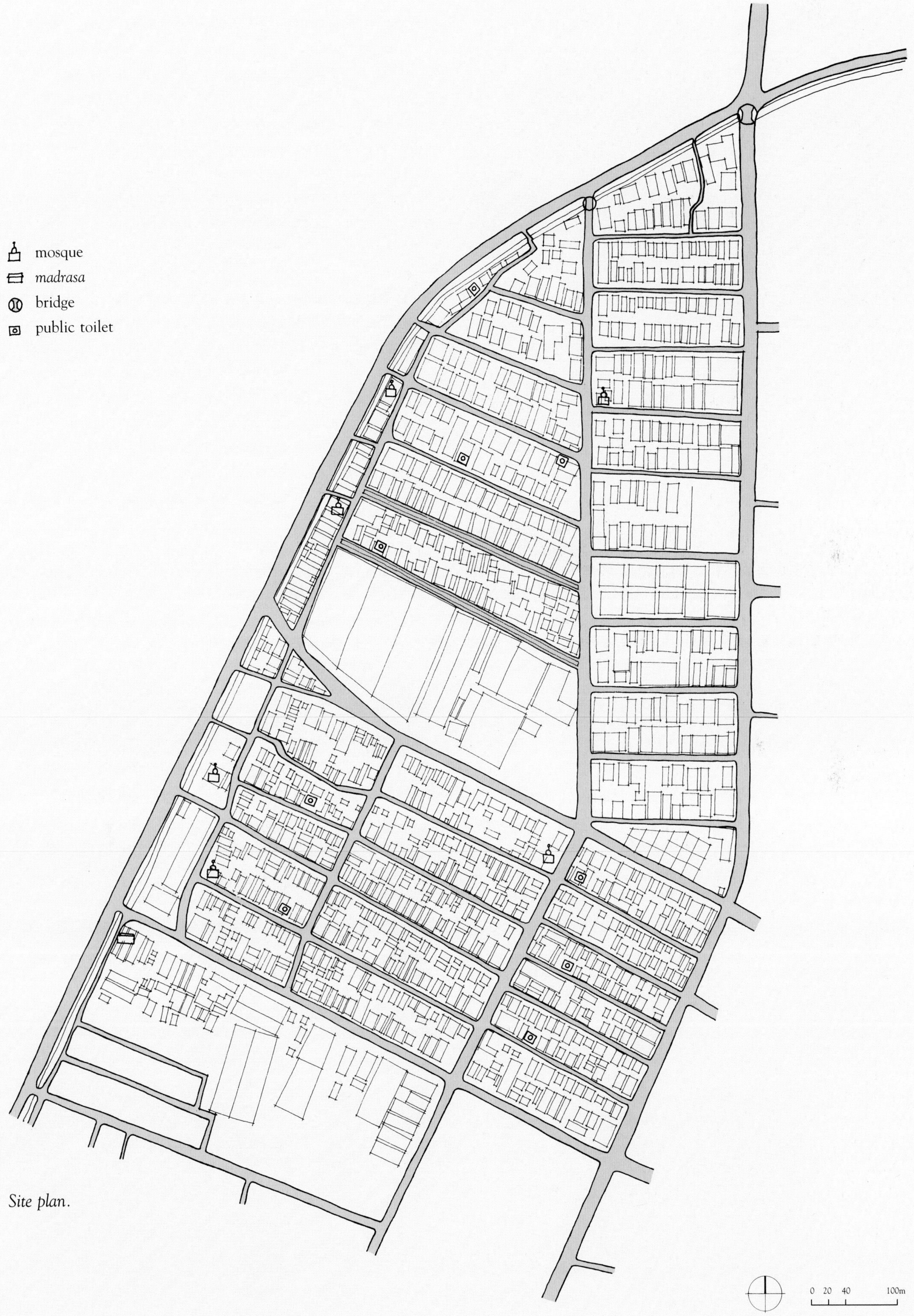

Site plan.

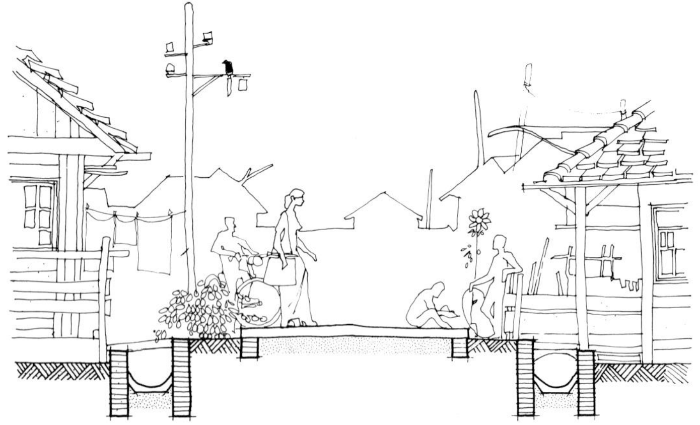

Section across typical lane.

The local communal water point (top) is made more inviting and easier to use. Typical houses (right and lower right) have been upgraded and the frontage landscaped by the owners.

LOCAL ARCHITECTURE. Kampungs are unplanned urban agglomerations that evolved out of villages and were bypassed by urban development. Mainly residential, they also house industries. They are generally built on flat ground a few metres above sea level.

Densely packed single storey houses within networks of narrow alleys characterise the kampung fabric. Housing types are difficult to classify in kampungs since development occurs rapidly according to the socio-economic circumstances and mobility of the family.

The front elevation is usually given special care, while side elevations can be finished in many ways with different building materials; a composite structure in the vertical as well as the horizontal surfaces is common. This type of structure is cheap in material and labour costs. It also offers many options for future adjustment. Multi-storey buildings are still rare in the kampungs of Surabaya.

The main determinants of the models of houses are climatic, economic and functional. The general architectural character of the kampung dwelling is a wooden or composite wooden/masonry construction with a sloping roof covered with reddish tiles.

DESIGN AND CONSTRUCTION. The design of the programme was influenced by the need for an inexpensive method of providing basic infrastructure with a minimum of technical and administrative resources. The premise was that the programme was the best way to improve the residential environment given the constraints and that better public infrastructure would encourage residents to improve their homes. The alternative was to put the limited resources into low cost housing construction schemes, benefitting few of those in need. The programme had to be easy and inexpensive to implement. This meant cheap, standardised components and a simple implementation procedure.

The inhabitants of the kampung were to be provided with the basic infrastructure including footpaths, drainage, water and proper sanitation.

The basic model used for the houses was made from bamboo. After the KIP's improvements, the inhabitants started to restore their houses with the available means and materials. The spaces, materials, and colours vary though the characteristics of the traditional Javanese house remain. The houses flank each other, and sometimes a narrow aisle leading to a private courtyard behind a house separates them.

TECHNICAL ASSESSMENT. The people are satisfied with the improvement of their living area.

The problem of flooding was resolved by the improved

drainage system. Inhabitants have enhanced the natural lighting and ventilation of their homes. Many have planted trees, flowers and shrubs.

Maintaining vehicular roads, schools, clinics, and garbage disposal is the responsibility of the public works, education, health and sanitation ministries. Cleaning, repairing footpaths, draining ditches, and collecting garbage are the responsibility of the kampung committee who are supposed to organise a maintenance squad from community members. Voluntary community funds pay for the squad. Individual households take care of footpaths and drains in front of their homes.

MATERIALS, TECHNOLOGY AND LABOUR. The technology used is characteristic of kampungs in Indonesia. Materials are almost exclusively cheap, locally produced bamboo and timber. The entire labour force is Indonesian. People from the kampung were actively involved in the construction process and choosing materials.

Ultimately, this project is about people. Street vendors and families (above) have reclaimed their environment and are now masters of their destiny. Most important, community pride in the achievements is evident everywhere (below).

CONCLUSION. The improvement of Kampung Kebalen started in 1980 and was completed in 1981. The programme development was initiated in 1976 and the design process was carried out in 1979. The improvements to Kampung Kebalen totalled U.S. $400,000. All funds were from the government of Surabaya with a loan from the World Bank. The large impact of this very small sum was made possible by the diligent collaboration of the municipality of Surabaya, the professors and students of the university and the inhabitants of the kampung.

Following the improvement of Kampung Kebalen, a revival has taken place in the cities of northern Surabaya. The constructive forces that the programme has released have begun to spill over generating broad-based community improvement programmes.

ISMAILIYYA DEVELOPMENT PROJECTS
ISMAILIYYA, EGYPT

Completed 1978, and ongoing.
Client: The Governorate of Ismailiyya.
Planners: Culpin Planning.

PROJECT BACKGROUND. The project demonstrates an alternative approach to deal with the problem of massive urban growth with its concomitant problems of inadequate shelter for the poor and the resulting unsanitary conditions. Rather than trying to build public housing which invariably proves too expensive and too small, this approach puts the emphasis on upgrading existing settlements, and on community self-help construction. The government is to provide the basic infrastructure and the access to land titles and credit. The result is not a project but a "process", that is making a real difference in the quality of the lives of the inhabitants. Not only is the environment upgraded, but the poor are now given some power to shape their own future and improve their lot. This increased self-reliance among the most economically vulnerable groups is as important an outcome as the improved sanitation systems.

The Ismailiyya Master Plan begun in 1974 addressed major land reclamation, rural settlement and development, tourism, and housing. It argued for an alternative to the conventional public sector social housing programme, which although in-

Left: The Hai el-Salaam district shows the consolidation proccess which is taking place. This is evident (centre right) where a single storey dwelling is being exterded upwards to create a three storey walkup unit. The pride of owners is exemplified by the fact that many have painted the façade of their individual dwelling.

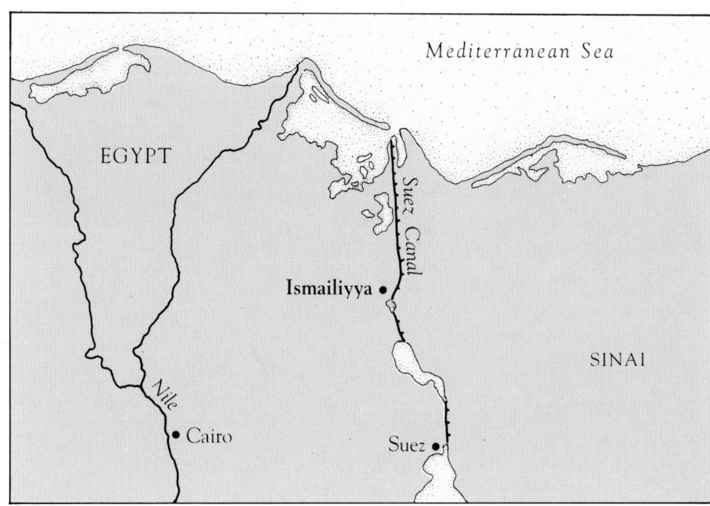

Left: Abu Atwa shows the same characteristic consolidation process from the simplest beginnings (foreground) to more elaborate, multi-storey structures in the background.
Above: The introduction of drainage is a key improvement and is at the heart of the success of this project.

tended for the poor could only be afforded by ten per cent of the population. An alternative use of the public subsidy was proposed to produce more social housing for the lowest income range. It would also encourage home ownership that has been prohibitively expensive except for the highest income families. An education programme was designed to train local administrators to implement the policies. Development was to be self-generative with gradual improvement of the service infrastructure, using income from land sales.

SITE. Ismailiyya is on the shores of Lake Timsah by the Suez Canal, about 135 kilometres from Cairo. Sweet water from the Nile is channeled into Ismailiyya through a canal that also irrigates mango and palms groves to the south and west. There is a dry, desert climate with hot summers, cool winters and only a few days of rain per year.

Hai el-Salaam is a northern extension of the city that had uncontrolled growth. Abu Atwa, formerly an agricultural settlement, is about four kilometres south of Ismailiyya. Both sites were planned and surveyed focusing on plot rationalisation. Existing settlers were given legal rights of occupation, frequently with adjusted plot boundaries. There were emergency relocations, where the owners of houses situated in road reserves or on sites needed for public purposes were given priority in the allocation of new plots. Public housing was provided for those who could not afford to build. Rules for allocation of new plots were drawn up and these were surveyed, demarcated and offered for sale.

HISTORICAL BACKGROUND. Ismailiyya was founded in the second half of the last century. It was originally the headquarters of the Suez Canal Authority and then became mainly a service centre. During the Arab-Israeli conflict, from 1967 to 1973, the Suez Canal region became a war zone. Consequently, people were evacuated, and Ismailiyya, like the other canal cities, was damaged.

After the hostilities subsided, the government resolved to reconstruct the canal cities and to undertake redevelopment programmes. Financial assistance from the United Arab Emirates went towards constructing 17,000 new apartments. Meanwhile, the government was funding 10 to 15 per cent of the housing units being built annually as public rental housing. Privileged Ismailiyyans, mainly government employees, had access to this housing. But many with low incomes were ineligible and could only get housing in the private rented sector or in squatter accommodation.

Almost half of the available housing was in "informal" areas mostly on government owned land near the desert. An annual *kehr* rent allowed use of the land, which in turn provided limited security of tenure.

LOCAL ARCHITECTURE CHARACTER. About 80 per cent of the Hai el-Salaam houses were individual homes built on plots averaging one hundred square metres. In "informal" areas, they are predominantly single storey, mud brick or rammed earth. In "formal" areas, they are baked brick, often with a reinforced concrete frame, allowing for future upward extension of the house.

In Abu Atwa, construction mostly followed a traditional village style, using a different technique (rammed earth) than most buildings in Hai el-Salaam.

DESIGN AND CONSTRUCTION. Security of tenure was the highest priority among households, followed by piped water, roads and sewage. Lack of security prohibited individual investment in buildings.

Those already living in the project areas were designated as the "target population" meaning that these income groups had to be able to afford access to the project. To upgrade areas, it was vital not to force out the population. In the new development, a mix of income groups were accommodated, giving low income groups at least their proportional share.

It was assumed that households would spend 20 per cent of their income on housing. It was concluded that full infrastruc-

Below left: Piped water makes the community standpipe a gathering place.
Below: Neighbours collaborate with small contractors to build the concrete and brick structures.

ture provision was not affordable and that initially only a minimum provision was possible without subsidy. Therefore, it was proposed that full provision be achieved incrementally, over a period corresponding to the population's ability to pay for this level of provision.

Residents preferred to negotiate block upgrading individually and not delegate important issues. Semi-independent project agencies with local officials were set up since the local government of Ismailiyya did not have administrative, financial or technical structures to manage the projects. These agencies were given the right to buy and sell land and to use the proceeds for infrastructure, management, and maintenance. They were responsible for the comprehensive planning of layouts and the survey, allocation and sale of plots. Negotiation with those agencies that provided the area's water, electricity and sewage was also their responsibility in addition to representing the people before authorities responsible for social facilities. Their further responsibilities included technical assistance to plot owners, landscaping and coordination with the city council. The agencies' staff received on-the-job training explaining detailed work procedures. In addition, seminars were held to explain why the works were being implemented.

The gradual improvements in the neighbourhood are reflected in the finished and painted façades.

ECONOMIC AND FINANCIAL CONSIDERATIONS. Plot pricing varied to enable affordable payments at low incomes. Good commercial locations commanded higher prices and open market prices were charged through auctioning for key location concession plots. This allowed internal cross-subsidy favouring low priced plots. Over half are in this category which thus increased the number of affordable plots.

In upgraded areas, land prices were set low (Egyptian pounds 2.25 per square metre) with repayment over 30 years. It was proposed that income from selling land go towards basic infrastructure as well as administration, services, and maintenance. In new settlement areas, income from selling land was also expected to pay for basic infrastructure. This meant that initially, infrastructure would be restricted to surveyed plots.

Public relocation housing was provided at a monthly rent of 14 Egyptian pounds per apartment and occupied by about five per cent of the population.

MATERIALS AND TECHNOLOGY. Building materials used in Hai el-Salaam, and Abu Atwa range from the cheapest solutions for construction to the higher standards of the formal sector. Modern building materials were favoured by the governor and the settlers, but a slow rate of construction in low income areas suggests that modern materials may be too expensive for immediate use.

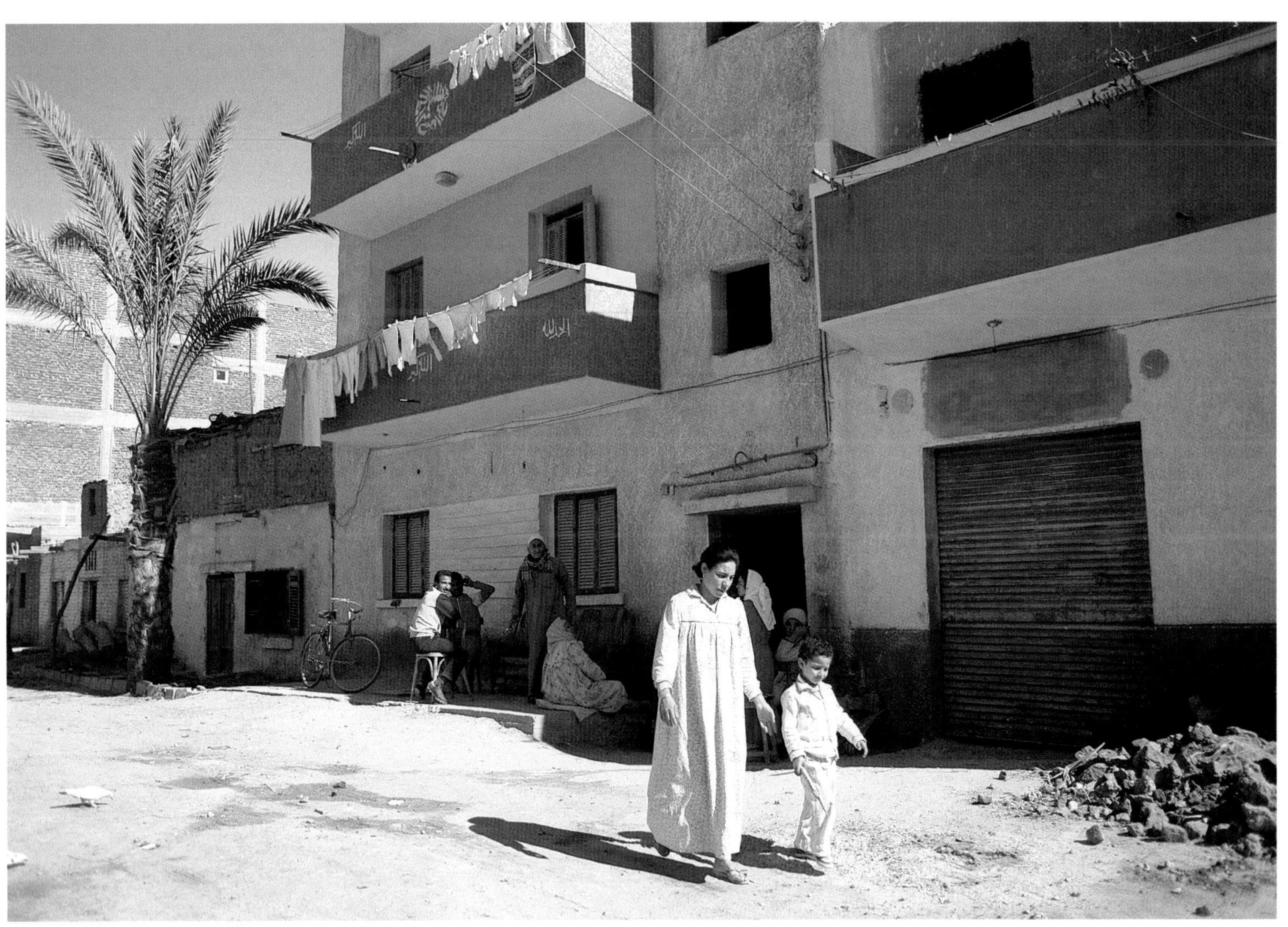

main new commercial/ industrial area
new concession areas
new low cost plot
social facilities
existing development
open space
special areas

Site plan, Hai-el-Salaam.

0 100 200 400m

Site plan, Abu Atwa.

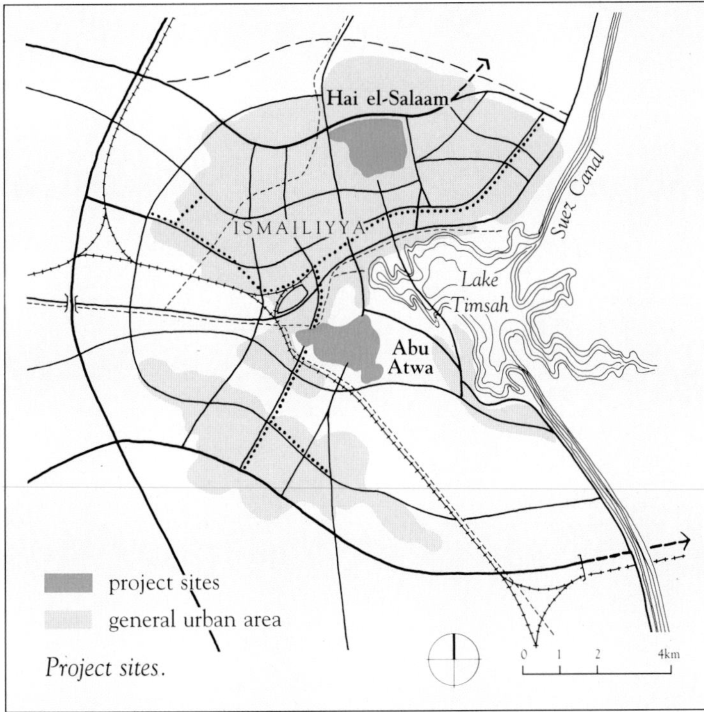

Project sites.

Baked brick production has been forbidden in Egypt, since it uses vegetal earth from agricultural land. Cement bricks have replaced them.

PLAN. The overall physical planning is a hierarchical arrangement of streets and avenues with a main centre and neighbourhood sub-centres. Shopping needs are met primarily by shops on housing plots except for a central market. Other centralised facilities include schools, community centres, a clinic, and a post office. Neighbourhoods tend to be defined by local mosques, as in the traditional Islamic urban pattern. The streets in the existing areas in each settlement being upgraded were adjusted to improve circulation and services, thus displacing some families to the new areas.

There are many advantages of combining upgrading with new development. It allows family relocation as near as possible to the original site. It allows improved social facilities which may not be possible in densely settled areas to be in the new area and to serve both. Utility networks can service the old and the new areas.

The Project Agency provided different house plans for families who could not afford to pay for professional assistance. Houses might be self-built or contracted to builders in the project. Control of lot types encouraged diversity of income level. For example, more expensive lots were allocated along the wider avenues and at intersections to ensure that the areas with strongest visual impact would appear completed early in the development.

CONCLUSION. Constructing the Hai el-Salaam extension of the city of Ismailiyya in 1978 represented a critical departure in the development of low-income housing in Egypt. It was one of a handful of areas where this new approach was applied. It has channelled public housing subsidies towards broadened local initiatives. For the first time in Egypt, physical and institutional guidelines for housing were established primarily to respond to the poor. In 1980, Abu Atwa commenced exploring the same strategy.

The Government donation of land was the largest single subsidy. A grant of 100,000 Sterling pounds from the British government provided the initial capital. Later, revenue to the agency amounted to almost 3,500,000 Egyptian pounds. This has been used for infrastructure and low income loans. So far, 90,000 people have been housed in Hai el-Salaam and Abu Atwa. They have achieved the security of titled ownership.

Hai el-Salaam and Abu Atwa housing is a personal endeavour controlled by local and personal decisions. The projects encouraged the input of thousands of families utilising their collective imagination, energy, time, and funds in order to create their own habitat.

Questions remain unanswered, related for example to the funding of the projects after income from land sales has ceased. There are reasons however, to be optimistic, and what has happened in Ismailiyya, and a few other pilot projects is influencing national housing policy elsewhere in the country.

Community life manifests itself in the newly established nurseries and playgrounds (below) as well as by the appearance and consolidation of small business (bottom).

SAID NAUM MOSQUE
JAKARTA, INDONESIA

Completed 1977.
Client: The Municipal Government of Jarkarta, and Yayasin Saïd Naum.
Architects: Atelier Enam, Architects and Planners.

OBJECTIVES. The Saïd Naum Mosque was part of a project resulting from a competition sponsored by the Jakarta Municipal Government in 1975. Eight prominent Indonesian firms were invited to enter. In addition to the mosque, the project included an ablutions building, a car park and landscaped areas. The criteria were, that the project should represent traditional character, suit the environment and use local materials. The jury selected the proposal of Atelier Enam who became the principal architects. It was intended to create a religious centre in the Indonesian Hindu-Javanese architectural tradition while retaining the spiritual concepts of Islamic philosophy. The goal was to create a refuge of peace and calm in a busy urban area and to provide a centre for social activity.

Left: The approach of the mosque building through the landscaped courtyard is inviting and unprepossessing.
Overleaf: The dramatic design of the roof structure recalls traditional buildings while allowing natural light for the centre of the prayer hall.

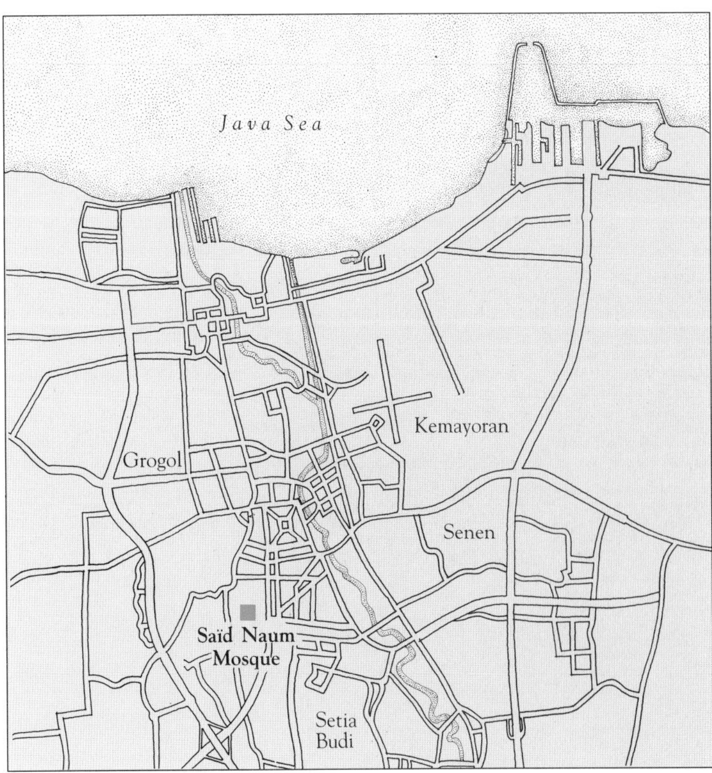

Cross section.

Diagonal section.

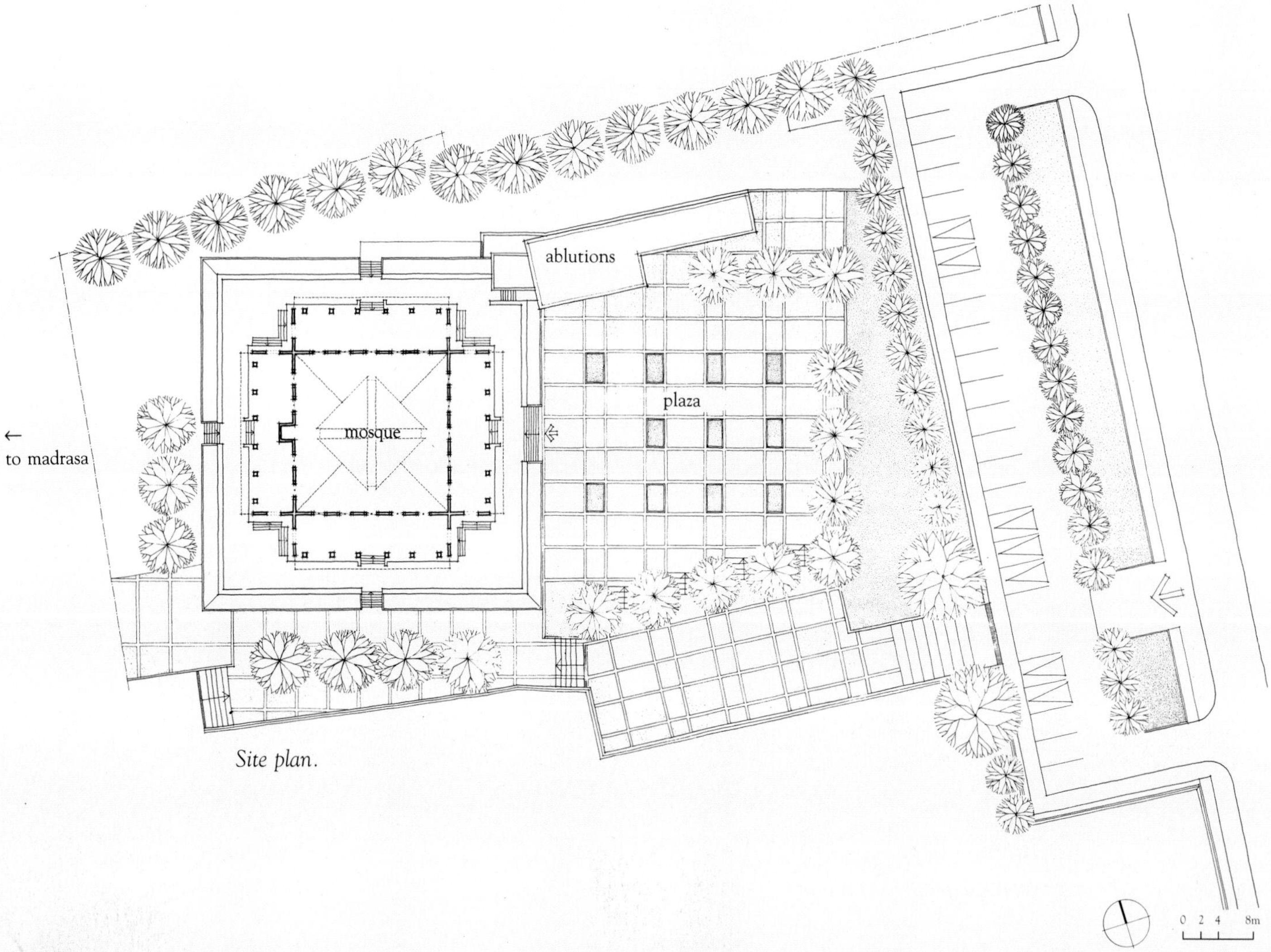

0 1 2 4m

ablutions

plaza

mosque

← to madrasa

Site plan.

0 2 4 8m

The main prayer hall is filled with worshippers (above left), but overflowing crowds are accommodated under overhanging external leaves (above right). Below: The entire composition is marked by an elegant simplicity, and a sensitive use of materials.

SITE. Saïd Naum Mosque is in a densely populated area in Jakarta. To its north is a middle-income housing area. To the south is a prefabricated, low cost housing zone built by the government. To the east and west are two roads. The entrance is from the east. On the other side of the eastern entrance road is another low-income, densely populated area and a low cost housing community. The west road is at the entrance of the *madrasa*, which is next to the mosque. A path connects the west road to the *madrasa* and the mosque.

HISTORICAL BACKGROUND. Jakarta was a port city in 1500 A.D. under the Hindu East-Javanese Pajaran reign. It was conquered in 1527 by the Banten Islamic Sultanate, whereupon its name was changed to Jakarta. The Dutch took over in 1615, renaming it Batavia. Dutch rule lasted nearly 350 years, manifesting itself in colonial buildings. The Dutch succumbed to the Japanese who occupied Indonesia during World War II. In 1945, Soekarno founded the independent Republic of Indonesia in Jakarta. Cities, villages and buildings in this archipelago have influences from China, India and Europe as well as the dominating influences of modern construction methods and technology.

The mosque and the *madrasa* were built on an area that had been a privately owned graveyard. The owner was an Egyptian, Saïd Naum, who donated the land. The rest of the site was owned by the city government who wanted to build on the entire site but considered the graveyard site unsuitable. Public protest emerged against building on the graveyard. After consulting religious leaders, it was agreed that a mosque and a *madrasa* could be built on the graveyard with the supervision of religious and social authorities.

LOCAL ARCHITECTURE. The local architecture consists mostly of small, individual houses with sloping roofs. Structures are usually made of wood and covered either with thatch or tiles. However, traditional rural building materials such as bamboo and native woods are being replaced with modern ones such as masonry walls, cement or brick floors, glazed doors, and tile or corrugated iron roofs.

ARCHITECTURAL CHARACTERISTICS. The mosque is square in plan. It is a symmetrical building with deep verandahs on all sides. The tiled, pitched roof has a lantern with patterned painted glass along its ridges. The space between the lantern and the roof has been left open, allowing for natural ventilation. Exposed timber rafters, concealing the steel-frame roof structure, run in pairs along the length of the roof. The walls are made of brick and plaster. Each wall has five wooden latticed, arched windows, some of which function as doors. In the west wall the central opening is the setting for the *mihrab*. Decorative tiles are used functionally on the floors to delineate praying rows.

The design retains characteristics of the traditional Javanese mosque, especially the roof which evolved from simple house forms. The main roof and lantern give a profile similar to the traditional *Sakaguru* type roof. There are differences however, including the elimination of the four central columns that normally support the second roof. This was done to clear the view of the *mihrab*, and provides clear prayer space for the worshippers.

Discarding the central columns required a steel frame roof instead of a wooden structure. The rotation of the central roof lantern also marks a departure from the typical multi-layered, *Meru* type roof characteristic of Javanese architecture.

TECHNICAL ASSESSMENT. The users are satisfied with the spaces of the mosque. Circulation is easy. During ceremonies, a curtain in the mosque is used to separate the space between men and women. The area around the mosque was landscaped with level changes and planting to differentiate each area. Trees planted around the site's periphery are also interspersed among the paving, providing shade and a relatively cool atmosphere. The mosque adapts well to the local climate: openings on all sides as well as on top are conducive to cross ventilation. The roof is well designed for heavy rain and the deep verandahs protect the interior from rain and excessive glare.

Natural lighting is low to promote an atmosphere for meditation. The light hanging from the centre of the roof lantern accentuates the unity and geometry while providing illumination. Nevertheless, lighting units were added to satisfy the request of users.

All materials were local except for the steel roof structure. The technology is well known and adapted to the local construction tradition. Ageing has been minimal and minor repairs are done regularly.

CONCLUSION. Most of the objectives were achieved. The client and the users are satisfied with the mosque. The mosque performs well as a place for prayer and reflection. It also houses conferences, social gatherings, communal discussions, charity funds, studying and sports. Children use the courtyard to play. The shaded verandah and the outdoor space are ideally suited for these purposes.

It took 15 months using local unskilled labour to build the mosque. Construction costs totalling U.S. $650,000 were low compared to local prices. Today the *Yayasin* or the mosque council is responsible for the mosque's upkeep using contributions from the community. These days the *Yayasin* is not as effective as in the past, and consequently there are fewer social and cultural activities. Maintenance of the mosque is not as complete or prompt as it used to be.

Nevertheless, the Saïd Naum Mosque is a notable structure that effectively galvanises the community of which it is the centrepiece. It is also an important example, in design terms, of a contemporary building echoing the traditional forms of a regional architecture. The design is based on the traditional architecture of Indonesia; that of the simplest Javanese house. The approach is innovative yet faithful to the region's indigenous architecture. What failings there may be in concept or execution are far outweighed by the courage of the architect and client in re-interpreting the traditional idiom and contributing to the production of an authentic yet modern regional architecture.

The functional lighting aspects of the roof structure show to dramatic effect in the main prayer hall (opposite). The fenestration at the centre of the ceiling is delicately coloured and carefully detailed (below).

HISTORIC SITES DEVELOPMENT
ISTANBUL, TURKEY

Completed 1974, and ongoing.
Clients and Planners: The Touring and Automobile Association of Turkey.

OBJECTIVES. Restoration and preservation of several historic buildings and neighbourhoods have concerned the Touring and Automobile Association (TAA) for several years. Many of the nineteenth and twentieth century kiosks and pavilions in the royal parks along the Bosporus have been neglected; and the remaining old residential districts are in danger of being razed to make room for apartment blocks. In 1979, the TAA signed an agreement with the city to lease specific buildings and parks to restore, to furnish, and to put them to profitable use. Each building is documented at the outset with maps, photographs and drawings.

The buildings restored by the TAA were originally constructed either with a wooden frame with brick and lime infill and clapboard façades, or with limestone blocks bonded with lime mortar. The association's projects fall into three categories: restoration works, demolition and reconstruction, and new structures patterned on historic models.

Left: The Malta pavilion in Yildiz Park was the first restoration completed by the Touring and Automobile Association (TAA).

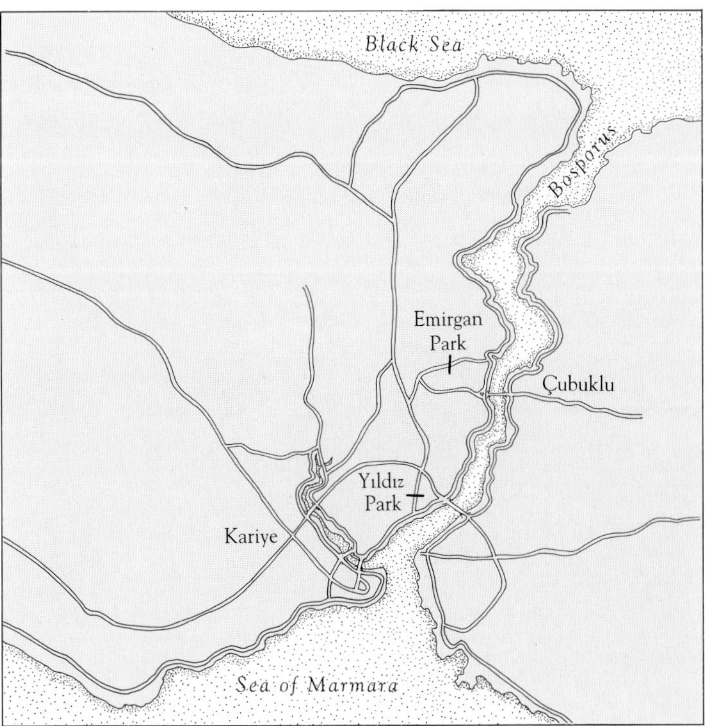

RESTORATION WORKS. This first category entails repairing and refurbishing a building using traditional methods of construction but occasionally strengthening with reinforced concrete or cement.

Yıldız Park. The park at Yıldız was first used by the Ottoman sultans in the early eighteenth century when Sultan Ahmet III built the wooden Çirağan Palace there. Sultan Abdulaziz built the Malta and Çadir pavilions between 1862 and 1871. The two pavilions were important in Ottoman history when they were used as the venue for the trial of Mithat Pasha by Sultan Abdulhamit II in 1881. During Abdulhamit's reign, many rare plants and trees were planted in the park. After the Turkish Republic was founded, government agencies took over the park, palaces, and pavilions. In 1979, the TAA leased the deteriorating pavilions and park to restore and revitalise them.

Malta Pavilion. The Malta Pavilion was the first restoration job completed by the TAA. Minor repairs were done on the exterior walls that were repainted bottle green with white trim. The interiors were restored and repainted; and the ceilings and the woodwork were restored to their former glory. Furnishings, paintings, chandeliers, and so on, were collected to fit the style of the rich, nineteenth century baroque building. It was designed to be re-used as a restaurant and conference facility. The patrons are mostly from the upper and middle classes who use the pavilion for opulent functions.

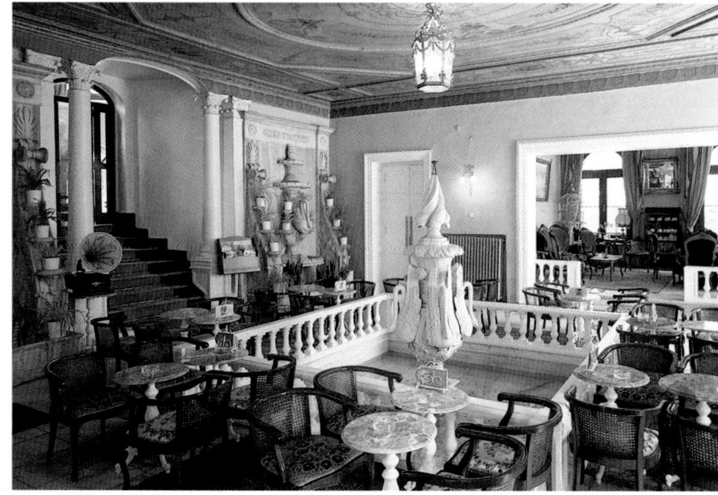

Çadir Pavilion. In 1983, the TAA made major repairs on the Çadir Pavilion. The outside was plastered and painted in a Bordeaux colour with white trimming. Richly painted ceilings inside were cleaned and painted also focusing on a Bordeaux colour scheme with silver and gold trimming. With panoramic views over the Bosporus, the pavilion is now used as a coffee house and has the atmosphere of an exclusive club.

Above: The Malta Pavilion. The interiors were restored to their original nineteenth century character, including fundamentally European furniture and balustrades.
Below: The Çadir Pavilion sits in a beautifully landscaped part of Yıldız Park with water significantly enhancing the ambiance.

Emirgan Park. This park is first mentioned during the reign of Murat IV when he presented the land to Prince Mir Gun of Persia, hence Emirgan Park. In the second half of the nineteenth century, it became the property of the Khedive Ismail Pasha who built a wooden *saray* on the Bosporus and the Pink, Yellow, and White Pavilions in the park. The Municipality of Istanbul bought the park and the pavilions allowing them to go into a state of disrepair until the TAA took over in 1979.

The White Pavilion. The White Pavilion was built in a monumental, neo-classical style around the 1880's. Minor repairs were needed on the exterior but the interiors had to be entirely renovated. Gardens famous for their tulips and terraces were landscaped and a marble pool was built. The building was converted into a concert hall and restaurant. Good acoustics make the building ideal for piano recitals and chamber music concerts. Clientele attend regularly for music, festivals, films, and other special functions.

The Pink Pavilion. This pavilion had been derelict for years. It was restored as a typical Bosporus house with appropriate Ottoman furnishings and woodwork. It is now open as a museum. The outside terrace is a cafe in the summer.

The Yellow Pavilion. The Yellow Pavilion was bought by the municipality in 1941. After a fire in 1954, it was rebuilt. The TAA leased the building in 1979 and converted it into a tea room and snack bar. Renovations and refurbishing dated back to the 1920's–1930's style with nineteenth century paintings of the Bosporous, an original woodburning stove, and a small library on the Bosporous. Only the ground floor is open to the public. The first floor is now used by the municipality as a conference centre.

Below left: The White pavilion in Emirgan Park reflects the late nineteenth century neo classical style.
Above: The Yellow pavilion has none of the monumentality of the White pavilion and now functions as a tea-room and snack-bar.
Below: The Pink pavilion has been restored as a museum. Its interior (bottom) has Ottoman furnishings. Note washbasin and samovar.

The Khedive's Palace at Çubuklu. In 1982, the TAA began restoration work on the summer palace of the Khedive at Cubuklu. It was built on the Asiatic side of the Bosporus between 1905 and 1910 by Abbas Hilmi Pasha II, Khedive of Egypt from 1892–1914. This building was built in the *Art Nouveau* style with lavish embellishments. A lift takes people up to a small platform at the top of a tower for a spectacular view of the Bosporus. Years were spent researching the history of the house to recreate its original form. Mirrored ceilings, wood work and a stained glass skylight were restored. Every piece of furniture was designed to fit into the rich, baroque style of the building. The floor and wall tiles are *Art Nouveau* originals imported from Denmark, and the textiles covering the walls were copied from the originals that were in poor condition. Today the palace functions as a hotel, accommodating about 50 people. The most expensive room in the palace is the Khedive's bedroom. The plethora of visitors to the palace and its grounds attest to its popularity.

Above left and above: The Khedive's Palace at Çubuklu, is a splendid art-nouveau structure which now functions as a hotel. A stained glass skylight in the dome (below) adds drama to the interior.
Opposite: The splendid hall has been meticulously restored into an inviting and elegant restaurant.

The Kariye Museum Neighbourhood. The Kâriye Museum is in a residential neighbourhood of dilapidating nineteenth century wooden houses. Visitors flock to the church to see its twelfth and fourteenth century mosaics and frescoes. In 1974, in an effort to rehabilitate the area, the TAA repaired and painted the facades of 12 houses on Bostan Sokak. Pavements were cemented, steps were rebuilt, iron grilles were restored, and rotten wood was replaced. No structural changes were made; interiors were untouched. The project included repairing the local fountain. Street were cobbled as well as the square in front of the museum. A few flower beds were planted and terraced steps were built up the hill. An open air cafe was installed on the terrace of a nearby house. The TAA is donating money to restore the Kariye Museum roof and to clean the wall painting inside. The project will continue indefinitely.

It is not hard to criticise the restorations and renovations at Kariye. Workmanship is poor — cracks are visible, roof tiles are already broken, iron grilles and brackets are rusting, and the gutters are placed incorrectly. A pudding shop the TAA built in front of the museum is an eyesore. But these negative aspects are offset by the paved and cobbled streets, a clean water fountain and advice the TAA gave to owners on improving their homes. Overall the renovation not only gave the houses a facelift, but also improved the physical conditions of local inhabitants who are pleased with the improvements. The entire district now wants to be included in the TAA project zone. Thus, it is unfortunate that the restorations were not done more professionally.

Opposite: The Kariye museum neighbourhood has been transformed by the cobbled streets and landscaping (top) and by the treatment of the wide stepped cobblestone paving (bottom).
Below: Restoration work on the individual houses was not of high quality, but the overall effect was still a dramatic improvement (bottom).

Above: The Konak Hotel was torn down and reconstructed in concrete and brick to meet firecode regulations. Clapboard façades were added to recreate the appearance of the wooden original structure.

Cedid Mehmet Efendi Madrasa. In 1984, the TAA started restoring the Cedid Mehmet Efendi Madrasa, a seventeenth century building. The limestone building was completely dilapidated with trees growing through the roof. Some rooms facing the street were closed off from the inside and rented out as retail shops.

The building was restored using original materials. An arched doorway connecting the *madrasa* with the Konak Hotel garden is being rebuilt using cement mortar. The shops will also be rebuilt using cement blocks and bricks. When completed, the *madrasa* will function as a crafts centre.

DEMOLITION AND RECONSTRUCTION. This category consists of wooden buildings, nineteenth century Istanbuli houses that were bought by the TAA with the intention of turning them into hotels or hostels. Hotels cannot be built of wood because of the risk of fire. These houses were torn down and rebuilt using a reinforced concrete frame, with breeze blocks or bricks as infill and cement mortar. Exterior façades are covered in clapboard that has been painted. Most of the interior spaces have also been changed. Thus, these structures are new with a veneer copied from an old model.

The Konak Hotel. The *Konak* or "noble mansion" was most recently the house of Şükrü Bey who held the tobacco monopoly under Sultan Abdulhamit II. This nineteenth century wooden mansion was bought by the TAA in the early 1970's. Since Istanbul law does not permit hotels to be built from wood, it was torn down and rebuilt using a concrete skeleton with brick infill and cement mortar. Façades were covered with clapboard duplicating original drawings and photographs. However, the interior spaces were changed — the separation of male quarters, *selamlık*, and female quarters, *haremlık*, was removed. New room divisions were created. The gardens and terrace at the rear were landscaped. A huge nineteenth century fountain was salvaged from another demolished mansion and installed. Pavements were covered in white marble.

Çamlıca Hill was completely landscaped, including building seven marble kiosks.

Soğukçeşme Sokaği. A dozen houses, a tiny *hammam* and a grand Byzantine cistern are situated along the Soğukçeşme Sokaği, a narrow alley way. TAA bought eleven houses, and is still negotiating the purchase of the twelfth house. Each house was drawn and photographed before it was pulled down and rebuilt using a concrete frame with brick infill and cement mortar. Clapboard will cover the exteriors. Interiors were transformed according to their new function. Most of them will be converted into hotels or hostels, and one building will house the *waqf* library. External embellishments and details make the reconstructed houses different from the original houses.

This is a controversial project. The Municipality wanted to pull the houses down because they were slums attached to the outer wall of the Topkapı Palace. But the TAA had already bought some of the houses and fought against their demolition. TAA won and then tore down the houses and rebuilt them again. Although these hotels will probably be popular with the tourists, the TAA cannot take credit for saving the traditional wooden houses.

NEW STRUCTURES. These are entirely new structures built on virgin sites. They are vaguely patterned after nineteenth century prototypes.

Çamlıca Hill. This hill site has a spectacular view of Istanbul. It was derelict until the TAA leased it. They landscaped the area, replanted the woods and made pathways. An eighteenth century style coffee house was built, along with seven marble kiosks. Thousands of people flock to this popular picnic and panoramic spot.

CONCLUSION. The pavilions at Yıldız and Emirgan Park and the Khedive's Palace on the Bosporus are well restored and beautifully maintained. But the renovations in the Kariye district are poor. Rebuilding the nineteenth century wooden houses with new materials and tacking a clapboard façade on them was controversial. Many people are irritated by the painted façades. However, these transformed houses make successful hotels. They are expected to pay back their cost which cannot be said of the pavilions or the Khedive Palace which have had enormous sums poured into them.

The work done by the TAA under Gülersoy has started a trend of saving threatened areas of old Istanbul.

CHAIRMAN'S AWARD

RIFAT CHADIRJI

Ministry of Municipal and Rural Affairs, Baghdad.

RIFAT CHADIRJI

CITATION. To Rifat Chadirji, Iraqi architect, critic and teacher, for a lifetime dedicated to the search for an appropriate contemporary architectural expression that synthesises elements of a rich cultural heritage and key principles of architecture in the twentieth century.

The exemplary dedication and tenacity, the intellectual and personal integrity, and the constant concern for teaching and communicating that have characterised this intellectual and artistic journey of over 35 years deserves world recognition and appreciation.

For the guiding principles of this search to produce an authentic regionalism are an important contribution to the universal cultural achievements of our age. They exemplify an openness to time and its imperatives, along with a deep appreciation of the ancient, Islamic and Arab cultural heritage of Iraq, generating a distinctive corpus of work, relevant well beyond the borders of Iraq.

Born in 1926 into a wealthy and intellectual environment in Iraq, Rifat Chadirji learnt to appreciate art and culture from his youth. These formative years are recorded with vivid realism in his autobiography *Taha Street and Hammersmith*. He travelled to England in 1946 where he completed his architectural education in 1952. He then returned to his native Iraq. Here he confronted the intellectual challenge posed by the contrast between the high technological development of building in the West and the situation in the Middle East where most building were still traditional. The Middle East was then in a state of flux as rapid modernisation was changing every facet of traditional life. The need to maintain this vibrant, modern drive without losing touch with the traditional roots

was to remain at the heart of Rifat Chadirji's work from that time to the present.

Chadirji maintains that the best architecture is the natural outcome of the interaction between social technology and social need. He argues that architecture's future lies in lessons learned from its past — where it can be categorised as man's most important way of dealing with regional variations in nature and his means of production.

Chadirji believed that every region should have its own modern architecture, that is, that modern architecture should be regionalised. Regionalisation should not imply a strict return to the past, or to a traditional architecture, since this in his view represented an anachronism. At the same time, he recognised the perils of adopting new building forms, already questionable in the West. However, the opportunities which the new technology offered were too important to ignore. Chadirji's concept of regionalisation required the abstraction of regional forms within the context of internationalism, that is, within the context of technology and aesthetic values generated by international architecture. The end result is an architecture that is international in its concepts and technology yet regional in its character.

His many projects serve as important examples for study, and they raise critical questions on architecture in Islamic society. Islamic architecture, he believes, is extremely varied and rich; and its values should form the basis of a contemporary Renaissance in architecture in the Islamic world.

Chadirji's contributions to built form transcend individual buildings. His influence on the urban form of Baghdad has been remarkable. In the last assignment he undertook in Iraq, he took over the responsibilities of Advisor to the Municipality of Baghdad for the most massive urban reconstruction in that city's history. With a boldness that matches that of Baron Hausmann's restructuring of Paris in the nineteenth century, Chadirji elaborated a vision of the future townscape that will mark that city forever. In executing his vision he invited some of the best architectural talent in the world to participate. Whatever becomes of that bold approach in the wake of a war-shattered economy, Chadirji's vision and drive have launched an architectural enterprise of epic proportions.

Chadirji's search for an effective synthesis of modernity and tradition that would enhance the architecture of the region is advanced through his contributions as teacher and critic, not just as practitioner.

In his analysis of architectural expression, Chadirji made many contributions to architectural thinking in the Arab world of which two are particularly noteworthy. First, he saw the evolving architectural form as mediating between societal needs and the prevailing social technology. This, he postulated, partly explained the rupture observed in post World War II Iraq's emergent built form. Secondly, Chadirji saw the relationship between the local architectural tradition and the internationalist modern movement as one where an authentic regionalism, based on the abstraction of classical forms and the internalisation of traditional building approaches and design concepts, was to be synthesised with the liberating concepts of the modern movement and with international building technology. This would produce an authentic, modern regionalism that would enrich the international movement rather than remain purely derivative from it.

By the 1970's, a critical perspective on the issue of "function" emerges in Chadirji's architecture, further separating plan from façade. In his theoretical writing, he turned further from accepted Western definitions of "function", which rely heavily on structure as the genesis of plan organisation and expression. He argued that this relationship was not deterministic or inevitable. These ideas led him to intensified plastic exploration, whose roots clearly were closer to his native culture than to Europe. At the same time, Chadirji did not lose his commitment to working within the context of an international discourse, and he did not slip into the realm of the provincial or sentimental. His recent text, *Concepts and Influences: Towards a Regionalised International Architecture*, has further advanced the concern of much of the most important critical theory of the past two decades. He has remained insistent in his criticism of "fashion" including regressive traditionalism. His voice has acted as a conscience for Arab and Muslim architects everywhere.

His work has been exhibited all over the world. He is an honorary fellow of the Royal Institute of British Architects, and has been a visiting scholar at Harvard University. He is currently devoting himself to research and writing and is pursuing his interests in affiliation with the Aga Khan Program for Islamic Architecture at Harvard University and M.I.T.

Villa Al Hamad, Kuwait.

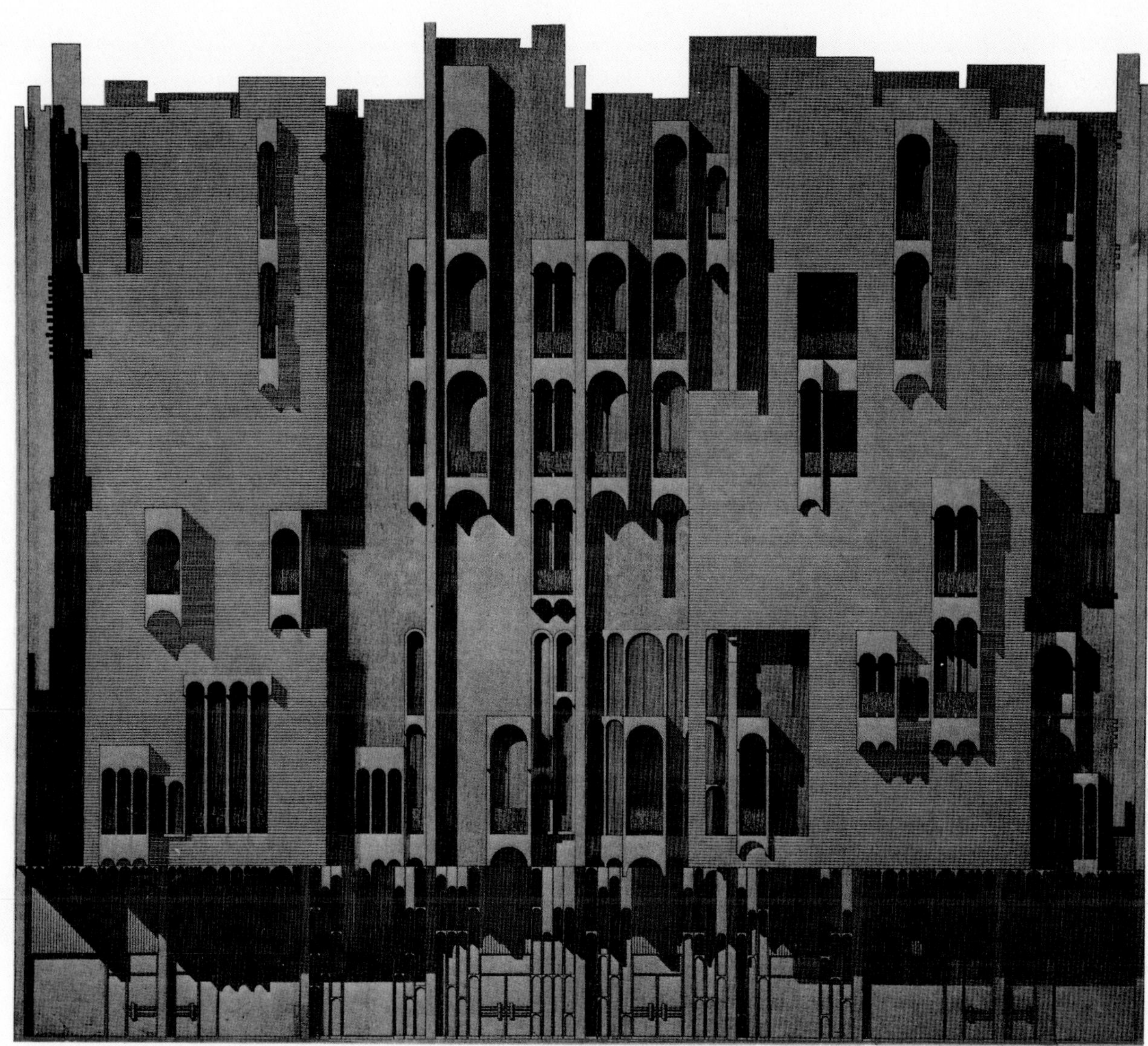

Federation of Industries, Baghdad.

Medical Auxiliary Training Centre, Baghdad.

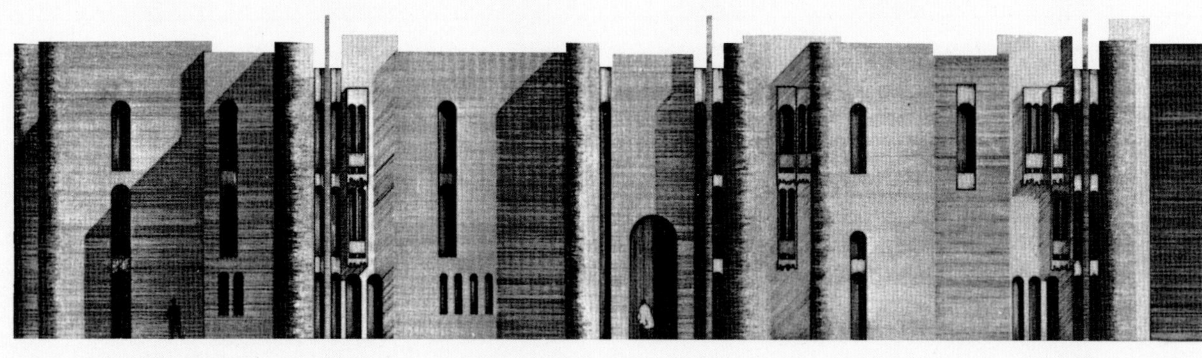

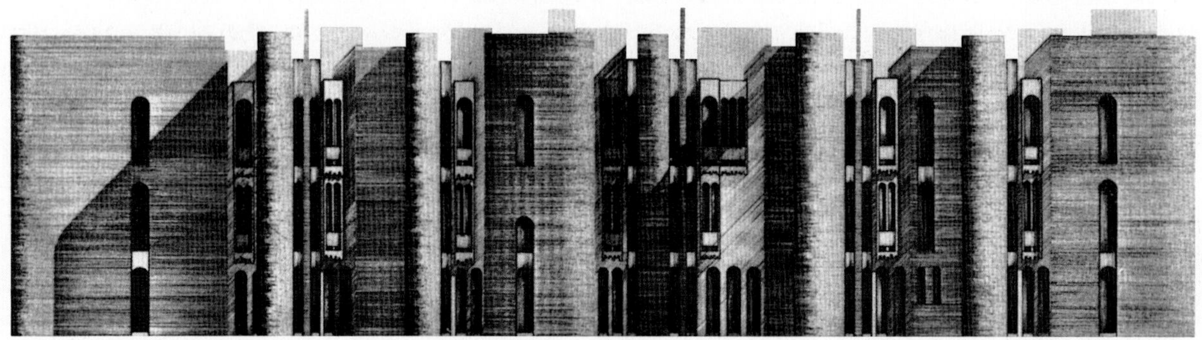

Tobacco Monopoly Offices and Stores, Baghdad.

CHADIRJI SPEAKS

Architectural Form, Modes of Production, Social Needs and Social Technology. Long before starting an architectural practice in 1952, I recognised that architectural form was not something static, apprehended passively, and describable from some singular underlying morphology. I was also aware of the nature of the modes of production and their effect on the creation and development of architecture. Therefore, I thought of architectural style in terms of the state and the properties of a mode of a production rather than as a series of stylistic events.

Architecture, or the material entity we perceive to be the form of architecture, is the manifestation, the end product in its state of repose, of a dialectical interaction between two opposing determinants: man's social needs and his social technology. Social need is composed of many constituents: the material and functional requirements of the society or individual, as well as the emotional and spiritual. Technology is also composed of many constituents: the availability of materials used in the production process, their natural properties and knowledge of these properties, the economic and social potential to interact with these materials and the manipulations to which they can be subjected. An equilibrium between the two determining poles of architecture — social need on one hand, social technology on the other — is a prerequisite for excellence in architecture.

Revolutionary Forces in the Development. Four new forces revolutionised social needs and social technology in the modern era. The first and most important of these new forces was the machine. It transformed production relationships. The second factor was the general abundance from the economic growth made possible by modern machine technology. It became possible to produce and distribute far beyond national and regional boundaries, which overwhelmed traditional values, creeds, faiths and political values. The third force was the standardisation of building elements and building systems. Because of economic necessity, competitive labour and lucrative markets, franchised production, and the universal dissemination of knowledge, structures and elements became increasingly homogenous. But it was an unorganised and unsystematised homogeneity, hectic and restless, directed chiefly by individual self-interest. Disseminated universally, it was partly responsible for the loss of national and regional character and the destruction of coherent styles that had been characteristic of architecture from the earliest times until the emergence of technology. The fourth force made itself felt through international media. These exerted a dichotomous influence on society. On one hand, the standardisation and internationalisation of science, art and academic training began to take place. On the other, aesthetic values became more heterogenous. Aesthetic values were no longer relegated to a unified style that regulated every kind of production — whether architecture, clothing, jewelry, furniture or domestic utensils — as they had in the past. The impact of these new forces — the widespread use of the machine, the heterogeneity of the new materials, the loss of a coherent and well-defined national style and the dichotomous influence of the new international media — threw the relationship between the two fundamental determinants of architecture, the needs and the technology, into confusion. This confusion introduced ambiguity into the processes of production, academic training and furthermore into architectural practice.

Dissemination of Architecture. Until the modern era, the dissemination and export of form from one culture to another was usually accepted or even sought by the receiving culture. The dissemination of culture usually became possible only when the receiving society was culturally prepared to absorb the new forms impinging on it. But since the universalisation of methods of production, the designer in an affected culture has been confronted with many stylistic options, technological methods, and materials from which he was forced to choose. Modern technology is not just development; it also carries with it all the prestige and improved welfare associated with modernisation. These are options that the designer cannot ignore but must interact with. Like it or not even outright rejection is a form of interaction.

Many of the choices available to the contemporary designer are both alien and novel to the extent that they have not yet been tried and tested in this culture. They are not the products of social and technological developments indigenous to the region — they are imports. Although they augur new kinds of production they cannot be absorbed immediately; nor have they yet been fully understood. The imported aesthetic and social values, technical knowledge and methods have still to be assimilated with the natural social potential of the receiving culture.

The modern designer has been deprived of his traditional technology because it is no longer economically viable. His aesthetic values are not equipped to satisfy contemporary daily needs, because his everyday life has been transformed and nourished by international standards and his own culture is too local and too stagnant. With no definite culture and technology of his own to act as a base from which to receive and absorb new influences, he must now choose between alternatives which he perceives as undifferentiated and unintegrated. His designs must be produced in conditions for which he is culturally unprepared. And because he cannot absorb the new input, cultural frustration and aesthetic collapse result.

Towards A Regionalised Architecture. By 1953, I thought modern architecture should be regionalised. In other words, I thought that every region should have its own modern architecture. But because I was convinced that architecture is the manifestation of a dialectical interaction, I believed that regionalisation should not imply a strict return to the past, or to a traditional architecture. Replication, a wholesale borrowing from traditional technology and aesthetics, represents an anachronism, a regression to the pre-machine-aesthetic era, and was therefore invalid.

I determined that my concept of regionalisation required the abstraction of regional forms — whether urban or rural, whether traditional or a definite past style — within the context of internationalism, that is, within the context of the technology and aesthetic values of international architecture.

By the mid-sixties, a new mode of production was emerging — the computer. The new phase this development heralded could not be determined because of the sheer magnitude of the potential involved and because of the opportunities the user would be given to participate in design and production. The opportunity for instantaneous participation in these processes reintroduces a continuous feedback relationship in architecture at a higher level, and new aesthetic values will be created in the future.

I was determined to follow a path that would synthesise concepts gleaned from the international avant-garde with abstract forms derived from tradition. I excluded from my experiments simplistic replicas of traditional elements or features. I also excluded conventional rural or primitive technologies, because neither is compatible with the mechanical-aesthetic mode. I hoped that my experiments would provide the raw materials for new architectural concepts, and thus leave a milestone on the road towards a regionalised international architecture.

PART THREE

A RISING EDIFICE

CONTRIBUTIONS TOWARDS A BETTER UNDERSTANDING OF ARCHITECTURAL EXCELLENCE IN THE MUSLIM WORLD

INTRODUCTION

Behind the Award Ceremonies lies a major effort at identification, documentation, analysis, and evaluation of a large number of projects, of which only a select few make it to the pinnacle of receiving an award. But beyond this vast enterprise, the Award staff and Steering Committee, under the guidance of His Highness the Aga Khan, undertake an ongoing search for excellence, and continue probing into a series of important issues that confront the Muslim world and its built environment. Their tools for so doing include small gatherings of specialists, referred to as *Think Tanks* for their free wheeling and far reaching debates, *regional seminars* that are more focused and structured in their approach and that deal with problems of immediate interest to a large community within a sub-region of the Muslim world, *international seminars* where luminaries from all over the world are brought to discuss themes of major interest, *research papers* that report upon faraway, misunderstood or little known parts of the Muslim world, as well as *think pieces* dealing with philosophical or technical issues of relevance to this ongoing search for a more meaningful architectural response to the needs of the built environment of the Muslim world. In this section, a sample of some of these activities will be reviewed. For purposes of clarity, the selections are grouped under four broad headings:

Conceptual Foundations. As was explained in Part One of this Book, the third cycle witnessed a renewed effort at probing the intellectual foundations of the Award's work. This enterprise involved two parallel streams of research and thinking: Firstly, philosophical issues related to Islam and the Muslim societies and their built environment; and secondly, the nature of the design process.

Cultural Continuity. An abiding concern of the Award, this set of issues is addressed both in terms of historical issues and in terms of active involvement in historic conservation efforts.

Social and Institutional Issues. No building activity takes place in a vacuum. The social context of architecture and the institutional framework within which decisions are made are fundamental dimensions of understanding the end result of the built form.

Contemporary Architectural Expression. So many of the Award's activities touch upon this that selections are difficult to make but key components of regionalism, building technology, and the cultural expression of particular Muslim communities are all represented here.

The extracts from this rich source of materials have been grouped under the main themes identified above. They represent only a very small part of the activities of the Award, but like the proverbial "tip of the iceberg", they indicate to the interested and the perceptive, the nature and extent of the remaining materials.

CONCEPTUAL FOUNDATIONS

PHILOSOPHICAL ISSUES ON ISLAM AND BUILDING

That everything changes is a truism. And yet, there are elements that are fixed and eternal, that help us, like compass points in the wilderness, to find our way and to remain true to our identity. Professor Arkoun addresses that question in his "Muslim Character: The Essential and the Changeable," an extract from his address to the Cairo seminar of November 1984.

In another extract from the same conference, Ismail Serageldin underscores the links between Islamic artistic and societal expression and that of contemporary Christian and Judaic communities, highlighting the similarities that point to a very cosmopolitan character in what we have come to consider the peak of medieval Islamic culture in Cairo.

But for those who would go back to the fundamental sources of Islamic doctrine with a view to define guidelines for action in the domain of architecture the task has been ardous.

Where are the sources of Muslim inspiration, and what does authentic Islam tell Muslims as to their built environment? Are there prescriptions in the *Quran*, the *Sunna*, or the early examples of the 'companions' that distinguish the original concerns of Islam as a system of values and ethics, from Islam as a culture practiced by Muslim societies whose manifestations of pomp and grandeur may well contrast with the simplicity, humility, and the directness that characterised the early Muslim eras? This has been one of the questions that has concerned a large number of Muslims practicing architecture, as well as those who practice architecture in the Muslim world. Clearly, there are no easy answers to these questions but, in a separate report for the Steering Committee, Ismail Serageldin has tried to address that question in looking at "Faith and the Environment" and reflecting on the built environment of Muslims. That unpublished report is reproduced in full here.

Muslim Character: The Essential and the Changeable*

Mohammed Arkoun

Rarely do we have enough time to deal with an aspect which is really essential to us in the framework of the Aga Khan Award for Architecture. Everything that has been said up to now, everything that we do in this great enterprise, is underlined by many problems related to what I call the Muslim character, to what is essential and what is changeable in the Muslim character.

How shall we approach this problem of the essential and the changeable in the context of the problems of urbanism and architecture? I shall put it first in an ontological way which is the approach given by the *Quran* itself, and then I shall consider it from an historical perspective.

The ontological way taught by the *Quran* could be summarised by one verse: "All that is on the earth will perish, and only that will survive which is under the care of the Lord, Majesty and Magnificence" (LV, 27–28).

We have in this verse two important words: *fana* and *baqa*. *Fana* is the annihilation of all existing beings on earth; and *baqa* means duration, eternity which applies to God. This is a way of looking at our existence, in a specifically religious way. We can say that *baqa*, the permanent and unchangeable, the essential, represents the way in which man viewed his existence, and all that he produced during his existence, through a vertical look at the transcendence of God.

What we call modernity...brings a historical way of looking at our problems which is a rupture with the ontological framework in which civilisations have developed according to the teaching of the revelation as they received it from the Bible, the Gospels, and of course, the *Quran*.

This change is fundamental. The problem for us is to face this rupture which is imposed on us from outside Islamic history. How do we face this rupture in terms of our own thinking? Do we face it with rich and original *munazarat* like the Muslim thinkers when they had to face, as we do today, modernity coming from the West? They had to face the philosophical thought coming from classical Greece which had nothing to do with the ontological framework of the revelation. Muslim thinkers faced this intellectually. But what do we do in our Muslim thinking and social behaviour today?

This is the main problem we are trying to discuss within the Steering Committee which is a very original gathering of specialists in history, sociology, architecture and urbanism. We try to develop a new vocabulary to approach the wide divergence between two frameworks of thinking. We find that we do not have an adequate vocabulary to express the problems of today. We try within the Steering Committee to provide these new ways of thinking and research and a new vocabulary. This is the original enterprise of the Aga Khan Award for Architecture, because we do not have this approach at all in the university, where we have a special academic approach to problems.

I would like to give you two examples to illustrate this rupture inside ourselves,

---

* Extract from Proceedings of *The Expanding Metropolis: Coping with the Urban Growth of Cairo*, Seminar Nine in the series – Architectural Transformations in the Islamic World, Cairo, Eygpt, Nov 11–15, 1984. Published by Concept Media for The Aga Khan Award for Architecture, Singapore, 1985, pp 233 – 236.

inside our traditions in Islamic thought; between the intellectual and the spiritual outlook on the one hand and the ideological outlook on the other. Take for example Gamaliya, a place which is exceptionally well preserved. The people of Cairo, love it; they want to live there; they are attached to it.

Why is there such a continuity in such a place, in such a quarter, in a Muslim town? I think that here we can touch upon one aspect of what could be considered as essential in our tradition. The essential here is the ethical force of Islamic tradition developed throughout history, especially in al-Azhar. There are leading Muslim figures symbolising religious values and attitudes, transmitting it to average people through schools, mosques, festivals, daily language, social institutions and relationships. All this has created a typical Islamic ethos which explains the particular attitude and sensibility we find in Cairo and in Egypt more than anywhere else. We are all struck by the dignity of Egyptians: even when they are very poor economically, they are so rich ethically. We do not find in Cairo the same violence that we find in other so-called very advanced cities.

Why is this? Because this ethos, this Islamic ethos exists here in Cairo. There is something essential which is linked to the environment, to the special design preserved in Cairo. We must pay attention to this through thinking that takes into account the special framework symbolising the whole existence of man with his built environment.

Today we do not adequately understand this richness of symbolism of Islamic thought as it has been developed and as we find it exceptionally preserved in such places. That is why I insist always on a framework for our thinking when we deal with designing, with planning and urbanism, because we are totally confused about this concept of symbol and symbolism. We, more often, use two other concepts: those of signs and signals. The former is essential to our thinking, since a place such as Gamaliya is becoming one of signs or even of signals more than of symbols. The whole framework of the city is destroyed but this place has tried to preserve the symbolic expressions taught by Islamic traditions. We do not pay enough attention to this rupture between the symbolic and the ideological expression of existence; the latter is now becoming more and more powerful, even among the intellectuals

The second example I would like to give you is two sentences we have heard and which we repeat very often. We have heard that Heliopolis has no Islamic character, and that it is a colonial creation. These two propositions are correct. But if we use these two sentences only and stop at that, then we are clearly looking at problems through an ideological framework, because the concept of colonialism is linked to our ideology of having to fight against colonialism. But today we have to consider the problem of Heliopolis within the context of the time in which it was created. We should not forget architectural and urban problems associated with Heliopolis just because we happen to think first of denouncing and rejecting the colonial aspect of the place. This is then one of the ways of distinguishing between the ideological approach on the one hand, and the technical, historical, symbolic approach to any city on the other hand.

As for the second proposition that Heliopolis has no Islamic character, it is true, but who knows, who can give us the definition today of an Islamic character? Do all the buildings in Cairo and other Muslim cities today, or Muslim cities themselves have an Islamic character? How does one define it?

When we start asking such questions, we reveal a set of problems which have not yet been previously raised, either in Islamic thought as such, or in the ways of thinking about Islam encountered in architectural conferences and seminars. We must underscore the fact that architects are trained as professionals in special programmes. We see over and over again that architects cannot speak: they cannot give any explanations without slides. I do not mean to criticise them but they need slides to point out problems.

Historians, philosophers, linguists, semioticians do not need slides; they speak with words; with concepts. Concepts have very, very precise contexts; they are instruments of thought. Here we have a problem of communication between architects and other specialists. I have experienced this problem as an historian. We cannot speak about any culture without a precise definition of what a myth and what a symbol are.

Many books are written about myths and symbols. We have not yet found an operational definition of these two concepts in spite of the fact that these concepts are keys to enter into any analysis of architectural, urban, artistic or historical problems. This is one of the greatest difficulties we face in trying to create the new space which we need in order to approach the problems raised with intellectual responsibility. These problems have been raised in connection with the architectural approach to the city of today, and I would even say in connection with the civilisation of today.

Tilework, Tomb of Shah Rukn-i-'Alam, Multan, Pakistan.

Islamic thought is cut-off from two dimensions which it is absolutely essential to restore and to revitalise. We are speaking of revitalising Gamaliya. We are speaking of rehabilitation of monuments. But we must first rehabilitate *our* tradition of thinking. We are cut-off from our tradition of thinking as it was established by Muslim thinkers in the classical age of Islam. One can go to all our universities and look at the programmes of teaching philosophy, theology, or Islamic thought. One will find them weak and irrelevant to the new ways of thinking which we need.

It is also a problem of historical research. We have not yet acquired historical knowledge of all the dimensions of thinking developed in the classical ages in what we call the *turath*, the legacy of Islamic thought.

The other point is that our Islamic ways of thinking developed today are much more under pressure from economic, political and social problems and are hence ideologically oriented. Islamic thought has not yet benefited enough from all the new trends of research that have appeared in these new sciences developed in the West. We must master all the methodologies developed in human and social sciences and think how it is relevant to apply them to make our Islamic thinking today operative. We must define problems correctly and analyse all the difficulties, such as the megalopolis and its related problems of demography and economy.

This problem of demography also has an impact on our way of thinking, in that it reinforces the pressure of ideology on Islamic thought. This is not conducive to the open way of scientific intellectual thinking. Today 50 per cent of our Muslim population are younger than 20 years of age. This young population has been brought up in an ideological atmosphere, created by political discourse and its well-known redundant slogans. They are not in touch with Islamic thinking in its tradition. The gap between classical Islamic thought, the present ideological thought and scientific thought has been increasing, especially since the 1970's, because political pressures are becoming stronger with the new regimes. Under these regimes, everything is controlled by the state, and the leaders are more oriented toward secularism than religious culture. At the same time, they claim to protect Islam and to restore its cultural and spiritual heritage. Intellectuals who could help to clarify this complex situation are very few in number, marginal in society and looked upon suspiciously by the ruling elites.

How can a new architecture linked to a new way of thinking and to culture appear in these conditions?

Faith and the Environment*

An Inquiry into Islamic Principles and the Built Environment of Muslims

Ismail Serageldin

INTRODUCTION: AN APPROACH TO THE SOURCES

As the Muslim world shakes and stirs in a fitful search to reaffirm its independent identity, it confronts the cultural as well as the political realities of a world dominated by the West generally and the United States specifically. This has lead many in the Muslim world to define their identities by emphasising the "otherness" of the Muslim being from the hegemonic world context.[1] Doubtless there is much truth to this "otherness", but emphasising it at the outset leads to a "rejectionist" approach which, to my mind, is narrow and constrictive and in fact does not do justice to the richness and variety that Muslim culture has achieved in the past, and can achieve again, by the more self-assured process of adaptive assimilation that characterised its confrontations with the Greek and Roman cultures at the time of the early Muslim conquests of the seventh and eighth centuries A.D.

The built environment, as it relates to Muslim societies and to the natural environment, is the main concern of this paper. It too has been subjected to this search for authentification, widely interpreted as "Islamisation". Strident cries have arisen to reject foreign "imported" models of architecture and development, and to return to the sources, unfortunately within the same narrow general conceptual framework that has guided many other aspects of the contemporary Islamic revival.

The basic approach proposed in this paper is different from this "rejectionist" mode of thinking. It returns to the original sources of Islamic doctrine: the *Quran* and the *Sunna* of the prophet, and relate these to the historical context of past experience and present realities. It seeks to derive an appropriate approach to dealing with the built environment of Muslim societies at the beginning of their fifteenth century (A.H.) and the end of the twentieth century A.D. regardless of how this derived approach is similar to, or different from, western experiences. On the other hand, there is a parallel and more subtle danger in initiating the search for a Muslim identity (in any specific domain of cultural expression) solely in terms of Muslim sources. This is the "bending" of source texts to provide literally specific detailed guides for contemporary actions, thus ignoring their context, to fit in a particular writer's viewpoint.

Return to the sources starts with reading the Quran.

I do not believe that any reading of the *Quran*, at any level[2], or a study of the *Sunna*, will provide detailed instructions on how to design a house in Morocco or Indonesia, or how to design the thoroughfares of Cairo or Istanbul. Those that have tried to derive specific examples from these sources are doing both themselves and the sources a disfavour. Themselves by ignoring the wider context in which we live and which must provide the major "givens" of the problems to be addressed, and the sources by demeaning them to the level of a "handbook" or "textbook" rather than treating the *Quran* as the eternal message of inspiration and guidance for all times and the *Sunna* of the Prophet as the embodiment of exemplary behaviour. If God had desired to give people specific instructions on how to build structures in the twentieth century, He could certainly have done so explicitly.

---

* Report No 27, Award Cycle III, AKKA, Geneva, Dec 1985. (Unpublished).

What then is the return to the sources likely to produce? Surely no instructions as to the size of rooms or height of doors. Rather, this systematic review of the sources should produce a general set of *principles* that should help guide the searcher towards what is an appropriate response to the problems confronting Muslim societies today and tomorrow.

In developing this appropriate response to contemporary problems, the past experience of Muslim societies must also be taken into account. Not only is it the basic determinant of the "heritage" which provides Muslims with exemplars of the achievement of past generations, but also it serves as the basis for defining the elements of a cultural continuity which are essential in any search for authenticity and assertion of self-identity. Nevertheless, one must be wary of accepting the actions of past generations too readily. The history of the Muslim peoples (like all other peoples) is one that is replete with failures to live up to the ethical and behavioural norms of their avowed credos. Sifting the wheat from the chaff is the task of the historian, the philosopher, the jurist and the theologian. Suffice to state this as an issue and proceed with our search for these general principles and our attempt to spell out their application to the problems confronting contemporary Muslim societies.

To develop the earth's bounty while remaining in harmony with nature. Yemen.

GENERAL PRINCIPLES

Stewardship of the Earth. The starting point of my search for a definition of the Muslim approach to the environment is based upon the intended role of man[3] in this world. I am firmly convinced that the intended role for humans is that of "stewards of the earth".

This concept of "stewardship of the earth" deserves elaboration. It plays a central role in the vision of spiritually guided material development advanced here, but it is curiously under-represented in the scholastic tradition of Islamic theology. Yet, the references to it are plentiful in the *Quran*.

In the original Arabic, the word is *Khalifa* (*istakhlafa*). It has appeared in various passages of the scriptures and has been translated by eminent scholars such as Yusuf Ali[4] variously as vice-regent (of God on earth), agent, inheritor, successor. To me, the concept of "stewardship" captures best the prismatic nature of this assignment.

It is apparent that this special assignment was central to the very role of man in the cosmos: Thus it is God's design that man should go to earth as his "vice-regent" as witnessed by this passage from the story of Adam:

> *"Behold, thy Lord said to the angels: "I will create*
> *a* VICE-REGENT ON EARTH." *They said:*
> *"Wilt Thou place therein one who will make*
> *Mischief therein and shed blood? —*
> *Whilst we do celebrate Thy praises*
> *And Glorify Thy holy (name)?"*
> *He said: "I know what ye know not."* (*Quran*, 2:30)

The intent that this injunction is universal comes through more clearly in the Arabic where the word (*Khalifa*) which here appears as "vice-regent" is the same as that used for "inheritors", "successors" in other passages addressed to all believers:

> *"He it is that has made*
> *You* INHERITORS IN THE EARTH:
> *If, then, any do reject*
> *(God), their rejection (works)*
> *Against themselves."* (*Quran*, 35:39)

And yet if there is a privilege attached to this assignment, it is hostage to the execution of special responsibilities, hence the stewardship concept:

"Then We made you heirs
In the land after them,
TO SEE HOW YE WOULD BEHAVE"[5] (*Quran*, 10:14)

Exercising that stewardship involves two complementary strands:

- The pursuit of "development of the earth", "taming" nature to serve man's purpose, cultivating its resources and increasing its bounty. This pursuit, is that of a steward, not a rapacious exploiter, i.e. it is balanced with limits imposed on greed and personal ambition, to nurture the underlying sustaining system.
- The society of men who work this earth and enjoy its fruits and bounty must be organised in a just and mutually supportive manner; a "justly balanced" society.

In the rest of this paper , these two themes recur in different forms. Some of the ways of the expected behaviour of the "stewards of the earth" are spelled out to the extent that they provide some guidance to the appropriate development of the natural as well as the built environment.

Insofar as one can identify such principles they can be grouped in a descending hierarchy based on scale:

- *Stewardship of the earth:* guiding principle of man's role in the cosmos.
- *Relationships with nature*: of particular relevance to rural settlement, ecological considerations in urban settlements, and conservation issues.
- *Relations between men*: of particular relevance in the congested, intricate patterns of settlements associated with urbanisation, where the organisation of space is closely tied to economic, financial and social issues.
- *Individual behaviour:* of particular relevance in the design of individual dwellings, choice of decorative expression, etc.

That the boundaries between these levels are not absolutely defined is self evident. Indeed, almost any issue is best studied by reference to more than one of these "levels" of principle. Their articulation in this manner here is merely a matter of convenience that facilitates and clarifies presentation.

The intricate and delicate balance of cosmological order is reflected in the elegant Muqarnas of Islamic architecture. Ali Qapu, Isfahan, Iran.

Relationship with Nature. The role of man in dealing with nature is guided by two general principles whose balance must be maintained at all times:

- There is an order and a balance in the cosmos and in this world which must be respected. This leads to the need for environmental protection, including wildlife of all types.
- It is the role of man to develop the natural resources of this world and to benefit from the rewards of this development. Thus a minimalist, anti-developmental approach cannot be maintained in the face of injunctions to the contrary.

The evidence for the need to respect the intrinsic balance in the natural order of things is sprinkled throughout the holy *Quran* in reference to God's meticulous order in all things, starting from the scale of the cosmos, of the sun and the moon:

"And the Sun
Runs his course
For a period determined
For him: that is
The decree of (Him)
The Exalted in Might,
The All-Knowing.

And the Moon,—
We have measured for her
Mansions (to traverse)..." (*Quran*, 36:38–39)

This meticulous order runs through all things,

"He to Whom belongs
The dominion of the heavens
And the earth...
It is He Who created
All things, and ordered them
In due proportions." (Quran, 25:2)

"...Every single thing is
before His sight in
due proportion." (Quran, 13:8)

"Verily, all things
Have We created
In proportion and measure." (Quran, 54:49)

Clearly, therefore, this implicit order that God created "in due proportion" in all things must be respected by those to whom he has granted stewardship of the earth. In today's jargon one would say that we are enjoined not to destroy the ecological balance, but to respect it.

Furthermore, we are reminded that our co-inhabitants on this planet are to be treated as communities like ourselves, i.e. the systematic destruction of species would be indefensible in this scheme of things:

"There is not an animal
(That lives) on the earth
Nor a being that flies
On its wings, but (forms
Part of) communities like you." (Quran, 6:38)

Thus, conservation of wildlife is part of our responsibilities on this earth. Elsewhere (*Quran, 6:59*) we are told that all things dry and green are of His domain, and not a leaf falls but by His will. Thus the protection of wildlife, vividly referred to as "communities like you" is expanded to all the natural environment.

Yet these injunctions should not lead us to fear the use of the world's resources for the benefit of mankind:

"Say: Who hath forbidden
The beautiful (gifts) of God,
Which He hath produced
For His servants,
And the things, clean and pure
(Which He hath provided)
For sustenance?" (Quran, 7:32)

"Lost are those who:...
...forbid food which
God hath provided for
them..." (Quran, 6:140)

"...Eat and drink: but waste not
by excess, for God loveth not
the wasters." (Quran, 7:31)

Thus the Muslim outlook is not one of withdrawal from this world to admire its unique balance from a distance, nor is it one of asceticism[6] and total rejection of the joys of the senses and the pleasures of possession and procreation:

"*Wealth and children are the allurements of the life of this world...*" (*Quran, 18:46*)

Mankind is enjoined to work to develop these wonderful endowments and enjoy the fruits of these labours, but they are enjoined to do so with respect for the environment and to partake of all things in moderation and under no circumstances to be wasteful. These are prescriptions that any rational human being would welcome, especially in the light of the environmental degradation that unchecked greed and thoughtless exploitation of resources have brought about.

Muslims undertake their work, whatever it might be, with precision and attention to quality. Multan, Pakistan.

Relationship between Men. The domain of *Mu'amalat* (transactions) that covers the relationships between humans in the context of a societal organisation has been particularly well elaborated in the scriptures, the *Sunna* and has constituted the bulk of the corpus of Islamic *Shari'a* law and *fatwa* rulings over the centuries. It is not necessary here to elaborately retrace these developments, rather we can sum up some of the more relevant highlights.

In any societal context guided by Islamic principles certain fundamental relationships vis-à-vis others in the community play a central organising role. All Islamic jurisprudence is based on the concept of the welfare of the community and the interest of the majority tempered by the protection of the rights of the minority.[7]

Since we shall return many times to the physical expression of the Islamic societal organisation it may be pertinent to spell out my understanding of the key aspects of this society. In general, in accordance with the principles of Islam, the organisation of society would have the following broad features:

- *Freedom:* Islam is an ideology of liberation. It sets the believer free from all the fears and shackles that can be imposed in this world. This freedom however is not complete license to rampage on earth where the strong destroy the weak. It is a freedom that is circumscribed by the bounds of law:

  "*O ye who believe! The law*
  of equality is prescribed to you...
  ...In the Law of Equality there
  is (saving of) Life, to you
  O ye men of understanding;
  That ye may restrain yourselves." (*Quran, 2:178–179*)

  It is imperative therefore that any society that tries to live with such Islamic principles be one where the freedom and dignity of all its members are carefully protected by a legal framework[8] that does not allow the humiliation of any minority or any individual, male or female. This freedom should be reflected in familial as well as societal contexts, and interpreted in its broadest sense.[9]
- *The Search for Knowledge ('Ilm) and Truth (Haq):* The pursuit of knowledge is the single most striking feature in a system of great revelation such as Islam. The word 'Ilm (knowledge) and its deriviatives occurs 880 times in the *Quran.* But knowledge is not perceived as neutral. It is the basis for better appreciating truth (Haq) which is revealed but which can be "seen" by the knowledgeable in the world around them. Indeed, believers are enjoined to look around and to learn the truth. The Prophet exhorted his followers to seek knowledge as far as China, then considered to be the end of the earth. Scientists are held in high esteem: the Prophet said that the ink of scientists is equal to the blood of martyrs. The very first word of the Quranic revelation was an order to r*ead* and then to learn, and to seek knowledge.
- *Action and Industry:* Action and industry are the way of salvation. The faithful are enjoined to Act: "*...and do good deeds, and your actions will be seen by God, His prophet and the believers.*" (*Quran, 9:105*)

Such actions should be for the common good, but even when the religious instructions are oriented towards one own's task then we are exhorted to undertake them with discipline and precision, and to produce quality work.

The Muslim faithful are told that they are responsible for their fellow men and they are asked to take an active role in redressing inequity where they see it to the full extent of their abilities (*Hadith:* If one of you sees something that is wrong, then let him set it right; first with his hand, and if he cannot then with his tongue, and if he cannot then with his heart, and that is the weakest of all possible forms of faith).

It clearly follows from the above that these exhortations place a heavy emphasis on being active *in this world* and acting well at all levels. Contemplative meditation is looked upon as a means of self renewal in order to be able to undertake more and better things in the future, not as an end in and of itself.

- *Justice:* The concept of justice is absolute in Islam and not relative as in some Christian theologies (due to the projection of the concept of responsibility for original sin). Muslims perceive all their actions as part of the great test in which they have to succeed by acting in a *just* manner. The worldly interpretation of this is Islamic legislation which seeks to set the limits for what is permissible between man and man. It defines the foundations of a theory of rehabilitation and punishment and the manner in which punishment should be meted out.[10] Jurists have to update and enforce the law in the pursuit of an idealised form of justice that should be as absolute as it can be on earth. Scholars still recognise that some things go beyond the means of the Muslim community and are in the hands of the creator (in the hereafter). But it is an essential feature of the Muslim society that it should seek to establish justice here on earth and not await the kingdom of heaven.
- *The Public Interest*: The concept of the public interest governs legislative innovation. It is perceived as a justification for changing the past forms and coping with an ever-changing present and future. The systematic means of introducing legislative innovation is both checked and helped by the pursuit of the public interest. It is aided by the liberal interpretation that "all that is not expressly forbidden is allowed."[11] Mechanisms and processes of introducing these innovations have been worked out in great detail in order to ensure that they are still consonant with the ethical principles of the *Quran* and that evolution does not, over time, lead to the abandonment of the basic ethical principles set out in the original seventh century society in Medina.
- *Concern for the Poor and the Weak:* Justice must be tempered by mercy, and compassion must be the prevalent feature of the Muslim community. The faithful are enjoined time and again to show mercy towards those who are less fortunate, to show compassion to the needy, and to be magnanimous in victory and forgiving when in power.[12] It is relevant that the Muslim system was the first to introduce a form of social security and welfare assistance whereby the poor and the weak had a *right* to part of the public treasury and did not have to rely on the charity of those who are more fortunate.[13]

In order to promote a development pattern consonant with the above, an entirely new approach is required. It is clearly beyond the scope of this paper to develop such an approach.

Nevertheless, and without falling prey to the excessive emphasis on "otherness" decried at the outset of this paper, it is still possible to mention the conceptual difference which this approach implies vis-à-vis the traditional western neo-classical economic approach:

- It requires a holistic view of development, social, political, cultural, physical and economic; and
- It is primarily focused on human beings, not on economics *per se*.

Individual Behaviour. Much of the behaviour demanded of Muslims is implicit in the preceding discussions in terms of relations with nature and relations with each other. Other aspects (piety, charity, etc.) are obvious and do not need restatement. Yet one additional aspect is of particular relevance to this discussion and that is a call for a certain *humility* in individual behaviour. This comes across clearly in many passages in the *Quran*, for example:

> "...*Nor exult over favours bestowed upon*
> *you for God loveth not any*
> *vainglorious boaster.*" (*Quran, 57:23*)

> "*And swell not thy cheek*[14]
> *(For pride) at men,*
> *Nor walk in insolence*
> *Through the earth;*
> *For God loveth not*
> *Any arrogant boaster.*" (*Quran, 31:18*)

> "...*For God loveth not the arrogant,*
> *the vainglorious*..." (*Quran, 4:36*)

> "...*Verily, He loveth not the arrogant.*" (*Quran, 16:23*)

These and many other passages when combined with other injunctions lead to a composite picture of the appropriate behaviour of the individual Muslim, which was summed up by one prominent Quranic scholar thus:

> "*And it flows naturally from a true understanding of our relation to God and His universe and to our fellow-creatures, especially man. In all things be moderate. Do not go the pace, and do not be stationary or slow. Do not be talkative and do not be silent. Do not be loud and do not be timid or half-hearted. Do not be too confident, and do not be cowed down. If you have patience, it is to give you constancy and determination, that you may bravely carry on the struggle of life. If you have humility, it is to save you from unseemly swagger, not to curb your right spirit and your reasoned determination.*"[15]

This moderation and humility is in sharp contrast to much of the ostentatious consumption and self-glorification that are found in the constructions of many Muslims, especially many of those who have exulted in new found wealth.

> "*Exult not, for God loveth not*
> *Those who exult (in riches).*
> *But seek, with the (wealth)*
> *Which God has bestowed on thee,*
> *The Home of the Hereafter*..." (*Quran, 28:76–77*)

THE BUILT ENVIRONMENT

Rural Settlements. The majority of Muslims today are rural dwellers. The vast mass of silently suffering impoverished peasants that constitutes the bulk of Muslim society today must be the starting point of our discussion, even if the urban scene is where the most exciting, innovating and challenging confrontations between Islamic values and westernisation are taking place.

In the rural world, the relationship with nature is essential. Carefully tilling the soil to produce its bounty and enjoying it, while being charitable towards others and husbanding these precious resources is vividly depicted in this passage:

"It is He who produceth
Gardens, with trellises
And without, and dates,
And tilth with produce
Of all kinds, and olives
And pomegranates,
Similar (in kind)
And different (in variety):
Eat of their fruit
In their season, but render
The dues that are proper
On the day that the harvest
Is gathered. But waste not
By excess: for God
Loveth not the wasters." (*Quran, 6:141*)

Garden with trellises — plants, shade, water and people. Harmony of the garden. Bagh-i Fin, Kashan, Iran.

The use of cattle is encouraged:

"Of the cattle are some
For burden and some for meat..." (*Quran, 6:142*)

Indeed this use of animals is elaborated in another passage very vividly:

"And cattle He has created
For you (men): from them
Ye derive warmth,
And numerous benefits,
And of their (meat) ye eat.

And ye have a sense
Of pride and beauty in them

And (He has created) horses,
Mules, and donkeys, doe you
To ride and use for show;
And He has created (other) things
Of which ye have no knowledge." (*Quran, 16:5, 6, 8*)

It is interesting to note in this passage animals are referred to as more than beasts of burden but indeed they may be pedigreed animals bred for beauty and show, for grace, elegance and refined enjoyment.

Thus the passage is in no way contrary to the large-scale mechanisation of agriculture, if this be feasible, or the modernisation of agricultural production with its consonant changes in the pattern of life of the rural built environment.[16]

So far there is no controversy. The heart of the issue of rural development, however, is the possession of land and the problem of land tenure. Here, Islam has a clear-cut preference to encouraging the development of fallow land and giving ownership to those who develop it.

(*Hadith*: "He who brings life to a dead piece of land owns it.")[17] The accumulation of vast land holdings is discouraged by the mechanism of the inheritance code. More generally the type of exploitation of peasants and share-croppers by absentee landlords that is so prevalent in much of the Third World has been thoroughly condemned by the more general recognition of the problems of poverty alleviation[18] on the one hand and by the consideration of property ownership as a social function, not an absolute right or privilege:

"...And spend out of the substance
whereof He has made you HEIRS *(stewards)..."* (*Quran, 57:7*)

These principles, I believe, mean a more equitable treatment of the rural (vis-à-vis the urban) world, and a more enabling environment for those who till the soil. Though their voices are seldom heard in the political arena's of today, they deserve our attention and respect. They should not be disenfranchised, as is often the case, rather they should be empowered to build the dignified productive environment to which they are entitled, and to live in that symbiotic harmony with the natural environment which is so characteristic of well-balanced rural societies.

This enabling environment, however, will mean that rural dwellers will respond to their changing socio-economic surroundings in a manner that is compatible with their own self-image, which may differ markedly from the romantic images of bucolic rurality that many contemporary architects hold. [19]

In terms of construction and building techniques, it is clear that the injunctions against waste and for a just balance argue in favour of what is today called the "appropriate technologies" approach. That is not only the outcome of this argument from the scriptures but also the course of practical wisdom. That such an approach can yield structures and compositions of outstanding beauty and evocative power, has been definitively demonstrated by the work of Hassan Fathy,[20] which stands as an exemplar for all designers who would tackle the problems of the rural world in Muslim societies.

Agreements between neighbours produced dense yet humane environments. Medina of Tunis, Tunisia.

Urban Settlement. Harking back to the principles governing the relations between men *(Mu'amalat)* they clearly come most acutely into play in the congested and contested articulation of urban spaces. Here, it is easy to see some applications of these principles in terms of urban form. Thus, property rights, while fully recognised and protected, are not absolute. For example, access to water cannot be denied. The right of first refusal of the neighbour in the disposal of neighbouring property *(shuf'a)* is a fundamental organising principle. Investment is encouraged and those who hoard gold and silver are warned of dire punishment.[21]

Within this broad framework, flexibility is the hallmark of guiding relations. *All that is not expressly forbidden is allowed.* Neighbours are encouraged to reach agreement by mutual consent rather than by arbitration. This approach has led to a variety of subtle and charming air-rights developments in old cities. It has also allowed organic linkages between different structures that abut, partly to accommodate expanding families and changing needs. It has therefore helped to create a living and changing environment that we have come to appreciate in the unique character of the old Medinas.

Indeed this emphasis on the relations between neighbours is exceptionally strong in Islam. Thus:

> *"And do good —*
> *To parents, kinsfolk,*
> *Orphans, those in need,*
> *Neighbours who are near,*
> *Neighbours who are strangers,*
> *The Companion by your side,*
> *The way-farer (ye meet),*
> *And what your right hands possess."* [22] *(Quran, 4:36)*

This is wider and more comprehensive than the general "Love thy neighbour" since it encompasses even animals and emphasises practical service above and beyond sentiment.

While this does not yield a specific *physical* prescription for the urban form of cities or even urban dwellings, it does encourage designers to create public spaces that enable *social interaction* between neighbours and way-farers, and immediately brings to mind images of a living, thriving dense townscape.

The key element in articulating this townscape becomes *the street*, its alignment, its scale, and its availability for pedestrian as opposed to motorised use. Broken *alignments* built at the *human scale*, with possible overhangs and air-right developments, and with adequately spaced enlarged areas for social interaction are characteristics to be encouraged. Activities allowed in the street are key determinants of the area's character: commercial, residential, mixed, etc. The *mixed use* pattern is again implied in the heavy emphasis on social interaction. It is interesting to note in this context that western town planning has now come full circle after experimenting for a century with exclusionary single use land zoning; it is now promoting mixed use developments that today carry a substantial economic premium for the developers. The United States has seen the emergence of the "Festival Market Place" of the Rouse Company as the saviour of downtown redevelopments. Boston's Faneuil Hall and Baltimore's new harbour are but artificially recreated modern versions of the old *suq's* and bazaars so characteristic of any old Muslim city.

For a variety of other reasons, not least of which is respect for *privacy*, this townscape should also enable a transition from the public domain to the private sphere without injury to either. When coupled with the general prohibition against ostentation and self-aggrandisement, I believe we are led to favour a *high-density low-rise residential environment*[23] which would also be quite economic in aggregate terms, (i.e. in the interest of the community as a whole).[24] It would also avoid much of the anomie that has accompanied large scale high-rise residential complexes[25] and has led in its extreme form to the destruction of Pruitt-Igoe.

The pattern of urban settlement is largely determined by a wide spectrum of technological and geographic considerations that have nothing to do with Islam *per se*.[26] Nevertheless, within the broad "skeleton" so determined, the "flesh" that is so definitive in determining character and defining the experiential aspects of architecture and urbanism, that "flesh" remains in the domain of the designer.

Yet one still stands confronted by the problem of the scale of the modern metropolis[27] and the problem of the tall building,[28] so characteristic of this century's technology and economics. On the former one must recognise the need to strike a balance between the imperative of rapid modernisation and growth on the one hand and the need to preserve historic districts[29] on the other. This can surely be done without losing sight of the *character* of new developments, avoiding what Charles Correa has rightly called the bureaucratic solutions of cloning structures.[30] On the question of tall buildings much remains to be said; although the new building for the National Commercial Bank in Jeddah (designed by SOM's Gordon Bunshaft) shows us that, with imagination, designers have a lot more to offer than the boxy curtain-walled pattern of the "typical" western office building. But more will be said on this subject later in this essay.

Discreet yet elegant touches are found everywhere in Muslim dwellings. Sidi Bou Said, Tunisia.

Individual Structures. When addressing individual structures we should first distinguish between individual dwellings and other types of structures. For *dwellings*, it behoves us to recall the injunctions on humility and the respect for privacy, as well as the sanctity of the home as the refuge of rest and peace and joy.

The physical layout of the house should provide for adequate articulation of public and private spaces and an appropriate transition to the public domain beyond (i.e. the street). The building should not be conspicuously projecting an image of wealth to generate the envy of neighbours and passers-by, but at the same time it should not be an ascetic structure devoid of decoration. On this latter point it is appropriate to note that outstanding Muslim scholars, including no less an authority than Muhammad 'Abduh[31] have ruled that paintings and sculptures are definitely acceptable in Muslim societies since the prohibitions against them derive primarily from the fear of idolatry. Since today this fear is irrelevant in the direct sense of idolatry, the prohibition is also irrelevant. Decoration and the use of paintings and sculptures, are all elements to be used by the Muslim in making his home a delightful place, along with the more traditional uses of plants and water.

In shaping the interior of his home to make it a place of restfulness, joy and beauty the Muslim is at liberty to do as he pleases, provided he observes the general dictum of *chastity*:

> *"To every religion there is a character*
> *and the character of Islam is chastity."* (*Hadith*)

Outside of dwellings, no discussion of individual structures in muslim societies can ignore the role of *the mosque*. It is central in the design of any Muslim agglomeration. It is not only the place of worship but also the key to community activities. Granted that the complexity of modern life has forced many communal public activities into specialised structures, the tendency towards limiting the mosque to its liturgical function, a "churchification of the mosque" is to be deplored. All the more so, since in western Christian cultures there is at present an active movement to open up churches as foci of community activity to improve the communications between the church organisation and the community and to better utilise the building at times where there are no religious services.

The architecture of the mosque is a complex subject which has received some critical attention, but certainly not enough. Some of the recent writing opens up avenues for speculation and reflection,[32] but considerably more needs to be done if we are to appropriately re-integrate the mosque building as an organising element in the increasingly complex patterns of contemporary settlements.

The *tall buildings* remains an important if puzzling question. Clearly there is nothing in Islamic teaching that prevents men from reaching for the stars and building ever higher structures if these are justified design solutions to particular problems, i.e. if the purpose of building such a tall structure is not mere self aggrandisement, but to provide an effective response to a set of economic, functional and technical criteria. Indeed old Islamic towns like Shibam and Sana'a are comprised of skyscrapers. One can easily visualise new problems arising in geographically constrained commercial downtown spaces under the pressure of an ever increasing urban population. Yet one must remain uneasy. To the extent that "skyscrapers" are indeed synonymous with the "zeitgeist" of this century, they have been the focus of much attention though relatively little critical concern.[33] The cultural dimensions of the tall building as an evocative work of art, an element of societal cultural expression rather than just as a symbol of commercial success and a projection of an "image of progress" remain tantalisingly unclear, insufficiently studied in the West and totally unstudied as they relate to the value structure and self-image of contemporary Muslim societies.

Tall buildings were the norm in many parts of the Muslim world, witness these ancient thirteen storey skycrapers in Shibam, Yemen.

In many ways, this unease is well expressed in three examples from Jeddah in Saudi Arabia. The Bugshan tower, is a tall curtain-walled structure which after completion with a conventional facade was then "Islamicised" by covering each element of the flat façade with a small "paste-on" arched window frame! The Rush Housing project is a complex of tower structures that make no attempt at developing or even hiding the conventional international modernist credentials of their façades. They have earned almost universal indifference if not scorn from the Saudi community of Jeddah. They remain vacant years after completion (although this is for other administrative reasons). The third example is Gordon Bunshaft's striking National Commercial Bank building,[34] which while remaining the epitome of modernism has nevertheless imaginatively dealt with the problems of sun and glare by a use of three inset atria that span eight to nine storeys each. This building has been generally very well received in the community although it has no "Islamic" decorative elements whatsoever. The purity of the forms and the elegance of the composition strike a responsive chord in almost all who have visited it.

Modern versions of the tall building must also be suited to the environment. SOM's dramatic National Commercial Bank building in Jeddah, Saudi Arabia, deals effectively with sun and glare.

What can one make of these three examples with respect to what the Muslim faith tells Muslims about tall buildings? Nothing. The universal truth is that imaginative design is better than uninspired imitation or kitsch. Muslim societies are as entitled as any other to have their sensibilities engaged by imaginative, beautiful landmark buildings, which if they eschew mere "vain-glorious", "arrogant" reasons for being and respond appropriately at the level of function will indeed fulfil part of the Islamic credo "God is beautiful and loves beauty". Indeed appreciation of beauty is one of the qualities that sets humans apart from the animal species.

CONCLUSIONS

The return to the sources which we have tried to undertake in this essay lead to guidelines for dealing with environment, both natural and man-made, that are broad and all encompassing. Some would argue that these broad guidelines are basically what rational minds would propose for sound design principles and are therefore not specifically "Islamic".[35] That is of course true. With the exception of some particularly value-specific injunctions such as chastity, humility and neighbourliness, most of the principles are those that rational humans would propose by themselves in order to maintain the natural habitat and develop enjoyable living surroundings. That is exactly what one would expect. It would have indeed been surprising if any reading of the sources had led to "irrational" instructions to despoil the natural environment and produce unpleasant, disfunctional living environments for humans!

The absence of discernible specific physical attributes of the architecture these principles imply, which could be seen as a weakness by those seeking cookbook recipes and simple answers, is in reality a very real strength. A strength because this is precisely what allows Islamic culture to be adapted to the cold climates of the Himalayas and the hot tropical forests of Indonesia as well as the deserts of Arabia. It is this subtle overlay of Islamic principles over regional particularism, the former fully recognising and working with the latter to help improve the inhabitants' response to it, that have enabled Islam to have its true universal impact creating the "diversity within a unity" that the flowering of Muslim culture has demonstrated through the ages.

Contrast this with the heavy-handed physical framework of the Roman *Castrum* — that outpost of Roman civilisation that was implanted, as if with a rubber stamp, from the cold forests of Britain and northern Europe to the deserts of Libya! Identical layouts incorporated the *Decumanus* and the *Cardo*. Identical elements including the forum, the temple, and the *thermae* were used. All of this was done without so much as a bow to the regional realities of climate and culture.

The Islamic essence of any building or set of buildings is much more subtle than to be captured exclusively by the physical attributes of these buildings. To seek to define any architecture as "Islamic" exclusively through the detailed analysis of the architectonic features of the building would be like trying to measure the temperature or the humidity of a room with a yardstick. The yardstick is a useful tool to capture one aspect of the reality of that room, but temperature and humidity are equally valid aspects of that same reality even if they totally escape the yardstick's ability to interpret them.

This analogy is indeed suitable for our subject. To the extent that (some aspects of) the suitability of the structure's design can be measured by the comfort of temperature and humidity, the specific materials, layouts, dimensions of the physical structure must be well adapted to geographic localism to achieve it. So it is with a truly successful Islamic architecture: its physical attributes will be primarily determined by the specificities of geographic localism, but the end product will produce a certain spiritual harmony and facilitate a pattern of social interaction that are truly in conformity with an Islamic world-view.[36]

Clearly, however, the application of these principles will be far from homogeneous throughout the Muslim communities of the world, and the quality of the results within each community will themselves show a very large degree of variability ranging from the absurd to the sublime. These results can indeed be plotted into the six-celled matrix proposed by Kamil Khan Mumtaz[37] which defines three "horizontal layers" (the architecture of the elite, that of the commercially dominant classes, and the anonymous vernacular architecture) and two "vertical streams" (the spiritual and the materialist). But the "quality" of the product in each cell, or its "Islamicity" is still an elusive property to assess. Here, there are no simple answers. There can only be an ongoing patient search to explore the essential nature of beauty which a work of art achieves through momentary fusion between artist and task, what Sir Kenneth Clark called "moments of vision"[38] and what is now being elucidated by an increasing number of Muslim scholars in the context of the Muslim world.[39] This self-knowledge, thus developed through painstaking analysis of past achievements and present realities, must then go to enrich the collective intellectual resources of architects practicing in the Muslim world. The myths, images and stimuli that they can bring to bear on any design problem must be enriched[40] with the type of concepts that transcend the simplistic physical reading of a monumental heritage and promote a deeper understanding of self and society within the context of an Islamic world view.

Only thus can we hope to promote a greater harmony between the built environments of Muslims and the eternal message of Islam.

Islamic Culture and Non-Muslim Contributions*

Ismail Serageldin

Let us look at some of the philosophical issues that are involved in dealing with the physical aspects of urbanisation and what the role of the architect should be.

The concerns of the architect and urban planner have been touched upon in a variety of ways including the very challenging question about the meaning of history to a contemporary architect. Not the technical issue of "How do we restore a building?", but rather "What is the meaning of a historical heritage to an architect practicing today?" Our heritage did not stop at the time of the Mamluks; we have subsequently had a large number of significant buildings. I think we have to take those two points together and address the question of the role of a heritage in inspiring architects to serve a contemporary society. But I would like to go back to the first question, that of history, and suggest that historical reality in Cairo is highly complex. I would invoke a comment made by Dr Salah Hejab in which he said there is not simply just an Islamic Cairo, or a Christian Cairo, but there is one Cairo that has gone on through time. I would like to highlight this to explain that Cairo through the ages has had a culture of its own. That culture may have been imbued with the spirit of Islam, but it also had the contributions of other religious faiths, welded together in a broader cosmopolitan urban culture that cannot be subsumed under any narrow label.

Fig. 1 Fig. 2

Patterns of dress were not dissimilar among different communities. Fig. 1: Rabbi Ibrahim ben Ezra (19th century). Fig. 2: Priest and Sheikh at the time of the 1919 Revolution.

Let me refer you to a few images, for which I must thank Professor Laila Ali Ibrahim, who has been able to dig up these very interesting examples from archival research. The distinguished gentleman portrayed in Figure 1 is not a Muslim scholar. He is the rabbi of the Jewish community in Cairo; but there was a commonality of dress and a commonality of behaviour that was shared in a wide variety of ways in a single community in the nineteenth century. There was a commonality of culture, manifested through clothes, habits and so on, that spread throughout the various communities within Cairo; it was not so dichotomised (into Muslim/non Muslim) as one would imagine. In fact Figure 2 is another striking picture of a priest and a sheikh sitting together at the time of the 1919 revolution; one would be hard-pressed to identify which is which.

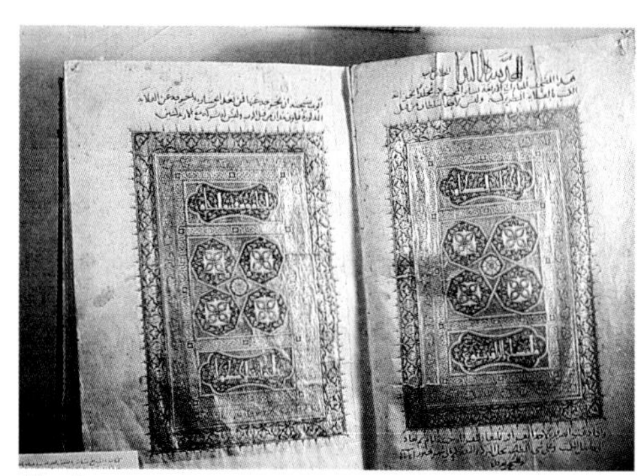

Fig. 3 Fig. 4

The careful and painstaking decoration of the Mamluk Quran (Fig. 3) is strikingly similar to that found in the Coptic Bible of the same period (Fig. 4).

Even in something that we consider as uniquely Islamic as the decoration of the cover of a *Quran* (Fig. 3), one would find a very strong resemblance to a contemporary picture of a Bible of the same Mamluk period (Fig. 4). Architecturally speaking, the magnificent decoration of the *minbar* of the Muayyad Mosque in Cairo (Fig. 5) can be found almost identically in the altar of the Abu Sirga Church (Fig. 6). And the doorway of the Mullaqa Church in Cairo is striking in its homogeneity and its closeness to the character of other parts of the Old City. In fact one cannot easily differentiate between a traditional *mihrab* and the apse of the Church of the Virgin in Zuwayla which is in the heart of Gamaliya.

I use these many examples to make the point that when we interpret (historic) culture we should not be obsessed with specific periods in history or with specific individual monuments, or with specific labels. Instead, we should take the broad product of Egyptian Cairene society which was truly predominantly Muslim; but which incorporated many talents and many geniuses in producing a magnificent heritage.

* Extract from Proceedings of *The Expanding Metropolis: Coping with the Urban Growth of Cairo*, Seminar Nine in the series – Architectural Transformations in the Islamic World, Cairo, Eygpt, Nov 11 – 15, 1984. Published by Concept Media for The Aga Khan Award for Architecture, Singapore, 1985, pp 209 – 211.

Fig. 5

Fig. 6

Architectural decoration used the same motifs in Christian and Muslim Cairo. The arabesques on the minbar of al-Muayyad Mosque (Fig. 5) are almost identical to those found on the altar of Abu Sirga Church (Fig. 6)

Fig. 7

Fig. 8

Architectural detailing was strikingly similar in medieval Cairene construction as can be seen in comparing the mihrab of the Sultan Hassan Mosque (Fig. 7) with the apse of the medieval Church of the Virgin in Zuwayla (Fig. 8).

Fig. 9

Fig. 10

The rich Cairene architectual heritage is considered a universal legacy. The recent Coptic Museum (Fig. 9) used the same ribbed arch motif found in the twelfth century Aqmar Mosque (Fig. 10).

On Creativity, Imagination, and the Design Process

The need for creativity and imagination in contemporary design cannot be overstated. The Award has addressed this subject through its think tanks.

That creativity and imagination permeate the design process is not in doubt. But probing what it is that constitutes a successful attack on a design problem, producing an innovative and creative solution that is then recognised as such, is a more difficult and troubling question. The Award devoted two separate think tanks to this question, combining prominent architectural critics, practitioners, and clients in a three-way interchange that tried to elucidate the illusive nature of the design process, and to identify the components of creativity and imagination that are brought to bear upon the practice of architecture.

These discussions are as yet not sufficiently advanced as a corpus of work to lead to a consensus of what is, or should be, involved beyond recognising that there is no easy formula that can be prescribed for architects to improve their performance in confronting difficult design problems. Yet, the theoretical efforts undertaken in these think tanks to develop a model of the design process, and to test some of the hypotheses of that model against the practice of prominent architects, deserve attention. The think tanks looked at the work both of prominent westerners practicing in the Muslim world as well as of prominent Muslim architects grappling with building in their own societies. These reviews have helped enrich our understanding of a difficult, if not intractable problem.

The discussions built upon a theoretical model presented by Ismail Serageldin. In a lengthy documented work (to be published separately), he argued that architects, when faced with a design problem, draw upon a wide array of myths, images and stimuli, as well as learned processes and techniques. They use these tools to confront the problem as they perceive it, within constraints that are both exogenous and endogenous, to arrive at a design solution. It follows, therefore, that efforts that enrich these myths, images and stimuli, as well as the techniques of problem solving that architects bring to bear upon their task, will enhance the possibilities of obtaining better architectural solutions. It is the subtlety of the procedures and processes of intermediation that take place in the mind of the architect moving from this first set of stimuli, images and myths to a design idea, that is most elusive. The understanding of the second intermediation from the design idea to the built reality is easier to comprehend. Here legal, technical, and economic reasons frequently can be identified as the causes of the changes that inevitably occur in translating a design concept to built reality.

It is impossible to reproduce here the full scope of what was covered in these lengthy and rich discussions. A few abstracts selected from these think tanks, fragmented as they appear here, do not do justice to the views and reasoned positions of the various individuals. Still, they convey some of the flavour of these discussions. They also reflect the breadth and variety of the Award's intellectual search and its deep and abiding commitment to the notion of *a space of freedom* for this ongoing search that can only be beneficial to those concerned with the built environment of the Muslim world today.

SERGE SANTELLI, *the talented French designer whose Résidence Andalous won an AKAA award in 1983, was asked to explain his own approach to design and the influences that have shaped his architectural sensibilities. The following are extracts from his comments.*

I feel that a very important influence on the creative aspect of my designs is my knowledge of North African building types, North African social patterns, the way people live in their houses and of the way they construct these houses.

There are many ideas that try to explain design and creativity. I prefer to talk about the collective aspects of a design process rather than about the creative aspects of the design process. These collective aspects refer to a common social content, to the cultural and social agreement existing among social groups and between individuals. What I try to express in these collective aspects of the design process are two basic elements. The first element is a kind of synchronic process between building types and society, between architect and client. The second element is the continuity between the present and the past through our historical understanding of cultures, connecting past and present architectural forms.

It is easy to define the professional aspects which are the proper domain of the architect. First, the architect has to develop a good knowledge of the brief and to provide a functional solution to the problem at hand. He has to be capable of building within financial constraints and he has also to be aware of the techniques of construction and to master them. These professional aspects are defined within precise social conventions which have to do with cultural habits, ways of living, technical tools used at a certain time, and so on. These social conventions were accepted by architects in the West until World War II. Architects expressed these social conventions as architectural conventions to respond to specific social needs. I am referring to "building types", a concept which connects social conventions, social practice and architectural work. It connects society and architecture.

In Europe, until the development of the Modern Movement in the period 1930–1940, architectural production was realised within building types and collective patterns. Architects used to work within the framework of existing building types. Therefore, their work was not opposed to society as the romantic views of some artists purported it to be. On the contrary, the architect was expressing the social and cultural values of his society, designing within building types and expressing the social values through constructing these building types. Thus, the architect has a modest role since he cannot or did not create *new* types.

This was equally true of Muslim societies, where historically there were no architects as we know them, with a few exceptions like Sinan in Turkey. There were master builders working with a client. They worked within identifiable types.

In North Africa, the traditional courtyard house is a specific building type, especially in Tunisia. It is easy to define and identify this kind of building. The North African mosque is also a strong and immutable type. The *hammams*, the public bath, the *fonduqs*, and the *madrasas* are others. The *madrasa* is a Muslim university building type.

The spaces and scale of the old funduqs (top) are reinterpreted in a simple modern idiom for the award winning Résidence Andalous (above).

If you go through the history of common architecture and not the history of monuments, you will see that architects do not have a role in designing types, since building types are social products created by the needs of people. Architects, however, have to adapt the building type to the site and environment, and can improve and perfect the type. An architect can express his personal talent by imbuing the type with his own architectural language. And what is architectural language? It is proportions, quality of light and spaces, compositions of rooms, relationships to structures. As Kahn would say, the relationship between the light and structure. This is architecture. The building type itself is not a matter of architecture.

This is different from the attitude of architects of the modern movement, supposedly the leaders of architecture. They said: "We have the freedom and the duty to create a new typology, a new type of building regardless of the people who live in them. We don't care about their views because we have the right. We belong to the avant-garde and people work for us because we are right, and our new typology will be the right typology in 50 years from now." All this still is very fashionable because 50 years after the modern movement began, the images of the modern building types are still not accepted by most of the people. If you ask the average Frenchman, for example, what is his image of a house, he would draw a house with a roof and a chimney, with classical windows and doors. He would not refer to the modern type of house described by Le Corbusier.

The open courtyard and the use of water in Résidence Andalous (top) give it a distinctly local flavour, even though decorative elements were used sparingly and in modern abstract designs (above).

A building type, however, is a social configuration but, it is not architecture. It does not have architectural manifestation or form. A problem in Western countries is what architectural language and vocabulary is the architect going to use working with a building type? How is he going to improve the type? What are the proportions, the quality of spaces and light? How are the plan and façades going to be composed? In short, what is he going to design?

The only way to do architecture for many is to refer to existing and past architecture, that is, the architecture that has been called the "Architect's reservoir." This reservoir contains all the buildings which are part of the history of architecture. It connects past and present thus building architectural memory. The modern movement destroyed this reservoir in Europe. In Europe, architects are reconstituting their reservoir again and learning their history of architecture again. Only then will they be able to borrow the language and the vocabulary they want from this reservoir.

These same problems exist in Muslim countries today. The first task of Muslim architects is to build a Muslim architectural reservoir and to have a profound understanding of the history of Muslim architecture. Unfortunately, in a North African school of architecture the history of Muslim architecture is hardly taught.

Coming to my own work, I can find avenues for creative expression within these collective aspects of the design process. A rough definition of creation is what remains personal or individual in connecting all these collective elements. The way to borrow a specific form from this architectural reservoir, the way to connect this form to another form, the way to express this grouping of forms, all this is the manifestation of a personal talent. This is part of one's creation.

I have practiced in Tunisia. Tunisia is open to Western influences and therefore is open to the myth of creativity. I am saddened by the absence of typological concern among practitioners in North Africa. That is why there are many "monsters" all over the country — the product of the high "creativity" of young architects who are fascinated by modern ideology, that values neglect of existing typologies.

This raises opposition between the architect and the typologies which are clear in Tunisia. But, the architect is recent. There were no architects until the nineteenth century, in the colonial period. Most of the houses in Tunisia are built without architects. Thus, Tunisia still retains powerful collective architecture.

Let me refer to my Apartment Hotel in Sousse, the Résidence Andalous. In Tunisia today, all public buildings and most large private buildings are now built by architects. Most are Tunisian, but some architects are French. These buildings refer to modern typologies and no longer refer to Tunisian typologies. However, the decoration of the façades refer to Muslim decoration. There are arcades, ceramic tiles, cupolas, and so on. These features give an Arabesque feeling to a building whose social, spatial structure is modern and does not refer to North African typologies. This situation arises because clients and architects are rejecting traditional values. They adopt modern, imported Western technologies like the pre-cast concrete panel, which is not well developed in Tunisia. Architects want to be modern and feel that to be modern is to use sophisticated technology.

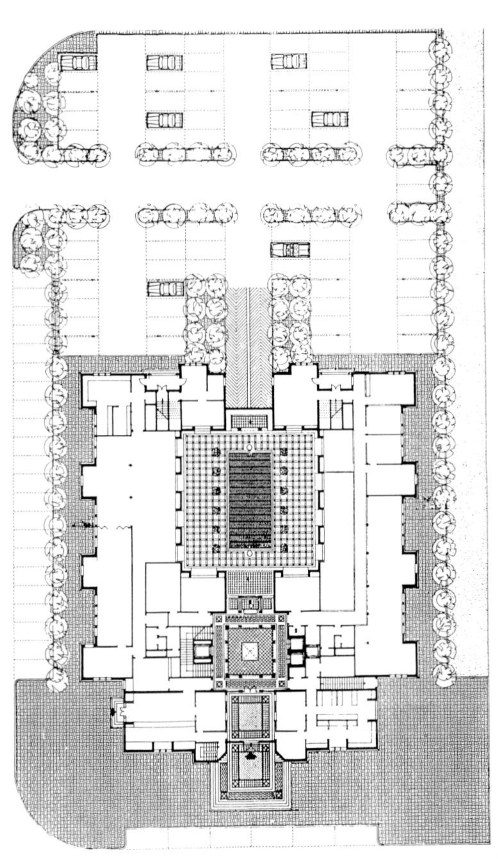

Plan, and exterior perspective.
Banque de Developpement Economique de la Tunisie. (S. Santelli with T. Ben Miled).

Contrary to this trend, our project tries to develop traditional and Tunisian typologies. When I talk about typologies, I am talking about space. For example, I believe that a building that does not have a courtyard is not really a Muslim building. When looking at the traditional typologies in Tunisia, all the buildings have a courtyard. So, the courtyard is a fundamental Tunisian architectural space. Because it belongs to this Muslim tradition of indoor architecture, it is in the courtyard that you will find the ornaments, the decorations, and the major rooms. We tried to include some rooms which would have traditional shapes. In long rooms, *iwans* were used. These niches are found in Morocco and in Egypt. We tried to use the gardens that are typical of the interior landscape of Muslim architecture. We also tried to use local products and craftsmanship in our projects. It is awful to import ceramic tiles to a country where there are fantastic local ceramics. We tried to be as close as possible to traditional building types.

I would like to refer to another project design. It is a competition entry for an office building for the *Banque de Developpement Economique de la Tunisie*. It is very difficult to do a traditional building with a new building type. There are strong elements which refer to Tunisian typologies; for example, the courtyards. Our building has a U-shape and encloses a courtyard which gives light to the offices. The monumental entrance refers to a large *iwan*, similar to Egyptian mosques. In the first entrance courtyard of the bank there are the staircases and the lifts, going up to the different offices. The offices around a second courtyard are designed in the traditional way with ceramic tiles and delicate Tunisian decorations which were used a long time ago. We tried to give a monumental feeling to this building.

I have been to the South of Spain and I have observed that in Seville and Grenada, there are many buildings where you can find Muslim spaces connected to Western spaces. It is a hybrid architecture. It is very difficult to connect and to mix traditional and modern building types. I have referred to two attempts to produce such a synthesis.

Model and analysis of the Justice Palace Grand Mosque, Riyadh, Saudi Arabia.

RASEM BADRAN, *the eminent Jordanian Architect, explained one aspect of his work which is particularly rich in symbolism: the design of the contemporary mosque.*

I find it appropriate to focus on one particular aspect of our work, which is the architecture of the mosque. These experiences started with our design for the Baghdad State Mosque in 1982. This was followed by the Royal Academy for Islamic Study in Amman, Jordan, in 1984, the Ali ibn Ali Taleb Mosque in Doha, Qatar, in 1985, and the Central Grand Mosque in Riyadh, Saudi Arabia, in 1985.

Let me firstly refer to the Baghdad City Mosque project. This mosque is about 30,000 square metres and can accomodate about 60,000 persons for prayers. There are additional facilities including a school, a library, a *Quran* school and accomodations for those who are working in the mosque or visiting *Imams*.

Initially we studied some plans of Iraqi mosques during the Abbasid period and other mosques from different parts of the Muslim world which we considered prototypical. But the real problem with the Baghdad City Mosque was the remoteness of the site called Bir Said. The mosque had to be integrated with its surroundings.

We tried to incorporate rivers and palm trees in the project since they are a significant part of the Iraqi landscape. Palm trees are arranged in an orderly manner surrounding the mosque to form a zone between the parking area and the mosque. In this zone, people can walk under the palm trees as if they were columns of nature. The main approach is lined on one side with trees. On the other side there is an artificial lake leading from a river on the *qibla* side of the site.

An artificial hill was built surrounding the mosque to try and get some sort of human relation between the individual coming for prayers and the high mosque wall. We had to consider the relationship between the individual as a single person entering a huge space. I thought of dividing this huge space into a small cubes to make some sort of separation. When combined, these geometrical cubes would form a regular form or a geometric form. These cubes are 20 square metres and you could have gaps between them that could be used for lighting and ventilation. Ventilation can be done simply without any technical effort. The tie beams had a dual function of structural support and of giving the large space a human scale.

Sometimes I am not convinced about using the dome as a form for such a mosque. It was a problem to decide what kind of dome and how many domes to use. We decided to place one of the domes in the centre of the mosque nearer to the *qibla* side and to emphasise the *mihrab* area. We tried to solve the space under the dome by using a big *muqarnas* composition which helps create light behind this big space in order to illuminate the *mihrab* and *Imam* areas.

I am also not convinced about using arches in such a mosque but I was trying to find meaning in using them. Another problem was the minarets which are still necessary symbols for a mosque.

WILLIAM J.R. CURTIS, *the emminent architectural historian and critic argued against the simplistic and superficial reproduction of past forms and stressed the need to transform the principles of tradition into vocabularies relevant to modern life. He also argued against the limitations of xenophobia.*

A tradition is rethought within an artist's imagination then exteriorised as a new form. One of the issues we have to examine is how the individual vocabulary of an architect joins forces with tradition and vice versa, and how this re-thinking, without which culture dies, takes place. Such re-invigoration is essential, especially in a period when traditional symbols are often reduced to the level of mere signs.

A design process is a way of understanding the world. It is a cognitive process: a way of proposing hypothetical models for reality which are tested against many things and thereafter translated into actuality. But a design process is also the very means through which the inheritance of forms is cast into a new pattern of meaning. This new order must be appropriate to the task at hand but must also transcend the particular case to touch upon matters of lasting human and aesthetic value.

Drawings are an essential tool in this act of transformation. They are used for the *prescription* of architecture — in the design process — but they can also be used for *description* of architecture, that is in the analysis of past forms. With the aid of sketches, tradition may be experienced, schematised, internalised then cross-bred with the artists evolving vocabulary.

We are talking about a process which cuts deeper than style, to the underlying order and principles of architecture: values which transcend time and place.

There is that certain magic which makes Ibn Tulun a perennial building, something that will communicate for as long as it stands. It possesses what I would call formal presence on the architectural level; it embodies a mythical quality and seems to touch substructures of great duration. In the re-thinking of these values there is the constant adjustment of trying to deal with present realities yet with reference to the substructure of past myths. The *aesthetic* problem of attaining the substructures, and the *mythical* problem of incorporating the best of the present culture, are related to one another. The design process explores the link between forms and meaning: it is an exercise in symbolism.

To understand why things happen and why forms are, or were, one gets involved in what I call the genetic problem of form. Where does form come from in relation to a society? A site? Traditions, both formal and social?

There are needs that come from a culture and are focussed via the client: they emerge eventually as a programme. The programme may already imply an *a priori* image of what ought to be; there may already by a clearly conceived building type for example. Other design processes are more fluid. Each designer has his way of doing things: he takes a programme and breaks it up, looking at it in a certain way. But he begins to categorise. There is already an aspect of an internalised style of thought in problem solving.

At an early stage, there are ways in which a design process can go seriously wrong in terms of inappropriate match. You can have an idea that is wrong from the practical point of view. There may be a conflict of form and function, or a form which is right for some aspects of the task, may express quite the wrong societal associations. The ideal aim of any design process is surely the resolution of the practical, the aesthetic and the symbolic. Tradition in the obvious sense of a visible past inheritance can only be partly helpful, for reality today is different. The architect must find what is right for the present circumstances and if he is sufficiently probing and profound he will make a valid addition to the stock of forms. There is no place for passeisme or for a bogus, revivalist sentimentality.

There is a whole world which has to do with the relation between not just social ritual and form but meaning and form; ideas in relation to expression and in relation to formal grammar. This is the beginning of a much larger historical investigation of how the mind interiorises forms. It concerns the grammatical rules of a tradition and a grasp of what is relevant to cultural conditions.

One of the attitudes you run into is that only Muslims can really understand Muslim problems. This is an ostrich's position. I think the best tall building in the Middle East was designed by a non-Muslim New Yorker, Gordon Bunshaft. This sky scraper in Jeddah, Saudi Arabia concerns a modern state of mind. It is consistent with a modern structural and social system, a geometry, an arrangement that is also adjusted to climate, wind and glare. But the building relies upon the basic principles of the *mashrabiyya* and of the wind tower, rethinking them in modern terms. A standard modern urban type has been critiqued in terms of a local tradition and climate. Yet there is no hankering after the bogus, frozen state of the past.

By using the term Islamic in a sloppy way historically, it is possible to treat the whole Muslim heritage as the expression of some supposed "immutable" religious essence. This can be very misleading especially in the atmosphere of current ideological distortions of "Islam". It is also possible to forget that many of the greatest past building complexes had primarily secular and mercantile functions. The superb markets at Aleppo, for example, were gorgeous displays of mundane wealth that were given an architectural framework of high quality. Why not the same today, but for the processes of modern commerce that are essential to the survival of many contemporary Middle Eastern societies? There is a hierarchy of building types and it

Sher-E Bangla Nagar, Dhaka, Bangladesh. The massive structure is stunning in the boldness and rigour of the abstract geometry employed on the façades (right). The interior spaces show dramatic lighting articulating voids and solids (above).

is misleading to speak of every modern office space as a kind of geiger counter of belief. If clients want a tall building for prestige or whatever other reason, and if the architect cannot persuade them otherwise, he can either resign or he can do it in a way that makes a substantial architectural statement that is qualitative in regional terms. Whether one likes it or not, the modern set up is what one is going to work with. It is a situation of increasing urbanisation, of larger organisations, of increasing mechanisation, of increasing abstraction, and of increasing links to the international monetary system. The special interest of Bunshaft's National Commercial Bank in Jeddah is that it addresses these developments head on.

A sensitive artist formed primarily in the West (wherever that is exactly), can certainly interact fruitfully with the multiple traditions of the world some now call "Islamic". Despite post-colonial sensitivities, it would be absurd to try and close the door on all occidental insights and examples. In fact some of the richest responses to regional culture constitute a cross fertilisation of modernism and local traditions.

Louis Kahn was an architect who learned a great deal from Islamic traditions, especially at the level of light, space, texture and geometry. In Dhaka he produced a masterly work which blended together the boldness of modern abstract form with a deep appreciation of the meaning of centralised tomb and mosque architecture in the Indian sub-continent. He was obsessed with the archetype of the central, ceremonial space surrounded by the fringe of shaded spaces – a pattern intrinsic to Islamic architecture in various places in India. The Dhaka building has a certain timeless quality and makes a strong and modern contribution to the architecture of the Muslim world and to international architecture as well. To learn from this substantial example does not imply mimicking its style.

Modern architecture in its profoundest manifestations has a level of abstraction and a level of depth and a level of compression of content which allows one to make contact with the substructures of tradition. The question is how best to combine these qualities with a relevant transformation of the principles of regional building.

It is important to the endeavour of the AKAA not to slip into a simplistic, anti-Western ideology, or a simple-minded conception of national, ideological or religious identity. The hope is to combine the best of the old and new, of regional and universal.

HALIM ABDEL-HALIM, *Professor of Architecture at Cairo University, is acutely aware of the need for Muslim architects to reinvigorate their contemporary culture. He described his search through the example of a small neighbourhood park and how his students are encouraged to decode and master the geometries of traditional forms.*

I wish to address myself to three questions: Firstly, the role of the architect and his responsibility to interpret, and understand culture and change society through his architecture. Secondly, the experiences and lessons learned from practice or actual activities in the Islamic world. The third question deals with the possible approaches and directions that can be pursued to move from the state that we are living in now to some other state that hopefully will be better.

Regarding the first question, I believe that the world is in a state of flux and that the laws of change are not explicit. Each segment of society attempts to identify these forces of change and whether we are architects, or lawyers, or philosophers, all must try to understand them.

There is a layer between the world as it exists and the world as we shape it. It is the layer of creation. This thin layer is coded historically through what I call the creative process of the community. Each community has its own way of decoding and coding reality. This pattern of coding and decoding might appear to be stagnant at times or active at other times.

One can think of ceremony or ritual as the unfolding of architecture. Every community has ceremonies and rituals that are related to the environment. Many communities still have rituals and ceremonies that are related to building production. One can identify those events; not only are they related to the process of building legally and economically, but culturally as well.

The helix of the Ibn Tulun minaret (above) is unfolded horizontally to create the geometry of the park (right) that is being created in its shadow.

The architect's ability to function in the state of flux in which the world continually operates depends on three realisations. The first two have to do with the preparation and education of the architect and the third one has to do with the practice. The first realisation is of the nature of the creative forces that are operating in the world, and that shape the overall environment. Second, is the realisation of the process by which this force is internalised and awakened in the creative person, the architect. In simpler terms the second realisation is the nature of practicing architecture. The third realisation deals with the community, in which this awakening is becoming real.

As a Muslim practitioner and designer, I am aware of the creative forces operating in the world. I am aware of my relation to those creative forces through work.

Returning ritual to architecture: community participation in the ceremony of laying the cornerstone for the park.

Cairo is a complex city in a state of decay. Monuments stand as a witness embodying a moment of creativity. That is a moment in which the realisation that I mentioned took their shape and remained. Egypt had rituals for building until the 1960's and 1970's. The location of the building and the division of the land were rendered through a ritual. Today you hardly find any such ritual.

We were asked to redesign a small park into a cultural park for children, near the Ibn Tulun Mosque. The site is surrounded by run down buildings of the *Sayyida Zeinab*, a sprawling community of over a million people.

The Ibn Tulun minaret was our starting point. We started a process of decoding; We began to understand the geometrical and mathematical laws behind the helix. The helix of the Ibn Tulun unfolds horizontally into a matrix of coordinates. These became the guiding pattern for the layout of the cultural park. At the entrance to the park is an exhibit, and a fountain from which water runs to irrigate the park. There is a theatre terraced into steps that marries the geometry of the thinking process to the elements of the site.

The architect has to put himself in the core of community events. We wanted to relate to the positive forces in the community. So, we used the occasion of laying the corner stone for the project (which is usually a big event in projects in Egypt). We convinced the Minister of Culture that we could design a ground breaking ceremony in which the future design of the park was the programme of the ceremony. We engaged hundreds of children into the ceremony. This was a way of actively linking the community to the project. It worked very well.

Student projects manipulate geometries to develop alternative forms and shapes.

Another project we did was a Presidential Residence. The scheme was an expression of two things: that there were laws behind tradition that could be embodied into work. The other, that there are elements in tradition that are private and can be reconstructed. For instance, the house of the president is constructed from reinterpreting the concept of a *qa'a*.

Another project, the Royal Academy for Islamic Culture in Jordan also shows the significance of geometry. Geometry in the cultural sense is much more important a matter than just the shaping of space. Our knowledge of geometry and transformation of geometry allows us to conceive the environment. Students in my classes are encouraged to manipulate the basic units of the traditional geometries to master the endless combinations that will ensue, thereby enriching their reservoir of forms and shapes.

Turning to the legacy of the past with its deep psychic roots for inspiration and achieving total mastery of the regional building crafts and techniques, El-Wakil's designs are outstanding contemporary works within the disciplined confines of tradition. Above: Minaret of King Saud Mosque, Jeddah, Saudi Arabia. Below: Elevation, King Saud Mosque. Opposite: Island Mosque, Jeddah, Saudi Arabia.

ABDELWAHED EL-WAKIL, *the distinguished Egyptian Architect, 1980 AKAA award winner, and member of the 1986 Master jury, forcefully expounded the virtues of adhering to tradition, and of reviving the traditional vocabulary. His corpus of work includes a large number of outstanding mosques.*

Modernity has destroyed hierarchy. It has created a nakedness, an obscenity because previously forms were adorning. A culture would seek forms. Modernity did away with forms.

The only difference between an African statue and Picasso's bull is that one is a reflection of the collective myth and the other is an individual expression. One is an established form of typology or has a story behind it that was collective. Picasso started giving a very big head to the bull and it became very heavy; Finally, at the end, the head disappeared completely and what was left of the bull was its fertile aspect. In that sense it represented in modern terms the rape; because what happened in modern times is that there was a rape. You can see a living symbol in the work of Picasso, It reflected something that he could feel was happening in modern times.

One of the things that the Modern Movement did was put a halo around art and call it art for art's sake.

If we analyse how the models of modern architecture tried to adapt typologies through the elements of structure, form and function we conclude that all of them did not have the mythical dimension, so critical to enriching works of art.

There are very few today in government who understand the role of architecture as the structuring of space that reflects our interaction with the exterior world and the inner world. Maybe an exception was Winston Churchill. When the House of Commons was destroyed during the Second World War and the architects wanted to make a modern building, he refused and said: "No, we will have the building as it was because we shape our buildings but later they form us."

In my work, I am proud to be traditional, to respect tradition, to study its forms and to use them creatively in a harmonious configuration that speaks to the hearts and souls of the Muslim peoples.

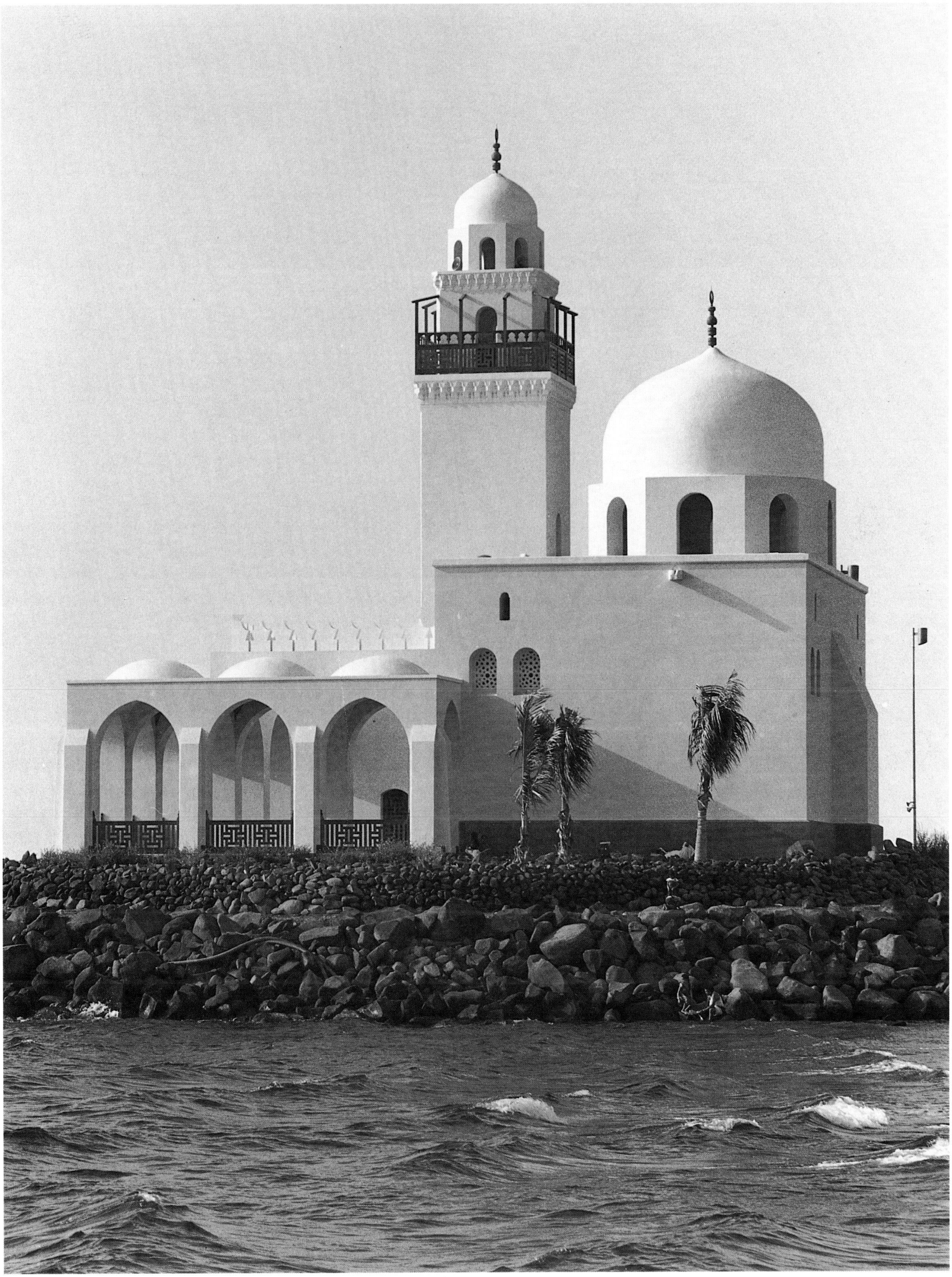

ON CULTURAL CONTINUITY

This important recurrent theme gets its very name from a deep sense of the 'rupture' that has permeated Muslim societies. The appreciation of this point is so essential that Mohammed Arkoun devoted several papers and interventions to it. An extract from one of these is reproduced here. It is only a small part of the lengthy and learned discourse in the original essay.

The extracts from the paper by Oleg Grabar, on the meaning of history in a city like Cairo, raise questions that transcend the domains of that particular city to what should be the relationship of the past to the present and the future, and what is the role of architects and practitioners in understanding the value of the past, but in contemporary terms.

The concern for historical conservation and cultural authenticity cannot be overlooked in the Award's activities, and a paper prepared jointly by Ismail Serageldin and Saïd Zulficar, Secretary-General of the AKAA, outlines the Award's concerns with these issues and how the different approaches found expression among its selected winners over the last three cycles.

Current Islam Faces its Tradition*

Mohammed Arkoun

RETHINKING ISLAMIC TRADITION IN ITS TOTALITY

Rethinking Islamic Tradition today is an intellectually urgent and necessary act, politically and culturally destabilising and psychologically and socially delicate. We are in fact obliged to uncover, much more clearly than did classic criticism, the ideological functions, semantic manipulations, cultural discontinuities, and intellectual inconsistencies that come together to delegitimise what over centuries we have been given to perceive and live as the authentic expression of Divine Will manifested in the Revelation. To rethink Islamic Tradition is to violate official prohibitions past and present, and the social censure that conspires to keep off limits the *unthinkable* questions that were asked at the early phase of Islam, but inquiry into which was closed off with the triumph of the official orthodoxy that was based on the classic texts.

But, how are we to rethink Tradition in positive terms that is, enabling it via constructive criticism to fulfill new functions in a socio-historical context radically changed in the last thirty years[1] Doubtless, we do not have to worry inordinately about the fate of the Tradition: it will always survive the most radical criticism and the most brutal revolution. As a mainspring of unity and continuity, it has over the centuries forged the collective sensibility and memory.

We must therefore borrow current ways of thinking opened up by the sciences of man and society. This being first a matter of *reading* the Scriptures (*Quran* and *hadith)*, we will begin by showing why it is advisable to base research on semiotics. We will then open the historical and sociological record, but from the perspective of a larger inquiry into the anthropology of tradition and modernity. On the basis of the information thus reunited, we may justifiably undertake inquiry on the new status of the theological attitude.

It goes without saying that such an itinerary cannot be followed to its end; it will be a matter, in this first effort, of establishing the necessity that Islamic thought must recover a tradition that safeguards the inherent richness suggested in the following definition:

> "*Tradition carries with it more than ideas capable of logical form: it embodies a life that includes at the same time sentiments, thoughts, beliefs, aspirations, and actions... Individual and collective effort can draw from it indefinitely without exhausting it. Consequently, it implies the spiritual communion of souls that feel, think, and will in the unity of a like patriotic or religious ideal; and by the same token, it is a condition of progress in so far as it permits some bits from the ingot of never-completely-coinable truth to be passed from Implicit Living to Explicit Knowledge; for tradition — well-spring of unity, continuity, and fecundity, and at the*

Sidi Bou Said, Tunisia.

* The original version of this essay was published in French in Aspects d'Islam (Brussels: Facultés Universitaires, Saint Louis, 1985). The study sheds light on the concept of "rupture" introduced by the author. This extract from the English translation is taken from the Proceedings of *Architectural Education in the Islamic World*, Seminar Ten in the series – Architectural Transformations in the Islamic World, Granada, Spain, April 21–25, 1986. Published by Concept Media for The Aga Khan Award for Architecture, Singapore, 1986, pp 92–103.

same time beginning, anticipatory, and final — precedes every constructive synthesis and outlives every reflective analysis".[2]

The Priority of the Semiotic Approach. It is now well established that semiotic analysis requires an indispensable exercise of intellectual self-discipline, a quality all the more precious when it comes to reading texts that for generations have forged individual and collective sensibility and imagination. We learn to introduce a methodological distance *vis-à-vis* "sacred" texts (the quotation marks are an expression of this distance) without pronouncing any of those theological or historical judgments that immediately block communication. This is what Orientalist historical criticism on the subject of the *Quran* and the *hadith* has never understood, and it continues to be unaware of the semiotic and anthropological approach, as is attested by the recent work of G.H.A. Juynboll.[3]

Ali Qapu, Isfahan, Iran.

The texts that are the point of departure and the inexhaustible source of the Tradition offer themselves as a perfectly defined cultural object.

This cultural object has been turned into a living *subject*, historically active through the reading-participation of the believers. By the process of selection, of decontextualisation, of recontextualisation, of retrospective and prospective projection, of literal or esoteric interpretation, and of semantic or mythical amplification, the readings of believers indefinitely go on creating secondary cultural objects, while being removed from the initial object due to its linguistic, historical, or sociocultural connection with a single space-and-time. The sum total of these operations constitutes *living* tradition. The empirical effectiveness of daily life bears on the cognitive aspects of the human condition. To paraphrase M. Blondel, *Implicit Living* expends effort in order to gain access to *Explicit Knowledge*.

How do we get back to the initial object in its genesis, its constituent parts and its own determining factors? This return to the source is a leitmotif of the Tradition, but it involves returning to the mythical founding age, a space-and-time transfigured by the traditional readings and modes of behaviour. Semiotics aspires to a summary criticism that at once goes beyond both the object that is read and all the second objects that are produced by the Tradition. How do the *signs* used in the texts signify? What linguistic mechanisms are used to produce *this* meaning and not another? For whom, and in what conditions, does *this* particular meaning arise?

These questions involve neither the revealed character of statements, nor their sacred charge, nor the results of their spiritual meaning for the believers. Instead, they concern the qualifications and functions of meaning as modalities of significance, the cognitive status of which must be established in a comprehensive approach to everything that has meaning.

It turns out that the texts we read are not preoccupied with distinguishing *knowing* from *believing*[4]. Instead, they teach that it is first necessary to *believe* — to open one's heart (in the Biblical and *Quranic* sense) — in order to gain access to perfect, complete, and totally true knowledge. Tradition takes form at just the moment when the members of a group (such as the first nucleus of believers, called *mu 'minun*, around Muhammad at Mecca and then Medina) gain access, aided by a foundation-laying account, to a common frame of perception and representation. Semiotically speaking, all of the Tradition — and every tradition — functions as a foundation-laying account perpetually enriched by the significant experiences of the group or the community.[5]

Addressing a greater number, the Tradition tends to function like the former model, rejecting in the name of orthodoxy both the plurality of meanings put forth by the exegeses and the various schools and the potential meanings not yet made actual by new readings of the Scriptures. I have already shown how the modern treatment of metaphor, symbol and myth authorise readings of the *Quran* quite different from all those bequeathed by the exegetic tradition.[6]

The Historical and Sociological Approach. Just as the Tradition implies a relationship of thought to language, as we have seen, so it imposes a vision of history, with a framework and writing adapted to its expression.

Modern authors — even Muslims such as Taha Hussein — who have taken the greatest interest in the critical revival of religious and/or cultural Tradition, have not known how to move the debate towards previous studies framed in socio-cultural terms of knowledge in the first two centuries of the Hijra. It is not enough to recall that oral transmission then prevailed over written transmission. More fundamentally, it must be shown how, in the formation and function of the social *imaginaire*, the dimension of the marvellous, the mythical, the symbolic, and the metaphorical prevailed over the rational categories and discursive procedures that would develop in relation to the invention of paper, the perfecting and diffusion of Arabic writing, and the expansion of Greek logocentrism. All cultural history of the Arab and Islamic domain must be reconsidered from this two-fold perspective of rivalry between oral and written, *mythos* and *logos*, marvellous and empirical, and sacred and profane. *Historically*, the Tradition, as textual form and meaning, bears the stamp of this rivalry; that is what today makes a re-evaluation of form and meaning indispensable, since all the determining concepts assumed in the *Implicit Living* of the believers (sacred, marvellous, mythical, oral, written, imaginary, rational, and irrational) are in the process of passing over the *Explicit Knowledge*, thanks to the new explorations of the sciences of man and society.

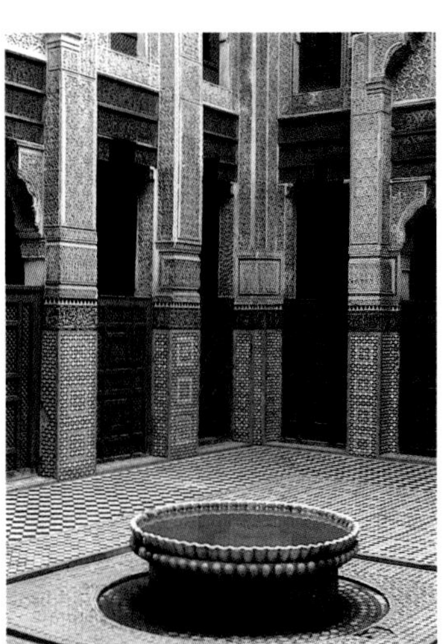

Madrasa of Bou Inan, Meknes, Morocco.

This position is new because it allows us to develop a common theory for what I prefer to call *societies of the Book*.[7] The concept of a society of the Book permits us to place emphasis on two dimensions of the Tradition minimised or transfigured by the advent of dogmatic theology: the *historicity* of all cultural processes, and the practical forms of conduct by which the Book is incorporated into the social body: the *sociology* of *reception*, by ethno-culturally diverse groups, of the Tradition. The concept of reception is complementary to that of historicity; I use it here from the theoretical perspective defined by Hans R. Jauss, one of the leaders of the "School of Constance", in his work *Pour une esthétique de la réception*.[8] The idea is that the literary work, or the work of art in general, exists and endures only with the active participation and continuous intervention, at multiple levels, of its successive publics. Now, that is *a fortiori* true in large degree of those literary and artistic works that are religious texts. In this sense, Tradition in societies of the Book is not just a "hoarded collection of testimony left to us by all those whom the Spirit of revelation has touched throughout history".[9] It is a collective creation of all those who draw their identity from it and contribute to its production-reproduction.

It is, therefore, no longer just the relationships between Scripture, Revelation, and Tradition that must be redefined from a perspective that is more concerned with explanatory adequacy than with edification; it is also the presence of belief, affected in the substance and functions that "the witnesses touched by the spirit of revelation" have always recognised in it. Without radically challenging the dynamic potential of this spirit, we may say that it is always mediated by social agents — that is, the sum total of amplifications, misrepresentations, semantic and textual manipulations, deviations, fabulations, mystifications and ideologisations — that are inherent in the reception and reproduction of the Tradition.

How is modernity to be worked into such an evolution of the Tradition? Are there some forms and contents that fit more easily than do others the most widespread traditional forms of behaviour?

Let us first observe that it is not a question today of opposing modernity that is eternally and totally positive and situated on the side of progress to a tradition rejected as archaic, obsolete, constraining and negative. Conversely, one cannot conform to the theology of the Tradition, which puts the latter on the side of the absolute, the transcendent, the sacred, and the revealed. The examination of current societies discloses three forces in competition:

- Tradition in the general and archaic sense, present in all societies, and preceding the scriptural Tradition of the revealed religions.
- Scriptural Tradition, which has occupied us to this point.
- Modernity, which tends to sanction rupture with the preceding forces without totally bringing it about. In reality, the three forces nourish the dialectic of any society via a stronger accentuation of one over the others, according to the socio-cultural setting and the historical circumstances.

The Scriptural Tradition, at its beginnings in the three monotheistic religions, appeared as modernity *par excellence*, because it consigned previous traditions to the darkness of ignorance and disorder *(jahiliyya)*.[10]

Modernity is transformed into tradition with the accumulation over time of events, works, values, success and trials significant for the collective subject. Since the 1950's, change has been so rapid, so profound, and so general that tradition has disintegrated and slipped away. In the so-called backward or traditional societies, in contrast to industrial or post-industrial ones, the presence and effects of material modernity are more obvious than those of intellectual modernity. I shall not reiterate the differences between these two aspects of modernity[11]; it will prove more illuminating to concentrate on the historical conditions of the production and repression of modernity in the West and in Islam.

In the West, material modernity and intellectual or cognitive modernity have received varied emphasis, according to historical circumstance.

Without anywhere constituting a social class homogeneous and influential enough to play a decisive mediating role, the community of scientists, thinkers, and artists, within the crisis of models of development, tends to set intellectual modernity, as a cognitive project of the spirit, above all the ideological formations that are enclosed within a national or community framework or even within the limits of a social class that still claims to incarnate the universal history of humanity.[12]

This new ambition of modernity, tied to the development of the community of scholars in the world, everywhere comes under the great historical and socio-cultural weight of each *national* context. Beyond the ideological cleavages that divide the contemporary world and favour, in particular, a negative perception of Islam, the most open-minded scholars continue to be prisoners of a linear, polemical and even theological vision of the West. The linear vision that springs from an image of Greco-Roman antiquity is separate from "the Muslim East" and traces a continuous evolution up to our day, while characterising as simple historical incident the role of Islam between the seventh and twelfth centuries. The polemic vision continues to perceive Islam first and foremost as an obstacle to reduce or shape in order to open up the imperial path of the West. The theological vision is due to Christian theology of the Revelation and the justification of the state of Israel that revive the old systems of reciprocal exclusion that have dominated the whole history of societies of the Book precisely since the appearance of Islam in the Mediterranean world.

In the grip of these visions that perpetuate and reinforce all sorts of collective phantasms, obsolete cultural schemes and epistemological barriers, cognitive modernity endeavours to reach a restored cognisance of what I have called Greco-Semitic space.

I have pointed out that this space in actuality extends from the Indus to the Atlantic; that Islam is not to be cast back into a romantic, dreamy, Bedouin, intolerant, or falsely spiritual "Orient".[13] On the contrary, it must be reintegrated as one of the historic factors that have contributed to the emergence of the cultural concept of the modern West.

The splitting of Greco-Semitic space into a modern West and an East devoted to Tradition, to traditionalisation, and to recurrence of archaic forms of behaviour begins with the Renaissance and the Reformation.

Islamic Tradition as I have presented it has remained rigorously separate from the Western adventure of man since the sixteenth century, and, more importantly, from that which, in this adventure, involves the destiny of man as such. I also want to note that, far from recognising and *rethinking* the reasons for and consequences of this exit from a history involving mind and consciousness, Islamic thought since the nineteenth century has been exclusively preoccupied with the defensive justification of its tradition, with polemic against the colonial and imperialist West and with the mythologising of its own history.

I am not saying, however, that the modern West, as its dominant classes claim, has forged a model of historical consciousness and action respectful of all the dimensions of man. But modernity is engaged in changing dimensions, ambitions, and horizons while opening up a new space of intelligibility and historical action, where not only the traditions of societies of the Book may be reintegrated in their totality, but also where historical totality, with all its cultural forms of expression in the world, may be explored and recapitulated by a cultural anthropology unrestricted to a single centre.

It is from this perspective that the project of a quest and re-examination of Islamic Tradition in its totality takes all its meaning, both for the Muslim Community and for contemporary thought engaged in exploring the universe, our planet and the human condition. The Tradition in its totality implies an exit from the framework of heresiographic thought set by the *hadith* cited above. All the familiar concepts of traditional theological discourse split apart and gain new dimensions, without losing their critical function concerning both scholastic traditions and provincial, ethnocentric, unitarian or positivist modernity. Among these concepts I shall cite religion and the religious in so far as they are tied to politics and to the secular world (*din, dawla, dunya*), the Revelation, the Book, the Scriptures, the sacred, the spiritual, the transcendent, and all the vocabulary of classical methaphysics, ethics, law, psychology and political economy. What are the local traditions if reduced to residue or relics by the Orthodox Tradition, and after that by unitarian modernity[14]? How does Orthodox Tradition itself tend to become repressed as obsolete, inadequate and archaic by material modernity in the absence of an intellectual modernity capable of reconsidering it? What mutilations has this same Orthodox Tradition inflicted on itself by eliminating the schools, works and thinkers that have come forth within Islam but that have been judged deviant or "heretic" — not by an entitled doctrinal tribunal but by the protagonists in a rivalry between professional categories, ethno-cultural groups or visions of the world?

These questions must first be answered historically, leaving aside any doctrinal judgement.[15] That current Muslim societies cannot accept the critical discourse of the historian does not mean that he has constructed a scientific object as abstract as that of the Orientalist philologists tracking down apocryphal *hadith*. To examine the Tradition in its totality in the sense I indicate here is to grapple directly with the roots of evil that undermine those confessional societies that are closed in what they believe to be their traditions. The function of history and cultural anthropology is to lay bare the realities travestied by the manipulators of the religious imagination.[16]

Is the notion we have just presented of the Tradition in its totality thinkable for a traditional theologian within the one framework of inherited theologies in each community based on the Book? What does theological attitude become in the new context created by the joint pressures of present-day history and of the cognitive strategies imposed by the sciences of man and society, themselves the product of this history and the answers to its challenge?

The Theological Attitude. "Ways of living and transforming the world": this is the fine title of the first section of *Initiation à la pratique de la théologie* (Initiation to the Practice of Theology).[17] This title and the whole book are the sign of an evolution that, like modernity, has taken place in the West but remains absent from Islam; an evolution limited, nevertheless, because the takeover by thought of the ways to live and transform the world remains strictly dependent on "the awareness of Faith (that) is tied to an institutional aggregate in the Church (scriptural canon, tradition, ministers) and around the university (diverse specialisations, centres of teachings, etc.)".[18] The psychologist and the psychoanalyst have shown us that under faith lie indistinct the most irrepressible compulsion of desire, the most complex contents of memory, the greatest phantasms of the imaginations, the most powerful impulses of the heart and the firmest demands of reason. The mastery of these different faculties depends on the forms of discipline of the spirit recognised and practised by each culture. No less does the theologian continue to presuppose in his discourse the existence and generalisation to all believers of a faith that is acquiescence, meet and right, to the Act of God that shows itself in the Revelation. One can conceive that the theologian aims to substantiate this ideal faith with a conscientious pedagogy of all the obstacles to be overcome, but one cannot forgive him for the constraints and confusions that he continues to force on this same human spirit that he claims to lead toward the absolute.

To state the matter clearly, religious thought is a quest of *independent* thinkers after having been, over the centuries, either the monopoly of zealous servants or the target of polemicists aiming at other objectives.

It will be understood, I hope, that I am not excluding theology from the field of investigating man and society; but theology must submit to rules common to every cognitive undertaking. For this, on *new* grounds, it must again raise the whole question of the revealed. It is not just a matter of *tolerating* the co-existence of discourse that each tradition pronounces about itself; it is necessary to explain first and foremost the historical, psychological and anthropological conditions of the emergence and functioning of any tradition, and then of the three monotheistic traditions. It will at that point be possible to envisage a theology of relations between Scripture, Revelation, and Tradition in societies of the Book.

The Meaning of History in Cairo*

Oleg Grabar

The purpose of this essay is to raise questions about the significance of the Cairene pecularity and to provoke a discussion on how to interpret it at two different levels. One is the level of perceiving, or reading, the city's static monuments as an integral component of the living fabric of the city. The second level is more of a query: assuming that a reasonable interpretation has been proposed for the monuments and therefore an adequate definition exists of the city's formal character, can and should this awareness be extended to the judgement of the modern city and become part of any planning of the future city?

The first historical question posed by Cairo is why it became so uniquely different. There is no clear answer to this question, but, I should like to propose the following explanation. Alone among the major urban centres of the mediaeval Muslim world, Cairo was provided with a combination of incentives for investment and expression in large scale architecture. The main ones are : continuous sources of wealth through trade for nearly half a millenium, whatever vagaries existed in commercial activities; absence of destructive invasions which had plagued most of western Asia until the sixteenth century; and an indigenous mix of religious and ethnic communities. It was also a consistent magnet for intellectual, social, and money-making institutions and activities which brought people from all over the Muslim world and, in a more controlled way, from the non-Muslim world as well. No other Muslim centre was provided with that many operative factors, creating in Cairo both a consistent patronage and the means to invest in building.

But the possibility of architectural investment does not compel its actuality. Something else triggered building as the major form of expression, as opposed to the manufacturing or collecting of objects, for instance (although both of these activities did take place). A partial answer to this second question emerges when we recall the remarkable conservatism of Cairene architectural forms. Whereas Iran and the Turkish beyliks, not to speak of Italy, embarked, from the thirteenth century onwards on major experiments with novel and sometimes striking ideas, Cairene architecture exploited and honed, lovingly and imaginatively, very traditional forms of spatial composition and surface decoration: courts, porticoes, domes, iwans, Muqarnas, geometric interlaces, large bands of writing, and so on. The Mamluk monuments of Cairo tell and tell again the same story in a by-then well established language, because the need had not arisen to seek a new idiom or to say something new. A culture at apparent peace with itself saw in the proclamations of buildings the best and most expressive way of reminding itself of its own accepted values and, a way of entering into a dialogue with whatever preceded them. They recall, it seems to me, the way in which the late nineteenth century mercantile civilisation of the West built, wherever it reached (including Cairo and Istanbul), its banks, insurance companies, museums and often universities in modified neo-classical style. I am arguing, in other words, that, beyond the existence of resources and of a

* Extract from Proceedings of *The Expanding Metropolis: Coping with the Urban Growth of Cairo*, Seminar Nine in the Series – Architectural Transformations in the Islamic World, Cairo, Eygpt, Nov 11–15, 1984. Published by Concept Media for the Aga Khan Award for Architecture, Singapore, 1985, pp 3–15.

patronage, there was in Cairo, especially in Mamluk times, a cultural self-assuredness and an unquestioning agreement on which forms are needed and why. It is this agreement which was necessary for the expression of resources and patronage in architecture and for the conservatism of that expression.

Historians may well refine these generalities, and pointing out certain exceptions to them like the *madrasa* of Sultan Hassan, identify many additional motivations and explanations for the buildings of Cairo between 1000 and 1500. They may pursue the multitude of descriptive, technical, archaeological, textual, formal and comparative analyses which are the requisites of a synchronic understanding of the monuments, that is to say of their meaning within their time, ideally coming as close as possible to the moment of their creation. However fascinating and important this knowledge may be for a proper awareness of the past, its pertinence for the contemporary world and especially for contemporary building is more difficult to ascertain. Only too often, as with the monument to Rifat Pasha, the direct mirroring of the past, even when well-done, gives a feeling of imitative emptiness, because it lacks the nexus of motivations, purposes, and ideological, functional or pious meanings which gave genuiness to the past. But, even if one is critical of the values of what has been called the neo-Mamluk style, it remains true that the genuine Mamluk style is an inescapable part of Cairo, deeply anchored in its very being, and therefore, that the contemporary city must come to grips with it without slavishly copying it.

Madrasa and Mausoleum of Sultan Qala'un, A.H. 684/1285 A.D.

A different kind of analysis of the classical, especially Mamluk, monuments of Cairo makes it possible to suggest a number of subtler and more profound ways in which the historical monuments of Cairo have in fact affected the physical fabric of the city and have created a specifically Cairene aesthetic, which may or may not be transferable into contemporary terms for new parts of the city, but which ought to be considered whenever the fate of the historic city is being debated. I shall limit myself to two points and develop some of their consequences.

The first point is that nearly all buildings of classical times are independent constructions and not major modifications of or additions to older buildings. There are exceptions, no doubt, as with the Mamluk additions to the mosque, and especially the Azhar complex. The latter is important, because it is the one example of a monument with a complex and idiosyncratic history which required constant modifications — as it is still modified today — because its living force and purpose overshadow its formal character and make its succession of synchronic meanings irrelevant as new ones come to the fore. Other exceptions are usually repairs or secondary reflections of a new taste, although further studies on individual monuments may modify this conclusion. Assuming, however, that it is valid, what are its implications for the history of Cairo, especially if one recalls that relatively few monuments (except for private dwellings or secular buildings) were systematically or willfully destroyed in order to be replaced by new ones?

Two implications strike me as particularly important. One is that the integrity of the monument was protected by much more than the legal deeds which assured, for a while at least, its proper utilisation. It was protected because, even when its initial functions had lessened in importance or dwindled to nothing, something else in it had become part of the fabric of its urban setting. On a pious and emotional level, it could be that so many of these monuments contained burial places and thus the fascinatingly complex relationship of the traditional Muslim ethos to the presence of the dead developed, nearly automatically, a web of constant associations with any monuments containing a mausoleum. I shall return shortly to a possible formal level of associations in a different context, but a second implication of this social protection of so many monuments may well be that, regardless of the formal differences which exist between them, they were always part of the visual code expected within traditional society. There would have been what may be called a semiotic contract between patrons, builders and the population which required certain functions to be performed. Certain forms were to be available regardless of the functions to which they were applied (Was there really a need for example for all the *madrasas* which existed in Cairo?).

It is much more difficult to identify the operation of a visual code in the past than to understand practical function, but (and this is my second point about the historic city of Cairo) the large number of monuments preserved as well as the literary and epigraphic sources available for them lead to a general hypothesis for discussion. It has often been noted that the specific function of many Mamluk buildings — *madrasa, khanqah, ribat, masjid, jami,* even at times hospital or warehouse — is difficult to identify by visual observation alone, by the simple perceptions of its gate or façade. Most of those buildings use a small number of architectural themes which are the ones dominating the city's landscape, most particularly minarets, domes and gates. They are the real, continuous, architecture of Cairo much more than the functions they house. The historian of society and of culture forgets the forms and discusses purposes, investments, economic and ideological contexts. The historian of art looks at them and determines stylistic evolution, technical quality and expressive power or else he points out that these and other similar features are related to each other in the sense that the mosque of Baybars recalls that of Al-Hakim, that Qaytbay's *madrasa* bears a relationship to Qala' un's or to al-Nasir's. These relations can be explained in terms of certain ideological or emotional objectives from the times of Baybars, Qala' un or Qaytbay, but these explanations do not operate for later times, when the contingencies of the thirteenth, fourteenth or fifteenth centuries are not meaningful. What still operates today is what I would like to call the rhythmic power of the monuments, whereby minarets (more accurately called towers) serve as a visual relay leading from one place to another, and elaborate gates request of the passerby that he stop and enter, or at least look. To the judgement of the historian of society or of art may be added the judgement of the Cairene urbanologist who seeks meanings from the point of view of the visual perception of the city.

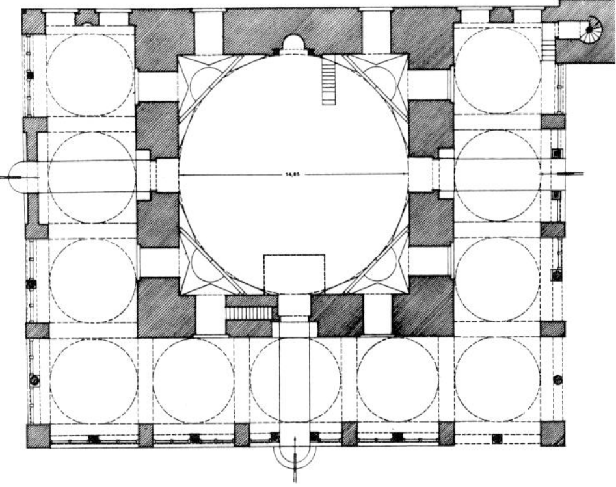

Mosque of Sinan Pasha, A.H. 979/1571 A.D., *elevation and plan.*

What has been provided in the city of Cairo is a network of visual signs which orders movement within the city and which makes it physically usable and understandable. These directions are given by permanent forms epistemologically independent of the functions to which they are attached.

Among the Islamic cities known to me, only Istanbul has a relatable rhythmic order, but it lacks the density of signs provided by Cairo and it is on a totally different scale. It no longer matters, at this level, what specific historical contingencies, functions or investments were needed for the creation of this visual network. What does matter is that a character has been given to a city in the latter part of the Middle Ages which has remained in function until today, but which has not been extended to the new areas of the city, where traffic circles and neon ads have replaced minarets as beacons, tall buildings took over from domes, and gateways have given way to window displays. This is indeed the language of the end of the twentieth century, but it may just be possible that a fuller understanding of what made Cairo unique in the past may help in keeping it unique in the future.

But the argument of this short essay in interpreting a city seeks to go beyond the specifics of the city of Cairo. Using a city unusually rich in mediaeval monuments, it suggests that, when a city has acquired the monumental density of Cairo, monuments escape the exclusive scrutiny of the historian; they become continuous factors in the life of the urban system because their real meaning is determined less by what happened in them than by how they act upon the total urban fabric.

A Living Legacy

The Aga Khan Award for Architecture and the Conservation of the Cultural Heritage

Ismail Serageldin and Saïd Zulficar

INTRODUCTION

From the very beginning, the Award wanted to recognise architecture that was responsive to contemporary Muslim societies and that solved the problems of today and tomorrow rather than being locked into sterile images of a bygone past. Nevertheless, the Award also recognised there can be no contemporary architecture of truly authentic cultural expression that is not rooted in the legacy of the past and that understands the messages of the cultural heritage of the evolving Muslim societies. Therefore, a significant part of the Award's endeavours must be oriented towards promoting a greater appreciation of this cultural heritage, especially at a time when the ravages of a wanton modernism and the assaults of economic and demographic pressure as well as environmental degradation are rapidly robbing Muslims of their best exemplars of past achievements.

In this essay we are concerned about the Aga Khan Award for Architecture's approach to the conservation of the cultural heritage. We intend to show that the Award has recognised different approaches to the problem with a view to encouraging all types of useful efforts for the preservation of the cultural heritage. Without this there cannot be the cultural continuity which is so necessary to define a better future for Muslim societies of today. Such efforts at preservation are a necessary corollary to all contemporary design efforts.

The multiplicity of projects that have been premiated and the diversity of approaches that they represent, collectively speak much for the richness of the stream dealing with historical preservation and the promotion of a cultural identity consonant with a traditional heritage.

Chehel Sutun, Isfahan, Iran.

From the earliest days of the Award, there was a concern for the creation of a special emphasis on historic preservation. Even more valuable would be those rare examples of sensitive adaptive re-use of traditional buildings of historic significance. Thus, the very first brochure that described the objectives of the Award in 1977, stated the following under the heading "Restoration and Re-Use":

> *"One aim of the Award is to highlight the role of architecture as a bridge between past, present and future.*
> *This bridge is also formed through the restoration and transformation of traditional buildings for modern usage, creating a challenge for adaptation as buildings are being given a new life and significance within the community they serve."*

Rüstem Paşa Caravanserai, Edirne, Turkey.

But translating this broad statement into an operational approach to promote conservation, preservation or adaptive re-use was not easy. A number of intellectual retreats, seminars and discussion groups were convened, most notably the seminar on "Conservation as Cultural Survival" (Istanbul, 1978). The theme returned many times in other seminars ostensibly discussing other subjects, from the very first seminar "Toward an Architecture in the Spirit of Islam" (Aiglemont, 1978) through "Development and Urban Metamorphosis" (Sana'a, 1983) and "The Expanding Metropolis: Coping with the Urban Growth of Cairo" (Cairo, 1984).

The key idea that emerged from these earnest discussions, that combined practitioners, scholars and decision-makers, is that a prerequisite for successful action in this difficult field, is to establish a common understanding. The various interested parties involved in any project must agree about some key philosophical questions that frequently remain not only unanswered, but even unasked.

First, what are we trying to preserve? A number of major buildings? The urban character? A way of life? Clearly each answer is going to generate a completely different set of solutions. Why do we want to preserve whatever it is we choose to preserve? Is it because it is part of our heritage? Then all citizens — and in some cases even the world at large — should be made to pay for it. Or is it to improve the lot of the inhabitants of the old city? Or is it to generate a new resource to earn money from tourism? Again, depending on how these questions are answered, the types of interventions to consider, the pattern of finance required, and the way to implement them will differ.

National Museum, Doha, Qatar.

Sidi Bou Said, Tunisia.

And then, who are we preserving for? Are the present users to be the prime beneficiaries of whatever intervention is to be made? Or the country at large? Or is it for the sake of future generations yet unborn? Again the responsibility for action will differ, depending on how these questions are answered. And unless they are answered, people will continue to talk at cross-purposes and confront administrative paralysis, if not outright opposition, when it comes to implementation.

At the same time, the Aga Khan Award for Architecture recognised that there cannot be single absolute answers to all these questions and hence evolved its own broad-based approach to reach out to the different contexts of the Muslim world.

THE APPROACH

The Aga Khan Award for Architecture recognised three different types of conservation efforts as worthy of support and recognition, each of which is judged by somewhat different criteria:

Conservation of Historic Monuments. Criteria in judging a restoration project include the technical difficulty, the quality of the detailing, and the adequacy and appropriateness of the methods and materials employed. Moreover, the revival of craftsmanship that the restoration work may engender is considered. And whether the restoration induces the society's awareness of its heritage is not overlooked.

Adaptive Re-Use. This approach combines restoration, if any, with the conversion of an old building from its traditional use to a new use (for example, an old palace converted to a cultural centre or a restaurant). In assessing the quality of an adaptive re-use project, due weight should be given to the imaginative and successful new uses, the extent to which the re-use assimilates the original surroundings, the technical difficulty of the adaptation, and the quality of the restoration work.

Area Conservation. The urban heritage of Islamic culture is not preserved merely by safeguarding individual buildings. We also need projects that address entire urban or rural settlements and preserve the character of the area by repaving, upgrading, and restoring, as well as forbidding the construction of inappropriate buildings.

Key considerations in such schemes are retaining the traditional street alignments, maintaining the scale and proportions of the built environment, providing intermingling uses, and protecting landmark buildings.

Preserving historic centres under enormous economic pressure as they are overtaken by urbanisation is specially challenging. Preserving the character and developing these centres includes protecting the historic monuments and upgrading the living conditions of its inhabitants.

In mounting efforts at preserving old centres, it is of paramount importance to avoid the twin polar problems of "ghetto-isation" and "gentrification". The most successful schemes are those that have carefully steered a middle course between the two extremes.

Even within each of these three broad categories different individual approaches are possible. The diversity of the AKAA winners in 1980, 1983 and 1986 makes this point most forcefully. It is therefore pertinent to review these outstanding projects to highlight their differences.

Two approaches to restoration: Externally the old and the new are clearly distinguished as in Darb Qirmiz, Cairo (top) or are indistinguishable, but are clearly labelled in unseen areas as in Multan, Pakistan (above).

Azem Palace, Damascus, Syria. More reconstruction than conservation.

A PARADE OF WINNERS

1980: When the first Master Jury met to premiate the first winners, it identified seven major themes or directions. Two of these dealt with conservation and accordingly were labeled "restoration" and "the search for the preservation of the traditional heritage".

Three projects won restoration awards in 1980. Of these, the restoration of the *Ali Qapu, Chehel Sutun, and Hasht Behesht* of Iran, demonstrated some of the finest delicate restoration work ever. The *Rüstem Paşa Caravanserai* in Turkey was upgraded from being badly mauled. The *National Museum in Qatar* was largely a reconstruction effort. The people of Qatar decided to rebuild the museum from an old ruined palace.

In the "search for the preservation of the traditional heritage," *Sidi Bou Said* of Tunisia won. In the integrated scheme, an entire community was responsible for maintaining the character of the village.

Two other themes identified by the first Jury were also close to the issues covered by the broad concerns of conservation. One was "the search for consistency with the historical context", that is, modern buildings that work closely within a historical context. In this category, the *Turkish Historical Society*, the *Mughal Sheraton Hotel*, and the *Ertegun House Project*, in Turkey, were awarded. The other theme was "the search for contemporary use of traditional language", that is, the reinterpretation of the historic idiom in contemporary terms. In this category, they awarded the *Halawa House* in Agamy, Egypt, the *Medical Centre* in Mopti, Mali, and the *Courtyard Houses* in Agadir, Morocco.

1983: The second Jury gave three of the eleven awards for conservation projects. Each of these winners represented a fundamentally different approach to the issues, a different philosophy of restoration.

The *Shah Rukn-i-'Alam Tomb in Multan, Pakistan*, is an outstanding example of a faithful restoration of a monument to the original design. The guiding philosophy was to restore the monument to its original grandeur. Even though every piece of material introduced in the project was precisely though invisibly labelled and dated for future restoration, the outside viewer would have trouble making that distinction. The monument stands in all its splendour as it must have when it was originally completed.

The Darb Qirmiz project in Cairo, Egypt tried to relate two different concepts of conservation and restoration. First, the concern was for area preservation using a complex of seven different structures as a starting point for renewal of the district. Restoring these seven monuments was done to exacting standards and with superb technical skills. The philosophy guiding the work was to distinguish between the new and the old. No effort was made to assimilate the old with the new. The patina of age shows to the casual observer where the old ends and the new begins.

The third selected project reflects a different approach which is more akin to reconstruction than to conservation or restoration. Thus the *Azam Palace* in Damascus, Syria required reconstruction of entire sections of the palace without detailed documentation of what existed before. Furthermore, over a period of 34 years, the conservationist took entire sections from another structure of a contemporary period and placed them in the reconstructed palace to recreate the former ambiance of the grandiose structure.

Despite their differences, the 1983 Jury felt that these three projects validated an approach for the Muslim world. Collectively, they show the importance of preserving the heritage as both witness to a glorious past and a continuing source of inspiration and pride.

Mostar, Yugoslavia: an imaginative institutional arrangement enabled the revitalisation of the old city centre.

Al-Aqsa Mosque, Jerusalem: technically outstanding restoration work carried out under exceptionally difficult circumstances.

1986: Two outstanding conservation schemes were among the six winners. The preservation of *Mostar Old Town in Yugoslavia,* has introduced an institutional dimension into the awards for conservation which until then had concentrated on the technical aspects of restoration. In Mostar, the Jury premiated a scheme that showed innovation and an ability to rechannel resources generated by the old city to restore its buildings. Thus, the old city was rejuvenated from the economic activities within its perimeter.

The restoration of *al-Aqsa Mosque in Jerusalem,* has shown tremendous technical ability, outstanding sensitivity, and staunch dedication in the face of much adversity.

A third project was also recognised. Though given the status of honourable mention, it deserves to be discussed here. This is the *Touring Club Restorations in Turkey*. While none of the structures in this project are especially notable and the technical work is not outstanding, two features deserve special recognition: First, this project was undertaken by the private sector and not by the government; and second, it includes some nineteenth century building which are not considered Islamic. This second point shows that Muslims are recognising that there is continuity between their past and their present and that all periods of their heritage are worthy of preservation.

TO THE FUTURE

After an outstanding array of winners over the three cycles, much can be asked about whether the Award has more to say on conservation issues. As we have seen, every cycle has brought new winners that had new things to tell the world. Perhaps the most outstanding achievement of the Award to date, and one which will continue, even if there were to be no future prizes for historic preservation, has been the enhancement of the importance of historic heritage in the thinking of planners and architects in the Muslim world who are grappling with contemporary problems. Through research, publication, and premiated winners, the Award has reminded architects practicing in the Muslim world that they have rich sources of inspiration, that they have a duty to protect as well as to use.

The Award will undoubtedly continue to be an ongoing process of thinking, research and dissemination of information about worthy efforts at maintaining our heritage. Only if we recognise our heritage as a living, evolving legacy will we be able to produce culturally, socially and ecologically relevant forms of contemporary architecture for the Muslim countries.

SOCIAL AND INSTITUTIONAL ISSUES

That architecture does not exist in a void, but is an ongoing enterprise that interacts with the societal context, is by now accepted by all. Yet, time after time we find difficulty in bringing to bear the notions of these concepts upon the training and organisation of curricula for the preparation of architects to face the challenge of practice in these evolving societies. From the Award seminar on Architectural Education (Granada, 1986), the paper by Ismail Serageldin on architecture and society illustrates some of these concerns.

The interaction between architecture and planning is at the nexus of public decision-making which is affected by the nature and extent of the pressures exerted by interested parties and by the objective realities of the urban condition.

This concern with the context in which contemporary activity takes place was manifested within different fora. The international seminar of 1984 dealt with the exploding metropolis, taking Cairo as a case study. Here, architects are trying to cope with a city that is growing by more than a thousand people a day. Its 12 million inhabitants are served by an infrastructure designed to cope with no more than a third of that number. The magnitude of the challenges, the compelling nature of the basic needs of providing water, sewage, transport, and decent shelter, compete for the attention of decision makers and the availability of resources. This tends to squeeze out the needs to preserve and protect one of the most outstanding historic heritages in the world, with unrivalled monuments that are falling prey to economic and demographic pressure and inappropriate uses, as well as a rising water table and environmental pollution. It is the reality of such a context that confronts the practitioners of architecture and urban planning in the Muslim world. It is in such contexts that one searches to find the meaning of history, to the present and the future, as well as the relationships between architects, their clients, and society.

The essay by Mona Serageldin deals with the institutional aspects of decision-making in Cairo, but it clearly has wider applicability.

Close to this reality and reflecting the concern with poverty and the issue of shelter, an extract from Charles Correa's *The New Landscape* shows how this important architect and member of the Steering Committee has addressed the issue of the social dimensions of design for shelter in a poor and overpopulated world.

Finally, the question of assessing the quality of projects in socially-oriented interventions is addressed in an extract of the Steering Committee's brief to the Master Jury of 1986.

Architecture and Society *

Ismail Serageldin

The Most Social of the Arts? There is no art form that is as completely intertwined with a particular society as its architectural expression: for it is art that is physically rooted in the geographic location of that society. For the members of that society — and this is to no way deny that the society may be far from an integrated entity — it reflects both their aspirations, their artistic sensibility, and their economic wealth; the level of advancement of their technology; the elements of climate and topography, and the structure of their social organisation. Not only does the architecture of any people physically express all this, being the net result of all the contradictions that society embodies, but is also helps shape the vision of the society of itself. It is both a mirror of that society's activities and an instrument shaping its identity.

Within this context, however, it is not clear to what extent the architectural profession, per se, is responsible for moulding taste, or merely for carrying it out. As Allsopp has stated: "*The failure of modern architecture in recent years is only partly the fault of architects. The main burden of blame for inhumane architecture must rest upon clients who have failed to educate themselves for the great responsibilities they undertake.*"[1] It is for this reason that the AKAA has consciously underlined the collective responsibility of all involved in the proccess of creating a building which is deserving of recognition.

It is undeniable that the taste of the governing elite is likely to dominate the pattern of buildings that give an area its easily identifiable character and that serve as landmarks and as exemplars of what the state's dominant elite promotes. As Oleg Grabar has noted, the form of the cities in the Muslim world was defined by the middle class, while the monuments were defined by the elite.[2] This is not to say that artistic expression is totally constrained by societal reality. Without question artists — be they architects, painters or sculptors — play a role in defining, articulating and improving society's perception of itself and its perception of its aesthetic reality. As Hamilton once put it: "*The artist, whether his medium is verbal, pictorial, plastic, or musical, is the man equipped with radar to penetrate the cultural fogs of the age.*"[3]

However, architects are more constrained than other artists. They have to contend with clients and financing, and they have to contend with the need for their creations to function properly and to meet a rigorous set of codes and restrictions. They interact with society much more than other artists, and they cannot function in isolation. Hence, architecture is by far the most closely linked of the arts to the reality of society in its multiplicity of dimensions, be they economic, social, cultural, political, institutional or religious.

View of Amran, Yemen. Architecture, whether done by the medium of architects or only builders, is by necessity a physical mirror of a society's social, economic, cultural, legal and technological realities as well as an adaptation to the physical environment.

Architecture and the "Image of Progress". In the context of the architecture of the Muslim world, I would like to emphasise that a central part of the problem which we confront in our Muslim culture today is that most of the ruling elites of our societies

* Extract from Proceedings of *Architectural Education in the Islamic World*, Seminar Ten in the series – Architectural Transformations in the Islamic World, Granada, Spain, April 21–25, 1986. Published by Concept Media for the Aga Khan Award for Architecture, Singapore, 1986, pp. 75–88.

have gone through a process of disassociation from their cultural roots. This has led to the *dichotomisation* of cultural perception, where the historic heritage — cultural, religious, spiritual — is identified with the past, backwardness and poverty, while the image of "progress" is borrowed from elsewhere, namely the West.

Unless and until architects and intellectuals generally succeed in providing the ruling elites of Muslim societies with an alternative image of progress, they will continue to pay lip service to the need for cultural authenticity while their actions will speak more loudly than their words as they hurry to adopt the most superficial aspects of Western culture.

Set of Metropolis. A particular architectural vision is associated with the "image of progress". In this century it has mostly been technology and skyscrapers that have captured the collective imagination.

Architecture and Changing Cultural Identity. As we have seen, the architect is responsible, by the variety of activities that he or she undertakes, for the definition or "image of progress" that a society, or at least its elite, holds of itself. The physical expression of that society today in most Third World countries is closely identified with the Manhattan skyline, and leaves little room for a more articulated and sensitive response that is more respectful of cultural continuity and more responsive to climatic and site requirements. Unless architects can successfully convince the elites of their societies to replace their imported image of progress with a more coherent and effective one, there is going to be little chance to reverse that widespread degradation of the urbanistic character and architectural expression that is so prevalent throughout the Muslim world and more generally the Third World.

The task of defining such an alternative reality for a contemporary image of progress in the Third World, of which the Muslim world is a part, is not an easy one. The designers who will cope with that task have to convince the "disassociated" decision-makers and the commercial elite of their societies of the superiority of the alternative that they present, to the imported model.

Only if this task can be done will the secondary effects of this new indigenous alternative reality be achieved. Namely, that the architectural expression of the whole society will be gradually affected. The lower middle classes aspire to have residences and to work in places that are comparable to those of the upper middle classes, and the upper middle classes to have residences and to work in places that are comparable to those of the prevailing elite. By changing the architecture of the elite, architects can indeed change the perception of large segments of society as to what is desirable as an expression of modernity and of social status.

It is unlikely that architects will be able to do this alone. A wide variety of disciplines have to interact in order to ensure that the visionary efforts of imaginative, sensitive architects are not left in isolation, but that the intellectual underpinnings that deal with abstractions and ideas, as well as with the social, economic and institutional realities of any societal system, are coherent and pull in the same direction. Without that, inherent tension is likely to continue and ruptures of a cultural and intellectual kind, at the very least, are bound to continue.[4] Architecture and urban planning will suffer in their inability to fulfill their assigned and noble mission of being the agents of progress rather than the servants of an elite.

APPRECIATING THE PAST

Preservation of the Heritage: What, Why, How, and for Whom? The preservation of tradition works at different levels, reflects if anything, differing contemporary functions and ideological needs (e.g. the need for legitimacy) by ascendant elites or their rivals. On one level, there is the effort to preserve the best examples of traditional buildings as exemplars, sources of contemporary inspiration and/or custodians of part of what its bearer regard as their contemporary cultural identity.

On a different level, the preservation and reuse of individual buildings in contemporary society raises serious functional and ideological problems. Yet, such adaptive reuse appears to be the only possibility of maintaining vitality for the buildings and avoiding the museum approach to important elements of an organic living city. Elsewhere, this author has analysed the approach and economics of dealing with adaptive reuse.[5] Whole seminars have been devoted to the subject[6] and many learned treatises have dealt with its different aspects[7] and, indeed, one is struck by the vast number of little noticed examples of such successful renovation and reuse found in any single country.[8]

The preservation of a single building, whether reused or not, is different from the preservation of the character of an area and, here, different criteria come into play. Of these, the sense of urban space is a fundamental one, as is the question of scale, proportions, street alignments, fenestration, articulation of volumes, relations between solids and voids, and, most of all, activities permitted in the public space and inter-relationship between the public and private domains.

This level of dealing with the historic past, underlines the types of skills that a practising architect should aquire to work in the Muslim world today, where ferment and change are important. In such situations of change and ferment society at large seeks to anchor its headlong rush into the future in its past and the assertion of its own individualism, i.e., its identity as witnessed by the greatness of its exemplars.

Decoding the Symbols of the Past. Architects must acquire the sophistication to read the symbolic content of this heritage in a manner that enriches their ability to produce relevant buildings for today and tomorrow, and to guide the "authentification" efforts between the twin shoals of *Kitsch* and alien inappropriateness.

This sophistication can only come through a strengthened educational process which engenders in future architects the critical sense required to decode the symbolic content of the past in a realistic, as opposed to an ideologically mystifying, fashion. This, of course, necessitates a broad knowledge of the methodology as well as the content of historical studies, a sense of the growth of societies as a process of successive attempts at totalisation and above all an ability to see the built environment of the past as it was perceived by contemporaries.

UNDERSTANDING THE PRESENT

Societies in Transition. The societies of the Muslim world are inescapably societies in transition, however much some members of those societies may try to avoid this basic process by denying it, or by absolutising a past which exists only in their own minds as a counterweight to the present reality they deny and the future which they fear. The demographic, technical, economic, cultural, political and ideological components of this transition process are well known. Drowning in a flood of Western technology and cultural imports that are frequently ill-matched to local conditions and insensitive to cultural traditions, Muslim societies are today struggling to create a cultural environment that provides them with a viable sense of self-identity and which is suited to regional and national conditions. Authenticity for an Indonesian will not be the same as authenticity for a Moroccan. Yet there is this fine thread of commonality of the nature of the search with variability of the conditions under which it is undertaken. This is part of the creative genius of the Muslim culture, whose hallmarks have always been unity with diversity. Contemporary "regionalism" must express itself in new and contemporary ways. This truism must be restated frequently in the face of a strong current that seeks refuge in perpetuating the myth that traditional vernacular architecture is enough. This "escape into the past" must be forced to recognise the scale and technology that increasingly link and undergird the urban built environment. Slavish copying of the past is not the answer. For those who would try, the dimensions of modern technology and its related infrastructural requirements will quickly remind them that the path of excellence requires creativity.

ANTICIPATING AND PREPARING FOR THE FUTURE

A Timeless Continuity: Reading the Signs. Architects must be masters of a wide range of skills and their deployment — a range far greater than architectural education currently prepares them for. First, architects must be able to decode the past so they can understand how their predecessors viewed *their* past, present, and future. Armed with this comparative knowledge, they must secondly attempt to read the signs and trends of the present. This is particularly tricky as, while buildings last a long time, current trends may prove ephemeral, and become so within the space of a few years. Third, architects must not only think of their single building, but of its relationship to the wider community. Fourth, and most significantly, they must pull all of this analysis together and design and implement a product which, over its lifetime, can justly win a place in the timeless continuity of world architecture, as have the great buildings of the past which, speak of excellence, not of an age, but for all time!

THE ROLE OF THE ARCHITECT IN SOCIETY

It flows from the above that the role of the architect in societies in transition such as the Muslim world is currently undergoing is indeed a pivotal one, both in defining the society's sense of its own reality, as well as in refining its perceptions of its taste and its authentic cultural expression.

There is much to learn from folk architecture but under no circumstance should we delude ourselves into trying to maintain and copy previous solutions that may have been perfectly rational and functional for social and economic circumstances that prevailed in society at a certain point in time. We must acknowledge the need for important changes in architectural forms as facets of the physical expression of the changes wrought by economic and social development.[9]

Architects, Builders and Planners. The architect, in my judgement, is the sole person capable of creating those unique structures that become landmarks in an environment and help identify and shape the collective image a society has of itself. Only the architect sets the tone for a new generation of buildings, and successfully reshapes a society's image of itself. The breakthrough innovative buildings are not produced without architects, they are produced as a result of the creative genius of a collectivity of individuals whose vocation is destined to become architecture.

At the same time, it is important to recognise that when architects have tried to build large numbers of houses, addressing those sets of buildings that constitute about 70 per cent of an average modern city's buildings, they have failed miserably. The blowing up of Pruitt-Igoe in the early 1970's, a celebrated symbol of urban failure, was, however, the condemnation of a *social policy* towards housing, of which the specific design of this public project was but a part. Given such a context, there is much to learn in the important warning of Fathy[10] that architects should limit themselves to working for individual clients and should try to uphold client-specific solutions in their designs.[11]

Planners are those who design the skeleton that helps shape a city; whether it be in terms of its transportation networks or its basic infrastructure or setting the

Mohammed 'Ali Mosque, Cairo, Egypt.

building codes, subdivision regulations, and zoning ordinances that make an urban environment what it is. Planners help shape the overall structure of the city, but they seldom have a major impact on the individual building except in very special cases. They bring all the overall concerns of topography, economic base, social structure, levels of service, financial health and viability of a municipality, to bear on the problem of the physical environment. Beyond that, their role is, and should be, limited. It has long been the view of this writer that only a public-private partnership can make for a viable attack on the problems of the urban environment and the planner's domain, the public one, is to be limited to those aspects of the overall problems that cannot and should not be handled by private initiative.[12]

Most of the remaining cityscape is filled in by anonymous architecture[13] that — although individually not distinguished — collectively provides the flesh over the planner's skeleton. It is the architect who provides the distinguished and distinguishing features. It is the architect who caps this collaboration between planners and non-architects by providing those buildings and those features that ultimately give an urban environment its landmarks and articulates its character. It is the architect who helps mould the major complexes in well designed urban planning schemes and who keeps rejuvenating cityscapes with new generations of buildings and structures that modify and improve as well as enrich, enhance and re-enforce the cultural identity of that environment.

National Commercial Bank in the context of the Jeddah skyline. Only architects can create landmark buildings that identify the image of a society and a period.

A Dual Function. The architect, therefore, must act on the one hand, as an instrument of change and a forward looking agent of the transformation of cultural identity, on the other hand as the keeper of existing identity, a preserver and extender of a heritage, and the molder and reinforcer of cultural authenticity. Just as architecture is inextricably entwined with society, so is the individual architect placed in a pivotal role in the society of which he or she is a member.

Certification, Registration and Professionalisation. Given the crucial dual function I have just mentioned, the reality of the role of the architect in today's society, limited as it becomes in relation to that of the many anonymous and the few well known builders, and circumscribed as it is by the work of the planners, is still sufficiently important in the broader context I have suggested to raise serious questions about qualifications and professionalism as they now exist.

Professional associations have consistently sought to seek broad acceptance of the "professional" status of the occupations or practices they represent.

In most of the Muslim world today, the problems of the architectural profession are somewhat different. They tend to fall into one or more of the following:
Firstly, architects impact on a very small part of the built environment. Charles Correa[14] estimates that architects interact with only one per cent or less of the society at large. Secondly, architects (and urban planners) tend to be subsumed under the broader professional grouping of engineering professions (e.g. Egypt, Saudi Arabia) where their concerns are seldom adequately reflected in the activities of the association. Finally, the views of architects and urban planners are frequently considered to be matters of "taste", i.e. much more discardable than, say, the views of structural engineers. This leads to a demobilisation of the professionals and a reduction of the professionalism in the practice of architecture and planning.

With few exceptions, the relationship between Muslim societies and their architects (and planners) needs to be upgraded. A deeper respect for the real contributions of the profession(s) will be achieved only if we upgrade the quality of the performance of the professionals. This means that in addition to the "certification" function of architecture schools, there must be a genuine nurturing of real talent, to produce the type of notable performance that can properly address the awesome challenge of building in the Muslim world today.

Planning and Institutional Mechanisms*

Mona Serageldin

Authorities dealing with urban development today are operating within the context of national policies over which they have limited influence. Priorities, criteria and budgets are set with reference to national development objectives rather than urban development needs.

Employment policies, labour laws, wage and salary levels, price controls and subsidies, and the relative importance given to the urban sector are all beyond the control of local authorities. In the case of Cairo, freedom of action is further constrained by sensitivity of the risks involved in tampering with the nation's political, economic and cultural nerve centre.

The system of local administration first introduced in 1960 sought to promote local participation through centralised planning and decentralised implementation. Commitment to the principle of local government was reaffirmed in 1971 and codified in 1975. It created a twin hierarchy of executive committees and popular councils to provide more administrative flexibility to municipal authorities and to give an active role to citizen participation.

The system was amended in 1979 to strengthen the authority of governors, who are now considered the direct representatives of the President. They have control over housing, public utilities, land development, slum up-grading, conservation, and most aspects of urban planning, design and project implementation.

Governorates lack adequate staff and resources to discharge their new responsibilities. In the case of Cairo the task is horrendous. Greater Cairo is one of the top ten most rapidly growing urban agglomerations in the world. Its needs are increasing at a rate far greater than the rate of growth of the Egyptian economy. Its management involves three administrative jurisdictions and complex interrelationships among a vast array of central agencies and special authorities.

Unregulated expansion of apartments in public housing blocks.

MASTER PLANS

In less than a hundred years, Cairo municipal authorities have evolved from a tiny Tanzim bureau attached to the Ministry of Public Works and mainly concerned with streets, parks and urban beautification to become the highest-order unit of local government in Egypt.

Over the same period, three master plans have been prepared, adopted and partially implemented. They have left a mixed legacy of real achievements and damaging results. On the positive side, they have contributed to improvements of infrastructure systems, introduction of modern transport technologies and new types of urban development. On the negative side, they have fostered enduring misconceptions, transplanted western models of dubious suitability, and adopted solutions which often proved counter-productive in the longer term.

---

* Extract from Proceedings of *The Expanding Metropolis: Coping with the Urban Growth of Cairo*, Seminar Nine in the series – Architectural Transformations in the Islamic World, Cairo, Eygpt, Nov 11 – 15, 1984. Published by Concept Media for the Aga Khan Award for Architecture, Singapore, 1985, pp 119 – 128.

Informal subdivisions on agricultural land.

TABLE 1 **Local Government**

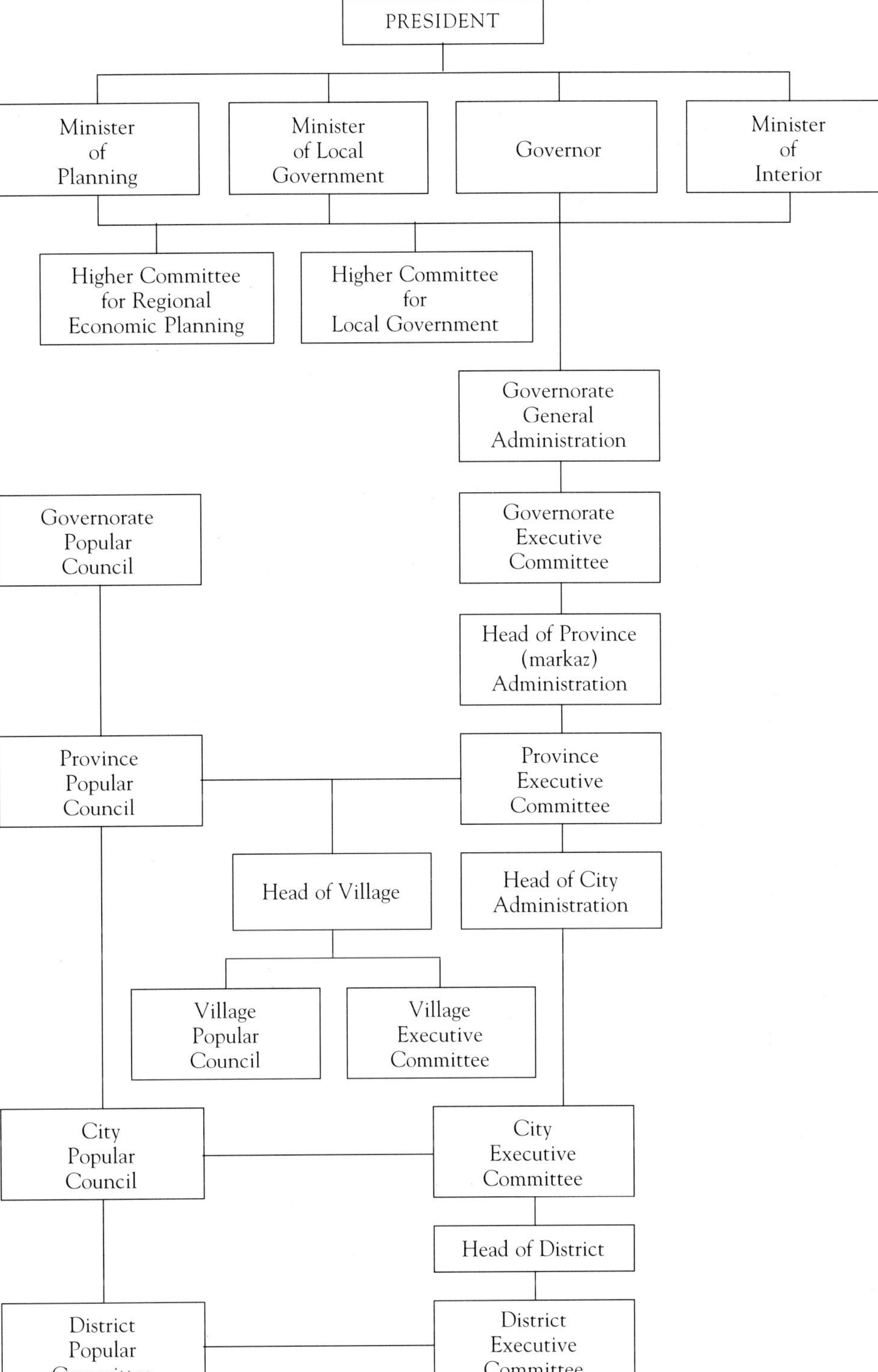

The 1974 plan, of clear Haussmannian inspiration, asserted that a basic incompatibility existed between the traditional and the modern. The old urban fabric could neither be modernised nor be integrated with the new. The plan introduced the vehicular avenue and the subdivision plat.

The 1956 plan followed the traditions of English town and country planning. It introduced the notions of ideal size, containment, development standards for new growth, and long-range (20 year) planning to guide and control development. Its most damaging legacy resulted from its major recommendation (that the industrial suburbs ought to absorb rural migrants) which ended up promoting development on agricultural land.

TABLE 2 **Conceptual Approach for Master Planning**

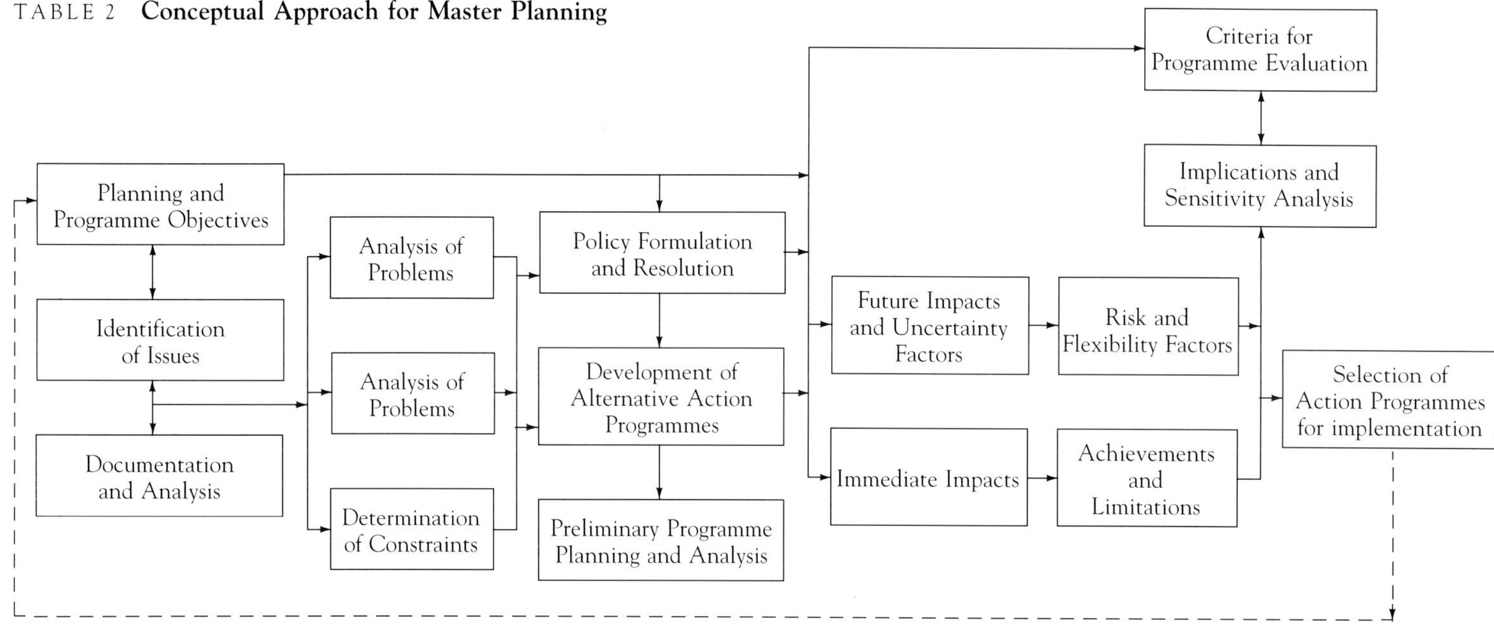

The master plan produced by the Greater Cairo Planning Commission in 1969 instituted an urban policy of "concentrated decentralisation." It retained some concepts from earlier plans: containment and ideal size, the view of the old city as a historic slum, and emphasis on large-scale projects requiring heavy investments and high levels of subsidy. Its important contributions were pointing out the problems of land consumption and housing shortage. It advocated planned satellite cities in the desert and vertical expansion within the existing urban area.

The fourth master plan was completed in 1982. It strengthened the approach of the 1969 plan by adding development corridors to link new towns and satellite cities to Cairo and recommended measures to rationalise growth patterns in the existing urban agglomeration.

DEVELOPMENT REGULATIONS

Government authorities at all levels are overwhelmed by the magnitude of the problems they face and frustrated by their inability to cope with the undesirable physical manifestations of an increasingly intensive use of land. The potential impact of public policies has been characterised by rigidity in legislation and leniency in enforcement.

Since 1960, an impressive body of laws, decrees and regulations has been enacted covering every aspect of urban development from master planning and land subdivision to building codes and standards of infrastructure. The frequency with which they have been updated, revised, amended and superceded testifies to their effectiveness. Despite wide powers to remove violations and impose sanctions on violators, local authorities have been unable to stem the tide of popular disregard of regulatory controls. The administrative procedures involved are so cumbersome, time consuming, and costly that they discourage compliance except for the most compulsively law-abiding citizens.[2]

Starting in the 1950's, disregard of regulatory measures quickly became widespread. Well over 60 per cent of the structures in the city harboured some violation of existing codes. Mounting pressure to regularise an uncontrollable situation could only end in legalising violations.This first occurred in 1956 and since then, periodic legalisations (1966, 1981 and 1984) have undermined the power of legislative controls and the credibility of the Tanzim (planning and building) authorities.

TABLE 3

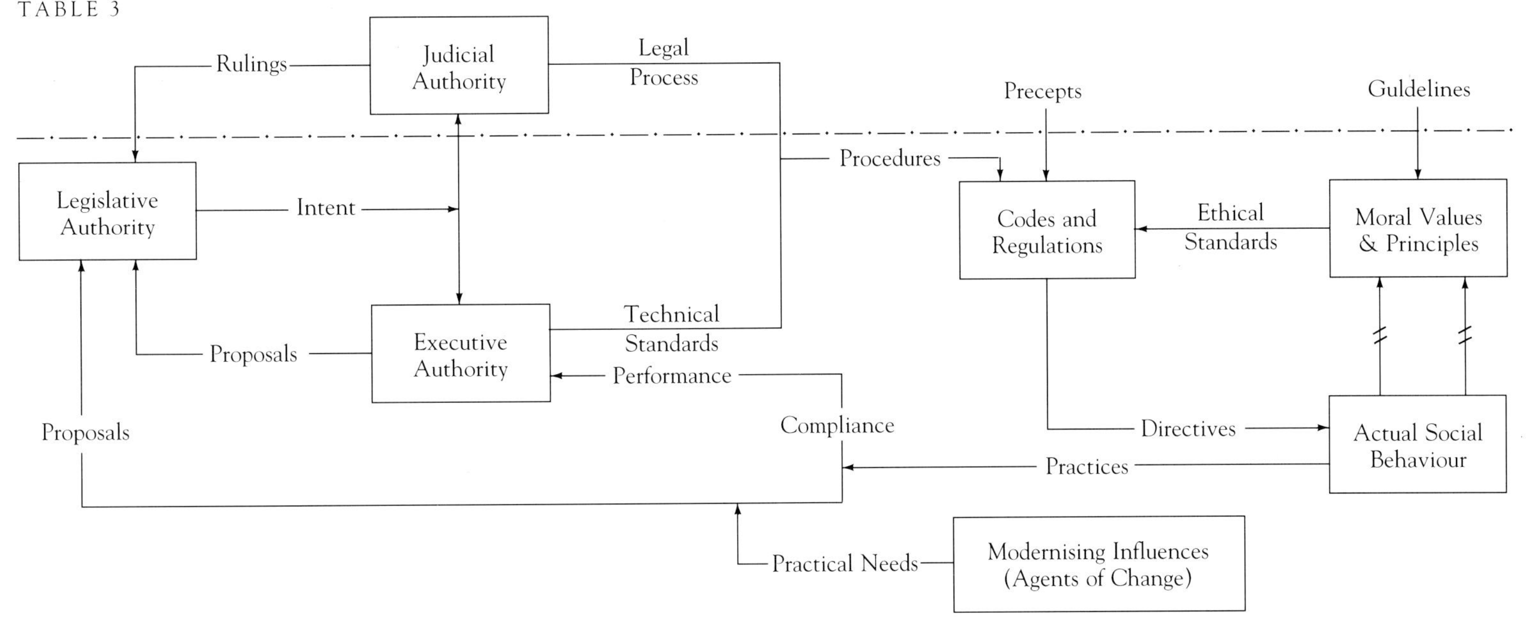

To remedy this chaotic situation, criteria, limitations and procedures for legalisation were promulgated early in 1984 — a gesture of dubious utility. The majority of violators have little incentive to engage in elaborate registration and appraisal processes which are bound to prove costly and time consuming (taking three to six months). Rather, they may be better advised simply to wait for the next round of blanket legalisation.

It is far more efficient to focus control on a few key factors (such as location and height) selected for their critical impact on urban growth and to enforce these measures with unfaltering determination.

The effectiveness of planning and regulatory measures is hampered by the difficulty of formulating and enforcing urban land policies. The incentive of potential profits from speculative transfers at the urban fringe easily override the deterrent of official pronouncements, particularly when adjustment of municipal boundaries will no doubt soon follow, regularising a *de facto* situation.

The badly needed reorientation of urban expansion onto desert land hinges on the ability of governorate authorities to adopt policies which allow a controlled but rapid release of land. The lack of experimentation with such options is attributable to earlier regulations, reaffirmed by the planning law of 1983, which prohibit the legal release of land unless it is fully serviced at the standards specified by law. These seemingly low standards require large front-end investments and result in financial burdens and delays which ensure that the amount of land marketed is insignificant compared to demand.

FINANCIAL CONSIDERATIONS

External factors and existing conditions have thus conspired to create inefficient and unproductive patterns of development for which there is no solution short of major restructuring. Unserviced areas are increasing at twice the rate of urban growth, and person-trips at a rate four times higher than in Europe due to cross-commuting patterns shaped by severe housing shortages, defective communication systems, and counter productive legislation. Since governorates finance 80 per cent of their budgets and 92 per cent of capital investments from national allocations, they are in a weak position to question the wider and long-term implications of policies which central authorities find expedient.

The growth discrepancy between the scale of the problems and the means of addressing them is disheartening and can easily engender a feeling of hopelessness or apathetic cynicism. Just to speak of 1,000 additional persons a day is a constant reminder of urgency or futility — depending on personal attitude.

The perennial lack of funds for both capital investments and operating expenditures beyond minimal levels has led to accelerated deterioration of the physical plan and reduced economic life of investments. National pricing policies based on social considerations set tariffs, charges and fees without reference to production and operating costs. The revenues raised are insufficient for adequate operation, let alone preventive maintenance. Greater Cairo has to subsist somehow with capital investments of less than U.S.$ 150 per person per year, when the amount needed is ten times as much.

Influx of workers at Cairo's railroad station.

Densification of informal settlements on the urban fringe.

Fiscal practices putting a premium on minimising immediate outlays resulted in over-extended infrastructure distribution networks and facilities operating at levels two to four times above design capacity. The dismal operating performance of public utilities and services is hardly surprising. The expansion of the urbanised area by some 600 hectares every year implies a growing backlog of unserviced developments. Capacity thresholds have long been crossed, and system indivisibilities entail substantial capital investment requirements totalling about U.S.$ 10 billion to bring Cairo's services up to acceptable standards. Constant break-downs, bottlenecks and shortages further add to the pressure on municipal authorities and to the overloading on their functional capacities.

The rate of increase in the cost of land and construction is quickly eroding the hope of broadening affordability through lower standards, better cost recovery, and wider use of "low-cost" technology. Dual levels of services (premium and popular) are not always a technically feasible alternative and are hardly ever a socially acceptable approach. The range of available options is very limited, and selection should emphasise flexibility and receptivity to incremental up-grading.

From the viewpoint of fiscal management, the problem is not so much competition for scarce resources as operational practices relying on subsidies. Gaps between expenditures and revenues are of little significance when receipts are recycled through central finance and disbursements are drawn against budget allocations set with reference to objectives other than financial viability. There is little reason to develop complicated programming and budgeting procedures when a simple accounting system is enough to assess operational cost efficiency.

INSTITUTIONAL ASPECTS

Problems of planning, implementation and inefficiency in the delivery of public services have been blamed on the quality of manpower in the public sector. Personnel is frustrated by inflation in numbers, despairingly slow advancement and low remuneration. Poor performance is hardly surprising in the face of such disincentives.

Managerial competence and technical expertise are certainly plentiful at the higher levels, but overall performance is hampered by inefficient and often unproductive support.

The result is an acute shortage of qualifications and experience for both programme planning and implementation. The inability to implement for lack of adequate support is, in fact, what underlies the seeming unwillingness to experiment with new approaches. Devising workable incentive programmes is a prerequisite for the success of any planning effort.

The involvement of a multiplicity of agencies and enterprises sharing control over sectors or specialised functions is not unique to Cairo. Administratively, the problem is not so much outright conflict stemming from divided responsibilities as

TABLE 4 ***Programme Planning and Crisis Management***

Issues	Determinants	
	Crisis Management	**Programme Planning**
Priority	Urgency	Desirability
	Time Horizon Immediate	5–20 Years
Important Geographic Areas	High Density Central	Vacant Peripheral
Focus of Strategy	Actions	Objectives
Criteria for Intervention	Trade-off Between Needs	Optimisation of Resource Use
Requirements		
Legislative	Operational Standards & Enforcement Procedures	Development Guidelines and Standards
Administrative	Manpower, Equipment & Materials	Design and Implementation
Fiscal	Support Budget & Foreign Exchange	Feasibility & Funding Sources
Technical	Procurement and Data Base Management	Information Gathering and Data Analysis
Investment Decisions	Initial Cost	Economic Life Cost

more subtle issues of rationalising and co-ordinating activities under management procedures based on centralised directives. Inter-agency co-ordination has to rely on organisational mechanisms which cut horizontally across the vertical chains of command. By definition, these mechanisms are weak.

Clearly, except at the highest ministerial levels, the capacity to achieve intersectorial rationalisation and coordination will remain limited by real or perceived constraints on mandate and leverage and by a tendency to focus on specific activities rather than on more general issues of policy.

Nonetheless, advisory, co-ordinating or special-purpose committees offer an excellent vehicle for:

- Overcoming the issue of inadequate compensation in the civil service by offering bonuses and honoraria for participation;
- Drawing on the expertise and dedication of private citizens and organisations irrespective of political affiliation;
- Promoting the potential effectiveness of public interventions as instruments for channelling urban growth in the desired direction;
- Bringing intersectorial linkages to bear on investment decisions;
- Setting in motion the mechanism for small, incremental changes which can be easily accepted, speedily implemented, and gradually result in marked improvement in effeciency.

Chief executive officers and key officials find it difficult to extricate themselves from the harrowing imperatives of crisis management in order to concentrate on the broader issues and longer term perspective of programme planning beyond the requirements of annual budgets. To reconcile these demands necessitates a political willingness to prevent the urgency of constant successions of crises from overwhelming other concerns and engulfing available time and energies. It implies an ability to reorient thought processes continually, shifting back and forth from a focus on immediate decisions to the frame of mind needed to contemplate the future.

The challenge is to develop strategies for growth and management in a situation for which there is no historical precedent. Innovation and experimentation are, per force, a key ingredient of urban policy. The implications of this are often overlooked in programme planning, while format and procedure are discussed endlessly. Disruption of existing modes of thought and procedure, inevitably generates controversy and opposition. Promoting acceptance of new concepts is of utmost importance; when necessary, the format should be reshaped to maximise the likelihood of successful achievement and visibility.

A system of internal evaluation should be established, specifically to assess the performance of institutional mechanisms introduced in conjunction with pilot projects. The key to capitalising on successful experience (regardless of its scale) lies in building an ability to quickly identify promising approaches, assess their potential replicability, and generalise their application.

CONCLUSION

Present institutional mechanisms are not geared to generating sweeping reform, even if it were desirable to do so. The urge to advocate radical changes must be tempered by the risks involved in failure. The concept of "absorptive capacity" which has long been used in relation to concrete physical variables can usefully be applied to the capacity of institutions to absorb varying degrees of change.

Cumulative, less ambitious incremental adjustments can often achieve very positive, though less spectacular results. Programmes focussing on issues of great concern provide the best vehicles for introducing institutional change because strong government support guarantees sustained implementation.

Planning is inherently an advisory function, in an ideal position for recommending bold innovative approaches but a weak one from which to implement restructuring concepts. Planning must be based on a vision of what the future should be, even when this implies a radical departure from prevailing trends. Pragmatism may dictate that the vision be tempered by the harsh economic and political realities of a nation engaged in a desperate race between population growth and resource development. Losing sight of these realities reduces planning to an academic exercise, but losing sight of the goals transforms it into mere public administration.

Monetary and other material rewards are powerful incentives, but they can overcome neither paralysing cautiousness nor sterility of thought. There is no substitute for a daring decision-maker willing to innovate, a skilled imaginative professional capable of generating ideas, and a persevering administrator with a sense of mission. When they have an optimistic view of the future and a firm belief that individual contributions can have an influence, such persons can be the catalysts needed to bring about institutional development.[3]

TABLE 5 **Implementation of Innovative Programmes and Activities**

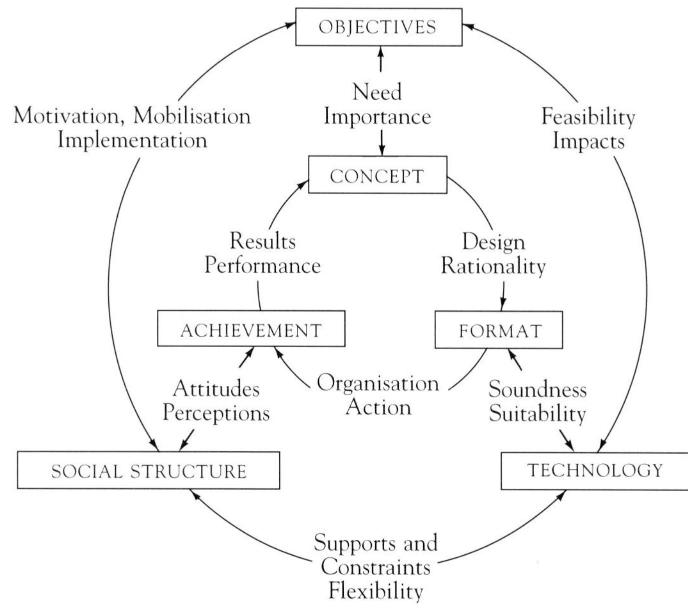

Scanning the Options

Charles Correa

Searching for a future.

The scale of the problem determines the solution. This is the key to the strategies we must develop over the next 25 years. If we succeed in our interventions, then we might actually be able to *use* the unprecedented growth of cities to our permanent gain, and emerge from the tunnel that lies ahead — so to speak — better off than when we entered. After all, most cities in the past have grown by continuous, incremental stages. Thus the authorities never perceived the opportunity to — "rearrange the scenery." Let us, for instance, turn the clock back to the time when New York had only one or two million inhabitants. If, at that stage, it was apparent that it would soon have to accommodate ten million people, then a lot of basic structural changes might have been not only financially possible but *politically* viable, and New York today would be a far more rationally organised city.

This, in the final analysis, is the advantage of our predicament. That, for the first time in history, we are able to perceive an enormous quantum leap in urban growth; a perception that should really prompt us to re-adjust this scenery we've inherited. Intelligently done, this could have staggering geo-political implications — for instance, the kind of leverage the U.S.A. gets from having an urban structure which spans a continent and connects two oceans. A little over a century ago, the U.S.A. was dominated by its Eastern seaboard cities (i.e. Boston, New York, etc.), facing only the Atlantic. The reason why that nation can now address the Pacific is that in the interim there has grown a matching set of urban centres along the West Coast (San Francisco, Los Angeles, etc.) — and also right across the continent (Detroit, Chicago, Denver). It is an organic interdependent urban structure generated by the enormous population growth that has taken place in the U.S.A. over the last 100 years. In contrast: Australia, a continent which was structured to face Britain through its south-eastern ports of Melbourne and Sydney; though it suspects that its future lies with its Asian neighbours to the immediate north and west, it does not have the dynamic population growth necessary to make such urban re-structuring possible. Where there's growth, there's hope.

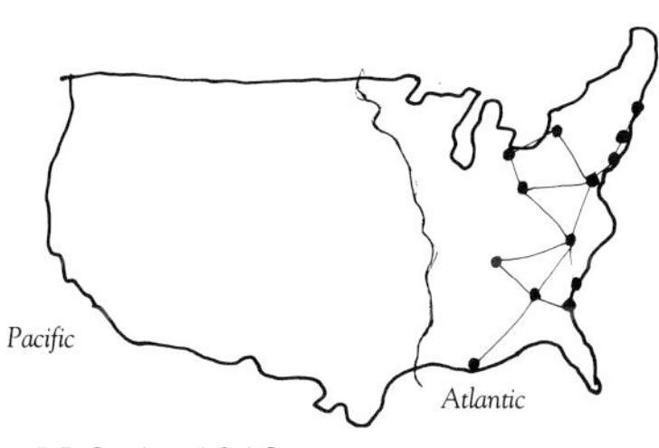

U.S.A. 1812.

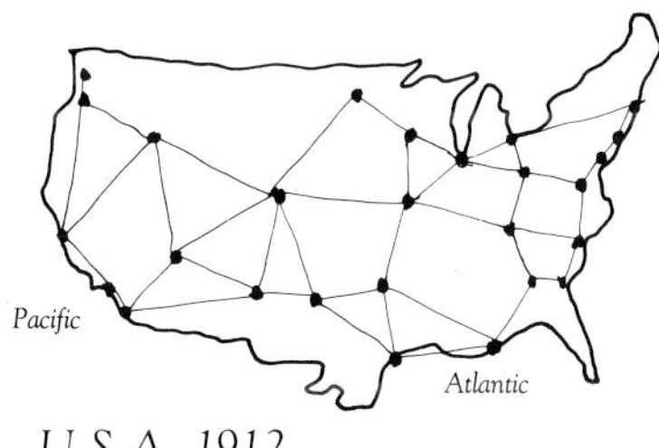

U.S.A. 1912.

This is not to say that the population should continue to grow in the Third World. It is merely to emphasise that in spite of anything we do, the population will in many cases double before they stabilise ("Enough girl babies have already been born, etc...") We do not have much choice about that. What we *do* have a choice about is in their distribution pattern across the nation — as well as the internal structuring within the urban centres. Future generations will certainly hold us accountable for missing that unique opportunity.

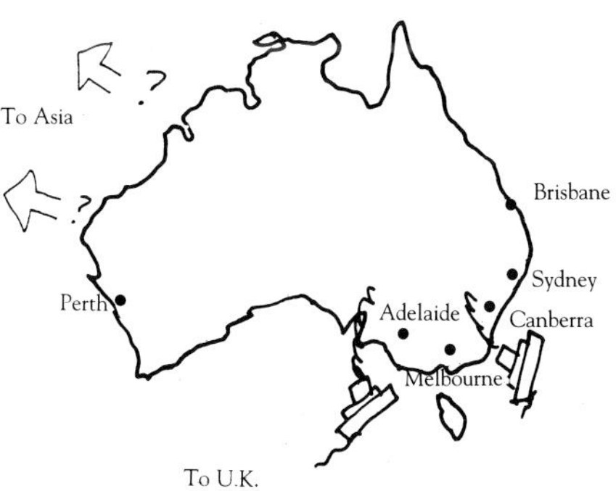

Australia. Slow population growth.

The colossal numbers involved need neither confuse nor intimidate us. True, a single city of ten million seems unmanageable — but what if the same population is distributed in a poly-centred system, of five or six centres, each of a reasonable size? Such urban structures already exist, for instance in the Bay Area in California where a number of separate centres (San Francisco, Oakland, Marine Country, etc.) all form one urban system involving over five million people — and yet San Francisco

---

* From Charles Correa, *The New Landscape*, Book Club of India, Bombay, 1985, pp 119–135. Reprinted by Concept Media. Singapore 1988.

itself has a population of under 900,000. In the same way, several Dutch cities (Amsterdam, The Hague, Rotterdam) all form a single poly-nucleated urban system, each unit of which still possesses a manageable and human scale. And in India itself: Kanpur, Allahabad, Lucknow, etc. form one urban system.

These kinds of models are certainly worth examining. In fact, it is disquieting to realise how seldom we stop to ponder how wide-open our options might really be. Perhaps what is needed is not just more towns and cities (in the conventional sense) but a new kind of community which is quasi-urban, quasi-rural; one which produces densities high enough to support an educational system and a bus service, yet low enough for each family to keep a buffalo or a goat — and a banana tree. In fact, if one can bring down the residential densities to about 50 households per hectare, it becomes feasible to dispense with central sewage systems and instead recycle waste matter (both human and animal) to considerable advantage: cooking gas, fertiliser, small vegetable gardens, etc. Under Indian conditions this would have the additional advantage of continuing the pattern of life to which people are accustomed — as though Mahatma Gandhi's vision of a rural India had an almost exact quasi-urban analogue.

Like gobar and bio-gas, the sun of course, to us in India is another great harbinger of the new landscape. For much of the Third World, the most cost-effective strategies for harnessing solar energy is not through gadgets like solar frying pans (expensive to produce and relatively inefficient) but through the setting up of biological cycles: for instance, shallow ponds to grow algae and plants which photosynthesise the solar energy incident on the water and which are then ingested by fish and other higher forms of life, and so forth, until we are the final recipients (though of course, in turn we must inevitably be consumed by something else in order to continue the cycle!). The employment-generating possibilities of such cycles are considerable, as in a pilot project in *New Bombay* where it was estimated that the building of the ponds would not only provide additional jobs, but also that the soil dug out of earth could be used to form simple sun-dried brick.

Such cycles will create not only the economic basis of communities, but will of necessity determine their physical pattern as well — just as today's cities have been generated by the carriage and the automobile. They constitute a new type of human settlement, using the Third World's unique combination of plentiful sunlight and abundant human labour.

If — and when — these settlements come into being, they will bring about two fundamental changes. First, since God's sunlight falls just about equally all over any of these Third World countries, the demographic pattern of population distribution will also follow suit, avoiding the centralisation and the large concentrations inherent in industrialisation. The second consequence follows from this pattern; for in such a world of evenly distributed self-contained communities the political power structure must change dramatically, since no one will be able to pull a lever in Delhi (or Lagos, or Sao Paolo, or Jakarta) and affect millions of people right across the country.

Yet obviously postulating these profoundly important prototypical settlements for the Third World is not merely a question concerning employment — what we need to metamorphosise is the social system, the life-style of the new settlements. After all, the communes of Mao are not just a legal contract binding a certain number of people to harvest together, but really the only political-social-human reality the commune members know (like fish know the water they swim in). It will take an effort of equivalent inventiveness to find the modus operandi for these new human settlements.

A commune in China.

In the past, such imaginative conceptualising was seldom lacking. For instance, in India since Vedic times, sacred diagrams called *mandalas* have formed the basis of architecture and city planning. These square *mandalas*, sub-divided in prescribed ratios (from 1 to 1024 sub-squares), represent a model of the cosmos — no less! The hierarchy they generate forms a matrix for locational decisions — whether of deities in a temple, or of the principal buildings in a city. They make explicit a Platonic ideal of built form which in turn reinforces and stabilises society.

Today such concepts are certainly not in current use. Furthermore, it would be foolish to think of invoking them unless we also subscribed to the underlying construct of the cosmos they are meant to represent. Yet, in a century when science has postulated an ever-expanding universe, it may be well worth considering the modelling of our central beliefs as the basis for structuring our environment.

Temple and kund at Modhera.

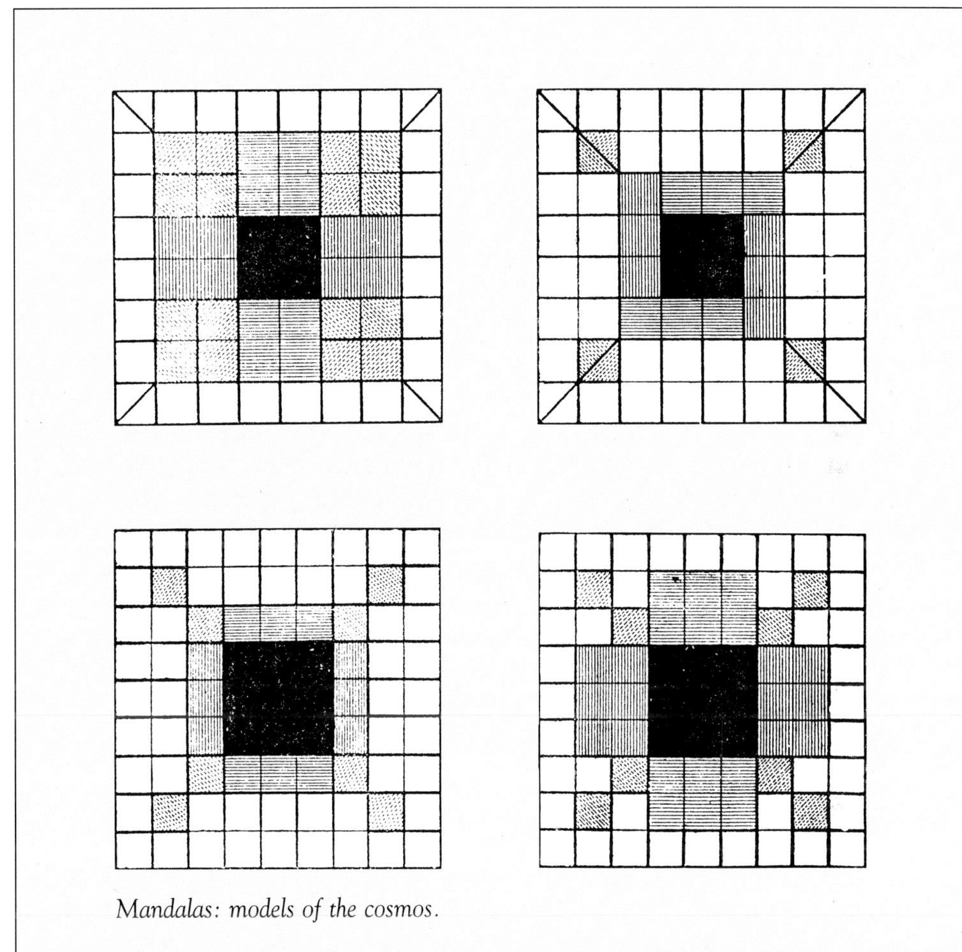

Mandalas: models of the cosmos.

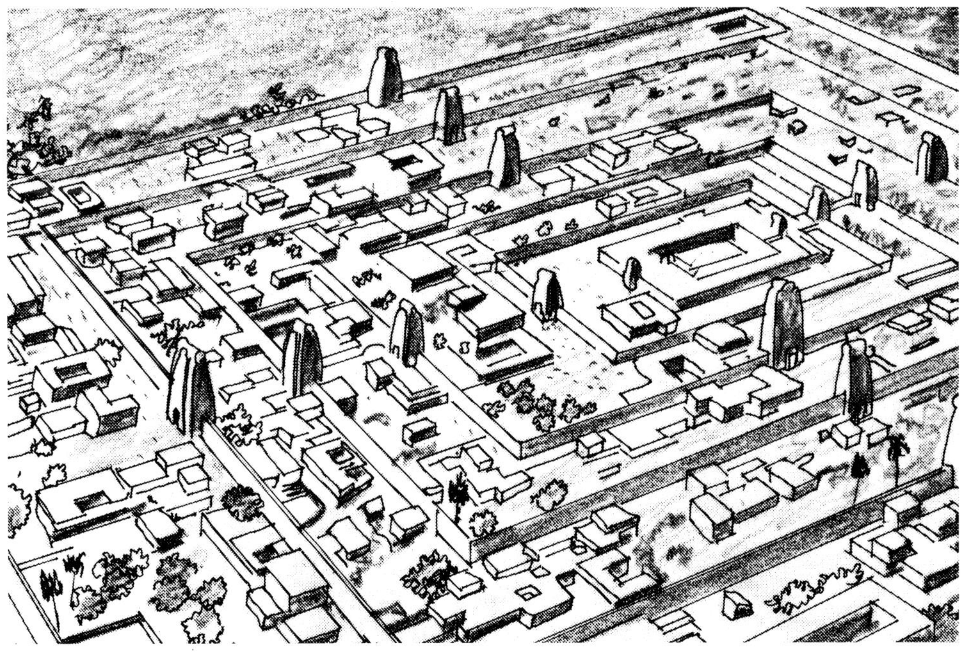

The mandala as temple town: Srirangam, South India.

At the other extreme, we must learn to be equally inventive about how we generate our habitat at the micro-scale. For instance, there is little relation between the form of our streets, and how we use them. Most sidewalks in Bombay are always crowded — during the day with hawkers, (forcing pedestrians onto the traffic lanes), and as evening falls, with people unfolding their beddings for a night's rest.

These night people are not pavement-dwellers, but mostly domestic servants and office boys who keep their belongings in a shared room, and use city pavements for sleeping at night. This pattern allows them to economise on living expenses (and thus maximise the monthly remittances sent back to their villages). What is dismaying is not that they sleep outdoors (on hot sultry nights, obviously a more attractive proposition than a crowded airless room), but that they have to do so under unhygienic conditions, with the public walking right amongst (and over!) them. Is there any way in which the city streets and sidewalks could respond to their needs?

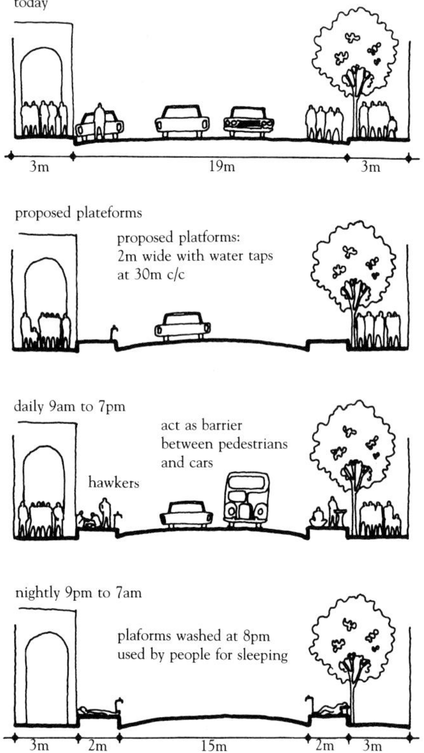

Modifying Bombay's streets with a line of platforms, 2m wide and 0.5m high, with water taps at 30m intervals. During the day these platforms would be used by hawkers — thus clearing the arcades for pedestrians. In the evening, water from the taps would wash the platforms clean — creating otlas for people to sleep on.

To be involved in these issues, the architect will have to act not as a *prima donna* professional, but one who is willing to donate his energy — and his ideas — to society. It is a role that has a very important historic precedent. For throughout most of Asia, his prototype in the past was the site *mistri,* i.e. an experienced mason/carpenter who helped with the design and construction of the habitat. Even today in the small towns and villages of India, the practice continues. Owner and *mistri* go together to the site, and with a stick scratch out on the earth the outline of the building they wish to construct. There is some argument back and forth about the relative advantages of various window positions, stairways, and so forth. But the system works because both builder and user share the same aesthetic, they are both on the *same* side of the table! It was exactly this kind of equation that produced the great architecture of the past, from Chartres to the Alhambra to Fatehpur-Sikri. (If the architect today cannot win an argument with a company executive, would he have been able to over-rule a Moghul Emperor 300 years ago — and survived?)

Today the situation is quite different. Not only has the shared aesthetic evaporated, but the interface has diminished. Only about ten per cent of the population have the resources to commission the kind of buildings the academically trained architect has learnt to design — and only a tenth of them would think of engaging him (the others would appoint a civil engineer, or perhaps a contractor directly). So there you have his interface with society: all of one per cent. This figure represents the people who commission the office buildings, apartments, luxury hotels, factories and houses that make up the bulk of the architect's practice. The situation is not to his making; it merely reflects the grotesque inequality within society itself. But of course it is the poor whose needs are the most desperate. Today in Rio or Lagos or Calcutta, there are millions living in illegal squatter colonies. Is the architect, with his highly specialised skills, going to find a way to be of any relevance to them?

Sharing the same aesthetic...

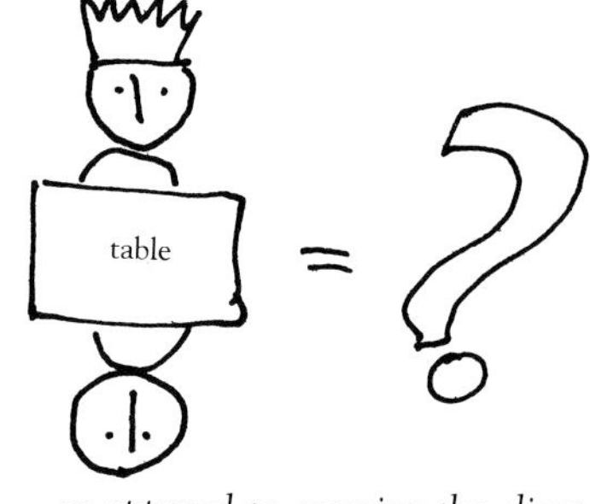

...as opposed to conning the client.

Unfortunately, even among those architects who have enough of a social conscience to want to reach out to the poor, many are really a-visual — in fact, in some cases, belligerently *anti-visual* — rejoicing (as they move among the poor like Florence Nightingale among the wounded) in the acres of ugliness/goodness of it all. What these communities need is not just our compassion, but our professional (i.e. visual and topological) skills. Without these, the squatter colonies will turn out to be nightmares — proliferating, over the next two decades, on a scale which boggles the mind. In turn, they will maim whole generations of Third World children, condemned to grow up in such environments.

We cannot just trust to luck and a blind faith in humanity; for every Mykonos history has created, there are ten other depressing towns. The stunningly beautiful handicraft and weaving of certain societies are the (fortunate!) result of a cumulative process, spread out over many decades — each generation making marginal improvements to the end-product. Without the benefit of such a heritage to provide context, people often opt for ugly things (it is the principle of Miami Beach); if we want to increase the probability of winding up with something as beautiful as Udaipur, then strategies for sites-and-services will have to be programmed accordingly. Perhaps by giving extra weightage to those of the inhabitants who are more visually sensitive, so as to hasten the process? (In a self-help scheme in New Bombay for instance, folk artists were brought in as catalysts, to work with the householders.)

To value the visual component, so obviously present in traditional habitat, is not to join the epicene enthusiasms of todays fashionable eclecticism. Far from it. We must understand our past well enough to value it — and yet also well enough to know why (and how) it must be changed. Architecture is not just a reinforcement of existing values — social, political, economic. On the contrary. It should open new doors — to new aspirations.

To reach the millions who lie on the pavements and in the shanty towns is to get involved in a whole new series of issues. Issues to which we must bring the instincts — and the skills — of the architect. I emphasise this again, because too often, in entering this arena, the architect leaves the best of himself behind. Hence the stultifying sites-and-services schemes — all 'justified' on the grounds that an aesthetic sense is something the poor cannot afford.

Why do we build this?....

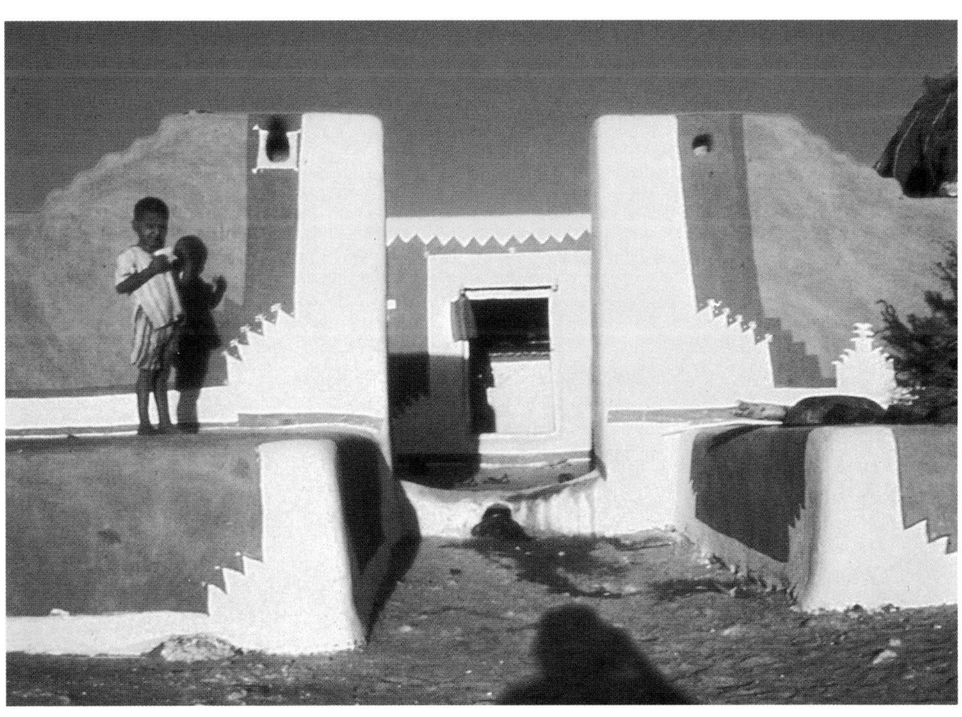

...when this already exists: low-energy high-visual habitat in Rajasthan.

Nothing, of course, could be further from the truth! Improving the habitat needs visual skills. The poor have always understood this. With one stroke of a pink brush, a Mexican artisan transforms a clay pot. It costs him nothing, but it can change your life. It is not a coincidence that the best handicraft comes from the poorest countries of this world — Nepal, Mexico, India. And the Arab had only the simplest tools: mud and sky, so he *had* to be inventive — in the process producing some of the most glorious oasis towns *(low-energy, high-visual!)* the world has ever seen.

From the Polynesian Islands to the Mediterranean hill-towns to the jungles of Assam, for thousands of years people have been building beautiful habitat.

Banni.

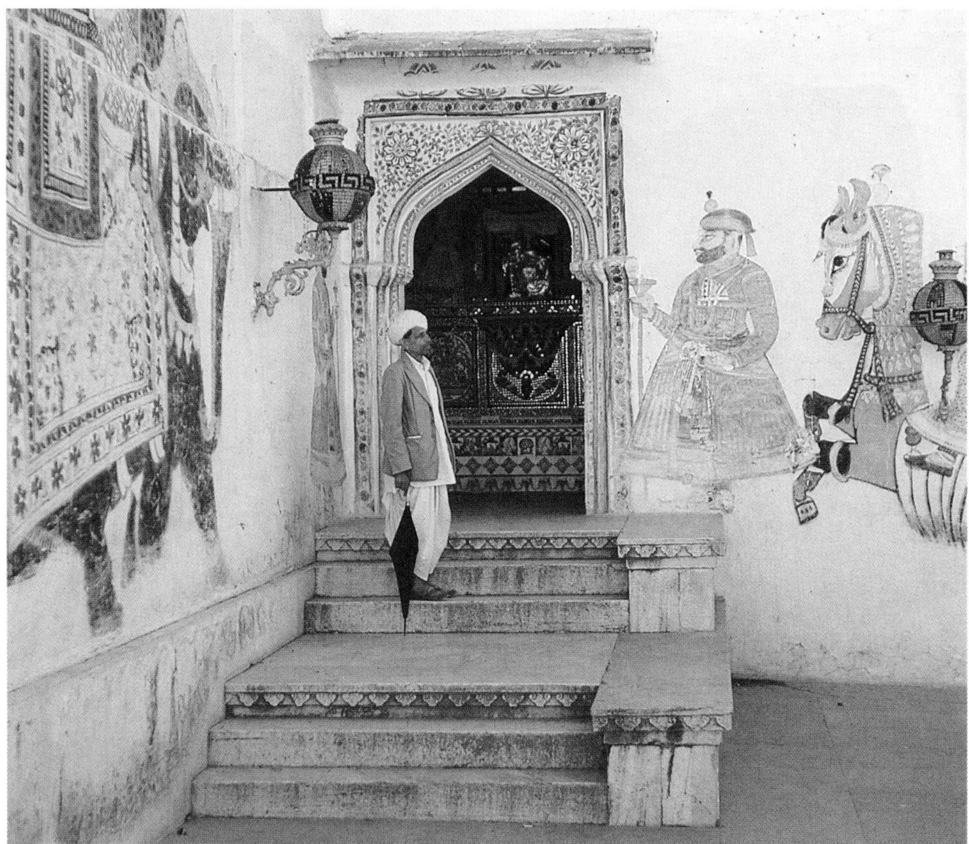

Udaipur.

In fact if we look at all the fashionable concerns of environmentalists today: balanced eco-systems, re-cycling of waste products, appropriate life-styles, indigenous technology, etc., we find that the people of the Third World already have it all. Ironically enough, that's the wonderful thing about the Third World: there is *no shortage* of housing. What there is a shortage of, most definitely, is the *urban context* in which these marvelously inventive solutions are viable.

This then is our prime responsibility: *to help generate that urban context.*

Architecture as an agent of change...which is why a leader like Mahatma Gandhi is called the Architect of the Nation. Not the Engineer, nor the Dentist, nor the Historian. But the Architect — i.e. the generalist who speculates on how the pieces could fit together in more advantageous ways. One who is concerned with *what well might be.*

To do this, in the context of the Third World, the architect must have the courage to face very disturbing issues. For what is your moral right to decide for ten thousand, for a hundred thousand, for two million people? But then what is the moral advantage in not acting, in merely watching passively the slow degradation of life around you?

This is indeed a cruel dilemma. To act, or not to act. On the one hand, the dangers of Fascism, on the other the paralysis of Hamlet. It is a profoundly disturbing issue, one which will define the key moral values of the first half of the twenty-first century. In this, the role of the architect will be central: can we really understand another's aspirations? In the 1960's, when European hippies first started coming to Bombay, a lot of rich Indians complained bitterly about them. At dinner parties they would refer to those "terrible, dirty people, with lice in their hair, lying on the pavements begging." In response one would say, "It doesn't bother you when you see a European?" Finally, a friend gave me the answer: "Naturally a rich Indian goes berserk when he drives his Mercedes and sees a hippie. The hippie is signalling him a message: I'm coming from where you're going — and it's not worth going there. That upsets him terribly."

But come to think of it, surely it is a message that should work the other way around as well! The hippie should realise that the Indian in his Mercedes, gross as he may be, is also sending a message, in fact, the very same one: *I'm coming from where you're going*.

The Metropolis as mirage.

We are but ships that pass in the night — as a photograph of Bombay's skyline illustrates so poignantly. Silhouetted in the foreground are the squatters. Behind them rises a bunch of new skyscrapers. To us the buildings are ugly and deplorable — but to them it is the surreal, mythic image of the city, which they yearn for, but which they may never attain.

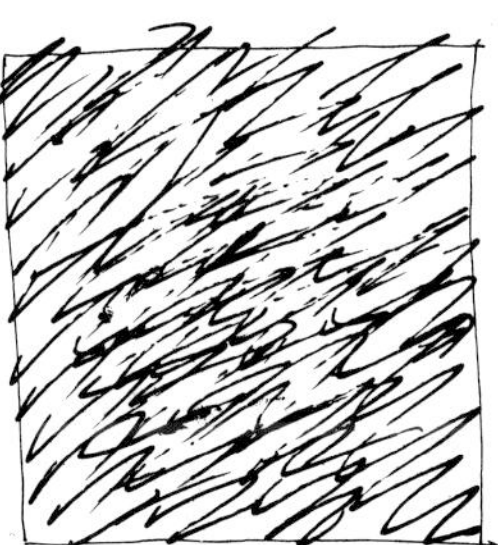

A twentieth century composer — I think it was Hindemith — was once asked the mind-boggling question: How do you compose your music? To which he gave an astonishingly evocative yet precise answer: It is like looking out of a window into the black night of a thunderstorm. Suddenly there is a flash of lightning, illuminating the entire landscape. In that one split second, one has seen everything — and nothing. What is called composition is the patient re-creation of that landscape, stone by stone, tree by tree.

Will the cities of the Third World survive the next few decades? The answer may well depend on whether or not we have the perspicacity to search out and recognise the stones and trees...as they gradually coalesce into the new landscape.

Assessing Social Housing and Community Building Efforts*

The Steering Committee

BACKGROUND

The Islamic world is on the whole poor, consisting of many demographically large countries (Bangladesh, Pakistan, Indonesia, Nigeria and Egypt comprise half of its total population) that rank among the lower-middle or low-income nations of the world. Being poor, this world cannot escape the challenge of shelter provision that confronts the developing world as a whole.

Shelter would seem reasonably simple to define: a roof over the individual's and his family's head, and protection from the elements, with, in Islamic societies, the need to meet the cultural requirement of privacy and other social aspects which the local community considers essential for a Muslim way of life. Along with food and clothing, shelter thus defined is always given prominence in any discussion of basic human needs, and the absolute right to it has been proclaimed in numerous international declarations. The shelter itself, be it a room in a crowded building or an illegal squatter shack, is but one aspect of a predominantly urban housing problem. The physical structure itself is part of an invisible web of relationships and services, the availability or lack of which have to be taken into account. Location is a key component of the problem. The poor themselves often prefer to live in overcrowded and expensive central locations which are nevertheless close to employment opportunities in both the formal and informal sectors of the urban economy rather than live on the urban periphery where they would have more space. If a shelter is to be healthy for those who dwell in it and for those who live in the community as a whole the water supply and the disposal of human wastes and refuse must be taken into consideration. Wider considerations involve the provision of power sources, access to and from the dwelling, and the provision of other facilities that fall within the framework of physical and social infrastructure and which range from transport to schools, markets, and mosques. Finally, if the dwellers are to survive, there is a need for opportunities to participate in income-generating labour. Housing, therefore, is far more than a material entity: individual dwellings are integrally related to the fortunes of the wider community.

The challenge of providing shelter for the absolute poor involves coping with the needs of some 800 million people, perhaps a third of whom are Muslim. These people, many of them children, are caught in a condition of life so limited by malnutrition, disease, illiteracy, short life-expectancy and high mortality as to be beneath any rational definition of human decency. Half of them are found in Southern Asia, mainly in India and Bangladesh; another sixth are in Eastern and South East Asia, mainly Indonesia; and a considerable proportion of the rest are in the Middle East and in sub-Saharan Africa. Only the poor of Latin America lie outside the Islamic world.

One simple set of statistics portrays the extent of the social challenge of shelter provision: In 1980, the number of poor households (with around seven people per

---

* Extract from a Memorandum from the Steering Committee of the Aga Khan Award for Architecture to the Master Jury, 1986.

household) in the developing world was about 120 million — 40 million in urban areas, and 80 million in rural areas. By the end of the century, however, given the immense surge in world population and especially in urban populations, the number of poor households will have risen to 130 million, according to even the most optimistic assumptions regarding development. This overall rise will conceal a dramatic drop in the number of poor rural households, from 80 million down to 56 million, and a startling rise in poor urban households, from 40 million to 74 million. The Muslim world itself will be growing: from 800 million to 1400 million by the end of the century. Many of the poor households will be squeezed into the unprecedentedly large cities that will develop in the Islamic world, such as Jakarta, Karachi, Tehran, Cairo and Lagos. The basic fact about the challenge of social housing is that, in the decades ahead, the Islamic world will be bigger, with more poor households, particularly in urban areas, creating immense needs for shelter. On a world scale, no less than 33 million new units will be required from 1980 to 2000, equivalent to the total stock of poor urban households in 1975.

Jakarta, Indonesia.

MEETING THE CHALLENGE

The magnitude of the problem requires a pragmatic approach that avoids expensive solutions which could only be applied on a limited scale. Reality requires that the programmes undertaken must be affordable to the final beneficiaries in order that sufficient resources can be mobilised by the communities and the countries concerned. The programmes must be replicable on the scale needed to address the vastness of the needs.

It follows that the single most important criteria in assessing the viability of a scheme dealing with the problem of mass housing for the poor is its replicability on a sufficiently large scale. This can best be tested in terms of relating costs, and hence the "affordability" of the units being provided, to the incomes of the target group.

A second fundamental aspect of meeting the challenge involved in providing mass housing and community facilities is the mobilisation of the people. No amount of well-intentioned government programmes organised and executed by technologists will be able to reach the totality of the rural and urban populations, targeted by such an approach. Mobilising the people has to be an important characteristic of appropriate schemes. This implies the involvement of the ultimate users in the design process and, more importantly, in the execution of part of the programmes, whether they be self-help or other community building ventures. There also exists the possibility of participation through financial payments and small-scale contractual arrangements.

No architecture or design can be disassociated from the human element which is the rationale of the design in the first place. Hence, creating a sense of self-worth and self-respect among the ultimate beneficiaries should be seen as an important part of the process. Some community building projects have been notably successful in generating this sense of self-worth and self-respect by involving the people in the design and construction processes.

It is important that such schemes do not deal solely with individual elements of the building or even one or two buildings, but rather with the generation of a process that upgrades the environment in which these masses of humanity live. The Kampung Improvement Programme, honoured in the first Award cycle, was precisely such a programme, where environmental improvements led to a massive upgrading by the inhabitants of their own homes. The programme managed to reach five million people in ten years, an astonishing achievement considering the real improvements introduced in the lives of so many with such limited resources.

Finally, beauty is not a commodity restricted to the rich. Hassan Fathy has showed us that the poor can aspire to beauty, and today the aesthetic quality of vernacular architecture is widely recognised.

The ability to design programmes that combine these different features, in varying degrees, is a measure of the extent to which the architectural and planning professions can address the magnitude of real problems facing the majority of Muslims today and that they are able to produce solutions of relevance to the Islamic world.

THE NEED FOR A SPECIAL AWARD

It is undeniable that schemes designated within this framework lack the visual impact of individual buildings designed by architects working under less stringent budgets and who are concerned with making a statement in terms of architectural expression. It is also undeniable that to exclude from the Master Jury's scope of concerns such socially motivated efforts as the Kampung Improvement Programme and the Pondok Pesantren Programme that effectively address these massive needs, and to deprive such efforts from being recognised and premiated, would send a wrong signal to the architectural and planning professions in the Islamic world. There is a definite need to alert aspiring young designers and planners, as well as dedicated practitioners, to both the relevance and importance of work that may have a more lasting effect on the lives of many. Finally, upgrading an environment is something which benefits all and too frequently have we focused on individual buildings without taking note of the rising sea of misery and degradation that overwhelms the cities where such jewels of architecture may be found.

CRITERIA FOR SELECTION

Against this background, the Master Jury is requested to address a number of social housing and community projects brought forth by the Nomination process and judge them with regard to the following criteria:

Relevance. The approach should be relevant to the nature of the problems being confronted. Frequently, one finds that it is the absence of an adequate economic base that destroys a particular project. Hassan Fathy's Gourna is an example where the most brilliant architecture was offset by the inadequacy and inappropriateness of the economic base of the target population.

Effectiveness. In the final analysis, the test of a successful approach to any problem is its effectiveness in meeting the challenge and, hopefully, its ability to create a multiplier effect that transcends the direct impact of the intervention. Thus, housing that is too expensive is not an effective means of coping with low-income requirements, no matter how beautiful it may appear in a physical sense. Likewise, a well-intentioned organisation of local citizens that is unable to achieve significant improvements in its physical environment is not an effective approach, no matter how attractive it may be on paper.

Sustainability. Sustainability is increasingly perceived as a measure of success in community building efforts. Frequently the architects, planners and other technicians who help to launch a project cannot indefinitely sustain the community building effort. Thus, one of the tests of the success of their intervention is the degree to which a community building effort is sustained by the community itself following their initial participation. It is important that the intended beneficiaries recognise the value of the intervention and internalise it, to make it their own.

Replicability. It is important to consider whether a scheme can be repeated again in coping with similar problems elsewhere in the same city, in the same rural environment, in the same country, or even in another country. This, after all, is the principal advantage of rewarding projects: they become models that can generate ideas which may inspire similar interventions (not copies) elsewhere.

Kampung Improvement Programme, Jakarta, Indonesia, before and after.

Impact. It is necessary to differentiate between various levels of impact. There is the impact on the residents and users themselves – undeniably an important criterion – as well as the impact on the environment surrounding the intervention, such as improvement and upgrading, protection of the natural habitat, protection of natural resources, limitation of pollution, etc. There is also the more subtle issue of the impact of the scheme on the national and international perceptions of practitioners, clients and the general public. Ideas are an integral part of award-winning designs and programmes; ideas that have generated a response on a national or international scale deserve greater attention and recognition by the Master Jury.

Aesthetic Quality. Good design can produce beautiful buildings inexpensively. The aesthetic quality of the design being considered is an important criterion in bestowing an award to a particular project.

Other Architectural Merits. These are the more common standards for judging good contemporary architecture and therefore need not be discussed here at length. These merits include such standards as the suitability of materials, quality of detailing, appropriateness of the building techniques and methods utilised, the functional qualities of the layouts, and so forth. These more conventional standards of architectural merit should, where applicable, be taken into account.

WEIGHTING FACTORS

The Master Jury may ascribe different weightage to the above criteria and may wish to add others of its own. Nevertheless, the intent outlined in this brief, concerning the nature and type of projects to be premiated, should be maintained. It is hoped that the Master Jury's choices will enhance the social consciousness of architects, designers and planners throughout the Islamic world and help to focus their talents on the enormous problems facing their countries in this sector as well as in the more traditional areas of architectural practice.

SELECTION

It is expected that the Master Jury will select one or two projects that deal directly with these issues. However, it is possible that no project will be recognised as having sufficient merit to receive an award. The Master Jury should, in that case, declare in its official statement that, while giving due importance to the issues of social housing and community building, and having searched for particular projects that deserved recognition, the Jury failed to find among the nominated projects any that achieved the standards of excellence required for the Aga Khan Award for Architecture. Such a statement would emphasise the importance of this sector without compromising the integrity and standards of the Award.

CONTEMPORARY ARCHITECTURAL EXPRESSION

Under this broad heading, so much of what the Award does could be fitted that selecting pieces and excluding others is a difficult exercise. Four selections are provided here.

The issue of regional identity manifests itself in different ways. It was the theme of the regional seminar held in Bangladesh in 1985 and the paper by Suha Özkan, Deputy Secretary General of the AKAA, provides an excellent overview. But it also manifests itself in the concern of the Award for the specific characteristics of regional sub-cultures in the Muslim world. The special report prepared by Oleg Grabar, on the Uzbek culture of the Muslims in Uzbekistan in the Soviet Union is a most interesting example where restoration efforts and new buildings try to maintain and create a unique cultural identity. The Award has enlarged that particular vein so that future scholars can mine the rich diversity of the many regional manifestations of Muslim culture.

Concern with technology cannot be ignored and the uses and abuses of such technology is one of the challenges that confronts contemporary designers. In a statement delivered before the Granada seminar dealing with architectural education, William Porter made some interesting observations that are summarised in the selection appended hereto. Finally Hasan-Uddin Khan's essay takes up the same themes of technology, form and culture in the context of the Architectural Education in developing countries, and rounds-off these selections. It must be emphasised that these selections are all extracts from longer and more complete presentations by the individual authors and therefore do not do full justice to the ideas and arguments elaborated in the original presentations.

Regionalism within Modernism*

Suha Özkan

With the all-obliterating spread of Modernism, the efforts which were made to highlight regional and local concerns were left without enough support to survive. Alvar Aalto, found a medium to exercise his own kind of regionalism which allowed it to exist within the parameters of modernism, but one can find few other references to regionalism until the early seventies. There are notable exceptions for, example the works of Jane Drew, Maxwell Fry, Hassan Fathy and Rifat Chadirji.

During the first regional seminar of the Aga Khan Award for Architecture in Kuala Lumpur, we discussed issues related to *Identity in Architecture*. As far as architecture and design are concerned, it is very hard to talk about identity — except the identity a particular architect brings to his designs — without going into regionalism. A geographical region defines many aspects of a society both culturally and environmentally. Culture includes aspects of life and prevalent modes of expression. Natural environment includes climate and topography. A region, when properly defined, represents all of these in a very complex amalgamate. Modernism, through its sub-theme of *internationalism* proclaimed universality and world-wide applicability of certain values of architecture and over the past sixty years, almost totally discarded all the "regional" building activity. The schools of architecture, the building industry and popular 'taste', all united in the reinforcement of internationalism until it became an ideology representing the aspirations of all sectors of modern society. For more than half a century internationalism in style became synonymous with the representation of contemporaneity.

The main critical movement as a reaction specifically to internationalism or implicitly to modernism, is regionalism. The regionalist approach recognises the vernacular modes of building at the one extreme, and abstract regionalism at the other. Even though it covers such a wide array of attitudes, regionalism has respect to the local culture, to climate and at times technology, at its core. If one has to classify the approaches, the following are the categories to be observed in regionalism though of course the boundaries of separation are not too distinct. Firstly Vernacularism and secondly Modern-Regionalism.

VERNACULARISM

Bernard Rudolfsky's *Architecture without Architects* exhibition at the Museum of Modern Arts and the catalogue, which subsequently became an indispensable reference of vernacular architecture, pointed out an area that had been ignored for a very long time. By the mid-seventies, vernacular architecture distinguished itself as an important source where the basic components of design such as climate, technology, culture and related symbolism have existed and matured over the centuries of man's involvement with architecture.

---

* Extracted from *Regionalism in Architecture*, Proceedings of Seminar No 2 in the series Exploring Architecture in Islamic Cultures II, Dhaka,, Bangladesh, 1986. Published by Concept Media for The Aga Khan Award for Architecture,. Singapore, 1987, pp. 8 – 16.

Paul Oliver's contribution in *Shelter and Society* and *Shelter, Sign and Symbol*, cultivated the theoretical grounds of vernacular architecture. He brought together the research of defined geographical areas of shelter in Africa, Greece and Afghanistan which displayed remarkable examples of these ignored area, not only as sources of inspiration for architect-designers but also as a viable alternative for solutions emerging in Third World countries.

The research continued, especially in the academic and research organisations in the West, and has grown by leaps and bounds since the mid-1970's onwards. There is now a fairly articulate stock of research covering the whole world. Both the vast research on vernacular modes of building and the cultures which generated it brought back genuine interest and admiration. The building tradition that has existed and excelled over centuries has been credited and recognised as a design approach within the realm of architectural design and its subsequent discourse.

Agricultural Training Centre, Nianing, Senegal, 1977. A labour intensive building system developed to generate a new and complete architectural language.

In a very broad classification we observe two approaches to vernacularism: first is the *conservative* attitude and second, the *interpretative* attitude. While both kinds of vernacularism have the ideals of bringing a new and contemporary existence to vernacular forms and spatial arrangements, they differ in the way they treat technology and community.

The most important contributor to conservative vernacularism is Hassan Fathy. He devoted more than half a century of his professional life to bringing back to the vernacular mode, building tradition in danger of extinction due to the massive post-World War II building activity. The architecture employed in this activity was indifferent to the community, its inherited traditional technology, local materials and the natural environment. Fathy, single-handedly, strived to revive a building tradition and tried to grasp it on the eve of its disappearance. He was firm and uncompromising, in incorporating the societal forces but was at the same time, innovative in bringing architects' know-how and design expertise on to the scene. He cherished the materials, technology and art of building of Egyptian society and throughout his work brought a new life and meaning to them. The success of his regionalism varies. It did not work out well in the rural communities, whose distorted aspirations and values attached to their understanding of contemporaneity did not match the environment that Fathy offered them. Nevertheless, the meticulous and sophisticated architectural design executed solely from local materials and means, displayed qualities for the generations to come. When Fathy adopted the same approach, but in a more durable material — stone instead of earth — this not only increased the acceptability but also offered him the opportunity to incorporate the finest examples of revived building crafts. Of course this category of building had to be private residences. While he displayed this design excellence in these buildings, the ideas he developed for the rural habitat echoed all over the world as a viable alternative solution for the action groups like Craterre Development Workshop and ADAUA who employed his ideas. Architects such as André Ravereau, Nader Khalili, Abdel Wahed El-Wakil, followed in his footsteps in vernacular technology.

The interpretative version of vernacularism is referred to here as *neo-vernacularism* which has emerged as an approach to bringing a new life to vernacular heritage for new and contemporary functions. The widest area of the application of this approach is obviously the architecture for tourism and culture. During the short term experience when tourists take their vacation the regional vernacular becomes an integral part of the anticipated ambience. Therefore tourist developments became the pioneering example of neo-vernacularism. Since modern comfort, ease of construction and maintenance are inevitably important factors, they utilised levels of technology which usually had nothing to do with those which existed regionally. Similarly with the infrastructure, heating, cooling, and technical services. In these efforts more of a lip service was given to the regional components, and therefore, architecture became more of an expression of local shapes and forms where culture is also reduced to souvenirs and folklore. Like any other architectural involvement, these attempts met with the varying degrees of success, depending on the sincerity of the designer-architect; on whether they wanted to simply design a stage-set with pastiche or if they wished to create genuine spatial and architectural experience.

Despite all the problems stemming from the preoccupation of image-making, these developments, being more in line with the local setting, created less oppressive environments. They also helped to develop a vocabulary of contemporary architecture which has its roots in the building tradition of a particular culture. In short, vernacularism and neo-vernacularism differ from each other mainly at the level of the user, labour for building, materials used and the construction technology employed. This means a lot of difference in reference to the societal context.

Neo-vernacularism approaches have dominated a vast amount of design activity to mainly accommodate habitation and tourism functions. It must be due to them being "taken for granted" or to their less innovative, more conformist nature that they did not generate any noteworthy or great architecture. The practitioners of this approach mainly became unknown or unnoticed architects.

The applicability of this mode of design has limited validity, however, especially when small scale units become a large building, e.g. a civic complex. The relevant guidance of vernacularism is limited, unless a reinterpretation is made or what has existed is stretched. Here the terminology has to be changed, as vernacularism represents only one, admittedly limited, section of regionalism.

M. Doruk Pamir, E. Gümrük Islamic Centre for Research and Training, Dhaka, 1982. A campus planned to introduce Islamic civic scale with local material and technology.

MODERN REGIONALISM

It should be repeated here again and must be clearly pointed out that what has been rejected by most of the regionalist architects is not modernism but internationalism. Modernism demands a respect for inherent qualities of building materials, expressiveness for structure, functional justifications for forms that constitute buildings. These abstract demands do not contradict much, in essence, with anything done by an architect who wishes to adopt a regionalist approach. Internationalism however, demanding the necessity to reduce the building to skin and bones has a completely different line of discourse which is a well accommodated sub-theme in modernism. Therefore, it would not be wrong to stress that the polarity is between *internationalism* which demands a global relevance for its existence and *regionalism* which seeks meaning and content under specific local conditions. To achieve the goals of the latter, modernism provides tools and techniques to cope with the problems. Additionally it also offers a code of ethics and categories of aesthetics by means of which the achievements can be assessed.

Unlike vernacularism, modern regionalism can be employed at all scales of building activity, since it derives from the monumental architecture of the past, as well as to the civil architecture to which vernacularism has to confine itself. Modern regionalism in very broad terms can be handled by employing two categories of reference: *concrete* and *abstract*. Concrete regionalism accommodates all approaches to regional expressions which copy features, fragments, or entire buildings, in the region. When these buildings are loaded with spiritual values of symbolic relevance, they become much more acceptable in their new form, owing to the values attached to the original. Of course it brings a comfortable defence in support of the new, backed by the qualities of the old. In many cases, when the existence of contemporaneity in new is stressed, they become so well accepted that they are considered as being "ideal". In this approach the mutual existence of rejection and acceptance of time has a "schizophrenic" mix. Contemporaneity is accepted by acknowledging the need to accommodate the requirements. This is further acknowledged by the use of contemporary materials and construction techniques. However the forms and spaces usually belong to the distant past.

The concrete replication of the motives and achievements of the past now has a very comfortable cover as they are interpreted as references to the past. There is however a wide spectrum of architectural involvement from a thoughtful eclecticism to a worthless pastiche. The ethos of both extremes has not been spelled out properly and it demands elaboration. Therefore the references for judgement remain vague, and seemingly, they will remain so for some time because a reaction to the Modern Movement and the achievements of post-modernism — which definitely covers what we call here concrete regionalism — has not yet developed its own ethos. To judge this against the ethics and aesthetics of Modernism would not be fair. The vacuum this creates is dangerous because it would lead to an "anything goes" situation which probably is what has been happening all over the world, especially in the Islamic world, in which many of the countries that are building nowadays are situated.

Henning Larsen, Ministry of Foreign Affairs, Riyadh, 1984. The fortress-like protected outside wall defines intricately detailed interiors.

Abstracting elements from the past in order to derive building form from it constitutes what we call "abstract regionalism". It is a very difficult and fine line to follow. It mainly incorporates the abstract qualities of a building, for example, massing, solids and void, proportions, sense of space, use of light, and structural principles in their reinterpreted form. It also endeavours to bring back to existence the cultural issues. An attempt is made to define in terms of design elements the prevalent culture of the region concerned. This is a long, tedious and sometimes endless devotion to an ideal. The line which separates a solemn, praiseworthy, regionalist achievement from a worthless pastiche or a pot-pourri of the past, is very thin and delicate. In the division of the two we still do not have any other criteria than that we have developed with modernism. To these, many of the contributors to regionalist endeavour have subscribed. These contributors to the regionalist modernism emphasised and developed certain important aspects of regionalism.

Charles Correa has put his endeavour into a nutshell by entitling his approach: "Form follows climate" where he gives priority to the macro environment which determines many aspects of the built form, Rifat Chadirji generated an articulate façadism which refers back to the architectural heritage in Iraq. Mohammad Makiya, another eminent Iraqi, especially in his earlier buildings, searched for sublime regional expressions for modern buildings. Sedad Eldem has coupled a continuous search into sources of traditional architecture with a modern practice which derives from, and reinterprets, the findings in these sources. From the younger generation, Raj Rewal brings a contemporary existence to the traditional understanding of space and to its cultural implication. Rasem Badran, Doruk Pamir, Charles Boccara, and many others, have elevated the quality of the contemporary architectural environment, by employing the regional idiom, regional input and environmental determinant. In Dhaka, the efforts of Muzharul Islam, from Bangladesh, to develop an architectural idiom from limited resources and technology, is a noteworthy contribution to regionalism for future generations to study, explore and develop.

Report on Soviet Central Asia*

Oleg Grabar

In May 1986 I accompanied a group of major donors to an American museum, some major collectors as well, to Tashkent, Bukhara, Panjikent, and Samarqand (as well as Vladimir and Suzdal not far from Moscow). The trip to the "Islamic" part of the Soviet Union lasted seven days and, as is nearly always the case in the Soviet Union, was in the hands of *Intourist* both for practical details of travel and for assistance in visiting monuments and sites, although we established from the beginning that, after the guide's explanations, I could add a few words of my own. These were all places I had visited more leisurely eleven years earlier and I am therefore able to draw certain conclusions about the changes which have occurred as well as about their implications for the future. Furthermore, I had written in advance to a colleague in Tashkent who had arranged special visits to the new museums in Tashkent and Samarqand.

Most of the trip was in Uzbekistan, the third largest and most rapidly growing Soviet republic; Panjikent alone was in Tajikistan, the Persian-speaking republic, but many Tajik speakers are found in Samarqand. I did not visit then or earlier Turkmenistan or Kazakhstan, nor the semi-autonomous Karaqalpak area. Uzbekistan, by accident, design, and in fact historical development since the sixteenth century, dominates most of the Turkic area of the Soviet Union (with the exception of Azerbaydzhan west of the Caspian sea) and forms the Soviet *pendant* to Xinjiang within the Chinese system.

I shall divide this report into two parts: firstly, a description of architecture and architecture related features with the aims of identifying what is available to be seen and of evaluating its quality and importance for architecture in the Muslim world; secondly, a discussion of a number of issues which affect our "intelligence" of the Muslim architectural heritage or contemporary creativity.

ARCHITECTURE AND PEOPLE

Bukhara. Bukhara was the last of the centres of Central Asian Islam to have been occupied by the West, as it was only after the success of the Bolshevik revolution (around 1920) that it lost its nominal independence; until that time, a small Russian settlement had been established nearby, mostly in relationship to the railroad station, but the local amir ruled quite independently. It contains two masterpieces of early Islamic architecture, the tenth century Samanid mausoleum and the twelfth century Kalayan minaret. There is one secondary early monument, the twelfth century Majok-i Altari Mosque façade. A fourteenth century funerary ensemble (Chashm Ayub) and a fifteenth century *madrasa* sponsored by Ulugh Beg, are of secondary importance. A sizeable group of mosques and *madrasas* (ten to my knowledge) of the sixteenth and seventeenth centuries exist for the most part arranged in clusters around open spaces or large pools within the city. There is a covered bazaar,

---

* Grabar, Oleg., Special Report No. 4, Award Cycle III, Aga Khan Award for Architecture, Geneva, June 1986.

of which only three or four domed crossroads have been preserved and a citadel so often redone that it reflects mostly a nineteenth century state. There are a number of monuments in outlying parts of the oasis, of which only one was visited, the quaint country villa built by the last amir as a sort of Trianon in a Petersbourg sauce, but interesting because a local craftsman was asked to decorate a westernised hall, while Russian designers were expected to do the "oriental" ones.

When I visited Bukhara eleven years earlier, most of the buildings were in an advanced state of decay and the large ones were used for squatter inhabitation. The Kalayan minaret and the Samanid mausoleum alone were in a reasonable state of preservation, while the Mir Arab Mosque was used (as it still is now) as the one major centre of Islamic learning in Central Asia; I could visit it in 1973 and speak in Arabic with its teachers; I did not try to do so this time, as the circumstances of my visit did not make it appropriate. Since 1973 Bukhara, together with Khiva, Suzdal, and perhaps other cities in the U.S.S.R. were proclaimed museum-cities and, in Bukhara, a massive programme of cleaning and restoration has begun. Thus the Kalayan Mosque is being repaired, the three buildings around the Liab pool have been for the most part (but not entirely) vacated, the streets cleaned to a sanitised degree, and a vast new rectilinear city of administration, institutions, and apartments built around the old city. The Samanid mausoleum has become the focal point of a handsome park with a Ferris wheel in the background and a new and fairly lively bazaar nearby. The Chashm Ayub ensemble has been repaired but is mostly used as a storage place whilst the Magok-i Attari Mosque has become the local discotheque, a rare instance of this type of adaptive reuse. There are street lights everywhere, buses circulate from one end of the city to the other. Every quarter is provided with a primitive dispensary. National costumes have almost disappeared except for the ubiquitous *ikat* fabric of women's clothes and the caps of men. The vast majority of the population is Uzbek and Europeans are quite clearly a minority.

Bukhara, remains of sixteenth century bazaar.

The work of restoration is done by students in a local art school; the idea is good, but there was very little supervision and the students had done little research. For instance, inscriptions were mirror-reversed instead of being copied, as no one knew the Arabic alphabet.

In a few years, the programme of restorations will be completed and Bukhara will become a true tourist city in the Soviet style; antiseptic and soulless monuments adapted to a city whose real life will for the most part have moved elsewhere.The emphasis will be on a vertical past emphasising local intellectual and folk heroes (it is curious that there is a life-size statue of Nasrettin Hoca on one of the main squares). Processions of buses with visitors will be given an explanation of history which is not so much inaccurate as partial; there will be thousands of postcards and folk dances for foreigners.

Samarqand. From the moment of arrival at the airport and especially during the short drive to the city, an entirely different atmosphere prevails. Samarqand is a large (400,000 inhabitants) and very active city on a much more uneven terrain with clearly demarcated areas. There are the immense ruins of the pre-Islamic and early Islamic city known as Afrasiyab. Ulugh Beg's stunning observatory is located at the edge of the ruins. There is the deep ravine, with the old cemetery and the moving sanctuary of Shah-i Sindah; also the "old city" which has lost nearly all of its traditional character, but whose imperial Timurid and later monuments (the Bibi Khanum Mosque, Registan, Gur-i Amir, traces of an old bazaar) dominate everything around them. A nineteenth – twentieth century city of wide tree-lined avenues with pre-revolutionary buildings alternates with new Soviet constructions which include a huge opera house, a university, the main hotel, and beyond it all apartment complexes and eventually outlying villages in the lush valley.

The main points of historical interest are:

- *Ulugh Beg's observatory*, part of whose immense underground sextant has been preserved in the midst of the foundations of the building. Nearby stands a well organised small museum on Ulugh Beg and astronomy. A project exists for rebuilding the observatory more or less according to the plans and calculations made by Prof. Bulatov, the most brilliant scholar of Uzbekistan. However well intentioned and probably attractive to visitors, the whole idea is a historical menace, as it would freeze a single and by necessity hypothetical reconstruction.
- *The Shah-i Sindah.* This is a series of private mausoleums of the fourteenth and early fifteenth centuries along a narrow path leading up to the sanctuary of Kutham b. c'Abbas, a relative of the Prophet alleged to have been killed during the conquest of Central Asia. It is still a holy place, although not officially. The anti-religious museum of atheism which had been set in the mosque at the entrance of the complex has been replaced by a souvenir shop. The monuments have for the most part been well repaired and are accessible throughout, including the sanctuary of the holy man which has been beautifully cleaned and in which a careful programme of restoration of paintings goes on. The Shah-i Sinda, with its festival of colour and of architectural techniques, is a true architectural masterpiece and a place of piety, whose transformation into a museum has in no way altered its emotional impact. It has been the subject of much archaeological work and of several excellent publications in Russian.

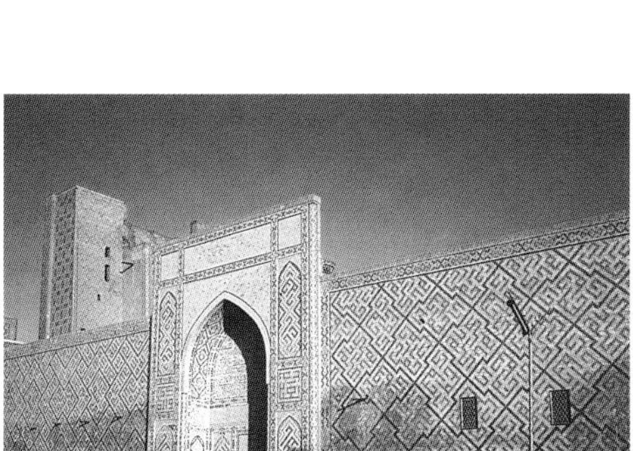

Samarqand, Ulugh Beg madrasa, side wall, early fifteenth century.

- *Bibi Khanum Mosque.* This was the somewhat megalomaniac congregational mosque built by Tamerlane. Eleven years ago it was in ruins and its façade as well as its sanctuary dome and *iwan* were standing impressively but precariously against the blue sky. An immense work of restoration is taking place there, with no less an objective than to rebuild the mosque almost entirely. Two of the *iwans* and one of the domes have already been redone in reinforced concrete and the process of covering up with copies of remaining designs is well under way. Although I realise that something major had to be done, I have the feeling that these restorations are overdone and that they will falsify the appearance of a grandiose mosque, perhaps because there was something totalitarian in its architectural grandeur. The technical work of restoration struck me as one of very poor quality in details, probably because of the absence of good craftsmen.
- *The Registan.* This is a complex of three buildings, one (Ulugh Beg's) of the fifteenth century, the other two of the sixteenth and seventeenth centuries, creating together a large open space which was the hub of the old city. The three buildings have been more or less entirely restored, on the whole well, especially Ulugh Beg's *madrasa,* which is a true masterpiece of elegance and refinement. A *son et lumiere* programme is given there at weekends, which recounts the history of the city up to the time in the 1920's when the women of Samarqand formally threw off their veils on the Registan. The space in front has been successfully designed for performances and as a park.
- *Gur-e Amir.* This is the majestuous tomb of Tamerlane, fully restored and with all exterior parts beautifully cleaned. I could not judge the quality of the work done in all details, but it struck me initially as very good.
- A newly built museum with a superb historical collection of paintings and ceramics, but also with excellent coverage of nineteenth and twentieth century popular art, especially textiles which are wonderfully exhibited. It has a large staff of six or seven curators, partly Russian and partly Uzbek. The museum is of excellent design but poor construction. It has an inadequate library.
- There are other buildings of interest in Samarqand and its region which are accessible on demand.

Panjikent. Here there are ruins in the process of excavation, some 80 kms to the east of Samarqand and some 300 km to the West of Kashgar, on the Silk Road. The excavations, whose finds are mostly in Leningrad, are among the most spectacular in Asia, as they, with a few others, led to a total re-evaluation of pre-Islamic Central Asia. The site itself is most spectacular in a setting with the snow-capped Altai beginning around it and leading eventually to the Hindu Kush and the Himalayas. In the village nearby, there is a museum of zoology, ethnography, and history.

I mention Panjikent for two reasons. One is that it is an occasion to see the fantastic urban transformation of a minute village of old with dozens of large buildings fulfilling new administrative, medical and educational functions.

The whole area has a strong Tadjik nationalism. The other reason for mentioning it is that the trip is a wonderful occasion to see the enormous development of irrigated agriculture and of sources of energy.

Tashkent. For the general purposes of the Award, Tashkent, the fourth city in the Soviet Union (1.8 million inhabitants and the capital of Uzbekistan), should be studied in great detail, because it is a model in the creation of a new metropolis in the style of the Second World. Nature helped with an earthquake in 1966 which destroyed most of the traditional city. The reconstruction was rapid and allowed for a restructuring of the town and for the dislocation of its traditional fabric. The sprawling traditional city of adobe houses, of which a few examples remain, was replaced by wide avenues, large and fancy official buildings, and parks, while enormous apartment complexes on the outskirts reorganised the social structure of the town. A subway of a luxury unknown even in Moscow relates the various parts to each other. As opposed to the drabness of so many Russian cities, here an effort was made to provide buildings with colour and with more original designs than is normally the case. With the monument to the earthquake, a visual symbolism based on contemporary events and their subsequent mythification is being created. The tight and small old native city is lost in the growth of a metropolis, as are the remains of a late nineteenth century Russian administration and garrison town.

The "monuments" of Tashkent are the opera, two hotels, the museum, a department store, and so on; the instruments of contemporary life. In a city which is two thirds Uzbek only, nearly all the slogans are in Uzbek, whereas in Bukhara they were in Russian. The new museum is of very high quality in design, technique of exhibition and pedagogical purposes. Its large staff is extremely competent. It is the pride of the academic Tashkent, which, through G.A. Pugachenkova, L.I. Rempel, and A. Bulatov, is a major school of historical and archaeological learning. Most of the exhibition space is once again devoted to the nineteenth and twentieth centuries. The detailing of the construction and the finish are mediocre, but not as bad as in hotels or in more provincial places.

In general, however, Tashkent seems to me to represent one model of modernisation, which, in spite of or because of its Second World methods, ought to be better known by the Award: it depicts the construction of a modern city with an ethnically mixed population in the process of cultural homogeneisation and with a "universal" ideology (Communism) in national (Uzbek) garb.

ISSUES AND QUESTIONS

Uzbekistan and I assume other republics of Central Asia as well as Azerbaydzhan have undergone an almost total physical and mental revolution, far greater than in Russia proper or anywhere else in the Muslim world. The technical, educational, and economic infrastructure for contemporaneity is in place, the emancipation of women irreversible, the building of spaces for modern activities on its way, if not already there. Tashkent or Samarqand seek comparison with the First World, not with the Third World, and the means to achieve all of that are those of the Second World. *Faust*, *Carmen*, and *Otello* were on the programmes of theatres, together with contemporary local plays, and Shakespeare was performed in Uzbek.

- All of this is accompanied by a true worship of the past and of its monuments, which are for the most part reconstructed and maintained. But this worship is couched almost exclusively in national terms, the Uzbegs being seen as the successors of the Soghdians, a kind of absurdity which amuses historians but which had parallels in imperial Iran. The means for the knowledge of the past are, however, almost entirely through scholarship in Russia, as there is very little knowledge left of Arabic, relatively little of Persian, and the cyrillisation of the alphabet has made access to old Turkish difficult. Islam is rarely talked about and knowledge of the faith or of its practices and implications is limited. What has replaced it all is, it seems to me, a sort of national communism which is seen as the motor for change and success. Traditional Islam is only visible in its most superstitious folk ways, at least in the large cities, and appears most of the time as a negative and obscurantist feature opposed to progress.
- In the area of building, the contrast is striking between the ambition of the projects, the often acceptable if pedestrian quality of the designs (with some exceptions in Tashkent or the Samarqand museum), and the miserable quality of execution, where even simple concrete T-blocks never seem to fit with each other. The state of plumbing is nearly disastrous and, with occasional exceptions, the finish of anything which requires craftsmanship is miserable. The process of construction is also rather curious, as the landscape is filled with cranes, most of which are not working, and with huge construction projects with only a dozen working people. I do not know the explanation for this phenomenon, but I am sure that formal Sovietologists do.
- It is a world trying to create visual symbols for itself. The means, however, are almost exclusively those of western sculpture and, except for the rather successful earthquake sculpture in Tashkent, most of these symbols are not inspiring. I have often wondered, as I watched people there, what in their own minds most easily identifies them as different or as themselves. It is probably clothes, as Uzbeks alone wear consistently their little skull caps and the *ikat* imitating dresses. It probably no longer is Islam, at least not in the large cities, but how easily and how well can a secular ideology of this type survive? And how exportable is it?
- The striking contrast between poor execution and high ambition in major restoration projects raises a fundamental question: does it matter? It seems to me that accuracy in reconstruction may only be a scholar's wish but not the expectation of a monument on the part of a culture. There is a subject for future discussion.
- Finally, I feel that it would be worthwhile to learn more about the issues of architecture, past and present, in Soviet Central Asia and I urge that the means to do so be developed. The reason is not simply that here is a large body of Muslims undergoing the most irreversible revolution of any Muslim land. Nor is it that the vehicle of the revolution, communism, is being exported elsewhere. It is rather that the Central Asian experience, in many ways like the Turkish one with which it has a lot in common, illustrates one of the available ways of modernisation and change, one which sees in national pride allied with a theoretical ideology a possible substitute for older ways. The problem is that both the ideology and the access to national pride have to go through an alien language and alien power. At this stage, I suspect, Russian control of the political process is a price that can be paid for material and educational progress, but can it last?

Technology Form and Culture in Architecture: Misconception and Myth*

William Porter

My intent in this paper is to engage issues that touch on architectural education when three concepts — technology, form and culture — intersect. First I shall touch on some aspects of that intersection and the architectural significance of technology, and then I shall look at some issues for architectural education that seem to emerge. I will deal chiefly with architecture in the West and with examples where technology has been consciously incorporated into the architectural aesthetic. Because architecture in the West is so often used to support various arguments about architecture in the Muslim world, I felt it essential to dispel certain misconceptions — that technology demands specific formal expression in architecture, or that its incorporation necessarily prohibits designs that are regionally and culturally appropriate — and to distinguish these misconceptions from myths that surround and project technology in architecture in the modern world. I believe that there are lessons for the education of architects in the Muslim world that can be drawn from this Western insider's story, and I shall try to indicate some of those possibilities.

ISSUES AT THE INTERSECTION

At the intersection of technology, form and culture are three apparent oppositions that will help to frame the rest of my discussion. These are: traditional versus modern technology, means versus ends, and centralisation versus regionalisation of the means of production.

Good building since the advent of modern construction technologies, and with increasing sophistication, has contained these oppositions, taking simultaneous account of traditional and modern techniques, engaging local enterprise in environmental improvement programmes and benefitting from the economies of centralisation without sacrificing regional specificity. Such possibilities rest in part on forces outside architecture, but they rest as well on architects' understanding that building functions as sign and symbol as well as to satisfy practical needs, and on architects' memory of good building of the past. The possibility of bad building, while it, too, depends on forces outside architecture, requires as well a naive and compliant semantically inept profession. It is to these that architectural education address themselves. Before discussing the architectural significance of technology, I need to develop a few ideas about significance in architecture more generally.

Great Mosque at Djenne, Mali. Men resurfacing mihrab tower.

ARCHITECTURAL SIGNIFICANCE OF TECHNOLOGY

Architecture is an internally ordered world. Its elements take on meaning in relation to one another and to the environment, both natural and architectural, in which they are located. Language has as its primary aim to convey meaning. It

* Extracts from Proceedings of *Architectural Education in the Islamic World* Seminar Ten in the series – Architectural Transformations in the Islamic World, Granada, Spain, April 21–25, 1986. Published by Concept Media for the Aga Khan Award for Architecture, Singapore, 1986, pp. 49–59.

signifies things outside itself. Of course, its internal structure must be consistent enough to make clear its reference to external things. Architecture can signify, too. The orientation of a mosque toward Mecca, which can make its street façade very different from the orientation of the rest of the street, signifies the presence of that institution. Minarets may convey the idea of a connection between heaven and earth, or, like the towers at San Gimignano, between wealth and a particular individual or family! Buildings like the Pantheon or Hagia Sophia have successfully supported a variety of associations and uses. The fact that many architecturally distinguished buildings have sustained a variety of different uses and meanings over time underlines the point that the life of architectural form does not depend primarily on its association with a specific use or meaning.

Like language, architecture has the capacity to define new ideas and to convey new meanings, but it also accumulates bits and structures of older languages that have unpredictable connotations when reused. Most architects are aware of this, and it affects the aesthetic attitudes that many architects and their clients have toward technology, and that arguably have driven the making of architectural form. *Bricolage* is the term sometimes used to refer to these cultural artifacts that in their reuse cause surprise, delight, and add meaning to the buildings in which they are found. *Bricolage*, if generously interpreted to include both elements and structures, can provide the chief connections to the past and to cultures elsewhere.

By rejecting the use of inherited architectural elements with their associated uses and meanings, the architect can demonstratively reject any past meanings and project a building that is intended to be entirely of its own time, without precedent, and embodying only the current and promised societal order. It is here that we turn back to questions of modernity in general and technology in particular.

Le Corbusier, inspired in part by environments like those of an ocean liner in which the design is determined in large part by forces that must be efficiently responded to, translated ordinary human activities like dwelling metaphorically into describable systems of forces for which designs can be sought.

From this came his "machine for living."[1] The idea was not, of course, to shape the house as precisely as a ship would be shaped. "Living" implied the user's adaptation of a basic form that modern construction would provide.[2]

His formulation of the "five points" for residential design, pilotis, free plan, free façade, long horizontal sliding window, and the roof garden that restored the ground were embodied in his project for the Stuttgart Weissenhofsiedlung of 1927 and the Villa Savoye at Poissy, 1929–1931. These could be thought to represent a transposition to architecture of the engineer's aesthetic and the products of the new modern construction technology that Le Corbusier had so long admired to at least the basic structural frame for living. In that transposition another important issue for modern architecture was dramatised: the opposition between freedom from place that modern technology implied and the locale-specific qualities that people bring to building and need in order to reinforce their own sense of identity.

There are many other examples that would display distinctive attitudes toward technology that formed a fundamental part of an architectural aesthetic. Mies Van der Rohe's corner of the Alumni Hall at Illinois Institute of Technology demonstrates an insistence to emphasise the materials of the building's making even though the actual structure lies behind the brick, mandatory for fire reasons. The truth of the condition is revealed by allowing the brick to pass under the steel corner elements, thus conveying their non-structural role.

The Centre Pompidou in Paris projects technology in a variety of ways that are much more complex. Severely functional to the point of exaggeration in its mechanical service systems, it does not pick up cornices, arcades or other features of building in the area.[3] Transparent, flexible and apparently functional, in clear distinction from its museum predecessors in Paris, it utilises a compulsively simple scheme, a metric repetition of steel trusses and columns that do not vary in their dimension and that convey the sense of anonymous and non-specialised building — a warehouse (or supermarket) of culture. But because of the extraordinary spans and because of the architects' wish to make these structural elements particularly expressive, columns, trusses and joints are all specially designed for this building and for this building only. Industrialisation and standardisation are here opposed to handcrafted, custom-built one-at-a-time objects. Through its structural exhibitionism it makes references to Notre Dame and the Eiffel Tower, both visible from the front and public façade; but neither of those buildings contains the obvious references to other buildings nor the complex and culturally contemporary equally important oppositions contained in the Centre Pompidou. Apparently simple, but semantically complex, this is an artifact to be "deconstructed" by our critics of contemporary art![4]

Otto Wagner, Postal Savings Bank, Vienna.

The grid is the last idea that I shall present as characteristic of how architects and artists have projected technology in modern times. The grid has been a much used figure of the avant-garde. *"The absolute stasis of the grid, its lack of hierarchy, of centre, of inflection, emphasises not only its anti-referential character, but — more importantly — its hostility to narrative."*[5] Krauss goes on to argue that the grid by virtue of its lack of reference emphasises not only the originality of the art work itself, but also its own organisation and its materiality.[6] By denying the possibility of signifying other architectures, times, cultures, and human events, the grid turned attention to the means of the building's own making — its technology — which, in turn, could then signify modern technology in general.

The grid struck at the heart of historicism and of eclecticism, and at the symmetries, axes, hierarchies, and other devices of formal organisation practiced by Beaux Arts and neo-classical architects. I say "struck" rather than "strikes" because, by now, the grid is so well established a figure in architecture and art that, when it is now used, it is often used demonstratively as in the case of Agnes Martin's paintings, and it is semantically much more complex than when it began to emerge earlier in this century.

TEACHING TECHNOLOGY

I have tried to put technology, especially modern technology, into an architectural perspective. I have not yet dealt with how technology should be taught. Too narrow a view of technology in architecture has probably dominated the teaching of technical subjects in architectural curricula. I am certain that technology must be taught by technically oriented faculty. I am equally certain that this, while necessary, is not sufficient. It is not sufficient, because technology is related to form and to culture in ways that are complex and subtle and that involve the insights of many, including architects, and theorists as well as those with specific technical competence. Several ideas follow that are rooted in an architectural understanding of technology and that could, I believe, affect how technology is taught.

Deep Understanding. It is not appropriate in architecture merely to teach the calculation of structures or mechanical systems and not the deep understanding such as that espoused by Robert Maillart. This is perhaps the most dominant criterion in good teaching of technical subjects, but one which is very difficult to achieve for most architecture students, and one which is best illustrated by bridges and other engineered structures. The structure of the Hajj Terminal Building in Jeddah, illustrating absolute fidelity to an idea of structure and aided by some of the most powerful computers in the world, gave rise to an extraordinarily powerful and evocative artifact, regardless of its presumed metaphoric origins in the desert tent.

Nature Revealed Through Purity of Form. Structure in the hands of master architects has taken various forms. In the quest for clarity in displaying the distribution of forces and in holding spaces for use, the buildings have approached the perfection of form that nature herself does not achieve in the visible everyday world. Mies Van der Rohe's early scheme for a skyscraper, for example, stands as an extraordinary analogue to the crystalline structure of matter. SOM's Jeddah National Commercial Bank building is a fine contemporary illustration of a search for geometrical perfection in another cultural context.

Nature Revealed Through Distortion. Structure is not the only source of inspiration for fidelity to the nature of things. Ralph Knowles allows the exterior envelope of the building to be shaped by the combination of sun position and the envelope's needs for light and shade. And others in the name of energy have sought systematic transformations that would reveal through form the resolution of forces at the boundary between man and nature. One can imagine pure forms that are distorted by natural forces, like wind or sun, expressing nature, and that at the same time retain their identity, ideas like those of Sir d'Arcy Thompson given architectural expression.[8]

National Commercial Bank, Jeddah, Saudi Arabia.

The Idea of Nature, Pursued. The idea of nature itself, as a source of energy and renewal of life, can inspire architectural solutions that themselves take on qualities that endure beyond their original inspiration. The Bagh-i Fin, the celebration of the water source at the low hills above Kashan in Iran, and Shah Jahan's great Shalimar Bagh at Lahore, not to mention the Alhambra itself, illustrate past accomplishments of supreme beauty and inspiration that utilise the technology of exploiting water to build the formal elements and structure of a place.[9]

Recognition of the Semantic Dimension. In architecture, even more than in engineering, it is important to understand meanings inherent in the forms that are taken by construction and other architectural technologies. In one of the more productive analogues with language, Panofsky observes that "To perceive the relation of signification is to separate the idea of the concept to be expressed from the means of expression. And to perceive the relation of construction is to separate the idea of the function to be fulfilled from the means of fulfilling it."[10] Caws observes that the practicing engineer as well as the architect "*...may well be part bricoleur. He may order his materials and calculate some components of his forms as an engineer, but he will almost certainly allow elements of bricolage into his design...*"[11] In the teaching of technology, if students became more aware of and adept at handling their inheritance in technical fields, it would help considerably in raising their awareness of that idea in architecture more generally.

Vernacular Reformed. The Halawa house, with careful insertion of modern techniques, conveys the look, and to a large extent the reality, of traditional methods of building in a house for the rich. The juxtaposition of vernacular forms with an upper class contemporary life-style strengthens the image of both. The Nianing Agricultural School was the result of a research effort at UNESCO that in a short time created a whole method of construction patterned after vernacular building, but adapted to modern space requirements for schools and other building types.

Tectonics and Experience. Construction systems only qualify for architectonic systems if, like Herzberger's Centraal Beheer in Amsterdam, they are used so that construction and experienced spatial definition merge. Making this distinction evident in alternative examples would also help the architecture student to make the bridge between the technology of structure, for example, and the art of architecture. Herzberger's Centraal Beheer and Louis I. Kahn's Richards Medical Research Towers in Philadelphia represent a relatively conservative view of how environments are to be experienced and read, because their spatial, functional, and structural systems are essentially congruent. In those buildings multiple and contradictory readings are not supported. Their architectonic systems are neither universal enough to be decoupled from the particular activity and seen in their more general frame of reference, nor specific enough to suggest alternative use associations. Furthermore, the semantic dimension was simply not tapped beyond a not-so-crude brutalism that signified the presence of an aggressive and dominant technology.

Hardy Holtzmann and Pfeiffer's Columbus, Indiana, Occupational Health Center exemplifies a dialectical relationship among architectonic systems, still in the modernist vein and tightly linked to the expression of modern technology and modes of production. Kallmann, McKinnell and Woods' American Academy of Arts and Sciences building in Cambridge, Massachusetts and, quite possibly, Henning Larsen's Ministry of Foreign Affairs building in Riyadh establish a powerful dialectic as well with vocabularies of the past.

Hardy, Holtzmann and Pfeiffer's Columbus, Indiana Occupational Health Centre.

CONCLUDING REMARKS

Many nations, caught up in the problems of their own development, may look to architecture to clarify their identity and express it to others. Many nations in the past have attempted this, with success ranging from the challenging and the beautiful in Chandigarh, the diplomatic quarter in Riyadh, and some of the recent planning for Baghdad, to the less obviously successful Algerian New Towns or King Khalid City in Saudi Arabia. Religion, too, may look to architecture to validate its claim on the lives and minds of the faithful and to exclude others. And private enterprise had made the same claims on the landscapes of our cities all over the globe by privatising the skyline and even parts of cities' public access system. Architecture has the capacity to support these objectives, but its greater force comes, in my view, from deeper linkages to the cultures that underlie businesses, nations, and religions.

Technology is caught up in this problem of emerging identity. If buildings in non-industrialised countries resemble too closely buildings in industrialised countries of the West, or utilise processes of production associated with those countries, they do not carry a forceful local identity. Moreover, the emerging nations of the Muslim world are not emerging in the vanguard of the new industrialisation, they are emerging as new and distinctive cultures. Technology, as expressed in the Centre Pompidou or the Hajj Terminal structure, or celebrating the machine as Chernikhov did, or any other of the several examples I have cited may not represent the right approach for the people and the institutions of these nations. Indeed, I suspect that too obvious a use of technology as the primary source of formal expression in building may not be appropriate in most countries of the world today, possibly for different reasons in each. But the more important point I have tried to make is that the formal language of architects must be able to support complex readings specific to where each building is built, and the architect must be able to manipulate that formal language in knowing ways.

The aim of this paper was to discuss linkages between technology, form and culture in the architecture of the West, and to distinguish in that discussion between misconception and myth.

Architectural Education: Learning from Developing Countries*

Hasan-Uddin Khan

A useful perspective for looking at architectural education in America or Europe may actually be from that of the Third World. In today's world there appear to be (to simplify and generalise) two major forces at work in all cultures — those of *universality* and *particularisation*. We are confronted with duality in our life and in our environment.

> *"On the one hand there is something specific to and inseparable from a given cultural and geographical situation (which we could call regionalism) whilst on the other hand there are developments which are global and uniform for all areas and mankind."*[1]

Universality can be said to be manifested in architecture through a form of Internationalism/Modernism and through building types such as airports and high-tech factories, whilst regionalism may be illustrated through tribal groups, vernacular building and religious institutions. These polar forces exist in a dialectic within which architects have to operate. It is impossible not to be influenced by international developments and to base an architecture strictly on a regional tradition.

This duality in architecture is important to tackle in terms of education. We have to prepare students to be able to work not only within their own cultures but also to give them the tools to understand other cultures, and therefore their manifestations of the modes of production, and aesthetic and symbolic values.

Whilst a broader-based education embracing cultural, demographic and economic influences should improve the student's general sensitivities, later in his or her career he or she is likely to need more specific training. Building types such as airports, hospitals, hotels and sports facilities have become so closely focused on the activities they support that each has its own specific technology. The architect's training must cater for both a wider basic learning and a narrowing specialisation.

Students who later practice outside their own countries or cultures will face unfamiliar considerations — whether they serve Hispanic, Far Eastern, or African communities in their own country, or whether they work abroad in the Islamic world or elsewhere, they will have to empathise with that civilisation's cultural base and to bridge a vast gap between it and the predominantly Western idioms and technology which have become the stock in trade of contemporary architecture. Concern with context and ritual, with uses and users cannot be minimised. I propose that the task of the architect as servant and interpreter needs to be more widely defined: educate individuals to use the vast spectrum of sources from which they can and should draw inspiration and train them to be aware of the *impact* their work will have on the future of the societies they serve.

Perhaps one can understand this process by using a construct which relates *technology*, *form* and *culture* — three major elements in the architect's arsenal — in the teaching of architecture.

In the past the horizons of formal academic architectural education in the West, as in the developing world, have in the main been limited to principles of construc-

* Extract from *Journal of Architectural Education*, Vol 40/2, 1987.

tion, the history of building and the aesthetics of design. It appears that in the West technology has been consciously incorporated into the design aesthetic giving rise to more or less appropriate forms. (This does not mean that it demands a specific formal expression). On the other hand, regionalism — a term with cultural implications — does not have to be taught in either design or technological terms. The recognition of style in architecture, beyond that of the classical periods delineated by historians such as Vasari, is also a recent phenomenon. Consciousness of style, which now obsesses designers and historians alike, was perhaps born with the periodical *Journal of Design and Manufacturing*, founded in London by Henry Cole in 1849. To develop such criteria as appropriateness to culture, ecological soundness, economy, as well as the identification of other bases on which to judge building, is also going to be a major educational task in parallel with an actual design education.

But to reduce architecture to its "essentials" or lowest common denominator: function and the use of materials alone, can only impoverish and restrict the practice of architects and deprive all of us of our individuality (regionalism) and commonality (universality).

> *"Too narrow a view of technology has probably dominated teaching of technological subjects in architectural curricula. It needs to be taught but does not come whole into architecture; it is mediated by form."*[2]

Therefore there is a real need for architects to develop greater sophistication in the handling and the manifestation of an architectural language. It is through an architectural language which is well understood and well handled that we stand a chance of modulating universal principles into regional ones.

The aesthetic and language of design in the West is often appropriate to the levels of technology, production of forms, climate, communication patterns, national identities, etc., found in these countries. However, these solutions of course pertain to the West which has over centuries been losing its regional and cultural variety. To make it more acceptable, to rediscover and reemphasise, some of that variation would, I propose, be a good thing.

The Western approach cannot be wholly applicable to developing countries, since the cultural milleu in the developing world is different and varied. It seems that in the Third World, there are two main reactions to the West's "leading edge": either the technological and formalistic solutions are embraced as being "progressive" or "modern", and are seen as symbols of dominant world culture: or, with rising nationalism and a search for a definition of self-identity, these manifestations are completely rejected and usually replaced with a nostalgic look at the past no longer entirely appropriate to the universal elements of life, even in a developing country.

Hence, the education of architects must embrace both the *universal* and the *specific* in order to come to terms with these different tendencies, both in the East and in the West. The *cross-cultural* nature of understanding design in today's multifaceted world seems to be crucially important everywhere. Le Corbusier's work in India and Hassan Fathy's galvanising of Western sensibilities are cases in point.

Should then architectural education, say in the Islamic world, be distinct from what it should be in the Western world? The answer is both yes and no. It could contain similar training in technology which would allow choices to be made between, say mud-brick and steel. Western solutions may be evaluated from a viewpoint based on regional specificities. Forms in relation to culture would be evaluated through a similar filter.

Therefore, how and where can such an education take place? The education of the architect is not solely a function of schools of architecture. The reliance of the architect on professional schools is relatively recent — and even more so in most Third-World countries. But schools are here to stay: the profession is far too complex to master empirically, unless practice is strictly limited. However, there is no substitute for experience: even the Beaux-Arts, Harvard, Cambridge and other famous schools cannot compensate. It is worth recalling the Roman Vitruvius' famous list of what an architect should be:

> *"Let him be educated, skillful with pencil, instructed in geometry, know much history, have followed the philosophers with attention, understand music, have some knowledge of medicine, know the opinions of the jurists, and be acquainted with astronomy and the theory of the heavens."*[3]

This is a tall order indeed! But one which includes much general *experience*. As Spiro Kostof has pointed out:

> *"The education of the architect is not exclusively, or even primarily, a function of schools of architecture...The process of professional initiation starts its course long before its formal unveiling at schools of architecture."*[4]

If we accept that environmental consciousness starts before architectural education, the teaching of architecture actually starts before a student enters an architectural school. It is often insufficient or ineffective. I suggest that environmental awareness should be intentionally inculcated as early as the primary-school level — which would benefit future *non*-architects as well in matters of aesthetic and functional appreciation — even in educated consumerism! Architecture school then provides the student with basic knowledge of architectural and design history, and how to find and apply the information in terms of technology and form. Due to the growing complexity of the profession, I would not be surprised to see the now normal five-year course extending to, say, a seven-year course. This is already happening as Master's and Doctoral programmes attempt to answer the need for specialisation, either in technology or form, or in a special interest in the need for a more regional or cultural input. But this lengthened academic training should not be a substitute for actual work experience as is currently needed in order to sit for professional practice exams. In fact it may be this facet of education that needs to be stressed further and integrated into academic education.

Perhaps regionalism, in cultural and technological terms, is stronger in the Third World because the latter has not yet reached the "advanced" stages of the West in terms of political stability, communications or technology, all of which permit greater universality. The advantage in the Third World is that universality of technological levels has not yet taken a complete hold and therefore regional variants are more appreciated, needed, and can be handled better. This actually means that an architectural education that deals with both regional and universal values, using technology, form and culture as a vehicle, may actually be easier to implement/realise in the developing world than in the West, which is much further along in its pattern of universality.

This dualistic approach — universality and regionalism — takes us back to the beginning: American or European education should actually be able to benefit by looking at regionally varied cultures and the possibilities of reciprocal exchange to their mutual gain.Architecture can then finally assume its inherent meaning as a fundamental discipline of human learning, and not only a profession.

REFERENCE NOTES

INTRODUCTION: THIS BOOK

1. From the first brochure of the Aga Khan Award for Architecture, Philadelphia, 1977.

2. Renata Holod, ed., with Darl Rastorfer, *Architecture and Community: Building in the Islamic World Today*, Aperture, New York, 1983.

3. Sherban Cantacuzino, ed., *Architecture in Continuity: Building in the Islamic World Today*, Aperture, New York, 1985.

PART ONE
SPACE FOR FREEDOM

THE AGA KHAN AWARD FOR ARCHITECTURE

1. *A Space of Freedom: The Aga Khan Award for Architecture*, from the first brochure of the Aga Khan Award for Architecture, Philadelphia, 1977, p. 1–2.

THE FIRST CYCLE: 1977–1980

2. His Highness The Aga Khan "Concluding Remarks", in the first proceedings of *Toward an Architecture in the Spirit of Islam*, Seminar One in the series-Architectural Transformations in the Islamic World, Aiglement, France, April 1978. The Aga Khan Award for Architecture, Philadelphia, 1978 and 1980, p. 114.

3. The spiritual view had already been addressed by Nader Ardalan in his book (written with Lailah Bakhtiar), *The Sense of Unity: The Sufi Tradition in Persian Architecture*, University of Chicago Press, Chicago, 1973. It also was explored within the Award context by S.H. Nasr in his paper, "The Contemporary Muslim and the Architectural Transformation of the Islamic Urban Environment", in the proceedings of *Toward an Architecture in the Spirit of Islam*, Seminar One in the series-Architectural Transformations in the Islamic World, Aiglement, France, April 1978. The Aga Khan Award for Architecture, Philadelphia, 1978 and 1980, p. 1–5. A more recent statement of this mystical view of the Islamic dimension in art is given in S.H. Nasr, *Islamic Art and Spirituality*, State University of New York Press, New York, 1987. Refer particularly to chapters I, III, XII and postscript. Titus Burckhardt's masterful work, *Art of Islam: Language and Meaning*, World of Islam Festival, London, 1976, also reflects what could be termed a generally "Mystical" view. At another level, one finds a discussion of the mystical dimension in the artistic expression of Muslims in Keith Critchlow, *Islamic Patterns: An Analytical and Cosmological Approach*, Schocken Books, New York, 1976. This book provides detailed analysis of the geometry of Islamic decorative patterns in addition to the (brief) text.

4. The Aga Khan Award for Architecture 1980, *Winners Brochure*.

5. This western recognition of Fathy was to come largely in response to the publication of his, *Architecture for the Poor: An Experiment in Rural Egypt*, University of Chicago Press, Chicago, 1973, originally published under the title: *Gourna: A Tale of Two Villages*, by the Ministry of Culture, Arab Republic of Egypt, 1969.

6. For an overall evaluation of Hassan Fathy's ideas and buildings, the reader is referred to J.M. Richards, Ismail Serageldin, and Darl Rastorfer, *Hassan Fathy*, A *Mimar* Book, Concept Media/Architectural Press, Singapore, 1985.

7. This side of Fathy is not sufficiently well known. The recent publication of his views on the subject should help remedy this. See Hassan Fathy, *Natural Energy and Vernacular Architecture*, The University of Chicago Press, Chicago, 1986.

8. *Architecture and Community, op. cit.*

THE SECOND CYCLE: 1980–1983

9. The unique features of sub-Sáharan African Islam have been noted by a few scholars as early as the nineteenth century, for example, Edward W. Blyden, *Christianity, Islam and the Negro Race*, Wittingham, London, 1888. The study of the subject received considerable impetus after the independence of the African states led to substantial interest in Islam as a socio-political force in these societies. For a good overview refer *inter alia* to "La Question Islamique en Afrique Noire" a special issue of *Politique Africaine* Vol. 1, No. 4, Edition Kathala, Paris, November 1981.

10. "Al-Hadatha wal Turath" Modernity and Tradition. Report in Arabic on the symposium of the Aga Khan Award for Architecture held in Sana'a May 25–30, 1983, in *Al-Mustaqbal Al-Arabi*, Beirut, No. 55, September 1983, p. 172–177.

11. The dichotomy between modernity, *al-hadatha*, and tradition, *al-turath*, was at the heart of the ongoing debates between architects especially in the Arab world. It was at the heart of two major international symposia held in Saudi Arabia in January 1980 and Feb/March 1981 in Dammam and Medina respectively. Each of these meetings was attended by approximately 1000 people. The Dammam symposium was sponsored by King Faisal University. Its proceedings were published in *Islamic Architecture and Urbanism: Selected Papers from a Symposium Organised by the College of Architecture and Planning*, Dammam, 1983. Also, see a review of these proceedings by Ismail Serageldin in *Mimar 18*, 1985, p. 65–66. The Medina symposium, sponsored by the Arab Towns organisation was attended by the mayors of some 600 towns and municipalities as well as by academics, practitioners and other interested parties. The proceedings were published in two volumes, one in Arabic and one in English (each covering different material). Both volumes were edited by Ismail Serageldin and Samir El-Sadek, *The Arab City: Its Character and Islamic Cultural Heritage*, Washington D.C. and Riyadh, Saudi Arabia: The Arab Urban Development Institute, 1982. The proceedings were also reviewed by Hasan-Uddin Khan in *Mimar 8*, 1983, p. 72–73.

12. See Mona Serageldin's paper on "New Popular Housing in the Middle East" in the proceedings of *Architecture and Identity*, AKAA Regional Seminar, Kuala Lumpur, July 1983. Published by Concept Media for the Aga Khan Award for Architecture, Singapore, 1983.

13. Jean-Jacques Guibbert, "Symbols, Signs, Signals: Walls of the City", in the proceedings of *Reading the African City*, Seminar Seven in the series-Architectural Transformations in the Islamic World, Dakar, Senegal, November 2–5, 1982. Published by Concept Media for the Aga Khan Award for Architecture, Singapore, 1983, p. 75–84.

14. This same debate can be found running through the last 75 years of western architectural thinking. Thus, the early modernists were concerned with designing appropriate environments for the working man, for example, the Weissenhofsiedlung projects. The relationship between industrial-age aesthetics and machine vs. artisanal production is found vividly in much of the Bauhaus literature. By the 1970s, Fathy's classic *Architecture for the Poor*

was but one of a rising tide of materials treating such concerns. For a sampling, see *inter alia,* Byron Mikellides, ed., *Architecture for People*, Holt, Rinehart and Winston, New York, 1980.

15. The Second International Congress of Architects and Technicians of Historic Monuments which met in Venice from May 25th to 31st, 1964, approved an International Charter for the Conservation and Restoration of Monuments and Sites.

16. For a discussion of these socio-economic aspects of the Hafsia project, and how they were to be handled in the second phase of the project, see Ismail Serageldin, "Financing the Adaptive Re-use of Culturally Significant Areas", in Yudishter Raj Isar, ed., *The Challenge to our Cultural Heritage: Why Preserve the Past,* Smithsonian Institute Press and Unesco, Washington and Paris, 1986, p. 67–95.

THE THIRD CYCLE: 1983–1986

17. For a discussion of these factors in the case of one such project, refer to Ismail Serageldin and Iain T. Christie, "Public Sector Management of Large-Scale Urban Development: El-Obour, a New Satellite City for Greater Cairo," in the proceedings of *Large Housing Projects*, Seminar Five offered by the Aga Khan Program for Islamic Architecture at M.I.T. and Harvard, Cambridge, 1985, p. 114–122.

18. On the proper link between art and technology, much has been said and the Granada seminar added much to that. A recent and brilliant presentation of the artistic possibilities that new technologies offer is found in Brian Winston, "A Mirror for Brunelleschi" in *Daedalus*, Vol. 116, No. 3, Summer 1987, p. 187–201.
Another example of the positive interaction between technology and art can be found in the work of Degas, whose innovative painting compositions were largely inspired by the nascent technique of photography. See: Elvire Perego "un peintre invente la photographie" in *Degas* sp. issue (Hors Serie) of *Beaux Arts magazine* (les grandes expositions) Paris, February 1988, p. 16–18.

19. For an eloquent statement of these issues refer to Mohammed Arkoun, *Pour une Critique de la Raison Islamique*, Maisonneuve et Larose, Paris, 1984; and see Arkoun's paper "Quelques Taches de L'intellectual Musulman, Aujourd'hui", 1988.

20. There is little doubt that these are the key themes of today. For example, in the Arab world: "Certain themes recur frequently - heritage, conservation, authenticity are the shared preoccupations of Arabs writing about their own problems and of non-Arabs writing about their concerns. The destruction of the Arab architectural heritage – the most tangible evidence of a traditional culture which once destroyed can never be recovered is a shared concern, as in the search for a style which will satisfy the demands of modern life and conserve or re-invent an Arab character." Cecil Hourani, introducing *The Arab Cultural Scene, A Literary Review Supplement*, Namara Press, London, 1982, p. 5. This issue is an excellent source for reviewing the various forms of artistic endeavours. A special mention is made of the AKAA on p. 95.

21. During the third cycle of the AKAA, Charles Correa, a member of the Steering Committee, wrote an outstanding book that became a best seller. *The New Landscape*, The Book Society of India, Bombay, 1985, effectively captures the essence of the arguments addressing the complex issues of mass shelter for the poor in a punchy, lucid and beautifully illustrated manner. A more conventional discussion of the subject can be found in Ismail Serageldin's "Housing the Urban Poor in Muslim Countries" in Yasmeen Lari, ed., *Challenges of Transformation: Built Environment in Islamic Countries*, Pakistan Council of Architects and Town Planners, Karachi, 1985, p. 156–186.

22. For a discussion of some of these issues, refer to I. Fethi, "The Mosque Today", R. Hillenbrand, "The Mosque in the Medieval Islamic World", both in Sherban Cantacuzino, ed., *Architecture in Continuity: Building in the Islamic World Today*, Aperture, New York, 1985.

23. For a critique of these approaches see William Curtis, "The Uses and Abuses of History", *Architecture Review*, August 1984.

24. Rifat Chadirji, *Concepts and Influences: Towards a Regionalised International Architecture*, KPI Limited, London, 1986.

A LIVELY DEBATE

25. William J.R. Curtis has written a number of outstanding papers on architectural criticism. His major work remains *Modern Architecture Since 1900*, Prentice-Hall, Inc., New Jersey, 1982.

26. The role of the architect as form-giver has been discussed elsewhere, see *inter alia* Ismail Serageldin "Architecture and Society" in the proceedings of *Architectural Education in the Islamic World*, Seminar Ten in the series-Architectural Transformations in the Islamic World, Granada, Spain, April 21–25, 1986. Published by Concept Media for the Aga Khan Award for Architecture, Singapore, 1986. The nature of this "heroic" architecture has been called into question by distinguished traditionalists such as Abdel Wahed El-Wakil. His views are broad enough to encompass both Mies and the local mason in his praise; see the interview "Abdel Wahed El-Wakil", *Mimar 1* 1981, p. 46–47, and intellectual post-modernists such as Robert Venturi; see R. Venturi, D. Scott Brown and S. Izenour *Learning from Las Vegas*, M.I.T. Press, Cambridge, 1972, 1977 and 1985, where "heroic" architecture is severely disparaged.

27. This point of view is expressed most clearly by Leo Steinberg who said: "Viewed from our elitist position, which makes excellence a defining trait of the class, it is not art that those others delight in; Just as devotion to folk astrology would not, in present company, qualify as love of science. It has to be good science to rank as science at all." L. Steinberg, "Art and Science: Do They Need to be Yoked?" *Daedalus*, Vol. 115, No. 3, Summer 1986, p. 7.

28. For a discussion of this issue of rupture, see Mohammed Arkoun in the proceedings of *Architectural Education in the Islamic World*, Seminar Ten in the series-Architectural Transformations in the Islamic World, Granada, Spain, April 21–25, 1986. Published by Concept Media for the Aga Khan Award for Architecture, Singapore, 1986, p. 15–21; and subsequent discussion on p. 22–25.

29. William Curtis, a more outspoken critic of the Bhong Mosque, said: "The Bhong Mosque obviously reflected a majority decision to enter the murky area of popular expression. One wonders what the idea was of promoting a solution like the Bhong Mosque that is really nothing more than a hackneyed formula coated in the sentimental perfume of orientalist kitsch." See William J.R. Curtis "AKAA 1986: A critical view", *Architectural Record*, January 1987, p. 104.

30. The Master Jury's majority report represents that point of view. More generally the feeling and exuberance of the approach is closer to the views of the post-modernists who have opposed the excessive "rationality" of the modern movement in architecture.

31. There have been a number of attempts by contemporary intellectuals to try to deal with symbolism and its application in contemporary society. Usually, however, these efforts limit themselves to trying to decode the past; for example, Zaki Naquib Mahmoud, *Qiyam min Al-Turath* (values from tradition), Dar Al-Shuruq, Cairo and Beirut, 1984, p. 49–90 on "Symbolism in Ibn Arabi's poetry: Turjuman Al-Ashwaq" (in Arabic) especially p. 60-69 which provide a dictionary or glossary of symbols (or sign-symbols) used by Ibn Arabi. Unfortunately, there is no comparable effort to define similar symbolic content in contemporary discourse, with the exception of the work of Arkoun and a few others.

32. Examples of these thought provoking reflections can be found in Brian Brace Taylor's "Reflections on the 1986 AKAA", *Mimar 22*, 1986, p. 50–52; and Shanti Jayewardene "A Search for Excellence", Ibid., p. 53–55.

THE COLLECTIVE MESSAGE OF THE AWARD

33. Ibid., p. 48–49.

34. There is a controversy between the francophone followers of Ferdinand de Saussure and the anglophone followers of Charles S. Pierce on the meaning and use of these terms. "In Pierce's terminology this word (symbol) has a precise meaning, referring to that type of sign which signifies by virtue of an arbitrary, conventional habit of usage. The Saussurean sign, in which signifier and signified are connected by convention only, in an arbitrary or `unmotivated' manner, is the equivalent of the Pierceian symbol. It is important that these two founders of semiotic study agree on this crucial matter. It is also important that Pierce goes on to name two sign-functions (iconic and indexical) that are not arbitrary or conventional, while Saussure's followers simply extend Saussure's notion of the linguistic sign or work to all signs, verbal and non-verbal. In the space opened up by this difference, much of the internal debate within semiotic studies now takes place. The word `symbol' is widely used with varying meanings, of course, and must always be interpreted with care". See Robert Scholes, *Semiotics and Interpretation*, Yale University Press, New Haven, Conn., 1982, p. 148.

35. Oleg Grabar, "The Iconography of Islamic Architecture" in Aydin Germen (ed.) *Islamic Architecture and Urbanism*, Dammam, Saudi Arabia, 1983, p. 11–13.

36. Mohammed Arkoun, "Background essay: Current Islam Faces its Tradition", in the proceedings of *Architectural Education in the Islamic World,* Seminar Ten in the series-Architectural Transformations in the Islamic World, Granada, Spain, April 21–25, 1986. Published by Concept Media for the Aga Khan Award for Architecture, Singapore, 1986, p. 92–103. Ismail Serageldin, "Individual, Identity, Group dynamics and Islamic Resurgence", in Ali Dessouki, ed., *Islamic Resurgence in the Arab World,* Praeger, New York, 1982, p. 54–66.

37. Indeed, the AKAA finds that even an orthodox ('Usuli) approach to the basic sources of Islam would not lead to a prescription to adopt past models, especially not in building. For a discussion of the part of the message of the scriptures and basic sources of Islamic authority that is of relevance to architects and planners, refer to Ismail Serageldin, "Faith and the Environment: An Inquiry into Islamic Principles and the Built Environment of Muslims", AKAA Award Cycle III, Report No. 27, Dec. 1985. The approach taken there is fundamentally different from the mystical approach taken by S.H. Nasr and N. Ardalan. It is also somewhat different from the more "philosophical" view presented by Muhsin Mahdi in his article: "Function: Concepts and Practice", in the proceedings *Architecture as Symbol and Self Identity*, Seminar Four in the series-Architectural Transformations in the Islamic World, Fez, Morocco, October 9–12, 1979. The Aga Khan Award for Architecture, Philadelphia, 1980.

38. See Oleg Grabar "From Utopia to Paradigms", *Mimar 18*, 1985, p. 41–45.

39. In discussing Muslim culture, one must always go back to the *Quran,* which is at the heart of all in Islam. For modern readings of the *Quran,* each of which is different in approach and construction, see: Mohammed Arkoun "Comment Lire le Coran?" introducing the Kasimirski translation of the *Quran: Le Coran,* Presses Garnier Flammarion, Paris, 1970, p. 11–36. And Regis Blachere, *Le Coran,* Presses Universitaires de France, Paris, 1966; and Mustafa Mahmoud, *Al-Quran: Muhawala Li Fahm 'Asriyye,* The Quran: An Attempt at a Contemporary Understanding, Al-Shuruq, Beirut, 1970.

AN AGENDA FOR THE FUTURE

40. See Mohammed Arkoun's paper "Quelques Taches de L'intellectuel Musulman, Aujourd'hui" to be published in 1988.

41. Some of the recent attempts to discuss these issues of cultural authenticity can be seen in Kamil K. Mumtaz, *Architecture in Pakistan,* a *Mimar* Book, Concept Media, Singapore, 1985, especially p. 191–196; and Abdel-Baki Ibrahim, *Ta'seel Al-Qiyam Al-Hadariyah Fi Bina' Al-Madina Al-Islamiya Al-Mu'asira.* The authentification of cultural values in the building of the contemporary Muslim city, CPAS, Cairo, 1982 (in Arabic).

42. "How to be a reactive thinking force today for all Muslim issues raised through architecture and planning?" One of the main features of Muslim societies today is the distance (growing) between the numerous and difficult issues imposed by historical evolution and the lack of appropriate thinking to deal adequately with these issues. The whole history of Islam needs to be written or rewritten according to the new procedures, interrogations and knowledge shared by the historians (new school of history). It is no more relevant to use traditional definitions of Muslim tradition, for example, when new interpretations are proposed by qualified scholars (cf. G.H. Juynboll: *Muslim Tradition,* Cambridge University Press, 1983). Here appears the intellectual responsibility of the Award as far as the ultimate aim is to give a spiritual impulse to an Islamic way of life and thinking. Spiritually, here, does not mean at all romantic, abstract, empty aspirations to restore so-called "Islamic values"; it is a rigorous discipline of mind to discover the right ways for producing the right knowledge and action through all the forces of oppression, error, disorder, rupture, failure, disintegration in history. Mohammed Arkoun, "Proposal for the Third Cycle of the AKAA", Cycle III, Report No. 1:1984.

43. This section is taken from Ismail Serageldin's memorandum to the Steering Committee dated July 5, 1986.

44. See Ralph Dahrendorf, *Life Chances: Approaches to Social and Political Theory,* University of Chicago Press, Chicago, 1979. Dahrendorf's concepts are very rich and insightful, though their presentation is somewhat complex. In summary: *"Life chances are the moulds of human life in society; their shape determines how and how far people can unfold. The specific combinations of options and ligatures, of choices and linkages which make up human life changes in society (also) ... provide the subject matter of judgments about the meaning of history."*

45. The concept of semantic disorder has received increasing attention in recent years. The advances in the application of semiotics to other domains combined with the structuralist efforts at understanding change and development in societies, which provided a rich mosaic in the late 1960's and throughout the 1970's, has now been challenged, or at least qualitatively added to, by the work of the post Levi-Strauss generation, especially Michel Foucault and Jacques Derrida. Many, however, have some concerned that much of the "deconstructionist" viewpoint of individuals like Derrida (which was very much in vogue in the late 1970's), is largely a form of inverted metaphysics of its own that precludes systematic recourse to evidence. The subject is broad, rich and quite complex. A good recent overview article is Frederick Crews, "In the Big House of Theory", in *The New York Review of Books,* May 29, 1986, p. 36–42.

PART TWO

MILESTONES AND LANDMARKS

THE SOCIAL SECURITY COMPLEX

1. Attilla Yücel, "Sedad Hakki Eldem", A *Mimar* Book, Concept Media, Singapore, 1987, p. 44–47.

PART THREE

A RISING EDIFICE

Faith and the Environment

Ismail Serageldin

1. For a discussion of how this process and its dynamics are affecting the self-image of Muslims, see among others Ismail Serageldin, "Individual Identity, Group Dynamics and Islamic Resurgence", in *Islamic Resurgence in the Arab World,* edited by Ali E.H. Dessouki, Praeger, New York, 1982, p. 54–66.

For an indication of the relationship between this process and the built environment, see Ismail Serageldin "Design and Social Change in the Contemporary Muslim Society" in Ekistics Vol. 47, No. 280, January 1980, p. 45–46.

2. There are several levels at which the *Quranic* text can be read. This is an issue that has concerned theologians, philosophers and mystics for many centuries, including most recently the work of such eminent scholars as Prof. Mohammed Arkoun who seeks to subject the text to a semiotic analysis. This search for understanding is enjoined by God: *"(Why) Do they not seek to ponder (understanding the meaning of) the Quran." (Quran, 47:24* and *4:82).*

3. The choice of the words "Man" and "his" does not connote any sexist bias, but simply is a shorter, more elegant stylistic convention than to refer to "Humans" and "his/her" throughout the essay. The *Quran,* however, goes out of its way to explicitly emphasise that these injunctions apply to all humanity men and women alike:

"For Muslim men and women,
For believing men and women,
For devout men and women,
For true men and women,
For men and women who are
Patient and constant, for men
And women who humble themselves,
For men and women who give
In charity, for men and women
Who Fast (and deny themselves),
For men and women who
Guard their chastity, and
For men and women who
Engage much in God's praise,
For them has God prepared
Forgiveness and great reward. (*Quran 33:35*)

4. Yusuf Ali, (The meaning of) *The Glorious Quran,* Dar Al-Kitab Al-Masri/ Dar Al-Kitab Al-Lubnani, Cairo/Beirut, N.D.

5. It is interesting to note the broad interpretation that prominent scholars like Yusuf Ali ascribe to this injunction:

> *"This is addressed to the Quraish in the first instance, for they had succeeded to the 'Ad of the Thamud heritage'. But the application is universal, and was true of the Abbasid Empire in the time of Harun-ar-Rashid, or the Muslim Empire in Spain or the Turkish Empire in its palmiest days and indeed, apart from political power, to the Muslims and non-Muslims of our own days." Yusuf Ali, op.cit. p. 487 (emphasis added).*

6. Indeed a prominent Islamic scholar goes further and notes that "asceticism often means the negation of *art and beauty*. It has no necessary sanctity attached to it". (Yusuf Ali, op.cit., p. 348, f.n. 1014).

7. This issue has been especially well discussed in relation to modes of governance, democracy, the Islamic state and the related literature. For a particularly pithy, short but thoughtful statement, see A.K. Aboul Magd, *Hiwar la Muwajaha* (Dialogue, Not Confrontation), Kitab Al-Arabi, Kuwait, 1985, p. 109–122 (in Arabic).

8. On this theme of basic human rights in Islam *see inter* alia Ali Abdel-Wahed Wafi, *Huquq Al-Insan fil Islam* (Human Rights in Islam), Cairo, Dar Al-Nahda, 1979 (in Arabic), and Mohamed Fathy "Uthman, *Taqrir Huquq Al-Insan bayn Al-Sharia Al-Islamiyya wal Fikr Al-Qanuni Al-Gharbi* (The affirmation of Human Rights in Islamic and Western Law), Imam Mohamed Ibn Saud Islamic University, Riyadh, Saudi Arabia, 1978.

9. Dahrendorf in developing his fascinating theory of social processes has rediscovered (unknowingly) these Islamic ideas and elaborated persuasively on the need for bonds (ligatures) as well as freedoms (options), in order to establish true happiness. See Ralph Dahrendorf, *Life Chances*, Univ. of Chicago Press, Chicago, 1979.

10. See *inter alia*: Mohamed Selim Al-'Awwa, *Fi Usul Al-Nizam Al-jana'i Al-Islami* (on the foundations of Islamic Criminal Jurisprudence), Dar Al-ma'aref, Cairo, 1979 (in Arabic).

11. "... He hath explained to you in detail what is forbidden to you ..." *(Quran 6:119)*. Hence anything not explicitly prohibited is allowed. For further discussions of this concept see *inter alia:*
- Abdel-Wahab Khallaf *Ilm Usul Al-Fiqh* (the Science of Jurisprudence) Darl Al-Qalam, Kuwait 1970 (originally publ. 1942 in Arabic) (esp. p. 115–116).
- Yusuf Al-Qaradawi, *Al-Halal wal Haram Fil Islam* (The accepted and the forbidden in Islam) Wahba, Cairo, 1980 (in Arabic) (esp. p. 18–21).

12. *"Those who spend (freely) whether in prosperity or in adversity; who restrain anger and pardon (all) men; – for God loves those who do good." (Quran 3:134)*

13. See *inter alia* Yusuf Al-Qaradawi *Mushkilat Al-faqr wa Kayf 'Alagaha Al-Islam* (The problem of poverty and how Islam dealt with it), Wahba, Cairo, 1980 (in Arabic).

Al-Qaradawi makes plain that these rights of the poor apply also to non-Muslims (see esp. p. 103) where he cites the treaty of Khalid Ibn Al-Walid with the Christians of Hira as it was reported in Abu-Yusuf's *Al-Kharaj*).

14. Yusuf Ali explains:

> *"The word cheek' in English, also means arrogance or effrontery, with a slightly different shade added, viz.: effrontery from one in an inferior position to one in a superior position. The Arabic usage is wider, and includes smug self-satisfaction and a sense of lofty superiority." (Yusuf Ali, op.cit., p. 1084, f.n. 3603).*

15. Yusuf Ali, *op.cit*; p. 1084, f.n. 3604.

16. For a discussion of some of these aspects see proceedings of *The Changing Rural Habitat*, Seminar Six in the series-Architectural Transformations in the Islamic World, Beijing, Peoples Republic of China, October 19–22, 1981. Published by Concept Media for the Aga Khan Award for Architecture, 2 Vols., Singapore, 1982.

17. For an elaboration of these concepts see Dr. Mustafa Al-Siba'i, *Ishtirakiyat Al-Islam* (The Socialism of Islam), Dar Al-Sha'b, Cairo, 1977, p. 141, *et.seq*.

18. See *inter alia Al-Qaradawi Mushkilat Al-Faqr. op.cit.* and Mohamed Abu-Zahra, *Al-Takaful Al-Ijtima'i fil Islam* (Social Solidarity in Islam), Dar Al-Fikr Al-Arabi, Cairo, n.d.

19. For an example of this interaction between the physical expression of rural architecture and the changing socio-economic determinants of that environment, see Ismail Serageldin. "Rural Architecture in the Yemen Arab Republic" in proceedings of *The Changing Rural Habitat*, Seminar Six in the series-Architectural Transformations in the Islamic World, Beijing, Peoples Republic of China, October 19–22, 1981. Published by Concept Media for the Aga Khan Award for Architecture, Volume 1 : Case Studies, Singapore, 1982, p. 1–10.

20. For a discussion of Fathy's life and work see J.M. Richards, Ismail Serageldin and Darl Rastorfer, *Hassan Fathy*, A *Mimar* Book, Concept Media, Singapore, 1985.

21. "... Those who bury (hoard) gold and silver and spend it not in the way of God: announce unto them a most grievous penalty." *(Quran 9:34)*.

22. Yusuf Ali explains the phrase:

> *"What your right hands possess: anything that has no civil rights. It includes captives or slaves (where they exist in any form whatever), people in your power, or dumb animals with whom you have to deal. They are all God's creatures and deserve our sympathy and our practical service. Cf. Coleridge's "Rime of The Ancient Mariner": "He prayeth best who loveth best, All things both great and small, For the dear God who loveth us, He made and loveth all." (Yusuf Ali, op.cit., p. 191, fn.n 553)*

23. For a compelling case see Charles Correa, *The New Landscape*, The Book Society of India, Bombay, 1985 (especially p. 51–53).

24. There is much evidence for this, including the famous United Nations Model Neighbourhood project in Peru (1968–1975). See *inter alia* Peter Land "The United Nations Model Neighbourhood project in Peru: prototype for Tomorrow?" in Frank P. Davidson, L.J. Giacoletto and Robert Salkeld (eds.) *Macro-Engineering and the Infrastructure of Tomorrow* (AAAS selected Symposium 23) Westview Press, Boulder, Colorado; 1978. p. 35–43. Also Peter Land "Houses for the Horizontal City" in *Process Architecture* No. 14, 1980, p. 121–159.

25. It is well established that human beings have emotional responses to their built environment, see for example Rikard Kuller "Architecture and Emotions" in Byron Mikellides (ed.) *Architecture for People;* Holt, Reinhart and Winston; New York, 1980, p. 87–100. For views on the mixture of awe and alienation inspired by Highrise structures see Donald J. Conway, ed., The Human Response to Tall Buildings, Community Development Series, Vol. 34. Van Nostrand Reinhold, New York, 1977.

26. See Ismail Serageldin "Infrastructure, Technology and the Pattern of Urban Settlement", in the proceedings of *Development and Urban Metamorphosis*, Seminar Eight in the series – Architectural Transformations in the Islamic World, held in Sana'a, Yemen Arab Republic, May 25–30, 1983. Published by Concept Media for the Aga Khan Award for Architecture, Volume 1 : Yemen at the Crossroads, Singapore, 1983, p. 27–32.

27. See proceedings of *The Expanding Metropolis: Coping with the Urban Growth of Cairo*, Seminar Nine in the series – Architectural Transformations in the Islamic World, Cairo, Eygpt, Nov 11–15, 1984. Published by Concept Media for the Aga Khan Award for Architecture, Singapore, 1985, p 3–15.

28. For an interesting essay on the subject see Ada Louise Huxtable, The *Tall Building Artistically Reconsidered: The Search for a Skyscraper Style*. Pantheon Books, New York, 1984.

29. See *inter alia*: Roger Kain, *Planning for Conservation*, New York, St. Martin's Press, 1981 and proceedings of *The Expanding Metropolis: Coping with the Urban Growth of Cairo*, Seminar Nine in the series – Architectural Transformations in the Islamic World, Cairo, Eygpt, Nov 11–15, 1984. Published by Concept Media for the Aga Khan Award for Architecture, Singapore, 1985, p. 3–15.

For a discussion of the economic and financial issues involved to make conservation measures feasible see also Ismail Serageldin "Project Finance, Subsidisation and Cost-recovery". AKPIA at Harvard University and MIT *Adaptive Reuse: Integrating Traditional Areas into the Modern Urban Fabric*, Cambridge, Mass., 1983, p. 92–102.

30. Charles Correa, *The New Landscape op.cit.*, p. 96–100.

31. At the time, (1903) Muhammad 'Abduh was Mufti of Egypt. See Mohammad 'Imara (ed.) *Al-A'mal Al-Kamila Lil Imam Muhammad'Abduh* (The Complete Works of Muhammad 'Abduh), Beirut, 1972, Vol. 2, p. 204–206 (in Arabic), see also Mohammed 'Imara, *Al-Islam wa Qadaya Al'Asr* (Islam and the issues of our time) Dar Al-Wahda, Beirut, 1980, p. 43–59.

32. See *inter alia*: Ihsan Fethi, "The Mosque Today", in S. Cantacuzino (ed.) *Architecture in Continuity: Building in the Islamic World Today*, Aperture, New York, 1984, p. 53–62.

33. One notable exception has been Ada Louise Huxtable, *op.cit.*, which compares very favourably with the lavishly illustrated piece by Charles Jencks *Skyscrapers — Sky Cities*, Rizzoli, New York, 1980.

34. See the eloquent description of that building in A.L. Huxtable, *op.cit.*, p. 61-62 and Arthur Drexler, *Three New Skyscrapers*, Museum of Modern Art, New York, 1983, p. 20–33.

35. For example, much of the same rational message of working with the environment can be found in Ian McHarg, *Design with Nature*, (Natural History Press, Philadelphia, 1969) Doubleday, New York, 1971 (paperback edition).

36. For a discussion of how this applies in the case of educational facilities, see Ismail Serageldin (rapporteur) "On Educational Facilities" in the proceedings of *Places of Public Gathering in Islam*, Seminar Six in the series-Architectural Transformations in the Islamic World, Amman, Jordan, May 4–7, 1980. The Aga Khan Award for Architecture, Philadelphia, 1980, p. 53–56.

37. See Kamil Khan Mumtaz, *Architecture in Pakistan*, a *Mimar* Book, Concept Media, Singapore, 1985, p. 192–193.

38. Kenneth Clark, *Moments of Vision and Other Essays*, Harper and Row, New York, 1981, p. 1–17. See also Kenneth Clark, *What is a Masterpiece* Thames and Hudson, New York, 1979, in which he sums up his answer to the title question: "*... it is above all the work of an artist of genius who has been absorbed by the spirit of the time in a way that has made his individual experiences universal.*" (p. 44).

39. See *inter alia*: N. Ardalan and L. Bakhtiar, *The Sense of Unity: The Sufi Tradition in Persian Architecture*, University of Chicago Press, Chicago and London, 1973. T. Burckhardt, *Art of Islam: Language and Meaning*, London, World of Islam Festival, 1976. Proceedings of *Architecture as Symbol and Self Identity*, Seminar Four in the series-Architectural Transformations in the Islamic World, Fez, Morocco, October 9–12, 1979. The Aga Khan Award for Architecture, Philadelphia, 1980.

40. See Ismail Serageldin, Creativity and Imagination in Architectural Design originally entitled *Towards a Model of the Design* Process, paper presented to AKAA Think Tank Seminar in January 1985 (to be published in 1989) which argues for the enrichment of the basis of myths, images and stimuli that the architect has at his or her command to draw upon when dealing with a problem. But a better understanding of evolving social realities is also called for. See Ismail Serageldin "Thoughts for the Education of Muslim Planners of the Future" in *Ekistics* Vol. 47, No. 285, Nov–Dec 1980, p. 428–432.

Current Islam Faces its Tradition

Mohammed Arkoun

1. Demographic pressure, secularisation, nationalisation, substitution of an economy of profit and productivity for the ethic of poverty and scorn for the world, the Western model of consumption, etc.

2. I cite this text for two reasons: first, I agree with the comments of Y. Congar on the pertinence of his vocabulary and approach to tradition faced with positivist criticism in the context of modernist crisis very closely related to that which Islam is at present undergoing; second, my objective is to use the example of Islam to work my way up to two levels of thought infrequently or never addressed until now;: the elaborating of the concept of Tradition in its totality for the three revealed religions *(ahl al-kitab)*, and the opening of the way to an anthropology of tradition and modernity.

3. Juynboll, G.H.A. Juynboll, *Muslim Tradition*, Cambridge University Press, Cambridge, 1983.

4. See A.J. Greimas, *Du sens* II, Seuil, Paris, 1983, p. 115–133.

5. See P. Ricoeur, *Temps et recit*, Seuil, Paris, 1983.

6. See Mohammed Arkoun, *Lectures du Coran*, Maisonneuve-Larose, Paris, 1982 and Mohammed Arkoun, *Pour une critique de la raison Islamique*, Maisonneuve-Larose, Paris, 1984.

7. See what I have said about this in "Autorite et pouvoir en Islam", in *Pour une critique op.cit.*

8. Gallimard, Paris, 1978.

9. Y. Congar, *La tradition et les traditions*, Vol. II "Essai Theologique" Paris, Fayard, 1963, p. 163. Compare the way in which Ibn Taymiyya and the Sunni tradition present the *Sahaba*: see my *Pensée arabe*, 2nd ed., P.U.F., Paris, 1979, p. 20.

10. In Christianity, *modernus* was employed for the first time around 480-500 to designate the passage from Roman antiquity to Christianity. See a good historical account of modernity in the West in H.R. Jauss, *Pour une esthétique de la réception*, Gallimard, Paris, 1978, p. 158–209, and what I have said on the subject of Islam in *L'Islam, hier, demain*, 2nd ed. Buchet-Chastel, Paris, 1982, p. 120–137.

11. *Ibid.*

12. Semiotics seems to me to be at present the discipline that crosses most effectively the national, ideological, and traditional frontiers of discourse with the knowledge it conveys.

13. M. Rodinson, *La fascination de l'Islam*, Maspero, Paris, 1980.

14. By unitarian modernity I mean the historical and cultural process by which Western thought, from the thirteenth-fourteenth century on, has imposed a model both explanatory and historically active, which sanctions the dissociation of the subject from his body and asserts a set of propositions and concepts summed up in *classical methaphysics:* transcendent ontology; Promethean time of Progress and Evolution and then Development; concrete space of productivity, legitimisation through Secular Reason, oppressive manipulation of groups with phantasmic constructions that allow the emergence of "great men": the state; the nation; democracy; universal suffrage; secularisation and separation of powers; equality; liberty; fraternity; the Great Leap Forward, and so on.

15. That is what I have tried to do in several essays in *Pour une critique de la raison Islamique, op.cit.*

16. I distinguish ideological manipulation from semiotic manipulation: the former is tactical, strategic, cynical; it controls all the strategics of domination in international life and political gamesmanship in order to obtain or keep power in the national sphere; the latter is inherent in every enunciation; it designates the operations of selection that every speaker performs in the language.

17. Under the direction of B. Lauret and F. Refoulé, 5 Vols., Cert, Paris, 1982–1983.

18. *Initiation*, Vol. 1, p. 12.

The Meaning of History in Cairo

Oleg Grabar

Sources

Abu-Lughod, Janet, Cairo: *One Thousand and One Years of the City Victorious*, Princeton, 1972.

Coste, Pascal. *L'Architecture arabe, ou monuments du Caire*, Paris, 1839.

Creswell, K.A.C. *Early Muslim Architecture*, Oxford, 1940 (EMA).

——. *The Mosques of Egypt*, Cairo, 1949 (ME).

——. *The Muslim Architecture of Egypt*, Oxford, 1952–1959 (MAE).

Henna, Nelly. "Bulaq: An Endangered Historic Area of Cairo" in *Islamic Cairo*, Michael Meinecke, ed. *AARP*, London, June 1980, p. 19–29.

Herz, Max. La Mosquee du Sultan Hassan au Caire, Cairo, 1899.

Raymond, Andre. "Les Bains Publiques au Caire a la fin du XVIIIe siecle." *Annales Islamologiqus* VII, 1967, p. 129–150.

Raymond, Andre. "Le Caire sous les Ottomans: 1517–1798" in *Palais et Maisons du Caire*, J. Revault and B. Maury, eds. Vol. 2, Paris, 1983.

Revault, J. and B. Maury, *Palais et Maisons du Caire*, Vol. 2, Cairo, 1977.

Architecture and Society

Ismail Serageldin

1. Bruce Allsopp, "Educating the Client" in Bryon Mikellides, ed., *Architecture for People*, Holt, Rinechart and Winston, New York, 1980, p. 43.

2. Oleg Grabar, "Cities and Citizens" in Bernard Lewis, ed., *Islam and the Arab World*, Knopf, New York, 1976, p. 89–100.

3. Kenneth Hamilton, *In Search of Contemporary Man*, Eerdmans, Grand Rapids, Michigan, 1967, p. 15.

4. See Ismail Serageldin, "Individual Identity, Group Dynamics and Islamic Resurgence" in A.E.H. Dessouki, ed., *Islamic Resurgence in the Arab World*, Praeger, New York, 1982, p. 54–66.

5. See Ismail Serageldin "Project Finance, Subsidisation and Cost Recovery", and (with Lewcock, Ronald) "Workshop 2; Conservation of the Old City of Sana'a". In the proceedings of *Designing in Islamic Cultures: Seminar Three – Adaptive Reuse: Intigrating Traditional Areas into the Modern Urban Fabric*, Aug. 16–20, 1982, Cambridge, Mass.The Aga Khan Program for Islamic Architecture, at Harvard and M.I.T., Cambridge, Mass.1983, p. 92–102 and 124–36. Also, Ismail Serageldin "Financing the Adaptive Reuse of Culturally Significant Areas". A paper presented at the Conference on "The Challenge of Our Cultural Heritage: Why Preserve the Past?" Co-sponsored by UNESCO and the Smithsonian Institution, in co-operation with the U.S. International Committee for Monuments and Sites (OS-ICOMOS) and the National Trust for Historic Preservation. Washington, D.C. April 9, 1984 (to be published in book form by UNESCO); and Ismail Serageldin "Organisation and Finance of Projects to Upgrade Older Areas". A paper presented at the seminar on "Adaptive Reuse: Integrating Traditional Areas into the Modern Urban Fabric". Sponsored by the Aga Khan Program for Islamic Architecture at Harvard University and M.I.T., Singapore, April 28-May 2, 1984.

6. e.g. The Aga Khan Program for Islamic Architecture seminar, *Designing in Islamic Cultures III*, 1983.

7. *Readings in Historic-Preservation: Why? What? How? op.cit.*

8. Barbara Lee Diamondstein, *Buildings Reborn*, Harper and Row, New York, 1978, provides a wealth of examples from the United States.

9. This argument has been vividly illustrated by the case of Yemen. See Ismail Serageldin, "Rural Architecture in the Yemen Arab Republic" in proceedings of *The Changing Rural Habitat*, Seminar Six in the series– Architectural Transformations in the Islamic World, Beijing, People's Republic of China, October 19–22, 1981. Published by Concept Media for the Aga Khan Award for Architecture, Volume 1 : Case Studies, Singapore, 1982, p. 1–10.

10. For a discussion of the man and his work see J.M. Richards, Ismail Serageldin and Darl Rastorfer, *Hassan Fathy*, A *Mimar* Book, Concept Media/ Architectural Press, Singapore, 1985, esp. p. 16–24.

11. See the excellent discussion of this point in Charles Correa, *The New Landscape*, The Book Society of India, Bombay, 1985, p. 96–100.

12. See *inter alia*, Ismail Serageldin, "Housing the Poor: The Role of the Public Sector" in the proceeding of *Designing in Islamic Cultures: Seminar Two – Urban Housing*, August 1981. The Aga Khan Program for Islamic Architecture at Harvard and M.I.T., Cambridge, Mass. 1982, p. 74–84; and Ismail Serageldin, "Private Sector Participation in Shelter Programmes: The Experience of The World Bank". Speech prepared for the International Shelter Conference of the National Association of Realtors, Washington, D.C., November 2–3.

13. This anonymous architecture has been the subject of much interest. It has been most powerfully projected onto the public consciousness by Bernard Rudofsky, *Architecture without Architects*, Doubleday & Co, New York, 1964. Squatter settlements have also been saluted by many, see also Bernard Rudofsky, *The Prodigious Builders*, Harcourt Brace Jovanich, New York, 1977, p. 340–351. A recognition of that dynamic role of private individuals and, hence, a construction of the public sector role is explained in Ismail Serageldin, "Housing the Poor: The Role of the Public Sector" *op.cit.*

14. Charles Correa, *The New Landscape*, *op.cit.*, p. 127.

Planning and Institutional Mechanisms

Mona Serageldin

1. Under any zoning classification the majority of buildings in Cairo would house at least one non-conforming use.

2. Official approvals needed to issue a building permit for a conventional walk-up apartment building can easily take up to four months, while the time expended to secure the approval and release of allocations of regulated building materials can add two months or more construction time, barring shortages and undue delays.

3. I use the term institutional development here in the sense defined by Edward Mason as "the creation of institutions capable of handling the needs of a changing society".

Technology, Form and Culture in Architecture: Misconception and Myth

William Porter

1. In *Vers Une Architecture* Le Corbusier wrote: "If we eliminate from our hearts and minds all dead concepts in regard to houses and look at the question from a critical and objective point of view, we shall arrive at the 'House Machine', the Mass production house, healthy (and morally so too) and beautiful in the same way that the working tools and instruments which accompany our existence are beautiful". Quoted by Frampton in his *Modern Architecture: A Critical History*, Thames and Hudson, New York, 1985, p. 153.

2. See S. Anderson, *"Architectural Research Programmes in the Work of Le Corbusier"*, *Design Studies*, Vol. 5, no. 3, July 1984.

3. Drawn in part from "Plateau Beaubourg" in *Essays in Architectural Criticism: Modern Architecture and Historical Change* by Alan Colquhoun.

4. "Deconstruction" is a term coined by Jacques Derrida to refer to a technique that makes evident that literature has always been structured in terms of dichotomies; life and death, good and evil, chaste mankind and wanton nature, etc. He argues that in the past the first term carried more positive moral force than the second, but implies that in the contemporary mind the second term need not be disadvantaged.

5. R. Krauss, *The Originality of the Avant-Garde and Other Modernist Myths*, M.I.T. Press, Cambridge, Massachusetts, 1985, p. 158.

6. "For those for whom art begins in a kind of originary purity, the grid was emblematic of the sheer disinterestedness of the work of art, its absolute purposelessness, from which it derived the promise of its autonomy ... While for those for whom the origins of art are not to be found in the idea of pure disinterest so much as in an empirically grounded unity, the grid's power lies in its capacity to figure forth the material ground of the pictorial object." Krauss, *op.cit.*, p. 158.

7. Robert Maillard as quoted in David Billington, "Meaning in Maillard" in *VIA*, Publications of the School of Fine Arts, University of Pennsylvania, Vol. 2.

8. A most eloquent and influential expression of how form and structure relate comes from Sir d'Arcy Wentworth Thompson in his book, *On Growth and Form*, 1917, revised 1942, and re-issued by Oxford University Press in 1961 who showed (first in 1917) "that in general no organic forms exist save such as are in confirmity with physical and mathematical laws ..." He introduced the concept of "Force" as the "symbol for the magnitude and direction of an action in reference to the symbol or diagram of a material thing" and argued that the form, then, of any portion of matter, whether it be living or dead ... may in all cases alike to be described as due to the action of force". His attention was caught by Harold Edgerton's photographs of splashes, and he noted that "There is nothing, then, to prevent a slow and lasting manifestation, in viscous medium such as a protoplasmic organism of phenomena which appear and disappear with evenescent rapidity". In his chapter on "Form and Mechanical Efficiency" Thompson shows that man-made structures and the flow of forces within them illustrate the same forces that occur in organic structures, particularly in cylindrical forms of plants and of bones in animals, and in the distribution of stresses more generally throughout the animal. And, reintroducing Descartes' "Method of Coordinates", he develops his now well known illustrations of deformations that allow the comparison of forms and the identification of families of form or 'types'. Thompson's ideas have been much used in the teaching of design and especially in the teaching of structures as an approach to understanding intuitively the links between natural and architectural form, and, by implication, between careful scientific inquiry and an insightful and penetrating process of design.

9. Nader Ardalan's design for a new town near Shiraz and for an ecological garden-park (with Ian McHarg) in Tehran, and Kamran Diba's gardens of Niavaran and Namaz Khaneh in Tehran are contemporary examples in this tradition.

10. Erwin Panofsky, *Meaning in the Visual Arts*, Anchor Books, 1955, p. 6.

11. Peter Caws, "Significant structures: Internal and External References" in *VIA*, University of Pennsylvania School of Fine Arts, 1973, p. 43.

Architectural Education: Learning from Developing Countries
Hasan-Uddin Khan

1. Hans Hollein, Preface to *Sedad Eldem*, A *Mimar* Book, Concept Media, Singapore, 1987.

2. William Porter, "Technology, Form and Culture in Architecture: Misconception and Myth" in the proceeding of *Architectural Education in the Islamic World*, Seminar Ten in the series-Architectural Transformations in the Islamic World, Granada, Spain, April 21–25, 1986. Published by Concept Media for the Aga Khan Award for Architecture, Singapore, 1986.

3. *Vitruvius d'Architecture*.

4. Spiro Kostof, "The Education of the Muslim Architect" in the proceedings of *Architectural Education in the Islamic World*, Seminar Ten in the series–Architectural Transformations in the Islamic World, Granada, Spain, April 21–25, 1986. Published by Concept Media, for the Aga Khan Award for Architecture, Singapore, 1986.

PROJECT DATA

SOCIAL SECURITY COMPLEX
Istanbul, Turkey

PERSONNEL. **Client:** Sosyal Sigortalar Kurumu (The Social Security Organisation). **Architect:** Sedad H. Eldem. **Consultants**: Erdal Erkunt and Orhan Günsoy, *Structural Engineers*; Joseph Kansun, *Electrical Engineer;* Anus Tekin Tokgöz, *Mechanical Engineer*. **Contractor:** Ismet Elbirlik.

TIMETABLE. **Definition:** 1962–1963. **Design:** 1965. **Construction:** 1966–1968. **Occupancy:** 1969.

DAR LAMANE HOUSING
Casablanca, Morocco

PERSONNEL. **Client:** Compagnie Générale Immobilière (C.G.I.), M'Fadel Lahlou, *Chairman;* Abderrahman, *Director General;* Mohamed Bastos, *Secretary General*. **Architects:** Abderrahim Charai, Aziz Lazrak. **Consultants**: Promoconsult, Omar Bannani.

TIMETABLE. **Design:** Commencement, November 1978. Completion, November 1980. **Construction:** Commencement, April 1981. Completion, June 1983. **Occupancy:** Beginning September 1982.

MOSTAR OLD TOWN
Mostar, Yugoslavia

PERSONNEL. **Client:** Ministry for the Protection of Monuments and Nature of the Republic of Herzegovina in Sarajevo. **Organisation in charge:** Stari-Grad Mostar, Dzihad Pasic, *Architect/Director*; Amir Pasic, *Architect/Assistant Director*.

TIMETABLE. **Restorations and Renovations:** The Bridge, Stari Most, 1970-present. Tower, Tara, 1882. Hadzi Mehmed Karadzozbeg Mosque and Madrasa, 7 months in 1978 & 1 month in 1985. Clock Tower, Sahat Kuly, 1982. Roznamedzi Ibrahim Efendi Mosque, 1978–present. **Major Buildings:** Koski Mehmed Pasha Madrasa and Embankments, 1989. Business District, Prijecka Carsija right bank, 1985–1986. Dzemal Bijedic House, Biscevica House and Tannery, Tabhana, 1982–1987.

AL-AQSA MOSQUE
Al-Haram Al-Sharif, Jerusalem

PERSONNEL. **Client/Owner:** Al-Aqsa Mosque and the Dome of the Rock Restoration Committee, H.E. Sheikh Ibrahim al-Katten, *Chairman* **Restoration:** Isam Awwad, Resident Architect. **Consultants:** Bernard Fielden, *ex-Director* and Paul Schwartzbaum, *Chief Conservator*, ICCROM, Rome, Italy. **Contractor:** The work was executed by foreign restoration teams organised and coordinated by P. Schwartzbaum in collaboration with a local team under the supervision of Isam Awwad. **Craftsman**: Adil Djabari.

TIMETABLE. **Restoration Work:** Commencement, November 1979; Completion, September 1983. **Stage I:** Removal of the earth, excavations, fortification of foundations, documentation, 1970–1975. **Stage II:** Restoration of interior and exterior domes and other works, including interior dome decoration, 1980–1983; carpenter's work, 1980; lead covering, 1980–1985; exterior walls, 1979–1983; interior works, 1975 and ongoing.

YAAMA MOSQUE
Yaama, Tahoua, Niger

PERSONNEL. **Client:** The Muslim Community of Yaama. **Master Mason:** Falké Barmou.

TIMETABLE. **Construction of Mosque's Main Prayer Hall:** 1962. **Major Modifications:** Arches and dome, 1975–1976. **Major Additions:** Corner towers, two-storey galleries and entrance building, 1978– 1982. **Modification of *Mihrab* Superstructure:** 1986.

BHONG MOSQUE
Bhong, Pakistan

PERSONNEL. **Patron:** The late Rais Ghazi Mohammad. **Master Craftsmen:** Abdul Ghani, *Stonework;* Wahid Bukhsh, *Woodwork;* Allah Bukhsh, *Frescoes;* Nabi Bukhsh, *Applied Painting Work;* Faiz Bukhsh and Ahmad Bukhsh, *Glass Mosaic Work;* Allah Diwaya, *Enameled Multan Tilework;* Hafiz Muhammad Anwar, *Stucco Tracery with Gilding;* Muhammad Alam, *Glazed Plaster Work;* Ahmad Hasan and Usam Ghani *Tilework Draftsmen*.

TIMETABLE. **Design:** Commencement, 1932; Completion, 1982 **Construction:** Took place simultaneously with the design. **Project Occupancy:** Since 1932.

SHUSHTAR NEW TOWN
Shushtar, Iran

PERSONNEL. **Client:** Karoun Agro Industries and Iran Housing Corporation. **Architects:** D.A.Z. Architects. **Planners and Engineers:** Kamran Diba, *President and Principal Designer;* Ahmad Kachanijou, *Partner*, Parviz Rezagholizadeh, *Project Management;* C.P. Sabberwal, S.K. Manchandra, Ghohamhossein Mamnoun, Parvin Pezeshki, *Architects on the Design Team;* Ravindram, Gibson, Sina Sadegh, *Planners*. **Structure:** Farzin Sadeghi, *Partner;* Kourosh Farnoush. **Infrastructure/Building Services:** Sica and Hinessy Company; Quadrate Company; Ali Akbar Vakili, *Mechanical Engineer;* Soroush Novini, *Electrical Engineer*. **Building Estimates, Contracts, Site Supervision:** Ahmad Amir Rezvani, *Partner;* Khosrow Taghizaoch, Hamid Farzib, Khosrow Eslampanah, *Site Engineers*.

TIMETABLE. **Programme Development:** 1974; **Design:** 1975. **Construction:** Completed 1978. **Occupancy:** 1978–1979.

KAMPUNG KEBALEN
Jakarta, Indonesia

PERSONNEL. **Client:** The Municipal Government of Surabaya, Mochadji Widjaja, *Mayor 1979–1984*. Poernono Kasidi, *Mayor 1984–present*. **Planners:** The Surabaya Kampung Improvement Programme, with the Surabaya Institute of Technology faculty and students, and the Kampung Kebalen Community, Zanuri Achmad, *Chairman of the Kampung Kebalen;* D.E. Anwari, *Vice Chairman of the Kampung Kebalen;* Chusen Chasbullah, *Overall Planning;* Eddy Indrayana, *Project Planning*. **Architect:** Johan Silas, *Faculty of Architect, Institute of Technology, Surabaya.* **Field Supervisor/ Engineer:** Bangbang Soegeng **Economist:** Hasyim Alhadad. **Technicians:** Koestope and Soetojo; Bob Soeroto, Drainage/Sanitation; Endang Titi Sunarti, Assistant Architect. **Contractor:** P.T. Suba Harkat Utama, A.M.M. Rifaddin, Director, Hananto, Civil Engineer, Takim Sutikno, Foreman.

TIMETABLE. **Programme Development:** 1976; **Design:** 1979. **Construction:** 1980. **Completion:** 1981. **Occupancy:** Continuous.

ISMAILIYYA DEVELOPMENT PROJECTS
Ismailiyya, Egypt

PERSONNEL. **Clients:** Ministry of Housing and Reconstruction, Osman Ahmad Osman, *Minister in 1974*: United Nations Development Programme; Ministry of Overseas Development, U.K., George Franklin, *Physical Plan Advisor*, Ernest Barnes, *Egypt Desk Officer;* Governorate of Ismailiyya, Abdel Moneim Emara, *Governor of Ismailiyya since 1978;* Hai el-Salaam Project Agency, Bayoumi Ahmed Bayoumi, *First Director;* Abu Atwa Project Agency, Habiba Mohammad Eid, *Former Director*, Salah Abdel Latif Damanhouri, *Present Director;* Ismailiyya Planning and Land Development Council, Ibrahim Rateb Ismail, *First Director*, Habiba Mohammad Eid, *Present Director*. **Consultants:** Culpin Planning, David Allen, *Project Partner;* Forbes Davidson, *Planner/Project Manager;* David Sims, *Urban Economist/Planner;* Ian Green, *Sociologist/Planner;* George Jelinck, *Housing Architect/Planner;* Alistair Blunt, *Planner/Acting Project Manager;* **Special Consultants to Culpin**: Roger Tym, *Urban Economist;* Alan Knight, *Housing Finance;* Ove Arup and Partners, Brian Campbell, *Engineer;* Roger Tomlinson, *Engineer;* Technical Assistance Programme Support Staff, Ibrahim Rateb Ismail, *Chief Liaison Officer*, Sayed Awad Hussein, *Assistant Liaison Officer;* Madiha Mahmoud Ali, *Accountant;* Egyptian Professional Counterpart, Aziz A. Yassin and Abdel Monem Osman, *Lead Counterparts;* William Gobran Daoud, *Legal Advisor;* Safwat Mina, *Roads Engineer*, Samir Abdel Mooty, *Architect.*

TIMETABLE. **Programme Development:** Commencement, 1975; Completion, 1976. **Design:** Commencement, May 1977; Completion, May 1978. **Construction:** Commencement, November 1978; Completion: Progressive from December 1978. **Occupancy:** Progressive from December 1978.

SAID NAUM MOSQUE
Jakarta, Indonesia

PERSONNEL. **Client/Owner:** The Municipal Government of Jakarta and Yayasin Daïd Naum. **Architect/Planner:** Atelier Enam, Adhi Moersid, *Managing Director*. **Consultants:** Teddy Boen & Associates, *Civil and Structural Engineers;* Joko Winarno & Associates, *Electrical Engineer*, Atchlier Enam, *Landscape and Site Planner*, Atelier Enam & Jaya Interior, *Interior Designer;* Satrio & Associates, *Sanitary Engineer*, P.T. Pembangunan Jaya, *Contractor*, P.T. Jaya Interior, *Master Craftsmen.*

TIMETABLE. **Programme Development:** Commencement, Preliminary Design Competition; Completion, First Prize Award, June 1975. **Design:** Commencement, 4 July 1975; Completion, 11 September 1975. **Construction:** Commencement, January 1976; Completion, April 1977. **Occupancy:** April 1977.

HISTORIC SITES DEVELOPMENT
Istanbul, Turkey

PERSONNEL. **Client and Planner:** The Touring and Automobile Association of Turkey, Celik Gülersoy, *Secretary General*. Consultants: Ertugrul Alparman, *Urban Planner;* Ersen Gürsel, Istanbul Yapi Sanayi ve Ticaret A.S., Mustafa and Vasif Pehlivanoglu, Gökhan Baydur, Gündogdu Akerzaman, Metin Sözen, Alpaslan Koyunlu, *Architects*. **TAA Site Supervisors:** Adnan Karlitepe, *Surveyor;* Sümer Atasoy, *Archaeologist;* Zeynep Aygen, *Architect;* Abdullah Yetkin, *Technician;* Esin Yücel, *Art Historian;* Gülbin Gönen and Ismail Hacioglu, *Landscape Architects*. **Craftsmen**: Mehmet Cakmak, *Stonemason;* Ziya Topcu, *Marble;* Bülent Güzel, *Decorator*, Mazhar, *Woodwork;* Muharrem Armgagan, *Gardener;* Döser Servet Seekinulus, *Furniture*.

TIMETABLE. The Association's Projects fall into three categories: Restoration, Rebuilding and New Structures. Timetables of specific projects are as follows: **Restorations**: Yıldız Park, 1979. The Malta Pavilion, 1979 (6 months). The Çadir Pavilion, 1980 and 1983 (it took 4 years for the building to be handed over, the restoration took altogether 2–3 months). Emigran Park, 1979. The White Pavilion, 1983. The Yellow Pavilion, 1979 (4 months). The Pink Pavilion, 1982 (5 months), the Khedive Palace at Çubuklu, 1982-1984. The Kariye Museum Neighbourhood (begun in 1974, ongoing). Cedid Mehmet Efendi Madrasa, 1984 (begun but held up now). **Rebuildings:** Komak Hotel, 1982–1984. Soğukçeşme Sokaği, ongoing. New Structures: Çamlica Hill, completed 1981. Muhalebici in the Kariye, 1983–1985. **Ongoing and Future Projects:** Kariye Museum Neighbourhood, Kariye Museum, Soğukçeşme Sokaği, Soğukçeşme Sokaği Byzantine Cistern.

PHOTOGRAPHIC CREDITS

Allam Abdallah: *p. 260.*

Halim Abdel-Halim: *p. 236–237.*

Kamran Adle: *p. 23, 31* (top), *41, 54, 132–138, 140–143, 156–159, 164, 165* (top), *166–167, 170, 171* (top left), *182–183, 186–187, 215, 221, 241–242, 250* (top).

AKAA Archives: *p. 63, 258.*

Joseph St. Anne: *p. 273* (left).

Art in America (May–June, 1979, p. 80): *p. 290.*

Atelier Enam: *p. 185* (bottom).

Chant Avedissian: *p. 172–173, 175, 176* (left), *177, 179.*

Rasam Badran: *p. 232.*

William Betsch: *p. 17–19.*

Jasques Bétant: *p. 12, 27, 30, 31* (bottom), *46, 55, 56* (bottom), *64, 66, 67, 70–73, 75, 76, 118–119, 122, 124* (all afters), *125–129, 130* (top), *144–151, 153–154, 212, 217, 252* (middle), *253* (bottom).

Jean-François Breton (*Mimar 18*, p. 12, 1985): *p. 223* (top).

Compagnie Générale Immobilière: *p. 98.*

Steven B. Cohen: *p. 56* (top), *206.*

Charles Correa: *p. 268, 269* (bottom), *271* (left), *272* (right).

Coste (Pl. XX): p. *248.*

Creswell (ME vol. 2, fig. 109, 110): *p. 249.*

CRY – Child Relief and You: *p. 267.*

Culpin Planning: *p. 174–175, 176* (right).

Farrokh Derakhshani: *p. 220, 243.*

Darab Diba: *p. 185* (left).

Argun Dündar: *p. 78–79, 82–83, 84* (left), *86–87.*

El-Wakil Associates: *p. 238.*

Ahmet Eyuce: *p. 239.*

Fritz Lang: *p. 256.*

Government of India Tourist Office: *p. 270* (bottom).

Oleg Grabar: *p. 284–285.*

J. J. Guibbert: *p. 28* (middle).

Reha Günay: *p. 6–7, 32–33, 35, 39* (top), *40, 44, 84* (right), *102–105, 109–117, 188–196, 252, 253* (top).

ICCROM: *p. 124* (all befores).

Anwar Hossain: *p. 281*

Leila Ibrahim Collection: *p. 226–227.*

K.B. Jain: *p. 272* (left).

Kulbhushan Jain: *p. 271* (right bottom).

Christian Lignon: *p. 91–93, 95–97, 99–101.*

Christopher Little: *p. 22* (bottom), *24, 26, 28, 42, 213–214, 222, 241, 251, 255, 275, 277* (bottom), *280.*

Pascal Maréchaux: *p. 44* (bottom), *45, 223* (bottom), *259.*

Rob Maulden: *p. 290.*

Robert Miller (*Mimar 19*, p. 4, 1986): *p. 294*

Saïd Mouline: *p. 94.*

M. Nalbandian: *p. 120–121.*

Gary Otte: *p. 16, 38, 199.*

Mustapha Pehlivanoglu: *p. 80–81, 88–89, 250* (bottom).

William Porter: *p. 20, 291, 292.*

Jacques Pérez: *p. 34* (bottom), *229* (bottom), *230.*

L. Prussin/AKP: *p. 289.*

Ram Rahman: *p. 269* (left).

Sabbour Associates: *p. 264* (top).

Samekto: *p. 180–181, 185* (top right).

Serge Santelli: *p. 229* (top).

Mona Serageldin: *p. 261, 264* (bottom).

Surabaya Kampung Improvement Programme: *p. 168, 277* (top).

The Hindu Temple (by Stella Kramrische, published by Motilal Banarsidass): *p. 269* (right top).

VBB: *p. 22* (top).

Atilla Yücel: *p. 130* (bottom).

Bijian Zohdi: *p. 39, 162–163, 165* (bottom).